D0139438

A SIMPLIFIED GUIDE TO
STRUCTURED COBOL PROGRAMMING

SECOND EDITION

DANIEL D. McCRACKEN
City College of New York

DONALD G. GOLDEN
Cleveland State University

JOHN WILEY & SONS, INC.

New York
Chichester
Brisbane
Toronto
Singapore

Editor: Gene A. Davenport

Design: Ann Renzi

Cover photograph: Marjory Dressler

Production supervision: Christopher Cosentino

Composition: Daniel D. McCracken and Helen E. Blumenthal
using Xerox Ventura Publisher
(Ventura™ Publisher is a trademark of
Ventura Software, Incorporated)

Library of Congress Cataloging-in-Publication Data
McCracken, Daniel D.
    A simplified guide to structured COBOL programming.

    Includes index.
    1. COBOL (Computer program language) 2. Structured
programming. I. Golden, Donald G. II. Title.
QA76.73.C25M42 1988   005.13'3   87-34608
ISBN 0-471-88658-0 (pbk.)

Printed in the United States of America

10 9 8 7 6 5

To

Grace Murray Hopper, Rear Admiral, U. S. Navy (Ret.)

The Grandmother of COBOL

And all the people who worked with her

PREFACE

This book is for the person who wants to learn what COBOL is, what programming is, and how to use COBOL in typical business data processing applications. It assumes no previous background in programming.

Each chapter is based on one or more example programs that present the programming concepts in a framework of meaningful applications. These examples are drawn from a variety of areas in business data processing: simple inventory and payroll calculations; validation of an order from a seed catalog; preparation of sales reports; and updating sequential, indexed, and relative files, among others. In fact, more than half the book consists of example programs and the discussion of them. All programs have been run, and actual computer output is displayed for all.

All chapters except the last two, "Additional COBOL Topics" and "Interactive COBOL," close with a set of review questions, both to reinforce the central concepts and to make the student aware of what may need more study; answers to all review questions are given immediately following the questions. There are many exercises, with answers to about half of them being given in Appendix IV. Most of the exercises call for writing partial or complete programs and are suitable for running on a computer. In several chapters there are exercises of sufficient size that they could be assigned either as homework or as projects; the solutions to these exercises are not given.

People learn programming by writing programs. Every experienced instructor knows that the sooner students see complete programs, no matter how simple, and begin writing and running them themselves, the quicker they begin to understand what programming is all about. This book supports that fact with plentiful exercises, with chapters in which the development of a program is shown in a process of stepwise refinement, and with a chapter that shows typical steps of program debugging. The first complete program appears on page 4. The initial chapters have exercises that can, and should, be run on a computer by the student.

The concepts of structured programming underlie the entire presentation: only a few simple logical control structures are used, and heavy emphasis is placed on writing programs so that they are easy to understand. The importance of easy (human) readability in facilitating program checkout and maintenance is stressed throughout. The use of meaningful data and paragraph names is encouraged and illustrated. Stepwise refinement is illustrated, and techniques of structured program design are presented in a complete chapter, then demonstrated in all following chapters.

No reader need be concerned, however, that the treatment is too difficult because of the emphasis on design technique. As it is used in this book, proper design is not an advanced topic; it is simply the right way to do the job in the first place. Students learning these methods from the outset develop habits of good programming that they can apply immediately. There is no need to develop poor programming habits and then be forced to unlearn them in advanced courses or on the job. However, statements such as GO TO, which is used relatively little in COBOL these days, and ALTER, which is almost universally discouraged but which may be encountered when maintaining older programs, are presented in Chapter 19 for those students who may need to know about them.

The material is organized so that most of the topics after Chapter 10 can be studied in any sequence that meets the needs of the class, although there are a few obvious dependencies. For example, Chapter 12 ("Updating Sequential Files") should be studied before Chapter 14 ("File Storage Devices and Programming"). On the other hand, an instructor who wants to cover the Report Writer early in the course should have no trouble doing so, although it is equally possible to cover the book without looking at the Report Writer at all.

Readers who know the first edition of this book will notice many familiar features as well as many new ones. We have tried to keep the features that have proven popular in the past, but COBOL has changed significantly since the book was first published, as have the ways in which COBOL programs are written. Perhaps the most noticeable change is that we have expanded the book by about 50 percent. The presentation of indexed files has been expanded significantly, and a new discussion of relative files has been added. The Report Writer has been given its own chapter and is presented in sufficient detail that it can be used throughout the course. We have also expanded the discussion of the SORT verb, including examples using the Input and Output Procedures. In keeping with current trends, we have added a chapter on the use of interactive COBOL, a concept that barely existed 12 years ago.

When the first edition was published the most common version of COBOL was COBOL-68, and COBOL-74 was just coming into use. Today, COBOL-68 has virtually disappeared, COBOL-74 is the common standard, and many vendors provide COBOL-85 compilers. The new edition reflects these changes. Most programs are in COBOL-74, a few use COBOL-85, and there are many examples of COBOL-85 syntax and code throughout the book. Of course, all references to punched cards have been eliminated.

Because of the many COBOL compilers available today ("All COBOLs are equal, but some COBOLs are more equal than others"), we tried to use a compiler that would be familiar to as many readers as possible. This, of course, led us to IBM OS/VS COBOL. Unfortunately, IBM has not been in the forefront of those developing COBOL-85 compilers, so we have had to make some exceptions. Where possible, we have tried to present programs that are compatible with the ANSI standards, both for 1974 COBOL and for 1985 COBOL. In a few specific cases, where IBM has introduced variations from these standards that have come into fairly common use, we have shown the variations and labeled them explicitly as being IBM-defined. To test COBOL-85 programs we used the TSCOB compiler produced by Taneco Systems. A few other programs, most notably the interactive COBOL examples shown in Chapter 20, were run using the REALIA COBOL 2.00 compiler produced by Realia, Inc.; this particular compiler has the advantage of being almost completely compatible with IBM OS/VS COBOL. It is hoped that the use of these compilers, and the policy of pointing out COBOL features that are specific to one compiler or computer, achieves a reasonable compromise between a rigid adherence to ANSI standards at one extreme, and an encyclopedic listing of both standards and numerous implementations at the other.

One of the important changes of the past decade is that structured programming is no longer a topic for debate; it is the accepted way of writing programs. To support this, virtually all program examples have been rewritten to use structured design with functionally oriented modules. Techniques of structured design appear in Chapter 4, immediately after the basic introduction to COBOL. All design is presented in terms of hierarchy charts and pseudocode, with emphasis on function and maintainability; and a number of the sample programs are developed from scratch, showing not only what the COBOL code looks like but how the design is created. In short, we not only show the finished COBOL programs, but how programs are actually developed. In the choice of illustrative material we also provide an overview of what COBOL is used for in industry.

We are indebted to the people who read the manuscript at various stages during its development and who made valuable suggestions for improvement: Norman D. Brammer, Colorado State University; Joseph J. Cebula, Community College of Philadelphia; Willard G. Crichton, University of Delaware; Charles E. Jackson and Karl J. Klee, Jamestown Community College; and Steven Stepanek, California State University, Northridge.

Locating these fine reviewers was just one of the many contributions made by our editor, Gene A. Davenport. We acknowledge both our debt and our gratitude to Gene.

Last, and most important, we wish to express our appreciation to Helen and Susan, each of whom, in her own way, contributed greatly to the development of this book.

December, 1987

Daniel D. McCracken
New York, NY

Donald G. Golden
Cleveland, OH

ACKNOWLEDGMENT

The following acknowledgement is reproduced from *American National Standard Programming Language - COBOL, ANSI X3.23-1985*, published by the American National Standards Institute, Inc.

COBOL is an industry language and is not the property of any company or group of companies, or of any organization or group of organizations.

No warranty, expressed or implied, is made by any contributor or by the CODASYL COBOL Committee as to the accuracy and functioning of the programming system and language. Moreover, no responsibility is assumed by any contributor, or by the committee, in connection therewith.

The authors and copyright holders of the materials used herein

FLOW-MATIC (trademark of Sperry Rand Corporation), Programming for the Univac I and II(R), Data Automation Systems copyrighted 1958, 1959, by Sperry Rand Corporation; IBM Commercial Translator Form No. F 28-8013, copyrighted 1959 by IBM; FACT, DSI 27A5260-2760, copyrighted 1960 by Minneapolis-Honeywell

have specifically authorized the use of this material in whole or in part, in the COBOL specifications. Such authorization extends to the reproduction and use of COBOL specifcations in programming manuals or similar publications.

CONTENTS

7 PICTURES AND RELATED TOPICS 117

8 DEBUGGING 157

14 FILE STORAGE DEVICES AND PROGRAMMING — 353

15 CHARACTER MANIPULATION — 402

16 THE REPORT WRITER — 414

CHAPTER 1

GETTING STARTED IN COBOL PROGRAMMING

1.1 INTRODUCTION

Computer programming is a human activity. A person who wants to use a computer to help solve a problem must develop a procedure consisting of the elementary operations that a computer is capable of carrying out. The procedure must be expressed in a language that the computer can "understand." COBOL is such a language, assuming that the computer in question is supplied with an appropriate compiler for translating from the COBOL language to the language of the particular computer. COBOL compilers are available for most computers, from microcomputers to mainframes.

It is worth pausing to emphasize that *people* have problems, whereas computers follow *procedures*. In spite of the almost-human computers that are seen so frequently on TV and in movies, a computer cannot really think or solve a problem. When we have a problem that we want to use a computer to help solve, we must first devise a precise method for solving it. The method chosen must, in principle, be something that a human being could do, if given enough time. In other words, it must be absolutely clear at every stage exactly what is to be done, and the exact sequence in which operations are to be carried out. The desired sequence of actions may be expressed in many ways: in English, in some form of program design language, or as a computer program. If the procedure is not expressed as a computer program in the first place, and usually it is not, the next step is to write a computer program that carries out the processing actions of the procedure.

1.2 THE LEARNING SEQUENCE

The objective of our work together—authors and reader—is that when you have completed the study through which the text will guide you, you should be able to write COBOL programs to solve problems in your area of interest. To do that, you will need to learn three broad areas of subject matter:

1. The **COBOL** *language*: what it is, what constitutes a valid **COBOL** program, and some of the things that distinguish a good program from one that is not so good.
2. *Coding*: how to write a **COBOL** program, given a road map of how the computer is to do the job that is expected of it.
3. *Program design*: how to prepare the road map; that is, how to go from a statement of *what* a program is supposed to do, to a statement of *how* it is to do it.

Here is our general plan for learning these things. In the first three chapters you will learn some of the most basic things about **COBOL** and about what a program is. In the exercises for these chapters you are required to make small changes in the illustrative programs described in the chapters, and to run the modified programs. In succeeding chapters, as you learn more of the elements of **COBOL** and some of the techniques for designing **COBOL** programs, your exercises will require you to write your own programs, beginning with quite simple tasks and working up to programs that are representative (in terms of techniques used although not in size) of what working programmers do. Beginning in Chapter 4 you will be introduced to the techniques used to design programs. In the following chapters and in the case studies you will learn more and more of the procedures used to design and implement **COBOL** programs.

The point is, there is a difference between knowing what a correct program is, and being able to write one. You will find yourself saying, "I understand the programs in the book and those presented in class, but when I sit down to write the homework programs I don't know where to begin." We understand! *Most* programmers feel that way to some degree, particularly when they are first learning a new language. The answer is to learn how best to go about the process of program design, to which we shall devote much attention as soon as we have covered enough material to make sense of the process.

That's the plan, in broadest outline. Now let's get started.

1.3   A SIMPLE PROGRAM

Let us begin the study of **COBOL** and of programming by considering a simple example of a program, one so short and simple that the "procedure" can be stated in a few sentences. The program required is merely to produce four lines giving the name and address of one of the authors, in this form:

```
DONALD G. GOLDEN
CIS DEPARTMENT
CLEVELAND STATE UNIVERSITY
CLEVELAND, OHIO 44115
```

We shall incorporate these lines into the program itself, so the program will not be required to read any data into the computer from input files. This is totally uncharacteristic of **COBOL** programs (you will probably never write a program that does not read data), but it lets us get into the subject of programming without becoming enmeshed in certain details that beginners often find confusing. You have probably noticed, for example, that the lines printed contain only capital letters. We will use this convention in all of our examples since many **COBOL** compilers only allow uppercase characters. If you are using a compiler that allows both upper- and lowercase, feel free to use lowercase wherever you wish in your output.

A complete program to print these lines is shown in Figure 1.1, as printed by the computer.

1.4   THE FOUR DIVISIONS OF A COBOL PROGRAM

A **COBOL** program consists of four major parts, the *Identification Division*, the *Environment Division*, the *Data Division*, and the *Procedure Division*. The four divisions must appear in the program in the order just stated. We see that in this program there is a blank line between divisions, which is recommended practice but not strictly required; blank lines can be inserted wherever one wishes to improve readability. The margins and indentations are discussed in Section 1.6. The Identification and Environment Divisions are not of much interest to us at this point, and they vary considerably from one computer installation to the next. Therefore, we shall postpone consideration of them until a later chapter. Your instructor or supervisor will tell you exactly what is to be done in these divisions in your first few programs.

The Data Division of a **COBOL** program is used to describe the information that the program processes and produces. In our case there is only one item of output, a line being printed, but ordinarily there will be data coming into the computer, intermediate results, and various kinds of output. Let us examine the five lines of the Data Division in succession.

The first line consists of just the words **DATA DIVISION** followed by a period. This line must always be written in exactly this way, that is, as two words followed by a period, with nothing else on the line. The **FILE SECTION** line must also be written just as shown. A *section* is simply part of a division; we shall learn later that there can be other sections in the Data Division, and that there can be sections in the Procedure Division.

The letters **FD** were devised as an abbreviation for "file description," but you do *not* have the option of spelling them out. (**COBOL**, like other programming languages, is very rigid about its rules for spelling words and for the order in which words may appear.) The name **LINE-OUT-FILE** is one the authors made up for the printed output that will be produced. In data processing terminology, a *file* describes any collection of related data that is organized into *records*. In our case, each line of printing will be a record, so that the file will consist of four records, one record for each line. For another example, we could have a file consisting of lines of text to be read as input; in that case, each line would be a record. We shall also learn about files consisting of records on magnetic tape or other storage media.

LINE-OUT-FILE, as noted, is a name devised by the authors. This is quite different from words like **DATA**, **DIVISION**, **FILE**, and **SECTION**, which have special meanings in the **COBOL** language and which cannot be used in any other way. Words like these are called *reserved words*. A list of **COBOL** reserved words appears in Appendix I. The list of reserved words is relatively constant, but does vary from compiler to compiler. To be completely informed, obtain a list for the compiler you are using. We must always be careful to avoid using reserved words for any purposes other than those specified in the **COBOL** rules.

```
IDENTIFICATION DIVISION.
PROGRAM-ID.
    CHAPTER1.
AUTHOR.
    D. GOLDEN.
DATE-WRITTEN.
    SEPTEMBER 29, 1986.

ENVIRONMENT DIVISION.
INPUT-OUTPUT SECTION.
FILE-CONTROL.
    SELECT LINE-OUT-FILE ASSIGN TO S-OUTPUT.

DATA DIVISION.
FILE SECTION.
FD  LINE-OUT-FILE
    LABEL RECORDS ARE OMITTED.
01  LINE-RECORD PICTURE X(26).


PROCEDURE DIVISION.
A000-WRITE-NAME-AND-ADDRESS.
    OPEN OUTPUT LINE-OUT-FILE.
    MOVE 'DONALD G. GOLDEN' TO LINE-RECORD.
    WRITE LINE-RECORD.
    MOVE 'CIS DEPARTMENT' TO LINE-RECORD.
    WRITE LINE-RECORD.
    MOVE 'CLEVELAND STATE UNIVERSITY' TO LINE-RECORD.
    WRITE LINE-RECORD.
    MOVE 'CLEVELAND, OHIO 44115' TO LINE-RECORD.
    WRITE LINE-RECORD.
    CLOSE LINE-OUT-FILE.
    STOP RUN.
```

FIGURE 1.1 A complete **COBOL** program to print a name and address on four lines.

Observe that although **FILE** is a reserved word, the name **LINE-OUT-FILE** is altogether different, and does not violate the rule against using **FILE** as the name of a file. The rules for making up names for things like files, records, and data items are collected at the end of the chapter, beginning on page 9.

The fourth line of the Data Division is the body of the file description (**FD**). It happens to be required by the **COBOL** rules; what a label record is will be described in Chapter 14. Certain other clauses may be required in the file description; the minimum requirement varies a bit. Note that there is a period only at the end of the entire **FD** entry. If you put a period at the end of the first line, the **COBOL** compiler will get completely confused and will be unable to translate your program.

The last line of the Data Division describes the record. The **01** is called the *level number*; we shall explore that concept in Chapter 3. **LINE-RECORD** is the name of the one type of record that makes up the file named **LINE-OUT-FILE**. Note that, although **LINE** and **RECORD** are both reserved words, **LINE-RECORD** is an acceptable name since the **COBOL** compiler treats it as a single eleven-character name. The **PICTURE X(26)** clause describes to **COBOL** what the record looks like: it consists of 26 characters, with each character permitted to be any letter, digit, or other symbol that can be represented in your computer. If we had wanted to specify that the record would contain only letters, we would have written **PICTURE A(26)**; if we had wanted to specify numeric digits only, we would have written **PICTURE 9(26)**.* An item that is described with an **X** in its **PICTURE** character string, and which may therefore consist of letters, digits, or special characters, is said to be *alphanumeric*.

The Procedure Division is used to tell the computer what is to be done and in what sequence. As with the words **DATA DIVISION**, the words **PROCEDURE DIVISION** must appear on a line by themselves, exactly as shown Figure 1.1.

This Procedure Division consists of eleven *statements*, one on each line. A **COBOL** *sentence* consists of one or more statements followed by a period. Here we have one statement per sentence in each case, but that will not always be true. Finally, by way of preliminary definitions, **COBOL** sentences are organized into *paragraphs*. A **COBOL** paragraph consists of a paragraph name followed by a period and one or more sentences. This program has only one paragraph (you may never see such a program again, certainly not in this book), but that one paragraph still needs a paragraph name. **COBOL** derives no meaning from paragraph names, which we devise to be helpful to us in understanding what paragraphs do and, when there are many of them, how they are related to each other. In fact, the first four characters of this paragraph name (**A000**) are used only to locate the paragraph within the program. The use of such prefixes will be discussed in Chapter 4, but it should be obvious that the prefix is useful only when your programs become larger.

Every **COBOL** statement begins with a verb that says what kind of action is to be carried out. The verbs in this program are **OPEN**, **MOVE**, **WRITE**, **CLOSE**, and **STOP**.

OPEN is a verb that applies to files, specifying some preparatory operations the nature of which is not interesting to us at this point. Suffice it to say for now that every file must be opened, in a statement that specifies whether it is an input or an output file.

The **MOVE** verb is one that we shall use a great deal, more than any other verb, in fact. Its function is to move information from one location in the computer to another. Frequently we shall use it in the general form

    MOVE data-name-1 **TO** data-name-2

where "data-name-1" stands for any name of data in our program, and "data-name-2" stands for some other data name in our program. We might have, for example,

    MOVE QUANTITY-ON-HAND TO OUTPUT-LINE-7

or

    MOVE GROSS-PAY TO GROSS-PAY-EDITED

---

*   Except for a detail: a numeric item in **COBOL** may not have more than 18 digits.

The word **MOVE** sometimes carries an implication that confuses new-comers; it seems to suggest that the information is erased from the sending location and rewritten in a new location, which does *not* occur. Actually, from this viewpoint a word like **COPY** might be preferable, since after a **MOVE** *the information exists in both places*. But the word **MOVE** has long usage behind it and is unlikely to be changed.

In our case, we are moving information that does not have a name but that is given right in the statement, in literal form. Such information is called a *literal*, in fact. Here we have an example of a *nonnumeric* literal, which must be enclosed in quotation marks as shown. **COBOL** permits using either single quotes (') or double quotes ("), but whichever you use you must use the same type of quote mark at both the start and end of the literal. For example, we could write

```
MOVE 'DONALD G. GOLDEN' TO LINE-RECORD.
MOVE "CIS DEPARTMENT" TO LINE-RECORD.
```

in the same program, but we could *not* write

```
MOVE 'CLEVELAND STATE UNIVERSITY" TO LINE-RECORD.
```

because the quote types do not match. (A numeric literal is not enclosed in quotes; numeric and nonnumeric literals are quite different, as we shall study in Chapter 3.) What the **MOVE** statement means is this: move all of the following characters

```
DONALD G. GOLDEN
```

including the period and the blank spaces but not the enclosing quotes that were in the literal in the program, to the record named **LINE-RECORD**.

The third statement says to write the record into which we have just placed a name. This means to produce a printed line containing the information now in the location identified by the name **LINE-RECORD**.

Next we say to move the first part of the address to **LINE-RECORD**. **LINE-RECORD** is, of course, the same name—and refers to the same location in the computer's memory—that we just used for the name. This action will, accordingly, destroy the previous contents of **LINE-RECORD**, replacing them with the new information. This is commonly done in programming. **LINE-RECORD**, in other words, is not the name of a *particular item* of information but is, instead, the name of a *place* where a variety of information may appear in the course of running a program.

It turns out that there are only 16 characters in this literal, including the blanks, whereas we said with our **PICTURE** clause that **LINE-RECORD** has room for 26. When a **MOVE** of this type is carried out, that is with the sending item being shorter than the receiving item, the sending item is placed at the *left* end of the receiving location and the extra positions on the right are filled with blanks. This is called left justification.

Now we write a line containing the information currently in **LINE-RECORD**, then place the third line of the address in **LINE-RECORD** and write it, and finally repeat the process to write the fourth line of the address. This completes the actions required in the specifications for the program, so we are ready to terminate program execution. Before we do this, however, it is necessary to write a **CLOSE** statement for all files, of which there is only one here. Note that with **CLOSE** it is not necessary to specify whether the file is input or output. Finally, we say **STOP RUN**, which tells the computer that we are finished and lets the computer go on to other work.

1.5   RUNNING A PROGRAM

This is the complete program. If we want to run it on a computer, we must enter it into the computer through a console or terminal; your instructor or supervisor can show you the specific method required for the computer you will be using. The program is then translated into the language of the computer by a **COBOL** *compiler* and the compiled program is *executed*, or run. When this program was run it produced this output:

```
DONALD G. GOLDEN
CIS DEPARTMENT
CLEVELAND STATE UNIVERSITY
CLEVELAND, OHIO 44115
```

In other words, it did operate as specified.

If you are in a programming course in which you will be running programs on a computer, you will probably be doing the exercise at the end of this chapter or the next. Since you do not know enough about **COBOL** or programming yet to do anything very substantial, the exercise asks you only to make a few rather small changes in this program and to run the slightly modified version. At this point, therefore, we pause to collect the information you will need to have to do that exercise, which includes the program format and the rules for forming identifiers.

1.6   THE COBOL CODING FORMAT

COBOL programs are generally entered into a computer through a terminal or computer console, frequently by the writer of the program (particularly in a programming course). However, **COBOL** still requires that programs be written according to a special format, and it is helpful to write a program out on paper before entering it into the computer. It is much easier to check your program and make corrections on paper than at a computer terminal.*

The format for **COBOL** statements was designed in the 1950s, at a time when data entry to computers was done almost entirely with punched cards. Most punched cards at the time had 80 *columns* in which characters could be punched; this is the origin of the term "columns" in the discussion that follows, and of the limit of 80 characters on a line.

Coding forms are available, with a small box for each character position in a line; your instructor may ask you to write your programs on such a form. Once your program has been entered into the computer, it is a simple matter to get a printed listing of it. (The techniques for doing all of this vary greatly with different computers; your instructor will give you the details.)

---

* Most schools have a legend about a student who never had to plan his or her programs, but who just sat down at the computer and entered the final version which, of course, worked perfectly the first time. Unfortunately, it always seems that this student graduated about two years earlier.

On each line, there are specific areas with special meanings that we must explore: sequence, continuation, Area A, Area B, and identification.

Columns 1-6 are used to number the lines in sequence, if one wishes. This capability was particularly useful when programs were commonly punched on cards. If one dropped a deck of cards, the sequence field made it possible to reassemble the deck in the proper order. Today, although the sequence field is still available in **COBOL**, it is commonly left blank. If you do use the sequence field, be sure to number the lines in multiples of 10 or 100, to leave room to insert new lines between old ones without having the new lines be out of order. Most **COBOL** compilers can be instructed to check whether lines of code are in sequence on the sequence numbers, and to give a warning if they are not.

Column 7 is used for two purposes. First, and least commonly, it is used in certain rare situations where a word or literal must be continued from a previous line in ways that would otherwise confuse the compiler. About the only circumstance where this makes any sense is the continuation of a long literal that does not fit entirely on one line. When this situation occurs, the literal is written to the end of the first line (column 72), a dash (-) is placed in column 7 of the next line, and the literal is continued beginning anywhere from column 12 on, starting with a new quote. This is sufficiently confusing and is so infrequently really necessary that most programmers avoid continuations altogether, as we shall almost always do.

A much more important use for column 7 is to serve as a *comment indicator*. Any program, no matter how well written, can usually benefit from comments to the reader describing what the program does and something about how it does it. These comments are ignored by the **COBOL** compiler and exist only to help a person trying to understand the program. To indicate that a line contains a comment, rather than a line of **COBOL** code, place an asterisk (*) in column 7. The **COBOL** compiler will then ignore everything else on the line. You can also use a slash (/) to indicate a comment line. In this case, however, when the compiler prints a listing of your program it will skip to the top of a new page before printing the comment line.

Column 8 is the beginning of *Area A*. The names of divisions, sections, and paragraphs must begin in this area, as must **FD**'s and **01** and **77** level entries in the Data Division (later, later!). *A statement must not begin in this area.* Column 8 is called the *A margin*.

Column 12 is the beginning of *Area B*; column 12 is called the *B margin*. Procedure Division statements may be written anywhere in this area. We shall ordinarily begin statements in column 12, unless they are subject to indentation rules that will be explained as we go along. (Indentation is used to make the program structure clearer.) The words of a statement must be separated by one or more spaces.

The B area ends in column 72. If a statement takes up too much space to fit in that area, we divide the statement after a complete word and simply proceed to the next line. Assuming that no word is broken in its middle—and we shall never do so—a dash in the continuation position of the next line is *not* required (and would cause an error if used). We shall never have more than one statement on a line, but one statement may—and often will—be spread over several lines.

The *identification area*, in columns 73-80, is available for anything the programmer pleases. The general idea is that it is sometimes helpful to be able to look at a program listing that has no other identifying information and find something that will tell what program this is. As with the sequence area, this area was much more useful when programs were commonly punched on cards. Some **COBOL** systems (compilers or source code editors) automatically insert part or all of the program name (taken either from the Identification Division or the file containing the program code) in this portion of the program listing if nothing else is written here.

1.7 RULES FOR FORMING DATA-NAMES

There are many occasions when it is necessary to devise names for files, records, items within records, and a variety of other things in a program. The formation of these programmer-supplied names, also called *identifiers*, is subject to the following rules.

1. A data-name may contain from 1 to 30 characters.
2. The characters of which a data-name is composed must be chosen from the 26 letters of the alphabet, the 10 decimal digits, and the hyphen.
3. A data-name must contain at least one letter.
4. A data-name must not begin or end with a hyphen.
5. A data-name must not be the same as any reserved word.
6. Each data-name must be unique; that is, it must not appear in the Data Division more than once. (This rule does not apply when data-name qualification is used, as described in Chapter 10.)

It is usual practice, and strongly recommended, to devise data-names that are mnemonic; that is, that remind a reader of what the data-names stand for. Thus, we might write names such as:

```
GROSS-PAY
QUANTITY-ON-HAND
REPORT-LINE-12
W-COST-1-UNADJUSTED
45-AUTHORIZATION
```

Here are some data-names that violate the rules.

`12-56`	Does not contain a letter
`-ABC-12`	Begins with a hyphen
`ACCOUNT/RECEIVABLE`	Contains a character other than a letter, digit, or hyphen
`FILE`	This is a reserved word
`AUTHORIZED-BY-DEPARTMENT-MANAGER-OR-DELEGATE`	
	More than 30 characters

"Cute" data-names are (marginally) acceptable in programs written for exercises, but they become a hindrance to easy understandability. Using the names of friends, rock stars, sports cars, or Doonesbury characters may be amusing to you, but such names don't convey meaning about the function of the program to another reader. After using cute names a few times, you will probably discover that they don't seem so funny as they did at first, and that they are an obstacle to good communication.

REVIEW QUESTIONS

1. Name the four divisions of a **COBOL** program.

2. Must the four divisions always appear in the same order?

3. Is it required, or only recommended, that a blank line be left between divisions?

4. What is the purpose of putting an asterisk in column 7 of a line? How does this differ from putting a slash in column 7?

5. In the program of Figure 1.1 we find the lines

```
INPUT-OUTPUT SECTION.
FILE-CONTROL.
FILE SECTION.
```

   Would it be permissible to change these lines to the following?

```
INPUT OUTPUT SECTION.
FILE CONTROL.
FILE-SECTION.
```

6. What would happen if you placed a period at the end of this line in the program?

```
FD  LINE-OUT-FILE
```

7. A sentence must end with a period, and putting periods where they are not called for can lead to lots of trouble. Then why is it permissible to have a period after the middle initial in this line?

```
MOVE 'DANIEL D. MCCRACKEN' TO LINE-RECORD.
```

8. Is it the **OPEN** or the **CLOSE** verb that requires us to specify whether the file is **INPUT** or **OUTPUT**?

9. Give two examples of files and the records of which they are composed.

ANSWERS

1. Identification, Environment, Data, and Procedure.

2. Yes.

3. Recommended, but rather strongly.

4. Both an asterisk and a slash in column 7 cause the **COBOL** compiler to treat the line as a comment. However, a slash will cause the compiler to skip to a new page before printing the comment line in a program listing.

5. Any of these changes would trigger all kinds of error messages, some of them possibly quite misleading. It is absolutely essential to write such things exactly as shown.

6. The compiler would probably complain that you had omitted the **LABEL RECORDS** clause (since it did not find one before the period ending the **FD** entry), then give error messages based on its inability to make sense of the **LABEL RECORDS** clause appearing where it was not expected. But the details depend on your **COBOL** compiler; diagnostic messages vary from one compiler to the next.

7. A period within a literal is part of the literal, and is not interpreted as ending the sentence.

8. OPEN.

9. A text file on a computer is a file, with each line of text being one record. A printed report can be thought of as a file, each line being a record.

EXERCISE

You are to make certain changes in the program shown in Figure 1.1, enter the program into your computer, and run it. Here are the changes.

1. To allow for longer names and address, change the **PICTURE** clause so that the lines are 40 characters long instead of 26.

2. Change the literals in the **MOVE** statements so that the program prints your name and address. If your address takes only three lines, you will of course need one less **MOVE**-and-**WRITE** combination.

3. Devise new names to replace **LINE-OUT-FILE** and **LINE-RECORD**, and replace all occurrences of these identifiers with your new names.

Now here are some things to keep in mind.

4. Your instructor or supervisor will specify a few *job control statements* that must be placed before your **COBOL** program, and probably some that must be placed at the end. These give the computer system information such as the account number that is to be charged for your usage of the computer, the fact that this is a **COBOL** job, and other information. These much be entered *exactly* as specified!

5. Your Identification Division, Environment Division, and **FD** entries may be different from those shown here, usually in rather minor but essential ways.

6. Your computer may not permit you to use both the double quote mark (") and the single quote mark ('). If so, just use whichever one is available.

7. If your name or address contains an apostrophe and your computer permits both double and single quote marks, simply use double quotes around the literal and a single quote to represent the apostrophe. For example, you could write something like

```
MOVE "SEAN O'REILLY" TO LINE-RECORD.
```

However, if your computer does not permit both double and single quote marks, you have a problem, because the computer cannot distinguish between a single quote and an apostrophe. If you write something like

```
MOVE 'SEAN O'REILLY' TO LINE-RECORD.
```

COBOL will interpret the second quote as the end of the literal and tell you that **REILLY** doesn't make sense at that point in a **MOVE** statement. There would likely be other error messages as well, some probably not making much sense.

CHAPTER 2

THE BASIC PROGRAM STRUCTURE

2.1 INTRODUCTION

As we noted in the previous chapter, it is highly unusual for a program not to involve the reading of data. All programs in the rest of the book will do so. Since data input is such an important part of **COBOL** programming, we turn immediately to an example of a program involving processing of data that comes from a simple text file rather than from the program itself.

The task to be performed is simplicity itself: read a file of text and, for each line in the file, print a line of output consisting of the information read. You should be aware that, although we will talk as though our text file is separate from the file containing the program, for many computers (such as IBM mainframes) both the program code and the lines of text can be written in the same file, with the text following immediately behind the program. In any case, whether the text is in the same file as the program or in a separate file, there is an important difference between this example and the one in the previous chapter. In the first example the data was coded within the program and did not need to be read. In the following example the data is separate from the program and will be read by the program.

The main thing to be learned in this chapter is the basic program structure that will be used in all programs in this book, whether there is only one input file or several, and whether there is one output file or several. This basic structure—it might be called a program skeleton—will require us to understand the functioning of two new **COBOL** verbs, **READ** and **PERFORM**. We shall also need to know the purpose of the Working-Storage Section in the Data Division.

2.2 THE PROGRAM

The complete program is shown in Figure 2.1. The Identification and Environment Divisions are much as before, the main difference being an additional **SELECT** clause in the latter. Again, you will get specific instructions on how to

```
IDENTIFICATION DIVISION.
PROGRAM-ID.
    COPIER.

ENVIRONMENT DIVISION.
INPUT-OUTPUT SECTION.
FILE-CONTROL.
    SELECT TEXT-IN-FILE     ASSIGN TO S-TEXTFILE.
    SELECT LINE-OUT-FILE    ASSIGN TO S-OUTPUT.

DATA DIVISION.
FILE SECTION.
FD   TEXT-IN-FILE
     LABEL RECORDS ARE OMITTED.
01   TEXT-IN-RECORD          PICTURE X(80).
FD   LINE-OUT-FILE
     LABEL RECORDS ARE OMITTED.
01   LINE-OUT-RECORD         PICTURE X(80).
WORKING-STORAGE SECTION.
01   OUT-OF-DATA-FLAG        PICTURE XXX.

PROCEDURE DIVISION.
A000-MAIN-LINE-ROUTINE.
    OPEN INPUT TEXT-IN-FILE
         OUTPUT LINE-OUT-FILE.
    MOVE 'NO' TO OUT-OF-DATA-FLAG.
    READ TEXT-IN-FILE
        AT END MOVE 'YES' TO OUT-OF-DATA-FLAG.
    PERFORM B010-PROCESS-WRITE-READ
        UNTIL OUT-OF-DATA-FLAG = 'YES'.
    CLOSE TEXT-IN-FILE
          LINE-OUT-FILE.
    STOP RUN.

B010-PROCESS-WRITE-READ.
    MOVE TEXT-IN-RECORD TO LINE-OUT-RECORD.
    WRITE LINE-OUT-RECORD.
    READ TEXT-IN-FILE
        AT END MOVE 'YES' TO OUT-OF-DATA-FLAG.
```

FIGURE 2.1   A program to read and print a text file.

write these divisions for your version of COBOL; we anticipate the discussion of the Environment Division in later chapters only to point out that there has to be a SELECT clause for every file that will be processed by the program. In this case we have an input file of text and an output file of printing.

2.3   THE DATA DIVISION

In the File Section of the Data Division we must have an FD entry for each file named in a SELECT clause in the Environment Division. The FDs here are just as simple as in the program of the first chapter, although slightly different. The PICTURE clause this time specifies 80 characters, corresponding to the 80 characters on a line of a typical text file. The PICTURE clause for LINE-OUT-RECORD is the same as that for TEXT-IN-RECORD.

2.4 THE WORKING-STORAGE SECTION

The first thing about this program that is really new is the Working-Storage Section. This section, which must follow the File Section, is used to describe information that is used by the program but that is not part of input or output and which, therefore, is not included in the FDs in the File Section. In this program we need to describe a data item that will be used as a *flag* to indicate whether we have yet come to the end of the text file. The word **NO** will be used to mean that we have not yet come to the end of the file, and the word **YES** will be used to mean that we have. Space for three characters is accordingly provided, using the **PICTURE** clause. Observe that we have written **PICTURE XXX**, which means three characters. We could also have written **PICTURE X(3)**. The choice is a toss-up in a case like this, but with **PICTURE**s describing more than three characters the parentheses form should be used.

A special word of warning: always be very sure to include the hyphen in **WORKING-STORAGE**! Most **COBOL** compilers will turn out a string of nearly meaningless and highly confusing diagnostic error messages if the hyphen is omitted.

2.5 THE PROCEDURE DIVISION

The Procedure Division begins as before with an **OPEN** statement for the files. Just as there has to be a **SELECT** clause in the Environment Division for each file and an **FD** in the Data Division for each file, so in the Procedure Division each file must be opened and later closed. We have a choice whether to have the **OPEN** containing the names of both files or to use two separate statements, each beginning with **OPEN**. Choose whichever alternative seems clearer to you.

The next statement, **MOVE**, is part of the scheme for reading data over and over until the end of the file is reached. We shall see how this works in a moment. Just bear in mind that as we proceed, the Working-Storage entry for **OUT-OF-DATA-FLAG** now contains the word **NO**.

2.6 THE READ VERB

Now we come to the first of our two new verbs: **READ**. The basic idea is simple enough. **READ** says to get one record from the file named. But there is a little more to it than that, because at some point we are going to attempt to read a record that isn't there, because we will have come to the end of the file. We don't know, as we write the program, how many records there will be. If the file contains four records, for instance, we want the program to execute four **READ**s and on attempting the fifth **READ** to discover that all the records have been read. If there are a thousand records, we want the **READ** to be executed a thousand times and on attempting to read the thousand-and-first record to find out that all the records have been read. And if, through some sort of mix-up, there aren't any records in the file at all, we need to be informed of that fact on attempting the first **READ** in the program.

COBOL provides the facility for handling this common data processing situation with the **AT END** phrase of the **READ** statement. The way it works is this. If, when the **READ** verb is executed, the computer does find a record, the record is placed in storage under the record name we have provided in the **FD** in the Data Division; the statement (or statements) written after the **AT END** is not executed. On the other hand, if when the **READ** is executed no records remain to be read in the file, nothing is placed in file storage and whatever statement is written after **AT END** is carried out. What we have done here is simply to move the word **YES** to the **OUT-OF-DATA-FLAG** item in working storage. We shall see very shortly what this accomplishes.

At least one statement must be written in the **AT END** phrase, but there may be more than one. The **AT END** controls all statements between the words **AT END** and the end of the sentence, which is marked by a period. One example of a situation where it is useful to have more than one statement in the **AT END** phrase is in the first **READ** in a program, where we might wish not only to set a flag but also to write a message noting that there was no data to be processed.

Perhaps needless to say, one must be very careful to put the period exactly where it is supposed to be. For instance, if the period after the **READ** statement is omitted, all statements after the **READ**, until the next period, will be taken to be part of the **AT END** phrase, and therefore not executed so long as there is data to be read. This can be a difficult error to locate.

It is essential to understand very clearly exactly when the **AT END** phrase comes into play. It *does not* become active on reading the last record of a file, but rather on attempting to read a record *after* the last record of a file. Students often wonder if it wouldn't have made more sense to design **COBOL** so that the **AT END** phrase comes into play on reading the last record. Occasionally this could, in fact, be useful—but not very often, as it turns out. Furthermore, if **COBOL** had been designed this other way, then the **AT END** would be of no help to us in detecting an empty file while executing the first **READ**.

2.7 THE PERFORM VERB

The **PERFORM** verb is one of the most powerful in the **COBOL** repertoire. What we are saying in this statement is that we want to carry out the instructions in another part of the program. They may be carried out just once, or a specified number of times, or—as in this case—repeatedly *until* a certain condition is true. We have two concepts here, both very important, that will be used in every program from now on, so it is important to understand them thoroughly. They are the idea of a paragraph and the idea of *conditional execution*.

2.8 THE COBOL PARAGRAPH

The first notion needing precise definition is that of a *paragraph*. A **COBOL** paragraph is simply a group of sentences preceded by a paragraph name. A paragraph name is defined according to the same rules that govern the formation of names for files, records, and data items—with the one additional flexibility that a paragraph name is not required to contain any letters. That is, it is permitted to consist of digits only or a combination of digits and hyphens only. This flexibility is seldom utilized in practice, however, and we shall never do so in this book. A paragraph name is required to begin somewhere in the A area, that is, in columns 8, 9, 10, or 11. We shall always begin paragraph names in column 8.

You have probably noticed that all of the paragraph names used in examples so far begin with a letter and three digits. This is not required by **COBOL**, but is a convention we shall use throughout this book. The purpose of this prefix code is to make it easier to locate a paragraph in the program listing. We shall talk more about the prefix convention in Chapter 4 when we discuss techniques of program design. For now, we will only state that if the prefix is used, paragraphs must *always* be written in sequence by prefix. For this reason prefix numbers should always be incremented in steps of at least ten to allow for the insertion of new paragraphs if the program is modified. That is, write **B010, B020, B030, . . .**, not **B001, B002, B003, . . .**.

A paragraph consists of all of the sentences from the one immediately following the paragraph name until the one just before the next paragraph name (or until the end of the program).

The only purpose in organizing statements into paragraphs that will be utilized in the body of this book is to permit the statements to be referred to by a **PERFORM** verb.* In our program we are saying that we want the paragraph named **B010-PROCESS-WRITE-READ** to be executed (that is, performed) over and over *until* a certain condition becomes true.

This paragraph is the one that, as its name is intended to suggest, basically does all the work of this program. Whenever this paragraph is about to be executed, there will always be one record from the input file that has not yet been written. The *first* time the paragraph is executed, that will be the record that was brought into the computer by the first **READ**. The first thing to be done is to move that waiting record from the input area (**TEXT-IN-RECORD**) to the output area (**LINE-OUT-RECORD**). Now we say to write that record to the output file, which will be sent to the printer. Finally we read—or perhaps *attempt to read*—another record from the input file. If there is such a record, the **AT END** phrase on this **READ** has no effect, just as before. And just as before, if this **READ** encounters the situation where no more records remain, then the statement in the **AT END** phrase will be carried out.

It should be noted that when we execute a **READ**, the information coming from the input file replaces whatever was in the record area for that file in the Data Division; the previous information in the record area is no longer available, unless it had previously been stored somewhere else as well.

2.9 THE OUT-OF-DATA-FLAG

Let us summarize what happens to the contents of the data item named **OUT-OF-DATA-FLAG** as the execution of the program proceeds. First, before encountering the first **READ**, we move the word **NO** to the flag. Then, for as long as there are records being read, neither the **AT END** phrase on the first **READ** nor the **AT END** phrase on the **READ** that is carried out repeatedly in the performed paragraph has any effect. In other words, as long as there are records, **OUT-OF-DATA-FLAG** will continue to contain **NO**. However, whenever either **READ** encounters the end of the file—whether that be the very first time or the ten-thousandth—the word **YES** will be moved to **OUT-OF-DATA-FLAG**.

---

* We will learn in chapter 19 that there is a statement called GO TO that is involved with paragraph names as well, but we shall have little occasion in this book to use the GO TO statement.

2.10 CONDITIONAL EXECUTION

Now, with one additional item of information, we can see how the whole program works. The crucial thing to know is that when the **PERFORM** statement is encountered, the condition after the word **UNTIL** is checked first, *before* performing the named paragraph. This means that if, in fact, there was *no* data to be read in the file, the **AT END** phrase on the very first **READ** will have moved **YES** to **OUT-OF-DATA-FLAG** and the paragraph named in the **PERFORM** is not executed. Instead, the statement after the **PERFORM** is executed.

The **CLOSE** verb names both files, and the **STOP RUN**, as before, says that the execution of this program should stop. Observe that **STOP RUN** is not required to be the last statement in the program. It will always be the last one *executed*, in point of time, but it is not required to be—and indeed, seldom will be—*physically* the statement on the last line of the program.

2.11 ANOTHER LOOK AT THE BASIC PROGRAM STRUCTURE

This program, simple as it is, exhibits the structuring technique that will be the basis for almost all programs in this book. It is, therefore, important to understand it thoroughly, so let's try to summarize it.

A program will always begin with a group of statements right at the beginning of the Procedure Division that we will call the main line routine. Something like **A000-MAIN-LINE-ROUTINE** is suitable for its name. Schematically it will usually consist of the following operations:

Preliminary operations
PERFORM
Wrap-up operations
STOP RUN

The preliminary operations will include things such as opening files and carrying out an initial **READ** for input files. This initial **READ** has the function of checking for the possibility of a missing or empty data file and of getting the basic process started. It is, accordingly, called a *priming* **READ**. The major work of the program is carried out in the paragraph named by the **PERFORM**. Within that paragraph is a **READ** with an **AT END** phrase that sets the flag to indicate when the file has been processed completely. The setting of this flag stops repeated execution of the paragraph by virtue of the testing carried out by the **PERFORM**.

It is helpful to display the sequence in which the verbs of this program will be executed for several small files. Here is a complete listing of all of the verbs executed if the data file is missing or empty.

OPEN
MOVE
READ (the priming **READ**; sets flag)
PERFORM (tests condition and does *not* give control to named paragraph)
CLOSE
STOP

It should be understood that we consider the **PERFORM** verb to have been "executed" even though, in this case, it did not cause the named paragraph to be carried out. The **PERFORM** verb was encountered and it carried out the testing, but on the basis of that testing did not call on the named paragraph. This is one form of its execution.

Here is the sequence of verb execution for a file containing one line:

```
OPEN
MOVE
READ (the priming READ; does not set flag)
PERFORM (tests condition and gives control to named paragraph)
MOVE
WRITE
READ (the performed READ; sets flag)
PERFORM (tests condition and does not give control to named paragraph)
CLOSE
STOP
```

Here is the sequence of statement execution for a file containing two lines:

```
OPEN
MOVE
READ (the priming READ; does not set flag)
PERFORM (tests condition and gives control to named paragraph)
MOVE
WRITE
READ (the performed READ; does not set flag)
PERFORM (tests condition and gives control to named paragraph)
MOVE
WRITE
READ (the performed READ; sets flag)
PERFORM (tests condition and does not give control to named paragraph)
CLOSE
STOP
```

The fundamental difference between this program and the one in Chapter 1 is in the conditional and repeated execution of the paragraph named in the **PERFORM** statement. Before, to print out four lines we had to put four **WRITE** statements in the program. Here, in the paragraph named **B010-PROCESS-WRITE-READ**, we have *one* **MOVE**, *one* **WRITE**, and *one* **READ**, all of which are executed as many times as necessary to process all of the lines in the data file. As we prepare the program we do not know—indeed, we *cannot* know—how many records there will be in the data file, but that doesn't matter. The program is designed to handle that variability correctly.

2.12 SAMPLES OF OUTPUT FROM RUNNING THE PROGRAM

This program was compiled, then run three times with three different data files. The first file consisted of one line; when the program was run with this file it produced this line of output:

```
THIS FILE CONSISTS OF ONE LINE. UNUSUAL, BUT NOT IMPOSSIBLE.
```

The program was next run with a different data file containing six lines, the fifth of which was entirely blank. Its output was this:

```
DONALD G. GOLDEN
CIS DEPARTMENT
CLEVELAND STATE UNIVERSITY
CLEVELAND, OHIO 44115

---FIRST CLASS MAIL---
```

(If there is any doubt in your mind, let us emphasize that a blank line is *not* the same thing as the end of the input!) Finally, the program was run with a data file of 14 lines, which produced this output:

```
LAST AMONG THE ESSENTIAL PERSONALITY TRAITS FOR
PROGRAMMING, WE MIGHT LIST SENSE OF HUMOR.  THE COMPUTER
"DOTH MAKE FOOLS OF US ALL," SO THAT ANY FOOL WITHOUT THE
ABILITY TO SHARE A LAUGH ON HIMSELF WILL BE UNABLE TO
TOLERATE PROGRAMMING FOR LONG.  IT HAS BEEN SAID WITH GREAT
PERSPICACITY THAT THE PROGRAMMER'S NATIONAL ANTHEM IS
"AAAAAHHHHH."  WHEN WE FINALLY SEE THE LIGHT, WE SEE HOW
ONCE AGAIN WE HAVE FALLEN INTO SOME FOOLISH ASSUMPTION,
SOME OAFISH PRACTICE, OR SOME WITLESS BLUNDER.  ONLY BY
SINGING THE SECOND STANZA, "HA HA HA HA HA," CAN WE LONG
ENDURE THE ROLE OF THE CLOWN.

GERALD M. WEINBERG, THE PSYCHOLOGY OF COMPUTER PROGRAMMING.
```

2.13 THE BASIC STRUCTURE AGAIN

This way of organizing the program will be the basis for just about everything we do in this book. Naturally, later programs will be much more complex than this, but you will still be able to see the same fundamental organization: a main line routine and one (or usually more) paragraphs called into play by **PERFORM**s in the main line routine. Very frequently there will be a number of levels of performed paragraphs, that is, a paragraph that has been activated by a **PERFORM** at a higher level will itself contain a **PERFORM** that activates a paragraph at a lower level. Sometimes there will be more than one input file and/or more than one output file. In such a case the condition for deciding when the job is finished will be more complex, but we shall learn how to write such programs so that they are not really too much harder to understand than this one. And that, of course, is a major reason for sticking with one basic structure in this way: to produce programs that are as simple as possible to understand, which makes them more likely to be correct and much easier to modify.

2.14 A CAUTION

Observe that in a **READ** statement we give the name of a *file*, whereas in a **WRITE** statement we give the name of a *record*. **COBOL** is designed this way because it is possible to read files that have several different formats of records in them, with some kind of information within the records used to let the program know which is which. When this is done, there will be a number of record descriptions following the **FD** entry. Since it is impossible to know before getting a record which format we have, **COBOL** specifies that we name the *file* in the **READ** statement. It is also possible to produce output files that have a variety of record formats, but when this happens, we can always know which kind of record it is we are writing. That is the reason for the difference between the **READ** and **WRITE** verb formats, but whether it makes sense to you or not, you have to do it! It may help to memorize the phrase "**READ** a file, **WRITE** a record."

REVIEW QUESTIONS

1. What is the difference between the File Section and the Working-Storage Section?

2. In both programs thus far, we have used file names that contain the word "file" and record names that contain the word "record." Does **COBOL** make any use of that information?

3. The Data Division for the program in this chapter contains two **FD** entries. Is it essential that they be written in the order given?

4. Is it required that the Working-Storage Section come after the File Section?

5. Suppose that the program did not contain the **MOVE** statement to put **NO** in **OUT-OF-DATA-FLAG**. What would the program do?

6. Literary usage in the United States is to place a period at the end of a sentence *inside* a closing quote. What would happen if we did that in the **PERFORM** statement in this program?

7. Is the blank line between the main line routine and the performed paragraph optional or required?

8. What is the difference in the naming rules for paragraphs compared with the rules for data-names?

9. Could a paragraph consist of only one sentence?

10. Suppose an input file has only one type of record. Could we not then specify the *record* name in the **READ** statement instead of the file name?

11. Would it have been permissible to have two **CLOSE** statements naming one file each, instead of one **CLOSE** statement naming both files?

ANSWERS

1. The File Section describes information in records coming directly into the computer from an input device such as a CRT, or going directly out of it to an output device such as a printer. The Working-Storage Section describes information that is not directly coming from or going to an

input or output device. We say "not directly" because we shall see that information in the Working-Storage Section can be transferred to an output area and then written, if we wish.

2. Not at all. If we were to use **TEXT-IN-RECORD** as the name of a file and **TEXT-IN-FILE** as the name of a record, the **COBOL** compiler would never know the difference. This would be a silly thing to do, however, since it is very important to try to write programs that are as easy as possible for a human being to read and understand easily.

3. No. Bear in mind, however, that the **01** entry giving the name and format of the record does have to come right after the **FD** for the file in which that record appears. In other words, a complete file description consists of the **FD** line, the various clauses such as **LABEL RECORDS ARE OMITTED** and others that we shall encounter later, and all record descriptions for that file. In later programs we shall see that the complete file description can easily run to dozens of lines.

4. Yes.

5. We can never assume anything about the contents of a data item unless we have put something there. Without the **MOVE**, **OUT-OF-DATA-FLAG** would contain whatever was in that part of the computer storage before our program came into the machine. Since it is unlikely that the previous program would have left the word **YES** in that spot, the program would probably work properly, but it would be extremely unwise to get in the habit of doing things that way. (We shall learn later that there is another and slightly simpler way to give a data item an initial value, using the **VALUE** clause.)

6. A compiler would consider the literal to consist of four characters including the period, and the sentence would not have a closing period. *As it happens*, the absence of the period for sentence punctuation would not hurt *in this case*, so the program would compile without an indication of error. However, this four-character literal—including the period—would never be equal to the three-character literal—without the period—so the program would not operate correctly. Specifically how it would work would depend on the particular **COBOL** compiler. With the system used to write and test programs for this book, the program would terminate with an error message when it tried to read past the physical end of the input file. Other systems might simply print the last line over and over, or print out meaningless garbage.

7. Optional, as blank lines always are, but strongly recommended for readability.

8. All data-names must contain at least one letter. Paragraph names have no such requirement.

9. Certainly.

10. No way. The specified formats must be adhered to in all cases, and **READ** statements must always name files.

11. Sure.

EXERCISE

You are to make the following changes in the program of Figure 2.1, enter the program into the computer, and run it. Here are the changes:

1. Change the **PICTURE** clause for **OUT-OF-DATA-FLAG** so that only one character is used instead of three, then change the **PROCEDURE DIVISION** in the appropriate places so that **Y** and **N** are used in place of **YES** and **NO**.
2. Change the program so that there is a separate **OPEN** for each file and a separate **CLOSE** for each file.
3. Devise new names to replace **TEXT-IN-FILE**, **TEXT-IN-RECORD**, **LINE-OUT-FILE**, and **LINE-OUT-RECORD**, and replace all occurrences of these identifiers with your new names.
4. Make up a new data file so that the printed output will be something of your choice.

Go back to the exercise in Chapter 1 and read the four "things to keep in mind," observing that the last one does not apply in this case, since quotes in data do not cause the problem discussed earlier. The Irish are in business this time!

CHAPTER 3

DATA DIVISION ELEMENTS AND THE ARITHMETIC VERBS

3.1 INTRODUCTION

In Chapter 1 we learned the fundamentals of what a **COBOL** program looks like and in Chapter 2 the basic program structure involved in reading data, processing it, and writing results. Building on this foundation, we are now ready to put a little flesh on the program skeleton and tackle a more difficult task than those in the previous chapters.

The processing task that we shall study in this chapter involves reading a file of data, and doing a bit of processing and writing one line for each input record. The information on a record describes one item in a simplified inventory control system. Each record contains a part number, a quantity on hand, a quantity received, and a unit price. For each record we are to print a line that contains all this information plus the new quantity on hand and the total value of this new quantity.

The main concepts to be studied in this chapter involve some of the basic elements of the Data Division, and the **COBOL** verbs for specifying arithmetic operations. There is nothing new about the basic program structure. The complete program is shown in Figure 3.1. Before studying it in detail, let us glance at it to get an idea of what is familiar and what is new.

There are four divisions as always, with no surprises in the first two. The Data Division contains a File Section and a Working-Storage Section as before. The presence of the **01** and **05** level numbers in the record description is new, and we shall discuss that in some detail shortly. Observe that a new convention has been employed in assigning data names, namely, all data names in the input record begin with the prefix **I**, all data names in the output record begin with the prefix **O**, and the one item in the Working-Storage Section begins with the prefix **W**. This is one possible data naming convention, among many others, that is intended to improve understandability of a program.

Notice that instead of **PICTURE** we have used the permissible abbreviation **PIC**. The word **PICTURE** must be written so many times—many hundreds in some program—that **COBOL** permits this abbreviation. There are a few other abbreviations of reserved words. *Only these few abbreviations are permitted.* You

may not abbreviate the word **PICTURE** as **PICT**, you may not abbreviate
PERFORM in any way whatsoever, etc. The other new features in the **PICTURE**
clause will be discussed in detail later.

The item for the **W-OUT-OF-DATA-FLAG** is only one character this time
instead of three; we are going to use the letters **Y** and **N** instead of **YES** and **NO** to
save a bit of space.

Within the Procedure Division there are three new features. One is that the
MOVE statement uses a new reserved word, **SPACES**, for blanking out the entire
contents of the **INVENTORY-OUT-RECORD**, for a reason that we shall discuss in
due course. The other two new items are the **ADD** and **MULTIPLY** verbs that we
shall also consider in detail later. Finally, although this is not a new feature, we
have changed the name of the second paragraph in the Procedure Division to
B010-LIST-INVENTORY-DATA. The reason we have made this change is to
emphasize the *function* that the paragraph performs, rather than just the
sequence of operations. In all future examples we shall try to follow this convention. That is, the name of a paragraph should identify the unique function
that the paragraph performs in the program, rather than just indicating what
processes are carried out.

```
IDENTIFICATION DIVISION.
PROGRAM-ID.
     INVENTRY.
DATE-WRITTEN.
     OCTOBER 24, 1986.

ENVIRONMENT DIVISION.
INPUT-OUTPUT SECTION.
FILE-CONTROL.
     SELECT INVENTORY-IN-FILE        ASSIGN TO S-INVENIN.
     SELECT INVENTORY-OUT-FILE       ASSIGN TO S-INVENOUT.

DATA DIVISION.
FILE SECTION.
FD   INVENTORY-IN-FILE
     LABEL RECORDS ARE OMITTED.
01   INVENTORY-IN-RECORD.
     05   I-PART-NUMBER              PIC X(6).
     05   I-QTY-ON-HAND              PIC 9(5).
     05   I-QTY-RECEIVED             PIC 9(4).
     05   I-UNIT-PRICE               PIC 9(3)V99.

FD   INVENTORY-OUT-FILE
     LABEL RECORDS ARE OMITTED.
01   INVENTORY-OUT-RECORD.
     05   O-PART-NUMBER              PIC X(6).
     05   FILLER                     PIC X(4).
     05   O-QTY-ON-HAND              PIC 9(5).
     05   FILLER                     PIC X(3).
     05   O-QTY-RECEIVED             PIC 9(4).
     05   FILLER                     PIC X(3).
     05   O-UNIT-PRICE               PIC 9(3).99.
     05   FILLER                     PIC X(3).
     05   O-NEW-QTY-ON-HAND          PIC 9(5).
     05   FILLER                     PIC X(3).
     05   O-COST                     PIC 9(6).99.
```

```
WORKING-STORAGE SECTION.
01  W-OUT-OF-DATA-FLAG              PIC X.

PROCEDURE DIVISION.
A000-MAIN-LINE-ROUTINE.
    OPEN INPUT INVENTORY-IN-FILE
        OUTPUT INVENTORY-OUT-FILE.
    MOVE 'N' TO W-OUT-OF-DATA-FLAG.
    READ INVENTORY-IN-FILE
        AT END MOVE 'Y' TO W-OUT-OF-DATA-FLAG.
    PERFORM B010-LIST-INVENTORY-DATA
        UNTIL W-OUT-OF-DATA-FLAG = 'Y'.
    CLOSE INVENTORY-IN-FILE
        INVENTORY-OUT-FILE.
    STOP RUN.

B010-LIST-INVENTORY-DATA.
    MOVE SPACES TO INVENTORY-OUT-RECORD.
    MOVE I-PART-NUMBER TO O-PART-NUMBER.
    MOVE I-QTY-ON-HAND TO O-QTY-ON-HAND.
    MOVE I-QTY-RECEIVED TO O-QTY-RECEIVED.
    MOVE I-UNIT-PRICE TO O-UNIT-PRICE.
    ADD I-QTY-ON-HAND, I-QTY-RECEIVED GIVING O-NEW-QTY-ON-HAND.
    MULTIPLY O-NEW-QTY-ON-HAND BY I-UNIT-PRICE GIVING O-COST.
    WRITE INVENTORY-OUT-RECORD.
    READ INVENTORY-IN-FILE
        AT END MOVE 'Y' TO W-OUT-OF-DATA-FLAG.
```

FIGURE 3.1   A program to perform a simple inventory control calculation for each record in an input file.

3.2   THE IDEA OF THE LEVEL STRUCTURE

The basic idea of the COBOL level structure is not very complicated. It is simply that we often want to be able to describe elements of data as being parts of larger groupings. In the case at hand, we have a file named INVENTORY-IN-FILE containing a record name INVENTORY-IN-RECORD, consisting, as it happens, of 20 characters. Sometimes we want to be able to refer to the entire 20 characters of the record by that one name. At other times we want to be able to refer to the individual items themselves, one at a time.

The COBOL scheme is that the first grouping of data, which is the most inclusive, must be given the level number 01; items within that group are given higher level numbers. Here we have used 05 as the higher number, but it could have been 02 or 10 or anything else up to a maximum of 49.

To show the level structure as clearly as possible, we indent the beginnings of lines so that all entries at a given level are aligned vertically. We shall ordinarily indent by four spaces.

An item that is further subdivided is called a *group item*. An item that is not further subdivided is called an *elementary item*. For instance, the 01 level item, INVENTORY-IN-RECORD, is a group item consisting of the four 05 level elementary items shown.

It will often happen that there will be levels within levels. For instance, consider the hypothetical portion of a record description shown at the top of the next page.

```
01  PAYROLL-RECORD.
    05  NAME.
        10  INITIAL-1               PIC X.
        10  LAST-NAME               PIC X(20).
    05  DATE-OF-HIRE.
        10  MONTH-OF-HIRE           PIC 99.
        10  DAY-OF-HIRE             PIC 99.
        10  YEAR-OF-HIRE            PIC 99.
    05  PAY-NUMBER                  PIC 9(6).
```

PAYROLL-RECORD is a group item consisting of three items at the 05 level, two of which are themselves group items. **NAME**, for instance, consists of two elementary items named **INITIAL-1** and **LAST-NAME**. **DATE-OF-HIRE** is a group item consisting of three elementary items for the month, day, and year. **PAY-NUMBER** is an elementary item, since it is not further subdivided—even though it has the same level number as group items elsewhere in the record.

The meaning of this record description can be shown graphically like this:

PAYROLL-RECORD						
NAME			DATE-OF-HIRE			PAY-NUMBER
INIT	LAST-NAME		MO	DAY	YR	

```
1  2  3  4  5  6  7  8  9 10 11 12 13 14 15 16 17 18 19 20 21  22 23  24 25  26 27  28 29 30 31 32 33
```

The first elementary item in the record is **INITIAL-1**, which is one character and occupies character position 1 in the record. The next elementary item, **LAST-NAME**, is 20 characters long and occupies positions 2-21. The group item consisting of these two elementary items, **NAME**, occupies character positions 1-21 and is 21 characters in length. The next elementary item after **LAST-NAME** is **MONTH-OF-HIRE**; its two characters therefore occupy positions 22-23. Likewise **DAY-OF-HIRE** takes up positions 24-25 and **YEAR-OF-HIRE**, positions 26-27. The group item **DATE-OF-HIRE** therefore occupies positions 22-27, and is 6 characters in length. The elementary item **PAY-NUMBER** is in positions 28-33 and is also 6 characters long.

It is always possible to determine the character positions occupied by each group and elementary item in a record by this kind of analysis. The key idea is that the first elementary item begins in position 1, and the successive elementary items after that occupy character positions in sequence. Knowing the character positions occupied by elementary items, it is possible to establish the character positions taken up by group items.

It is instructive to note that the **COBOL** compiler has to go through an analysis of exactly the sort just sketched, since it must translate all data-names into references to character positions in the internal storage of the computer.

A fundamental Data Division rule says that elementary items must have **PICTURE** clauses and group items must not. Conceivably **COBOL** could have been designed to permit or require **PICTURE** clauses for group items, but it would have been pointless, since the compiler can always determine the size of a group item by adding up the number of characters in the elementary items of which it is composed.

Another basic rule says that group items are always considered by the compiler to be alphanumeric. Group items do not have PICTUREs, of course, so this is simply a rule of the language. This is true even if all of the elementary items in the group are numeric. The rule makes complete sense in terms of the way group items are moved, but there is no need at this time to become enmeshed in the details.

The programmer has no choice in assigning 01 as the level number for the most inclusive group item, which is the entire record. However, whether to assign the successive subdivisions the level numbers 05, 10, 15, 20, etc., as we shall do in this book, or to use 02, 03, 04, etc., or some other way, is a matter of free choice. The way we are doing it is traditional in many programming installations, presumably because at one time it was thought that programmers would occasionally want to insert new group items between existing levels when they made program modifications. It turns out that this is done very infrequently, but the pattern has caught on.

3.3 NEW PICTURE CLAUSE FEATURES

There are three new features in the PICTURE clause for this program, two for describing the internal representation and arrangement of data within the computer, and one for describing how information is to be prepared for output. This last is called *editing*. In the programs in Chapters 1 and 2, there was no processing of information other than to move it without change from one place in the computer to another. When this is done, each character of information is described in the PICTURE clause by the letter X. We recall that any information described with the letter X is called alphanumeric, which can include letters, digits, the character "blank," and all of the special characters (such as punctuation) that a particular computer is capable of representing. Now it is perfectly possible for an alphanumeric item, designated as such by Xs in its PICTURE clause, to consist of numeric digits only. This would be true of a United States Social Security number, for instance, so long as it is written without hyphens as it ordinarily would be in a computer. However, *any time arithmetic operations of any type are to be done on an item the item must be described as numeric*, which is done by using 9's in its PICTURE clause instead of X's. Each 9, however many there are, stands for one decimal digit. For example, the item named I-QTY-ON-HAND is seen to be described as having five digits: the 9 designates numeric digits and the 5 says there are five of them. This, of course, could also have been written 99999. The item I-QTY-RECEIVED has four digits. Observe that the item named I-PART-NUMBER is described as having six *alphanumeric* characters. Even though the part number may, in fact, be entirely numeric, as its name would seem to suggest, we never do arithmetic with it, so it is designated as alphanumeric. This also points out that it is by no means necessary that the elementary items within a record be all numeric or all alphanumeric.

3.4   THE ASSUMED DECIMAL POINT

We have set up this application on the assumption that the quantities involved are always whole numbers. We can have 12 hammers or 143 feet of wire, but not 63.4 pounds of lead. (This is, of course, an unrealistic assumption, made as usual to keep things simple for the time being.) But what is to be done when we have an item like price, where it is really not possible to assume that items always have prices that are whole dollars?

The answer is that we have a way of telling **COBOL** that an item is to be treated *as though* it had a decimal point in a specified position. Not an *actual* decimal point, mind you, but rather an *assumed* or *implied* decimal point. We are thinking of a typical situation where a four-column field in an input record might contain the digits 6397. We want to tell the **COBOL** compiler to treat that as if it stands for 63.97, which might be a price in dollars and cents. *This does not mean that there is a decimal point typed in the record.*

Common practice in writing numeric quantities that contain assumed decimal points is to write a caret (a sort of upside-down **v**) in the desired position like so:

$$63_\wedge 97$$

In the **COBOL PICTURE** clause, this assumed decimal point is represented by a **V** (presumably chosen because it looks like an upside-down caret!) which is inserted into the **PICTURE** clause in the desired position. It is very important to understand that whereas the **V** in the **PICTURE** clause takes up one character space in the **PICTURE** clause, the assumed decimal point in the data item is still *assumed: it does not take up space in the input record*. In our case, with the item **I-UNIT-PRICE**, we are describing a five-column elementary item with a decimal point assumed between the third and fourth digits to make a dollars-and-cents amount. There is no decimal point keyed in the record. (In fact, it is fairly difficult in **COBOL** to read data values that contain actual decimal points.) The **COBOL** compiler, in setting up the computer program to handle arithmetic on this item, will take into account all of the proper decimal point considerations.

3.5   THE ACTUAL DECIMAL POINT

When it comes time to print an item such as a dollars-and-cents amount, we do want the program to produce an actual dot on the printed listing. This is done by placing an actual decimal point in the **PICTURE** clause in the desired position. We see this in the items **O-UNIT-PRICE** and **O-COST**. When an item such as unit price is moved from **I-UNIT-PRICE** to **O-UNIT-PRICE**, the **COBOL** program will take into proper account the relationship between the assumed decimal point and the actual decimal point and put the digits of the item into the correct positions.

One more bit of information, hopefully not too confusing, and we can set aside the decimal point question for the time being. It must be understood that arithmetic can be done only on *numeric* items, by which is meant items containing only digits. The **PICTURE** for a numeric item must contain **9**'s, not **X**'s, and the **PICTURE** must *not* contain an actual decimal point. An item that contains an *actual* decimal point is *not* numeric and therefore may not be used in arithmetic operations. Thus, once **I-UNIT-PRICE** has been moved to **O-UNIT-PRICE** it is not permissible to carry out arithmetic operations on it there. Of course, it still exists as a numeric item in **I-UNIT-PRICE** and can still be used in that form in arithmetic operations.

3.6 LEADING BLANKS IN DATA

It should be realized that an item containing blanks is *not* numeric and, therefore, cannot be used in arithmetic operations. This means that, in general, leading zeros in values in input records *cannot be replaced by blanks*, unless appropriate measures are taken in the Procedure Division as discussed in Chapter 15. Although some versions of **COBOL** will accept leading blanks, in other versions failure to heed this advice will cause the program to fail, with not-very-helpful messages on the order of "data exception." Key in all of those leading zeros!

3.7 THE FILLER ITEM

It commonly happens that we need to describe characters in a record that we never refer to by name. Sometimes these are positions that are to contain blanks, as in our case. Sometimes they are elementary items that will receive information when something is moved to the group of which they are a part. In any event, they do describe character positions within the record and are counted in determining how many characters the record contains, but they do not have a name, and therefore cannot be referenced except as part of the group item that contains them.

In our situation all that is involved is that when we print the line for each inventory item, we don't want the individual numbers bunched up together, but rather want some blank spaces between them. The amount of space to be provided is a decision of the person who designs the format of the output report. These decisions depend on questions of making the printing fit a preprinted form, general questions of pleasing appearance, and the like. We see that in this program four spaces have been provided in one place and three in others.

The insertion of **FILLER** characters implies nothing whatsoever about the contents of those characters. In our case, it *may not* be assumed that those positions will automatically be blank. We shall take care of that question later, in the Procedure Division, and we shall see in Chapter 6 how it might have been done with a **VALUE** clause in the Working-Storage Section of the Data Division.

FILLER is a **COBOL** reserved word, not a programmer-supplied data-name. The word **FILLER** accordingly can, and usually does, appear many times in a program, since it is not subject to the uniqueness rule that applies to data-names.

COBOL-85

In **COBOL-85** the word **FILLER** can actually be omitted. Thus, for example, in this version of **COBOL** we can write the definition of **INVENTORY-OUT-RECORD** as follows:

```
01   INVENTORY-OUT-RECORD.
     05   O-PART-NUMBER              PIC X(6).
     05                              PIC X(4).
     05   O-QTY-ON-HAND              PIC 9(5).
     05                              PIC X(3).
     05   O-QTY-RECEIVED             PIC 9(4).
     05                              PIC X(3).
     05   O-UNIT-PRICE               PIC 9(3).99.
     05                              PIC X(3).
     05   O-NEW-QTY-ON-HAND          PIC 9(5).
     05                              PIC X(3).
     05   O-COST                     PIC 9(6).99.
```

This is *exactly* equivalent to the version shown in Figure 3.1 and either approach may be used.

END COBOL-85

3.8   THE MAIN LINE ROUTINE

The main line routine is just the same (except for data-names) as that of the program in Chapter 2, with the minor difference that we are using **Y** and **N** as the values for the out-of-data flag instead of **YES** and **NO**.

3.9   THE PROCESSING PARAGRAPH

The processing paragraph involves a number of new features, the most important of which are the verbs for specifying arithmetic, **ADD** and **MULTIPLY** in this program. First, however, there are certain preliminary operations.

The first of these is a **MOVE** statement that puts spaces (blanks) in all character positions of the output record. **SPACES** is a new type of reserved word called a *figurative constant*. When the **COBOL** compiler encounters this word, it supplies as many of the character *blank* as there are characters in the receiving item. We have designated the entire record in this case, which happens to contain room for 51 characters. Observe incidentally that this is a *group* **MOVE**, which places blanks in all 11 of the elementary items in the group item. (The **FILLER** items are considered to be elementary items since they have **PICTURE**s, even though they cannot be referred to by name.)

The purpose of moving spaces to this record is to get blanks into all of the **FILLER**s. This is necessary because, as we noted previously, setting aside storage locations in the **FILLER** items does not tell us anything about what those positions will contain. If we do not move spaces to this record, those positions would contain whatever was left there by the program that used the computer before this one. By sheerest accident that might happen to be blanks, but it would be foolish to assume so. Without this **MOVE** statement, our printed output would accordingly contain miscellaneous garbage in the positions between fields that should have been blank.

3.10   THE PROCESSING

The processing of the data on an input record begins with moving the four items on the record to their desired positions in the output record that will later be written. There is nothing really new about them except that when the unit price is moved from the input record to the output record, editing is performed, namely, the insertion of an actual decimal point into the dollars-and-cents unit price.

3.11   THE ADD STATEMENT

Now we come to something quite new, a statement that calls for two numbers to be added, in this statement:

        ADD I-QTY-ON-HAND, I-QTY-RECEIVED GIVING O-NEW-QTY-ON-HAND.

This means: form the sum of **I-QTY-ON-HAND** and **I-QTY-RECEIVED**, and place that sum in **O-NEW-QTY-ON-HAND**. Neither **I-QTY-ON-HAND** nor **I-QTY-RECEIVED** is changed by this action. The comma is entirely optional; the action of the statement would be exactly the same without it. It may be used as one wishes if it is thought to improve readability. Many programmers never use the optional commas, however, since they are an additional source of possible error and since they are sometimes hard to distinguish from periods in printed listings.

(There is much more to be said about the **ADD** statement. We shall devote considerable time to the different forms of this verb and the other arithmetic verbs after seeing how the rest of the program works.)

3.12   THE MULTIPLY STATEMENT

The **MULTIPLY** statement that comes next computes the total cost of the new amount of inventory on hand for this item. As with the **ADD** statement, neither of the quantities in this computation is changed as a result. We shall see shortly that this is true when any of the arithmetic verbs are used with the **GIVING** option.

It should be pointed out that we are making an assumption about the relative size of the quantities that go into this multiplication. According to the input **PICTURE**s, the largest possible quantity on hand would be 99999 and the largest possible unit price would be 999.99. If both of these maximum sizes occurred for any inventory item the product—the total cost for that item—would be $99,998,000.01. That would lead to a problem because in the Data Division for **O-COST** we specified only six digits before the decimal point, not eight. The **COBOL** compiler will accordingly produce a warning message indicating the possibility that high order digits can be lost in this multiplication.

However, it is reasonable to assume that the two factors in the multiplication would not both take on the maximum sizes for any one inventory item.

An item that the company would stock in very large quantity would tend to have a low unit price, and conversely an item with a high unit price would tend to be stocked in low quantities. The assumption made in setting up this program is that the total cost of any one inventory item will never exceed $999,999.99. So long as that assumption is justified, the compiler's warning message about the possibility of lost digits need not concern us. Naturally, such assumptions must not be made casually. If we were talking about IBM's stock of microcomputers, for example, this would presumably be a very bad assumption.

This completes the processing that is done by this program, so we may proceed to write the record that has now been developed, get another input record, and repeat the process.

3.13 THE OUTPUT

The program was run with a small sample file of data and produced the following output:

```
123456    00012    0003    010.00    00015    000150.00
123459    11111    0022    001.00    11133    011133.00
234567    00005    0006    340.44    00011    003744.84
23AAX4    00400    0148    001.54    00548    000843.92
23AAX5    00023    0012    433.00    00035    015155.00
```

Looking at any one line, we see that the value in column 2 plus the value in column 3 equals the value in column 5; this is the result of the statement

```
ADD I-QTY-ON-HAND, I-QTY-RECEIVED GIVING O-NEW-QTY-ON-HAND
```

Also, the value in column 6 on any line is the product of the values in columns 4 and 5, resulting from

```
MULTIPLY O-NEW-QTY-ON-HAND BY I-UNIT-PRICE GIVING O-COST
```

Thus we see that the arithmetic was carried out as desired.

It is always necessary to compare at least a few typical results with hand-calculated values to establish that the program has no obvious errors.

As soon as we have learned the necessary techniques, in Chapter 7, we shall see how to handle a number of matters that would normally be done a bit differently. Ordinary practice would include at least column headings, the deletion of leading zeros, and the provision of appropriate dollar signs and commas to improve readability. We shall also see that it will ordinarily be unusual to do arithmetic on an item after it has been moved to an output record, which is legal in this case only because we did not perform the normal action of replacing leading zeros with blanks.

3.14 GENERAL FORMATS FOR COBOL STATEMENTS

A good deal of flexibility is available in writing many of the COBOL statements, but there are rules that must be followed with great care. It is accordingly necessary for the programmer to be able to determine readily exactly how a given statement may be written. This need is answered by a way of showing the available options that is called the *general format*. Here, for example, is the format for the form of the **ADD** statement that we have just used.

$$
\underline{\text{ADD}} \left\{ \begin{array}{l} \text{identifier-1} \\ \text{literal-1} \end{array} \right\} \left\{ \begin{array}{l} \text{identifier-2} \\ \text{literal-2} \end{array} \right\} \left[\begin{array}{l} \text{identifier-3} \\ \text{literal-3} \end{array} \right] \cdots
$$

$$
\underline{\text{GIVING}} \text{ identifier-m } [\underline{\text{ROUNDED}}] \text{ [identifier-n } [\underline{\text{ROUNDED}}] \text{] } \cdots
$$

$$
[\underline{\text{ON}} \underline{\text{SIZE}} \underline{\text{ERROR}} \text{ imperative-statement}]
$$

We shall consider this carefully after discussing a number of conventions that are used in writing all such formats.

1. All words printed entirely in capital letters are reserved words. All such words have preassigned meanings in **COBOL** and, as we have noted earlier, may not be used in any other way. In a general format, words in capital letters represent an actual occurrence of those words. That is, nothing else may be substituted for them. Reserved words must be spelled exactly as shown. They must not be abbreviated unless an abbreviation is specifically permitted, and plurals of words must not be used unless the plural is specifically allowed.

2. All underlined reserved words are required unless the portion of the format containing them is itself optional. These words are *key words*. If any such word is missing or incorrectly spelled, it is an error and the program cannot be compiled correctly. Reserved words not underlined may be included or omitted at the option of the programmer. These words are used only for the sake of readability and are called *optional words*. However, if they are used, they must be spelled correctly.

3. The characters +, -, <, >, and =, when appearing in formats, are required although they are not underlined.

4. All punctuation and other special characters (except certain symbols discussed below) represent the actual occurrence of those characters. Punctuation is essential where it is shown. Additional punctuation can sometimes be inserted according to rules specified elsewhere. The comma in our **ADD** statement is an example of additional punctuation.

5. Words that are printed in lowercase letters represent information to be supplied by the programmer. In the case of the **ADD** format, in place of identifier-1 we are to write the name of a data item such as **I-QTY-ON-HAND**, and in place of literal-1 we could write 12.6 or 2 or any other number as needed.

6. In order to facilitate references to them in describing the format, some lowercase words are followed by a hyphen and a digit or letter. This modification does not change the meaning of the word. For example, in our **ADD** format identifier-1, identifier-2, identifier-3, etc., are all simply identifiers that are to be supplied by the programmer. It is also not to be inferred by this convention that the identifiers are required to be different. It would be perfectly legitimate to write a statement such as

ADD HOURLY-USAGE, HOURLY-USAGE GIVING USAGE-LIMIT.

This would have the result of putting two times **HOURLY-USAGE** into **USAGE-LIMIT**.

7. Square brackets [ ] are used to indicate that the enclosed item may be either used or omitted depending on the requirements of the particular program. When two or more items are stacked within brackets, one or none of them may be used. In the format at hand, for example, either identifier-3 or literal-3 may be used, or neither. In the **ADD** statement in our program we used neither.

8. Braces { } enclosing vertically stacked items indicate that exactly one of the enclosed items must be chosen. For example, immediately after the word **ADD** one must write either an identifier or a literal and following that one must again write an identifier or a literal. This is simply a precise way of stating the fairly obvious fact that there must be at least two things to be added. One is *not* permitted to write a statement such as

ADD GROSS-PAY GIVING STARTING-VALUE

in an attempt to get the same effect as a **MOVE**.

9. The ellipsis ... indicates that the immediately preceding unit may occur once or any number of times in succession. A *unit* means either a single lowercase word or a group of lowercase words and one or more reserved words included in brackets or braces. In the **ADD** format the ellipsis means that we could have identifier-4 or literal-4, identifier-5 or literal-5, etc.

3.15 BACK TO THE ADD STATEMENT

Now that we have explored the symbolism to be used in presenting the options available in writing **COBOL** statements, let us return to the case at hand, the **ADD** verb. Here it is again, for easy reference, and this time we identify it as Format 2, since in fact it is one of two ways of writing an **ADD**, and the one that is usually given second in reference manuals.

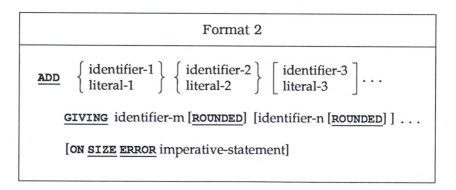

We see that the word **ADD** is underlined, meaning that it must be present; that is only reasonable since all **COBOL** statements must begin with a verb that specifies the action to be performed. Then we have braces enclosing identifier-1 and literal-1; this means that we must make a choice from those two possibilities. Similarly, braces tell us that we must choose between an identifier and a literal for what to write next. Note that braces mean that we are forced to pick one of the items enclosed; we do not have the option of writing neither. The square brackets enclosing identifier-3 and literal-3, however, give us precisely that option: *if we wish to write additional operands*, then the choice once again is between an identifier and a literal. The ellipsis indicates that the previous unit, in this case the choice indicated by the square brackets, may be repeated as many times as desired. What this means is that we may add up as many identifiers and/or literals as we please, simply writing their names or values before the word **GIVING**. Since the word **GIVING** is underlined, it too is required in this format of the **ADD**.

3.16 THE ROUNDED OPTION

Observe that the key word **ROUNDED** is optional in the **ADD** statement, since it appears in square brackets. When used, this applies to a situation where the sum has more decimal places than are provided in the item to which the sum is being sent. This, of course, would not be an oversight (hopefully!), but a deliberate design decision. In our program, for example, management might specify that the cost was to be reported in whole dollars. To accomplish this we would write the **PICTURE** for **O-COST** with no digits to the right of the actual decimal point, and then use the **ROUNDED** option on the **MULTIPLY** verb. Then if the cost turns out to have a cents figure of 49 or less, the cents are dropped and the dollar is left unchanged. If the cents figure comes out to 50 or greater, the cents are still dropped but the dollar amount is increased by 1. This is all that rounding means.

3.17 THE ON SIZE ERROR OPTION

This option permits us to make provision for the possibility that the addition will produce a quantity too large to fit in the space provided for it. If we write this option, we are free to put any sort of statement(s) we wish in the place shown as imperative-statement. This statement could stop the program, or terminate processing of this record after writing an error message, or could call for almost anything we please.

The **ON SIZE ERROR** option is seldom used because there are usually better ways to deal with the problem that it is designed to handle. As we shall learn, it is strongly recommended practice to check input data extensively for validity. If this has been done, the programmer will seldom be in any doubt about whether a result is going to fit in the space provided.

3.18 THE FORMAT 1 ADD

The form of the **ADD** statement that we have just studied is usually listed second in reference manuals. (There is also a third format, the **ADD CORRESPONDING**, but this is seldom used.) The other permissible form of the **ADD** statement is as shown at the top of the next page.

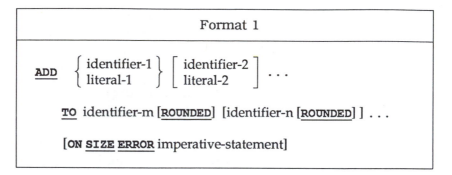

This means to form the sum of all of the quantities listed, including the original value of identifier-m, with the sum replacing the previous value of identifier-m. The difference between the **ADD TO** and **ADD GIVING** forms, therefore, is that with the **ADD TO** the original value of identifier-m is included in the sum, whereas with **ADD GIVING** it is not. If more than one identifier appears after the word **TO**, then the meaning is that the sum of all of the quantities before the word **TO** is added to each of these others separately.

Identifiers appearing in arithmetic statements must always be elementary items. (This does not apply to **ADD CORRESPONDING** and **SUBTRACT COR-RESPONDING**, but as noted previously these will seldom be used.)

Examples of the ADD statement

	Before				After			
	A	B	C	D	A	B	C	D
ADD A TO B	3	6			3	9		
ADD A, B TO C	1	4	7		1	4	12	
ADD A, B TO C, D	1	4	7	22	1	4	12	27
ADD A, B GIVING C	1	4	7		1	4	5	

3.19 THE FORMAT 2 ADD IN COBOL-85

In **COBOL-85** Format 2 has been extended to eliminate an error which occurred commonly in earlier versions of **COBOL**. This extension allows you to insert "**TO** identifier-m" before the word **GIVING**; the resulting format is shown below. In this format the values of all literals and identifiers preceding the word **TO** are added together. The total is then added to the literal or identifier between **TO** and **GIVING**; the result is stored as the new value of identifier-m, identifier-n, etc. Since the word **TO** is not underlined it may be omitted, in which case this version of the Format 2 **ADD** reduces to the older version.

Examples of the extended format 2 ADD statement

	Before				After			
	A	B	C	D	A	B	C	D
ADD A TO B GIVING C	1	4	7		1	4	5	
ADD A, B TO C GIVING D	1	4	7	22	1	4	7	12

```
┌─────────────────────────────────────────────────────────────────────┐
│                        Format 2 - COBOL-85                          │
├─────────────────────────────────────────────────────────────────────┤
│                                                                     │
│         ┌ identifier-1 ┐         ┌ identifier-2 ┐                    │
│  ADD    │              │  ...  TO │              │                   │
│         └ literal-1    ┘         └ literal-2    ┘                    │
│                                                                     │
│     GIVING  identifier-m [ROUNDED]  [identifier-n [ROUNDED] ]  ...   │
│                                                                     │
│     [ON SIZE ERROR imperative-statement]                            │
│                                                                     │
└─────────────────────────────────────────────────────────────────────┘
```

END COBOL-85

3.20   THE SUBTRACT STATEMENT

The two formats for the **SUBTRACT** statement are as shown below.

```
┌─────────────────────────────────────────────────────────────────────┐
│                            Format 1                                 │
├─────────────────────────────────────────────────────────────────────┤
│                                                                     │
│              ┌ identifier-1 ┐  ┌ identifier-2 ┐                      │
│   SUBTRACT   │              │  │              │  ...                 │
│              └ literal-1    ┘  └ literal-2    ┘                      │
│                                                                     │
│     FROM  identifier-m [ROUNDED]  [identifier-n [ROUNDED] ]  ...     │
│                                                                     │
│     [ON SIZE ERROR imperative-statement]                            │
│                                                                     │
└─────────────────────────────────────────────────────────────────────┘
```

```
┌─────────────────────────────────────────────────────────────────────┐
│                            Format 2                                 │
├─────────────────────────────────────────────────────────────────────┤
│                                                                     │
│              ┌ identifier-1 ┐  ┌ identifier-2 ┐                      │
│   SUBTRACT   │              │  │              │  ...                 │
│              └ literal-1    ┘  └ literal-2    ┘                      │
│                                                                     │
│              ┌ identifier-m ┐                                       │
│     FROM     │              │                                       │
│              └ literal-m    ┘                                       │
│                                                                     │
│     GIVING  identifier-n [ROUNDED]  [identifier-o [ROUNDED] ]  ...   │
│                                                                     │
│     [ON SIZE ERROR imperative-statement]                            │
│                                                                     │
└─────────────────────────────────────────────────────────────────────┘
```

In Format 1 the values of all literals or identifiers preceding the word **FROM** are added together and this total is then subtracted from the value of identifier-m and from the value of identifier-n (if stated), etc. The result of the subtractions are then stored as the new values of identifier-m, identifier-n, etc.

In Format 2 the values of all literals or identifiers preceding the word **FROM** are added together, and this total is subtracted from the value of literal-m or identifier-m. The result of the subtraction is then stored as the new value of identifier-n, and, if specified, identifier-o, and so on.

Examples of the SUBTRACT statement

	Before A	B	C	D	After A	B	C	D
SUBTRACT A FROM B	5	9			5	4		
SUBTRACT A, B FROM C	1	4	15		1	4	10	
SUBTRACT A FROM B GIVING C	1	4	15		1	4	3	
SUBTRACT A, B FROM C GIVING D	1	4	15	22	1	4	15	10
SUBTRACT A, B FROM C, D	1	4	15	22	1	4	10	17
SUBTRACT 3 FROM A	12				9			
SUBTRACT A, B FROM 22 GIVING C	2	3	47		2	3	17	

3.21 THE MULTIPLY STATEMENT

The **MULTIPLY** statement also comes in two forms, with and without the word **GIVING**.

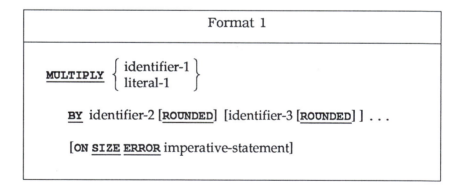

```
┌─────────────────────────────────────────────────────────────┐
│                          Format 1                           │
├─────────────────────────────────────────────────────────────┤
│                                                             │
│  MULTIPLY  { identifier-1 }                                 │
│            { literal-1    }                                 │
│                                                             │
│     BY identifier-2 [ROUNDED] [identifier-3 [ROUNDED] ] ... │
│                                                             │
│     [ON SIZE ERROR imperative-statement]                    │
│                                                             │
└─────────────────────────────────────────────────────────────┘
```

When Format 1 is used, the value of identifier-1 (or literal-1) is multiplied by the value of identifier-2. The value of identifier-2 is then replaced by the product. If identifier-3 is present, the value of identifier-1 or literal-1 is multiplied by identifier-3 and the result placed in identifier-3, and so on. (It may seem to some readers as though normal English usage would suggest that the product should replace the value of identifier-1, but this is not so.)

When the **GIVING** form is used, Format 2, the value of identifier-1 (or literal-1) is multiplied by the value of identifier-2 (or literal-2) and the product is placed in identifier-3, identifier-4, etc. Identifier-2 is unchanged.

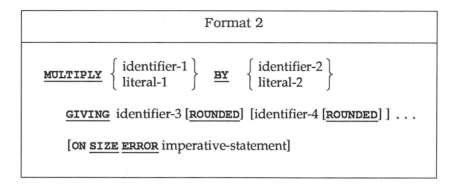

Format 2
MULTIPLY { identifier-1 / literal-1 } BY { identifier-2 / literal-2 }
GIVING identifier-3 [ROUNDED] [identifier-4 [ROUNDED]] . . .
[ON SIZE ERROR imperative-statement]

Examples of the MULTIPLY statement

	Before				After			
	A	B	C	D	A	B	C	D
MULTIPLY A BY B	2	4			2	8		
MULTIPLY A BY B, C	2	4	6		2	8	12	
MULTIPLY A BY B GIVING C	2	4	17		2	4	8	
MULTIPLY A BY B GIVING C, D	2	4	17	20	2	4	8	8
MULTIPLY 4 BY A	3				12			
MULTIPLY A BY 6 GIVING B	3	4			3	18		

Notice in the sixth example that there is a literal after the word **BY**. This is acceptable because the **GIVING** clause places the result of the multiplication in B. We could *not*, however, write the fifth example as

MULTIPLY A BY 4

because we would be trying to place the result in the literal 4!

3.22   THE DIVIDE STATEMENT

This verb has three formats, which are as shown below and on the next page.

In Format 1 the value of identifier-1 or literal-1 is divided into the value of identifier-2, and the value of identifier-2 is replaced by the value of the quotient. If identifier-3 is present, identifier-1 or literal-1 is divided into the value of identifier-3 and the quotient is placed into identifier-3, and so on.

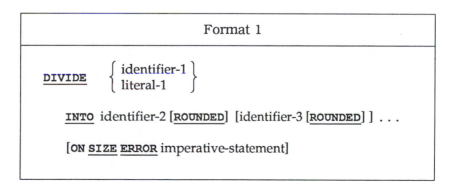

Format 1
DIVIDE { identifier-1 / literal-1 }
INTO identifier-2 [ROUNDED] [identifier-3 [ROUNDED]] . . .
[ON SIZE ERROR imperative-statement]

In Format 2 the value of identifier-1 (or literal-1) is divided into or by the value of identifier-2 (or literal-2). The quotient is stored in identifier-3, identifier-4, etc.

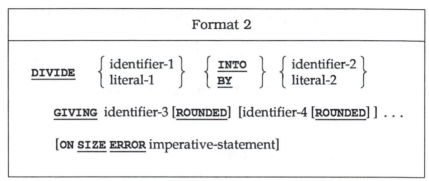

In Format 3 the value of identifier-1 (or literal-1) is divided into or by the value of identifier-2 (or literal-2). The quotient is stored in identifier-3 and the remainder is optionally stored in identifier-4. The remainder is defined as the result of subtracting the product of the quotient and the divisor from the dividend. If the ROUNDED option is also specified, the quotient is rounded after the remainder is determined. The REMAINDER option is seldom used.

```
┌─────────────────────────────────────────────────────────────┐
│                          Format 3                            │
├─────────────────────────────────────────────────────────────┤
│           ⎧ identifier-1 ⎫  ⎧ INTO ⎫  ⎧ identifier-2 ⎫       │
│   DIVIDE  ⎨ literal-1    ⎬  ⎨ BY   ⎬  ⎨ literal-2    ⎬       │
│           ⎩              ⎭  ⎩      ⎭  ⎩              ⎭       │
│                                                              │
│     GIVING identifier-3 [ROUNDED]                            │
│                                                              │
│     [REMAINDER identifier-4]                                 │
│                                                              │
│     [ON SIZE ERROR imperative-statement]                     │
└─────────────────────────────────────────────────────────────┘
```

Examples of the DIVIDE statement

	Before				After			
	A	B	C	D	A	B	C	D
DIVIDE A INTO B	3	15			3	5		
DIVIDE A INTO B, C	3	15	21		3	5	7	
DIVIDE A INTO B GIVING C	3	15	4		3	15	5	
DIVIDE A INTO B GIVING C, D	3	15	4	6	3	15	5	5
DIVIDE A BY B GIVING C	24	12	19		24	12	2	
DIVIDE 2 INTO A	18				9			
DIVIDE A BY 3 GIVING B	24	2			24	8		
DIVIDE A BY B GIVING C REMAINDER D	19	7	0	0	19	7	2	5
DIVIDE A BY B GIVING C REMAINDER D	7	19	0	0	7	19	0	7

3.23 THE HANDLING OF ALGEBRAIC SIGNS

COBOL makes provision for handling signed quantities correctly. That is, if two negative quantities are multiplied, the product is positive; if two quantities having different signs are added, the effect is that of a subtraction, etc.

3.24 MOVING NUMERIC QUANTITIES

Whenever a numeric quantity is placed in an elementary item, either as a result of an arithmetic operation or in a simple MOVE, certain rules govern what is done when the quantity being sent is not the same size as the receiving field.

1. If the receiving field has fewer positions to the right of the decimal point than the item being sent, the extra digits are simply dropped and no warning is given. Thus, if we sent the quantity 1234.567 to a field described by

   PICTURE 9999.99

   the stored result would be 1234.56. Notice that there is *no* automatic rounding; the 7 is simply dropped.

2. If the receiving field has more positions to the right of the decimal point than the item being sent, zeros are supplied. Thus, if the quantity 1234.567 is sent to a field described by

   PICTURE 9999.9999

   the result will be 1234.5670.

3. If the receiving field has more positions to the left of the decimal point than the item being sent, then again zeros are supplied. Thus, if the quantity 1234.567 is sent to a field described by

   PICTURE 9(6).999

   the result will be 001234.567.

4. For the case where the receiving field has fewer positions to the left of the decimal point than the item being sent, we have to distinguish between the case where this is the result of a MOVE and where it is the result of an arithmetic operation.

   a. On a MOVE, the extra digits simply are dropped. Thus if the quantity 1234.567 is sent to a field described by

      PICTURE 99.999

      the result will be 34.567. In this case some compilers will give a warning that significant digits can potentially be lost, but the program will be compiled. If we ignore the compiler's warning and run the program, no additional warning will be given when significant digits are actually lost. Except in highly unusual cases, this will be a very serious error. That is why it is so important to be absolutely certain that any assumptions about maximum sizes of results are justified.

   b. For an arithmetic result, the precise outcome is not predictable, which is to say that it will certainly be wrong, but there is no way of knowing exactly what will be placed in the receiving field. Again, the compiler will issue a warning but if the warning is ignored, there will be no notification of the problem when the program is run. If there can be legitimate questions about the assumptions on the sizes of results, we have an occasion for the use of the ON SIZE ERROR option.

3.25 THE HANDLING OF DECIMAL QUANTITIES IN ARITHMETIC OPERATIONS

The **COBOL** compiler automatically takes care of most of the problems having to do with decimal points. For example, if two numbers to be added do not have the same number of digits after their decimal points, **COBOL** will provide for correctly aligning the quantities before adding. Similarly, the results of arithmetic operations are stored with proper allowance for the relationship between the decimal point location of the result and the decimal point location shown in the Data Division for the item where that result is stored. (In almost all cases in a discussion such as this, we are talking about *assumed* decimal points. Quantities involved in arithmetic operations *must not* have actual decimal points. The result of an arithmetic operation may be placed in an elementary item that has an actual decimal point, if the **GIVING** form of the arithmetic statements are used, but such a data item may not be used in any further arithmetic.)

COBOL-85

However, in **COBOL-85**, the edited result may be moved back to a numeric field and the data is converted back to numeric format. For example, suppose we have three fields defined as follows:

```
01  A       PIC 99V9.
01  B       PIC 99.9.
01  C       PIC 99V9.
```

If we move **A** to **B**, then move **B** to **C**, the results will be as follows.

	Before			After		
	A	B	C	A	B	C
MOVE A TO B.	12ᴧ3	00.0	00ᴧ0	12ᴧ3	12.3	00ᴧ0
MOVE B TO C.	12ᴧ3	12.3	00ᴧ0	12ᴧ3	12.3	12ᴧ3

We must emphasize that this will work only in **COBOL-85**! In earlier versions of **COBOL**, moving **B** to **C** will cause an error; in these versions it is not possible to "unedit" numeric data.

END COBOL-85

It is not quite sufficient, however, to say simply "**COBOL** will take care of the decimal point," and forget about the subject. The problem is that in setting up the Data Division we have to know in complete detail what the various quantities are going to look like. This is particularly true with regard to providing enough space for the maximum size that any arithmetic result could assume. Let us accordingly study this subject a little more closely.

3.26 DECIMAL LOCATION IN ADDITION AND SUBTRACTION

Addition and subtraction do not present too much of a problem. The **COBOL** compiler arranges to align decimal points automatically if the quantities involved do not have the same number of digits after the decimal point. This may involve extra operations for the computer, which will sometimes slow things down, but the change in speed is usually too small to measure and in any case we are not concerning ourselves about such efficiency considerations for now.

Elaborate rules can be devised for determining the maximum size of the result of an addition or subtraction, but the following procedure is recommended. Simply write down all of the operands in the form of all **9**'s, with decimal points properly aligned, and perform the addition using pencil and paper or a pocket calculator. The result will be the biggest number you could ever get. Naturally, if any of the numbers being added are negative, or if we are talking about a subtraction of numbers having the same sign, then the result will be smaller than that. And as noted in connection with the program in Figure 3.1, we may know something about the application that will tell us that the result just could never be that large.

3.27 THE DECIMAL LOCATION ON MULTIPLICATION

The situation with regard to multiplication is a little more complicated than for addition and subtraction, but not much. The rule is this: the product of multiplying two factors has as many digits to the right of the decimal point as the sum of the number of digits to the right of the decimal point in the two factors, and likewise it may have as many digits to the left of the decimal point as the sum of the number of digits to the left of the decimal point in the two factors. That is a mouthful but it is not really too difficult to understand. Consider, for example, the multiplication of 12.345 by 9.87. One of the factors has three digits after the decimal point and the other has two, so the result will have five. One of the factors has two digits before the decimal point and the other one has one, so the product will have three. The product of these two numbers is, in fact, 121.84515.

It must be understood, or course, that we are talking about the *maximum possible* size of results. For instance, if a number is described in the Data Division as having four digit positions before the decimal point, but the actual number has three leading zeros, then of course there will be leading zeros in the product. Somewhat similarly, if we multiply 1.23 by 2.3 the rule tells us that the product *could* have two digits to the left of the decimal point, but the *actual* product is 2.829. This does not mean that the rule is wrong, however, since the rule speaks about *maximum* possible sizes. If we multiply 7.89 by 6.7, then we get 52.863, a product that does indeed have two digits to the left of the decimal point.

3.28 DECIMAL LOCATION ON DIVISION

Division is an altogether different story for two fundamental reasons having to do with mathematics and not COBOL. The first is that the quotient of two numbers does not necessarily have a finite decimal representation. The simplest example is the division of 1 by 3, the result of which cannot be represented exactly in any finite number of decimal digits, but only as a string of as many 3's as we wish to write following the decimal point. The second problem is that it is not possible to state the maximum size of a quotient without knowing both the maximum value of the dividend and the minimum value of the divisor. For example, suppose we have a dividend described by

PICTURE 9999V99

a divisor described by

PICTURE 99V99

and a quotient described by

PICTURE 99999.999

Now, if we do this division

$$\frac{0412.58}{55.11}$$

the stored result will be 00007.486. No problem. But suppose we do this division

$$\frac{7359.10}{00.34}$$

The result this time is 27648.260, which just barely fits in the space allocated for the quotient. And if we do this division

$$\frac{6359.10}{00.05}$$

the result is 127182.000, and there is insufficient room to store the result.

Mathematically, the extreme case of this problem is in the attempt to divide by zero. If we really don't know anything about what the possible number of sizes is, we have to take the largest possible dividend and the smallest possible divisor and provide space for the quotient that would result. In many cases this is far too conservative and will result in considerable wasted space. Again, the proper approach is to know as much as possible about the data and either test your data to be sure your assumptions are justified, using techniques shown in following chapters, or else use the **ON SIZE ERROR** option.

REVIEW QUESTIONS

1. In the program in Figure 3.1 we used prefixes (**I**, **O**, and **W**) to designate the nature of the data items (input, output, and Working-Storage, respectively). Do these prefixes have any meaning in **COBOL**?

2. You are given that each of the three parts of a date takes up two digits, and that regular and overtime hours are both three digits with one place after the assumed decimal point. Is this a legal Data Division structure for these items?

```
01  PAY-DATA-RECORD.
    05  PAY-DATE.
        10    MONTHS          PIC 99.
        10    DAYS            PIC 99.
        10    YEARS           PIC 99.
    05  HOURS.
        10    REGULAR-HOURS   PIC 99V9.
        10    OT-HOURS        PIC 99V9.
```

3. How many characters are there in the record described by these Data Division entries?

```
01   DATA-RECORD.
     05   ONE                    PIC X(10).
     05   TWO.
          10   THREE             PIC XXX.
          10   FOUR              PIC XXXX.
     05   SIX.
          10   SEVEN.
               15   EIGHT        PIC XXX.
               15   NINE         PIC X.
          10   TEN               PIC XX.
```

4. Consider the following illustrative portion of a Data Division:

```
01   FIRST.
     05   SECOND                 PIC XX.
     05   THIRD.
          10   FOURTH            PIC X(10).
          10   FIFTH             PIC X(12).
     05   SIXTH                  PIC X.
```

Name the group items and the elementary items. Is it possible for a group item to be a part of a more inclusive group?

5. An elementary item may be numeric, alphabetic, or alphanumeric. What can you say about group items?

6. Can a data item having a level number of **01** be an elementary item?

7. The letter **v** for an assumed decimal point and a decimal point itself representing an actual decimal point both take up space in a **PICTURE** clause. Do they also both describe a character that takes up space in the data items to which they refer?

8. Could **FILLER** ever be used as the name of a data item in the Procedure Division? We understand that **FILLER** is a reserved word, but if it occurred only once in the Data Division, could we not refer to that data item by that name **FILLER**?

COBOL-85

In **COBOL-85** you need not use the word **FILLER** at all. Could you then use it as a data name?

END COBOL-85

9. Locate errors in these Data Division entries.

```
a.   01   SAM                    PIC X(20).
          05   JOE               PIC X(12).
          05   BILL              PIC X(8).


b.   01   DAN.
          05   TOM               PIC X(20).
               10   ONCE         PIC X(10).
               10   TWICE        PIC X(10).
          05   RACHEL            PIC X(30).
```

```
C.  01   JUNE
         05  GINI               PIC X(10)
         05  CINDY              PIC X(23)
```

10. How many characters are there in the record described by these entries?

```
01  GEORGE.
    05  BETTY               PICTURE X(3).
    05  GLORIA              PICTURE XX.
    05  LIZ.
        10  ED              PICTURE X(12).
        10  LEO             PICTURE X(8).
    05  NAN.
        10  LEN             PICTURE X.
        10  ZEB             PICTURE XX.
```

11. Suppose a program contains the following statement:

    ```
    ADD REGULAR-HOURS OVERTIME-HOURS GIVING TOTAL-HOURS
    ```

    If you are told the values of REGULAR-HOURS and of OVERTIME-HOURS before execution of this statement, but not the value of TOTAL-HOURS, can you tell exactly what the statement will do?

12. Suppose you are given the following statement:

    ```
    SUBTRACT A, B, C FROM D GIVING E
    ```

    Write a formula that expresses what will be placed in E in terms of the values of the other four data items.

13. One statement was removed from the program in Figure 3.1 and the modified program run with the same data used previously. Here is the output that the modified program produced.

    ```
    12345630   00012 AD0003 B 010.00   00015   000150.00
    12345930   11111 AD0022 B 001.00   11133   011133.00
    23456730   00005 AD0006 B 340.44   00011   003744.84
    23AAX430   00400 AD0148 B 001.54   00548   000843.92
    23AAX530   00023 AD0012 B 433.00   00035   015155.00
    ```

    What was the one statement removed?

14. What is wrong with this statement?

    ```
    ADD A TO B GIVING C
    ```

15. For each statement, fill in the "after" positions for items that have a "before" entry.

	Before				After			
	A	B	C	D	A	B	C	D
ADD A TO B	12	14						
ADD A, B TO C	1	2	14					
ADD A B TO C D	2	4	6	10				
ADD A, B, C TO D	1	2	3	4				
ADD A B C GIVING D	1	2	3	4				
ADD 12 TO A	13							

```
SUBTRACT A FROM B                   2    8

SUBTRACT A FROM B GIVING C          1    2   12

SUBTRACT A, B FROM C                1    2   12

SUBTRACT A, B FROM C GIVING D  1    2   12   39

SUBTRACT 5 FROM A                   8

SUBTRACT A FROM 35 GIVING B    25   99

MULTIPLY A BY B                     6    3

MULTIPLY A BY B GIVING C            6    3   29

MULTIPLY 4 BY A GIVING B            5   21

DIVIDE A INTO B                     2   12

DIVIDE A INTO B GIVING C            2   12   23

DIVIDE A BY B GIVING C             12    4   98

DIVIDE A BY 12 GIVING B            36    7

DIVIDE A BY B GIVING C             23    7    8    6
    REMAINDER D
```

ANSWERS

1. None whatever. Experienced programmers recommend such conventions, but they are for the benefit of human readers (including the writer) of the program, not the **COBOL** compiler.

2. Yes.

3. 23.

4. The group items are **FIRST** and **THIRD**; the elementary items are **SECOND**, **FOURTH**, **FIFTH**, and **SIXTH**. A group item certainly can be part of a larger group. **THIRD** is such a case.

5. Group items are always treated as if they are alphanumeric. That statement can be misleading, however, since the elementary items *within a group* can be numeric.

6. Certainly, so long as it is not further subdivided. In the program in Chapter 2, for example, we read an entire record and printed all the contents. The entire record was described by

   PICTURE X(80)

   making the contents of the record one elementary item.

7. Absolutely not. An assumed decimal point is *assumed*, not stored explicitly! This has a crucial bearing on such things as alignment of operands for arithmetic operations, but an assumed decimal point does not exist as a character in the data item.

8. No way. A practical problem is that ordinarily the word **FILLER** will appear many times, so the **COBOL** compiler would have no way of knowing which one you meant. But in any event, this is illegal.

COBOL-85

This is true in **COBOL-85**, as well as older versions of **COBOL**, even if you do not use the word **FILLER** more than once. It is still a reserved word and may not be used as a data name.

END COBOL-85

9. a. **SAM**, as a group item, must not have a **PICTURE**!
    b. Ditto for **TOM**.
    c. There are no periods after the entries.

10. Twenty-eight, the sum of the number of characters in each of the **PICTURE** clauses.

11. Certainly. Using the **GIVING** option, the previous value of the data item named after the word **GIVING** is simply replaced by the result of the arithmetic operation.

12. $E = D - (A + B + C)$

The point is that in any **SUBTRACT** the values of all of the items before the word **FROM** will first be added together and then that result subtracted from the value of the item named after the word **FROM**. This is true whether or not the **GIVING** option is used.

13. **MOVE SPACES TO INVENTORY-OUT-RECORD.**

The modified program thus did not blank out the positions associated with the **FILLER** item in the output record. After doing some other work with the computer the same modified program was run again with the same data, producing these results:

```
1234563XOU00012 P10003CER010.00 IK000152MO000150.00
1234593XOU11111 P10022CER001.00 IK111332MO011133.00
2345673XOU00005 P10006CER340.44 IK000112MO003744.84
23AAX43XOU00400 P10148CER001.54 IK005482MO000843.92
23AAX53XOU00023 P10012CER433.00 IK000352MO015155.00
```

This demonstrates that when we don't put anything in a given location, we simply don't know what is going to be there.

14. This is actually a trick question, because the answer depends on which version of **COBOL** you are using. In **COBOL-85** the statement is perfectly acceptable. In older versions of **COBOL**, however, the **GIVING** option does not permit the **TO**. (But even some of the older compilers simply issue a warning, then compile as though the **TO** were not there.)

15.

	Before				After			
	A	B	C	D	A	B	C	D
ADD A TO B	12	14			12	26		
ADD A, B TO C	1	2	14		1	2	17	
ADD A B TO C D	2	4	6	10	2	4	12	16
ADD A, B, C TO D	1	2	3	4	1	2	3	10
ADD A B C GIVING D	1	2	3	4	1	2	3	6

ADD 12 TO A	13				25			
SUBTRACT A FROM B	2	8			2	6		
SUBTRACT A FROM B GIVING C	1	2	12		1	2	1	
SUBTRACT A, B FROM C	1	2	12		1	2	9	
SUBTRACT A, B FROM C GIVING D	1	2	12	39	1	2	12	9
SUBTRACT 5 FROM A	8				3			
SUBTRACT A FROM 35 GIVING B	25	99			25	10		
MULTIPLY A BY B	6	3			6	18		
MULTIPLY A BY B GIVING C	6	3	29		6	3	18	
MULTIPLY 4 BY A GIVING B	5	21			5	20		
DIVIDE A INTO B	2	12			2	6		
DIVIDE A INTO B GIVING C	2	12	23		2	12	6	
DIVIDE A BY B GIVING C	12	4	98		12	4	3	
DIVIDE A BY 12 GIVING B	36	7			36	3		
DIVIDE A BY B GIVING C REMAINDER D	23	7	8	6	23	7	3	2

EXERCISES

*1. A record named **ACCOUNTS** consists of three elementary items named **RECEIVABLE**, **PAYABLE**, and **PAST-DUE**, each of which is a dollars-and-cents amount with five digits before the assumed decimal point. Write Data Division entries describing this record.

2. A record named **INVENTORY** consists of elementary items named **ON-HAND** and **ON-ORDER**, each of which contains five digits before the assumed decimal point and three digits after, together with a 25-character alphanumeric item named **DESCRIPTION**. Write Data Division entries describing this record.

*3. Here is the description of an input record. Its name is **ALPHA-INPUT**. The first item in the record is a group item, named **A**, consisting of a four-character item named **B** and a five-character item named **C**. Next after **A** is a six-character elementary item named **D**, and finally a seven-character elementary item named **E**. All characters are alphanumeric. Write suitable Data Division entries describing the record.

4. Here is the description of an input record. The name of the record is **INPUT-RECORD**. The first 10 characters make up an alphanumeric data item named **A**. The next 8 characters make up a numeric data item named **B**. The next 9 characters make up an alphanumeric item named **C**, that is further divided into a three-digit numeric item named **D**, a two-digit numeric item named **E**, and a four-digit item named **F**. The last 53 characters make up an alphanumeric item named **G**. Write a suitable Data Division entry for this record.

* Answers to starred exercises will be found in Appendix IV at the end of the book.

*5. An output record named **NORMAL-LINE-OUT** contains the following fields:

A three-character alphanumeric item named **IDENT**, followed by space for three blanks (which would be inserted by a **MOVE SPACES TO NORMAL-LINE-OUT** statement in the Procedure Division).

A group item named **COSTS**, consisting of elementary items named **OUT-GOING** and **RETURNING**, each of which is a dollars-and-cents amount with a maximum size of 9999.99. These items are to be printed with decimal points, and each is to be followed by space for two blanks.

An elementary item named **TOTAL-MILES**, which has five numeric digits without a decimal point.

Write suitable Data Division entries describing this record.

6. An output record named **ERROR-LINE-OUT** contains the following fields.

NAME, which consists of **INITIAL-1** and **INITIAL-2**, each one character followed by space for one blank, and **LAST-NAME**, which is 20 characters, followed by space for four blanks.

REST-OF-RECORD, which is 43 alphanumeric characters.

Write suitable Data Division entries.

*7. Refer to the schematic representation of a record shown below. The essential information about each elementary item is as follows:

PREFIX	2 letters
BIN-NUMBER	4 digits
QTY	6 digits
DOLLARS	7 digits with 2 assumed decimal places
DESCRIPTION	15 alphanumeric characters
WHERE-MADE	1 letter
MFG-PURCH	1 digit
HI-LO-USAGE	1 digit
QOH	5 digits

Level

Level									
01	INVENTORY								
05	PART		YTD-USAGE		DESCRIPTION	CODES			QOH
10	PREFIX	BIN-NUMBER	QTY	DOLLARS		WHERE-MADE	MFG-PURCH	HI-LO-USAGE	

Write a complete record description entry.

8. Refer to the schematic representation of the record shown on the next page. The essential information about each elementary item is as follows:

DEPT	2 letters
PERSON	5 digits
RATE	5 digits, 4 decimal places
SEX	1 letter
MONTH	2 digits
DAY-NO	2 digits
YEAR	2 digits
GROSS	6 digits, 2 decimal places

SS-TAX	3 digits, 2 decimal places
WITHHOLDING	6 digits, 2 decimal places
PENSION	5 digits, 2 decimal places

Level

Level											
01	PAYROLL										
05	EMPLOYEE		RATE	SEX	SERVICE-DATE			YTD			
10	DEPT	PERS			MONTH	DAY-NO	YEAR	GROSS	SS-TAX	WITHHOLDING	PENSION

Write a complete record description.

*9. Write a description, in words, of the record represented by the following Data Division structure. How many characters are there in the record?

```
01   PREMIUM-LINE-1.
     05   POLICY-NUMBER       PIC X(7).
     05   FILLER              PIC X(3).
     05   AMOUNTS.
          10   PREMIUM        PIC 9(4).99.
          10   FILLER         PIC XX.
          10   DIVIDEND       PIC 9(4).99.
          10   FILLER         PIC XX.
          10   INTEREST       PIC 9(4).99.
          10   FILLER         PIC XX.
          10   AMOUNT-DUE     PIC 9(4).99.
          10   FILLER         PIC XX.
```

10. Write a word description of the record represented by the following Data Division structure. How many characters are there in the record?

```
01   PREMIUM-LINE-2.
     05   NUMBER-OF-MONTHS    PIC XX.
     05   FILLER              PIC XX.
     05   DATE-DUE.
          10   MONTH-DUE      PIC XX.
          10   FILLER         PIC X.
          10   DAY-DUE        PIC XX.
          10   FILLER         PIC X.
          10   YEAR-DUE       PIC XX.
     05   FILLER              PIC X(38).
     05   LOAN-BALANCE        PIC 9(5).99.
```

*11. State in words what these statements do.

a. ADD R, S TO T.

b. ADD R, S GIVING T.

c. SUBTRACT A, B, C FROM D.

d. SUBTRACT A, B, C FROM D GIVING E.

e. MULTIPLY 12.3 BY FACTOR-9.

f. DIVIDE M INTO N.

g. DIVIDE M INTO N GIVING Q ROUNDED.

12. State in words what these statements do.
    a. ADD X TO Y.
    b. ADD X, Y GIVING Z.
    c. SUBTRACT G, H FROM P.
    d. SUBTRACT G, H FROM P GIVING Q.
    e. MULTIPLY FACTOR-1 BY FACTOR-2 ROUNDED.
    f. MULTIPLY MONTHLY-USAGE BY 12 GIVING YEARLY-USAGE.
    g. DIVIDE 12 INTO YEARLY-USAGE GIVING MONTHLY-USAGE.
    h. DIVIDE 24 INTO TOTAL-HOURS GIVING DAYS REMAINDER HOURS.

*13. Write single arithmetic statements that will have the effect of carrying out each of the following actions.
    a. Add the values of JAN, FEB, and MAR, and place the sum in 1-QUARTER.
    b. Add the values of YEAR-1 and YEAR-2, with the sum replacing the value of YEAR-2.
    c. Add 13.45, the value of ABC, and the value of DEF, with the sum going to DEF.
    d. Same as c., except that the sum goes to GHI.
    e. Decrease the value of Q-1 by 12.
    f. Form the sum of Y-88 and Y-89, and subtract that sum from the value of YEARS.
    g. Multiply the value of FINAL-TOTAL by the value of RATE-ADJUSTMENT, with the rounded product being placed back in FINAL-TOTAL.
    h. Multiply the value of MONTHLY-USAGE by 12, with the product placed in YEAR-TOTAL.
    i. Multiply the value of MILES-PER-HOUR by the value of HOURS, to get the value of DISTANCE.
    j. Divide the value of YEAR-TOTAL by 12, to get the value of MONTHLY-AVERAGE.
    k. Divide the value of MACHINE-UTILIZATION by the value of OVERLAP-FACTOR, with the rounded quotient replacing the previous value of MACHINE-UTILIZATION.
    l. Divide the value of TOTAL-TIME by 60; place the quotient in HOURS and the remainder in MINUTES.

14. Write arithmetic statements to carry out the following actions.
    a. Place the sum of the values of REG-HOURS and OT-HOURS in TOTAL-HOURS.
    b. Increase the value of Q-1 by 12.
    c. Add the values of MON, TUES, WED, THUR, and FRI, and place the sum in WEEK.
    d. Add the value of MON-1, MON-2, and MON-3; place the sum in MON-3.
    e. Subtract 69.3 from the value of FACTOR-3.
    f. Add the values of QTY-1 and QTY-2, subtract that sum from QTY-3, and place the final result in FINAL-VALUE.

g. Add 39 to the sum of the values of **F-6** and **F-8**, subtract that sum from **F-10**, and place the result in **F-10**.

h. Multiply the values of **OT-HOURS** by 1.5 and place the product in **TEMP-STORAGE**.

i. Multiply the value of **S** and **Y** and place the product back in **S**.

j. Divide the value of **SUMMATION** by the value of **N** and place the quotient in **AVERAGE**, rounded.

k. Divide the value of **KW-USAGE** by 1.2, with the quotient replacing the previous value of **KW-USAGE**.

l. Divide the value of **AMOUNT** by 5; place the quotient in **NICKELS** and the remainder in **PENNIES**.

*15. In each part of this exercise you are given an arithmetic statement and a **PICTURE** clause for each item entering into the arithmetic.
Find the **PICTURE** clause for **RESULT** that will permit the largest possible result to be placed in **RESULT**, without wasting space.

```
ADD A B GIVING RESULT.

    05  A         PICTURE 99V9.
    05  B         PICTURE 9(3)V99.

MULTIPLY A BY B GIVING RESULT.

    05  A         PICTURE 9(3).
    05  B         PICTURE 99V9.

MULTIPLY A BY 12.34 GIVING RESULT.

    05  A         PICTURE 9(3)V9(4).
```

16. Same as Exercise 15.

```
ADD A B GIVING RESULT.

    05  A         PICTURE 9(3)V99.
    05  B         PICTURE 9V9.


MULTIPLY A BY B GIVING RESULT.

    05  A         PICTURE 9V9(3).
    05  B         PICTURE 9(3)V9(3).
```

*17. You are given a data file. Each record in the file contains payroll information about one employee, in the following format:

Columns 1-5	Identification number
Columns 6-8	Hours worked, to tenths of an hour
Columns 9-12	Pay rate, in dollars and cents

You are to write a program that will read the data records, compute the employee's pay (hours multiplied by rate), and print the following information on a line for each worker:

Positions 1-5	Identification number
Positions 9-12	Hours worked, with a decimal point
Positions 16-20	Pay rate, with a decimal point
Positions 24-30	Pay, with a decimal point

Be sure to blank out the **FILLER** positions between items in the output.

Your program is to include all four divisions, and you should compile it and run it with sample data. Compare your results with hand-calculated test cases.

18. You are given a data file whose records contain the following information:

Columns 1-7	Identification number
Columns 8-10	Hours worked on Monday, to tenths of an hour
Columns 11-13	Hours worked on Tuesday
Columns 14-16	Hours worked on Wednesday
Columns 17-19	Hours worked on Thursday
Columns 20-22	Hours worked on Friday
Columns 23-25	Hours worked on Saturday

You are to write a program that will read these records, and for each record compute the total hours worked and the average hours worked (the total divided by 6). For each record, a line is to be printed giving the following information:

Positions 1-7	Identification number
Positions 12-15	Total hours worked, with a decimal point
Positions 17-21	Average hours worked, to hundredths of an hour

Be sure to blank the positions between items in the output line. Use rounding on the average. Compile and run your program with illustrative data.

19. (This exercise is suitable for use as a small project.)

Assume you are developing a sales and inventory report for the National Widget Corporation. Input records for the report have the following format:

Columns 1-5	product code (alphanumeric)
Columns 6-30	product description (alphanumeric)
Columns 31-35	sales for three weeks ago
Columns 36-40	sales for two weeks ago
Columns 41-45	sales for last week
Columns 46-50	inventory level
Columns 51-57	selling price in dollars and cents

For each record in this inventory you are to produce a line on the report that shows all of the data in the record. In addition, you are to calculate and print several pieces of information. First, the company would like to have a forecast of next week's sales. (All sales figures are recorded in units sold.) Basically, this is calculated as an average of the past three weeks' sales. However, since it is assumed that current data is more likely to reflect current sales conditions than older data, the company uses a *weighted* average. That is, if **WEEK1** represents the sales for three weeks ago and **WEEK3** represents the sales for last week, then the forecast is computed as

forecast = (**WEEK1** + 2×**WEEK2** + 3×**WEEK3**) / 6

The result is to be rounded to the nearest unit.

In addition to the forecast for next week's sales you are to compute the current value of each item in inventory. An item's value is defined to be the quantity in inventory times the selling price of the item.

Finally, the company wants to know the average value of an item in inventory. This is defined to be the total value of all items divided by the number of different products in the warehouse. The average product value is to be printed at the end of the report.

The headings shown on the sample report below are for explanation only and you need not produce any headings in your program. However, each column should be separated from the following column by a blank space.

Prod Code	Product Description	3 wk Sales	2 wk Sales	Last week Sales	Curr Inv	Product Price	F'cst Sales	Product Value
AA123	SNOW BLOWER	00002	00000	00005	00022	00299.95	00003	0006598.90
BB345	LAWN CHAIR	01050	02577	00933	09515	00017.50	01501	0166512.50
	AVERAGE VALUE							0086555.70

CHAPTER 4

PROGRAM DESIGN

4.1 INTRODUCTION

Developing a computer program requires two steps: first, you must plan what the program is to do and how it is to do it; second, you translate this plan into the actual program. Although you may not believe it now, writing the program is the easier of the two tasks. Unfortunately, it is not possible to skip the planning step. At some point you *must* decide how the program is to work. If you don't do it before you start writing the **COBOL** code you will find yourself doing it while you try to write the program. The result will be a program that is harder to write, harder to debug, and much more complicated than one that is carefully designed in advance.

Learning all of the techniques for designing large programs is beyond the scope of this book. Our objective in this chapter is simply to present the basic tools of program design. You will be introduced to *hierarchy charts*, which are used to design the overall structure of a program, and *pseudocode*, which lets you define what each part of the program is to do. We will discuss the basic method for designing a program and show an example of how a simple program might be designed. Keep in mind that we have not yet covered enough **COBOL** to actually *implement* all of the programs we will design. This doesn't matter! Eventually you will learn the necessary **COBOL**, and in any case the design techniques you will learn are independent of the language used to write the program.

4.2 PROGRAM FUNCTION

We begin the design of a program by recognizing that every program performs a *function*, or task. Therefore, we must try to think about a program in terms of this function, *not* in terms of the detailed steps that must be performed to carry out the function. This is not a natural way for a beginner to think about a program. At this point you are very likely overwhelmed by the complexities of what you have learned about COBOL, to say nothing of what will be covered in the remainder of this book. When you start to think about how to write a program such as the one presented in Chapter 3, you are likely to start with something like "Well, first I have to read a record. Now what do I do with it? Oh yes, I had better go back and open the files I need...." This approach is very natural and quite common. It really has only one serious flaw—it won't work! Even if you have been able to design your first few programs this way (and you may already have run into trouble!) it will become harder and harder to use this method as your programs become larger and more complex. Although you may get the program working eventually, it will take longer and produce a much more complicated program than if you do it the right way. So let's begin by remembering that we want to think in terms of the *functions* that a program performs, and go on to see how we can put these functions down on paper.

4.3 HIERARCHY CHARTS

If programmers could picture the operation of an entire program all at once, the task of writing a program would be simple. Unfortunately, the human mind is capable of dealing with only a limited number of concepts at one time, and research has shown that this limit runs between five and nine concepts, depending on the person and the difficulty of each concept. If you try to deal with a problem that has more factors than this, you start to forget about parts of the problem and to make mistakes in your solution; the more factors you try to deal with at one time the more mistakes you make. Unfortunately, most computer programs involve many more than nine factors, which leads us to a serious conflict. On the one hand, we cannot deal with all of the factors necessary to develop most programs. On the other hand, we *must* be able to deal with large problems if programming is to be a useful activity.

The solution to this conflict is to divide the original problem into several smaller problems, which, if carried out correctly, solve the original problem. We don't have to decide how the smaller problems will be solved yet; that can be done later on. Right now all we must do is be certain that *if* the smaller problems can be solved, then we will have solved the original problem. Later on we can worry about how to solve each of the smaller problems. For example, if I were to try to plan my day minute by minute from the time I wake up in the morning until the time I go to sleep at night, I probably wouldn't have too much success. I would omit details, then remember things that I had to do earlier, make corrections to my schedule, and so on. Instead, I can start by listing major activities like this:

1. Shower
2. Get dressed
3. Have breakfast
4. Go to office
5. Check mail
6. Review output from last night's computer runs
7. Continue design of sales report program
   .
   .
   .

If I wanted to, I could go on to divide each of these activities into still smaller tasks. For example, I could divide "have breakfast" into "pour juice, prepare cereal, make coffee, . . . ," and I could further divide one of these steps into the detailed activities required, for example, to make coffee. In a similar manner, instead of trying to understand all of the details needed to make a typical program work, we divide the program into the major tasks required to accomplish the basic function of the program, then as necessary divide each of these tasks into smaller tasks, and so on. At each stage, we don't have to decide exactly how to carry out the tasks we are listing; we only need to be certain that if we get the proper tasks listed then the program will accomplish the original task. Eventually we will have the program broken down into a number of tasks, each of which is small enough that we can deal with it.

In order to keep track of these tasks and how they relate to each other, we use a hierarchy chart. (You may find hierarchy charts referred to elsewhere by other names, such as *structure charts*. The style may vary slightly but the concept is the same.) For example, Figure 4.1 shows part of a hierarchy chart that documents the daily activities listed above.

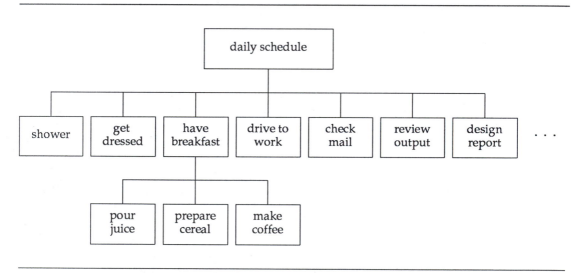

FIGURE 4.1 Hierarchy chart of day's schedule.

This hierarchy chart tells us that the daily schedule consists of the activities "shower," "get dressed," and so on; and that the activity "have breakfast" consists of three more detailed activities. Notice that we can show lower levels of detail for one activity without showing them for all activities. If we wished, we could even show lower levels of detail for preparing cereal and making coffee.

4.4 A HIERARCHY CHART FOR A SIMPLE PROGRAM

We are ready now to develop a simple hierarchy chart for a program. The particular program we are going to design is the one shown in Figure 3.1. We begin the design by considering just what task this program is trying to accomplish. Basically, the function of the program is to produce an inventory report. This function, then, becomes the top box, or *module*, of the hierarchy chart.

```
+------------------+
|     PRODUCE      |
|    INVENTORY     |
|      REPORT      |
+------------------+
```

The next question is, what tasks must be performed in order to produce the inventory report? Keep in mind that we aren't at all concerned with the details of the **COBOL** code that must be written to carry out these tasks. Suppose all of the inventory records were printed on three-by-five-inch cards, and the report was to be computed by hand and written on a printed form, one line for each item in inventory. How would you describe what had to be done to produce the report?

Your description would probably go something like this: "First I get an inventory record. I copy the part number, quantity on hand, quantity received, and unit price to the report. Then I compute the new quantity on hand and put it on the report, and finally I compute the value of the item and write it on the report. When I'm done with this I repeat the whole process for the next inventory record."

If you look at this description you can see that producing the inventory report consists of four tasks:

1. get the next inventory record;
2. copy the item data to the report;
3. compute the new quantity on hand (QOH);
4. compute the item value.

Notice that we have not shown any of the details of how these tasks are performed. We have not, for example, shown that task 3 is the result of an addition. All we are trying to do at this point is describe the *function* of the task. Later we will tell how the task is actually carried out.

Based on this list of tasks we can now expand the hierarchy chart for the program, producing the version shown in Figure 4.2.

At this point we should review the hierarchy chart to see if there are any details that we have forgotten. In this case, there is one more task that we should add that did not show up in the manual preparation of the report. That task is writing the report record. When we described the manual activities, we assumed that each piece of data was being written by hand in its proper place on the report form. In **COBOL**, of course, we must use a **WRITE** statement. The final version of the hierarchy chart is shown in Figure 4.3. Each module contains a *brief* (a few words) statement of the function that the module performs, including a *precise verb* that tells what the major action of the module is, such as *get, copy, compute,* or *write*.

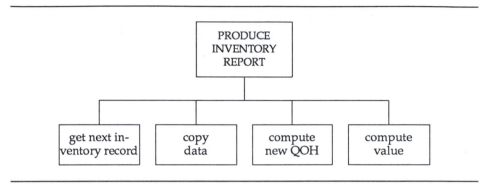

FIGURE 4.2 Expanded version of a hierarchy chart for an inventory report program.

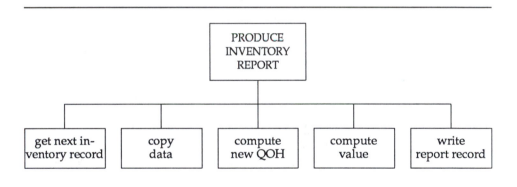

FIGURE 4.3 Final version of a hierarchy chart for an inventory control program.

We have one question left to resolve in preparing hierarchy charts. When do we *stop* adding more levels of detail? In this example that was no problem because the tasks being performed were very simple. In more complicated programs, however, the problem is not so easily resolved. Is it necessary, for example, to continue until each module consists of only one **COBOL** statement? The answer is, No! We can stop adding more detail when the lowest level of modules describes basic tasks. In some cases each of these tasks may consist of only one **COBOL** statement. More likely, a task will represent an entire paragraph containing a number of statements. The main requirement is that you must be able to visualize clearly how the task is to be carried out.

4.5 CONTROL OF EXECUTION

Although a hierarchy chart will show you what functions a program must perform to accomplish its basic task, it will not show the order in which these functions must be performed, whether some functions are performed repeatedly, or what details are actually carried out to accomplish each function. The tool that we shall use to specify in detail what each module actually does is called *pseudocode*. The name is meant to suggest that the notation of pseudocode is similar to program code such as **COBOL**; but the "pseudo" part of the name means that although there are similarities, the two are not identical. In particular, we are not bound by the rules for writing **COBOL** statements and, in fact, are free to use abbreviations and ordinary English where appropriate.

The statements in a **COBOL** program (and in the pseudocode specifications for a **COBOL** program) can be divided into two basic types. First, there are the statements such as **READ, WRITE, ADD, MOVE**, etc., which carry out the detailed work of the program. Second, there are statements such as **PERFORM** and others we shall encounter shortly that control the execution of the program. For example, in Figure 3.1, the **PERFORM** statement in paragraph **A000-MAIN-LINE-ROUTINE** controls whether paragraph **B010-LIST-INVENTORY-DATA** and the statements inside this paragraph get executed. In most programs, the control statements are by far the most important of the two types. If the control statements are designed correctly, the remainder of the program can be written in a fairly straightforward manner. If the control structure of a program is poorly designed, no amount of effort will produce a good program.

Any computer program, whether in **COBOL** or some other language, can be written using only the following three types of control structures:

1. *Sequence*. This is the basic mode of operation of any program. Unless specified otherwise, operations are carried out from top to bottom in the order written.
2. *Selection*. This means to select one of two alternative courses of action, depending on whether some condition is true or not. For example, in planning my schedule for the day I might say "If I have to visit a client's office, today then I will drive to work; if not, then I will take the bus."
3. *Iteration*. This means to perform some action repeatedly until a stated condition terminates the repetition. For example, in Figure 3.1 paragraph **B010-LIST-INVENTORY-DATA** is performed repeatedly until we run out of inventory records. As is the case in this program, the number of "repeats" can be zero.

There is also a fourth type of structure that is frequently used, called the *case* structure. The case structure is actually just a special type of selection, so it is sometimes omitted from pseudocode specifications. However, since **COBOL-85** includes a statement that supports the case structure, we shall include the structure here.

4. *Case*. This means to perform one of several alternative actions, depending on the value of some variable. For example, a delivery service might charge $7.50 for a delivery within 5 miles of the center of town, $10 for a delivery over 5 miles but within 10 miles, and $1/mile for deliveries over 10 miles.

4.6 PSEUDOCODE STRUCTURES

As in **COBOL** itself, the sequence structure requires no special notation. It is simply a series of statements written one after the other.

The selection structure is indicated by an IFTHENELSE pseudocode statement. For example, the selection statement given above would be written as:

```
IF have to visit client's office THEN
    drive to work
ELSE
    take bus to work
ENDIF
```

The interpretation of this statement is fairly simple. If the condition specified between IF and THEN is true, execute the statement (or statements) between THEN and ELSE. If the condition is false, execute the statement(s) between ELSE and ENDIF. Optionally, the word ELSE and the statements following it may be omitted. In this case if the condition following IF is false, we do nothing and go on to the next statement.

The ENDIF part of the IFTHENELSE statement is very important, especially if there are several statements following ELSE, since the word ENDIF defines very clearly where the entire structure ends. This is particularly important if one of the statements to be executed is itself an IFTHENELSE structure. Consider the following example.

```
IF employee is salaried THEN
    set gross-pay to weekly-salary
ELSE
    set base-pay to hours-worked x pay-rate
    IF hours-worked are greater than 40 THEN
        set overtime-pay to 1.5 x pay-rate x (hours-worked - 40)
    ELSE
        set overtime-pay to zero
    ENDIF
    set gross-pay to base-pay + overtime-pay
ENDIF
```

The use of the ENDIFs makes clear where each IF structure terminates.

We also want to call your attention to the format of the structure. The words ELSE and ENDIF are aligned under the IF, and the action statements are indented. Following this format makes the pseudocode much easier to read than if we wrote it something like this:

```
IF have to visit client's office THEN drive to work ELSE take bus to work ENDIF
```

The meaning of the statement hasn't changed, but the ease of understanding certainly has!

For the iteration structure, we shall take into account the fact that in **COBOL** iteration is expressed with the PERFORM...UNTIL statement, and we shall use a very similar format, PERFORM-UNTIL, in our pseudocode. Just as we use the ENDIF to show explicitly the end of the scope of influence of the IF structure, we shall use an ENDPERFORM for the same function with iteration. The statements controlled by the PERFORM-UNTIL will be indented and shown right in the same place as the PERFORM-UNTIL. Although this is not the same as the **COBOL** PERFORM...UNTIL statement, it matches common program design usage. The following example shows the PERFORM-UNTIL structure in use:

```
move 'N' to flag
get record; at end move 'Y' to flag
PERFORM-UNTIL flag = 'Y'
    process record
    get record; at end move 'Y' to flag
ENDPERFORM
```

The case structure has numerous formats in general program design, so we shall again borrow from **COBOL** and use a format based on the equivalent statement in **COBOL-85**. For example, the evaluation of the delivery service fee described above could be written as follows:

```
EVALUATE distance from center of town
    WHEN less than or equal to 5 miles
        fee is $7.50
    WHEN more than 5 miles but less than or equal to 10 miles
        fee is $10
    WHEN more than 10 miles
        fee is $1/mile
ENDEVALUATE
```

The EVALUATE structure begins with an expression following the word EVALUATE, and contains a series of WHEN clauses, each of which begins with a possible value for the expression. We evaluate the expression, then compare this value to each of the values in the WHEN clauses. If we find a value that matches the current value of the expression, the statement or statements following the WHEN value are executed and we go on to the next statement. At most, one WHEN clause is executed in the structure. If none of the values in WHEN clauses matches the current value in the expression, no action is taken and the EVALUATE statement is ignored.

The EVALUATE structure has two optional features that are not shown in this example. First, we can have more than one value in each WHEN clause. Second, we can follow the *last* WHEN clause with the word OTHERWISE. In this case, if no WHEN clause is executed, the statement(s) following OTHERWISE will be executed. For example, consider the following specification for evaluating a student's standing in a class:

```
EVALUATE quiz-grade
    WHEN 10
        class-standing is excellent
    WHEN 8 or 9
        class-standing is above-average
    WHEN 5 or 6 or 7
        class-standing is average
    WHEN 3 or 4
        class-standing is below-average
    OTHERWISE
        class-standing is failing
ENDEVALUATE
```

With the EVALUATE structure, as with the IF and PERFORM structures, we have an END word, in this case ENDEVALUATE, to mark the end of the scope of the structure.

4.7 SPECIFICATION OF THE INVENTORY REPORT PROGRAM

We are now ready to complete the design of the inventory report program by providing pseudocode specifications for each of the modules on the hierarchy chart. In many cases each module is treated as though it were a separate paragraph in a **COBOL** program. In this case, however, each second-level module will consist of only a few statements, so we shall treat the entire second level as a single "paragraph."

We begin with the basic specifications for the top module, "**PRODUCE INVENTORY REPORT**." This module reads an inventory record, then for every inventory record in the file it processes the record and reads another record. So far, the specifications to perform this task look like the following:

```
Read an inventory record; at end move 'Y' to flag
PERFORM-UNTIL flag = 'Y'
      process the inventory record
      read an inventory record; at end move 'Y' to flag
ENDPERFORM
stop
```

Next we expand the design by replacing the "process" statement, which really doesn't tell much about what the program is to accomplish, with the names of the remaining modules on the hierarchy chart:

```
Read an inventory record; at end move 'Y' to flag
PERFORM-UNTIL flag = 'Y'
      copy data
      compute new quantity on hand
      compute value
      write report record
      read an inventory record; at end move 'Y' to flag
ENDPERFORM
stop
```

Finally, we can complete the specification by replacing the names of the processing modules with pseudocode that tells what each module is to do:

```
Read an inventory record; at end move 'Y' to flag
PERFORM-UNTIL flag = 'Y'
      move spaces to output record
      move part-number to output record
      move qty-on-hand to output record
      move qty-received to output record
      move unit-price to output record
      compute new qty-on-hand as the sum of the qty-on-hand and
             the qty-received
      compute value by multiplying the new qty-on-hand
             by the unit-price
      write report record
      read an inventory record; at end move 'Y' to flag
ENDPERFORM
```

For all practical purposes the specification of the inventory report program is now complete. If you wish, you may add statements to open and close the input and output files, and to set the initial value of the flag to '**N**'. These changes are left as an exercise for the student.

We do, however, wish to show an enhancement to this program to demonstrate how various types of control structures can be combined in a specification. Let us assume that it is possible to have a quantity-received of zero. In this case, we will leave the qty-received and new qty-on-hand fields of the output record blank, and we will compute the value as the product of the old qty-on-hand and the unit price. If the qty-received is greater than zero, the revised program is to produce the same results as the original one. The pseudocode for this enhanced program is as follows:

```
Read an inventory record; at end move 'Y' to flag
PERFORM-UNTIL flag = 'Y'
    move spaces to output record
    move part-number to output record
    move qty-on-hand to output record
    move unit-price to output record
    IF qty-received > 0 THEN
        move qty-received to output record
        compute new qty-on-hand as the sum of the qty-on-hand
            and the qty-received
        compute value by multiplying the new qty-on-hand
            by the unit-price
    ELSE
        compute value by multiplying the old qty-on-hand
            by the unit-price
    ENDIF
    write report record
    read an inventory record; at end move 'Y' to flag
ENDPERFORM
stop
```

We have not yet studied the COBOL statements necessary to implement this enhanced program, but the meaning of the pseudocode should still be clear. If necessary, study the example until you understand what the revised program will do when we write it. We will study the required COBOL code in the following chapter.

4.8 PROGRAMMING STANDARDS

Up to now your primary objective with any COBOL programs you have written is simply to get the program to work, and at this stage in your education that is not an unreasonable objective. However, you must now begin to look ahead to the time when you will be writing COBOL programs for an employer. What is acceptable in a beginning COBOL class is not acceptable in the workplace!

The classroom environment is not a very realistic one as far as programming is concerned. In most of your programming assignments you will be writing relatively small programs (even if they don't seem small at the time), you will be working alone, and you will need to get your programs to work only *once*; after your program is graded by your instructor neither you nor anyone else will look at it again. In the typical work environment, your programs may be thousands of lines long, you will likely be working on a team with other programmers, and the programs you write will be in use for years and may very well be modified by other programmers long after you have gone on to other work. In this type of environment it is vital that programs be written to be as clear and readable as possible. Consider the plight of the poor programmer who is awakened at 2 a.m. to come into the office to fix a program that blew up, and whose output *must* be available for a 9 a.m. management meeting! (What if that programmer is *you*?)

We made a start in developing good programs when we studied techniques for designing programs instead of just letting them happen. Another important step toward creating good software is to write the COBOL code according to standards. The objective of programming standards is not to make your program look exactly like everyone else's. There is plenty of room for individuality of technique, and it is highly unlikely that any two people will produce exactly the same program for a given problem. However, if you hold to a standard style in your programs, it becomes much easier for someone else to read your code and follow what you are trying to do.

In Appendix III you will find suggested COBOL programming standards. The basic goal of these standards is to promote a style of coding that makes the code as easy to read as possible. These standards are not unique, and your instructor or supervisor may wish to modify them or use other standards entirely. In any case, remember that the function of programming standards is to make your code readable; making sure that the code *means* something is another problem entirely.

We recommend this point of view: if your program can't be understood by another human being, you may as well not have written it.

One part of the suggested programming standards that may require special explanation is the use of prefixes such as A000 or B010 in paragraph names. These prefixes serve two purposes. First, they indicate the relative position of a paragraph in a hierarchy chart of the program. A paragraph beginning with A is on level one, a paragraph beginning with B is on level two, and so on. Second, since paragraphs are *always* written in prefix-number sequence in the program, the prefix makes it much easier to find a paragraph when you are trying to read a program. This may not mean much to you yet, since the programs you have encountered up to now only contain two or three paragraphs, but consider the problem of trying to find a paragraph quickly when your program contains twenty or thirty paragraphs! (That is intended to sound large to you; in "real life," programs of hundreds of paragraphs are routine, and programs of thousands of paragraphs are not rare.)

4.9 SUMMARY

In this chapter you have learned five new concepts:

1. Programs must be *designed*, not just thrown together;
2. Every program performs a *function*, every paragraph in the program performs a specific task that is part of this function, and the design of the program should be based on these tasks;
3. A *hierarchy chart* is a tool that is used to document the tasks that a program performs and their relationship to each other;
4. *Pseudocode* is used to specify the way in which each task, or *module*, on a hierarchy chart performs its function;
5. Programs should be written to be as readable as possible by other people, and to help achieve this goal they should be written following *standards*.

We have used these concepts in developing the programs in the first three chapters, and we will continue to demonstrate techniques for designing and writing good COBOL code throughout the remainder of this book.

REVIEW QUESTIONS

1. What are the two basic program design tools introduced in this chapter? Describe the function of each.

2. Name the four basic control structures that were described in the chapter and state the function of each.

3. Why do we need program design aids? Why can't we simply sit down and start writing the COBOL code directly?

4. What is wrong with the following hierarchy chart?

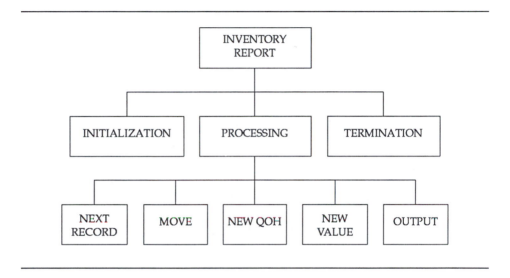

5. What, if anything, is wrong with the following pseudocode?

```
EVALUATE flag
    WHEN 'Y'
        write "The flag is set to 'Y'."
    OTHERWISE
        write "The flag is not set to 'Y'."
ENDEVALUATE
```

6. Are the following pseudocode statements equivalent?

```
EVALUATE amount
    WHEN greater than zero
        add amount to positive-total
    WHEN less than zero
        add amount to negative-total
    WHEN equal to zero
        write "The amount is zero.
ENDEVALUATE
```

```
        IF amount > zero THEN
            add amount to positive-total
        ELSE
            IF amount < zero THEN
                add amount to negative-total
            ELSE
                write "The amount is zero."
            ENDIF
        ENDIF
```

7. What, if anything, is wrong with the following pseudocode?

```
    move 'N' to flag
    read an input record; at end move 'Y' to flag
    PERFORM-UNTIL flag = 'Y'
        IF record is a sales record THEN
            move the seller's name to the output record
            move the sale amount to the output record
            write the output record
        read an input record; at end move 'Y' to flag
    ENDPERFORM
```

8. What is the reason for using programming standards?

ANSWERS

1. Hierarchy charts and pseudocode. The hierarchy chart defines the structure of the program in terms of the basic functions the program performs and the relationship of these functions to each other, and the pseudocode defines the detailed actions required to perform each function.

2. *Sequence.* The basic top-to-bottom mode of operation of any program or program specification.
   Selection. Choose between two alternative actions depending on whether some condition is true or false.
   Iteration. Repeat an action until some condition becomes true.
   Case. Choose one of several alternative actions depending on the value of a variable or expression.

3. We need design aids because the human mind cannot deal with all of the factors that are needed to write a typical program. If you try to keep more than nine or ten concepts in mind at the same time, you will forget details and make mistakes. The design tools help the programmer break a program into manageable pieces.

4. The module names don't tell anything about the functions of the modules, and most of the names don't specify an action. The name of a module should always consist of a brief (a few words) statement that describes the action that the module is to perform.

5. The statement is perfectly correct, although it is more common to use an IFTHENELSE structure if you are only choosing between two alternatives.

6. Yes.

7. The ENDIF, which should follow the write statement, is missing. From the indentation we assume that what the PERFORM-UNTIL loop was

intended to do is to process the current record, then read a new record, repeating until flag becomes equal to '**Y**'. However, as the specifications stand the read statement inside the PERFORM-UNTIL is within the scope of the **IF** statement and will only be executed if the record is a sales record. If a program written according to these specifications ever encountered a record other than a sales record, the read would not be executed and the program would loop forever (or until someone or some part of the operating system stopped its execution).

8. Programming standards are used to improve program readability. Standards generally prohibit coding styles that lead to overly complex code, and they make it easier for a programmer to read programs written by other people in his/her organization.

EXERCISES

*1. Write pseudocode statements to carry out the following operations.

   a. Add 1 to an item named **LEGAL-ADULT** if **AGE** is 18 or greater.

   b. Print **STOCK-ITEM** if **PART-1-A** contains the letter **S**.

   c. Add 1 to **BIG** if **SIZE-A** is greater than 800; add 1 to **LITTLE** if **SIZE-A** is less than or equal to 800.

   d. If the item in **NAME-A** is greater than the item in **NAME-B**, move the contents of **NAME-A** to **TEMPORARY**; if the item in **NAME-A** is less than the item in **NAME-B**, move the contents of **NAME-B** to **TEMPORARY**; if the two are equal, move either of them to **TEMPORARY**.

   e. If the value of the item named **HOURS-WORKED** is *anything but* 40, print "**NON-STANDARD HOURS**".

2. Write pseudocode statements to carry out the following operations.

   a. Add 1 to an item named **MAJOR-BILLING** if **ACCOUNT-TOTAL** is greater than 1000.00.

   b. Determine whether the value of the item named **FINAL-BILL** is greater than 999.99 and, if so, print "**SPECIAL APPROVAL REQUIRED**".

   c. If the item named **CODE-A** contains the characters **AB47Z**, move the characters **APPROVED** to the item named **APPROVAL**.

   d. Move zero to **SIGNAL** if **MEASUREMENT** is zero, and move 1 to **SIGNAL** if **MEASUREMENT** is not zero.

   e. Print "**CODE-A IS INVALID**" if **CODE-A** contains anything but letters and spaces.

3. Each student in a class has a grade record containing the student's name (contained in a field named **STUDENT-NAME**) and three examination grades named **GRADE-1**, **GRADE-2**, and **GRADE-3**. For each student, the three grades are to be added and their sum divided by 3, giving the average grade. If the average grade is 65 or more, the word **PASS** is to be placed in the item named **FINAL-GRADE**; otherwise, the word **FAIL** is to be placed in **FINAL-GRADE**. In either case a record containing the student's name, all three grades, and the contents of **FINAL-GRADE** are to

---

* Answers to starred exercises will be found in Appendix IV at the end of the book.

be printed. After all students have been graded, a count of the number of passing students and a count of the number of failing students are to be printed. Design a program to produce this grade report. Show both a hierarchy chart and a pseudocode for every module.

*4. Suppose that a salesperson's commission is based on a **PRODUCT-CODE**, as follows.

PRODUCT-CODE	Commission Formula
1	$0.15 \times$ **SALE-PRICE**
2	$0.40 \times ($**SALE-PRICE** $-$ **BASE-PRICE**$)$
3	$0.10 \times$ **BASE-PRICE** $+ 0.50 \times ($**SALE-PRICE** $-$ **BASE-PRICE**$)$
4	$\$25 + 0.05 \times$ **BASE-PRICE**
5	$\$75$

For every sale there is a **SALE-RECORD** containing **SELLER** (the salesperson's name), **PRODUCT-CODE**, **SALE-PRICE**, and **BASE-PRICE**. Design a program that reads all sales records and, for each record, writes a record containing the salesperson's name, the product code, sale price, base price, and commission. If **PRODUCT-CODE** is anything but 1, 2, 3, 4, or 5, set the commission to zero and add the message **"ERRONEOUS PRODUCT CODE"** to the end of the output record, following the normal fields.

5. Each record in a data file has the following format.

Columns 1-5:	Cost center code
Columns 6-11:	Budgeted expense, dollars
Columns 12-17:	Actual expense, year to date, dollars

Design a program that reads such a file and, for each record, prints a line giving the information read together with a comment **EXCEEDS BUDGET** if the actual expense is greater than the budgeted amount.

*6. Each record in a file contains an alphanumeric identification in columns 45-50 and a gross pay in dollars and cents in columns 70-76. A city tax is to be computed for each, the tax being 4% of the amount (if any) over $2000. For each record, a line is to be printed containing the input data and the computed tax. Design a suitable program.

7. Each record in a file contains an alphanumeric identification in columns 40-47 and a total price in columns 31-36 in dollars and cents. For each record a discount is to be computed and printed, along with the input data. The discount is 2% if the amount is over $1000, and zero if it is not. Design a suitable program.

*8. A file contains records having the following format:

Columns 1-8	**IDENT**	Alphanumeric
Columns 9-15	**DOLLARS**	**9(5)V99**
Columns 16-80	**OTHER-INFO**	Alphanumeric

The contents of each record are to be listed; the amount in the **DOLLARS** field from each record should be added to a total (which is initially set to zero); when the end of the file is detected, this total should be printed. Design a suitable program.

9. Extend the program of Exercise 8 as follows. First, any record in which the dollar amount is zero should not be printed. Second, you are to keep a count of the number of records having a zero dollar amount and the number having a nonzero amount; both of these counts should be printed on the final total line, together with their sum (the total number of records), and the average of the nonzero amounts (which is the total of the dollar amounts divided by the number of nonzero records).

CHAPTER 5

COBOL STRUCTURE STATEMENTS

5.1 INTRODUCTION

In Chapter 4 we introduced some of the techniques used to design COBOL programs. In particular, we looked at the basic control structures: sequence, selection, iteration, and case. In this chapter we present COBOL statements that correspond to these structures. The sequence structure, of course, requires no special statement since it represents simply the standard order in which COBOL statements are executed. Each of the other control structures has a COBOL statement that implements that structure. We shall examine each of these statements, beginning with the IF statement.

5.2 THE IF STATEMENT

The IF statement, which is very similar to the pseudocode IF structure, is used to specify that a condition is to be evaluated and to specify what is to be done for each outcome of the evaluation. The most common format of the statement is this:

```
IF condition
    statement-1
ELSE
    statement-2.
```

In this format the *condition* is usually a test of the relationship between two items. For example, we can have IF statements with conditions like these:

```
IF HOURS-WORKED IS GREATER THAN 40.0

IF CODE-1 = '2'

IF QTY-ON-HAND IS LESS THAN REORDER-QTY
```

We shall study the possible types of relation conditions after getting an idea of the general nature of the IF statement.

Following the condition comes a statement of what is to be done when the condition is true. This can be any **COBOL** statement or group of statements. Continuing with the examples above, we might have:

```
IF HOURS-WORKED IS GREATER THAN 40
    PERFORM OVERTIME-ROUTINE
    MOVE 'X' TO OVERTIME-FLAG

IF CODE-1 = '2'
    MOVE NAME-AND-ADDRESS TO PAGE-AREA-1

IF QTY-ON-HAND IS LESS THAN REORDER-QTY
    PERFORM REORDER-ROUTINE
    MOVE ORDER-QTY TO QTY-ON-ORDER
    ADD 1 TO ORDER-RECORD-COUNT
```

Next comes the word **ELSE** followed by a statement(s) specifying what is to be done when the condition is not true. We might have:

```
IF HOURS-WORKED IS GREATER THAN 40
    PERFORM OVERTIME-ROUTINE
    MOVE 'X' TO OVERTIME-FLAG
ELSE
    PERFORM NORMAL-TIME-ROUTINE
    MOVE SPACES TO OVERTIME-FLAG.

IF CODE-1 = '2'
    MOVE NAME-AND-ADDRESS TO PAGE-AREA-1
ELSE
    MOVE NAME-AND-ADDRESS TO PAGE-AREA-2.

IF QTY-ON-HAND IS LESS THAN REORDER-QTY
    PERFORM REORDER-ROUTINE
    MOVE ORDER-QTY TO QTY-ON-ORDER
    ADD 1 TO ORDER-RECORD-COUNT
ELSE
    SUBTRACT TRANSACTION-QTY FROM QTY-ON-HAND.
```

Finally, there is a period. The position of the period is crucial! Since this format of the **IF** statement has nothing that corresponds to the ENDIF of the IF pseudocode structure, there *must* be a period at the end of the **IF** statement and there *must not* be a period anywhere else in the **IF** statement.

The general format of the **IF** statement has been shown with the components written on separate lines. Actually, the **COBOL** compiler will permit the parts to be written on one line if they will fit. However, we shall always write **IF** statements with their parts on different lines, with indentation of the statements that are controlled by the decision, to make the meaning of the program easier to understand. **IF** statements are of central importance in most programs, and it is worthwhile doing anything we can to make their meaning and operation as clear as possible.

Here is another example of a complete **IF** statement:

```
IF W-GROSS-PAY IS GREATER THAN W-EXEMPTION-TOTAL
    SUBTRACT W-EXEMPTION-TOTAL FROM W-GROSS-PAY
        GIVING W-TAXABLE
    MULTIPLY W-TAXABLE BY C-TAXRATE GIVING W-TAX ROUNDED
ELSE
    MOVE ZERO TO W-TAX.
```

This statement comes from a program that we shall be studying in the next chapter. It determines whether the gross pay for a worker is greater than his or her exemption. If this condition is true, then the worker has tax to pay, which we proceed to calculate with the arithmetic statements shown, and the statement shown after the **ELSE** is not executed. On the other hand, if the worker's gross pay is not greater than the exemptions, then he or she is not required to pay tax and we set the tax to zero (note the new figurative constant **ZERO**). In this case the statements before the **ELSE** are not executed.

The format of the **IF** statement is, as you have probably noticed, almost identical to that in the IF pseudocode structure. The major difference between the two is that the IF terminates with ENDIF, while the **COBOL IF** simply terminates with a period. If the operations to be performed by the **IF** statement are complicated, then the **COBOL** code required to execute them can also become extremely complicated. In this case we can write the **IF** statement as in the following example:

```
IF HOURS-WORKED IS GREATER THAN 40
    PERFORM OVERTIME-ROUTINE
ELSE
    PERFORM NORMAL-ROUTINE.
```

There is now only one statement to be executed for the true path and only one for the false path. These happen to be **PERFORM** statements, which would call into play complete paragraphs.

Observe here the use of the **PERFORM** statement in a new form, without the **UNTIL** phrase. This means to carry out the named paragraph exactly once. The paragraphs **OVERTIME-ROUTINE** or **NORMAL-ROUTINE** might contain complex code, but by moving this code away from the **IF** statement we have achieved two results. First, we can focus our attention on designing each of the paragraphs separately, without having to worry about how one paragraph relates to the other or about how either paragraph relates to the **IF** statement. Second, we can put periods at the end of every statement in the paragraphs, which we could not do if the code were part of the **IF** statement, since the only period permitted in an **IF** statement is at the end of the statement. As we shall see in later examples, this can simplify the **COBOL** code considerably.

5.3 THE IF STATEMENT WITHOUT AN ELSE

Sometimes it happens that we have something to be done when a condition is true, but when that condition is false no other action is required. In this case we have two choices. The first is simply to omit the word **ELSE** and the statement(s) following it altogether. When the condition is true the statement(s) will be executed and when the condition is false, they will not be.

The second choice is to write **ELSE NEXT SENTENCE**, which has exactly the same effect. Some people recommend this form as promoting clarity in complex programs. However, we shall simply omit the **ELSE** in this situation.

5.4 THE COMPLETE GENERAL FORMAT OF THE IF STATEMENT

The general format shown at the start of Section 5.2 for the **IF** is actually a condensation, for the sake of simplicity in a first look. Here is the complete general format of the statement:

$$\text{IF condition} \left\{ \begin{array}{l} \text{statement-1} \\ \text{NEXT SENTENCE} \end{array} \right\} \left\{ \begin{array}{l} \text{ELSE statement-2} \\ \text{ELSE NEXT SENTENCE} \end{array} \right\}$$

We see that **NEXT SENTENCE** may be written for the true path as well as the false path. This has little point for the kind of **IF** statement we shall be considering for the next few chapters, but is occasionally useful. Observe in this format that the choice between **ELSE** statement-2 and **ELSE NEXT SENTENCE** is in braces, not square brackets. Under the rules for general formats that were given in Chapter 3, this would seem to mean that we must pick one of the two and that we cannot omit both. The format is given this way to make it apply to the more complex **IF** statements that will be taken up later. The general format (in a reference manual) is accompanied by a statement that the words **ELSE NEXT SENTENCE** may be omitted if they immediately precede the period at the end of the sentence. Here is an example of an **IF** statement without an **ELSE** phrase:

```
IF TRANSACTION-CODE = '1'
    PERFORM ADDITION-ROUTINE.
```

Here is another example of an **IF** statement without an **ELSE**, based on the program that will be discussed in the next chapter:

```
IF I-HOURS-WORKED IS GREATER THAN 40
    SUBTRACT 40 FROM I-HOURS-WORKED GIVING W-OVERTIME-HOURS
    MULTIPLY 0.5 BY W-OVERTIME-HOURS
    MULTIPLY W-OVERTIME-HOURS BY I-PAYRATE
        GIVING W-OVERTIME-PAY ROUNDED
    ADD W-OVERTIME-PAY TO W-GROSS-PAY.
```

This says to test whether the hours-worked item is greater than 40. If so, the four statements shown are carried out; otherwise, the calculations are not carried out.

5.5 THE IMPORTANCE OF THE PERIOD IN AN IF STATEMENT

It is of crucial importance that the period of an **IF** statement appear *exactly where it is intended* because, unlike the IF pseudocode structure, the **COBOL IF** statement has nothing that corresponds to ENDIF. Suppose, for example, that in the last example we absentmindedly put a period at the end of the **SUBTRACT** statement. That would tell the **COBOL** compiler that the end of the **IF** statement had been reached. The effect would be to make the execution of the **SUBTRACT** conditional, but the two **MULTIPLY** verbs and the **ADD** would not be controlled by the **IF** and would, in fact, *always* be carried out. The pseudocode corresponding to the two different statements is shown in Figure 5.1 and Figure 5.2.

Obviously, the misplaced period destroys the intended effect of the program. This error can sometimes be rather difficult to locate. It is not possible for the compiler to flag this error, which has nothing to do with the rules of **COBOL**; the erroneous program would be entirely legal—it would just not do what we wanted it to do.

IF the hours-worked exceeds 40 THEN
    set overtime-hours to hours-worked - 40
    multiply overtime-hours by 0.5
    set overtime-pay to overtime-hours times payrate
    add overtime-pay to gross-pay
ENDIF

FIGURE 5.1   Pseudocode corresponding to correct **IF** statement.

IF the hours-worked exceeds 40 THEN
    set overtime-hours to hours-worked - 40
ENDIF
multiply overtime-hours by 0.5
set overtime-pay to overtime-hours times payrate
add overtime-pay to gross-pay

FIGURE 5.2   Pseudocode corresponding to erroneous **IF** statement.

Leaving off the period at the end of an **IF** is also disastrous. This has the effect of making everything that was supposed to *follow* the **IF**, up to the next period, part of the **IF** statement. Occasionally this error will create an illegal program that can be caught by the compiler, but in most cases not. The results of this error can also be difficult to diagnose.

Similar comments apply to the period at the end of the **READ** statement. If there are several statements in the **AT END** phrase, placing a period after any except the last will remove the statement(s) after the period from control of the **AT END**. Omit the period following the **AT END** phrase, and all statements up to the next period will be part of the **AT END** and, therefore, will be executed only on detecting the end of the file.

It is also essential to be careful about a **READ** statement within an **IF**. The problem is that there is no way to indicate that the end of the statements in the **AT END** phrase has been reached, other than by writing the period at the end of the sentence. What this means, in short, is that if a **READ** appears in an **IF**, everything in the rest of the sentence will be considered part of the **AT END** phrase of the **READ**. If this is not what is desired, the **READ** must be put into a separate paragraph and executed with a **PERFORM**.

5.6 RELATION CONDITIONS

We have been using relation conditions in programming since Chapter 2, where we had a statement

```
PERFORM B010-PROCESS-WRITE-READ
    UNTIL OUT-OF-DATA-FLAG = 'YES'.
```

The part of this statement following the **UNTIL** is a simple example of a relation condition. (We see in this **PERFORM**, incidentally, that conditions appear in statements other than the **IF**.) Now we need to be more precise about the concept of a relation condition, which we have used intuitively so far.

The general format of a relation condition is:

$$\left\{ \begin{array}{l} \text{identifier-1} \\ \text{literal-1} \\ \text{arithmetic-expression-1} \end{array} \right\} \text{relational-operator} \left\{ \begin{array}{l} \text{identifier-2} \\ \text{literal-2} \\ \text{arithmetic-expression-2} \end{array} \right\}$$

We see that a relation condition involves a comparison between two items. The first is called the *subject* and the second the *object*. For example, in the relation condition

```
IF MORE-DATA-FLAG = 'NO'
```

MORE-DATA-FLAG is the subject, the equal sign is the relational operator, and the alphanumeric literal **'NO'** is the object. Both subject and object may be either identifiers, literals, or arithmetic expressions (see Chapter 19). One combination is not permitted, however, and that is the comparison of two literals. Since literals never change value, such a relation condition would be either always true or always false, which means that it would not really be conditional. For example, the relation condition

```
IF 12 IS GREATER THAN 10
```

would always be true, making the test pointless, so this kind of comparison is not allowed.

5.7 RELATIONAL OPERATORS

There are three relational operators that may be used in forming relation conditions. These are used to determine whether the object is greater than, less than, or equal to the object. The permissible ways of writing these relational operators are shown in the following table.

Relational-operator	Meaning
IS [NOT] GREATER THAN IS [NOT] >	Greater than or not greater than
IS [NOT] LESS THAN IS [NOT] <	Less than or not less than
IS [NOT] EQUAL TO IS [NOT] =	Equal to or not equal to

COBOL-85

COBOL-85 supports two additional operators:

Relational-operator	Meaning
IS <u>GREATER THAN OR EQUAL</u> TO IS >=	Not less than
IS <u>LESS THAN OR EQUAL</u> TO IS <=	Not greater than

As you can see from the meaning of these new operators, they do nothing that could not be done with the older operations. They simply provide a more natural (and occasionally shorter) way of expressing certain relations.

END COBOL-85

We see that the words **IS**, **THAN**, and **TO** are always optional, and that the word **NOT** may be used if it is desired to reverse the effect of a comparison. The two forms of each relational operator are equivalent so that, for instance, we have complete freedom either to write **IS GREATER THAN** or the symbol >, which means the same thing. The mathematical symbols may not be familiar or comfortable to some programmers or it may be felt desirable to keep the program as close to ordinary English as possible. We shall use both forms.

Every relational operator must be preceded by and followed by a space.

5.8 THE COLLATING SEQUENCE

The comparison of numeric items determines which of two numbers is larger; this involves no new concepts. The comparison of two nonnumeric items, however, requires that we know how the computer treats such items. Is the digit 7 "more" or "less" than the letter K? Mathematically the question has no meaning, but such tests are very commonly required in data processing, and we must know how our computer operates. The question is answered by knowing the *collating sequence* for the machine; that is, the sequence in which the computer will rank characters, from smallest to largest, in a relation test.

With regard to certain types of nonnumeric comparisons, all computers work the same way. Letters of the alphabet are compared according to their ordinary alphabetic sequence; the character "blank" (space) is less than any letter. Unfortunately, however, computers are not all the same with regard to other types of nonnumeric comparisons. For instance, in some computers the numeric digits are considered to be smaller than the letters, but in others it is just the reverse. It is necessary for you to know how the particular computer you are using operates. However, almost all computers use one of two common collating sequences: EBCDIC (Extended Binary-Coded-Decimal

Interchange Code, pronounced "EB-cee-dick") or ASCII (American Standard Code for Information Interchange, pronounced "AS-key"). These collating sequences are shown in the following table, along with the most common names for the characters.

		EBCDIC		ASCII
1.		(space)		(space)
2.	¢	(cent sign)	!	(exclamation point)
3.	.	(period, decimal point)	"	(double quote)
4.	<	(less-than sign)	#	(number sign, pound sign)
5.	(	(left parenthesis)	$	(dollar sign)
6.	+	(plus sign)	%	(percent sign)
7.	|	(vertical bar, logical OR)	&	(ampersand)
8.	&	(ampersand)	'	(apostrophe, single quote)
9.	!	(exclamation point)	(	(left parenthesis)
10.	$	(dollar sign)	)	(right parenthesis)
11.	*	(asterisk)	*	(asterisk)
12.	)	(right parenthesis)	+	(plus sign)
13.	;	(semicolon)	,	(comma)
14.	¬	(logical not)	-	(minus, hyphen)
15.	-	(minus, hyphen)	.	(period, decimal point)
16.	/	(slash)	/	(slash)
17.	,	(comma)	0–9	(digits)
18.	%	(percent sign)	:	(colon)
19.	_	(underscore)	;	(semicolon)
20.	>	(greater-than sign)	<	(less-than sign)
21.	?	(question mark)	=	(equal sign)
22.	:	(colon)	>	(greater-than sign)
23.	#	(number sign, pound sign)	?	(question mark)
24.	@	(at sign)	@	(at sign)
25.	'	(apostrophe, single quote)	A–Z	(uppercase letters)
26.	=	(equal sign)	[	(left bracket)
27.	"	(double quote)	\	(reverse slash)
28.	a–z	(lowercase letters)	]	(right bracket)
29.	A–Z	(uppercase letters)	^	(caret)
30.	0–9	(digits)	_	(underscore)
31.			`	(grave accent)
32.			a–z	(lowercase letters)
33.			{	(left brace)
34.			|	(vertical bar, logical OR)
35.			}	(right brace)
36.			~	(tilde)

These collating sequences are given in *ascending* sequence. For example, a blank (space) is smaller than any other character in either of the sequences, while the digit 9 is the largest EBCDIC character and the tilde (~) is the largest ASCII character. If your computer does not use one of these collating sequences, you will need to obtain the collating information from a reference manual for your computer. In many applications it is not essential to know the details of the collating sequence so long as we can be assured—as we are—that any given computer will always perform comparisons the same way. In fact, in most current **COBOL** compilers you can set the collating sequence to be anything you want. However, this is not a topic we shall discuss in this book.

It is often necessary to compare nonnumeric items that are not of the same length. When this is done, the effect is as though the shorter item had additional blanks on its right to make it the same length as the longer. This simply means that normal alphabetization rules apply. For example, the name **DAN** is considered "smaller" than the name **DANDRUFF**.

5.9 CLASS CONDITIONS

The relation condition that we have presented so far is only one of four types of conditions, all of which we shall find useful. We now consider the *class condition*, which determines whether the contents of a data item are alphabetic or numeric. The general format is:

$$
\text{identifier IS } [\underline{\text{NOT}}] \left\{ \begin{array}{l} \underline{\text{NUMERIC}} \\ \underline{\text{ALPHABETIC}} \end{array} \right\}
$$

Class conditions are used primarily to test input data. The full story would get us into the question of representation of information inside the computer, which we shall consider more fully in Chapter 10; for now we will simply say that the numeric class test cannot be used with an alphabetic item (only **A**s in its **PICTURE**) and the alphabetic test cannot be used on a numeric item (only **9**s in its **PICTURE**). Either one may be used with an alphanumeric item (**X**s in its **PICTURE**).

The purpose of this test is to be sure that items that are supposed to be numeric do in fact contain only digits, and that items that are supposed to be alphabetic contain only letters. For the purpose of a class test, an item is considered to be numeric if it consists of nothing but digits. In particular, if it contains any blanks it is *not* numeric. This, in fact, is one of the most common uses of the class test: to determine whether an input item contains blanks where the user may have intended zeros. In the absence of appropriate corrective measures that we shall consider in later chapters, this condition can cause the program to abort (that is, stop unexpectedly), since arithmetic cannot be done on items containing blanks.*

An item is considered to be alphabetic only if it consists of nothing but letters and spaces. Here, in other words, the character "space" is considered to be part of the alphabet. We shall have less occasion to use this test.

---

* Some compilers are partially "forgiving" in this matter. Some IBM compilers, for example, will treat blanks in a numeric item as zeros for arithmetic *so long as there is not a blank in the rightmost digit position*. It is inadvisable to rely on such quirks in compilers, however. The same characteristics that allow the IBM compilers to treat most blanks as zeros also cause them to treat letters as digits, but give meaningless results if the data is used for arithmetic operations.

COBOL-85

Since **COBOL-85** recognizes the distinction between lowercase and upper-case letters, it supports two additional tests, **ALPHABETIC-LOWER** and **ALPHABETIC-UPPER**. The format for the class conditions with these additions is as shown here:

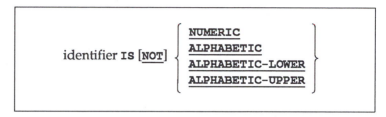

The **ALPHABETIC-LOWER** and **ALPHABETIC-UPPER** tests are used in the same way as the **ALPHABETIC** test. However, **ALPHABETIC-LOWER** is true only if the identifier contains nothing but "a" through "z" or blank, and **ALPHABETIC-UPPER** is true only if the identifier contains nothing but "A" through "Z" or blank. **ALPHABETIC** will accept either lowercase or uppercase.

END COBOL-85

As the formats show, any of the class condition tests may be reversed by use of the word **NOT**.

5.10 COMPOUND CONDITIONS

It often happens that we wish to combine several conditions in one test. Did the employee work more than 40 hours *and* is he or she on the weekly payroll? Is the first item *or* the second item nonnumeric?

Very complex compound conditions can be built up following rules that we shall examine later. We shall also consider at a later time how it is some-times possible to simplify the way that compound conditions are written. For now, we restrict ourselves to just two types of compound conditions, those in which the simple conditions are connected by **OR** and those in which the simple conditions are connected by **AND**.

5.11 THE LOGICAL OPERATOR OR

A compound condition made up of two or more simple conditions connected by the logical operator **OR** is true if any one or more of the simple conditions is true. For example, consider this statement

```
IF      ACCOUNT-AGE IS GREATER THAN 90
    OR CREDIT-CODE = '6'
    PERFORM CREDIT-ROUTINE.
```

The true path on this **IF** statement (**PERFORM CREDIT-ROUTINE**) will be taken if either condition is true or if both are.

We shall ordinarily use indentation, as illustrated here, to align corresponding items vertically, but this is a matter of programming style, not **COBOL** requirements. In fact, it is permissible to write a compound condition all on one line—but at the expense of ease of understanding.

5.12 THE LOGICAL OPERATOR AND

A compound condition made up of two or more simple conditions connected by the logical operator **AND** is true if *all* of the simple conditions are true. For example, we might write

```
IF      HOURS-WORKED IS NUMERIC
    AND HOURS-WORKED IS LESS THAN 80
    AND HOURS WORKED IS GREATER THAN ZERO
        PERFORM NORMAL-PROCESSING
ELSE
        PERFORM HW-ERROR-PROCESSING.
```

This compound condition is true if and only if all three of the simple conditions are satisfied.

5.13 THE PERFORM...UNTIL STATEMENT

The pseudocode structure PERFORM-UNTIL is, of course, implemented in **COBOL** by the **PERFORM...UNTIL** statement. We have used this statement in several examples in preceding chapters and have discussed it in connection with these examples, so no extensive explanation is required here. However, we do wish to emphasize the fact that the condition that follows **UNTIL** is tested *before* the named paragraph is executed. This is very important in determining how many times a loop will be executed. For example, consider the following **COBOL** code, where the dots indicate other statements that do not concern us in this discussion:

```
MOVE 1 TO COUNT.
PERFORM B010-PROCESS
    UNTIL COUNT = 10.
    .
    .
    .

B010-PROCESS.
    READ INPUT-FILE AT END MOVE 'Y' TO FLAG.
    MOVE INPUT-RECORD TO OUTPUT-RECORD.
    WRITE OUTPUT-RECORD.
    ADD 1 TO COUNT.
```

Paragraph **B010-PROCESS** will be executed *nine* times, not ten. When **COUNT** becomes equal to ten after execution of the **ADD** statement, the **PERFORM** statement finishes execution of **B010-PROCESS**, then tests the **UNTIL** condition to determine whether to execute the paragraph again. Since this happens *before* the tenth execution of **B010-PROCESS**, the loop terminates before the tenth execution of the paragraph.

If you have any question in your mind about how this works, try it out with paper and pencil. Make one column to show the current value of **COUNT** and one column to count the number of times **B010-PROCESS** has been executed. Mark down the initial value of **COUNT** in the first column, then trace through the code, following the sequence of steps the computer would take in executing the loop. Each time you enter **B010-PROCESS** make a mark in the second column, and each time you get to the **ADD** statement write down the new value of **COUNT** in the first column. This technique of "playing computer" can be a very useful tool in trying to understand exactly what a program is doing as loops execute. One useful tactic: test that the loop works correctly for zero executions and for one execution; if it does, you have greatly increased your confidence that it will work correctly for any other number of executions.

In any case, it is absolutely essential that you know exactly how many times any loop will be executed. One good building block is to be positive that you understand clearly how the **PERFORM** statement works.

5.14 THE CASE STRUCTURE

Most versions of **COBOL** have no statement that corresponds directly to the CASE structure. However, we can accomplish the same results using other **COBOL** statements. Although there are several ways in which this can be done, the simplest makes use of what is called a *nested* **IF**. This refers to an **IF** statement in which the statement following **ELSE** is itself an **IF** statement. The appropriate format can best be demonstrated by means of an example.

Suppose we are designing part of a payroll system for a company whose employees work in one of four departments. As part of the payroll reporting, we want to determine how much of the total payroll is to be charged to each department. Therefore, after we have computed the gross pay for an employee we will add the amount to a total for the department in which the employee works. The pseudocode for this process is as follows:

```
EVALUATE department number
    WHEN 1
        add gross pay to dept-1-total
    WHEN 2
        add gross pay to dept-2-total
    WHEN 3
        add gross pay to dept-3-total
    WHEN 4
        add gross pay to dept-4-total
    OTHERWISE
        the department number is in error
ENDEVALUATE
```

COBOL code to implement this structure looks like the following:

```
IF      DEPT-NBR = 1
    ADD GROSS-PAY TO DEPT-1-TOTAL
ELSE IF DEPT-NBR = 2
    ADD GROSS-PAY TO DEPT-2-TOTAL
ELSE IF DEPT-NBR = 3
    ADD GROSS-PAY TO DEPT-3-TOTAL
ELSE IF DEPT-NBR = 4
    ADD GROSS-PAY TO DEPT-4-TOTAL
ELSE
    PERFORM X100-DEPT-NBR-ERROR.
```

Observe the structure of this example carefully. What we have done is to insert an **IF** statement as the action to be executed in the false path of another **IF** statement, and repeat this process of nesting the **IF** statements for each additional case. The condition of each **IF** statement tests the CASE variable against a different value, and the final **ELSE** takes care of the **OTHERWISE** action. We can also write a compound condition if two or more case values require the same action, as in the following example:

```
IF      DEPT-NBR = 1 OR DEPT-NBR = 2
    ADD GROSS-PAY TO DEPT-1-2-TOTAL
ELSE IF DEPT-NBR = 3
    ADD GROSS-PAY TO DEPT-3-TOTAL
ELSE IF DEPT-NBR > 3 AND DEPT-NBR < 100
    ADD GROSS-PAY TO OTHER-TOTAL
ELSE
    PERFORM X100-DEPT-NBR-ERROR.
```

In general, nested **IF** statements tend to be a source of trouble in COBOL and must be used with care. However, they do provide a simple way of implementing the case structure if you are careful to follow two rules:

1. Use the conditional phrase after an **IF** only to test values for the case variable, such as "**IF DEPT-NBR = 1 OR DEPT-NBR = 2**".
2. Use only simple, unconditional statements for the case actions. In particular, *never* use an **IF** statement for one of the action statements. If it is necessary to execute an **IF** statement as part of a case action, set up a separate paragraph and use the case action to **PERFORM** the paragraph.

We will discuss the use of nested **IF** statements again in Chapter 8. For now, we will restrict the use of the nested **IF** to implementation of the CASE structure.

COBOL-85

5.15 END STATEMENTS IN COBOL-85

Up to this point, although we have presented some new features of COBOL-85, the differences between COBOL-85 and earlier versions of COBOL have been relatively minor. With the introduction of structure statements, however, we encounter enhancements that are perhaps the *major* difference between COBOL-85 and its predecessors.

We mentioned before that although the conditional structure terminates with an ENDIF, COBOL has no such statement to terminate the **IF** statement. What we have not emphasized, however, is how serious a problem this can be. For example, consider the following pseudocode:

```
set counter to 0
PERFORM-UNTIL counter = 10
    IF rec-code = 'A'
        read data record; at end set flag to 'Y'
        add 1 to counter
        process the record
    ENDIF
ENDPERFORM
```

You might be tempted to use the following **COBOL** code to implement this specification:

```
MOVE ZERO TO COUNTER.
PERFORM B010-PROCESS
    UNTIL COUNT = 10.
    .
    .
    .

B010-PROCESS.
    IF REC-CODE = 'A'
        READ DATA-FILE
            AT END MOVE 'Y' TO FLAG
        ADD 1 TO COUNTER
        PERFORM C050-PROCESS-RECORD.
```

Unfortunately, as we indicated in Section 5.5, this would produce an error. The program would continue to execute **B010-PROCESS** until the end of file was reached, then would keep on executing the paragraph causing an error when the computer tried to read the nonexistent records following the end of the file. The problem is that the **IF** statement cannot contain a period until the end of the statement, and the **AT END** clause does not terminate *until* a period is encountered. Therefore, **COUNTER** is incremented only when the **AT END** phrase is executed.

This type of problem occurs frequently in older versions of **COBOL** and has no clean solution. **COBOL-85**, however, introduces **END** phrases to terminate statements such as **IF** and **PERFORM**, and to terminate phrases such as the **AT END** phrase in the **READ** statement. The use of these **END** phrases is always optional, so any code we have shown up to now is still valid in **COBOL-85**. However, there are situations where the use of an **END** phrase can clarify and simplify your program.

5.16 THE READ STATEMENT WITH END-READ

The problem we encountered trying to implement the previous example occurred because we had no way of terminating the **AT END** phrase of the **READ** statement without also terminating the entire **IF** statement. In **COBOL-85** we can write the paragraph as follows:

```
B010-PROCESS.
    IF REC-CODE = 'A'
        READ DATA-FILE
            AT END MOVE 'Y' TO FLAG
        END-READ
        ADD 1 TO COUNTER
        PERFORM C050-PROCESS-RECORD.
```

This is an accurate implementation of the pseudocode specification given for the problem. The **COBOL** compiler can tell that the **AT END** action terminates with the **END-READ** phrase, and executes the **ADD** statement regardless of whether or not the end of file has been reached. This new feature of the **READ** statement is very useful in implementing certain types of programs. It is typical of the **END** phrases in **COBOL-85** in that it allows you to specify clearly where a conditional statement or phrase ends and the next statement begins.

5.17 THE ARITHMETIC VERBS WITH END PHRASES

Just as the **READ** statement has a conditional phrase, **AT END**, so the arithmetic statements (**ADD**, **SUBTRACT**, **MULTIPLY**, and **DIVIDE**) have a conditional phrase, the **ON SIZE ERROR** phrase. As you might expect, **COBOL-85** has an **END** phrase for each of these statements. For example, we can change the previous example to the following:

```
B010-PROCESS.
    IF REC-CODE = 'A'
        READ DATA-FILE
            AT END MOVE 'Y' TO FLAG
        END-READ
        ADD 1 TO COUNTER
            ON SIZE ERROR MOVE 'Y' TO ERROR-FLAG
        END-ADD
        PERFORM C050-PROCESS-RECORD.
```

In this example, the program will read a record from **DATA-FILE**, add 1 to **COUNTER**, then perform **C0500-PROCESS-RECORD**. If the end of the file is encountered in the **READ**, **FLAG** is set to **'Y'**. If a size error is detected as a result of the **ADD**, **ERROR-FLAG** is set to **'Y'**. In any case, however, all three statements are executed any time **REC-CODE** is equal to **'A'**.

Just as there is the **END-ADD** phrase for the **ADD** statement, so there is **END-SUBTRACT**, **END-MULTIPLY**, and **END-DIVIDE** for the other arithmetic statements. Their formats are very similar to that of the **ADD** and **END-ADD** and, although we will demonstrate the use of these **END-STATEMENTS** in future examples, we will not show the complete formats here.

5.18 THE IF STATEMENT WITH END-IF

The format of the **IF** statement in **COBOL-85** is as follows.

$$
\underline{\text{IF}} \text{ condition-1 } \underline{\text{THEN}}
\left\{
\begin{array}{l}
\{\text{statement-1}\} \ldots \\
\underline{\text{NEXT SENTENCE}}
\end{array}
\right\}
\left\{
\begin{array}{l}
\underline{\text{ELSE}} \{\text{statement-2}\} \ldots [\underline{\text{END-IF}}] \\
\underline{\text{ELSE}} \ \underline{\text{NEXT SENTENCE}} \\
\underline{\text{END-IF}}
\end{array}
\right\}
$$

The major difference between this format of the **IF** statement and the format shown in Section 5.4 is the addition of the **END-IF** phrase. This enhancement of the **IF** statement makes its structure identical to that of the pseudocode IF structure, which greatly improves the flexibility and readability of the statement. The use of **END-IF** delimits the scope of all statements within the **IF** very clearly, and makes it easier to change a program without causing errors. The real advantage of this capability comes when we use nested **IF** statements for something other than implementing the case structure. However, we will defer detailed discussion of the nested **IF** until Chapter 8.

There is one more change in the **COBOL-85** version of the **IF** statement, the word **THEN** after the condition. Since the **THEN** is not underlined it is not required and, in fact, has no effect on the meaning of the **IF** statement. However, some programmers feel that its use improves the readability of the **IF** statement. We will generally not use **THEN** in an **IF** statement, if only to maintain compatibility with earlier versions of **COBOL**.*

5.19 THE PERFORM STATEMENT WITH END-PERFORM

Frequently, when you design a program you will specify a module that, in addition to other statements, contains a simple iteration specification. When this is implemented in **COBOL**, however, it has always been necessary to create a separate paragraph because the **PERFORM** statement would execute only named paragraphs. With the addition of the **END-PERFORM** phrase in **COBOL-85**, it is now possible to execute many loops "in-line," without creating a new paragraph. For example, consider the following pseudocode specification:

```
set counter to zero
PERFORM-UNTIL counter = 10
     add 1 to counter
     move counter to line-number
     write the print line
ENDPERFORM
```

In **COBOL-85** we can implement this as

```
MOVE ZERO TO COUNTER.
PERFORM UNTIL COUNTER = 10
     ADD 1 TO COUNTER
     MOVE COUNTER TO LINE-NUMBER
     WRITE PRINT-LINE
END-PERFORM.
```

It is obvious that this capability simplifies the **PERFORM** statement. However, there is an important restriction on the in-line loop. The statement(s) following the **UNTIL** phrase must be an *unconditional* statement(s). For example, the following code is *not* legal:

```
MOVE ZERO TO COUNTER.
PERFORM UNTIL COUNTER = 10
     ADD 1 TO COUNTER
     READ DATA-FILE
         AT END MOVE 'Y' TO FLAG
     END-READ
     MOVE COUNTER TO LINE-NUMBER
     WRITE PRINT-LINE
END-PERFORM.
```

The problem is that the **AT END** phrase makes the **READ** statement a *conditional* statement: the **AT END** code is executed sometimes but not always. Other conditional statements that we have encountered so far are the **IF** statement, any arithmetic statement that uses the **ON SIZE ERROR** phrase, and of course the **PERFORM...UNTIL** statement. However, in spite of this limitation, the **END-PERFORM** will generally save you work and make your program easier to read.

---

* *Some* earlier versions of COBOL accept the use of THEN in the IF statement, but this is by no means universal.

PERFORM...UNTIL statement. However, in spite of this limitation, the **END-PERFORM** will generally save you work and make your program easier to read.

There are two more restrictions on the use of the **END-PERFORM**. First, you cannot specify the name of a paragraph to be performed (between **PERFORM** and **UNTIL**) *and* specify in-line code and **END-PERFORM** as well. You must choose one or the other. Second, if you use in-line code, the **END-PERFORM** phase is *not* optional.

5.20 THE EVALUATE STATEMENT

In addition to improving the control structure of **COBOL** by adding the **END** phrases, **COBOL-85** has added a new statement that implements the case structure directly instead of through other statements. This new statement is the

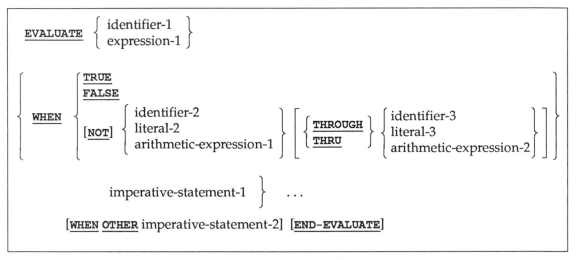

EVALUATE statement (hence the name for our pseudocode structure), and a simplified version of its format is as shown.

Even this version of the **EVALUATE** statement, which is simplified considerably over the complete statement, is quite a bit to handle, so let's look at a few examples to see what this really means. The **COBOL** statements that correspond to the examples of the **EVALUATE** pseudocode structure in Section 4.6 (page 63) are shown in Figures 5.3 and 5.4.

```
EVALUATE DIST-FROM-TOWN
     WHEN 0 THRU 5
          MOVE 7.50 TO FEE
     WHEN 5 THRU 10
          MOVE 10.00 TO FEE
     WHEN OTHER
          MOVE DIST-FROM-TOWN TO FEE
END-EVALUATE.
```

FIGURE 5.3 **EVALUATE** statement corresponding to first case example in Chapter 4.

```
EVALUATE QUIZ-GRADE
    WHEN 10
        MOVE 'EXCELLENT' TO CLASS-STANDING
    WHEN 8 THRU 9
        MOVE 'ABOVE-AVERAGE' TO CLASS-STANDING
    WHEN 5 THRU 7
        MOVE 'AVERAGE' TO CLASS-STANDING
    WHEN 3 THRU 4
        MOVE 'BELOW-AVERAGE' TO CLASS-STANDING
    WHEN OTHER
        MOVE 'FAILING' TO CLASS-STANDING
END-EVALUATE.
```

FIGURE 5.4   **EVALUATE** statement corresponding to second case example in Chapter 4.

subject. Following each occurrence of **WHEN** we have specified either a single value or a range of values; these are the *selection objects*. The program computes the current value of the selection subject, then compares it to each of the selection objects in turn. If the value of the selection subject matches the value(s) specified by the selection object, then the statement following the selection object is executed. (Of course, although these examples show only one imperative statement for each selection object, you can have a series of imperative statements just as in **PERFORM**.) If no selection object matches the value of the selection subject, the **WHEN OTHER** statement is executed. If no **WHEN OTHER** phrase is specified, the **EVALUATE** statement causes no action. In any case, no more than *one* **WHEN** statement will be executed. If more than one selection object would match the value of the selection subject, only the statement following the *first* selection subject to make the match is executed.

Notice that the format of the **EVALUATE** statement includes the words **TRUE** and **FALSE**. These are two new reserved words whose values match the values that can be taken by a conditional expression such as "**AMOUNT > 1000**". **TRUE** and **FALSE** are *not* general purpose constants and may *not* be used in any statement except **EVALUATE**. The following example shows how these values might be used.

```
EVALUATE DIST-FROM-TOWN > 10
    WHEN TRUE
        MULTIPLY DIST-FROM-TOWN BY 2 GIVING FEE
    WHEN FALSE
        MOVE 12.50 TO FEE
END-EVALUATE.
```

Of course, this example could also be written as

```
IF DIST-FROM-TOWN > 10
    MULTIPLY DIST-FROM-TOWN BY 2 GIVING FEE
ELSE
    MOVE 12.50 TO FEE
END-IF.
```

Rather than going through more examples here, we shall wait to demonstrate the use of **EVALUATE** and the other **COBOL-85** enhancements throughout the following chapters.

END COBOL-85

REVIEW QUESTIONS

1. What is the function of the period in the **IF** statement?

2. What does **NEXT SENTENCE** accomplish?

3. What happens if you omit the **ELSE** part of an **IF** statement? Will you get an error?

4. Is there more than one category of condition?

5. What is the function of the relation condition?

6. List the relational operators. Your answer will depend on whether or not you are using **COBOL-85**. Give the answer for your version.

7. What is the collating sequence of a computer? What is its function?

8. What will these statements do?

   a. ```
      PERFORM NORMAL-SALE
           UNTIL COLUMN-1 = '6'
              OR COLUMN-2 = '7'
              OR COLUMN-7 = 'A'.
      ```

   b. ```
      PERFORM LO-EQUAL-ROUTINE
           UNTIL KEY-1 > PREVIOUS-KEY-1.
              OR TRANS-EOF = 'Y'
      ```

   c. ```
      READ TRANSACTION-FILE
           AT END WRITE MESSAGE-RECORD-5
                MOVE 'Y' TO TRANSACTION-EOF-FLAG.
      ```

   d. ```
      READ TRANSACTION-FILE
           AT END WRITE MESSAGE-RECORD-5.
                MOVE 'Y' TO TRANSACTION-EOF-FLAG.
      ```

9. Point out any errors in syntax in the following **IF** statements, that is, any violations of the rules for writing legal **COBOL** statements, without regard for what the statements might mean.

   a. ```
      IF A = B
           WRITE EQUAL-RECORD.
      ELSE
           WRITE UNEQUAL-RECORD.
      ```

   b. ```
      IF HOURS-WORKED IS GREATER THAN 40
           SUBTRACT 40 FROM HOURS-WORKED GIVING OT-HOURS
           MULTIPLY 0.5 BY OT-HOURS.
           ADD OT-HOURS TO HOURS-WORKED.
      ```

   c. ```
      IF 24.0 GREATER THAN 37.0
           MOVE 'STRANGE' TO COMMENT-1.
      ```

   d. ```
      IF A IS LESS THAN B MOVE X TO Y ELSE
      MOVE X TO Z.
      ```

   e. ```
      IF ON-HAND IS
                          LESS   THAN
      REORDER-POINT ADD 1 TO ORDER-COUNT MOVE REORDER-QTY TO
      RECORD-AREA-6 WRITE ORDER-RECORD
      ELSE
           WRITE NORMAL-LINE.
      ```

10. Name two figurative constants.
      ```

11. Each record in a payroll file is supposed to contain either a **C**, an **H**, or an **S** in field 8. Any other character would give erroneous results. Would the following **IF** statement correctly check for the possibility of error?

```
IF      FIELD8 IS NOT EQUAL TO 'C'
     OR FIELD8 IS NOT EQUAL TO 'H'
     OR FIELD8 IS NOT EQUAL TO 'S'
     PERFORM X100-BAD-FIELD8.
```

12. Given the following code, how many records would be written to the output file?

```
          MOVE 1 TO COUNT.
          PERFORM D010-WRITE
              UNTIL COUNT = 100.
            .
            .
            .

     D010-WRITE.
          WRITE OUTPUT-RECORD.
          ADD 1 TO COUNT.
```

13. How many records would this code write to the output file?

```
          MOVE 1 TO COUNT.
          PERFORM D010-WRITE
              UNTIL COUNT = 100.
            .
            .
            .

     D010-WRITE.
          WRITE OUTPUT-RECORD.
          ADD 2 TO COUNT.
```

ANSWERS TO REVIEW QUESTIONS

1. The period marks the end of the **IF** statement. If you omit the period, everything following the **IF** statement becomes part of the **IF** statement.

2. It does nothing, which sometimes is precisely what you want to do. For example, if you want to perform some action if the **IF** condition is false but do nothing if the condition is true, writing **NEXT SENTENCE** for the "true action" will produce the result you need.

3. Omitting the **ELSE** part of an **IF** statement will certainly not cause an error. It simply means that if the condition is false, you don't want the computer to do anything.

4. Yes. So far we have encountered the *class* condition and the *relation* condition. Eventually we shall study four categories of conditions.

5. The relation condition compares two values. These values may be identifiers, literals, or arithmetic expressions (but you can not compare two literals).

6. The relational operators are:

```
IS GREATER THAN              >
IS NOT GREATER THAN          NOT >
IS LESS THAN                 <
IS NOT LESS THAN             NOT <
IS EQUAL TO                  =
IS NOT EQUAL TO              NOT =
```

If you are using **COBOL-85**, you also have

```
IS GREATER THAN OR EQUAL TO      >=
IS LESS THAN OR EQUAL TO         <=
```

7. The collating sequence of a computer is the order in which it will rank characters in a comparison. It is used to determine the value of a comparison in a relation condition.

8. **a.** The paragraph named **NORMAL-SALE** will be performed repeatedly until any one or more of the relations shown is true.

   b. If the program could be compiled, the paragraph named **LO-EQUAL-ROUTINE** would be performed until **KEY-1** is greater than **PREVIOUS-KEY-1**; but the period at the end of this relation, which presumably is not intended, makes the next line illegal. No **COBOL** statement begins with **OR**.

   c. A record from the file named **TRANSACTION-FILE** is read. If this is the end of file, two statements are carried out, writing a message and setting the flag.

   d. A record from the file named **TRANSACTION-FILE** is read. If this is the end of file, a message is written. Unconditionally, the end of file flag is set. Presumably the extra period after the first relation is unintended, but the resulting sequence of statements is completely legal from the standpoint of the **COBOL** rules. The end of file flag will be set after reading the first record, and succeeding statements will presumably stop program execution before processing the first record. *The compiler could not give any warning!*

9. **a.** A statement beginning with the word **IF** and ending with the first period is syntactically legal. However, the first period makes the material beginning with **ELSE** syntactically illegal.

   b. Presumably the period at the end of the **MULTIPLY** is unintended, but there are no syntactic errors here. The **SUBTRACT** and the **MULTIPLY** would be conditional but the **ADD** would always be performed.

   c. A relation condition may not compare two literals.

   d. This is syntactically legal according to the rules of **COBOL**. The fact that the **IF** statement is written on two lines instead of four violates the programming standards followed in this text, but no **COBOL** rules are broken.

   e. This also contains no syntactic errors. The point here is to demonstrate how very difficult it can be to read programs that do not follow sensible conventions about the form in which statements are written.

10. **SPACES, ZERO**.

11. **X100-BAD-FIELDS** would *always* be performed. **FIELD8** cannot possibly be equal to *all three* of **C**, **H**, and **S** on any one record, so at least two of the simple conditions connected by the ORs would always be true. This error, which is very common, is probably the result of confusion between the rather loose usage of the words "and" and "or" in English usage and the very precise way the logical operators **AND** and **OR** are used in **COBOL**.

The desired result can be obtained by replacing the **ORs** in the statement with **ANDs**, or perhaps more understandably, writing

```
IF    FIELD8 IS EQUAL TO 'C'
   OR FIELD8 IS EQUAL TO 'H'
   OR FIELD8 IS EQUAL TO 'S'
   NEXT SENTENCE
ELSE
   PERFORM X100-BAD-FIELD8.
```

12. 99. Since the **UNTIL** condition is tested *before* **D010-WRITE** is executed, the 100th record is never written. A better way to write this type of code is to change the first line to

```
MOVE ZERO TO COUNT
```

This makes **COUNT** a count of how many records have actually been written, rather than having it indicate which record is *going* to be written.

13. The code would continue forever (or until some other condition terminated the program). **COUNT** is initially set equal to 1, and since the paragraph adds 2 each time it is executed, **COUNT** always has an odd value. Therefore, it will never be equal to 100, which is even. The point is that you must be very careful when designing a loop that it is always possible to reach the termination condition.

EXERCISES

*1. Write statements to carry out the following operations.

   a. Add 1 to an item named **LEGAL-ADULT** if **AGE** is 18 or greater.

   b. Perform a paragraph named **D050-PROCESS-STOCK-ITEM** if **PART-1-A** contains the letter **S**.

   c. Add 1 to **BIG** if **SIZE-A** is greater than 800 and add 1 to **LITTLE** if **SIZE-A** is less than or equal to 800.

   d. If the item in **NAME-A** is greater than the item in **NAME-B**, move the contents of **NAME-A** to **TEMPORARY**; if the item in **NAME-A** is less than the item in **NAME-B**, move the contents of **NAME-B** to **TEMPORARY**; if the two are equal, move either of them to **TEMPORARY**.

   e. If the value of the item named **HOURS-WORKED** is *anything but* 40, perform **C035-NON-STANDARD**.

   f. Perform the paragraph named **X020-BAD-CODE** if **CODE-X** contains anything but digits.

2. Write statements to carry out the following operations.

   a. Add 1 to an item named **MAJOR-BILLING** if **ACCOUNT-TOTAL** is greater than 1000.00.

   b. Determine whether the value of the item named **FINAL-BILL** is greater than 999.99 and, if so, perform the paragraph named **D035-SPECIAL-APPROVAL**.

* Answers to starred exercises will be found in Appendix IV at the end of the book.

   c. If the item named **CODE-A** contains the characters **AB47Z**, move the characters **APPROVED** to the item named **APPROVAL**.

   d. Move zero to **SIGNAL** if **MEASUREMENT** is zero, and move 1 to **SIGNAL** if **MEASUREMENT** is not zero.

   e. Perform the paragraph named **C055-REGULAR** if the value of **HOURS-WORKED** is exactly 40.0.

   f. Perform the paragraph named **Y030-BAD-CODE** if **CODE-A** contains anything but letters and spaces.

*3. Given the appropriate Data Division entries, write statements that will move either **REORDER-QTY** or zero to **ORDER-AMOUNT**, depending on whether the sum of **ON-HAND** and **ON-ORDER** has or has not fallen below **REORDER-POINT**.

4. Three examination grades are named **GRADE-1**, **GRADE-2**, and **GRADE-3**. The three are to be added and their sum divided by 3, giving the average grade. If the average grade is 65 or greater, the word **PASS** is to be placed in the item named **FINAL-GRADE**; otherwise the word **FAIL** is to be placed in **FINAL-GRADE**. Write appropriate statements.

*5. Suppose that a salesperson's commission is based on a **PRODUCT-CODE**, as follows:

PRODUCT-CODE	Commission Formula
1	0.15 × SALE-PRICE
2	0.40 × (SALE-PRICE - BASE-PRICE)
3	0.10 × BASE-PRICE + 0.50 × (SALE-PRICE - BASE-PRICE)
4	$10.00 + 0.05 × BASE-PRICE
5	$35.00

Given **PRODUCT-CODE**, **SALE-PRICE**, and **BASE-PRICE**, write statements to compute **COMMISSION**. If **PRODUCT-CODE** is anything except 1, 2, 3, 4, or 5, move zero to **COMMISSION** and move **X** to **BAD-PRODUCT-CODE-FLAG**.

6. Given **ANNUAL-EARNING**, write statements that will compute **TAX** according to the following table.

ANNUAL-EARNINGS	TAX
Not over $5000	Zero
Over $5000 but not over $15,000	2% of the amount over $5000
Over $15,000	$200 plus 5% of the amount over $15,000

*7. Each record in a data file has the following format:

Columns 1-20	Name
Columns 21-25	Blank
Columns 26-27	Years of service

Write a program to read the data file, print the data from each record and, if the years of service are greater than 40, write the comment **AN ABC COMPANY VETERAN**.

8. Each record in a data file has the following format:

Columns 1-5	Cost center code
Columns 6-11	Budgeted expense, dollars
Columns 12-17	Actual expense, year to date, dollars

Write a program that will read such a file and, for each record, print a line giving the input data together with a comment **EXCEEDS BUDGET** if the actual expense is greater than the budgeted amount.

*9. Each record in a data file contains an alphanumeric identification in columns 45-50 and a gross pay in dollars and cents in columns 70-76. A city tax is to be computed for each, the tax being 2% of the amount (if any) over $2000. For each record, a line is to be printed containing the input data and the computed tax. Write a suitable program.

10. Each record in a data file contains an alphanumeric identification in columns 40-47 and a total price in columns 31-36 in dollars and cents. For each record a discount is to be computed and printed, along with the input data. The discount is 2% if the amount is over $1000, and zero if it is not. Write a suitable program.

*11. You are to read a file whose records have the following format:

Columns 1-8	IDENT	Alphanumeric
Columns 9-15	DOLLARS	9(5)V99
Columns 16-80	OTHER-INFO	Alphanumeric

The contents of each record are to be listed with three blanks between fields. The amount in the **DOLLARS** field from each record should be added to a total (that is initially set to zero); when the end of the file is detected, this total should be printed.

12. Extend the program of Exercise 11 as follows. First, any record in which the dollar amount is zero should not be printed. Second, you are to keep a count of the number of records having a zero dollar amount and the number having a nonzero amount; both of these counts should be printed on the final total line, together with their sum (the total number of records), and the average of the nonzero amounts (which is the total of the dollar amounts divided by the number of nonzero records).

13. (This exercise extends the project-level Exercise 19 in Chapter 3.)
Assume that the inventory record has been modified as follows:

Columns 1-5	product code
Columns 6-30	product description
Columns 31-35	sales for three weeks ago
Columns 36-40	sales for two weeks ago
Columns 41-45	sales for last week
Columns 46-50	inventory level
Columns 51-57	selling price in dollars and cents
Columns 58-62	standard inventory level

The standard inventory level for a product is the ideal number of units that the company would like to have in stock for that product. (This may be changed at any time by management, such as for seasonal products.) If a product's inventory level has fallen below the standard level, then the company needs to order more of the product from their supplier. The quantity to be ordered is determined by the following function:

reorder qty = predicted sales + (standard level - inventory) where "predicted sales" is the sales predicted for the following week (see Exercise 3.19), "standard level" is the standard inventory level for the product, and "inventory" is the current inventory level for the product.

Modify the program of Exercise 3.19 so that if the inventory level of a product has fallen below the standard inventory level, the program will calculate the quantity to be ordered and print a message on the report. The message should consist of the word **REORDER**, followed by a single space, then the reorder quantity. The standard inventory level should also be printed, between the columns for current inventory and selling price. Here is a sample of the revised report:.

```
                        Last
Prod  Product        3 wk  2 wk  week   Curr   Std  Product  F'cst Product
Code  Description    Sales Sales Sales  Inv    Inv  Price    Sales Value

AA123 SNOW BLOWER    00002 00000 00005 00022  00025 00299.95 00003 0006598.90 REORDER 00006
BB345 LAWN CHAIR     01050 02577 00933 09515  08500 00017.50 01501 0166512.50

      AVERAGE VALUE                                                   0086555.70
```

14. (This exercise is suitable for a small project.)

Write a program that uses records in a payroll file to produce a payroll report. The payroll records have the following format:

Column 1	not used
Column 2-6	employee number
Column 7-11	department number
Column 12-17	not used
Column 18-21	hours worked; numeric, 2 decimals
Column 22-25	base pay rate; numeric, 2 decimals
Column 26-27	municipality code

For each employee compute the employee's gross pay as hours worked times base pay rate for the first 37.5 hours, then base rate times 1.5 times hours worked in excess of 37.5 hours. For example, if an employee worked 41.50 hours with a base pay rate of $10.00 the gross pay would be $435.00 ($375 for the first 37.5 hours, plus $60 for the remaining 4 hours).

In addition to computing the employee's gross pay you are to compute the employee's deductions. Deductions consist of federal tax (25% of gross pay), state tax (5% of gross pay), and city tax. City tax varies depending on where the employee lives; this is coded in the "municipality code" field. Using the municipality code, city tax is calculated as follows:

Municipality	Tax
03	1.50% of gross pay
07	2.00%
15	5.25%
23	3.75%
77	2.50%

The employee's net pay is the gross pay minus the sum of all deductions.

Print a report showing the following information for each employee:

Column 1-5	employee number
Column 8-12	hours worked
Column 15-19	base pay rate
Column 22-28	gross pay
Column 31-37	federal tax
Column 40-45	state tax
Column 48-53	city tax
Column 56-62	net pay

All decimal fields should show the actual decimal point.

CHAPTER 6

A SIMPLE PAYROLL PROGRAM

6.1 INTRODUCTION

In the preceding chapters we showed how to design a program, then introduced the **COBOL** statements that implement the basic control structures. It is now time to see these tools used in a complete program. We shall design an illustrative program, then show code that implements the design. Finally, we shall make some revisions to the program, first changing the design specifications, then changing the program.

6.2 REQUIREMENTS OF THE PROGRAM

The function of the program is to accept a file of records, each of which contains information about one worker, in a payroll system. We are required to compute the gross pay, tax, and net pay for each worker and to print a line for each. The basic program structure—that is, a main line routine and a performed paragraph that is executed for each record—is the same as in previous chapters. However, within the performed paragraph we shall perform lower-level paragraphs to carry out details, and shall have **IF** statements that determine whether there is overtime pay to be calculated and whether the worker has any taxable income.

The input to the program consists of one record for each employee. The fields in a record give the employee's payroll number (5 alphanumeric characters), name (20 alphanumeric characters), hours worked to tenths (three digits), hourly pay rate with three decimals (five digits), and a two-digit number giving the number of dependents. The record layout is:

Columns 1-5	Payroll number	**X(5)**
Columns 6-25	Name	**X(20)**
Columns 26-28	Hours worked	**99V9**
Columns 29-31	Not used	
Columns 32-36	Hourly pay rate	**99V999**
Columns 37-38	Number of dependents	**99**

For each record we are required to carry out the following calculations. The number of hours worked is to be multiplied by the pay rate, giving gross pay. If the person worked more than 40 hours, time-and-a-half is to be paid for hours over 40. The employee is allowed an exemption of $50.00 for each dependent; if the gross pay is greater than the total of the exemptions, a tax of 21% is assessed against the taxable amount (the difference between gross pay and the total of exemptions). A line is to be printed for each record, giving all of the input data and calculated results. The format in which the results are to be presented may be seen in the sample output in Figure 6.4.

6.3 DESIGNING THE PROGRAM

We begin the design process by determining what the major functions of the program are. The basic function of the program is to *produce payroll calculations*. This can be accomplished if we can *calculate the payroll for one employee*, then do this repeatedly for all employees. Based on the program requirements given in Section 6.2, we have the following functions that must be performed for an employee:

1. Get a payroll record;
2. Compute gross pay (including overtime pay);
3. Compute exemptions;
4. Compute tax;
5. Compute net pay;
6. Print output line.

From these functions we can produce the hierarchy chart that is shown in Figure 6.1. You may wish to add modules to open and close the files, subordinate to the main module.

The next design step is to write pseudocode specifications for each module. These are shown in Figure 6.2.

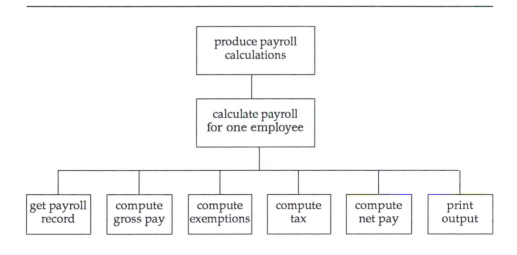

FIGURE 6.1 Hierarchy chart for a payroll program.

PRODUCE PAYROLL CALCULATIONS:
open files
set eof-flag to 'N'
get payroll record
PERFORM-UNTIL eof-flag = 'Y'
    calculate payroll for employee
ENDPERFORM
close files

CALCULATE PAYROLL FOR EMPLOYEE:
compute gross-pay
compute exemptions
compute tax
compute net pay
print output line
get payroll record

GET PAYROLL RECORD:
read payroll-record; at end set eof-flag to 'Y'

COMPUTE GROSS PAY:
gross-pay = hours-worked x pay-rate
IF hours-worked is greater than 40 THEN
    overtime-hours = hours-worked - 40
    multiply overtime-hours by 0.5
    overtime-pay = overtime-hours x pay-rate
    add overtime-pay to gross-pay
ENDIF

COMPUTE EXEMPTIONS:
exemptions = 50.00 x number-dependents

COMPUTE TAX:
IF gross-pay is greater than exemptions THEN
    tax = 0.21 x (gross-pay - exemptions)
ELSE
    tax = 0
ENDIF

COMPUTE NET PAY:
net-pay = gross-pay - tax

PRINT OUTPUT LINE:
move payroll-number, employee-name, hours-worked, pay-rate,
    number-dependents, gross-pay, tax, and net-pay
    to output-record
print output-record

FIGURE 6.2 Pseudocode specifications for a payroll program.

We must emphasize that it is *not* necessary to go into this level of detail when designing most programs. Most of the modules defined in Figure 6.2 will be implemented by only one or two lines of **COBOL** and can certainly be written in-line, without creating a separate paragraph for each module. In fact, *all* of the modules on the bottom level of the hierarchy chart can be implemented as in-line code (see Exercise 6.2). However, we will show each module as a separate paragraph in the program to emphasize the modularity and the relationship between the hierarchy chart and the final program.

Observe that the higher level modules emphasize control of execution and the overall logic of the program, while the lower level modules show the details of computation. This division of activity is common in most programs. In the higher levels we concentrate on *when* things are done, and leave the details of *how* they are done for lower levels.

6.4   THE PAYROLL PROGRAM

The complete payroll program is shown in Figure 6.3.

The File Section contains no new concepts. Prefixes are used to indicate input and output, as in Chapter 3. However, notice the **FILLER** field at the end of **PAYROLL-RECORD**. The computer used to implement this program requires that simple input files be 80 characters long, so it was necessary to pad the record to 80 characters. This is a requirement of the computer, not **COBOL**, and other computers will not necessarily have this requirement; be sure that you know what your computer requires.

```
IDENTIFICATION DIVISION.
PROGRAM-ID.
     PAYROLL1.
DATE-WRITTEN.
     JANUARY 29, 1987.

ENVIRONMENT DIVISION.
INPUT-OUTPUT SECTION.
FILE-CONTROL.
     SELECT PAYROLL-FILE        ASSIGN TO S-PAYROLL.
     SELECT REPORT-FILE         ASSIGN TO S-REPORT.

DATA DIVISION.
FILE SECTION.
FD   PAYROLL-FILE
     LABEL RECORDS ARE OMITTED.
01   PAYROLL-RECORD.
     05   I-PAYROLL-NUMBER       PIC X(5).
     05   I-NAME                 PIC X(20).
     05   I-HOURS-WORKED         PIC 99V9.
     05   FILLER                 PIC X(3).
     05   I-PAYRATE              PIC 99V999.
     05   I-DEPENDENTS           PIC 99.
     05   FILLER                 PIC X(42).
```

```
FD   REPORT-FILE
     LABEL RECORDS ARE OMITTED.
01   REPORT-RECORD.
     05  O-PAYROLL-NUMBER      PIC X(5).
     05  FILLER                PIC XX.
     05  O-NAME                PIC X(20).
     05  FILLER                PIC XX.
     05  O-HOURS-WORKED        PIC 99.9.
     05  FILLER                PIC XX.
     05  O-PAYRATE             PIC 99.999.
     05  FILLER                PIC XX.
     05  O-DEPENDENTS          PIC 99.
     05  FILLER                PIC XX.
     05  O-GROSS-PAY           PIC 999.99.
     05  FILLER                PIC XX.
     05  O-TAX                 PIC 999.99.
     05  FILLER                PIC XX.
     05  O-NET-PAY             PIC 999.99.


WORKING-STORAGE SECTION.
01   C-EXEMPTION              PIC 99V99      VALUE 50.00.
01   C-TAXRATE                PIC V999       VALUE   .210.
01   W-EXEMPTION-TOTAL        PIC 999V99.
01   W-GROSS-PAY              PIC 999V99.
01   W-NET-PAY                PIC 999V99.
01   W-OUT-OF-RECORDS-FLAG    PIC X          VALUE 'N'.
01   W-OVERTIME-HOURS         PIC 99V9.
01   W-OVERTIME-PAY           PIC 999V99.
01   W-TAX                    PIC 999V99.
01   W-TAXABLE                PIC 999V99.


PROCEDURE DIVISION.
A000-PRODUCE-PAYROLL-CALC.
    OPEN INPUT PAYROLL-FILE
         OUTPUT REPORT-FILE.
    PERFORM C010-GET-PAYROLL-REC.
    PERFORM B010-CALC-EMP-PAYROLL
        UNTIL W-OUT-OF-RECORDS-FLAG = 'Y'.
    CLOSE PAYROLL-FILE
          REPORT-FILE.
    STOP RUN.


B010-CALC-EMP-PAYROLL.
    PERFORM C020-COMPUTE-GROSS-PAY.
    PERFORM C030-COMPUTE-EXEMPTIONS.
    PERFORM C040-COMPUTE-TAX.
    PERFORM C050-COMPUTE-NET-PAY.
    PERFORM C060-PRINT-OUTPUT.
    PERFORM C010-GET-PAYROLL-REC.


C010-GET-PAYROLL-REC.
    READ PAYROLL-FILE
         AT END MOVE 'Y' TO W-OUT-OF-RECORDS-FLAG.
```

```
C020-COMPUTE-GROSS-PAY.
    MULTIPLY I-HOURS-WORKED BY I-PAYRATE
            GIVING W-GROSS-PAY ROUNDED.
    IF I-HOURS-WORKED IS GREATER THAN 40
        SUBTRACT 40 FROM I-HOURS-WORKED
            GIVING W-OVERTIME-HOURS
        MULTIPLY 0.5 BY W-OVERTIME-HOURS
        MULTIPLY W-OVERTIME-HOURS BY I-PAYRATE
            GIVING W-OVERTIME-PAY ROUNDED
        ADD W-OVERTIME-PAY TO W-GROSS-PAY.

C030-COMPUTE-EXEMPTIONS.
    MULTIPLY C-EXEMPTION BY I-DEPENDENTS
        GIVING W-EXEMPTIONS-TOTAL.

C040-COMPUTE-TAX.
    IF W-GROSS-PAY IS GREATER THAN W-EXEMPTIONS
        SUBTRACT W-EXEMPTIONS-TOTAL FROM W-GROSS-PAY
            GIVING W-TAXABLE
        MULTIPLY C-TAXRATE BY W-TAXABLE
            GIVING W-TAX ROUNDED
    ELSE
        MOVE ZERO TO W-TAX.

C050-COMPUTE-NET-PAY.
    SUBTRACT W-TAX FROM W-GROSS-PAY GIVING W-NET-PAY.

C060-PRINT-OUTPUT.
    MOVE SPACES              TO REPORT-RECORD.
    MOVE I-PAYROLL-NUMBER    TO O-PAYROLL-NUMBER.
    MOVE I-NAME              TO O-NAME.
    MOVE I-HOURS-WORKED      TO O-HOURS-WORKED.
    MOVE I-PAYRATE           TO O-PAYRATE.
    MOVE I-DEPENDENTS        TO O-DEPENDENTS.
    MOVE W-TAX               TO O-TAX.
    MOVE W-GROSS-PAY         TO O-GROSS-PAY.
    MOVE W-NET-PAY           TO O-NET-PAY.
    WRITE REPORT-RECORD.
```

FIGURE 6.3 A program to calculate weekly pay, including overtime, for all of the employee records in an input file.

6.5 THE VALUE CLAUSE IN THE WORKING-STORAGE SECTION

It frequently happens that data items in Working-Storage need to be loaded into a computer with specified initial values. We recall that it is impossible to know what a location in computer storage contains unless we specifically put something there. In past programs we have done this by means of MOVE statements in the Procedure Division. That is a bit awkward, however, in many cases, and an alternative method has been provided, the VALUE clause.

In order to give a starting value to a data item in the Working-Storage section, we follow its **PICTURE** clause with the word **VALUE** and a literal. This literal value is assigned to the data item when the program is first loaded into storage. If the item is numeric, the literal must be numeric, that is, written without quotes. For example, in our program we give the data item **C-TAX-RATE** the numeric value .210, written without quotes. If the item is non-numeric, then a nonnumeric literal—with quotes—is required. In our program, the data item **W-OUT-OF-RECORDS-FLAG** is given the nonnumeric value **'N'**.

VALUE clauses should be written for elementary items only. Although they can be used on group items, doing so tends to decrease program flexibility and tends to be a source of errors as well. Therefore, in this book we use **VALUE** items only on elementary items. Observe, too, that **VALUE** clauses may be written for items in Working-Storage only; they may not be used this way on File Section items.

The value given to a Working-Storage item by a **VALUE** clause may be changed later by a Procedure Division statement, if the programmer wishes. In the program shown, the value for the flag certainly will be changed from **N** to **Y** by the action of the **AT END** phrase on the **READ**.

The first two items in Working-Storage are never changed by the program. These items, the tax rate and the exemption rate, could have been replaced by numeric literals wherever they are used in the Procedure Division. However, if we had done that, it would be necessary to search through the entire Procedure Division looking for numbers that need to be changed every time the tax laws change. By creating the Working-Storage entries, we only need to change the two **VALUE** clauses to install any tax changes. Since the items never change in the Procedure Division they are called constants, and we suggest this by using a prefix of **C** in their names.

We strongly urge adherence to this rule: no Procedure Division literals! Zero and one, used to initialize and increment counters, are a permissible exception, as is 100 when used to convert from a fraction to a percentage, and *possibly* a very few others. For anything else, the voice of experience says: make named constants out of them. "Constants" have an uncanny way of not staying constant very long! No magic numbers! (A "magic number" is a constant appearing in the Procedure Division without any explanation of what it is. Pity the poor maintenance programmer!)

It is important to realize that a value is given to a Working-Storage item by a **VALUE** clause *only at the time the program is loaded into the computer*. If this value is changed later by a Procedure Division action, there is no way to get the **VALUE** clause to "do its job" again—at least not until the program is run from scratch again. If the item must be returned to its initial value after having been changed, a Procedure Division statement must be provided to do that.

6.6 THE PROCEDURE DIVISION

The main module for this program is essentially the same as the one we have studied previously, with the slight difference that we perform a paragraph to get the first record instead of coding the **READ** directly in the module. In the paragraph executed by the **PERFORM...UNTIL** we compute the gross pay and the exemptions, then compute the tax. Finally, we compute the net pay, print the input data and results, and get the next payroll record.

The structure of this paragraph is simple, easy to code, and easy to understand, because we used **PERFORM** statements to execute all of the calculation details. Of course, it is not really necessary to use **PERFORM** statements in a program as simple as this one, and we did so only to emphasize the structure of the program. In actual practice, if a module contains only a few lines of code, it is not usually coded as a separate paragraph.

The next paragraph simply reads a record from the payroll file, setting a flag when the end of file is reached. Following that is the paragraph that computes the employee's gross pay. We begin by multiplying the hours worked by the worker's pay rate to get a "provisional" gross pay. It is provisional because if the **IF** statement established that the worker put in more than 40 hours, this gross pay figure must be adjusted upward.

We have already seen the **IF** statement in the examples in Chapter 5. The specification for this program requires that any hours beyond 40 are to be paid for at the rate of one-and-one-half times the normal pay rate. There are various ways to arrange this calculation. The way that is used here is to get the number of overtime hours by subtracting 40 from the hours worked, and then to multiply the difference by 0.5 to get what might be called the premium hours. When this number is multiplied by the pay rate, we have the overtime premium, which is then added to the gross pay. Regardless of the number of hours that the employee worked, the gross pay in dollars and cents is now in the item named **W-GROSS-PAY**.

The following paragraph computes the total exemption for the employee by multiplying the number of dependents by the exemption allowed for each dependent. As we mentioned in the previous section, we have used a data name, **C-EXEMPTIONS**, to represent the exemption rate rather than coding the actual value in the **MULTIPLY** statement. This has two advantages. First, it presents a descriptive name to indicate what values are being multiplied, rather than just showing the "magic" number 50.00. Second, if the exemption rate changes, it is much easier to change the value clause in the Data Division than to search through the Procedure Division looking for "50.00".

After we have computed the exemptions we compute the tax. If the gross pay exceeds the exemptions, the employee owes tax, so we subtract the total exemption from the gross pay to get the amount of the pay that is taxable, then multiply that amount by the tax rate to get the tax; notice that we round the multiplication to the nearest cent. Of course, if no tax is owed we simply set the tax to zero. Once we have the tax, we compute the net pay by subtracting the tax from the gross pay.

The final paragraph begins by moving spaces to the output record, moves the input data and computed results to their locations in the output record, and writes the output record.

6.7   THE OUTPUT OF THE FIRST VERSION OF THE PROGRAM

The program was compiled and run with sample data. Figure 6.4 contains the output it produces. The text over each column was not produced as part of the program; it was inserted in this listing to identify the data.

Payroll Number	Name	Hrs	Pay Rate	Nbr Dep	Gross Pay	Tax	Net Pay
12345	THOS H. KELLY	20.0	05.350	00	107.00	022.47	084.53
12401	HENRY JENSEN	40.0	07.500	01	300.00	052.50	247.50
12511	NANCY KAHN	40.0	07.500	03	300.00	031.50	268.50
26017	JANE MILANO	10.0	06.875	03	068.75	000.00	068.75
26109	PETER W. SHERWOOD	40.0	10.000	05	400.00	031.50	368.50
26222	GEORGE M. MULVANEY	41.0	10.000	05	415.00	034.65	380.35
27511	RUTH GARRISON	50.0	10.000	04	550.00	073.50	476.50
28819	LEO X. BUTLER	40.1	10.000	02	401.00	063.21	337.79
29000	ANNE HENDERSON	40.2	10.000	03	403.00	053.13	349.87
29001	JULIA KIPP	40.3	10.000	01	404.00	074.34	329.66
99999	IMA TESTCASE	99.9	99.999	99	979.87	006.27	973.60

FIGURE 6.4 Output from the payroll calculation program.

Looking at the first line, we see that Kelly worked 20.0 hours at a pay rate of $5.35 per hour, earning a gross pay of $107.00. He claimed no dependents, so his entire gross pay was taxable at the 21% rate, for a tax of $22.47. His net pay was thus $84.53. Jensen earned $300.00 for his week's work; after subtracting his $50.00 exemption, the remaining $250 was taxable, for a tax of $52.50 and a net pay of $247.50. Jane Milano worked only 10 hours, and did not earn enough to have any taxable amount. The tax is accordingly zero, and her gross and net pay are equal.

The first worker in this sample to earn overtime is Mulvaney: he received $10 per hour for the first 40 hours, and 1.5 times that rate for the one hour over 40, for a gross pay of $415.00. The next employee, Garrison, received time-and-a-half for 10 hours.

Look closely at the results for Butler, however. He worked 40.1 hours; at $10 per hour that would give him $401.00, plus overtime. The overtime is 0.1 hours. This is multiplied by 0.5, which ought to give 0.05. This is multiplied by the pay rate, which ought to give $0.50, for a total pay of $401.50. So, why did the program print $401.00? The answer is the automatic dropping of digits in the multiplication of **W-OVERTIME-HOURS** by 0.5, which should have given 00.05—but the **PICTURE** for this item is **99V9**. The last digit is simply dropped, without rounding. Adding **ROUNDED** would not be much of a solution since the stored result would then be 00.1, resulting in an overpayment of 50 cents. The proper solution is to write **PICTURE 99V99**. The second version of the program, shown later in the chapter, incorporates this change; the results of that program for Butler are correct.

The last "worker," Ima Testcase, was placed there to demonstrate the consequences of not having enough space to the left of the decimal point. The 99.9 hours at $99.999 per hour with overtime should result in a gross pay of $12,984.87, but at various points in the calculation the items are too small for the intermediate and final results to be stored. Digits were dropped at different stages and in obscure ways, so that there is no obvious relationship between the correct results and what was printed.

Some compilers will produce a warning message for this program such as: "An intermediate result or a sending field might have its high order digit position truncated." If this warning is ignored on the assumption that no worker would ever earn more than $999.99 in one week, the program will produce nonsense when such a case is tried. We shall consider in later chapters what can be done to guard against this situation and to take appropriate action if it occurs, either because of correct input that does not match our assumptions or because of bad data.

6.8   THE PAYROLL CALCULATION WITH OVERTIME—VERSION TWO

The program we have just studied has a number of limitations, some of which we can remedy now and some of which will have to wait until the next chapter when we shall learn how to present the results in a fashion that is easier to read and use. For now, we examine the problem that the program is easily disrupted by bad data; just one nonnumeric character in any field that has been described as supposedly being entirely numeric, and the program will have serious problems. On some computers it will blow up, frequently giving no meaningful notification as to the cause of the termination; if this happens, subsequent good records will not be processed. Even worse, the program may continue to run but produce erroneous results with no indication that an error has occurred. (To get some idea of the problem involved in detecting this kind of error, consider the fact that Butler is not the only employee whose gross pay is short by 50 cents. Did you spot the second error when you first looked at Figure 6.4?) This is hardly an acceptable state of affairs. Therefore, we seek ways to revise the program to detect these conditions and handle them more gracefully. In general, a good programmer is a firm believer in Murphy's Law: Anything that can go wrong, will (especially with data)! A correctly written program should *never* permit an erroneous calculation or abnormal termination due to incorrect data.

6.9   REVISING THE PROGRAM SPECIFICATIONS

Basically, the change that we want to make to the program is this: if the record read from the payroll file contains errors in any of the data fields, then we want to print an error message and go on to the next record; otherwise, we process the record just as in the original version of the program. In other words, instead of simply getting the next payroll record to process, we want to get the next *valid* payroll record. To incorporate this function into the program, we change the hierarchy chart as shown in Figure 6.5.

The module labeled "get valid pay record" does more than just read the next record from the payroll file. After it reads the record, it *edits* the data fields in the record to check for invalid data; if one or more bad fields are found, the edit module writes an error message and the entire process must be repeated for the next record, or until the end of file is encountered. The pseudocode for the module is shown in Figure 6.6.

The module begins by setting the valid record flag to **N**, in effect saying, "No, we do not yet have a valid payroll record." The module will continue looking for a valid record until it finds one, or until it runs out of records in the payroll file. To find a valid record, the module first gets a record from the payroll file. If the end of file was not encountered, the module edits the record just read. If the edit module detects errors it prints a message; otherwise, it sets

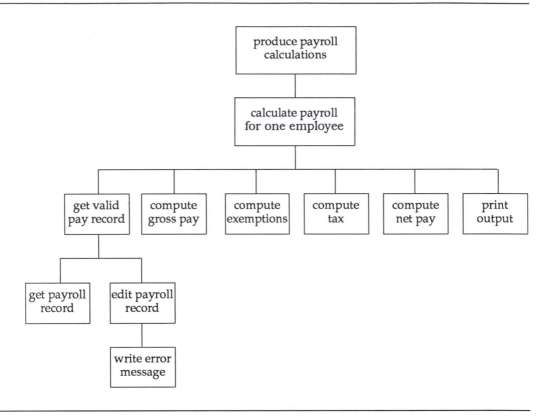

FIGURE 6.5 Hierarchy chart for revised payroll program.

```
GET VALID PAY REC:
set valid-rec-flag to 'N'
PERFORM-UNTIL valid-rec-flag = 'Y' or eof-flag = 'Y'
        get payroll-record
        IF eof-flag = 'N' THEN
              edit payroll-record
        ENDIF
ENDPERFORM
```

FIGURE 6.6 Pseudocode for revised payroll input module.

the valid record flag to **Y**. If neither the valid record flag nor the end of file flag have been set to **Y**, the loop will be repeated; otherwise, the loop terminates and we have either a valid record or the end of the file.

The module "get payroll record" is the same as it was in the first version of the program. The next module, "edit payroll record," requires that we decide what the editing should involve. In this case, we will simply test every numeric field to make sure that it actually contains only numeric data. Although the employee payroll number is defined as alphanumeric, notice in Figure 6.4 that it actually contains only numeric values. Therefore, we shall also test the payroll number for nonnumeric data.

The last new module, "write error message", will require some new concepts when we write the **COBOL** code, but conceptually there is nothing difficult in the design. The pseudocode specification of these last few modules, therefore, is left as an exercise (see Exercise 6.1). The revised payroll program is shown in Figure 6.7.

```
IDENTIFICATION DIVISION.
PROGRAM-ID.
    PAYROLL2.
DATE-WRITTEN.
    JANUARY 29, 1987.

ENVIRONMENT DIVISION.
INPUT-OUTPUT SECTION.
FILE-CONTROL.
    SELECT PAYROLL-FILE     ASSIGN TO S-PAYROLL.
    SELECT REPORT-FILE      ASSIGN TO S-REPORT.

DATA DIVISION.
FILE SECTION.
FD  PAYROLL-FILE
    LABEL RECORDS ARE OMITTED.
01  PAYROLL-RECORD.
    05  I-PAYROLL-NUMBER    PIC X(5).
    05  I-NAME              PIC X(20).
    05  I-HOURS-WORKED      PIC 99V9.
    05  FILLER              PIC X(3).
    05  I-PAYRATE           PIC 99V999.
    05  I-DEPENDENTS        PIC 99.
    05  FILLER              PIC X(42).

FD  REPORT-FILE
    LABEL RECORDS ARE OMITTED.
01  REPORT-RECORD           PIC X(69).

WORKING-STORAGE SECTION.
01  NORMAL-OUTPUT-LINE.
    05  O-PAYROLL-NUMBER    PIC X(5).
    05  FILLER              PIC XX.
    05  O-NAME              PIC X(20).
    05  FILLER              PIC XX.
    05  O-HOURS-WORKED      PIC 99.9.
    05  FILLER              PIC XX.
    05  O-PAYRATE           PIC 99.999.
    05  FILLER              PIC XX.
    05  O-DEPENDENTS        PIC 99.
    05  FILLER              PIC XX.
    05  O-GROSS-PAY         PIC 999.99.
    05  FILLER              PIC XX.
    05  O-TAX               PIC 999.99.
    05  FILLER              PIC XX.
    05  O-NET-PAY           PIC 999.99.
```

```
01   ERROR-RECORD.
     05   BAD-DATA            PIC X(38).
     05   FILLER             PIC(4)           VALUE SPACES.
     05   ERROR-MESSAGE      PIC X(27)
          VALUE 'INVALID DATA IN THIS RECORD'.

01   C-EXEMPTION            PIC 99V99        VALUE 50.00.
01   C-TAXRATE              PIC V999         VALUE .210.
01   W-EXEMPTION-TOTAL      PIC 999V99.
01   W-GROSS-PAY            PIC 999V99.
01   W-NET-PAY              PIC 999V99.
01   W-OUT-OF-RECORDS-FLAG  PIC X            VALUE 'N'.
01   W-OVERTIME-HOURS       PIC 99V99.
01   W-OVERTIME-PAY         PIC 999V99.
01   W-TAX                  PIC 999V99.
01   W-TAXABLE              PIC 999V99.
01   W-VALID-RECORD-FLAG    PIC X.

PROCEDURE DIVISION.
A000-PRODUCE-PAYROLL-CALC.
    OPEN INPUT PAYROLL-FILE
         OUTPUT REPORT-FILE.
    PERFORM C010-GET-VALID-PAY-REC.
    PERFORM B010-CALC-EMP-PAYROLL
        UNTIL W-OUT-OF-RECORDS-FLAG = 'Y'.
    CLOSE PAYROLL-FILE
          REPORT-FILE.
    STOP RUN.

B010-CALC-EMP-PAYROLL.
    PERFORM C020-COMPUTE-GROSS-PAY.
    PERFORM C030-COMPUTE-EXEMPTIONS.
    PERFORM C040-COMPUTE-TAX
    PERFORM C050-COMPUTE-NET-PAY.
    PERFORM C060-PRINT-OUTPUT.
    PERFORM C010-GET-VALID-PAY-REC.

C010-GET-VALID-PAY-REC.
    MOVE 'N' TO W-VALID-RECORD-FLAG.
    PERFORM D010-VALID-RECORD-LOOP
        UNTIL    W-VALID-RECORD-FLAG = 'Y'
             OR W-OUT-OF-RECORDS-FLAG = 'Y'.

C020-COMPUTE-GROSS-PAY.
    MULTIPLY I-HOURS-WORKED BY I-PAYRATE
          GIVING W-GROSS-PAY ROUNDED.
    IF I-HOURS-WORKED IS GREATER THAN 40
        SUBTRACT 40 FROM I-HOURS-WORKED GIVING W-OVERTIME-HOURS
        MULTIPLY 0.5 BY W-OVERTIME-HOURS
        MULTIPLY W-OVERTIME-HOURS BY I-PAYRATE
            GIVING W-OVERTIME-PAY ROUNDED
        ADD W-OVERTIME-PAY TO W-GROSS-PAY.

C030-COMPUTE-EXEMPTIONS.
    MULTIPLY C-EXEMPTION BY I-DEPENDENTS
          GIVING W-EXEMPTIONS-TOTAL.
```

```
C040-COMPUTE-TAX.
    IF W-GROSS-PAY IS GREATER THAN W-EXEMPTION-TOTAL
        SUBTRACT W-EXEMPTIONS-TOTAL FROM W-GROSS-PAY
            GIVING W-TAXABLE
        MULTIPLY C-TAXRATE BY W-TAXABLE GIVING W-TAX ROUNDED
    ELSE
        MOVE ZERO TO W-TAX.

C050-COMPUTE-NET-PAY.
    SUBTRACT W-TAX FROM W-GROSS-PAY GIVING W-NET-PAY.

C060-PRINT-OUTPUT.
    MOVE SPACES              TO NORMAL-OUTPUT-LINE.
    MOVE I-PAYROLL-NUMBER    TO O-PAYROLL-NUMBER.
    MOVE I-NAME              TO O-NAME.
    MOVE I-HOURS-WORKED      TO O-HOURS-WORKED.
    MOVE I-PAYRATE           TO O-PAYRATE.
    MOVE I-DEPENDENTS        TO O-DEPENDENTS.
    MOVE W-TAX               TO O-TAX.
    MOVE W-GROSS-PAY         TO O-GROSS-PAY.
    MOVE W-NET-PAY           TO O-NET-PAY.
    WRITE REPORT-RECORD FROM NORMAL-OUTPUT-LINE.

D010-VALID-RECORD-LOOP.
    PERFORM E010-GET-PAYROLL-RECORD.
    IF W-OUT-OF-RECORDS-FLAG = 'N'
        PERFORM E020-EDIT-PAYROLL-RECORD.

E010-GET-PAYROLL-RECORD.
    READ PAYROLL-FILE
        AT END MOVE 'Y' TO W-OUT-OF-RECORDS-FLAG.

E020-EDIT-PAYROLL-RECORD.
    IF      I-PAYROLL-NUMBER IS NOT NUMERIC
        OR I-HOURS-WORKED    IS NOT NUMERIC
        OR I-PAYRATE         IS NOT NUMERIC
        OR I-DEPENDENTS      IS NOT NUMERIC
        MOVE PAYROLL-RECORD TO BAD-DATA
        WRITE REPORT-RECORD FROM ERROR-RECORD
    ELSE
        MOVE 'Y' TO W-VALID-PAYROLL-RECORD.
```

FIGURE 6.7 A program to calculate weekly pay, including overtime, for all employee records in an input file; provides some validation of the input.

6.10 THE REVISED PROGRAM—THE WRITE FROM OPTION

The revised version of the program requires that we be able to produce either of two rather different output records, one for a normal line and one for an error line. This problem can be handled in any of several ways; we have chosen the one that will prove most convenient in the applications of later chapters. The technique is to provide, in the File Section, for a record consisting of just one long elementary item, REPORT-RECORD. The name of the record is accordingly the name of this one item. Within the Working-Storage Section we provide space to set up the two types of records that we are required to be able to write, **NORMAL-OUTPUT-LINE** and **ERROR-RECORD**. (**ERROR-RECORD** is not subdivided into fields, as are the input record and the normal output record, because some kinds of errors—such as omitting one character early in the record—would make the output more difficult to read than if it is simply printed in an unbroken string.) Within the Procedure Division we make the decision as to which one is to be printed and on the basis of that decision move the information from the input record to the appropriate output record, in the Working-Storage Section.

At this point it is not possible simply to say **WRITE**, because nothing has been placed in the record *in the File Section*. We must either move the chosen record from the Working-Storage Section to the File Section, using a group **MOVE** followed by a **WRITE**, or else use the **WRITE FROM** option. We have

```
WRITE REPORT-RECORD FROM ERROR-RECORD.
```

where **REPORT-RECORD** is the name of the record in the File Section and **ERROR-RECORD** is the name of the record in the Working-Storage Section. The effect of this statement is *exactly* the same as if we had written

```
MOVE ERROR-RECORD TO REPORT-RECORD.
WRITE REPORT-RECORD.
```

6.11 THE DATA DIVISION

Aside from the changes described in the previous section, there are two changes in the Data Division, both in the Working-Storage Section. First, we have added the flag **W-VALID-RECORD-FLAG** to be used in editing the input payroll record. We have not initialized this flag with a **VALUE** clause because it is always initialized at the start of **C010-GET-VALID-PAY-REC**. Second, the **PICTURE** for **W-OVERTIME-HOURS** has been changed to **99V99**, to take care of the problem with overtime calculation noted in the first version of the program.

6.12 THE PROCEDURE DIVISION

This version of the program has several more levels of code than the first version, corresponding to the additional levels of hierarchy shown in the hierarchy chart. There are two structural differences between the actual program and the hierarchy chart, however. First, we were forced to create a separate paragraph, **D010-VALID-RECORD-LOOP**, because **COBOL** requires the paragraph for the **PERFORM** statement. Second, although we showed "write error message" as a separate module on the hierarchy chart, we simply wrote it as in-line code in the program. These changes emphasize the fact that although the hierarchy chart is used as a guide in designing the program, it should not be treated as a straitjacket. Certain changes in the structure of the program are mandated by the requirements of **COBOL**, while others can be made to simplify the program code.

Compare the final structure of the program to the hierarchy chart and to the revised pseudocode, then compare the revisions to the specifications and code for the first version of the program. Be certain that you understand what changes were made, why they were made, and what design principles were used.

6.13 THE OUTPUT OF THE SECOND VERSION OF THE PROGRAM

This version of the program was compiled and run, using the same sample data as before with some erroneous records added. The output it produced is shown in Figure 6.8.

Payroll Number	Name	Hrs	Pay Rate	Nbr Dep	Gross Pay	Tax	Net Pay
12345	THOS H. KELLY	20.0	05.350	00	107.00	022.47	084.53
12401	HENRY JENSEN	40.0	07.500	01	300.00	052.50	247.50
12511	NANCY KAHN	40.0	07.500	03	300.00	031.50	268.50
UILKMB. R. BROOKS		400	0575002	INVALID DATA IN THIS RECORD			
26017	JANE MILANO	10.0	06.875	03	068.75	000.00	068.75
12 4KAY DELUCCIA		400	0600004	INVALID DATA IN THIS RECORD			
26109	PETER W. SHERWOOD	40.0	10.000	05	400.00	031.50	368.50
26222	GEORGE M. MULVANEY	41.0	10.000	05	415.00	034.65	380.35
26500A. W. ENWRIGHT		40	0545001	INVALID DATA IN THIS RECORD			
27511	RUTH GARRISON	50.0	10.000	04	550.00	073.50	476.50
28819	LEO X. BUTLER	40.1	10.000	02	401.50	063.32	338.18
28820D. X. IANNUZZI		450	4.50003	INVALID DATA IN THIS RECORD			
28821K. L. NG, JR.		350	450003	INVALID DATA IN THIS RECORD			
28822DANIEL REINER		350	045000C	INVALID DATA IN THIS RECORD			
28822L. E. SIMON		388	06000 3	INVALID DATA IN THIS RECORD			
2883QA. REAL BAD-ONE		3 8	4.5KJXX	INVALID DATA IN THIS RECORD			
7HGV6GARBAGE-CASE-1		..M.,M.,M.,M.		INVALID DATA IN THIS RECORD			
NJI9GARBAGE-CASE-2		GV 6 46 8 H		INVALID DATA IN THIS RECORD			
GARBAGE-CASE-3		----------+++++,M		INVALID DATA IN THIS RECORD			
29000	ANNE HENDERSON	40.2	10.000	03	403.00	053.13	349.87
29001	JULIA KIPP	40.3	10.000	01	404.50	074.45	330.05
99999	IMA TESTCASE	99.9	99.999	99	984.87	007.32	977.55

FIGURE 6.8 Output from the revised payroll calculation program.

Note that Butler's overtime pay is now correctly computed, so we have solved that problem. Ima Testcase, on the other hand, is still wrong; we will have to take that case up again later.

The records that triggered the error messages have a variety of types of bad data—blanks for zeros, alphabetic characters, special characters. Observe the payroll number for B. R. Brooks: UIKLM is what you get on some data entry keyboards if you forget to hold down the numeric key while trying to enter 12567. The record with the name A. Real Bad-One contains errors in all four fields that are checked, to demonstrate that the compound condition does respond to one *or more* of the simple conditions.

Three records with the name Garbage-Case were inserted as a matter of policy. The objective of running test data is to detect any possible errors in the program. This means that we must make certain that erroneous data items are detected and dealt with, and that valid data items are processed correctly. We encountered a case of this second type of error in the first version of the program when we realized that certain overtime pay was not being calculated correctly. In this test run we are primarily concerned with detecting errors in input data. The problem with this type of error checking is to try to anticipate every conceivable error that could occur, which is impossible. In a small attempt to force out errors that we might not have thought of, we put in some test cases consisting of random data, just to satisfy ourselves that the program will indeed reject bad data. In this program it is hard to see how we might have overlooked types of bad data, but these random tests sometimes can turn up errors we have missed.

This is not to say that program testing is merely a matter of putting in random data and seeing what happens. It is absolutely necessary to determine that the program does produce correct results for cases that have been calculated by hand, and that it specifically rejects all the kinds of bad data that it is designed to check for. We suggest a small amount of testing with random data only because of the difficulty of anticipating all of the strange things that can happen. In any case, however, you must be certain that you know what results to expect for every input record. If you don't know how the program *should* process a record, you can't tell if the results are wrong.

We shall consider the requirements of error handling and bad data throughout the remainder of the book, but since it is an important part of data processing you should be thinking about it in testing *all* of your programs.

REVIEW QUESTIONS

1. What is the purpose of editing input data?
2. Is the **VALUE** clause used correctly in each of the following examples?

   a. `01   COUNTER              PIC 9(3) VALUE ZERO.`

   b. `01   FLAGS                        VALUE SPACES.`
        `05   EOF-FLAG     PIC X.`
        `05   ERR-FLAG     PIC X.`

   c. `01   COUNTERS.`
        `05   GOOD-RECS    PIC 9(3) VALUE SPACES.`
        `05   BAD-REC      PIC 9(3) VALUE SPACES.`

3. Is it acceptable to use *only* randomly chosen data values as test values? Explain your answer.
4. What two classes of errors should testing try to detect?
5. The program of Figure 6.7 contains a deviation from our usual punctuation standards. Can you find it?

ANSWERS TO REVIEW QUESTIONS

1. To be certain that a program does not try to process data that was entered with errors. Obviously there are limits to this objective. The

program will probably not be able to tell that you meant to enter 3 when you typed 2, but it can tell if there is, for example, nonnumeric data in a field that should be numeric.

2. **a.** Yes.

   b. Yes, but we do not recommend using the **VALUE** clause at the group level.

   c. No. The constant following **VALUE**, whether it is a figurative constant or a literal, must be compatible with the **PICTURE** of the variable. In this case we are trying to initialize a numeric variable with a nonnumeric value.

3. No. Randomly chosen test data may be used to try to catch errors that you had not thought of in planning your tests, but the bulk of the test cases should be planned carefully to test specific actions in the program.

4. The first class consists of errors that occur when valid data is processed and the program generates incorrect results. An example of this is the incorrect processing of overtime pay in the first version of the payroll program. The second class consists of errors that occur when the program tries to process invalid data, such as nonnumeric values in a numeric field.

5. The third **PERFORM** statement in **B010-CALC-EMP-PAYROLL** does not have a period. Hard to see, isn't it? What if that had been syntactically legal but logically incorrect?

EXERCISES

1. Write the pseudocode for the "edit" and "write" modules in Figure 6.5.

*2. Rewrite the program in Figure 6.3 so that all C-level paragraphs are coded in-line; i.e., the program should consist only of paragraphs **A000-PRODUCE-PAYROLL-CALC** and a revised version of **B010-CALC-EMP-PAYROLL**.

3. Rewrite the program in Figure 6.7 so that all paragraphs below the B-level *except* those needed for **PERFORM** loops are recoded as in-line code.

*4. Modify the program of Figure 6.3 so that it produces a final line at the end of the report, giving the total number of input records processed.

5. Modify the program of Figure 6.7 so that it produces a final line at the end of the report, giving the number of good records processed and the number of records in which errors were detected.

6. (The next two exercises are suitable for small projects.)
   Modify the program in Exercise 13 of Chapter 5 to meet the following new specifications.
   Assume that inventory records may contain errors. Edit the data as follows:

   1. The first two characters of the product code must be alphabetic;
   2. The last three characters of the product code must be numeric;
   3. All three sales fields must be numeric;

---

* Answers to starred exercises will be found in Appendix IV at the end of the book.

4. both current inventory and standard inventory levels must be numeric;
5. selling price must be numeric;
6. no item's inventory value should exceed $2,000,000.00.

If a record is found to be in error, do not print the product in the normal format. Instead, print the record image with a simple error message similar to the format shown in Figure 6.8.

7. Modify Exercise 14 of Chapter 5 according to the following specifications.

The payroll system is now required to handle both salaried and hourly employees. For this reason the payroll record has been modified as follows:

Column 1	pay code; **H** for hourly, **S** for salaried
Column 2-6	employee number
Column 7-11	department number
Column 12-17	for hourly employees the field contains zero; for salaried employees the field contains the weekly salary; numeric, 2 decimals
Column 18-21	for salaried employees the field contains zero; for hourly employees the field contains the hours worked; numeric, 2 decimals
Column 22-25	for salaried employees the field contains zero; for hourly employees the field contains the base pay rate; numeric, 2 decimals
Column 26-27	municipality code

For salaried employees gross pay is simply the weekly salary. Deductions and net pay are calculated as in Exercise 5.14 for all employees.

Assume that payroll records may contain errors. A valid record must meet the following requirements:

1.The pay code must be **H** or **S**;
2.The employee number must be numeric;
3.The first character of the department number must be alphabetic;
4.The last four characters of the department number must be numeric;
5.The salary of a salaried employee must be numeric;
6.The salary of a salaried employee must not exceed $3000;
7.The hours worked for an hourly employee must be numeric;
8.The hours worked for an hourly employee must not exceed 80 hours;
9.The base pay rate of an hourly employee must be numeric;
10.The municipality code must be 03, 07, 15, 23, or 77.

If a payroll record is in error do not perform any calculations on it. Instead, print the record and a simple error message using the general format shown in Figure 6.8.

CHAPTER 7

PICTURES AND RELATED TOPICS

7.1 INTRODUCTION

We begin this chapter with a study of the full power of the **PICTURE** clause, which finds heavy use in preparing output so that it is pleasing in appearance and convenient to use. Then we look again at the payroll program and use the program to introduce several other topics; for example, level **77** and **88** entries in the Data Division, and obtaining the current date for use in the program. We will also discuss how to read numeric data that has arithmetic signs.

7.2 THE PICTURE CLAUSE

A **PICTURE** clause, consisting of the word **PICTURE** or **PIC** and an appropriate character string, is required for all elementary items with a very few exceptions that will be discussed in later chapters. The character string in a **PICTURE** clause describes to the **COBOL** compiler two related but somewhat different aspects of an elementary data item.

- It conveys information about the form in which the data item is stored inside the computer. For example, if a **PICTURE** clause contains only **9**s, the compiler knows that the item is expected to be numeric and is capable of being used in arithmetic operations. If such an item contains a **V**, designating an assumed decimal point, the compiler takes that information into account in setting up decimal point alignment for any computations involving the item. If the item contains **X**s or **A**s, the compiler knows that it is not numeric and that arithmetic will therefore never be done using it.

- It conveys information about the external representation of an item that receives values from input or that is sent to output. For example, if an item in an input record is described with **PICTURE 999**, we (and the **COBOL** compiler) know that when typed at a terminal the item takes up exactly three characters, and by inspecting the **PICTURE** clauses for the rest of the record, we can tell exactly which three characters. If the **PICTURE** clause for an item that will be printed contains a decimal point, then a decimal point will appear at that point in the printed representation of the item.

All items described in the Data Division have an internal representation within the computer. All items in the File Section of the Data Division either come from input or go to output. Items in the Working-Storage Section may receive values that have first been read into the File Section; they may be sent to output, also through the File Section; or they may be intermediate results of computations and never see the light of day in the outside world.

All of this needs to be said in order to provide a basis for distinctions we will have to make in what follows, as we talk about the movement of data within a computer and the preparation of results for printing.

Let us now consider in detail the various characters that may be used in **PICTURE** clauses and something about how they may be combined.

7.3 THE SYMBOL S IN A PICTURE CHARACTER STRING

The symbol **S** is used in a **PICTURE** character string to indicate the presence of a sign on a numeric data item. This is called an operational sign. It has nothing whatever to do with the ways in which a sign may be represented in typed input or printed output, which we shall study later. A numeric item that has an **S** in its **PICTURE** character string is allowed to be either positive or negative, whereas an item without an **S** in its **PICTURE** character string is always positive. When the **S** is used, it must be the leftmost character in the **PICTURE**.

Experienced **COBOL** programmers often put an **S** in the **PICTURE** string for numeric items even if they know that the items should never be negative. For one thing, it saves having to make a decision for each numeric item as to whether or not the item should be signed. For another, if an error occurs in the program, or if the program specifications change, it is much easier to spot a negative result that should be positive than to figure out why an item that is always positive has the wrong value. We shall ordinarily put a sign on numeric items in programs from now on. For example, in the program shown later in the chapter, we have two numeric constants that are entered as items in Working-Storage. Neither would have any meaning as a negative number, yet we will still make them signed numbers by the use of the **S** in the **PICTURE** clauses, like this:

```
PIC S99V99 VALUE +50.00.
PIC SV999  VALUE +.210.
```

An important characteristic of the operational sign is that it takes no additional space in memory. For example, the following **PICTURE**s take exactly the same amount of memory:

```
PICTURE S999V99.
PICTURE  999V99.
```

7.4 THE ALLOWABLE SIZE OF A PICTURE CHARACTER STRING

A **PICTURE** character string may not contain more than 30 characters. This will be far more than adequate for all but very unusual circumstances, in which case the field might have to be defined as two separate data items. It should be understood clearly that *this limitation applies to the* **PICTURE** *character string itself*, not to the item described by the character string. For instance, this **PICTURE** character string

        PICTURE X(71).

contains 5 characters but describes an item that takes 71 characters. On the other hand, the character string here

        PICTURE S999V99.

contains 7 characters but describes an item that has only 5, since the **S** and the **V** do not describe character positions in the representation of the item.

Quite apart from the number of characters in its **PICTURE** character string, remember that a numeric item may not have more than 18 digits in it.

7.5   THE PICTURE CHARACTER STRING FOR EDITING

The **PICTURE** clause, as we have just discussed it and in most of the ways we have used it thus far in the book, provides information to the compiler about how to set up storage for data. It describes how many characters there are, where an assumed decimal point is, and something about the kind of internal representation to be used. A **PICTURE** character string for editing goes a considerable step further: applied to an item that receives a value as a result of a **MOVE** or an arithmetic operation, it specifies action to be taken when the object program is run. The precise nature of the action taken depends on the value of the data item. This is called an *editing* **PICTURE**. Editing, in this context, refers to the preparation of data for printing in a more easily readable form than the way it appears in storage, and to the insertion of dollar signs, commas, etc.

Editing actions, which may refer to elementary items only, must refer to a *receiving area*, that is, a data item that receives data as the result of a **MOVE** statement or an arithmetic statement. In a statement such as **MOVE A TO B**, **A** is called a *sending item* and **B** is called a receiving item. The editing that is called for by an editing **PICTURE** clause takes place at the time the object program is run, when a data value is transmitted to the item by a **MOVE** statement or an arithmetic statement with a **GIVING** phrase.

Most editing actions in **COBOL** are applied to numeric information, but some limited editing can be done on nonnumeric items. That is, in a statement such as **MOVE A TO B**, if the **PICTURE** character string for **B** specifies editing, then **A** must almost always be numeric. In any event, after editing the resulting item will automatically be an alphanumeric item whether a value was placed there by a **MOVE** or by an arithmetic statement. *Further arithmetic cannot be done on an edited item.*

COBOL-85

Ordinarily, once an item has been edited it is not possible to "unedit" the data. However, **COBOL-85** allows you to MOVE data from an edited field to an unedited field (containing only **9**s, **V**, and **S** in its **PICTURE**), in which case the result is once more numeric and can be used in arithmetic.

END COBOL-85

7.6 THE SYMBOL Z IN A PICTURE CHARACTER STRING

The character **z** specifies suppression of leading zeros. (A leading zero is one that does not have a nonzero digit to the left of it. Thus, the number 00102 contains two leading zeros.) Whenever the character in the data item corresponding to a **z** in the picture contains a leading zero, the data character is replaced by a space. If all character positions of the data item correspond to **z**s in the **PICTURE** character string, and the item in fact contains all zeros, then the edited item will be blank.

Examples

SENDING ITEM		RECEIVING ITEM	
PICTURE	SAMPLE DATA	PICTURE	EDITED RESULT
9(5)	12345	ZZ999	12345
9(5)	01234	ZZ999	1234
9(5)	00001	ZZ999	001
9(5)	00000	ZZ999	000
9(5)	10023	ZZ999	10023
9(5)	10000	ZZ999	10000
9(5)	00010	Z(5)	10
9(5)	00000	Z(5)	

7.7 THE SYMBOL $ IN A PICTURE CHARACTER STRING

A single dollar sign (or other currency symbol as appropriate) as the leftmost character of a **PICTURE** character string specifies that a dollar sign should be placed in the edited item *in that position*. This is generally called a *fixed dollar sign*.

Examples

SENDING ITEM		RECEIVING ITEM	
PICTURE	SAMPLE DATA	PICTURE	EDITED RESULT
9(4)	1234	$9(4)	$1234
9(4)	0023	$9(4)	$0023
9(4)	0023	$ZZ99	$ 23
9(4)	0004	$ZZ99	$ 04
9(4)	0050	$Z(4)	$ 50
9(4)	0000	$Z(4)	

Observe the blank in the space for the edited item on the last line. This is correct: for the **PICTURE** shown, a zero sending item produces all blanks.

Zero suppression with a floating dollar sign is specified by placing a dollar sign in each leading position to be zero suppressed; the rightmost character suppressed will be replaced by a dollar sign in the edited result. Zero suppression with the floating dollar sign is specified only if *more than one* dollar sign is written.

To avoid truncation of the sending item, the **PICTURE** character string for floating dollar sign insertion must contain space for all of the characters of the sending item *plus one position for the dollar sign*. Thus, in the example above and in those that follow, the four-character sending items are sent to receiving items having five-character pictures.

Examples

SENDING ITEM		RECEIVING ITEM	
PICTURE	SAMPLE DATA	PICTURE	EDITED RESULT
9(4)	0123	$$999	$123
9(4)	0002	$$999	$002
9(4)	1234	$(5)	$1234
9(4)	0000	$$$99	$00
9(4)	0000	$(5)	
9(4)	0102	$$$99	$102

7.8   THE COMMA IN A PICTURE CHARACTER STRING

When a comma is written in a **PICTURE** character string, it will be inserted in the position shown without loss of digits from the sending data item. If all characters to the left of the comma(s) in the sending data item are zeros, and zero suppression is called for, the comma(s) will be replaced by space(s).

Examples

SENDING ITEM		RECEIVING ITEM	
PICTURE	SAMPLE DATA	PICTURE	EDITED RESULT
9(6)	123456	999,999	123,456
9(6)	000078	999,999	000,078
9(6)	000078	ZZZ,ZZZ	78
9(6)	000000	ZZZ,ZZZ	
9(6)	001234	ZZZ,ZZZ	1,234
9(6)	000123	ZZZ,ZZZ	123
9(6)	000030	ZZ,9999	0030

7.9 THE DECIMAL POINT IN A PICTURE CHARACTER STRING

This is one feature of the editing **PICTURE** that we have already seen, beginning in Chapter 3. When a decimal point is written in a **PICTURE** character string, it is inserted into the position shown without loss of digits from the sending data item. This, as we have discussed, is an *actual* decimal point, which occupies a character position in the edited result. An item may never contain more than one decimal point, actual or assumed.

When data from a sending item is moved to a receiving item for which the **PICTURE** character string contains a decimal point, the assumed decimal point of the sending item is taken into account. That is, the sending value is placed in the receiving item with the actual decimal point in the receiving item aligned with the assumed decimal point in the sending item. This may cause insertion of zeros in the edited result, as shown in the third example. If the receiving item is smaller than the sending item, the decimal point alignment may also cause *truncation, without any warning whatever!* This is shown in the fourth example. Carets denote assumed decimal points in the sending items.

Examples

SENDING ITEM		RECEIVING ITEM	
PICTURE	SAMPLE DATA	PICTURE	EDITED RESULT
9(4)V99	1234ᴧ56	9(4).99	1234.56
99V9(4)	01ᴧ2345	99.9(4)	01.2345
9V9(5)	1ᴧ23456	99.9(6)	01.234560
99V9(4)	12ᴧ3456	9.999	2.345
99V9(4)	00ᴧ0123	99.9(4)	00.0123
99V9(4)	10ᴧ0000	99.9(4)	10.0000

It is entirely possible to combine different types of editing in one **PICTURE** clause. For example, zero suppression may be combined with decimal point insertion. A very common operation combines floating dollar sign insertion, conditional comma insertion, and decimal point insertion. A few of the possibilities are illustrated in the following examples.

Examples

SENDING ITEM		RECEIVING ITEM	
PICTURE	SAMPLE DATA	PICTURE	EDITED RESULT
9(4)V99	0100ᴧ00	ZZZ9.99	100.00
9(4)V99	0041ᴧ09	ZZZ9.99	41.09
9(6)V99	123456ᴧ78	$ZZZ,ZZ9.99	$123,456.78
9(6)V99	000044ᴧ44	$ZZZ,ZZ9.99	$ 44.44

9(6)V99	000000ˆ01	$ZZZ,ZZ9.99	$ 0.01
9(6)V99	123456ˆ78	$$$$,$$9.99	$123,456.78
9(6)V99	012000ˆ00	$$$$,$$9.99	$12,000.00
9(6)V99	000012ˆ00	$$$$,$$9.99	$12.00
9(6)V99	000000ˆ12	$$$$,$$9.99	$0.12
9(6)V99	000000ˆ00	$$$$,$$9.99	$0.00

7.10 THE SYMBOL - (MINUS SIGN) IN A PICTURE CHARACTER STRING

The symbol **s** in a **PICTURE** character string designates an *operational* sign. An operational sign is not counted in determining the number of characters in an item, and we need not concern ourselves with the way it is represented inside the computer. A display sign, on the other hand, which has to do only with data items intended for output, does take up space.

If a single minus sign is written as the first or last character of a **PICTURE** clause and if the data item is negative, a display minus sign will be inserted into the edited item where written. If the data item is positive or if it is unsigned, a space is inserted into the same position.

None of this says anything about how signed quantities are represented when typed into a record at a terminal. We will delay this topic for a bit, and simply assume that the signs have somehow been placed in the data items, perhaps as the result of an arithmetic operation. In the examples that follow, the operational sign of the sending item is represented by a plus or minus sign over the rightmost character.

Examples

SENDING ITEM		RECEIVING ITEM	
PICTURE	SAMPLE DATA	PICTURE	EDITED RESULT
S999	12̄3	-999	-123
S999	12̄3	999-	123-
S999	12⁺3	-999	123
S999	12⁺3	999-	123
S999	00̄0	-999	000
S999	00⁺0	999-	000

It is possible to combine the operations of zero suppression and sign insertion by writing more than one minus sign at the beginning of a **PICTURE** clause. When this is done, the rightmost character suppressed will be replaced by a minus sign in the edited result if the sending item is negative. As with the floating dollar sign, be sure to allow one extra position in the receiving field for the sign itself.

Examples

SENDING ITEM		RECEIVING ITEM	
PICTURE	SAMPLE DATA	PICTURE	EDITED RESULT
S9(4)	$\overline{1234}$	---99	-1234
S9(4)	$\overline{0012}$	----9	-12
S9(4)	$\overset{+}{0012}$	----9	12
S9(4)	$\overline{0008}$	---99	-08
S9(4)	$\overset{+}{0000}$	---99	00
S9(4)	$\overset{+}{0000}$	-----	
S9(4)	$\overline{0012}$	-----	-12

7.11 THE SYMBOL + (PLUS SIGN) IN A PICTURE CHARACTER STRING

If a single plus sign is written as the first or last character of a **PICTURE** character string, a display plus sign is inserted into the edited item where written if the data item is positive; if the data item is negative, a minus sign is inserted. If the sending item has no sign (that is, if its **PICTURE** character string does not contain an **S**), it is considered to be positive.

Examples

SENDING ITEM		RECEIVING ITEM	
PICTURE	SAMPLE DATA	PICTURE	EDITED RESULT
S9(5)	$\overline{12345}$	+9(5)	-12345
S9(5)	$\overset{+}{12345}$	+9(5)	+12345
S9(5)	$\overline{12345}$	9(5)+	12345-
S9(5)	$\overset{+}{12345}$	9(5)+	12345+
S9(5)	$\overset{+}{00000}$	+9(5)	+00000
S9(5)	$\overline{00000}$	9(5)+	00000-
S9(5)	$\overline{00123}$	+Z(4)9	- 123

Zero suppression may be combined with the insertion of a floating plus or minus sign by placing a plus sign in each leading position to be suppressed. The rightmost character suppressed will be replaced by a plus sign if the sending item is positive or has no sign, and by a minus sign if the sending item is negative. As with the floating minus sign, this applies only if more than one plus sign is written.

Examples

SENDING ITEM		RECEIVING ITEM	
PICTURE	SAMPLE DATA	PICTURE	EDITED RESULT
S9(4)	+1234	+++99	+1234
S9(4)	+0023	+++99	+23
S9(4)	−0023	+++99	−23
S9(4)	+0004	+++99	+04
S9(4)	+0000	+(5)	

7.12 THE SYMBOLS CR AND DB IN A PICTURE CHARACTER STRING

The combination **CR** and **DB**, for credit and debit, may appear *only as the rightmost two characters* of a **PICTURE** character string. If the sending item is negative, the edited result will contain whichever of these pairs of symbols is written. If the sending item is positive or has no sign, these symbols will be replaced by spaces. Although it might seem reasonable, it is not possible to get both **CR** and **DB** from one picture, such as **CR** if negative and **DB** if positive. If output so labeled is required, it can be managed, but only by some additional effort including an **IF** statement in the Procedure Division.

Examples

SENDING ITEM		RECEIVING ITEM	
PICTURE	SAMPLE DATA	PICTURE	EDITED RESULT
S9(4)	+1234	9(4)CR	1234
S9(4)	−1234	9(4)CR	1234CR
S9(4)	−0002	9(4)DB	0002DB
S9(4)	−0002	Z(4)CR	2CR
S9(4)	+0000	Z(4)CR	

We may summarize the actions for the various types of display signs for positive and negative data as follows:

PICTURE characters	Edited result if data is positive	Edited result if data is negative
−	blank	−
+	+	−
CR	2 blanks	CR
DB	2 blanks	DB

7.13 THE CHARACTER * (ASTERISK) IN A PICTURE CHARACTER STRING

The asterisk in a **PICTURE** character string is used for check protection, to make it difficult for numbers to be altered fraudulently by inserting leading digits. (For this reason, the asterisk is frequently referred to as the check protect character.) The action with this symbol is a combination of insertion and zero suppression. Any leading zero in the sending item that corresponds to an asterisk in the picture is replaced by an asterisk in the receiving item. This is different from the various floating insertion symbols that we have seen previously, where only the rightmost character suppressed is replaced by the symbol. Here *all* suppressed characters are replaced. If only asterisks or other suppression characters are used and the data item is zero, the edited result will be all asterisks except for an actual decimal point.

Examples

SENDING ITEM		RECEIVING ITEM	
PICTURE	SAMPLE DATA	PICTURE	EDITED RESULT
9(4)	1234	**99	1234
9(4)	0023	**99	**23
9(4)	0000	**99	**00
9(4)	0000	****	****
9(4)	0080	***9	**80
9(4)	0080	**99	**80
9(4)	0080	*999	*080

7.14 THE CHARACTER 0 (ZERO) IN A PICTURE CHARACTER STRING

The character zero in a **PICTURE** character string is a straight insertion symbol. It causes a zero to be inserted into the corresponding position in the receiving item without loss of characters from the sending item.

Examples

SENDING ITEM		RECEIVING ITEM	
PICTURE	SAMPLE DATA	PICTURE	EDITED RESULT
9(4)	1234	990099	120034
9(4)	1234	099990	012340
9(4)	0012	ZZZZ0	120
9(4)	1234	$$,$$9.00	$1,234.00
9(4)	0080	$$,$$9.00	$80.00

7.15   THE CHARACTER B IN A PICTURE CHARACTER STRING

The character **B** causes the insertion of a space (blank) in the corresponding position of the receiving item without loss of characters from the sending data item.

The insertion of blanks will more often be useful than the insertion of zeros. The next-to-last line of the following examples, for instance, shows a Social Security number, written without spaces as it would normally appear in file storage, and grouped in the ordinary way in the edited result by the insertion of blanks. Note that since the dash (-) is *not* an insertion character, we cannot use the **PICTURE** clause to print the Social Security number in the format 999-99-9999. We can obtain this format, but we will have to wait until Chapter 15 to learn the technique.

Examples

SENDING ITEM PICTURE	SAMPLE DATA	RECEIVING ITEM PICTURE	EDITED RESULT
9(6)	123456	99BBB9999	12 3456
X(6)	ABCDEF	XXBBBXXXX	AB CDEF
999	123	90B90B90	10 20 30
X(9)	123456789	999B99B9999	123 45 6789
X(7)	FTBAKER	XBXBX(5)	F T BAKER
X(7)	DANIELD	X(6)BX	DANIEL D
X(7)	DONALDG	X(6)BX	DONALD G

7.16   THE CHARACTER / (SLASH) IN A PICTURE CHARACTER STRING

The character / in a **PICTURE** character string is still another insertion symbol. It is used primarily for printing the date in numeric format, but may actually be used in any **PICTURE**. It causes no loss of characters from the sending item.

Examples

SENDING ITEM PICTURE	SAMPLE DATA	RECEIVING ITEM PICTURE	EDITED RESULT
9(6)	103188	99/99/99	10/31/88
9(6)	070488	99/99/99	07/07/88
9(6)	070488	Z9/99/99	7/04/88
X(8)	JMWILSON	X/X/X(6)	J/M/WILSON
X(8)	MMDDYY	XX/XX/XX	MM/DD/YY

7.17 THE CHARACTER P IN A PICTURE CHARACTER STRING

The character **P** in a **PICTURE** character string is used differently from the characters we have just seen. It does not cause editing of the data field; instead, it is used to *scale* numeric data for use in calculations. Suppose, for example, that a company is preparing a sales report for management. If the company is large, the sales figures are generally not reported to the last cent, but are shown to the nearest thousand dollars for ease of comparison. If we have the following code, the value stored in **SALES-87** is 075, not 075000, but for arithmetic operations it is still treated as 75,000.

```
01  SALES-87      PIC 999PPP.
    .
    .
    .
    MOVE 75000 TO SALES-87.
```

The character **P** may be placed in a **PICTURE** character string only at the beginning of the string or at the end of the string. If the string begins with **P**, then the decimal point is assumed to be immediately to the left of the first **P**; optionally, an **S** and a **V** may appear to the left of the first **P**. In each of the following pairs, the pictures are equivalent.

```
PIC PPP999.
PIC VPPP999.

PIC SPP9(5).
PIC SVPP9(5).
```

If the **PICTURE** character string ends with **P**, the decimal point is assumed to follow the last **P**; optionally, **V** may follow the last **P**. For example, **99PPP** is equivalent to **99PPPV**.

The character **P** does *not* take up space in memory, but it *does* count as one digit in determining the maximum size (18 digits) of numeric items. For example, **SVP(10)99** only takes up *two* characters in memory, but represents a *twelve* digit number. Each position represented by a **P** in a **PICTURE** character string is considered to contain the value zero.

Examples

SENDING ITEM		RECEIVING ITEM	
PICTURE	SAMPLE DATA	PICTURE	EDITED RESULT
999PPP	075	ZZZ,ZZ9	75,000
PPP999	075	9.9(6)	0.000075
PPP999	075	9.9(5)	0.00007
9(6)	150000	999PPP	150
9(6)	123456	999PPP	123
V9(6)	˄001234	PP99	12

The data given for the first three sending items in these examples shows what the items would look like if you could somehow look directly at the computer's memory, but not how the sending items were initialized. As the edited output for the receiving items shows, the first sending item (for example), has a value of 75,000 *not* 75. To initialize this sending item it would be necessary to use a statement such as the following:

```
MOVE 75000 TO SENDING-ITEM-1.
```

Likewise, to initialize the second sending item we might use a statement such as this:

```
MOVE 0.000075 TO SENDING-ITEM-2.
```

Remember: the **P** character in a **PICTURE** character string does not affect the value stored in the data item, it simply allows **COBOL** to save space by not storing leading or trailing zeros in memory.

7.18   A SUMMARY OF PICTURE RULES

Here is a summary of rules governing the use of the **PICTURE** clause.

1. A **PICTURE** character string may not contain more than 30 characters.
2. A **PICTURE** character string may contain no more than one sign designation and no more than one actual or assumed decimal point. (This does not contradict the principle of floating sign insertion; multiple plus signs or multiple minus signs are considered as *one* "sign designation.")
3. A numeric literal or an operand in any arithmetic operation may not exceed 18 digits, including any digits represented by the character **P**. All **PICTURE** character strings, whether for editing or not, must reflect this restriction—although in practical commercial applications it would be extremely unusual to have any occasion to exceed this limit. (For example, in 18 digits you could represent a number several orders of magnitude greater than the Gross National Product of the United States.)
4. An edited item may at a later time become a sending item. This would usually happen through movement of the group item of which the edited item is one of the elementary items, but it may occasionally happen that an edited item becomes a sending elementary item. When this is done, it must be remembered that *edited items are always nonnumeric and may not be used in arithmetic.* Also, the edited item—which is now alphanumeric—may not be moved to a receiving item that calls for further numeric editing. In other words, for purposes of arithmetic or further editing, an edited item should be treated as though its **PICTURE** contained only **X**s.

COBOL-85

5. In **COBOL-85** only, an edited numeric item may be de-edited by moving it to a numeric item.

END COBOL-85

6. Zero suppression may not be employed more than once in one **PICTURE** character string. For example, the following **PICTURE** is illegal.

   PICTURE Z9/Z9/99

   However, one type of zero suppression may be combined with other types of insertion, such as the insertion of space.

7. The **PICTURE** character string for a receiving item must provide enough space for the largest number that is expected to be placed there. This, of course, is true whether or not editing is involved. It is mentioned here because when a floating dollar sign is used, one of the dollar signs is an insertion character and the rest stand for digits. The dollar sign for insertion must be considered in determining the amount of space required. For instance, if the **PICTURE** character string for a sending item were **9999** and we sent it to a receiving item having a **PICTURE** of **$$$$**, the compiler might warn us of a possible truncation of high order digits: after using one dollar sign for insertion, we have provided only three characters for the possible four nonzero digits of the sending item.

8. The insertion of zeros, blanks, and slashes are the only editing operations that may be applied to alphabetic and alphanumeric items as well as to numeric items.

One final reminder on two matters that beginners frequently forget: one cannot do arithmetic on an edited item, and one cannot do any editing on group items.

7.19 COMBINING EDITING OPERATION

We have already seen that it is possible to combine editing operations in one **PICTURE** character string. Figure 7.1 shows a variety of applications of the **PICTURE** clause, including a number that combine operations.

SENDING ITEM		RECEIVING ITEM	
PICTURE	SAMPLE DATA	PICTURE	EDITED RESULT
9(6)	123456	$ZZZ,ZZZ.99	$123,456.00
9999V99	123456	$ZZZ,ZZZ.99	$ 1,234.56
9(4)V99	000123	$ZZZ,ZZZ.99	$ 1.23
9(4)V9(2)	000006	$ZZZ,ZZZ.99	$ .06
9(4)V99	000123	$$$$,$$$.99	$1.23
9(4)V99	000000	$$$$,$$$.99	$.00
9(4)V99	000000	$$$$,$$$.$$	
9(6)	102030	$ZZZ,ZZZ.ZZ	$102,030.00

9(6)	000100	$$$$,$99.99	$100.00
9(6)	000008	$$$$,$99.99	$08.00
9(4)V99	123456	$***,***.99	$**1,234.56
9(4)V99	000123	$***,***.99	$******1.23
9(4)V99	000098	$***,***.99	$*******.98
9(4)V99	000000	$***,***.99	$*******.00
9(4)V99	000000	$***,***.**	********.**
9(5)V9	001234	$$$$,$$$.99	$123.40
9(4)V99	000123	Z,ZZZ.ZZ	1.23
9(4)V99	000123	Z,ZZZ,ZZZ.ZZ	1.23
9(6)	123456	-999999	123456
S9(6)	$\overline{123456}$	-9(6)	-123456
S9(6)	$\overline{000123}$	-9(6)	-000123
S9(6)	$\overline{000123}$	-(6)9	-123
S9(6)	$\overline{000123}$	9(6)-	000123-
S9(6)	$\overline{000123}$	Z(6)-	123-
9(6)	123456	+9(6)	+123456
S9(6)	$\overline{123456}$	+9(6)	-123456
S9(6)	$\overline{000012}$	+(6)9	-12
S9(4)V99	$\overline{001234}$	$*,***.99CR	$***12.34CR
S9(4)V99	$\overline{001234}$	$*,***.99DB	$***12.34DB
S9(4)V99	$\overline{001234}$	$$,$$$.99CR	$12.34CR
S9(4)V99	$\overline{000000}$	$$,$$$.99CR	$.00CR
S9(4)V99	$\overline{000000}$	$$,$$$.$$CR	
9(6)	001234	ZZZBBB999	1 234
9(6)	123456	9B(4)9(5)	1 23456
X(6)	ABCDE5	XXBXXXBBX	AB CDE 5

FIGURE 7.1 Examples of the actions of a variety of editing **PICTURE**s.

7.20   THE PAYROLL CALCULATION WITH OVERTIME - VERSION THREE

We now take up still another version of the payroll calculation that we studied in Chapter 6. There are two new requirements for the program. First, the printed output must include headings over the columns before the first output; the format of these headings is shown in the sample output in Figure 7.5. Second, the numeric quantities in the body of the report are to be edited. Leading zeros are to be suppressed and dollar amounts are to have a floating dollar sign inserted.

We begin as always with a program design. Figure 7.2 shows the revised hierarchy chart.

There is only one change in this chart: a module has been added, directly subordinate to the main module, which will print column headings before any other processing is done. The rest of the changes will affect the **COBOL** code but do not show up in the design. For convenience, the pseudocode for the program is reproduced in Figure 7.3, with the slight changes required for the column headings.

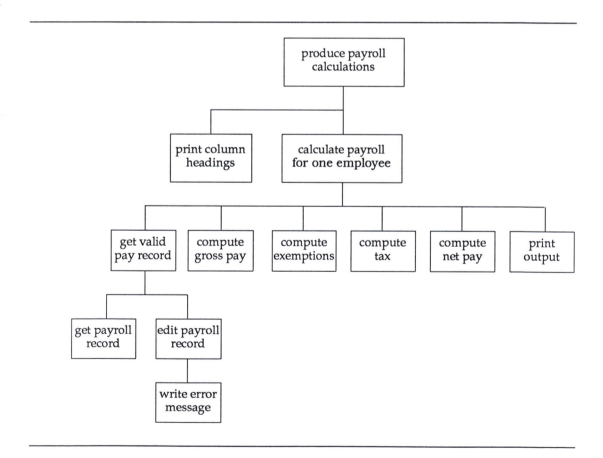

FIGURE 7.2 Hierarchy chart for third version of payroll program.

```
PRODUCE PAYROLL CALCULATIONS:
open files
print column headings
set eof-flag to 'N'
get valid payroll record
PERFORM-UNTIL eof-flag = 'Y'
      calculate payroll for employee
ENDPERFORM
close files


PRINT COLUMN HEADINGS:
get today's date
print date line
print heading text lines


CALCULATE PAYROLL FOR EMPLOYEE:
compute gross-pay
compute exemptions
compute tax
compute net pay
print output line
get valid payroll record


GET VALID PAY REC:
set valid-rec-flag to 'N'
PERFORM-UNTIL valid-rec-flag = 'Y' or eof-flag = 'Y'
      get payroll record
      IF eof-flag = 'N' THEN
            edit payroll-record
      ENDIF
ENDPERFORM


GET PAYROLL RECORD:
read payroll-record; at end set eof-flag to 'Y'


EDIT PAYROLL RECORD:
IF any of payroll-number or hours-worked or pay-rate or dependents
            is not numeric THEN
      write the error message
ELSE
      set valid-rec-flag to 'Y'
ENDIF


WRITE ERROR MESSAGE:
move the payroll record to the output line
move the error message text to the output line
print the output line
```

```
COMPUTE GROSS PAY:
gross-pay = hours-worked x pay-rate
IF hours-worked is greater than 40 THEN
        overtime-hours = hours-worked - 40
        multiply overtime-hours by 0.5
        overtime-pay = overtime-hours x pay-rate
        add overtime-pay to gross-pay
ENDIF


COMPUTE EXEMPTIONS:
exemptions = 50.00 x number-dependents


COMPUTE TAX:
IF gross-pay is greater than exemptions THEN
        tax = 0.21 x (gross-pay - exemptions)
ELSE
        tax = 0
ENDIF


COMPUTE NET PAY:
net-pay = gross-pay - tax


PRINT OUTPUT LINE:
move payroll-number, employee-name, hours-worked, pay-rate,
        number-dependents, gross-pay, tax, and net-pay
        to output-record
print output-record
```

FIGURE 7.3 Pseudocode specifications for version three of the payroll calculation program.

As you can see, the changes from version two are slight. Most of what needs to be done to meet the revised specifications will show up in the COBOL program rather than in the design.

7.21 THE PAYROLL PROGRAM

A revised payroll program is shown in Figure 7.4. It includes several new features, the first of which is illustrated at the beginning of the Working-Storage Section. Any time we have elementary items in Working-Storage that we do not wish to organize into any larger group, we may indicate this fact by using a special level number, 77. Level 77 entries, if any, are generally placed at the start of the Working-Storage Section. Earlier versions of COBOL required this placement and, although the requirement does not exist in current versions of the language, the convention is often still followed. In any case, level 77 items must begin in the A margin.

As a practical matter, there is really no strong incentive to use a level 77 entry, which does nothing that cannot be done by using an elementary item at level 01. Nevertheless this feature is used in many existing programs and the reader should be aware of it. To show it in action, we have placed all of the items used for temporary storage, as well as the two constant items, into level **77** entries in this program. The only advantage you may find in using level **77** items is that in some computers they will use slightly less space than the same item written as level **01**. Also, bear in mind that level **77** entries may not be used in the File Section.

```
IDENTIFICATION DIVISION.
PROGRAM-ID.
     PAYROLL3.
DATE-WRITTEN.
     JANUARY 29, 1987.


ENVIRONMENT DIVISION.
INPUT-OUTPUT SECTION.
FILE-CONTROL.
     SELECT PAYROLL-FILE        ASSIGN TO S-PAYROLL.
     SELECT REPORT-FILE         ASSIGN TO S-REPORT.

DATA DIVISION.
FILE SECTION.
FD   PAYROLL-FILE
     LABEL RECORDS ARE OMITTED.
01   PAYROLL-RECORD.
     05   I-PAYROLL-NUMBER      PIC X(5).
     05   I-NAME                PIC X(20).
     05   I-HOURS-WORKED        PIC 99V9.
     05   FILLER                PIC X(3).
     05   I-PAYRATE             PIC 99V999.
     05   I-DEPENDENTS          PIC 99.
     05   FILLER                PIC X(42).


FD   REPORT-FILE
     LABEL RECORDS ARE OMITTED.
01   REPORT-RECORD             PIC X(75).

WORKING-STORAGE SECTION.
77   C-EXEMPTION               PIC  S99V99    VALUE +50.00.
77   C-TAXRATE                 PIC     SV999  VALUE +.210.
77   W-EXEMPTION-TOTAL         PIC S999V99.
77   W-GROSS-PAY               PIC S999V99.
77   W-NET-PAY                 PIC S999V99.
77   W-OUT-OF-RECORDS-FLAG     PIC X          VALUE 'N'.
     88   OUT-OF-RECORDS                       VALUE 'Y'.
77   W-OVERTIME-HOURS          PIC  S99V99.
77   W-OVERTIME-PAY            PIC S999V99.
77   W-TAX                     PIC S999V99.
77   W-TAXABLE                 PIC S999V99.
77   W-TODAYS-DATE             PIC 9(6).
77   W-VALID-RECORD-FLAG       PIC X.
     88   VALID-RECORD                         VALUE 'Y'.

01   HEADING-LINE-1.
     05   FILLER                PIC X(26)
          VALUE 'PAYROLL CALCULATION REPORT'.
     05   FILLER                PIC X(41)      VALUE SPACES.
     05   REPORT-DATE           PIC 99/99/99   VALUE ZERO.
```

```
01   HEADING-LINE-2.
     05  FILLER                 PIC X(42)
         VALUE 'NUMBER            NAME            HOURS   RATE
     05  FILLER                 PIC X(29)
         VALUE '  DEP   GROSS       TAX      NET'.


01  NORMAL-OUTPUT-LINE.
     05   O-PAYROLL-NUMBER       PIC X(5).
     05   O-NAME                 PIC BBX(20).
     05   O-HOURS-WORKED         PIC BBZ9.9.
     05   O-PAYRATE              PIC BBZ9.999.
     05   O-DEPENDENTS           PIC BBZ9.
     05   O-GROSS-PAY            PIC BB$$$9.99.
     05   O-TAX                  PIC BB$$$9.99.
     05   O-NET-PAY              PIC BB$$$9.99.


01  ERROR-RECORD.
     05  BAD-DATA                PIC X(38).
     05  FILLER                  PIC X(4)        VALUE SPACES.
     05  ERROR-MESSAGE           PIC X(27)
         VALUE 'INVALID DATA IN THIS RECORD'.



PROCEDURE DIVISION.
A000-PRODUCE-PAYROLL-CALC.
    OPEN INPUT PAYROLL-FILE
         OUTPUT REPORT-FILE.
    PERFORM B010-PRINT-COLUMN-HEADINGS.
    PERFORM C010-GET-VALID-PAY-REC.
    PERFORM B020-CALC-EMP-PAYROLL
        UNTIL OUT-OF-RECORDS.
    CLOSE PAYROLL-FILE
          REPORT-FILE.
    STOP RUN.


B010-PRINT-COLUMN-HEADINGS.
    ACCEPT W-TODAYS-DATE FROM DATE.
    MOVE W-TODAYS-DATE TO REPORT-DATE.
    WRITE REPORT-RECORD FROM HEADING-LINE-1.
    MOVE SPACES TO REPORT-RECORD.
    WRITE REPORT-RECORD.
    WRITE REPORT-RECORD FROM HEADING-LINE-2.
    MOVE SPACES TO REPORT-RECORD.
    WRITE REPORT-RECORD.
    MOVE SPACES TO REPORT-RECORD.
    WRITE REPORT-RECORD.


B020-CALC-EMP-PAYROLL.
    PERFORM C020-COMPUTE-GROSS-PAY.
    PERFORM C030-COMPUTE-EXEMPTIONS.
    PERFORM C040-COMPUTE-TAX.
    PERFORM C050-COMPUTE-NET-PAY.
    PERFORM C060-PRINT-OUTPUT.
    PERFORM C010-GET-VALID-PAY-REC.


C010-GET-VALID-PAY-REC.
    MOVE 'N' TO W-VALID-RECORD-FLAG.
    PERFORM D010-VALID-RECORD-LOOP
        UNTIL   VALID-RECORD
             OR OUT-OF-RECORDS.
```

```
C020-COMPUTE-GROSS-PAY.
    MULTIPLY I-HOURS-WORKED BY I-PAYRATE
            GIVING W-GROSS-PAY ROUNDED.
    IF I-HOURS-WORKED IS GREATER THAN 40
        SUBTRACT 40 FROM I-HOURS-WORKED GIVING W-OVERTIME-HOURS
        MULTIPLY 0.5 BY W-OVERTIME-HOURS
        MULTIPLY W-OVERTIME-HOURS BY I-PAYRATE
                GIVING W-OVERTIME-PAY ROUNDED
        ADD W-OVERTIME-PAY TO W-GROSS-PAY.

C030-COMPUTE-EXEMPTIONS.
    MULTIPLY C-EXEMPTION BY I-DEPENDENTS
            GIVING W-EXEMPTIONS-TOTAL.

C040-COMPUTE-TAX.
    IF W-GROSS-PAY IS GREATER THAN W-EXEMPTION-TOTAL
        SUBTRACT W-EXEMPTIONS-TOTAL FROM W-GROSS-PAY
                GIVING W-TAXABLE
        MULTIPLY C-TAXRATE BY W-TAXABLE GIVING W-TAX ROUNDED
    ELSE
        MOVE ZERO TO W-TAX.

C050-COMPUTE-NET-PAY.
    SUBTRACT W-TAX FROM W-GROSS-PAY GIVING W-NET-PAY.

C060-PRINT-OUTPUT.
    MOVE SPACES               TO NORMAL-OUTPUT-LINE.
    MOVE I-PAYROLL-NUMBER      TO O-PAYROLL-NUMBER.
    MOVE I-NAME               TO O-NAME.
    MOVE I-HOURS-WORKED        TO O-HOURS-WORKED.
    MOVE I-PAYRATE            TO O-PAYRATE.
    MOVE I-DEPENDENTS          TO O-DEPENDENTS.
    MOVE W-TAX                TO O-TAX.
    MOVE W-GROSS-PAY           TO O-GROSS-PAY.
    MOVE W-NET-PAY            TO O-NET-PAY.
    WRITE REPORT-RECORD FROM NORMAL-OUTPUT-LINE.

D010-VALID-RECORD-LOOP.
    PERFORM E010-GET-PAYROLL-RECORD.
    IF NOT OUT-OF-RECORDS
        PERFORM E020-EDIT-PAYROLL-RECORD.

E010-GET-PAYROLL-RECORD.
    READ PAYROLL-FILE
            AT END MOVE 'Y' TO W-OUT-OF-RECORDS-FLAG.

E020-EDIT-PAYROLL-RECORD.
    IF      I-PAYROLL-NUMBER IS NOT NUMERIC
        OR I-HOURS-WORKED   IS NOT NUMERIC
        OR I-PAYRATE        IS NOT NUMERIC
        OR I-DEPENDENTS      IS NOT NUMERIC
        MOVE PAYROLL-RECORD TO BAD-DATA
        WRITE REPORT-RECORD FROM ERROR-RECORD
    ELSE
        MOVE 'Y' TO W-VALID-PAYROLL-RECORD.
```

FIGURE 7.4 A program to calculate weekly pay, including overtime, for all employee records in an input file; provides some validation of the input. Headings are printed and output fields are edited.

7.22   LEVEL 88 ENTRIES

A level **88** entry makes it possible to give a name to a value or set of values for an elementary item anywhere in the Data Division. This name, more precisely called a *condition name*, may then be used anywhere that a condition is required in writing Procedure Division statements.

All of this is much easier to present through an example than through abstract descriptions. Consider the flag that we have named **W-OUT-OF-RECORDS-FLAG**. In the first two versions of the payroll program, we gave this flag an initial value of **N**, set it to **Y** upon detecting the end of file, and used a **PERFORM** statement with an **UNTIL** phrase that read

```
UNTIL W-OUT-OF-RECORDS-FLAG = 'Y'.
```

Now we shall use a level **88** entry in the Working-Storage area where the flag is defined to give a name to the value **Y**. An obvious name is **OUT-OF-RECORDS**. Here are definitions of two level **88** entries.

```
77   W-OUT-OF-RECORDS-FLAG        PIC X      VALUE 'N'.
     88  OUT-OF-RECORDS                      VALUE 'Y'.
77   W-VALID-RECORD-FLAG          PIC X.
     88 VALID-RECORD                         VALUE 'Y'.
```

Then in the Procedure Division we write

```
PERFORM B020-CALC-EMP-PAYROLL
    UNTIL OUT-OF-RECORDS.
```

The effect is exactly the same as what we did in Chapter 6 except that the new form is perhaps easier to read. Naturally, it is easier to read *only if we take the trouble to devise meaningful names*. This condition could also be named **XQ13G**; the program would work correctly but program readability would take a giant step backward.

Also notice the entry for **W-VALID-RECORD-FLAG** that is used to check for valid records.

A level **88** entry may have, besides the name of the condition it defines, only a **VALUE** clause. It *must not* have a **PICTURE** clause. On the other hand, the elementary item to which a level **88** item refers *must* have a **PICTURE** clause; it may or may not have a **VALUE** clause, as circumstances dictate. The elementary item to which the condition name refers may be a level **77** item, but it may also be at any other level. For example, we could have written the flag definitions in the payroll program as follows:

```
01   FLAG-AREA.
     05   W-OUT-OF-RECORDS-FLAG     PIC X      VALUE 'N'.
          88   OUT-OF-RECORDS                  VALUE 'Y'.
     05   W-VALID-RECORD-FLAG       PIC X.
          88   VALID-RECORD                    VALUE 'Y'.
```

In fact, a condition name may even be associated with a group item; we shall discuss this usage in Chapter 11.

Level **88** entries are permitted in both the File Section and the Working-Storage Section of the Data Division. It is only in level **88** entries that **VALUE** clauses are permitted in the File Section.

Finally, a level **88** entry may specify not only a single value but also a range of values, as suggested in the following example:

```
05   PRODUCT-CODE          PIC X.
       88 HOUSEWARES                 VALUE 'A' THRU 'F'.
       88 AUTOMOTIVE                 VALUE 'G' THRU 'Q'.
       88 DRY-GOODS                  VALUE '7'.
       88 NOTIONS                    VALUE '8' 'J' 'R' THRU 'W'
                                           '1' THRU '4'.
```

We should mention that some programmers dislike the use of condition names because reference to a name such as **AUTOMOTIVE**, for example, in the Procedure Division does not document the fact that the *field* being examined is **PRODUCT-CODE**. This is a valid point and not to be ignored. Nonetheless, we can argue that the term **AUTOMOTIVE** tells the reader what the program is looking for more effectively than simply testing if the **PRODUCT-CODE** is in the range **G** through **Q**. In the end, the deciding factor should be one of the basic rules of programming: write the program in the way that conveys the most information to a human reader.

7.23   THE PROGRAM OUTPUT

There are two basic changes in the output for this version of the payroll program. First, we have headings at the start of the output, and second, the numeric data values have been edited for easier reading. The changes in the program code begin with two new entries in the Working-Storage Section, **HEADING-LINE-1** and **HEADING-LINE-2**. These structures will be printed at the start of the Procedure Division to create the heading text. Basically, there is nothing new about the structures. Their elementary fields have been initialized with text using **VALUE** clauses, just as we did with the constants in the previous version of the program. Notice that it is not necessary to define a heading line as a single elementary item; we can break it up into pieces in a structure in whatever manner is most convenient.

NORMAL-OUTPUT-LINE is almost the same as it was in Chapter 6, except that we have changed the numeric **PICTURE**s to suppress leading zeros and insert floating dollar signs where appropriate. We have also used the **B** insertion character to put blank spaces between columns instead of having to use **FILLER** entries. This method works equally well; the choice between the two is a matter of personal preference.

In the beginning of the Procedure Division we have added a statement to **PERFORM** the module that prints the column headings, and renumbered the **CALC-EMP-PAYROLL** paragraph to make sure that the paragraph prefixes remain in ascending sequence. Of course, we could have placed the new paragraph after **CALC-EMP-PAYROLL** and given it the **B020** prefix, but the order shown is more in keeping with the hierarchy of the program, and it is generally not wise to bend the structure of a program to fit the convenience of the moment.

Paragraph **B010-PRINT-COLUMN-HEADINGS** begins with a new statement, the **ACCEPT** statement. This statement is used to obtain the date or time from the hardware of the computer. It may also be used to obtain small quantities of input data from sources such as a terminal keyboard, but we will not use this feature. The format of the **ACCEPT** statement is as shown at the top of the next page.

$$\text{\underline{ACCEPT} identifier \underline{FROM}} \left\{ \begin{array}{l} \text{\underline{DATE}} \\ \text{\underline{DAY}} \\ \text{\underline{TIME}} \end{array} \right\}$$

The identifier may be any data item whose format is consistent with the particular data source chosen. **DATE** gives the current date in the form **YYMMDD** (year, month, day), and has the implicit format **9(6)**; for example, July 4, 1981 is given as 810704. **DAY** contains the year and day of the year in the form **YYDDD**, and has the implicit format **9(5)**; July 4, 1981 is expressed as 81185. **TIME** contains the time of day in the form **HHMMSSHH** (hours, minutes, seconds, hundredths of a second), and has the implicit format **9(8)**. For example, 30 seconds after 3:45 p.m. is expressed as 15453000. (Note the use of the 24-hour clock.)

The data names **DATE**, **DAY**, and **TIME** are reserved words that may be used only with the **ACCEPT** statement. You could *not*, for example, write

```
MOVE TIME TO TIME-OF-DAY.
```

COBOL-85

COBOL-85 provides a fourth data source, **DAY-OF-WEEK**. **DAY-OF-WEEK** has the implicit format **9**, and its value is an integer between 1 and 7 whose value represents the current day of the week; Monday is day 1, and Sunday is day 7. For example, if a program were run on July 4, 1990, **DAY-OF-WEEK** would have the value 3, representing Wednesday.

END COBOL-85

Notice that **DATE** presents the date in the order year, month, and day, and that we have not changed this order in moving the data into **REPORT-DATE**. There are several ways in which we could have reordered the data fields into the more familiar month/day/year sequence, but for now we will leave the order unchanged. The reason we accepted the date into **W-TODAYS-DATE** instead of accepting it directly into **REPORT-DATE** is to get the slashes edited into the field. The **ACCEPT** verb treats **DATE** as though it were a character field and performs no editing.

The remainder of **B010-PRINT-COLUMN-HEADINGS** holds no surprises. Notice that in order to print blank lines we had to move **SPACES** into **REPORT-RECORD** before writing it. There is a better way to do this, which we shall discuss in Chapter 9.

Other than these changes, the current version of the payroll program is exactly the same as the previous one. It was run with the same test data and produced the output shown in Figure 7.5.

It is clear that we have accomplished our objectives. The report heading appears at the top of the report, with the current date on the first line and

```
PAYROLL CALCULATION REPORT                                        87/02/12

NUMBER        NAME              HOURS   RATE   DEP   GROSS      TAX      NET

12345    THOS H. KELLY          20.0   5.350    0  $107.00   $22.47   $84.53
12401    HENRY JENSEN           40.0   7.500    1  $300.00   $52.50  $247.50
12511    NANCY KAHN             40.0   7.500    3  $300.00   $31.50  $268.50
UILKMB.  R. BROOKS        400   0575002       INVALID DATA IN THIS RECORD
26017    JANE MILANO            10.0   6.875    3   $68.75    $0.00   $68.75
12   4KAY DELUCCIA         400   0600004       INVALID DATA IN THIS RECORD
26109    PETER W. SHERWOOD      40.0  10.000    5  $400.00   $31.50  $368.50
26222    GEORGE M. MULVANEY     41.0  10.000    5  $415.00   $34.65  $380.35
26500A.  W. ENWRIGHT       40    0545001       INVALID DATA IN THIS RECORD
27511    RUTH GARRISON          50.0  10.000    4  $550.00   $73.50  $476.50
28819    LEO X. BUTLER          40.1  10.000    2  $401.50   $63.32  $338.18
28820D.  X. IANNUZZI       450   4.50003       INVALID DATA IN THIS RECORD
28821K.  L. NG, JR.        350    450003       INVALID DATA IN THIS RECORD
28822DANIEL REINER         350   045000C       INVALID DATA IN THIS RECORD
28822L.  E. SIMON          388    06000 3      INVALID DATA IN THIS RECORD
28883QA. REAL BAD-ONE      3 8    4.5KJXX       INVALID DATA IN THIS RECORD
7HGV6GARBAGE-CASE-1         ..M.,M.,M.,M.       INVALID DATA IN THIS RECORD
 NJI9GARBAGE-CASE-2        GV 6 46  8  H        INVALID DATA IN THIS RECORD
     GARBAGE-CASE-3   ----------++++++,M        INVALID DATA IN THIS RECORD
29000    ANNE HENDERSON         40.2  10.000    3  $403.00   $53.13  $349.87
29001    JULIA KIPP             40.3  10.000    1  $404.50   $74.45  $330.05
99999    IMA TESTCASE           99.9  99.999   99  $984.87    $7.32  $977.55
```

FIGURE 7.5   Illustrative output of the program in Figure 7.4.

descriptive text over each column. The numeric fields, except for the payroll number, have had leading zeros suppressed; and the fields that represent dollar amounts have dollar signs preceding each amount. However, the last line, for Ima Testcase, is still in error; the fact that the numbers look prettier doesn't alter the fact that they are wrong! We will learn how to deal with this last problem in the next chapter.

7.24 READING SIGNED DATA

We have one last topic to consider relating to data pictures: How do we read signed numeric data? If we simply define a numeric item with an operational sign, such as **S999**, the sign is assumed to be stored *within* the numeric field, generally associated with the rightmost digit. This makes no difference within the computer (after all, as long as the compiler knows where the sign is, it usually doesn't make any difference to us what the details are), but it becomes immensely important when we need to type a negative number to be entered into the computer as data.

In earlier versions of **COBOL** the problem could be resolved fairly easily. Since data was entered on punched cards, you could simply type *both* the digit and the sign in the same column on the card. This technique doesn't work too well with a computer terminal.

You might consider using the display sign, + or –, but this won't work either. Although the display sign is treated as a separate character in **COBOL**, it is used for output only and cannot be used to read data.

The solution to the problem is to use the **s** picture in combination with a new clause, the **SIGN** clause. For example, suppose we want to read a record for a retail sales operation. This record contains the date, the customer's name and address, and a transaction amount. If the transaction represents a sale, the amount is positive, but if the transaction is for returned merchandise, then the amount is negative. The following structure definition could be used for this record:

```
01   TRANSACTION-RECORD.
     05   TR-DATE              PIC 9(6).
     05   TR-NAME              PIC X(20).
     05   TR-STREET-ADDR       PIC X(20).
     05   TR-CITY              PIC X(10).
     05   TR-STATE             PIC XX.
     05   TR-ZIP               PIC 9(5).
     05   TR-AMOUNT            PIC S9(4)V99
                               SIGN IS TRAILING SEPARATE.
```

The **SIGN** clause tells the compiler that the sign is to be treated as a separate character which, in this example, follows the amount field. This means that the **TR-AMOUNT** is a *seven*-character item: 4 digits before the decimal point, an implied decimal point (which takes no space), 2 digits after the decimal point, and a sign.

The complete format for the **SIGN** clause is

If the **SEPARATE** phrase is omitted, the sign is stored within the item and the **s** character does not occupy a separate position in the computer; this is essentially the situation that normally exists, when no **SIGN** clause is used. However, if the **SEPARATE** phrase is present, the sign is treated as a separate character, either preceding or following the number, depending on whether **LEADING** or **TRAILING** is used. Although the syntax seems to imply that either **LEADING** or **TRAILING** must always be selected, in fact both may be omitted if the **SEPARATE** phrase is used. In this case, the decision as to whether the sign precedes or follows the number depends on what default is selected by the compiler. On IBM mainframe computers, for example, the default is equivalent to **TRAILING**.

REVIEW QUESTIONS

1. Fill in the edited result column for each of the following.

SENDING ITEM		RECEIVING ITEM	
PICTURE	SAMPLE DATA	PICTURE	EDITED RESULT
9(6)	000123	ZZZ,999	
9(6)	000008	ZZZ,999	
9(6)	123456	ZZZ,ZZZ.00	
9(4)V99	123456	ZZZ,ZZZ.ZZ	
9(4)V99	001234	$$,$$9.99	
9(4)V99	000078	$$,$$9.99	
9(4)V99	000078	$Z,ZZ9.99	
S9(4)V99	000078 (+)	$Z,ZZ9.99CR	
S9(4)V99	045678 (−)	$Z,ZZ9.99CR	
S9(6)	123456 (−)	−999,999	
S9(6)	123456 (+)	−999,999	
S9(6)	123456 (+)	+999,999	
S9(6)	123456 (−)	+999,999	
S9(6)	123456 (−)	−−−−,−−9	
S9(6)	000123 (+)	−−−−,−−9	
S9(6)	001234 (+)	++++,++9	
9(6)	123456	99B99B99	
9(6)	123456	99/99/99	
9(6)	001234	Z(6)0	
9(6)	000092	ZZZ,ZZZ00	
999PPP	123	9(8)	
X(6)	123ABC	XBXBXBBXXX	
X(6)	123ABC	X/X/X//XXX	

2. For each of the following entries, supply the character that is used in a PICTURE character string to designate the function.

   a. Assumed decimal point.

   b. Actual decimal point.

    c. Zero suppression without insertion of any other character.

    d. Numeric digit.

    e. Alphanumeric character.

    f. Alphabetic character.

    g. Zero suppression and check protection.

    h. Presence of a sign.

    i. Zero suppression with floating dollar sign insertion.

    j. Credit.

    k. Debit.

    l. Scale factor.

3. True or false:

    a. An assumed decimal point takes up no space in storage and is therefore not counted in determining the size of an item.

    b. A display decimal point takes up no space in storage and is therefore not counted in determining the size of an item.

    c. A scale factor (character **P**) takes up no space in storage and is therefore not counted in determining the size of an item.

    d. Given the following Data Division entry

```
05  FIELD-R        PICTURE X(5).
```

    we could legally write

```
ADD 3 TO FIELD-R.
```

    e. Given the following Data Division entry

```
05  FIELD-X        PICTURE 999.
```

    we could legally write

```
MOVE 'ABC' TO FIELD-X.
```

    f. **PICTURE 99,99Z.99** could be used to zero-suppress a field up to and including the decimal point.

4. Which of the following may appear more than once in a **PICTURE** clause?

    a. Actual decimal point.

    b. Assumed decimal point.

    c. Dollar sign.

    d. Scale factor.

    e. Comma.

    f. Sign designation.

    g. Minus sign.

    h. Plus sign.

5. Identify any errors in the following **PICTURE** character strings.

    a. **99.99.99**

    b. **99,99,99**

c. `-Z,ZZ9.99CR`

d. `$$$Z.99`

e. `ZZZ,ZZ9.Z9`

f. `$**,***.99`

g. `+++,$$$.99`

h. `999,PPP,999`

6. For each of the following, supply a **PICTURE** clause that could produce the edited results from the data shown. There will not, in most cases, be just one correct answer, since you will not know how other data might be treated. On the first entry, for example, the **PICTURE** could be `Z9.9999` or `ZZ.9999` and give the same result with the data shown.

SENDING ITEM		RECEIVING ITEM	
PICTURE	SAMPLE DATA	PICTURE	EDITED RESULT
99V9(4)	013579		1.3579
99V9(4)	011111		001.11110
9(6)	000000		
9(6)	000001		1
9(4)V99	000123		$ 01.23
9(4)V99	000123		$1.23
9(4)V99	001234		$***12.34
9(6)	000005		$5.00
S9(6)	000014 (+)		*****14+
S9(6)	000014 (+)		+ 14
S9(6)	000014 (−)		14CR
S9(6)	000014 (+)		+14
S9(6)	000014 (−)		014−
S9(6)	009876 (+)		+9,876
S9(4)V99	012345 (−)		$123.45DB
S9(4)V99	123456 (+)		$1,234.56+
S9(4)V99	000123 (−)		$****1.23−
X(6)	USARMY		U S ARMY
9(6)	123456		1,23,456
9(6)	123456		123 4560

7. Identify errors in each of the following.

a. 05 SALARY-CODE.
    88 MONTHLY   PIC X VALUE '1'.
    88 WEEKLY   PIC X VALUE '2'.
    88 SPECIAL   PIC X VALUE '3'.
    88 ERROR-CODE   PIC X VALUE '0' '4' THRU '9'.

b. 01 CODES.
    77 CODE-1   PIC X.
    77 CODE-2   PIC X.

c. 01 FLD-9   PIC -9(5) SIGN IS LEADING SEPARATE.

d. 77 TODAYS-DATE   PIC Z9/99/99.
        .
        .
        .
     ACCEPT TODAYS-DATE FROM DATE.

ANSWERS

1.

SENDING ITEM		RECEIVING ITEM	
PICTURE	SAMPLE DATA	PICTURE	EDITED RESULT
9(6)	000123	ZZZ,999	123
9(6)	000008	ZZZ,999	008
9(6)	123456	ZZZ,ZZZ.00	123,456.00
9(4)V99	123456	ZZZ,ZZZ.ZZ	1,234.56
9(4)V99	001234	$$,$$9.99	$12.34
9(4)V99	000078	$$,$$9.99	$0.78
9(4)V99	000078	$Z,ZZ9.99	$ 0.78
S9(4)V99	000078 (+)	$Z,ZZ9.99CR	$ 0.78
S9(4)V99	045678 (−)	$Z,ZZ9.99CR	$ 456.78CR
S9(6)	123456	−999,999	−123,456
S9(6)	123456 (+)	−999,999	123,456
S9(6)	123456 (+)	+999,999	+123,456
S9(6)	123456 (−)	+999,999	−123,456
S9(6)	123456 (−)	----,--9	−123,456
S9(6)	000123 (+)	----,--9	123
S9(6) (+)	001234	++++,++9	+1,234
9(6)	123456	99B99B99	12 34 56
9(6)	123456	99/99/99	12/34/56

9(6)	001234	Z(6)0	12340
9(6)	000092	ZZZ,ZZZ00	9200
999PPP	123	9(8)	00123000
X(6)	123ABC	XBXBXBBXXX	1 2 3 ABC
X(6)	123ABC	X/X/X//XXX	1/2/3//ABC

2. **a.** V
   b. .
   c. Z
   d. 9
   e. X
   f. A
   g. *
   h. S
   i. $
   j. CR
   k. DB
   l. P

3. **a.** True.
   b. False.
   c. True. The scale factor affects the number of *digits* the item represents, but not the amount of space the item occupies.
   d. False. Arithmetic may not be done on alphanumeric items.
   e. False. Alphanumeric data may not be stored in a numeric item.
   f. False. Zero suppression applies only to *leading zeros,* so if a picture has both 9s and Zs, the Zs must be to the left of any 9s.

4. **a.** May not appear more than once, since decimal point alignment would be ambiguous.
   b. Ditto.
   c. More than one dollar sign specifies floating dollar sign.
   d. Any number may be written, but must be either at the left end of the picture or the right end.
   e. Any number may be written.
   f. Only one permitted.
   g. More than one calls for floating sign insertion.
   h. Ditto.

5. **a.** A decimal point may not appear more than once in a PICTURE character string.
   b. No error.
   c. A PICTURE string may not have both a minus sign and CR or DB.

    d. Only one form of zero suppression is permitted in one **PICTURE** character string.

    e. A **9** may not precede a **z** which, if permitted, would describe separate zero suppression operations within one item.

    f. No error.

    g. Two different floating string characters are not permitted in the same **PICTURE** character string.

    h. The scale factor must be at one end or the other of the **PICTURE** character string, not in the middle.

6.

SENDING ITEM		RECEIVING ITEM	
PICTURE	SAMPLE DATA	PICTURE	EDITED RESULT
99V9(4)	013579	Z9.9(4)	1.3579
99V9(4)	011111	999.9(5)	001.11110
9(6)	000000	ZZZ,ZZZ	
9(6)	000001	ZZZ,ZZZ	1
9(4)V99	000123	$Z,Z99.99	$ 01.23
9(4)V99	000123	$$,$$9.99	$1.23
9(4)V99	001234	$*,**9.99	$***12.34
9(6)	000005	$$$$,$$9.00	$5.00
S9(6)	000014 (+)	***,**9+	*****14+
S9(6)	000014 (+)	+ZZZ,ZZ9	+ 14
S9(6)	000014 (−)	ZZZ,ZZ9CR	14CR
S9(6)	000014 (+)	++++,++9	+14
S9(6)	000014 (−)	ZZZ999−	014−
S9(6)	009876 (+)	++++,+++	+9,876
S9(4)V99	012345 (−)	$$,$$9.99DB	$123.45DB
S9(4)V99	123456 (+)	$$,$$9.99+	$1,234.56+
S9(4)V99	000123 (−)	$*,**9.99−	$****1.23−
X(6)	USARMY	XBXBX(4)	U S ARMY
9(6)	123456	9,99,999	1,23,456
9(6)	123456	0999B9990	0123 4560

7. a. The elementary item to which a level **88** entry refers must have a **PICTURE** clause; a level **88** entry itself must not have a **PICTURE**.

    b. Level **77** entries cannot be parts of group items.

   c. If the **SIGN** phrase is used, the **PICTURE** character string must contain an operational sign character, not a display sign character.

   d. The **ACCEPT** statement simply moves the contents of **DATE** into the identifier, **TODAYS-DATE** in this case, so the editing implied by the **Z** and the slashes in the picture would not be performed.

EXERCISES

*1. In each of the five parts of this exercise you are given four sending items, a **PICTURE** character string that describes all of them, and corresponding edited receiving items. For each part write a **PICTURE** clause for the receiving area that would edit the sending items as shown.

   a. 9(5)

```
12345      12345
01234       1234
00123        123
00012        012
```

   b. 9(6)

```
012345     $12345
000123       $123
000001         $1
000000
```

   c. 9(4)V99

```
012345     $123.45
000123     $  1.23
000001     $  0.01
000000     $  0.00
```

   d. 9(4)

```
    +
1234       +1234

    -
0012        -12
    +
0004         +4
    +
0000
```

   e. S9(5)

```
01462       1   462
00192       0   192
10004      10   004
98765      98   765
```

2. Same as Exercise 1.

   a. 999

```
   +
123        123

   -
123       -123

   -
002        -2
   +
000         0
```

---

* Answers to starred exercises will be found in Appendix IV at the end of the book.

b. `9(4)V99`

```
123456    1,234.56
001234       12.34
000123        1.23
000012        0.12
```

c. `9(4)`

```
1234    1234.00
0012      12.00
0001       1.00
0000       0.00
```

d. `999V99`

```
12345    $123.45
00012    $***.12
00001    $***.01
00000    ****.**
```

e. `9(4)`

```
1234    $1234
0123    $123
0012    $12
0001    $01
```

*3. Study the input record format shown and the printed output produced from it for sample data. Supply the **PICTURE** clauses for **I-RECORD** and **O-DETAIL-LINE** that would properly describe such a record and produce such output. On the output provide five blank spaces between columns.

Input record format:

Columns 1-5	Customer Number	numeric
Columns 6-25	Customer Name	
Columns 6	First Initial	
Columns 7-25	Last Name	
Columns 26-31	Amount of Sale	dollars and cents; negative for refund
Columns 32-37	Product Code	mixed letters and numbers
Columns 38-79	Blanks	
Columns 80	Record Code	A-Z

Sample output:

```
12 345      J DOE                $1,012.09      CD149A      S
23 456      R ROE                   $4.79-      PQ276C      R
34 567      J SMITH                  $.84       CX726X      S
```

```
01    I-RECORD.
      05    I-CUST-NO
      05    I-CUST-NAME
      05    I-AMT-SALE
      05    I-PROD-CODE
      05    FILLER
      05    I-RECORD-CODE
```

```
01   O-DETAIL-LINE.
     05   O-CUST-NO
     05   FILLER
     05   O-CUST-NAME
     05   FILLER
     05   O-AMT-SALE
     05   FILLER
     05   O-PROD-CODE
     05   FILLER
     05   O-RECORD-CODE
```

(Suggested by Professor Stuart J. Travis, Ferris State College.)

4. Supply **PICTURE** clauses for the following record format.

Record format:

Columns 1-5	Cust No.	numeric only
Columns 6-65	Cust. Address	
Columns 6-25	Name	
Columns 26-45	Street Address	
Columns 46-65	City and State	
Columns 66-72	Amount of Sale	
Columns 73-79	Not Used	
Columns 80	Code	A-Z only

```
01   DATA-RECORD.
     05   CUST-NO
     05   CUST-ADDRESS
          10   NAME
          10   STREET
          10   CITY
     05   SALE-AMT
     05   FILLER
     05   REC-CODE
```

In the following two exercises you are given a File Section description of a number of sending items that are to be edited for printing in a specified format. The format required is described and a sample of the described output is shown. You are to prepare the entries, including all necessary **PICTURE** clauses, for a record named **OUTPUT-LINE**. You are not required to write any Procedure Division entries, but it is assumed that for each exercise there would be **MOVE** statements of the form

```
MOVE ITEM TO ITEM-OUT
```

for each item to be printed.

*5. (See general description above.) The output goes on a preprinted form (see next page), so decimal points are not required and most items are to be printed without spaces between adjacent fields. Specifically, the items from **ID-NUMBER** through **REFERENCE** have no spaces between them. Between **REFERENCE** and **GROSS** there is one blank space, between **GROSS** and **DISC-OR-DEDUC** there is one, and between **DISC-OR-DEDUC** and **AMOUNT-PAYABLE** there are two.

ANYVILLE UNIVERSITY						DETACH THIS STUB BEFORE CASHING					E 431861

REFERENCE		FUND	DEPT	B	P. O. NUMBER	YOUR REFERENCE	GROSS	DISCOUNT OR DEDUCTIONS	AMOUNT
NUMBER	REQ.								
508397		0100	2104	02		HONORARIUM	250 00	0 00	250 00

Please direct any correspondence regarding this payment to ACCOUNTS PAYABLE, BUSINESS OFFICE, ADMINISTRATIVE SERVICES BLDG.
2810 University Place, Gotham City, XX 12345 OR TELEPHONE 212-345-6789

```
01  INPUT-RECORD.
    05  ID-NUMBER            PIC X(6).
    05  REQUISITION          PIC X(6).
    05  FUND                 PIC X(4).
    05  DEPARTMENT           PIC X(4).
    05  B                    PIC XX.
    05  PURCHASE-ORDER       PIC X(6).
    05  REFERENCE            PIC X(18).
    05  GROSS                PIC 9(5)V99.
    05  DISC-OR-DEDUC        PIC 999V99.
    05  AMOUNT-PAYABLE       PIC 9(5)V99.

01  OUTPUT-LINE.
    05  ID-NUMBER-OUT
    05  REQUISITION-OUT
    05  FUND-OUT
    05  DEPARTMENT-OUT
    05  B-OUT
    05  PURCHASE-ORDER-OUT
    05  REFERENCE-OUT
    05  FILLER
    05  GROSS-OUT
    05  FILLER
    05  DISC-OR-DEDUC-OUT
    05  FILLER
    05  AMOUNT-PAYABLE-OUT
```

6. (See general description before Exercise 5.) The output goes on a preprinted form, but of a different design with more room. There are eight items to be printed; the number of blank spaces between them, reading from left to right, are two, three, two, two, one, one, and one. The item named **LEASE-BEGAN** consists of five characters including the slash. Zero suppression is to be applied only to the three dollar amounts, which are to have decimal points inserted but not dollar signs.

Lease began	Lease term	Payable	Equipment Description	Lease Number	Current Rent	Sales Tax	Current Amount Due
08/87	36	M	PHOTOCOPIER	38459	162.43	13.40	175.83

```
01    INPUT-RECORD.
      05    LEASE-BEGAN           PIC X(5).
      05    LEASE-TERM            PIC XX.
      05    PAYABLE               PIC X.
      05    DESCRIPTION           PIC X(21).
      05    LEASE-NUMBER          PIC X(5).
      05    CURRENT-RENT          PIC 999V99.
      05    SALES-TAX             PIC 99V99.
      05    CURRENT-AMT-DUE       PIC 999V99.

01    OUTPUT-LINE.
      05    LEASE-BEGAN-OUT
      05    FILLER
      05    LEASE-TERM-OUT
      05    FILLER
      05    PAYABLE-OUT
      05    FILLER
      05    DESCRIPTION-OUT
      05    FILLER
      05    LEASE-NUMBER-OUT
      05    FILLER
      05    CURRENT-RENT-OUT
      05    FILLER
      05    SALES-TAX-OUT
      05    FILLER
      05    CURRENT-AMT-DUE-OUT
```

*7. Prepare a hierarchy chart and pseudocode to design a program that will prepare an accounts receivable report, then write a program to implement your design.

The input consists of records having the following format:

Columns 1-5	Customer number
Columns 6-25	Customer name
Columns 26-30	Invoice number
Columns 31-36	Invoice date
Columns 37-42	Invoice amount in dollars and cents, with an assumed decimal point

The problem is to produce a report with page and column headings of the following form. (You may ignore the requirement to limit the number of detail lines; come back to this after you have studied the **ADVANCING** clause and line spacing.)

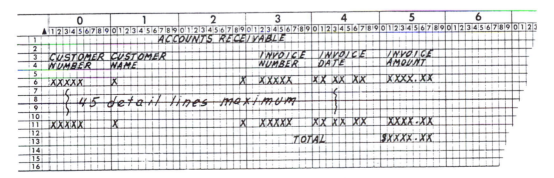

The report is to start with the 5 lines (including blanks) of the heading, as shown. As the accounts receivable records are read and printed, a final total of the invoice amounts is to be accumulated. When the last record has been read, this total should be printed following the body of the report.

Here is sample input for the exercise:

```
12810AMERICAN CAN        11223112387157468
12810AMERICAN CAN        12336123087040902
21654APPLEBEE MFG.       09852010588033000
22873BAKER TOOL          12453112687057690
24251C.F.B. FREIGHT      13342010688130076
```

For this input, the program should produce the following output.

```
                      ACCOUNTS RECEIVABLE


CUSTOMER  CUSTOMER                INVOICE  INVOICE   INVOICE
NUMBER    NAME                    NUMBER   DATE      AMOUNT

12810     AMERICAN CAN            11223    11 23 87  1574.68
12810     AMERICAN CAN            12336    12 30 87   409.02
21654     APPLEBEE MFG.           09852    01 05 88   330.00
22873     BAKER TOOL              12543    11 26 87   576.90
24251     C.F.B.  FREIGHT         13342    01 06 88  1300.76

                                  TOTAL       $4,191.36
```

(Adapted, by permission of the author, from Joan K. Hughes, *PL/I Programming*. New York: Wiley, 3rd edition, 1985.)

8. Design (hierarchy chart and pseudocode) and implement a program to produce proof totals for a weekly payroll.

You are given a file whose records have the following format.

Column 1	Record Type
	1 = regular pay
	2 = overtime pay
	3 = bonus pay
	4 = other pay
Columns 2-6	Employee Number (numeric)
Columns 7-11	Earnings in dollars and cents, with an assumed decimal point.

The function of the program is to produce four totals, one for each type of earnings. For each type of earnings, the program is to print a count of the number of records of that type. For instance, the total for regular earnings consists of the sum of the earnings amount on all records having the record type of 1.

The printer layout should be as follows:

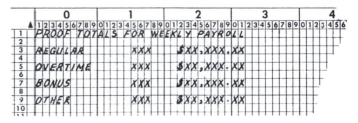

Here is some sample data:

```
11111118542
21111101465
11111229011
21111201200
11111340000
31111308000
41111450000
11111538065
11111642000
21111612376
41111601000
11111729999
11111868011
31111910500
```

For this input, the program should produce this output:

```
PROOF TOTALS FOR WEEKLY PAYROLL

REGULAR          7      $2,656.28

OVERTIME         3       $138.41

BONUS            2       $185.00

OTHER            2       $510.00
```

(Adapted, by permission of the author, from Joan K. Hughes, *PL/I Programming*. New York: Wiley, 3rd edition, 1985.)

*9. Modify the program in Figure 7.4 so that it treats the data as invalid and prints the message **GROSS PAY SUSPICIOUSLY LARGE** if the computed gross pay exceeds $600.

10. Modify the program in Figure 7.4 so that it produces the **INVALID DATA** message if the payroll number is less than 23000, the number of dependents is greater than 15, or the number of hours worked is greater than 80. Create test data to test each of these errors individually and in combination with others.

*11. Modify the program in Figure 7.4 so that at the end of the listing, it produces a count of the total number of input records processed, the number having invalid data, the total of the gross pay on all valid records, the total of the tax on all valid records, and the total of the net pay on all valid records.

*12. A United States company pays taxes in 10 different states. In a certain tax summarization program it is desired to be able to write statements like

```
IF ALABAMA
    PERFORM D010-ALABAMA-TAX-COMP.
```

rather than

```
IF STATE-CODE = '01'
    PERFORM D010-ALABAMA-TAX-COMP.
```

Show how this can be accomplished.

13. Continuing with Exercise 12, suppose that the 50 states are to be referenced in three categories:
    a. Those that have a condition name consisting of their name, of which there are only 4: California, Michigan, Illinois, and Florida;
    b. Any of the other 6 states to which the company pays taxes, referred to by a condition name of OTHER-STATE;
    c. Any of the other 40 states, referred to by INVALID-STATE.
       Show how this can be accomplished.

*14. All of the examples of the actions of various PICTURE characters were produced by COBOL programs. Write a program to produce the examples in Section 7.7.

15. Same as Exercise 14, except write the program to produce the examples in Section 7.10. Be sure to include code that will write the sign of each sending item above the item, as shown in the examples.

CHAPTER 8

DEBUGGING

8.1 INTRODUCTION

By now you have probably discovered that it is almost impossible to write a program, in COBOL or any other language, without making *some* kind of error. The objective of this chapter is to study various types of errors that occur in a COBOL program, and to find ways of dealing with them.

Errors in COBOL programs can be divided into two types: *compile-time* and *run-time*. Recall that the function of the COBOL compiler is to take the *source code* that you write and turn it into *machine code*, also called *object code*, that can be executed by the computer. (This is a slight simplification, since there is usually a second step needed to create the actual machine code that the computer executes, but we can ignore this for our purposes.) Compile-time errors are those that occur during the compilation process, that is, errors in your COBOL code that are detected by the COBOL compiler. Run-time errors are those that occur when the program executes. In other words, you have written a syntactically correct COBOL program but it doesn't produce the proper results. An example of this type of error is the output produced for Ima Testcase in the payroll program of the previous chapters. The program compiled correctly and executed, but the results for this test case were incorrect.

The methods we use for dealing with the two types of errors are completely different. Compile-time errors are detected by the COBOL compiler, which produces a message indicating that an error has been made and where it is located in the program. The general nature of this type of error is always the same: something you have written does not obey the rules of COBOL. The problem is simply a matter of determining why the code is illegal, and then correcting it.

Run-time errors are generally much more difficult to deal with. In the first place, the computer frequently will not tell you that an error has occurred. (Consider the first version of the payroll program; it ran and produced output, and nothing the computer did informed us that part of the output was incorrect.) We must learn how to tell if the output the computer produces is invalid.

However, even if the computer does tell you that *something* has gone wrong, it usually does not do a very good job of telling you exactly what caused the problem and where the error is located in the program. It is your job as the programmer to find the answers to these questions, then determine how to correct the problem.

8.2 THE EFFECT OF PROGRAM DESIGN ON DEBUGGING

The best way to fix program errors is not to put them in the program in the first place. Although this may seem to be a rather sarcastic comment ("Of course I don't want to put errors into my program!"), the intent is quite serious. The place to start debugging a program is with the design. If the design of the program is clear and logical, and if the specifications are complete and free of errors, then the program will probably not have serious problems. However, no amount of work will make a good program from a poor design. *If you don't understand how to solve the problem, the computer won't figure it out for you!*

We discussed the basics of program design in Chapter 4, and now we see more of the motive for the techniques used. It is not sufficient simply to produce a program; we must be able to develop a program that works correctly, with a minimum of debugging, and (as we shall see throughout the book) that can be modified with a minimum amount of effort. The design techniques presented in Chapter 4 serve this goal.

What we did not stress in Chapter 4, however, is the need to review the design for completeness and accuracy. Do not expect that the first attempt at designing a program will be the final attempt. One almost never creates an acceptable design with the first try. After you create the initial versions of the hierarchy chart and pseudocode, review them carefully to make sure that they say what you want them to; that is, if you write a program exactly according to those specifications, will it do what it should? In all likelihood you will realize that you have forgotten something or made some kind of error, or simply that there is a better structure for the design. This is not unreasonable. It is necessary to study a problem repeatedly until you learn enough about it to be able to design a good program. The more effort you put into the program design, the more you will understand the problem, and the more likely that your program will be free of serious errors.

8.3 PROGRAMMING STYLE

A good design is not all that is necessary to develop a good program. The coding style that is used in writing a program also affects the number of errors to be found in the program, which is why in our example programs we use the coding standards given in Appendix III. The objective of these standards is to present the program in such a way as to make its statements as clear as possible to the reader. We have mentioned some of these standards in previous chapters and will continue to mention coding technique wherever it is appropriate. Remember: the easier it is for you to read what you have written, the less likely you are to miss errors in the code.

Once the program has been entered into the computer, begin your error checking by getting a listing of the program using whatever file listing procedure your computer provides. Although the listing should be used to check for simple typing errors, its main purpose is to give you a clean, readable version of the program that can be studied for design errors. In particular, verify that the structure of the program matches the structure of the hierarchy chart, and that this structure is a logical one. One of the most important program characteristics to check for is to make certain that each paragraph performs a single, well-defined function. For example, suppose we modified the payroll program slightly so that it counts the number of valid records processed (see Exercise 5 in Chapter 6). We could accomplish this by changing paragraphs `E010-GET-PAYROLL-RECORD` and `E020-EDIT-PAYROLL-RECORD` as follows:

```
E010-GET-PAYROLL-RECORD.
    READ PAYROLL-FILE
            AT END MOVE 'Y' TO W-OUT-OF-RECORDS-FLAG.
    ADD 1 TO VALID-RECORD-COUNT.

E020-EDIT-PAYROLL-RECORD.
    IF      I-PAYROLL-NUMBER IS NOT NUMERIC
        OR  I-HOURS-WORKED   IS NOT NUMERIC
        OR  I-PAYRATE        IS NOT NUMERIC
        OR  I-DEPENDENTS     IS NOT NUMERIC
        MOVE PAYROLL-RECORD TO BAD-DATE
        WRITE REPORT-RECORD FROM ERROR-RECORD
        SUBTRACT 1 FROM VALID-RECORD-COUNT
    ELSE
        MOVE 'Y' TO W-VALID-PAYROLL-RECORD.
```

There are two problems with this code, however. First, each paragraph performs two or more unrelated activities. The activities performed by `E010-GET-PAYROLL-RECORD`, reading a record and incrementing the counter, have nothing to do with one another since one involves getting the next record (valid or not) and the other is related only to valid records. The statements performed in `E020-EDIT-PAYROLL-RECORD` when the condition is true all relate to processing an *invalid* record, except for the **SUBTRACT** statement that is related to processing *valid* records. The task of counting the number of valid records is split over two paragraphs, and the part in each paragraph doesn't really make much sense where it is.

The second basic problem with this version of the program is simply that it will give incorrect results. If the value of **VALID-RECORD-COUNT** is printed at the end of the program, it will not give an accurate count of the number of valid records. The precise nature of the error is left as an exercise (see Exercise 1 at the end of this chapter).

A much better solution to the problem is the following:

```
B020-CALC-EMP-PAYROLL.
    PERFORM C020-COMPUTE-GROSS-PAY.
    PERFORM C030-COMPUTE-EXEMPTIONS.
    PERFORM C040-COMPUTE-TAX.
    PERFORM C050-COMPUTE-NET-PAY.
    PERFORM C060-PRINT-OUTPUT.
    ADD 1 TO VALID-RECORD-COUNT.
    PERFORM C010-GET-VALID-PAY-REC.
```

This approach is based on the fact that counting the number of valid records is related to processing those records, which is controlled by paragraph **B020-CALC-EMP-PAYROLL**. The first version tried to associate counting *valid* records with reading *any* record, then found it necessary to fudge the count when an invalid record was detected, and still did not arrive at an error-free solution. In general you will find that the more closely related the statements in a paragraph are, and the more you place the actions needed to carry out a function in the same paragraph, the more likely you are to have a well-designed program without major errors.

8.4 NESTED IF STATEMENTS

There are several statements or structures in **COBOL** that cause a disproportionately large number of programming problems, particularly for beginning **COBOL** programmers. One of the ways to minimize errors in a **COBOL** program is to avoid using these statements or, if they must be used, to be aware of the problems they can cause.

The first of these "dangerous" constructions that we will look at is the nested **IF**. We have already encountered the nested **IF** in Section 5.14 as a means of implementing the case structure. We now want to see some of the uses of the nested **IF** beyond this one format, and to learn the dangers that the structure presents. Most of the problems that we will discuss apply only to versions of **COBOL** prior to **COBOL-85**. If you are using **COBOL-85**, read the remainder of this section to see how nested **IF** statements are used, but remember that the problems we will be discussing can usually be cured with the **END-IF** phrase.

Recall that a nested **IF** exists when one of the actions of an **IF** statement is itself an **IF** statement. In the following discussion we will use the letter **C** to stand for a Condition, and the letter **S** to stand for a Statement. There will generally be one or more of each, so we shall number them. Thus, we might write

```
IF C1
   IF C2
      S1.
```

to stand for a simple nested **IF** statement such as

```
IF ACCOUNT-NO IS EQUAL TO PREVIOUS-ACCT-NO
   IF DISTRICT IS EQUAL TO PREVIOUS-DISTRICT
      PERFORM C040-PROCESS-DETAIL-RECORD.
```

Another statement that could be represented by the same shorthand is

```
IF HOURS-WORKED IS EQUAL TO 40
   IF REGULAR-PAY
      MOVE 'X' TO NORMAL-PROCESSING-FLAG.
```

In other words, **C1** and **C2** can be any conditions, including condition names from **88** level entries (such as **REGULAR-PAY**). Furthermore, any time we indicate one statement, by writing **S**, any number may be written. Thus the skeleton above would also describe

```
IF A = B
    IF C = D
        MOVE 'X' TO ABCD-FLAG
        PERFORM D055-BOTH-EQUAL.
```

It is always possible to represent the logic of a nested **IF** by one or more simple **IF**s having compound conditions. The statement just given, for example, has exactly the same effect as

```
IF A = B  AND  C = D
    MOVE 'X' TO ABCD-FLAG
    PERFORM D055-BOTH-EQUAL.
```

The more complex nested **IF** statements that we shall study later, if translated to unnested form, become many **IF**s, sometimes with very complicated compound conditions. The choice between nested **IF**s vs. simple **IF**s with compound conditions is, to a certain extent, a matter of taste. However, remember that you should always try to make the program as straightforward and readable as possible.

Here is a slightly more complicated nested **IF**:

```
IF C1
    IF C2
        S1
    ELSE
        S2.
```

When written without the nested **IF**, it becomes these two statements:

```
IF C1 AND C2
    S1.
IF C1 AND NOT C2
    S2.
```

This is a good place to mention once again the crucial importance of putting the periods of **IF** statements in the right place. For instance, if the first period in the two unnested **IF**s just shown were omitted, the result would be syntactically correct, but it would represent altogether different logic. The pseudocode for the statements above is shown in Figure 8.1, while the pseudocode for the statements without the first period is shown in Figure 8.2.

```
IF C1 and C2 THEN
    S1
ENDIF
IF C1 and not C2 THEN
    S2
ENDIF
```

FIGURE 8.1 Pseudocode for correctly written **IF** statements.

The "true" path for the first decision in Figure 8.2 will be taken only if **C1** and **C2** are both true. But if this is the case, it cannot also be the case that **C1** is true and **C2** is false—so **S2** would never be executed. (A "smart" compiler would be able to detect that **S2** is *dead code*, meaning that it can never be reached, but most compilers are not that sophisticated.)

```
IF C1 and C2 THEN
    S1
    IF C1 and not C2 THEN
        S2
    ENDIF
ENDIF
```

FIGURE 8.2. Pseudocode for incorrectly written IF statements.

It might be argued that without the period after the first **IF** the indentation of the **COBOL** code is wrong, since then the second **IF** is controlled by the first **IF** and ought to be indented. This, of course, is true, but we must always remember that the compiler knows nothing about indentation rules. These are of great importance for clarity of communication between human beings, but the compiler takes no information from them. In fact, even deeply nested **IF**s may all be written on one line if the data names are short enough. That is not an intelligent way to write code, but it is legal.

An alternative way to write statements such as the ones above is to use a separate paragraph for the nested **IF**. For example, we could write

```
IF C1
    PERFORM NESTED-PARA.
    .
    .
    .
NESTED-PARA.
    IF C2
        S1
    ELSE
        S2.
```

This approach has the advantage that we don't have to worry about omitting the first period, but this comes at the cost of splitting the function to be performed over two paragraphs, which might be pages apart on the listing. Again, within limits, the decision is largely a matter of personal taste.

Now consider the following **IF** statement, and the matching pseudocode:

```
COBOL                   PSEUDOCODE

IF C1                   IF C1 THEN
    IF C2                   IF C2 THEN
        S1                      S1
    ELSE                    ELSE
        S2                      S2
ELSE                        ENDIF
    S3.                 ELSE
                            S3
                        ENDIF
```

Here each **IF** has a matching **ELSE**. The next step in this progression is to have decisions on both branches of the first decision:

```
        COBOL              PSEUDOCODE
IF C1                      IF C1 THEN
    IF C2                      IF C2 THEN
        S1                         S1
    ELSE                       ELSE
        S2                         S2
ELSE                           ENDIF
    IF C3                  ELSE
        S3                     IF C3 THEN
    ELSE                           S3
        S4                     ELSE
                                   S4
                               ENDIF
                           ENDIF
```

We have now reached a level of complexity where it is necessary to have rules telling us exactly what is meant by certain forms of nested **IF** statements.

The first rule governing the meaning of nested **IF**s is this:

Rule 1: Every statement within a nested **IF** is controlled by the most recent **IF** or **ELSE**.

Here is an **IF** statement where this rule causes no problem:

```
        COBOL              PSEUDOCODE
IF C1                      IF C1 THEN
    S1                         S1
    IF C2                      IF C2 THEN
        S2                         S2
    ELSE                       ELSE
        S3                         S3
ELSE                           ENDIF
    S4                     ELSE
                               S4
                           ENDIF
```

On the true path from the **C1** decision we have first an unconditional statement, then another decision. This is perfectly legal.

Here is an **IF** statement that is also legal but that does not do what is suggested by the indentation. Notice the difference between the two pseudocode specifications. (The heading INDENTATION PSEUDOCODE is meant to suggest that this is what the **COBOL** codes *looks* like it means, as contrasted with what it really means, as shown in the column headed ACCURATE PSEUDOCODE.)

```
        COBOL         INDENTATION        ACCURATE
                      PSEUDOCODE         PSEUDOCODE

IF C1                 IF C1 THEN         IF C1 THEN
    IF C2                 IF C2 THEN         IF C2 THEN
        S1                   S1                 S1
    ELSE                 ELSE               ELSE
        S2                   S2                 S2
    S3                   ENDIF                  S3
ELSE                     S3                 ENDIF
    S4                 ELSE               ELSE
                           S4                 S4
                       ENDIF              ENDIF
```

The presumed intention of the indentation in the **COBOL** code is that the action should be as shown in the column headed INDENTATION PSEUDOCODE. The idea is that if **C1** is true, then **S3** is always carried out, regardless of the outcome of the **C2** decision. This is done easily in **COBOL-85** by using the **END-IF** phrase in a manner identical to that shown in the pseudocode. However, in earlier versions of **COBOL** that do not have the **END-IF**, Rule 1 specifies that each statement is controlled by the most recent **IF** or **ELSE**. This means that to describe the action of **COBOL** correctly, **S3** should have been indented exactly the same as **S2**. Regardless of the indentation, however, the action of the **COBOL** statement written will be as shown by the pseudocode in the column marked ACCURATE PSEUDOCODE. **S3** will be carried out only on the false path of **C2**.

This is not an unsolvable problem. One simple solution is to make a performed paragraph out of the **C2** decision. Now the scope of the inner **IF** is contained completely within a performed paragraph; all that appears in the outer **IF** is a **PERFORM**. Statement **S3** can follow this **PERFORM** with no problems as to which **IF** controls it; the outer **IF** does. The code, in skeleton form, would be like this:

```
IF C1
    PERFORM INNER-IF-PARAGRAPH
    S3
ELSE
    S4.
    .
    .
    .

INNER-IF-PARAGRAPH.
    IF C2
        S1
    ELSE
        S2.
```

It is very important in interpreting the meaning of **IF**s to know which **IF** goes with which **ELSE**. This is true even if there is an **ELSE** for every **IF**, and it is made even more urgent by the fact that **COBOL** does not require every **IF** to have an **ELSE** path. The meaning of a nested **IF** in this regard is governed by the following rule:

Rule 2   Each **ELSE** in a nested **IF** is matched with the most recent **IF** that does not already have an **ELSE**.

The simplest violation of Rule 2 is shown in this example:

COBOL	INDENTATION PSEUDOCODE	ACCURATE PSEUDOCODE
IF C1	IF C1 THEN	IF C1 THEN
IF C2	IF C2 THEN	IF C2 THEN
S1	S1	S1
ELSE	ENDIF	ELSE
S2.	ELSE	S2
	S2	ENDIF
	ENDIF	ENDIF

The indentation suggests the interpretation shown in the column headed INDENTATION PSEUDOCODE, with the **ELSE** matching the first **IF**. Rule 2, however, states that the actual meaning is that of the column headed

ACCURATE PSEUDOCODE. Once again this is an error in the semantics of **COBOL** (the *meaning* of the statement), not an error in the *syntax* (the rules for writing a correct **COBOL** statement). The statement as written will be compiled without diagnostic error indications, since in fact it breaks no rule of **COBOL**; it simply doesn't do what the programmer wanted.

Happily this problem has an easy solution, the **NEXT SENTENCE** feature. At any point in an **IF** statement where there is nothing to be done and we wish simply to "escape" from the logic of the **IF**, we may write **NEXT SENTENCE**. In the example just shown, this permits us to write:

```
IF C1
    IF C2
        S1
    ELSE
        NEXT SENTENCE
ELSE
    S2.
```

The effect is now precisely what is suggested by the indentation.

It occasionally will happen that a set of nested **IF**s will require no action when the **IF** conditions are true, but will call for various actions on each of the **ELSE** paths. In this case we can use the **NEXT SENTENCE** feature where we would otherwise execute a statement controlled by the "true" path of the innermost **IF**.

It is possible to write **IF** statements that are nested as deeply as one wishes, certainly deeper than is generally advisable from the viewpoint of clarity. Consider the following example:

```
IF C1
    S1
    IF C2
        IF C3
            S2
        ELSE
            S3
    ELSE
        S4
        IF C4
            S5
        ELSE
            S6.
```

This example clearly shows the danger that a very complex, deeply nested **IF** can present, namely that it is easily subject to misinterpretation. Since the compiler can give us no help with semantic errors that are not also syntactic errors, serious mistakes can sometimes go undetected. This suggests that great care should be exercised in determining that nested **IF**s really do what they are supposed to do, and it also suggests some kind of common sense limit on how complex such statements should be allowed to become. It is difficult to say what constitutes "too complex" but, as a general indication, we suggest that the last example is too error-prone for safety.

We cannot ignore the fact that some programs require complex condition testing simply because of the nature of the problems they deal with. What we can do, however, is to present the code in a manner that is less prone to error than deeply nested **IF**s. For instance, the example above could be written as shown on the next page.

```
       IF  C1
            PERFORM  D010-NESTED-FUNCTION-1.
            .
            .
            .

   D010-NESTED-FUNCTION-1.
       S1.
       IF  C2
            PERFORM  E010-NESTED-FUNCTION-2.
       ELSE
            PERFORM  E020-NESTED-FUNCTION-3.
            .
            .
            .

   E010-NESTED-FUNCTION-2.
       IF  C3
            S2
       ELSE
            S3.

   E020-NESTED-FUNCTION-3.
       S4.
       IF  C4
            S5
       ELSE
            S6.
```

Of course, in a real program the paragraph names for the inner functions would indicate the task that each function is to perform. If the statements being executed, such as **S1** and **S4**, are complex, this approach to coding the program can be much easier to write correctly than trying to create a deeply nested **IF**. Remember, no one gives extra points (or bonuses!) for writing a program with fewer paragraphs. Clarity and correctness are what count.

8.5 OTHER COMMON CODING PROBLEMS

Although the **IF** statement is one of the largest sources of errors in **COBOL**, there are other statement structures that are also common trouble spots. One of these, which we have mentioned before, comes from the fact that conditional clauses in **COBOL** statements can be terminated only by a period. If the conditional clause occurs in the middle of an **IF** statement, which *must not* have a period before its end, we have a problem. Countless hours of debugging time have been spent trying to figure out why code such as the following does not work as expected:

```
   MOVE ZERO TO COUNTER.
   MOVE 'N' TO EOF-FLAG.
   READ INPUT-FILE
           AT END MOVE 'Y' TO EOF-FLAG.
   PERFORM B035-PROCESS-RECORD
       UNTIL EOF-FLAG = 'Y'.
       .
       .
       .
```

```
B035-PROCESS-RECORD.
    PERFORM C020-EDIT-RECORD.
    IF EDIT-FLAG = 'Y'
        WRITE OUTPUT-LINE FROM ERROR-MESSAGE
        READ INPUT-FILE
            AT END MOVE 'Y' TO EOF-FLAG
        ADD 1 TO COUNTER
    ELSE
        PERFORM C030-PROCESS-VALID-RECORD
        READ INPUT-FILE
            AT END MOVE 'Y' TO EOF-FLAG.
```

After the program is executed, COUNTER will have a value of 0 or 1—depending on which READ triggers the AT END—not the number of invalid records detected. The problem, of course, lies with the first READ statement in B035-PROCESS-RECORD. Since there is no period following the AT END clause of this statement, the ADD statement is treated as part of the AT END action and is executed only once, when the end of file is detected.

Another common error involving the READ statement occurs in code such as this:

```
MOVE ZERO TO RECORD-COUNT.
MOVE 'N' TO EOF-FLAG.
PERFORM B010-PROCESS-RECORD
    UNTIL EOF-FLAG = 'Y'.
    .
    .
    .

B010-PROCESS-RECORD.
    READ INPUT-FILE
        AT END MOVE 'Y' TO EOF-FLAG.
    ADD 1 TO RECORD-COUNT.
    PERFORM C050-PROCESS-DATA.
```

This program will produce two errors. First, RECORD-COUNT will indicate one more record than is actually in the input file. Second, an erroneous record will be processed in C050-PROCESS-DATA. The problem here is that while the AT END clause signals the end of file, processing still continues within B010-PROCESS-RECORD. That is, even when the end of file is detected, the ADD and PERFORM statements are still executed.

There are two cures for this problem. First, a priming record can be read in the driver paragraph before the PERFORM...UNTIL statement, and the READ can be moved to the end of B010-PROCESS-RECORD. This means that the AT END action is executed just before the PERFORM...UNTIL statement tests to see whether the loop condition is true, thereby ensuring that no action takes place inside the loop after the end of file. The second cure involves changing B010-PROCESS-RECORD as follows:

```
B010-PROCESS-RECORD.
    READ INPUT-FILE
        AT END MOVE 'Y' TO EOF-FLAG.
    IF EOF-FLAG = 'N'
        ADD 1 TO RECORD-COUNT
        PERFORM C050-PROCESS-DATA.
```

Now the **ADD** and **PERFORM** are executed only if the end of file has not yet been detected.

Still another common error involving the **READ** statement occurs when the program attempts to read a record even after the end of file has been encountered. Consider the following example. We want to read a maximum of ten records, but stop processing if the end of file is encountered first.

```
MOVE ZERO TO COUNTER.
MOVE 'N' TO EOF-FLAG.
PERFORM B010-PROCESS-RECORD
    UNTIL EOF-FLAG = 'Y'  AND  COUNTER = 10.
   .
   .
   .

B010-PROCESS-RECORD.
    READ INPUT-FILE
           AT END MOVE 'Y' TO EOF-FLAG.
    IF EOF-FLAG = 'N'
        ADD 1 TO COUNTER
        PERFORM C010-PROCESS-DATA.
```

What we wanted to say was that the loop should terminate either if the end of file was reached or the counter was equal to ten. What the code actually says is that the loop will continue until *both* these conditions occur. If the input file contains anything but ten records, the program will attempt to read past the end of the file, generally with fairly disastrous results. While this is one example of how a program might try to read past the end of a file, it is certainly not the only way the problem might occur. Be certain in every program that detecting an end of file will actually cause the program to stop reading from that file.

The example above demonstrates another common **COBOL** error, confusing the use of **AND** and **OR** in a compound condition. Remember that a compound condition using **AND** is true only if *all* of its components are true, while a compound condition using **OR** is true if *any* of its components are true. In the example, what was desired was that the loop should terminate if either of the conditions **EOF-FLAG = 'Y'** or **COUNTER = 10** are true; what was written required that both the conditions must be true to stop the loop.

A very serious type of **COBOL** error involves a particular misuse of the **PERFORM** statement. Since Chapter 4, when we introduced the use of hierarchy charts in program design, we have always used the **PERFORM** statement in such a way that a module on one level of the chart always performed a module on a lower level of the chart. If this approach is followed consistently, we avoid violating one of the restrictions on the use of the **PERFORM** statement: the paragraph named in the **PERFORM** statement cannot be the paragraph containing the **PERFORM** statement. In other words, a statement such as the following is illegal:

```
B010-PROCESS-DATA.
    PERFORM B010-PROCESS-DATA.
```

This particular example is not too serious a problem since most **COBOL** compilers will detect an error this obvious and generate a warning. However, the restriction on the use of the **PERFORM** actually goes a bit further than this.

The complete form of the restriction is this: the paragraph named in a **PERFORM** statement may not be the paragraph containing the **PERFORM** statement, nor may the **PERFORM** statement perform any paragraph that results in a **PERFORM** of the original paragraph. For example, the following code is illegal:

```
PARA-1.
    PERFORM PARA-2.

PARA-2.
    PERFORM PARA-3.

PARA-3.
    PERFORM PARA-1.
```

This type of procedure is called *recursive*. In languages like Pascal and many others, recursion is legal and often useful for solving the type of problems best attacked with such languages. However, in **COBOL** recursive programming is illegal. If you use the design techniques we have shown in this book, it is unlikely you will need to use recursion. In any case, it is not supported by **COBOL** and will cause an abnormal termination sooner or later. Unfortunately, the termination frequently occurs in such a way that the cause is not obvious.

The last common error we wish to mention is one we have already discussed. It occurs when a program tries to execute with data containing errors, such as nonnumeric data in a (supposedly) numeric field. This type of error sometimes will cause abnormal program termination, but more commonly simply gives results that are incorrect, and not always obviously so. It is vital that your program validate any input data that could contain errors, if at all possible. Most commonly this involves testing numeric fields to be certain that their contents actually are numeric. Other times it will involve testing data to be certain that it is within an acceptable range, or that a value can be found on a list of legal values. The exact nature of the validation will depend on the program and the data involved, but it must be done. There is no excuse for a program that "blows up" because of invalid input data.

We should add two warnings, however. First, it is not always necessary that data validation and data processing be done in the same program. For example, in a payroll system one might wish to validate the payroll records in one program, then process the valid records in a second program. This gives the people who use the program an opportunity to correct errors before payroll checks are actually produced. The second warning is that there are some fields that cannot be edited by a program. For example, it is difficult to come up with a formula for validating a person's name without rejecting names that are perfectly correct; the name "John P. O'Malley, Jr." is correct, but contains several nonalphabetic characters. This simply means that you should validate the fields that you can, but not force validation on those fields that can't be edited.

The errors that we have discussed in this section are common **COBOL** errors, but they are certainly not the only errors you may encounter. We will discuss other potential errors as we present new material; in the remainder of this chapter we discuss ways of locating and dealing with various general types of errors.

8.6 COMPILE-TIME ERRORS

COBOL compilers are designed to identify code that is not legal COBOL (syntax errors). Of course, no two compilers use exactly the same format for reporting these errors. In some cases, the error messages are printed in the middle of the program listing, immediately following the line(s) of code containing the error(s). In other cases, all error messages are printed at the end of the program listing along with line or statement numbers to identify the code in error. In some cases, with microcomputers in particular, the compiler may not print a program listing, relying on your ability to use a source code editor to look at the program. The following discussion will be based on an example run on an IBM mainframe computer using the IBM OS/VS COBOL compiler. Although this is a common compiler, it is obviously not universal, and you will need to adapt the following material to fit the compiler you are using.

8.7 AN EXAMPLE OF COMPILE-TIME ERRORS

The payroll program presented in Chapter 7 (Figure 7.4) was modified to intentionally create syntax errors. Because of the seriousness of some of these errors, the COBOL compiler was not able to produce an object program. It is instructive to examine the diagnostic error messages in Figure 8.4 to see how they can help in developing a correct program. Naturally, no other compiler would give *exactly* this list of messages. Nevertheless, readers not using this compiler will find the following discussion useful, since the general principles are valid even though details differ.

```
00001          IDENTIFICATION DIVISION.
00002          PROGRAM-ID.
00003              PAYROLL4.
00004          AUTHOR.
00005              D. GOLDEN.
00006          DATE-WRITTEN.
00007              FEBRUARY 23, 1987.
00008      *
00009      *    THIS PROGRAM CONTAINS MANY DELIBERATE ERRORS.
00010      *    A CORRECT VERSION OF THE PROGRAM IS SHOWN IN FIGURE 8.5.
00011      *
00012
00013          ENVIRONMENT DIVISION.
00014          FILE-CONTROL.
00015              SELECT PAYROLL-FILE       ASSIGN TO S-PAYROLL.
00016              SELECT REPORT-FILE        ASSIGN TO S-REPORT.
00017
00018          DATA DIVISION.
00019          FILE SECTION.
00020          FD  PAYROLL-FILE.
00021              LABEL RECORDS ARE OMITTED.
00022          01  PAYROLL-RECORD.
00023              05  I-PAYROLL-NUMBER      PIC X(5).
00024              05  I-NAME                PIC X(20).
00025              05  I-HOURS-WORKED        PIC 99V9.
00026              05  FILLER                PIC X(3).
00027              05  I-PAYRATE             PIC 99V999.
00028              05  I-DEPENDENTS          PIC 99.
00029              05  FILLER                PIC X(42).
00030
```

```
00031          FD  REPORT-FILE
00032              LABEL RECORDS ARE OMITTED.
00033          01  REPORT-RECORD          PIC X(75)          VALUE SPACES.
00034
00035          WORKING STORAGE SECTION.
00036          77  C-EXEMPTION            PIC S99V99         VALUE +50.00.
00037          77  C-TAXRATE              PIC  SV999         VALUE   +.210.
00038          77  W-EXEMPTION-TOTAL      PIC S999V99.
00039          77  W-GROSS-PAY            PIC S999V99.
00040          77  W-NET-PAY             PIC S999V99.
00041          77  W-OUT-OF-RECORDS-FLAG  PIC X              VALUE 'N'.
00042              88  OUT-OF-RECORDS                        VALUE 'Y'.
00043          77  W-OVERTIME-HOURS       PIC  S99V99.
00044          77  W-OVERTIME-PAY         PIC  S999V99.
00045          77  W-TAX                  PIC  S999V99.
00046          77  W-TAXABLE              PIC  S999V99.
00047          77  W-TODAYS-DATE          PIC  9(6).
00048          77  W-VALID-RECORD-FLAG    PIC X.
00049              88  VALID-RECORD                          VALUE 'Y'.
00050
00051          01  HEADING-LINE-1.
00052              05  FILLER             PIC X(26)
00053                  VALUE 'PAYROLL CALCULATION REPORT'.
00054              05  FILLER             PIC X(41)          VALUE SPACES.
00055              05  W-TODAYS-DATE      PIC 99/99/99       VALUE ZERO.
00056
00057          01  HEADING-LINE-2.
00058              05  FILLER             PIC X(42)
00059                  VALUE 'NUMBER      NAME             HOURS  RATE  '.
00060              05  FILLER             PIC X(29)
00061                  VALUE '  DEP  GROSS     TAX     NET'.
00062
00063          01  NORMAL-OUTPUT-LINE.
00064              05  O-PAYROLL-NUMBER   PIC X(5).
00065              05  O-NAME             PIC BBX(20).
00066              05  O-HOURS-WORKED     PIC BBZ9.9.
00067              05  O-PAYRATE          PIC BBZ9.999.
00068              05  O-DEPENDENTS       PIC BBZ9.
00069              05  O-GROSS-PAY        PIC BB$$$9.99.
00070              05  O-TAX              PIC BB$$$9.99.
00071              05  O-NET-PAY          PIC BB$$$9.99.
00072
00073          01  ERROR-RECORD.
00074              05  BAD-DATA           PIC X(38).
00075              05  FILLER             PIC X(4)           VALUE SPACES.
00076              05  ERROR-MESSAGE      PIC X(27)
00077                  VALUE 'INVALID DATA IN THIS RECORD'.
00078
00079
00080          PROCEDURE DIVISION.
00081          A000-PRODUCE-PAYROLL-CALC.
00082              OPEN  INPUT PAYROLL-FILE
00083                    OUTPUT REPORT-FILE.
00084              PERFORM B010-PRINT-COLUMN-HEADINGS.
00085              PERFORM C010-GET-VALID-PAY-REC.
00086              PERFORM B020-CALC-EMP-PAYROLL
00087                  UNTIL OUT-OF-RECORDS.
00088              CLOSE PAYROLL-FILE
00089                    REPORT-FILE.
00090              STOP RUN.
00091
```

```
00092            B010-PRINT-COLUMN-HEADINGS.
00093               ACCEPT W-TODAYS-DATE FROM DATE.
00094               MOVE W-TODAYS-DATE TO REPORT-DATE.
00095               WRITE REPORT-RECORD FROM HEADING-LINE-1.
00096               MOVE SPACES TO REPORT-RECORD.
00097               WRITE REPORT-RECORD.
00098               WRITE REPORT-RECORD FROM HEADING-LINE-2.
00099               MOVE SPACES TO REPORT-RECORD.
00100               WRITE REPORT-RECORD.
00101               MOVE SPACES TO REPORT-RECORD.
00102               WRITE REPORT-RECORD.
00103
00104            B020-CALC-EMP-PAYROLL.
00105               PERFORM C020-COMPUTE-GROSS-PAY.
00106               PERFORM C030-COMPUTE-EXEMPTIONS.
00107               IF W-GROSS-PAY IS GREATER THAN W-EXEMPTION-TOTAL
00108                   PERFORM C040-COMPUTE-TAX
00109               ELSE
00110                   MOVE ZERO TO W-TAX.
00111               PERFORM C050-COMPUTE-NET-PAY.
00112               PERFORM C060-PRINT-OUTPUT.
00113               PERFORM C010-GET-VALID-PAY-REC.
00114
00115            C010-GET-VALID-PAY-REC.
00116               MOVE 'N' TO W-VALID-RECORD-FLAG.
00117               PERFORM D010-VALID-RECORD-LOOP
00118                   UNTIL   VALID-RECORD
00119                       OR OUT-OF-RECORDS.
00120
00121            C020-COMPUTE-GROSS-PAY.
00122               MULTIPLY I-HOURS-WORKED BY I-PAYRATE
00123                   GIVING W-GROSS-PAY ROUNDED.
00124               IF I-HOURS-WORKED IS GREATER THAN 40
00125                   SUBTRACT 40 FROM I-HOURS-WORKED GIVING W-OVERTIME-HOURS
00126                   MULTIPLY 0.5 BY W-OVERTIME-HOURS
00127                   MULTIPLY W-OVERTIME-HOURS BY I-PAYRATE
00128                       GIVING W-OVERTIME-PAY ROUNDED
00129                   ADD W-OVERTIME-PAY TO W-GROSS-PAY.
00130
00131            C030-COMPUTE-EXEMPTIONS.
00132               MULTIPLY C-EXEMPTION BY I-DEPENDENTS
00133                   GIVING W-EXEMPTION-TOTAL.
00134
00135            C040-COMPUTE-TAX.
00136               SUBTRACT W-EXEMPTION-TOTAL FROM W-GROSS-PAY
00137                   GIVING W-TAXABLE.
00138               MULTIPLY C-TAXRATE BY W-TAXABLE GIVING W-TAX ROUNDED.
00139
00140            C050-COMPUTE-NET-PAY.
00141               SUBTRACT W-TAX FROM W-GROSS-PAY GIVING W-NET-PAY.
00142
00143            C060-PRINT-OUTPUT.
00144               MOVE SPACES            TO NORMAL-OUTPUT-LINE.
00145               MOVE I-PAYROLL-NUMBER  TO O-PAYROLL-NUMBER.
00146               MOVE I-NAME            TO O-NAME.
00147               MOVE I-HOURS-WORKED    TO O-HOURS-WORKED.
00148               MOVE I-PAYRATE         TO O-PAYRATE.
00149               MOVE I-DEPENDENTS      TO O-DEPENDENTS.
00150               MOVE W-TAX             TO O-TAX.
00151               MOVE W-GROSS-PAY       TO O-GROSS-PAY.
00152               MOVE W-NET-PAY         TO O-NET-PAY.
00153               WRITE REPORT-RECORD FROM NORMAL-OUTPUT-LINE.
00154
```

```
00155          D010-VALID-RECORD-LOOP.
00156              READ PAYROLL-FILE
00157                  AT END MOVE 'Y' TO W-OUT-OF-RECORDS-FLAG
00158          IF NOT OUT-OF-RECORDS
00159              PERFORM E020-EDIT-PAYROLL-RECORD.
00160
00161          E020-EDIT-PAYROLL-RECORD.
00162              IF      I-PAYROLL-NUMBER IS NOT NUMERIC
00163                  OR  I-HOURS-WORKED   IS NOT NUMERIC
00164                  OR  I-PAYRATE        IS NOT NUMERIC
00165                  OR  I-DEPENDENTS     IS NOT NUMERIC
00166              MOVE PAYROLL-RECORD TO BAD-DATA
00167              WRITE REPORT-RECORD FROM ERROR-RECORD
00168          ELSE
00169              MOVE 'Y' TO W-VALID-RECORD-FLAG.
```

FIGURE 8.3 A modification of the payroll program. *This program contains many deliberate errors.*

The program listing in Figure 8.3 was taken directly from the output of the **COBOL** compiler; notice the line numbers at the left, generated by the compiler. These line numbers will be used for reference by the error messages in Figure 8.4, also taken directly from the output of the compiler. Remember as you study these errors that the program basically is well-designed. The only errors in the program are of the type that might be created in entering the program into a computer.

CARD	ERROR MESSAGE	
15	IKF1002I-W	INPUT-OUTPUT SECTION HEADER MISSING. ASSUMED PRESENT.
15	IKF2133I-W	LABEL RECORDS CLAUSE MISSING. DD CARD OPTION WILL BE TAKEN.
21	IKF1004I-E	INVALID WORD LABEL . SKIPPING TO NEXT RECOGNIZABLE WORD.
35	IKF1087I-W	' WORKING ' SHOULD NOT BEGIN A-MARGIN.
35	IKF1004I-E	INVALID WORD WORKING . SKIPPING TO NEXT RECOGNIZABLE WORD.
33	IKF2125I-W	VALUE CLAUSE TREATED AS COMMENTS FOR ITEMS IN FILE LINKAGE, OR COMMUNICATION SECTIONS, EXCEPT FOR FIRST RECORD DESCRIPTION UNDER CD.
33	IKF2030I-C	77 ITEM PRECEDED BY 01-49 ITEM OR 77 IN FILE SECTION. 77 CHANGED TO 01.
36	IKF2125I-W	VALUE CLAUSE TREATED AS COMMENTS FOR ITEMS IN FILE LINKAGE, OR COMMUNICATION SECTIONS, EXCEPT FOR FIRST RECORD DESCRIPTION UNDER CD.
36	IKF2030I-C	77 ITEM PRECEDED BY 01-49 ITEM OR 77 IN FILE SECTION. 77 CHANGED TO 01.
37	IKF2125I-W	VALUE CLAUSE TREATED AS COMMENTS FOR ITEMS IN FILE LINKAGE, OR COMMUNICATION SECTIONS, EXCEPT FOR FIRST RECORD DESCRIPTION UNDER CD.
37	IKF2030I-C	77 ITEM PRECEDED BY 01-49 ITEM OR 77 IN FILE SECTION. 77 CHANGED TO 01.
38	IKF2030I-C	77 ITEM PRECEDED BY 01-49 ITEM OR 77 IN FILE SECTION. 77 CHANGED TO 01.
39	IKF2030I-C	77 ITEM PRECEDED BY 01-49 ITEM OR 77 IN FILE SECTION. 77 CHANGED TO 01.
40	IKF2030I-C	77 ITEM PRECEDED BY 01-49 ITEM OR 77 IN FILE

		SECTION. 77 CHANGED TO 01.
41	IKF2125I-W	VALUE CLAUSE TREATED AS COMMENTS FOR ITEMS IN FILE LINKAGE, OR COMMUNICATION SECTIONS, EXCEPT FOR FIRST RECORD DESCRIPTION UNDER CD.
42	IKF2030I-C	77 ITEM PRECEDED BY 01-49 ITEM OR 77 IN FILE SECTION. 77 CHANGED TO 01.
43	IKF2030I-C	77 ITEM PRECEDED BY 01-49 ITEM OR 77 IN FILE SECTION. 77 CHANGED TO 01.
44	IKF2030I-C	77 ITEM PRECEDED BY 01-49 ITEM OR 77 IN FILE SECTION. 77 CHANGED TO 01.
45	IKF2030I-C	77 ITEM PRECEDED BY 01-49 ITEM OR 77 IN FILE SECTION. 77 CHANGED TO 01.
46	IKF2030I-C	77 ITEM PRECEDED BY 01-49 ITEM OR 77 IN FILE SECTION. 77 CHANGED TO 01.
47	IKF2030I-C	77 ITEM PRECEDED BY 01-49 ITEM OR 77 IN FILE SECTION. 77 CHANGED TO 01.
52	IKF2125I-W	VALUE CLAUSE TREATED AS COMMENTS FOR ITEMS IN FILE LINKAGE, OR COMMUNICATION SECTIONS, EXCEPT FOR FIRST RECORD DESCRIPTION UNDER CD.
54	IKF2125I-W	VALUE CLAUSE TREATED AS COMMENTS FOR ITEMS IN FILE LINKAGE, OR COMMUNICATION SECTIONS, EXCEPT FOR FIRST RECORD DESCRIPTION UNDER CD.
55	IKF2125I-W	VALUE CLAUSE TREATED AS COMMENTS FOR ITEMS IN FILE LINKAGE, OR COMMUNICATION SECTIONS, EXCEPT FOR FIRST RECORD DESCRIPTION UNDER CD.
58	IKF2125I-W	VALUE CLAUSE TREATED AS COMMENTS FOR ITEMS IN FILE LINKAGE, OR COMMUNICATION SECTIONS, EXCEPT FOR FIRST RECORD DESCRIPTION UNDER CD.
60	IKF2125I-W	VALUE CLAUSE TREATED AS COMMENTS FOR ITEMS IN FILE LINKAGE, OR COMMUNICATION SECTIONS, EXCEPT FOR FIRST RECORD DESCRIPTION UNDER CD.
75	IKF2125I-W	VALUE CLAUSE TREATED AS COMMENTS FOR ITEMS IN FILE LINKAGE, OR COMMUNICATION SECTIONS, EXCEPT FOR FIRST RECORD DESCRIPTION UNDER CD.
76	IKF2125I-W	VALUE CLAUSE TREATED AS COMMENTS FOR ITEMS IN FILE LINKAGE, OR COMMUNICATION SECTIONS, EXCEPT FOR FIRST RECORD DESCRIPTION UNDER CD.
93	IKF3002I-E	W-TODAYS-DATE NOT UNIQUE. DISCARDED.
94	IKF3002I-E	W-TODAYS-DATE NOT UNIQUE. DISCARDED.
94	IKF3001I-E	REPORT-DATE NOT DEFINED.
95	IKF4100I-W	IDENTIFIER FOLLOWING INTO (FROM) IN READ (WRITE) STATEMENT SHOULD NOT BE DEFINED UNDER SAME FD AS RECORD-NAME. STATEMENT ACCEPTED AS WRITTEN.
98	IKF4100I-W	IDENTIFIER FOLLOWING INTO (FROM) IN READ (WRITE) STATEMENT SHOULD NOT BE DEFINED UNDER SAME FD AS RECORD-NAME. STATEMENT ACCEPTED AS WRITTEN.
153	IKF4100I-W	IDENTIFIER FOLLOWING INTO (FROM) IN READ (WRITE) STATEMENT SHOULD NOT BE DEFINED UNDER SAME FD AS RECORD-NAME. STATEMENT ACCEPTED AS WRITTEN.
158	IKF4086I-C	CONDITION USED WHERE ONLY IMPERATIVE STATEMENTS ARE LEGAL MAY CAUSE ERRORS IN PROCESSING.
167	IKF4100I-W	IDENTIFIER FOLLOWING INTO (FROM) IN READ (WRITE) STATEMENT SHOULD NOT BE DEFINED UNDER SAME FD AS RECORD-NAME. STATEMENT ACCEPTED AS WRITTEN.

FIGURE 8.4 The diagnostic messages produced when the program of Figure 8.3 was processed by an IBM **COBOL** compiler.

In addition to the text of the message and the line number on which the error occurred, each message contains an error code. The alphanumeric part of the code preceding the dash is of little interest to us, but the **w**, **c**, and **E** suffixes indicate the seriousness of the error. The suffix **w** denotes a warning of a condition that did not cause the compilation to fail, but which may indicate an error. We see that the very first message here, for line 15, refers to a missing section header that the compiler was able to compensate for. (It points to line 15 because that is where it detected the omission.) This warning, in other words, describes an "error" of the least possible seriousness: if this had been the only problem, the compiler would have been able to proceed without incident. A suffix of **c** denotes a *conditional* error, one that is possibly serious enough to make the compiled program unworkable. The suffix of **E** denotes a *serious* error, which would almost always cause the object program either not to be compiled or to be incorrect.

Writing a compiler is a difficult task, and writing diagnostic routines to anticipate *every* possible error in a source program is essentially impossible. This is said in apology for the fact that diagnostic messages are not always directly indicative of the problem, and to indicate that detective work is sometimes required. The second error message for line 15, for example, refers to a missing **LABEL RECORDS** clause, which may seem puzzling since a **SELECT** clause would never have such a thing. What this really refers to is an error in the file description entry for that file; the actual error is later, but the compiler reported it here, where that file name first appears in the program. Such slightly misleading diagnostic messages are usually not much of a problem if we simply keep on reading. Here, the very next error message points out what the real problem is, namely the improper period in line 20.

The missing hyphen in **WORKING-STORAGE** was mentioned in Chapter 2 as being a potential source of lots of problems. In this program it triggered, directly or indirectly, 29 out of a total of 36 error messages, some of which could seem to a novice to be a bit mysterious. The messages for line 35 are fairly clear, but the messages for lines 33 through 76 are not. Since a **VALUE** clause is allowed in the File Section only in a level **88** entry, the first error message for line 33 (**IKF2125I-W**) is correct. However, all later instances of this error message are caused by the fact that, because of a missing hyphen, the compiler never saw the beginning of the Working-Storage Section and, hence, took the entire contents of the Data Division to be part of the File Section. The second message for line 33 (**IKF2030I-C**) is caused by the same problem. **COBOL** does not permit level **77** items in the File Section, so it tries to convert the level **77** to level **01**. These messages are repeated throughout the remainder of the Data Division, through line 76.

The first errors in the Procedure Division are found on lines 93 and 94. By mistake, we typed **W-TODAYS-DATE** on line 55 where we should have typed **REPORT-DATE**, which created two errors and three messages. The first error is that **W-TODAYS-DATE** is defined twice, and the second error is that **REPORT-DATE** is not defined at all. The mistake in the Data Division did not trigger an error message because what we did is not actually a syntactic error. It is permissible to have the same data name in two different group items—which leads to the subject of data qualification, to be discussed in Chapter 10.

Message `IKF41009-W`, encountered on lines 95, 98, 153, and 167, is somewhat obscure. This, too, is caused by the missing hyphen in Working-Storage in line 35, which caused everything after line 31 to be considered part of the `FD` for `REPORT-FILE`. We will discuss files that have more than one record format in Chapter 14.

Missing or extra periods are a very common problem for beginners (and sometimes for experienced `COBOL` programmers as well). For example, the missing period at the end of line 157 means that the following `IF` statement is part of the `AT END` phrase. Since an `IF` statement in an `AT END` phrase is illegal, we get a conditional error message on line 158—which is lucky, because if the statements after the `READ` had been something other than the `IF` statement, there would have been no error message at all.

8.8   RUN-TIME ERRORS

The `COBOL` compiler helps you find syntax errors in your program at compile time. Unfortunately, even a program that is syntactically correct may contain errors that appear when it runs. These run-time errors show up in two different ways. First, a run-time error may cause abnormal program termination; this is also known as an *abend*. An abend typically occurs when the computer hardware can detect an abnormal condition. For example, if you attempt to perform a division by zero, most computers will detect the error and terminate the program.

Although it may be difficult to track down the cause of an abend, at least you know that an error has occurred. The second type of run-time error simply produces results that look valid but are logically or arithmetically incorrect. Not only do you have the problem of determining the cause of this type of error, you must first detect that the error has occurred!

8.9   PROGRAM TESTING

The first step in dealing with run-time errors is to test the program *thoroughly* to locate all bugs. Testing does *not* mean just running one set of test data, then assuming that everything is okay if no abend occurs. Unfortunately, the most common homework policy for programming courses is for students to run programs using standard data prepared by the instructor. The testing procedure used by most students in this situation is to compare their output to that of other students in the class; if two programs produce the same output then the programs must both be correct! Aside from the value (or lack thereof) of using this highly unreliable technique in the classroom, it won't do you much good on the job. Employers don't assign two or three programmers to write the same program just so they can compare results.

Testing a program is not a casual activity and, especially for large programs, requires careful planning. The testing activity can be divided into two types of testing which, for historical reasons, are called *black box* testing and *white box* testing. Black box testing involves testing a program based solely on the specifications of the problem it is supposed to solve. For example, the payroll program is supposed to perform certain calculations based on data found in records having a predefined format. To do black box testing on the payroll program we would try to list all the possible mistakes that could occur in the input data, then run tests to see what the program would do if it actually encountered such data. This is essentially what we did in Chapter 6.

White box testing involves studying the program source code, then using our knowledge of how the program is actually written to try to find more weaknesses. For example, if you notice that a **READ** statement was written without an **AT END** clause you might try running the program with no records in the input file. This approach gives you an idea of what the basic objective of testing really is: to make a program fail! When you test a program you are not trying to prove that it works. You can run test files for years and they won't *prove* that the program works; after all, the very next test might find an error. The only thing that a well-designed test can really accomplish is to locate another error. Eventually, if you are unable to locate more errors, you can stop testing the programs. (This doesn't necessarily mean that there aren't any more errors in the program. It means only that you haven't found them.)

If your instructor will permit it, one of the most effective ways of locating errors is to swap programs with a friend. You try to find the errors in your friend's program, and your friend tries to find the errors in yours. The difficulty in finding errors in your own program is that you *know* what it is *supposed* to do, which makes it hard for you to see what it *really* does, which may be quite different. This psychological blindness to mistakes doesn't apply in the same way in reading another person's program.

Many commercial programming organizations take this principle a step further. Each programmer is required to present his or her program to a small group of colleagues, simply explaining what the program does and how it does it. Such a presentation is called a *walkthrough*. The colleagues, who are seeing the program with a fresh view, can often spot mistakes or unwarranted assumptions that the writer would have caught only with much greater effort.

Whether in the formal structure of a walkthrough or just getting a friend to help, you will be surprised how often you will see your own mistake as you try to explain your logic and your coding to someone else. It happens all the time: you ask a friend to help with your program, start to explain it, suddenly see the problem, and exclaim, "Gee, thanks for your help!" The friend can only laugh and say, "You're welcome!"—he or she hadn't even started to get an idea of what you were doing!

One final word on testing: you must examine the output from your tests *carefully* to determine whether the results of the run contain errors or not. There are far too many times when a programmer, either student or professional, declares a program ready for use, only to have someone later point out blatant inconsistencies in the output. For example, consider the payroll program. Suppose you have modified the program to print total net pay for the company, and the value printed is $890.28. Is this reasonable? The sample data contains 11 valid records (including the record for Ima Testcase), whose values appear to average around three hundred dollars. Obviously then, the total payroll should be about $3300. Clearly our result is unreasonable, and the printed value seems to indicate that a leading digit has been dropped.

If our test run had printed a net payroll of $2912.73 it would not be immediately obvious whether this was correct or not, although in light of our rough estimate it seems a bit low. In any case, there is no obvious indication as to what the error actually is, if indeed there is an error. What we must do is to add the individual net pay amounts with a pocket calculator, then compare this total with the computer's output. If this is done, you will find that the total net pay should be $3890.28, so we have dropped $977.55. Does this amount give any clue as to where the error lies? The general conclusion is clear. Not only is it necessary to examine the results of your test runs in detail, you must know what to expect from these tests. If you have not calculated what the results *should* be, you can't really tell if they are wrong.

8.10 DEBUGGING AIDS

Once you detect an error in a **COBOL** program, you must locate the cause of the error. **COBOL** contains several statements that can assist you in this process, and we shall discuss these debugging aids in the remainder of this chapter.

The first and most important debugging aid is not a feature of **COBOL**; it is *you*. There is no magic technique, no wonderful tool in any programming language that will automatically find the cause of an error. You must begin the debugging process by *thinking* about the error and its possible causes. For example, in the payroll errors we discussed in the previous section, a study of the nature of the error should give you several clues as to the cause of the problem. If the amount printed is almost correct but has one or more leading digits omitted, look for a field that is too small for the result placed in it. If the total was close to the correct value but a bit short of it, see if the missing amount is equal to the net pay for one of the employees. You may also find the reverse situation; the total may be too high, with the excess equal to the pay for an employee. In either case, if you can detect the case, or cases, which contributed to the error you have made a good start in locating the bug.

Whatever the nature of an error and whatever the cause, the responsibility for finding the cause rests with you. You may choose to use some of the **COBOL** debugging aids for help, but the most these aids can do is provide you with supplementary data. Analyzing and interpreting these results require human action. After all, if you wrote the program you know more about it than anyone else. It is not a mysterious box whose contents are unknown. Think about the program's structure and what functions each part performs, then try to determine how these functions might relate to the symptoms of the error.

8.11 THE ON SIZE ERROR PHRASE

One of the basic steps in locating a program error is to determine if intermediate calculations are producing unexpected results. You will recall from the discussions of arithmetic operations in earlier chapters that a result that is too large for its receiving field will normally be truncated, with no warning of the loss of data. This, for example, is the cause of the errors in the payroll program for Ima Testcase. We can detect this type of truncation in arithmetic operations by using the **ON SIZE ERROR** phrase.

The **ON SIZE ERROR** phrase was mentioned in Chapter 3. It may optionally be written with any of the arithmetic verbs (and, as we shall see later, with the

COMPUTE statement). Its effect is very similar to the AT END phrase on a READ: if the condition arises, then all of the statement(s) in the ON SIZE ERROR phrase are executed. If the condition does not arise, they are ignored. The condition that the program is directed to test for is the existence of an arithmetic result that is too large to fit into the space provided for it. In the payroll program, for example, we allowed for a week's gross pay that can be no larger than $999.99. We have already seen that if the data values are such as to generate an amount larger than this, the program produces gibberish.

The rules of COBOL permit any *imperative* statement to be written in an ON SIZE ERROR phrase. An imperative statement is defined as one that specifies *unconditional* action. This obviously excludes the IF statement, but it also excludes the READ (since its AT END phrase is conditional), and it excludes any arithmetic operation that has an ON SIZE ERROR phrase.

COBOL-85

As with any conditional phrase or statement, COBOL-85 provides END phrases for the arithmetic verbs to be used with the ON SIZE ERROR phrase. The following example shows how this might be used:

```
IF VALID-RECORD-FLAG = 'Y'
    ADD AMOUNT TO TOTAL-AMOUNT
        ON SIZE ERROR MOVE 'Y' TO SIZE-ERROR-FLAG
    END-ADD
    READ INPUT-FILE
        AT END MOVE 'Y' TO EOF-FLAG
    END-READ
END-IF.
```

There is an END phrase for each of the arithmetic verbs: END-ADD, END-DIVIDE, END-MULTIPLY, and END-SUBTRACT. In each case the format is the same as in the example.

END COBOL-85

There is one common type of arithmetic truncation which, unfortunately, will not create a size error. This is truncation that occurs as a result of a MOVE statement. For example, consider the following code:

```
77  FLD-1             PIC 9(5)V999.
77  FLD-2             PIC Z(4).99.
        .
        .
        .
    MOVE FLD-1 TO FLD-2.
```

The MOVE statement will truncate the leftmost and rightmost digits of FLD-1 with no warning whatever, nor is it possible to ROUND the result in FLD-2. Although some compilers may give a warning that truncation of the leading digit might occur, basically it is the responsibility of the programmer to be aware of this problem and guard against it.

8.12 A REVISED VERSION OF THE PROGRAM

A revised version of the payroll program is shown in Figure 8.5. In this version, if the on size error condition arises, the entire record will be rejected from further processing and the notice "gross pay suspiciously large" will be printed. There are several changes you should study. First, an error flag was added to tell of the size error condition that was detected. Also, **ERROR-RECORD** was changed to eliminate the text of the message, and two new structures were added for the two possible error messages. In the Procedure Division, **B020-CALC-EMP-PAYROLL** and **C020-COMPUTE-GROSS-PAY** were modified to test and set the size error flag. Notice that it is not necessary to test for a size error on all arithmetic statements, only where there is a possibility of overflowing the receiving field.

```
IDENTIFICATION DIVISION.
PROGRAM-ID.
    PAYROLL4.
DATE-WRITTEN.
    JANUARY 29, 1987.

ENVIRONMENT DIVISION.
INPUT-OUTPUT SECTION.
FILE-CONTROL.
    SELECT PAYROLL-FILE      ASSIGN TO S-PAYROLL.
    SELECT REPORT-FILE       ASSIGN TO S-REPORT.

DATA DIVISION.
FILE SECTION.
FD  PAYROLL-FILE
    LABEL RECORDS ARE OMITTED.
01  PAYROLL-RECORD.
    05   I-PAYROLL-NUMBER    PIC X(5).
    05   I-NAME              PIC X(20).
    05   I-HOURS-WORKED      PIC 99V9.
    05   FILLER              PIC X(3).
    05   I-PAYRATE           PIC 99V999.
    05   I-DEPENDENTS        PIC 99.
    05   FILLER              PIC X(42).

FD  REPORT-FILE
    LABEL RECORDS ARE OMITTED.
01  REPORT-RECORD            PIC X(75).

WORKING-STORAGE SECTION.
77   C-EXEMPTION            PIC  S99V99      VALUE +50.00.
77   C-TAXRATE              PIC    SV999     VALUE    +.210.
77   W-EXEMPTION-TOTAL      PIC S999V99.
77   W-GROSS-PAY            PIC S999V99.
77   W-NET-PAY              PIC S999V99.
77   W-OUT-OF-RECORDS-FLAG  PIC X            VALUE 'N'.
     88   OUT-OF-RECORDS                      VALUE 'Y'.
77   W-OVERTIME-HOURS       PIC  S99V99.
77   W-OVERTIME-PAY         PIC S999V99.
77   W-SIZE-ERROR-FLAG      PIC X.
     88   NO-SIZE-ERROR                        VALUE 'N'.
77   W-TAX                  PIC S999V99.
```

```
77   W-TAXABLE                 PIC S999V99.
77   W-TODAYS-DATE             PIC 9(6).
77   W-VALID-RECORD-FLAG       PIC X.
     88   VALID-RECORD                          VALUE 'Y'.

01   HEADING-LINE-1.
     05   FILLER               PIC X(26)
          VALUE 'PAYROLL CALCULATION REPORT'.
     05   FILLER               PIC X(41)        VALUE SPACES.
     05   REPORT-DATE          PIC 99/99/99     VALUE ZERO.

01   HEADING-LINE-2.
     05   FILLER               PIC X(42)
          VALUE 'NUMBER         NAME            HOURS  RATE  '.
     05   FILLER               PIC X(29)
          VALUE ' DEP  GROSS      TAX      NET'.

01   NORMAL-OUTPUT-LINE.
     05   O-PAYROLL-NUMBER     PIC X(5).
     05   O-NAME               PIC BBX(20).
     05   O-HOURS-WORKED       PIC BBZ9.9.
     05   O-PAYRATE            PIC BBZ9.999.
     05   O-DEPENDENTS         PIC BBZ9.
     05   O-GROSS-PAY          PIC BB$$$9.99.
     05   O-TAX                PIC BB$$$9.99.
     05   O-NET-PAY            PIC BB$$$9.99.

01   ERROR-RECORD.
     05   BAD-DATA             PIC X(38).
     05   FILLER               PIC X(4)         VALUE SPACES.
     05   ERROR-MESSAGE        PIC X(30).

01   MESSAGE-1                 PIC X(30)
     VALUE 'INVALID DATA IN THIS RECORD'.
01   MESSAGE-2                 PIC X(30)
     VALUE 'GROSS PAY SUSPICIOUSLY LARGE'.


PROCEDURE DIVISION.
A000-PRODUCE-PAYROLL-CALC.
     OPEN INPUT PAYROLL-FILE
          OUTPUT REPORT-FILE.
     PERFORM B010-PRINT-COLUMN-HEADINGS.
     PERFORM C010-GET-VALID-PAY-REC.
     PERFORM B020-CALC-EMP-PAYROLL
          UNTIL OUT-OF-RECORDS.
     CLOSE PAYROLL-FILE
           REPORT-FILE.
     STOP RUN.


B010-PRINT-COLUMN-HEADINGS.
     ACCEPT W-TODAYS-DATE FROM DATE.
     MOVE W-TODAYS-DATE TO REPORT-DATE.
     WRITE REPORT-RECORD FROM HEADING-LINE-1.
     MOVE SPACES TO REPORT-RECORD.
     WRITE REPORT-RECORD.
     WRITE REPORT-RECORD FROM HEADING-LINE-2.
     MOVE SPACES TO REPORT-RECORD.
     WRITE REPORT-RECORD.
     MOVE SPACES TO REPORT-RECORD.
     WRITE REPORT-RECORD.
```

```
B020-CALC-EMP-PAYROLL.
    PERFORM C020-COMPUTE-GROSS-PAY.
    IF NO-SIZE-ERROR
        PERFORM C030-COMPUTE-EXEMPTIONS
        PERFORM C040-COMPUTE-TAX
        PERFORM C050-COMPUTE-NET-PAY
        PERFORM C060-PRINT-OUTPUT
    ELSE
        MOVE PAYROLL-RECORD TO BAD-DATA
        MOVE MESSAGE-2 TO ERROR-MESSAGE
        WRITE REPORT-RECORD FROM ERROR-RECORD.
    PERFORM C010-GET-VALID-PAY-REC.

C010-GET-VALID-PAY-REC.
    MOVE 'N' TO W-VALID-RECORD-FLAG.
    PERFORM D010-VALID-RECORD-LOOP
        UNTIL    VALID-RECORD
             OR OUT-OF-RECORDS.

C020-COMPUTE-GROSS-PAY.
    MOVE 'N' TO W-SIZE-ERROR-FLAG.
    MULTIPLY I-HOURS-WORKED BY I-PAYRATE
            GIVING W-GROSS-PAY ROUNDED
            ON SIZE ERROR MOVE 'Y' TO W-SIZE-ERROR-FLAG.
    IF NO-SIZE-ERROR
        IF I-HOURS-WORKED IS GREATER THAN 40
            SUBTRACT 40 FROM I-HOURS-WORKED GIVING W-OVERTIME-HOURS
            MULTIPLY 0.5 BY W-OVERTIME-HOURS
            MULTIPLY W-OVERTIME-HOURS BY I-PAYRATE
                    GIVING W-OVERTIME-PAY ROUNDED
            ADD W-OVERTIME-PAY TO W-GROSS-PAY
                    ON SIZE ERROR MOVE 'Y' TO W-SIZE-ERROR-FLAG.

C030-COMPUTE-EXEMPTIONS.
    MULTIPLY C-EXEMPTION BY I-DEPENDENTS
            GIVING W-EXEMPTIONS-TOTAL.

C040-COMPUTE-TAX.
    IF W-GROSS-PAY IS GREATER THAN W-EXEMPTION-TOTAL
        SUBTRACT W-EXEMPTIONS-TOTAL FROM W-GROSS-PAY
                GIVING W-TAXABLE
        MULTIPLY C-TAXRATE BY W-TAXABLE GIVING W-TAX ROUNDED
    ELSE
        MOVE ZERO TO W-TAX.

C050-COMPUTE-NET-PAY.
    SUBTRACT W-TAX FROM W-GROSS-PAY GIVING W-NET-PAY.

C060-PRINT-OUTPUT.
    MOVE SPACES             TO NORMAL-OUTPUT-LINE.
    MOVE I-PAYROLL-NUMBER   TO O-PAYROLL-NUMBER.
    MOVE I-NAME             TO O-NAME.
    MOVE I-HOURS-WORKED     TO O-HOURS-WORKED.
    MOVE I-PAYRATE          TO O-PAYRATE.
    MOVE I-DEPENDENTS       TO O-DEPENDENTS.
    MOVE W-TAX              TO O-TAX.
    MOVE W-GROSS-PAY        TO O-GROSS-PAY.
    MOVE W-NET-PAY          TO 0-NET-PAY.
    WRITE REPORT-RECORD FROM NORMAL-OUTPUT-LINE.
```

```
D010-VALID-RECORD-LOOP.
    PERFORM E010-GET-PAYROLL-RECORD.
    IF NOT OUT-OF-RECORDS
        PERFORM E020-EDIT-PAYROLL-RECORD.

E010-GET-PAYROLL-RECORD.
    READ PAYROLL-FILE
            AT END MOVE 'Y' TO W-OUT-OF-RECORDS-FLAG.

E020-EDIT-PAYROLL-RECORD.
    IF      I-PAYROLL-NUMBER IS NOT NUMERIC
        OR  I-HOURS-WORKED   IS NOT NUMERIC
        OR  I-PAYRATE        IS NOT NUMERIC
        OR  I-DEPENDENTS     IS NOT NUMERIC
        MOVE PAYROLL-RECORD TO BAD-DATA
        WRITE REPORT-RECORD FROM ERROR-RECORD
    ELSE
        MOVE 'Y' TO W-VALID-PAYROLL-RECORD.
```

FIGURE 8.5 A revised payroll program utilizing the ON SIZE ERROR test.

When this version of the program was run with the data file used before, the output shown in Figure 8.6 was produced. Observe that we have finally found a way of detecting the error for Ima Testcase.

8.13 THE DISPLAY STATEMENT

Once an error has been identified in a program, either an abend or incorrect results, the next step is to locate the bug that caused the error. Begin by studying the nature of the error, the structure of the program, and the COBOL source code. If this is not sufficient to locate the bug, the next step is to look at the results of preliminary calculations that lead to the final output. For example, in the payroll program we now see that the calculated results for Ima Testcase are incorrect, but this may give you no idea of what caused the error. It might be that the data values were read incorrectly (although this is unlikely considering the fact that the program worked correctly for all the other test cases), or there might be a calculation or logic error at any of several steps. What we would like to be able to do is see the step-by-step operation of the program as it processes the data.

One way we could accomplish this is to set up a new output record in Working-Storage, then use it to print the data values we need to see. This has several flaws, however. First and most obvious is the effort of setting up an output record, particularly one that is flexible enough to show the variety of data fields that need to be studied. The second problem is that the error may involve an incorrect format for an output data field; if we repeat the same format in the new record we have accomplished nothing. Last, and perhaps most important, is the fact that on many computers an abend will destroy as much as several pages of output waiting to be printed.

Fortunately, COBOL provides a much more effective way to show intermediate data: the DISPLAY statement. The DISPLAY statement allows us to print any combination of literals and variables. For example, look at paragraph C020-COMPUTE-GROSS-PAY in Figure 8.7.

```
PAYROLL CALCULATION REPORT                                        87/02/12

NUMBER        NAME            HOURS  RATE   DEP   GROSS      TAX      NET

12345  THOS H. KELLY          20.0   5.350   0  $107.00   $22.47   $84.53
12401  HENRY JENSEN           40.0   7.500   1  $300.00   $52.50  $247.50
12511  NANCY KAHN             40.0   7.500   3  $300.00   $31.50  $268.50
UILKMB. R. BROOKS        400    0575002  INVALID DATA IN THIS RECORD
26017  JANE MILANO            10.0   6.875   3   $68.75    $0.00   $68.75
12  4KAY DELUCCIA         400    0600004  INVALID DATA IN THIS RECORD
26109  PETER W. SHERWOOD      40.0  10.000   5  $400.00   $31.50  $368.50
26222  GEORGE M. MULVANEY     41.0  10.000   5  $415.00   $34.65  $380.35
26500A. W. ENWRIGHT       40    0545001  INVALID DATA IN THIS RECORD
27511  RUTH GARRISON          50.0  10.000   4  $550.00   $73.50  $476.50
28819  LEO X. BUTLER          40.1  10.000   2  $401.50   $63.32  $338.18
28820D. X. IANNUZZI       450    4.50003  INVALID DATA IN THIS RECORD
28821K. L. NG, JR.        350    450003   INVALID DATA IN THIS RECORD
28822DANIEL REINER        350    045000C  INVALID DATA IN THIS RECORD
28822L. E. SIMON          388    06000 3  INVALID DATA IN THIS RECORD
28883QA. REAL BAD-ONE     3 8    4.5KJXX  INVALID DATA IN THIS RECORD
7HGV6GARBAGE-CASE-1       ..M.,M.,M.,M.   INVALID DATA IN THIS RECORD
 NJI9GARBAGE-CASE-2       GV 6 46  8   H   INVALID DATA IN THIS RECORD
    GARBAGE-CASE-3  ----------++++++,M   INVALID DATA IN THIS RECORD
29000  ANNE HENDERSON         40.2  10.000   3  $403.00   $53.13  $349.87
29001  JULIA KIPP             40.3  10.000   1  $404.50   $74.45  $330.05
99999IMA TESTCASE         999    9999999  GROSS PAY SUSPICIOUSLY LARGE
```

FIGURE 8.6 Illustrative output of the program in Figure 8.5.

For Ima Testcase, the first **DISPLAY** statement will print

A: (GROSS PAY) 98990

This is the literal '**A: (GROSS PAY)** ', followed immediately by the current value of **W-GROSS-PAY**. There are no spaces between the literal and the value of the variable, and the variable displayed is unedited. By looking at the definition of **W-GROSS-PAY**, however, we see that there is an assumed decimal between the third and fourth digits. The complete **DISPLAY** output for Ima Testcase is shown in Figure 8.8.

By following this output and comparing it to the code in paragraph **C020-COMPUTE-GROSS-PAY** we can see how the output shown in previous chapters was computed. Truncation at each of several steps (**A**, **D**, and **E**) leads to the final incorrect result.

Using the **DISPLAY** statement to show this output has several advantages over using a **WRITE** statement. First, of course, it is much easier to set up a **DISPLAY** than to set up a **WRITE**. Not only does the **WRITE** statement necessitate defining a new record, but the data to be printed must be moved to the output fields; also, the **DISPLAY** statement allows us to print *any* data, even data defined in the Working-Storage Section. Second, the **DISPLAY** statement shows the data *exactly* as it appears in the computer's memory. This avoids any error that may be caused by an incorrect **PICTURE** in the output record. Finally, because of the way in which **DISPLAY** statements are processed by the computer, an abend will not affect output from a **DISPLAY** unless it occurs while the **DISPLAY** statement is being executed.

```
C020-COMPUTE-GROSS-PAY.
    MULTIPLY I-HOURS-WORKED BY I-PAYRATE
            GIVING W-GROSS-PAY ROUNDED.
    DISPLAY 'A:   (GROSS PAY) ', W-GROSS-PAY.
    IF I-HOURS-WORKED IS GREATER THAN 40
        SUBTRACT 40 FROM I-HOURS-WORKED GIVING W-OVERTIME-HOURS
        DISPLAY 'B:   (OVERTIME HOURS) ', W-OVERTIME-HOURS
        MULTIPLY 0.5 BY W-OVERTIME-HOURS
        DISPLAY 'C:   (OVERTIME HOURS) ', W-OVERTIME-HOURS
        MULTIPLY W-OVERTIME-HOURS BY I-PAYRATE
                GIVING W-OVERTIME-PAY ROUNDED
        DISPLAY 'D:   (OVERTIME PAY) ', W-OVERTIME-PAY
        ADD W-OVERTIME-PAY TO W-GROSS-PAY.
    DISPLAY 'E:   (GROSS PAY) ', GROSS-PAY.
```

FIGURE 8.7 The paragraph to compute gross pay, taken from Figure 8.5 and modified to display intermediate results.

There are several features of the **DISPLAY** statement that require a bit of care. First, notice in the example above that we began each **DISPLAY** statement with a literal containing a letter followed by the name of the variable being displayed. The **DISPLAY** statement gives no indication of what data is being printed, or where in the program the statement is located. The function of the literal is twofold: it tells us *which* **DISPLAY** statement is responsible for producing a particular line of output, and it identifies the data being printed. If you omit this information you may find yourself staring at a page of numbers with no easy way to match them to specific statements in your program.

The second feature of the **DISPLAY** statement is that it does not provide any spaces between output fields; this is why each literal had a space before the closing apostrophe. If you have several variables printed by the same **DISPLAY**, their values will be run together unless you specifically place spaces between the data names. For example, you could write:

```
DISPLAY 'A:   ' FIELD-1 ' ' FIELD-2 SPACES FIELD-3.
```

In this example we have not used commas between output items; as always in a **COBOL** list the commas are optional. Also, the figurative constant **SPACES** is equivalent to a single space and can be used interchangeably with the literal ' '.

We should point out that although the example for the payroll problem showed output for only one test record, in an actual run the **DISPLAY** output would be printed for *every* record in the input file. In addition to the data we showed, you might wish to display the employee number so that you know which record is being processed.

```
A:   (GROSS PAY) 98990
B:   (OVERTIME HOURS) 5990
C:   (OVERTIME HOURS) 2995
D:   (OVERTIME PAY) 99497
E:   (GROSS PAY) 98487
```

FIGURE 8.8. **DISPLAY** output for "Ima Testcase" from the paragraph shown in Figure 8.7.

Finally, we must consider the question of where the output printed by the **DISPLAY** statement will actually appear. That is, to which file is the **DISPLAY** output assigned? The answer is that although every computer has a standard default file for **DISPLAY** output, this file varies from machine to machine. On the IBM mainframe computers, for example, **DISPLAY** output goes to a file called **SYSOUT**. On microcomputers **DISPLAY** output generally goes to the CRT. You must determine where the output is sent on the computer you are using. On all computers, however, not only are you not *required* to define a file for the **DISPLAY** statement, you are not *permitted* to define one. There is an option on the **DISPLAY** statement to change the output device, but we will have no occasion to use this feature.

8.14 THE EXHIBIT STATEMENT

To simplify identification of the output printed in a debugging statement, the IBM **COBOL** compiler (and several other **COBOL** compilers as well), supports the **EXHIBIT** statement. The **EXHIBIT** statement works very much like the **DISPLAY** statement with one change: the name of every variable is printed just before the variable's value, and a space is automatically inserted between one value and the next. For example, we could rewrite **C020-COMPUTE-GROSS-PAY** as shown in Figure 8.9. The corresponding output is shown in Figure 8.10.

We have still included a literal to identify the statement that produced each line, but now the **EXHIBIT** statement identifies the variable for us. The literal is simply printed as a comment and is followed by a space. The output from the **EXHIBIT** statement goes to the same default file as the **DISPLAY** output, but there is no option to change the file.

In the example in Figure 8.9 we always followed the word **EXHIBIT** with the word **NAMED**. This is because the **EXHIBIT** statement has several options that we have not discussed here. The format shown in Figure 8.9 is the easiest to use for the beginning **COBOL** programmer.

```
C020-COMPUTE-GROSS-PAY.
    MULTIPLY I-HOURS-WORKED BY I-PAYRATE
            GIVING W-GROSS-PAY ROUNDED.
    EXHIBIT NAMED 'A:  ', W-GROSS-PAY.
    IF I-HOURS-WORKED IS GREATER THAN 40
        SUBTRACT 40 FROM I-HOURS-WORKED GIVING W-OVERTIME-HOURS
        EXHIBIT NAMED 'B:  ', W-OVERTIME-HOURS
        MULTIPLY 0.5 BY W-OVERTIME-HOURS
        EXHIBIT NAMED 'C:  ', W-OVERTIME-HOURS
        MULTIPLY W-OVERTIME-HOURS BY I-PAYRATE
                GIVING W-OVERTIME-PAY ROUNDED
        EXHIBIT NAMED 'D:   ', W-OVERTIME-PAY
        ADD W-OVERTIME-PAY TO W-GROSS-PAY.
    EXHIBIT NAMED 'E:  ', GROSS-PAY.
```

FIGURE 8.9 The paragraph to compute gross pay, using the **EXHIBIT** statement to show intermediate results.

```
A:     W-GROSS-PAY = 98990
B:     W-OVERTIME-HOURS = 5990
C:     W-OVERTIME-HOURS = 2995
D:     W-OVERTIME-PAY = 99497
E:     W-GROSS-PAY = 98487
```

FIGURE 8.10 **EXHIBIT** output for "Ima Testcase" from the paragraph shown in Figure 8.9.

8.15 THE TRACE STATEMENT

Another debugging statement that is supported by IBM but not by standard **COBOL** is the **TRACE** statement. When the **TRACE** mode is enabled, the **COBOL** program will automatically print the name of every paragraph as it is executed, which allows you to follow the execution of the program paragraph by paragraph. **TRACE** mode is turned on by executing the statement **READY TRACE**; it is turned off by executing **RESET TRACE**. The names of the paragraphs are printed on the same default file used by **DISPLAY** and **EXHIBIT**. Figure 8.11 shows code to turn on **TRACE** at the start of the payroll program and turn it off at the end. Figure 8.12 shows the trace output for Ima Testcase.

Some programmers, especially beginning **COBOL** programmers, look on the **TRACE** statement as the solution to all their debugging problems. They seem to feel that if only they stare at the **TRACE** output long enough it will tell them what is wrong with their program. In point of fact, the **TRACE** tells you nothing that you can't discover using the **DISPLAY** or **EXHIBIT** statements, and it produces *much* more paper. Although a trace of the program will tell you *where* the execution went, it will not tell you *why* it went there, which is usually much more important. Most of the time, careful use of **DISPLAY** or **EXHIBIT** statements will give you the most useful information with the least amount of output, which is really what you need in order to understand the program. However, if you do decide to use **TRACE**, use **READY TRACE** and **RESET TRACE** very carefully to turn on the trace only where you think the problem is located. If you simply enable the **TRACE** mode at the start of the program, you may have so much output you can't separate the useful information from the junk.

```
PROCEDURE DIVISION.
A000-PRODUCE-PAYROLL-CALC.
     READY TRACE.
     OPEN INPUT PAYROLL-FILE
          OUTPUT REPORT-FILE.
     PERFORM B010-PRINT-COLUMN-HEADINGS.
     PERFORM C010-GET-VALID-PAY-REC.
     PERFORM B020-CALC-EMP-PAYROLL
          UNTIL OUT-OF-RECORDS.
     CLOSE PAYROLL-FILE
          REPORT-FILE.
     RESET TRACE.
     STOP RUN.
```

FIGURE 8.11 Driver paragraph to turn **TRACE** on and off in payroll program.

```
B010-PRINT-COLUMN-HEADINGS ,C010-GET-VALID-PAY-REC ,
D010-VALID-RECORD-LOOP ,E010-GET-PAYROLL-RECORD ,
E020-EDIT-PAYROLL-RECORD ,B020-CALC-EMP-PAYROLL ,
C020-COMPUTE-GROSS-PAY ,C030-COMPUTE-EXEMPTIONS ,
C040-COMPUTE-TAX ,C050-COMPUTE-NET-PAY ,C060-PRINT-OUTPUT ,
C010-GET-VALID-PAY-REC , D010-VALID-RECORD-LOOP ,
E010-GET-PAYROLL-RECORD ,
```

FIGURE 8.12 Output from **TRACE** for a file containing one payroll record.

REVIEW QUESTIONS

1. In what way is program design related to program errors?
2. How does programming style affect the likelihood of finding errors in a program?
3. Does the indentation of the following nested **IF** statements correspond to the way a **COBOL** compiler would interpret the statements?

a.
```
IF C1
    S1
    IF C2
        S2
    ELSE
        IF C3
            S4
ELSE
        S5.
```

b.
```
IF C1
    IF C2
        IF C3
            S1
        ELSE
            S2
    ELSE
        S3
ELSE
    S4.
```

c.
```
IF C1
    S1
ELSE
    IF C2
        S2
    ELSE
        S3.
```

d.
```
IF C1
    S1
    IF C2
        S2
    ELSE
        S3
    S4
ELSE
    S5.
```

```
e.  IF C1
        IF C2
            S1
        ELSE
            IF C3
                S2
            ELSE
                S3
    ELSE
        S4.
```

4. Rewrite each of the following nested **IF** statements as several unnested **IF** statements, some of which have compound conditions; that is, use **AND** and **NOT** operators.

```
a.  IF C1
        IF C2
            S1
        ELSE
    ELSE
        S3.
```

```
b.  IF C1
        IF C2
            IF C3
                S1
            ELSE
                NEXT SENTENCE
        ELSE
            S2.
```

```
c.  IF C1
        S1
        IF C2
            NEXT SENTENCE
        ELSE
            S2.
```

```
d.  IF C1
        IF C2
            S1
        ELSE
            IF C3
                S2
            ELSE
                NEXT SENTENCE
    ELSE
        S3.
```

5. The following program, based on an example we shall study in the next chapter, contains 14 syntactic errors, all of which were diagnosed by a compiler, and one very serious punctuation error that was not diagnosed because it did not create a syntax error. Find the errors.

```
00001      IDENTIFICATION DIVISION.
00002      PROGRAM-ID.
00003          FINDERRS.
00004
00005      DATE-WRITTEN.
00006          MARCH 3, 1987.
00007
```

```
00008          ENVIRONMENT DIVISION.
00009          INPUT-OUTPUT SECTION.
00010          FILE-CONTROL.
00011              SELECT INPUT-FILE           ASSIGN TO S-INPUT.
00012              SELECT REPORT-FILE          ASSIGN TO S-REPORT.
00013
00014          DATA DIVISION.
00015
00016      FD  INPUT-FILE
00017          LABEL RECORDS ARE OMITTED
00018      01  INPUT-RECORD.
00019          05  ACCOUNT-NUMBER          PIC X(5).
00020          05  ACCOUNT-DOLLARS         PIC 9(5)V99.
00021          05  FILLER                  PIC X(68).
00022
00023      FD  REPORT-FILE
00024          LABEL RECORDS ARE OMITTED.
00025      01  REPORT-RECORD               PIC X(132).
00026
00027      WORKING-STORAGE SECTION.
00028
00029      01  FLAGS.
00030          05  MORE-DATA-REMAINS-FLAG.
00031              88  MORE-DATA-REMAINS              VALUE 'YES'.
00032              88  NO-MORE-DATA-REMAINS           VALUE 'NO'.
00033
00034      01  LINE-AND-PAGE-COUNTERS.
00035          05  LINE-NUMBER             PIC S99    VALUE +1.
00036          05  PAGE-NUMBER             PIC S999   VALUE +1.
00037
00038      01  SAVE-ITEM.
00039          05  PREVIOUS-ACCOUNT-NUMBER PIC X(5).
00040
00041      01  TOTALS.
00042          05  ACCOUNT-TOTAL           PIC S9(6)V99 VALUE ZERO.
00043          05  FINAL-TOTAL             PIC S9(6)V99 VALUE ZERO.
00044
00045      01  DETAIL-LINE.
00046          05  ACCOUNT-NUMBER-OUT      PIC Z(4)9.
00047          05  FILLER                  PIC X(3).
00048          15  ACCOUNT-TOTAL-OUT       PIC $$$$,ZZ9.99.
00049          05  FILLER                  PIC X(8).
00050          05  FINAL-TOTAL-OUT         PIC $$$$,$$9.99.
00051
00052      01  HEADING-LINE.
00053          05  FILLER                  PIC X(48)
00054              VALUE 'ACCOUNT    TOTAL           FINAL TOTAL        PAGE.
00055          05  PAGE-NUMBER-OUT         PIC Z(6)9.
00056
00057      PROCEDURE DIVISION.
00058      A000-PREPARE-SALES-REPORT.
00059          OPEN INPUT-FILE
00060               REPORT-FILE.
00061          READ INPUT-FILE
00062              AT END MOVE NO TO MORE-DATA-REMAINS-FLAG.
00063          IF MORE-DATA-REMAINS
00064              MOVE ACCOUNT-NUMBER TO PREVIOUS-ACCOUNT-NUMBER
00065              PERFORM B010-PROCESS-INPUT-RECORD
00066                  UNTIL NO-MORE-DATA-REMAINS-FLAG
00067              PERFORM B020-FINAL-TOTAL-PROCESSING.
```

```
00068                    CLOSE INPUT-FILE
00069                          REPORT-FILE.
00070
00071            B010-PROCESS-INPUT-RECORD.
00072                    IF ACCOUNT-NUMBER IS NOT EQUAL TO PREVIOUS-ACCOUNT-NUMBER
00073                        PERFORM C010-PROCESS-ACCOUNT-TOTAL
00074                    ADD ACCOUNT-DOLLARS TO ACCOUNT-TOTAL
00075                                        FINAL-TOTAL
00076                    READ INPUT-RECORD
00077                        AT END MOVE 'NO' TO MORE-DATA-REMAINS-FLAG.
00078
00079            B020-FINAL-TOTAL-PROCESSING.
00080                    PERFORM C010-PROCESS-ACCOUNT-TOTAL.
00081                    MOVE SPACES TO DETAIL-LINE.
00082                    MOVE FINAL-TOTAL TO FINAL-TOTAL-OUT.
00083                    PERFORM C020-LINE-OUT.
00084
00085            C010-PROCESS-ACCOUNT-TOTAL.
00086                    MOVE SPACES TO DETAIL-LINE
00087                    MOVE PREVIOUS-ACCOUNT-NUMBER TO ACCOUNT-NUMBER-OUT
00088                    MOVE ACCOUNT-TOTAL TO ACCOUNT-TOTAL-OUT
00089                    PERFORM C020-LINE-OUT
00090                    MOVE ACCOUNT-NUMBER TO PREVIOUS-ACCOUNT-NUMBER
00091                    MOVE ZERO TO ACCOUNT-TOTAL
00092
00093            C020-LINE-OUT.
00094                    IF LINE-NUMBER EQUALS 1
00095                        MOVE PAGE-NUMBER TO PAGE-NUMBER-OUT
00096                        WRITE REPORT-RECORD FROM HEADING-LINE
00097                        MOVE SPACES TO REPORT-RECORD
00098                        WRITE REPORT-RECORD
00099                        MOVE 2 TO LINE-NUMBER
00100                        ADD 1 TO PAGE-NUMBER.
00101                    WRITE REPORT-RECORD FROM DETAIL-LINE.
00102                    IF LINE-NUMBER = 66
00103                        MOVE 1 TO LINE-NUMBER
00104                    ELSE
00105                        ADD 1 TO LINE-NUMBER.
```

6. A programmer has stated that the purpose of testing a program is to prove that it contains no errors. Do you agree with this statement? Why or why not?

7. Which of the following statements describes what happens as a result of an arithmetic statement that includes the SIZE-ERROR phrase, when a size error occurs.

   a. The run is terminated and the words SIZE-ERROR are printed.

   b. A partial result is stored and then the truncated high order digits are saved in a special storage location.

   c. Nothing is stored and the imperative statements in the SIZE-ERROR phrase are executed.

   d. The receiving field is enlarged to accommodate the high order digits.

   e. None of the above.

8. Can the DISPLAY statement be used for output other than debugging? That is, could we eliminate the output files in our programs and simply use DISPLAY to print results?

ANSWERS

1. A well-designed program will have few, if any, serious program errors. Conversely, a poorly designed program is likely to contain serious problems and, even if they are fixed, the program will probably continue to cause maintenance problems throughout its lifetime.

2. If a program is written in a style that makes the code easy to read, it is easier to spot typing errors, simple logic errors, and so on. If the code is hard to read, these errors can slip by even the most careful checking.

3. Statements **b**, **c**, and **e** are correct. The second **ELSE** in statement **a** violates the rule that an **ELSE** matches the most recent **IF** that does not already have an **ELSE**; the second **ELSE** accordingly should be indented to match **IF C3**. In statement **d** the indentation of **S4** violates the rule that every statement is controlled by the most recent **IF** or **ELSE**; it should be aligned with **S3**.

4. **a.**
```
IF C1 AND C1
      S1.
   IF C1 AND NOT C2
      S2.
   IF NOT C1
      S3.
```
   b.
```
IF C1 AND C2 AND C3
      S1.
   IF C1 AND NOT C2
      S2.
```
   c.
```
IF C1
      S1.
   IF C1 AND NOT C2
      S2.
```
   d.
```
IF C1 AND C2
      S1.
   IF C1 AND NOT C2 AND C3
         S2.
   IF NOT C1
      S3.
```

5. In the following error listing, observe that the diagnostic message for line 47 is actually caused by an error on line 48; that the messages for lines 53, 54, and 55 are caused by the absence of a closing quote on line 54; that the error for line 83 is the substitution of zero for the letter **o**; that the message for line 88 relates to the action taken by the compiler in response to the error on line 48. The strange-looking symbols in the message for line 76 (**DNM=1-207**) are the compiler's internal name for the structure **INPUT-RECORD**; some compilers will supply the actual name, but the one that was used for this program does not.

   The logic error is the absence of periods at the ends of lines 73 and 75, which puts the **ADD** and **READ** statements into the **IF** statement. This is not a syntactic error. As soon as the program comes across a situation in which the **IF** condition becomes false (a very common occurrence for this program), it would be in an *infinite loop*: the main line routine says to perform **B010-PROCESS-INPUT-RECORD** until the end of file flag has been set, but because the **READ** is in an unsatisfied **IF** and is therefore not executed, the flag can never be set.

CARD	ERROR MESSAGE	
16	IKF1002I-W	FILE SECTION HEADER MISSING. ASSUMED PRESENT.
11	IKF2049I-C	NO OPEN CLAUSE FOUND FOR FILE.
18	IKF1043I-W	END OF SENTENCE SHOULD PRECEDE 01 . ASSUMED PRESENT.
12	IKF2049I-C	NO OPEN CLAUSE FOUND FOR FILE.
30	IKF2141I-C	LENGTH OF LITERAL IS MORE OR LESS THAN LENGTH OF GROUP. LENGTH OF LITERAL ASSUMED.
47	IKF2034I-E	GROUP ITEM HAS PICTURE CLAUSE. CLAUSE DELETED.
48	IKF2094I-C	NUMERIC EDITED PICTURE - FLOATING STRING PRECEDES * OR Z. PICTURE REPLACED BY 9(1).
54	IKF1098I-C	ALPHA LITERAL NOT CONTINUED WITH HYPHEN AND QUOTE. END LITERAL ON LAST CARD.
55	IKF1007I-W	05 NOT PRECEDED BY A SPACE. ASSUME SPACE.
55	IKF1043I-W	END OF SENTENCE SHOULD PRECEDE 05 . ASSUMED PRESENT.
53	IKF2126I-C	VALUE CLAUSE LITERAL TOO LONG. TRUNCATED TO PICTURE SIZE.
60	IKF1017I-E	INPUT-FILE INVALID IN OPEN CLAUSE. SKIPPING TO NEXT CLAUSE.
62	IKF4004I-E	NO IS ILLEGALLY USED IN MOVE STATEMENT. DISCARDED.
65	IKF3001I-E	NO-MORE-DATA-REMAINS-FLAG NOT DEFINED. TEST DISCARDED.
76	IKF4050I-E	SYNTAX REQUIRES FILE-NAME . FOUND DNM=1-207 . STATEMENT DISCARDED.
83	IKF3001I-E	C020-LINE-OUT NOT DEFINED. STATEMENT DISCARDED.
88	IKF5011I-W	AN INTERMEDIATE RESULT OR A SENDING FIELD MIGHT HAVE ITS HIGH ORDER DIGIT POSITION TRUNCATED.
93	IKF1043I-W	END OF SENTENCE SHOULD PRECEDE C020-LINE-OUT . ASSUMED PRESENT.
94	IKF3001I-E	EQUALS NOT DEFINED.
94	IKF4013I-C	RELATIONAL MISSING IN IF OR CONDITIONAL STATEMENT. 'EQUAL' ASSUMED.
105	IKF5019I-W	NO STOP RUN, GOBACK, OR EXIT PROGRAM STATEMENTS ENCOUNTERED IN SOURCE.

6. This is not the objective of testing. Unless we are able to run test cases that cover *all possible paths through the program*, an activity that would take years even for relatively small programs, we cannot *prove* that a program is correct through testing. A more reasonable goal of testing is to find the errors in the program. If, after a thorough job of testing, we can find no more errors we can say that there are probably no *major* errors left in the program.

7. c.

8. Yes, but we don't advise it. In the first place, you would still have to set up edited fields in Working-Storage, or the printed results would be very hard to read. More important, however, is the fact that different **COBOL** compilers send the output from **DISPLAY** to different places. If you move your program to a new computer you may discover that your output is going someplace totally unexpected (such as an operator's console in the main computer room). There are other serious limitations on the **DIS-PLAY** statement. In general it should not be used for any output except debugging. We will discuss some specific exceptions to this policy in Chapter 20.

EXERCISES

*1. The first example in Section 8.3 contains a bug. Identify the bug and modify the code shown to correct the error. Do not rewrite the entire example—just modify to code shown, doing as little as necessary to make the correction.

COBOL-85

2. If you are using **COBOL-85**, insert **END-IF** phrases in parts **a** and **d** of Review Question 3 so that the indentation matches the way a **COBOL** compiler would interpret the statements.

END COBOL-85

*3. Write a nested **IF** statement that will do the following. A marital status code has level **88** entries defining condition names **SINGLE**, **MARRIED**, **DIVORCED**, and **WIDOWED**. Depending on the value of the code, it is necessary to perform **D010-SINGLE-ROUTINE**, **D020-MARRIED-ROUTINE**, **D030-DIVORCED-ROUTINE**, or **D040-WIDOWED-ROUTINE**. If the code is not any of these, **D050-ERROR-ROUTINE** should be performed. Assume that for the employee group involved, the most common status is married, then single, then divorced, and the least frequent is widowed; write the statement so that it is as efficient as possible in view of these frequencies.

4. A certain company manufactures electric motors in the range of 1 to 99 horsepower. Three different departments are involved, and a nested **IF** statement must choose an appropriate order routine according to the following table:

If the value of **HORSEPOWER** is:	**PERFORM:**
Less than 1	D040-ERROR-ROUTINE
At least 1 but less than 5	D010-DEPT-23-ORDER
At least 5 but less than 20	D020-DEPT-26-ORDER
At least 20 but less than 100	D030-DEPT-39-ORDER
100 or over	D040-ERROR-ROUTINE

(This can be done with one nested **IF** containing no **AND**s.)

*5. Write a nested **IF** statement to perform a routine named **E050-EXCESSIVE-PAY-POSSIBLE** if any one of the following conditions is true:

The value of **SALARY-CODE** is **W** and **GROSS-PAY** is greater than **500**.
The value of **SALARY-CODE** is **S** and **GROSS-PAY** is greater than **1400**.
The value of **SALARY-CODE** is **M** and **GROSS-PAY** is greater than **4500**.

Perform **X030-ERROR-ROUTINE** is **SALARY-CODE** is not **W**, **S**, or **M**.

* Answers to starred exercises will be found in Appendix IV at the end of the book.

6. Write a nested **IF** statement to carry out one of four routines according to the following combinations of the value of the two items named FLD-1 and **FLD-2**:

FLD-1	A	A	A	B	Anything but **A** or **B**
FLD-2	1	2	Anything but **1** or **2**	3	Doesn't matter
PERFORM:	A-1-RTN	A-2-RTN	ERROR-RTN	A-3-RTN	ERROR-RTN

*7. Modify the program in Exercise 7 of Chapter 7 to print an error message if the total of the invoice amounts overflows the total field. The program should continue to run until all data has been processed, and the error message should be printed once, in place of the normal total.

8. Modify the program in Exercise 8 of Chapter 7 so that if any of the total fields overflows, an error message is printed for that field in place of the total at the end of the output. The overflow could occur for none of the fields, one of the fields, etc., and only the affected totals should show the error message.

CHAPTER 9

CONTROL BREAKS

9.1 INTRODUCTION

The primary topic for this chapter is the processing of a file that is in sequence on some field in each record, building a report that is organized according to the changes in that field. A change from one account group to the next is called a *control break*, hence the title of the chapter.

The vehicle for this study will be an application of broad general interest. Starting with a file of sales data that is in ascending sequence, we are to produce a summary of the data by region, seller, and account. The techniques involved in processing such a file are of fundamental importance (they will concern us in future chapters as well), and summarization is a basic computer application. The program will be developed in two stages, starting first with a simpler task.

In the course of this study we also examine several new COBOL features. The first is the content of the Identification Division, which is much simpler and shorter than the Data and Procedure Divisions and which does not require a great deal of effort. The second is the use of techniques that allow us to skip lines between lines of output and to skip to the top of a new page. We will present some additional examples of debugging, and discuss the handling of requests for program modification.

9.2 THE SALES STATISTICS APPLICATION

Suppose we have an input file of information about the previous month's sales of some company. The company has a number of sales regions; within each region there are a number of salespeople; each salesperson handles a number of accounts. We are required to produce a sales summary that shows the total sales for the entire company for the month, the total sales for each region, the total sales for each salesperson, and the total sales for each account. Figure 9.1 indicates the general layout of the report that we are to produce and helps to clarify the hierarchical nature of the data organization.

REGION	TOTAL	SALESPERSON	TOTAL	ACCOUNT	TOTAL	FINAL TOTAL	PAGE	1
				20	$17.00			
				24	$36.00			
				27	$184.00			
		1	$237.00					
				17	$26.00			
				24	$266.90			
		2	$292.90					
				10	$87.50			
				16	$54.75			
		12	$142.25					
1	$672.15							
				40	$50.12			
				41	$105.99			
		4	$156.11					
				44	$1,594.14			
		39	$1,594.14					
2	$1,750.25							
				30	$1,180.94			
				35	$69.26			
				38	$157.43			
				49	$45.00			
				60	$1,234.56			
				78	$276.02			
		15	$2,963.21					
3	$2,963.21							
						$5,385.61		

FIGURE 9.1 Illustrative output of a program to produce three-level control totals.

When faced with a programming task that is too complex for us to solve in a single step, we can approach it by first determining if there is a related but simpler task that we can do. Once we have found a workable approach to the simpler job, we can build on that foundation to complete the task we really want to accomplish. In the assignment for this chapter, an obvious simplification is to deal first with only one level of control totals rather than three.

Suppose that the input file for a one-level version of our program is this:

ACCOUNT	AMOUNT
20	$ 12
20	18
20	4
24	72
27	40
27	26
27	218
27	2
27	82

We see that there are three transactions for account 20, totaling $34. Account 24 has only one transaction, so its account total is just the $72 for that one transaction. Account 27 has five transactions for a total of $368. The final total is for all transactions, which is also equal to the sum of all account totals.

The purpose of the program is to prepare summary totals from the input file of such transactions. The output of the program that we shall develop for this one-level version, given this input file, would be as follows:

ACCOUNT	TOTAL	FINAL TOTAL	PAGE	1
20	$34.00			
24	$72.00			
27	$368.00			
		474.00		

9.3 SEQUENTIAL FILE PROCESSING

It is certainly possible to prepare summaries of this type when the transactions appear in random order, although the program might get rather cumbersome if we were dealing with 30,000 accounts instead of only three. In this chapter, however, we are assuming a file in which the records appear in ascending sequence on the account numbers contained in them. For our example file this means that, since 20 is the smallest account number, all the transactions for that account must appear together at the beginning of the file; since 24 is the next larger account number, its transaction must appear next; all of the transactions for account 27 must appear at the end of the file. We don't care at all what the order of the transactions is within any one account number; reverse the first two transactions, for instance, and the program should produce the same result.

It is not to be expected that the sales records will already be in proper ascending sequence on the account number. Getting the records into sequence requires a preliminary operation called sorting, which is done with an appropriate program. We shall learn in Chapter 17 how this can be done by using the **COBOL** verb **SORT**.

The value of knowing that the records appear in ascending sequence is that we are able to write a program that never has to deal with more than two transaction records at any one time. After getting the process started, by a method that we shall investigate shortly, we always ask whether the transaction just read has the same account number as the transaction before this one. If not, then the previous transaction was the last one (or the only one) for an account number group, and we can produce the group's total. When we discover that the account number for the transaction just read is different from the account number of the previous transaction, we have what is called a control break. If the account number for the current transaction is the same as that for the previous one, then there is nothing to be done except add the dollar amount for this transaction to the account total. This contrasts sharply with what the situation would be if the transactions could arrive in random sequence. Then we would have to keep a separate total for each account number, since it would be impossible to print any of the totals until reaching the end of the file; there would be no way of knowing until then that any of the account groups was complete. The extra storage required could present a problem, especially on small computers, if the number of account groups was large. Of course, we would gain the advantage of not having to sort the transactions into ascending sequence before doing the process.

Sequentially and randomly accessed files both have their place, depending primarily on the needs of the application. After studying the use of sequentially accessed files in Chapters 9 and 12, we shall study randomly accessed files in Chapter 14, where trade-offs between the two will be considered more fully.

9.4   A PROGRAM DESIGN FOR THE ONE-LEVEL VERSION

We begin the design of this program by looking at the structure of the two files being processed, the data file and the report file. Each file consists of individual records—account records for the data file and lines of print for the report file—but this doesn't really help us very much. What does help is to observe that both files contain sets of records for account groups. In the input file the account group consists of one or more records having the same account number; in the report file an account group is just one line. The basic task of the program, therefore, is to process account groups until all groups have been processed, then produce a final total. Processing an account group is simple: all we have to do is add the amount on the current record to the group total. The tricky part is to determine when we have reached the end of a group, and to initialize a new account group. The hierarchy chart for the program is shown in Figure 9.2, and the basic pseudocode is in Figure 9.3.

The basic structure of this design follows the structure of the data files. In the main program we execute a priming **READ**, then process account groups until we run out of data, at which time we print the final total. At this level we are not really concerned with what an account group is or what the individual input records look like. However, if the input file is empty, the program will not process any account groups, which is what we would want.

In any program such as this, which processes successive data groups, the most difficult task usually is dealing with the end of one group and the start of

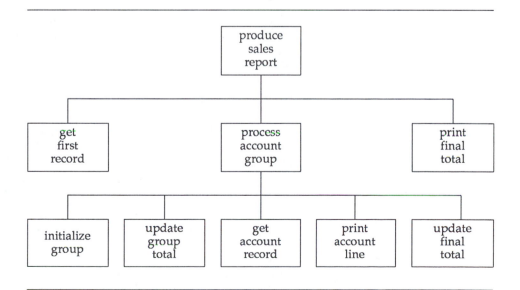

FIGURE 9.2   Hierarchy chart for a one-level control break program.

```
PRODUCE SALES REPORT:
open files
set final total to zero
set more-data-flag to 'Y'
get account record; at end set more-data-flag to 'N'
PERFORM-UNTIL no more data
     process account group
ENDPERFORM
print final total
close files

PROCESS ACCOUNT GROUP:
initialize account group
PERFORM-UNTIL
          current account number is not equal to previous account number
                 or
          no more data
     update account total
     get account record; at end set more-data-flag to 'N'
ENDPERFORM
print account line
update final total

INITIALIZE ACCOUNT GROUP:
set account total to zero
set previous account number to account number of current record
```

FIGURE 9.3. Basic pseudocode for one-level control break.

the next. We would like to have a general technique for this situation, one that does not require special handling for special cases. The basic approach we will use is to have two variables, one to identify the group to which the *current* record (the one we are working with now) belongs, and one to identify the group to which the *previous* record (the one we just finished with) belongs.

As long as these two variables have the same value, everything is easy; we simply continue processing the current data group. When the variables have different values, however, we know that we are at the end of one group and the start of another. We terminate the current group, then start the new one. In the pseudocode for PROCESS ACCOUNT GROUP, this means that we terminate the PERFORM-UNTIL loop, print the account line, and update the final total. This completes the old group, and we go through the PERFORM-UNTIL loop of PRODUCE SALES REPORT once more (assuming there is still more data).

Up to this point, nothing in the pseudocode has changed the value of "previous account number." Now, however, we begin execution of PROCESS ACCOUNT GROUP again, which requires that we execute INITIALIZE ACCOUNT GROUP. Here we set the total for the new group to zero, then take the account number of the record we just read and save it as the "previous account number." We are now ready to process the new data group.

Notice that each time we start a group, the record we use as the first record of the group is the one that was read when we *ended* the previous group.

There are two special groups to deal with: the first group in the file and the last group in the file. The last group is easy. Both PERFORM-UNTIL loops will terminate when an end-of-file is encountered, so we simply print the final total, close the files, and stop the run. The first group is a bit more complex because there is no previous group to start it off. We can solve this problem rather easily, however, by reading a priming record before we start the main PERFORM-UNTIL loop in PRODUCE SALES REPORT. This record becomes the current record that is used to set the previous account number in INITIALIZE ACCOUNT GROUP.

This technique is very general, and can easily be adapted to any system where the input file is structured as a sequence of data groups.

The hierarchy chart and pseudocode imply that the program should have about nine modules (although we have not actually shown the pseudocode for all nine modules). In point of fact, we shall not actually use this many paragraphs in the **COBOL** program. Most of the modules are very simple and are coded in-line. The code for the program is shown in Figure 9.4.

```
IDENTIFICATION DIVISION.
PROGRAM-ID.
    ONELEVEL.
AUTHOR.
    D. GOLDEN.
INSTALLATION.
    CLEVELAND STATE UNIVERSITY.
DATE-WRITTEN.
    MARCH 4, 1987.
DATE-COMPILED. MAR  5,1987.
SECURITY.
    NON-CLASSIFIED.
*
*    THIS PROGRAM PRODUCES A SIMPLE ONE-LEVEL SUMMARY REPORT FOR A
*    SALES ACCOUNTING SYSTEM
*

ENVIRONMENT DIVISION.
CONFIGURATION SECTION.
SPECIAL-NAMES.
    C01 IS TO-TOP-OF-PAGE.
INPUT-OUTPUT SECTION.
FILE-CONTROL.
    SELECT ACCOUNT-FILE         ASSIGN TO S-ACCOUNT.
    SELECT REPORT-FILE          ASSIGN TO S-REPORT.

DATA DIVISION.
FILE SECTION.

FD  ACCOUNT-FILE
    LABEL RECORDS ARE OMITTED.
01  ACCOUNT-RECORD.
    05   ACCOUNT-NUMBER         PIC X(5).
    05   SALE-AMOUNT            PIC 9(5)V99.
    05   FILLER                 PIC X(68).

FD  REPORT-FILE
    LABEL RECORDS ARE OMITTED.
01  REPORT-RECORD               PIC X(133).
```

```
WORKING-STORAGE SECTION.

77  ACCOUNT-TOTAL                PIC S9(6)V99.
77  FINAL-TOTAL                  PIC S9(6)V99.
77  LINE-NUMBER                  PIC S99.
77  MORE-DATA-FLAG               PIC X.
    88  NO-MORE-DATA                              VALUE 'N'.
77  PAGE-NUMBER                  PIC S999.
77  PREVIOUS-ACCOUNT-NUMBER      PIC X(5).


01  DETAIL-LINE.
    05  CARRIAGE-CONTROL         PIC X.
    05  ACCOUNT-NUMBER-OUT       PIC Z(4)9.
    05  FILLER                   PIC XXX.
    05  ACCOUNT-TOTAL-OUT        PIC $$$$,$$9.99.
    05  FILLER                   PIC X(8).
    05  FINAL-TOTAL-OUT          PIC $$$$,$$9.99.


01  HEADING-LINE.
    05  CARRIAGE-CONTROL         PIC X.
    05  FILLER                   PIC X(48)
        VALUE 'ACCOUNT    TOTAL           FINAL TOTAL      PAGE'.
    05  PAGE-NUMBER-OUT          PIC Z(6)9.

PROCEDURE DIVISION.
A000-PREPARE-SALES-REPORT.
    OPEN  INPUT ACCOUNT-FILE
          OUTPUT REPORT-FILE.
    MOVE ZERO                    TO FINAL-TOTAL.
    MOVE 'Y'                     TO MORE-DATA-FLAG.
    MOVE 55                      TO LINE-NUMBER.
    MOVE ZERO                    TO PAGE-NUMBER.
    READ ACCOUNT-FILE
            AT END MOVE 'N' TO MORE-DATA-FLAG.
    PERFORM B010-PROCESS-ACCOUNT-GROUP
        UNTIL NO-MORE-DATA.
    MOVE SPACES TO DETAIL-LINE.
    MOVE FINAL-TOTAL TO FINAL-TOTAL-OUT.
    PERFORM X010-LINE-OUT.
    CLOSE ACCOUNT-FILE
          REPORT-FILE.
    STOP RUN.


B010-PROCESS-ACCOUNT-GROUP.
    MOVE ZERO TO ACCOUNT-TOTAL.
    MOVE ACCOUNT-NUMBER TO PREVIOUS-ACCOUNT-NUMBER.
    PERFORM C010-PROCESS-ACCOUNT-RECORD UNTIL
            ACCOUNT-NUMBER IS NOT EQUAL TO PREVIOUS-ACCOUNT-NUMBER
        OR NO-MORE-DATA.
    MOVE SPACES TO DETAIL-LINE.
    MOVE PREVIOUS-ACCOUNT-NUMBER TO ACCOUNT-NUMBER-OUT.
    MOVE ACCOUNT-TOTAL TO ACCOUNT-TOTAL-OUT.
    PERFORM X010-LINE-OUT.
    ADD ACCOUNT-TOTAL TO FINAL-TOTAL.


C010-PROCESS-ACCOUNT-RECORD.
    ADD SALE-AMOUNT TO ACCOUNT-TOTAL
    READ ACCOUNT-FILE
            AT END MOVE 'N' TO MORE-DATA-FLAG.
```

```
X010-LINE-OUT.
    ADD 1 TO LINE-NUMBER.
*           SEE IF WE ARE AT THE END OF THE PAGE
*           IF SO, PRINT A NEW PAGE HEADING
    IF LINE-NUMBER IS GREATER THAN 55
        ADD 1 TO PAGE-NUMBER
        MOVE PAGE-NUMBER TO PAGE-NUMBER-OUT
        WRITE REPORT-RECORD FROM HEADING-LINE
              AFTER ADVANCING TO-TOP-OF-PAGE
        MOVE SPACES TO REPORT-RECORD
        WRITE REPORT-RECORD
              AFTER ADVANCING 2 LINES
        MOVE 4 TO LINE-NUMBER.
    WRITE REPORT-RECORD FROM DETAIL-LINE
          AFTER ADVANCING 1 LINE.
************************ END OF PROGRAM ************************
```

FIGURE 9.4 A program to produce one-level control totals for a sales accounting system.

Some readers may not have noticed that in Figure 9.4 there is no period after the **ADD** statement in paragraph **C010-PROCESS-ACCOUNT-RECORD**. Since neither the **ADD** nor the **READ** is subordinate to a conditional statement, they were simply carried out in order. With only one period at the end of the paragraph, this became a one-sentence paragraph with two statements in it, instead of a two-sentence paragraph, each with one statement. Under these conditions, the missing period is completely legal and, in fact, causes no trouble.

We do not recommend taking advantage of this flexibility, however. It is better to learn good habits and stick with them. The omission has been to demonstrate—to some readers at least—how difficult it can be to "see" an omission that, when it is later pointed out, is perfectly obvious. Here the omission triggered no diagnostic messages and caused no trouble. The problem is that things like this will sometimes trigger no diagnostic messages but will cause a great deal of trouble.

9.5 THE IDENTIFICATION DIVISION

This program contains several new features, beginning with a full-scale Identification Division, the only one that appears in the book. The Identification Division is by far the simplest of the four divisions of a **COBOL** program. We shall be able to cover its one required entry and the various optional entries rather briefly.

The Identification Division is considered to be organized into paragraphs with paragraph names. **PROGRAM-ID**, for example, is a paragraph name. The balance of a paragraph is supposed to be written according to the rules for the formation of sentences and paragraphs that apply elsewhere in a **COBOL** program. However, most compilers will accept almost anything that is written within a paragraph in the Identification Division as a comment entry. That means that since the compiler takes no meaning from it, anything at all may be written there.

A few simple rules cover the syntax of the Identification Division.

1. *The* **PROGRAM-ID** *entry must be present.* The entry in this paragraph becomes the name by which the compiler and other components of the operating system refer to the program. If the entry contains more characters than the operating system allows for a program name, the computer will ignore the balance. If the entry contains characters that the operating system does not allow in a program name (such as a dash), the compiler will either give you an error message or automatically change the characters to acceptable ones. If this sounds at all complex, it is only because there is a certain degree of variability from one compiler to the next. The rules for your system will be very simple, and if you have been writing **COBOL** programs for the exercises, you probably know them by now anyway.
2. All other entries in the Identification Division are optional. If present, however, they must be written in the order shown in this program. The paragraph names must be spelled correctly.
3. If the Date-Compiled entry is present, it is normal to leave the paragraph empty because the compiler will replace any written comments with the date on which the compilation was done in any case.

We see in this entry that the compiler has inserted the compilation date on the same line as the paragraph name. Recall from Chapter 1 that the first sentence of any paragraph in a **COBOL** program is permitted to begin on the same line as a paragraph name, but that in the interest of readability and maintainability we never exercise that option in this book.

It is common for any installation to have simple rules as to what should be written in the Identification Division. Besides the required program identification, it is usual to include the author's name and the date compiled. The latter is useful when, as frequently happens, there are multiple versions of a program in existence and it becomes important to know whether you have the latest one.

Although all entries shown in the program are supported by **COBOL-85**, the **COBOL-85** standard has specified that all paragraphs in the Identification Division *except* the **PROGRAM-ID** paragraph will be deleted whenever the *next* standard is issued. Although this may not be for several years, **COBOL** programs frequently have a lifetime of well over a decade, so it is probably a good idea to start using alternatives to these "comment" paragraphs now.

9.6 COMMENTS

The alternative to using the optional entries in the Identification Division is demonstrated in the four lines following the Security paragraph. These lines are *comment lines.* As we mentioned in Chapter 1, a comment line is a line beginning with an asterisk in column 7. Comments are ignored by the compiler and may be placed anywhere in the program that you wish to include a note to the reader. If you place a slash ("/") in column 7, the line is still treated as a comment, but the printer will skip to the top of a new page before printing that line when the compiler prints a listing of the program.

It is common to place a comment at the end of the Identification Division to give a brief statement of what the program is to do. Comments are frequently used in the Procedure Division to explain a particularly tricky piece of code, or in the Data Division to document the use of data fields. Although many programs can benefit from the use of thoughtfully placed comments, we recommend sparing use of them since a well-written program ought to be largely self-documenting; too many comments can hide the actual code.

9.7   THE CONTROL OF LINE SPACING

The next new feature of **COBOL** demonstrated by this program involves several different parts of the program. In the programs up to this point we have taken no special measures to control the vertical spacing of lines on printed output. The result has been to get an automatic single spacing of all lines, with no attention paid to where one page stops and the next one begins.

Often this is not adequate. Sometimes we wish to guarantee that a line of column headings will be printed at the top of a new page; other times we may wish to double or triple space; on rare occasions we may wish to suppress spacing and print two lines in the same position. **COBOL** makes provision for all of these operations in a fairly simple way that we now investigate.

9.8   THE COMPLETE WRITE STATEMENT

Two types of options are available in using the **WRITE** statement. We have already seen how to utilize the **WRITE FROM** capability and now we look into the **ADVANCING** feature. Here is the complete general format of the **WRITE** verb as it is used for the kind of files we know about thus far:

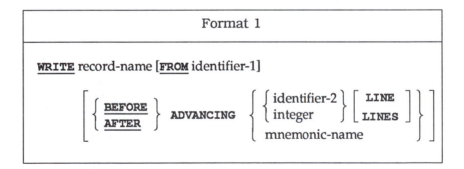

We see that it is possible to specify that the printing of a line take place either before or after actions having to do with the vertical positioning of the paper and, therefore, the printing. We might say, for instance,

`WRITE OUTPUT-RECORD AFTER ADVANCING 2 LINES.`

This would mean to double-space before printing the line specified by **OUTPUT-RECORD**. We might also say

`WRITE MESSAGE-LINE AFTER ADVANCING NUMBER-OF-LINES LINES.`

This would mean to space as many lines as the current value of the item named **NUMBER-OF-LINES**.

The number of lines is allowed to be *zero*. When this is done, the printer is not advanced at all and the line prints in the same position as the previous line. The facility may be used to print the same line twice and gain a bold-faced effect, or it may be used to obtain underlining.

A basic rule of **COBOL** states that if *any* of the **WRITE** statements for a file employ the **ADVANCING** option, then *all* **WRITE** statements for that file must have it. This means that if we use the option to get spacing to the top of the page or for any other purpose, then we must also use it when we want normal single-spacing. This requires us to write things like

```
WRITE OUTPUT-RECORD AFTER ADVANCING 1 LINE.
```

A word of caution is in order at this point. Although **COBOL** allows you to use both **BEFORE ADVANCING** and **AFTER ADVANCING** for the same file (that is, sometimes write one and sometimes the other), it is generally not advisable to do so. The program will work, but the results of this type of mixing are not always what you might expect. If you must mix the two options on the same file, do so with care.

The option mnemonic-name refers to names that we may apply to certain hardware functions that are built into the mechanisms that control spacing in printers. The primary example is moving the paper so that the next line will print at the top of a new page. All computer printers provide this feature, but the exact details of how it is specified vary from one machine to the next.

The specification of aspects of a program that depend on the nature of the equipment is precisely the function of the Environment Division. This is not the time for a complete study of that subject, even though it is not very extensive, but we do need to pause long enough to learn how to get spacing to the top of a new page.

9.9 THE CONFIGURATION SECTION OF THE ENVIRONMENT DIVISION

All the programs that we have studied thus far have contained only an Input-Output Section in the Environment Division. Within that, there has been the File-Control paragraph with **SELECT** clauses. Now we add a Configuration Section, which must be at the beginning of the division, and within it a paragraph named **SPECIAL-NAMES**. The details of what is written in this paragraph will differ from one machine to the next. On the IBM computer used to test the programs in this book, we insert here a statement of the form

```
C01 IS mnemonic-name
```

The mnemonic-name here is thus defined as specifying a skip to the top of a new page if written in an **ADVANCING** phrase. The **C01** specifies the appropriate printer action; this code would be different for other computers. To make this operation truly mnemonic ("aiding the memory"), we shall ordinarily use the mnemonic-name **TO-TOP-OF-PAGE** so that our **WRITE** statements for this purpose will have the form

```
WRITE OUTPUT-RECORD AFTER ADVANCING TO-TOP-OF-PAGE.
```

9.10 THE CARRIAGE CONTROL CHARACTER

With a number of **COBOL** compilers (IBM in particular), when the **ADVANCING** option is used it is necessary to provide space for one character at the beginning of each record to be printed. This is called the *carriage control character*, because it controls the part of a mainframe printer (the carriage) that advances the paper. We are not required to place anything in this character position; that is done as a consequence of whatever we write in the **ADVANCING** phrase. Indeed, if we do place anything in the carriage control character, it is overwritten by the action of the **ADVANCING** phrase. The character that is placed there by the object program is not printed but is, instead, used to control the line spacing on the printer.

There are three points about which you should be very careful. First, the carriage control character is not a standard **COBOL** feature and is only used on some compilers. If you are using a computer that does not require a carriage control character, do not leave space for one. Second, if you are using a computer that requires a carriage control character, the **ADVANCING** phrase will *always* use the first character of the output record for the carriage control character. If you don't allow space for this character, then the first character of your output data will be overwritten. Finally, whatever computer you are using, if you don't use the **ADVANCING** option on the **WRITE** statements for a file, then don't leave space for a carriage control character. It is only used by the **ADVANCING** phrase, which is why we have not needed it until now.

All of the variations of the **ADVANCING** feature we shall ordinarily need are illustrated in our program. When a heading is to be written, the heading line employs the form **AFTER ADVANCING TO-TOP-OF-PAGE**. To get two blank lines between the heading line and the first detail line we place spaces in the output record and then write that blank line with the **AFTER ADVANCING 2 LINES** option. Finally, detail lines are written with the **AFTER ADVANCING 1 LINE** form.

9.11 PRINTING HEADINGS

The need to print headings in a report is a very common one, and the code used in Figure 9.4 is typical. The problem we have to deal with is simple. Because we only want a certain number of lines on a page (55 in this example), we count the lines each time an output line is written. When this count exceeds our limit we skip to a new page, print the heading, print the detail line, and reset the line counter. While we could update the line counter and test for the end of the page every place in the program that we write an output record, this would add quite a bit to the size of the program and would be prone to error. It is much simpler to have a single paragraph that does all the work, then perform this paragraph whenever we want to print a line. Notice, however, that **X010-LINE-OUT** can write records only from **DETAIL-LINE**. If, as in the payroll program, we had to write several different records to the report, it would be necessary to move the record to **DETAIL-LINE** before performing **X010-LINE-OUT**.

Notice that **X010-LINE-OUT** has an **X** prefix instead of **C** or **D**. This is because the paragraph is not part of the main structure of the program. Since it may be performed from any level of the hierarchy to accomplish the task of printing a line of output, it is considered to be a utility paragraph and is given a prefix code outside the normal hierarchical sequence.

9.12 DESIGN OF THE THREE-LEVEL VERSION

The full problem that we set out to solve involves three levels of control totals. What is called the major level is a summary by sales region. Within each region there are several salespeople; salesperson is called the *intermediate* level; finally, each salesperson has several accounts and this is called the minor level. To summarize each level, input records for this version must contain the region number, the salesperson number, the account number, and the dollar amount of the sale.

The sales records are required to be in sequence (after a preliminary sort) on all three control fields. Thus all the records must be in ascending sequence on region number, the major control. Within any one region, all the records in that group must be in sequence on salesperson number, the intermediate control. For any one salesperson, all the records in that group must be in sequence on account number, the minor control. The records can be put into order on three control fields this way with just one sort, as we shall learn in Chapter 17.

The logic of the three-level program we must now develop, as shown in Figure 9.5, will be a bit more complex than that of the one-level program we studied at the start of this chapter. Somehow, the program must handle each level of control break properly. If there has been a break on the minor control, for example, it must produce a minor total but not a major or intermediate one. If there has been a break on the intermediate control, it must produce minor and intermediate totals but not a major one. Finally, if there has been a break on the major control, it must produce all three totals.

Much of the logic of this version of the program is the same as or very similar to that for the one-level version. This similarity, of course, is the reason it is worthwhile approaching the full job in two steps as we have done.

Notice that the bottom three levels of the chart are almost identical. Module names are slightly different, and the lowest level contains an extra module, but the similarities in structure are very strong. Basically, this structure states that to produce the sales report, we must process all regions within the company, then print the final total; to process a region, we must process all sellers within the region, then print the region total; to process a seller, we must process all accounts for the seller, then print a seller total; and to process an account, we process all sales records for that account, then print the account total.

What does not show up on the hierarchy chart is how we know when we have finished processing a group. In the one-level case this was easy; if the account number changed, we were starting a new group. In the three-level case things are a bit more tricky. For example, suppose a salesperson moved from one region to another during the month. Then the seller number for two consecutive records is the same, but the region numbers are different. This means that we have finished both the seller group and the region group. The technique for dealing with this problem is to realize that a control break for a level occurs not only when the group number for that level changes, but also if the group number for any higher level changes.

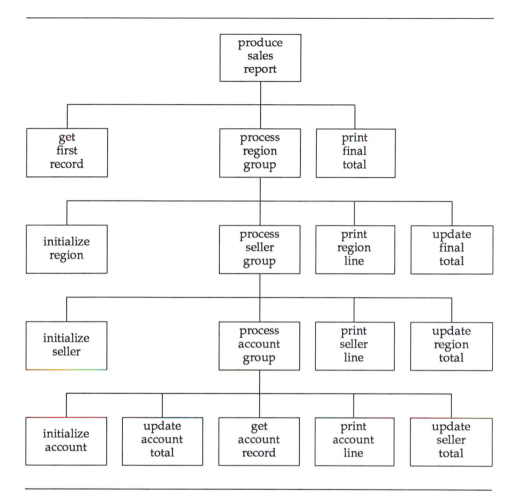

FIGURE 9.5 Hierarchy chart for a three-level control break program.

The pseudocode for this program is shown in Figure 9.6.

Again observe the similarities between the module specifications. Except for the control variable involved, the PROCESS specifications are all essentially the same, as are the INITIALIZE specifications. Using these specifications as a basis, we can easily produce the program shown in Figure 9.7.

```
PRODUCE SALES REPORT:
open files
set final-total to zero
set more-data-flag to 'Y'
get account record; at end set more-data-flag to 'N'
PERFORM-UNTIL no-more-data
    process region group
ENDPERFORM
print final-total
close files
```

PROCESS REGION GROUP:
initialize region group
PERFORM-UNTIL
      current region number is not equal to previous region number
         or
      no-more-data
    process seller group
ENDPERFORM
print region line
update final-total

PROCESS SELLER GROUP:
initialize seller group
PERFORM-UNTIL
      current seller number is not equal to previous seller number
         or
      current region number is not equal to previous region number
         or
      no-more-data
    process account group
ENDPERFORM
print seller line
update region-total

PROCESS ACCOUNT GROUP:
initialize account group
PERFORM-UNTIL
      current account number is not equal to previous account number
         or
      current seller number is not equal to previous seller number
         or
      current region number is not equal to previous region number
         or
      no-more-data
    update account total
    get account record; at end set more-data-flag to 'N'
ENDPERFORM
print account line
update seller-total

INITIALIZE REGION GROUP:
set region-total to zero
set previous region number to region number of current record

INITIALIZE SELLER GROUP:
set seller-total to zero
set previous seller number to seller number of current record

INITIALIZE ACCOUNT GROUP:
set account-total to zero
set previous account number to account number of current record

---

FIGURE 9.6 Basic pseudocode of the logic for a three-level control break.

```
IDENTIFICATION DIVISION.
PROGRAM-ID.
    THREELVL.
AUTHOR.
    D. GOLDEN.
DATE-WRITTEN.
    MARCH 6, 1987.
*
*    THIS PROGRAM PRODUCES A SIMPLE THREE-LEVEL SUMMARY REPORT FOR
*    A SALES ACCOUNTING SYSTEM
*

ENVIRONMENT DIVISION.
CONFIGURATION SECTION.
SPECIAL-NAMES.
    C01 IS TO-TOP-OF-PAGE.
INPUT-OUTPUT SECTION.
FILE-CONTROL.
    SELECT ACCOUNT-FILE         ASSIGN TO S-ACCOUNT.
    SELECT REPORT-FILE          ASSIGN TO S-REPORT.

DATA DIVISION.
FILE SECTION.

FD  ACCOUNT-FILE
    LABEL RECORDS ARE OMITTED.
01  ACCOUNT-RECORD.
    05  REGION-NUMBER           PIC X(5).
    05  SELLER-NUMBER           PIC X(5).
    05  ACCOUNT-NUMBER          PIC X(5).
    05  SALE-AMOUNT             PIC 9(5)V99.
    05  FILLER                  PIC X(58).

FD  REPORT-FILE
    LABEL RECORDS ARE OMITTED.
01  REPORT-RECORD               PIC X(133).

WORKING-STORAGE SECTION.

77  LINE-NUMBER                 PIC S99.
77  MORE-DATA-FLAG              PIC X.
    88  NO-MORE-DATA                            VALUE 'N'.
77  PAGE-NUMBER                 PIC S999.
77  PREVIOUS-ACCOUNT-NUMBER     PIC X(5).
77  PREVIOUS-REGION-NUMBER      PIC X(5).
77  PREVIOUS-SELLER-NUMBER      PIC X(5).

01  DETAIL-LINE.
    05  CARRIAGE-CONTROL        PIC X.
    05  REGION-NUMBER-OUT       PIC Z(4)9.
    05  REGION-TOTAL-OUT        PIC BBB$$$$,$$9.99.
    05  SELLER-NUMBER-OUT       PIC B(5)Z(4)9.
    05  SELLER-TOTAL-OUT        PIC BBB$$$$,$$9.99.
    05  ACCOUNT-NUMBER-OUT      PIC B(5)Z(4)9.
    05  ACCOUNT-TOTAL-OUT       PIC BBB$$$$,$$9.99.
    05  FINAL-TOTAL-OUT         PIC B(8)$$$$,$$9.99.
```

```
01   HEADING-LINE.
     05   CARRIAGE-CONTROL         PIC X.
     05   FILLER                   PIC X(40)
          VALUE 'REGION       TOTAL      SALESPERSON     TOTAL'.
     05   FILLER                   PIC X(46)
          VALUE '       ACCOUNT      TOTAL              FINAL TOTAL'.
     05   FILLER                   PIC X(10)
          VALUE '       PAGE'.
     05   PAGE-NUMBER-OUT          PIC Z(6)9.

01   TOTALS.
     05   ACCOUNT-TOTAL            PIC S9(6)V99.
     05   SELLER-TOTAL             PIC S9(6)V99.
     05   REGION-TOTAL             PIC S9(6)V9
     05   FINAL-TOTAL              PIC S9(6)V99.

PROCEDURE DIVISION.
A000-PREPARE-SALES-REPORT.
     OPEN  INPUT ACCOUNT-FILE
           OUTPUT REPORT-FILE.
     MOVE ZERO                     TO FINAL-TOTAL.
     MOVE 'Y'                      TO MORE-DATA-FLAG.
     MOVE 55                       TO LINE-NUMBER.
     MOVE ZERO                     TO PAGE-NUMBER.
     READ ACCOUNT-FILE
          AT END MOVE 'N' TO MORE-DATA-FLAG.
     PERFORM B010-PROCESS-REGION-GROUP
         UNTIL NO-MORE-DATA.
     MOVE SPACES TO DETAIL-LINE.
     MOVE FINAL-TOTAL TO FINAL-TOTAL-OUT.
     PERFORM X010-LINE-OUT.
     CLOSE ACCOUNT-FILE
          REPORT-FILE.
     STOP RUN.


B010-PROCESS-REGION-GROUP.
     MOVE ZERO TO REGION-TOTAL.
     MOVE REGION-NUMBER TO PREVIOUS-REGION-NUMBER.
     PERFORM C010-PROCESS-SELLER-GROUP UNTIL
          REGION-NUMBER IS NOT EQUAL TO PREVIOUS-REGION-NUMBER
         OR NO-MORE-DATA.
     MOVE SPACES TO DETAIL-LINE.
     MOVE PREVIOUS-REGION-NUMBER TO REGION-NUMBER-OUT.
     MOVE REGION-TOTAL TO REGION-TOTAL-OUT.
     PERFORM X010-LINE-OUT.
     ADD REGION-TOTAL TO FINAL-TOTAL.


C010-PROCESS-SELLER-GROUP.
     MOVE ZERO TO SELLER-TOTAL.
     MOVE SELLER-NUMBER TO PREVIOUS-SELLER-NUMBER.
     PERFORM D010-PROCESS-ACCOUNT-GROUP UNTIL
          SELLER-NUMBER IS NOT EQUAL TO PREVIOUS-SELLER-NUMBER
         OR REGION-NUMBER IS NOT EQUAL TO PREVIOUS-REGION-NUMBER
         OR NO-MORE-DATA.
     MOVE SPACES TO DETAIL-LINE.
     MOVE PREVIOUS-SELLER-NUMBER TO SELLER-NUMBER-OUT.
     MOVE SELLER-TOTAL TO SELLER-TOTAL-OUT.
     PERFORM X010-LINE-OUT.
     ADD SELLER-TOTAL TO REGION-TOTAL.
```

```
D010-PROCESS-ACCOUNT-GROUP.
    MOVE ZERO TO ACCOUNT-TOTAL.
    MOVE ACCOUNT-NUMBER TO PREVIOUS-ACCOUNT-NUMBER.
    PERFORM E010-PROCESS-ACCOUNT-RECORD UNTIL
            ACCOUNT-NUMBER IS NOT EQUAL TO PREVIOUS-ACCOUNT-NUMBER
        OR SELLER-NUMBER IS NOT EQUAL TO PREVIOUS-SELLER-NUMBER
        OR REGION-NUMBER IS NOT EQUAL TO PREVIOUS-REGION-NUMBER
        OR NO-MORE-DATA.
    MOVE SPACES TO DETAIL-LINE.
    MOVE PREVIOUS-ACCOUNT-NUMBER TO ACCOUNT-NUMBER-OUT.
    MOVE ACCOUNT-TOTAL TO ACCOUNT-TOTAL-OUT.
    PERFORM X010-LINE-OUT.
    ADD ACCOUNT-TOTAL TO SELLER-TOTAL.


E010-PROCESS-ACCOUNT-RECORD.
    ADD SALE-AMOUNT TO ACCOUNT-TOTAL.
    READ ACCOUNT-FILE
            AT END MOVE 'N' TO MORE-DATA-FLAG.


X010-LINE-OUT.
    ADD 1 TO LINE-NUMBER.
*           SEE IF WE ARE AT THE END OF THE PAGE
*           IF SO, PRINT A NEW PAGE HEADING
    IF LINE-NUMBER IS GREATER THAN 55
        ADD 1 TO PAGE-NUMBER
        MOVE PAGE-NUMBER TO PAGE-NUMBER-OUT
        WRITE REPORT-RECORD FROM HEADING-LINE
                AFTER ADVANCING TO-TOP-OF-PAGE
        MOVE SPACES TO REPORT-RECORD
        WRITE REPORT-RECORD
                AFTER ADVANCING 2 LINES
        MOVE 4 TO LINE-NUMBER.
    WRITE REPORT-RECORD FROM DETAIL-LINE
            AFTER ADVANCING 1 LINE.


************************ END OF PROGRAM *************************
```

FIGURE 9.7   A program to produce three-level control totals.

When this program was run, it produced the output shown earlier, in Figure 9.1.

9.13   A SPECIFICATION CHANGE

Any program that is used for any length of time can be expected to change. Management may request new information; tax laws may change; new computer equipment may require partial reprogramming; long-standing errors in a program may finally surface and have to be corrected. We can't predict when, or where, or how the program will have to be changed, but we can guarantee that *most programs will require change eventually!* The work of installing such changes is called program maintenance and is a major activity in most data processing installations. In fact, it has been estimated that maintenance accounts for two-thirds or more of the typical data processing budget.

For some practice in dealing with maintenance, let us suppose that the "customer," or "user," the person or organization using the sales report, asks us to make the following changes:

1. The customer informs us that we misunderstood the desired arrangement of the printed report: the account and region totals are reversed from their desired positions.
2. The customer has decided that the final total should be printed in the same column as the region total, which is now the rightmost column. Furthermore, the final total should be identified by the words FINAL TOTAL printed to the left of the dollar amount. Finally on this point, the customer is concerned that it could occasionally happen that the final total would be the only line printed after the heading line at the top of a new page. Therefore, the final total should always be printed at the bottom of the last page even if that makes the last page run over 55 lines.
3. Another column is to be added to the report, printed between the account number and the account total, giving the number of sales in that account group.
4. If any individual sale exceeds $1000, an asterisk is to be printed after the count of transactions for that group.
5. The customer indicates that the company is considering a reorganization of the sales division that would make it possible for an account to be serviced by more than one salesperson. We have been asked if this would cause any problems in reporting the sales summary.

9.14 RESPONDING TO THE SPECIFICATION CHANGES

Some of these changes are simple, but the last one is very difficult and raises serious problems.

Reversing the position of the region and account totals is a simple matter of modifying the arrangement of the elementary items in DETAIL-LINE, and changing the heading.

Making sure that the final total prints at the bottom of the last page requires us to sidestep the logic of X010-LINE-OUT, which is a simpler solution than inserting new logic to handle the final total line separately within that routine. Rather than develop new logic, we simply put a WRITE statement in A000-PREPARE-SALES-REPORT instead of performing X010-LINE-OUT.

Counting the transactions is a matter of setting up a data item to hold the count, modifying DETAIL-LINE to provide space for it, adding a statement in E010-PROCESS-ACCOUNT-RECORD to add 1 to this total for each transaction, and inserting a statement in D010-PROCESS-ACCOUNT-GROUP to move it to its position in DETAIL-LINE.

Generating an asterisk for a large transaction means providing space for it in DETAIL-LINE, inserting an IF statement in E010-PROCESS-ACCOUNT-RECORD, and adding another IF in D010-PROCESS-ACCOUNT-GROUP.

The last thing that the customer would like to do really cannot be done, at least not without showing the figures for one account in more than one place. For instance, if sellers 1 and 2 can both service account 17, say, then there will be a total for account 17 under seller 1 and another total for account 17 under seller 2. Nowhere will there be one single number giving the total—by all salespeople—for account 17.

The best we can do for the customer in this case is to point out what the organization of the sales report will be if this change is made and suggest that, if summarizations of sales by account are really needed, it will be necessary to go through another processing stage altogether and to produce a separate document. This would require re-sorting the input file so it is in sequence on region number as the major control, account number as the intermediate, and salesperson as the minor. Now a program like this one but with slightly different logic and output will produce a report giving the total for each account and within that, the amount sold by each person who services the account.

9.15 RUNNING THE REVISED REPORT

The necessary changes were made in the program of Figure 9.7, and the revised program was run with the same data as before. The output is shown in Figure 9.8.

ACCOUNT	TOTAL	NUMBER	SALESPERSON	TOTAL	REGION	TOTAL	PAGE	1
20	$17.00	3						
24	$36.00	4						
27	$184.00	9						
			1	$237.00				
17	$26.00	11						
24	$266.90	14						
			2	$292.90				
10	$87.50	15						
16	$54.75	18						
			12	$142.25				
					1	$672.15		
40	$50.12	20						
41	$105.99	21						
			4	$156.11				
44	$1,594.14	27						
			39	$1,594.14				
					2	$1,750.25		
30	$1,180.94	31						
35	$69.26	34						
38	$157.43	36						
49	$45.00	38						
60	$1,234.56	39*						
78	$276.02	51*						
			15	$2,963.21				
					3	$2,963.21		
				FINAL TOTAL		$5,385.61		

FIGURE 9.8 The output of a modified version of the program of Figure 9.7. The modified version contains errors, and the output is not correct.

It seems to be about what we want, except that the figures for the number of transactions are wrong, and there are asterisks in some wrong places. (In fact, since we have not shown the sample data, it is conceivable that these counts could be correct, but, in fact, they are wrong. In any case, even without seeing the data, it seems unlikely that *every* account will have more records than the previous one.) We seem to be having logic trouble again. What happened? The first thing to check is to make sure that the locations for the total named **NO-OF-TRANSACTIONS** is initialized to zero. This was done, but unfortunately in the wrong place. The initialization statement had been placed in **A000-PREPARE-SALES-REPORT**. While this set the field to zero once, it was never reset to zero after printing each account total line. This is a very common type of mistake, which frequently involves data initialized by **VALUE** clauses; this is why we tend to use **VALUE** clause only for "constant" types of data items. The solution to the problem is to move the initialization statement from **A000-PREPARE-SALES-REPORT** to the start of **D010-PROCESS-ACCOUNT-GROUP**.

The problem with the extra asterisks is that once the asterisk flag was set, it was never reset to a blank. The resetting needs to be done as part of the initialization in **D010-PROCESS-ACCOUNT-GROUP**.

A final corrected program is shown in Figure 9.9; it produced the output of Figure 9.10.

```
IDENTIFICATION DIVISION.
PROGRAM-ID.
     3LEVEL2.
AUTHOR.
     D. GOLDEN.
DATE-WRITTEN.
     MARCH 6, 1987.
*
*    THIS PROGRAM PRODUCES A SIMPLE THREE-LEVEL SUMMARY REPORT FOR
*    A SALES ACCOUNTING SYSTEM
*

ENVIRONMENT DIVISION.
CONFIGURATION SECTION.
SPECIAL-NAMES.
     C01 IS TO-TOP-OF-PAGE.
INPUT-OUTPUT SECTION.
FILE-CONTROL.
     SELECT ACCOUNT-FILE          ASSIGN TO S-ACCOUNT.
     SELECT REPORT-FILE           ASSIGN TO S-REPORT.

DATA DIVISION.
FILE SECTION.

FD   ACCOUNT-FILE
     LABEL RECORDS ARE OMITTED.
01   ACCOUNT-RECORD.
     05   REGION-NUMBER           PIC X(5).
     05   SELLER-NUMBER           PIC X(5).
     05   ACCOUNT-NUMBER          PIC X(5).
     05   SALE-AMOUNT             PIC 9(5)V99.
     05   FILLER                  PIC X(58).
```

```
FD   REPORT-FILE
     LABEL RECORDS ARE OMITTED.
01   REPORT-RECORD               PIC X(133).


WORKING-STORAGE SECTION.

77   ASTERISK-FLAG               PIC X.
     88  ASTERISK-FLAG-ON                        VALUE 'Y'.
77   LINE-NUMBER                 PIC S99.
77   MORE-DATA-FLAG              PIC X.
     88  NO-MORE-DATA                            VALUE 'N'.
77   PAGE-NUMBER                 PIC S999.
77   PREVIOUS-ACCOUNT-NUMBER     PIC X(5).
77   PREVIOUS-REGION-NUMBER      PIC X(5).
77   PREVIOUS-SELLER-NUMBER      PIC X(5).


01   DETAIL-LINE.
     05  CARRIAGE-CONTROL        PIC X.
     05  ACCOUNT-NUMBER-OUT      PIC Z(4)9.
     05  ACCOUNT-TOTAL-OUT       PIC BBB$$$$,$$9.99.
     05  NO-OF-TRANSACTIONS-OUT  PIC BBZZ9.
     05  ASTERISK-OUT            PIC X.
     05  SELLER-NUMBER-OUT       PIC B(5)Z(4)9.
     05  SELLER-TOTAL-OUT        PIC BBB$$$$,$$9.99.
     05  REGION-NUMBER-OUT       PIC B(5)Z(4)9.
     05  REGION-TOTAL-OUT        PIC BBB$$$$,$$9.99.


01   FINAL-TOTAL-LINE.
     05  CARRIAGE-CONTROL        PIC X.
     05  FILLER                  PIC X(44) VALUE SPACES.
     05  FILLER                  PIC X(11) VALUE 'FINAL TOTAL'.
     05  FINAL-TOTAL-OUT         PIC B(7)$$$$,$$9.99.



01   HEADING-LINE.
     05  CARRIAGE-CONTROL        PIC X.
     05  FILLER                  PIC X(41)
         VALUE 'ACCOUNT     TOTAL     NUMBER  SALESPERSON '.
     05  FILLER                  PIC X(39)
         VALUE 'TOTAL        REGION    TOTAL      PAGE'.
     05  PAGE-NUMBER-OUT         PIC Z(6)9.

01   TOTALS.
     05  ACCOUNT-TOTAL           PIC S9(6)V99.
     05  SELLER-TOTAL            PIC S9(6)V99.
     05  REGION-TOTAL            PIC S9(6)V99.
     05  FINAL-TOTAL             PIC S9(6)V99.
     05  NO-OF-TRANSACTIONS      PIC S999.

PROCEDURE DIVISION.
A000-PREPARE-SALES-REPORT.
     OPEN  INPUT ACCOUNT-FILE
           OUTPUT REPORT-FILE.
     MOVE ZERO                   TO FINAL-TOTAL.
     MOVE 'Y'                    TO MORE-DATA-FLAG.
     MOVE 55                     TO LINE-NUMBER.
     MOVE ZERO                   TO PAGE-NUMBER.
     READ ACCOUNT-FILE
             AT END MOVE 'N' TO MORE-DATA-FLAG.
```

```
        PERFORM B010-PROCESS-REGION-GROUP
            UNTIL NO-MORE-DATA.
        MOVE FINAL-TOTAL TO FINAL-TOTAL-OUT.
        WRITE REPORT-RECORD FROM FINAL-TOTAL-LINE
                AFTER ADVANCING 3 LINES.
        CLOSE ACCOUNT-FILE
              REPORT-FILE.
        STOP RUN.


    B010-PROCESS-REGION-GROUP.
        MOVE ZERO TO REGION-TOTAL.
        MOVE REGION-NUMBER TO PREVIOUS-REGION-NUMBER.
        PERFORM C010-PROCESS-SELLER-GROUP UNTIL
                REGION-NUMBER IS NOT EQUAL TO PREVIOUS-REGION-NUMBER
            OR NO-MORE-DATA.
        MOVE SPACES TO DETAIL-LINE.
        MOVE PREVIOUS-REGION-NUMBER TO REGION-NUMBER-OUT.
        MOVE REGION-TOTAL TO REGION-TOTAL-OUT.
        PERFORM X010-LINE-OUT.
        ADD REGION-TOTAL TO FINAL-TOTAL.


    C010-PROCESS-SELLER-GROUP.
        MOVE ZERO TO SELLER-TOTAL.
        MOVE SELLER-NUMBER TO PREVIOUS-SELLER-NUMBER.
        PERFORM D010-PROCESS-ACCOUNT-GROUP UNTIL
                SELLER-NUMBER IS NOT EQUAL TO PREVIOUS-SELLER-NUMBER
            OR REGION-NUMBER IS NOT EQUAL TO PREVIOUS-REGION-NUMBER
            OR NO-MORE-DATA.
        MOVE SPACES TO DETAIL-LINE.
        MOVE PREVIOUS-SELLER-NUMBER TO SELLER-NUMBER-OUT.
        MOVE SELLER-TOTAL TO SELLER-TOTAL-OUT.
        PERFORM X010-LINE-OUT.
        ADD SELLER-TOTAL TO REGION-TOTAL.


    D010-PROCESS-ACCOUNT-GROUP.
        MOVE ZERO TO ACCOUNT-TOTAL.
        MOVE ZERO TO NO-OF-TRANSACTIONS.
        MOVE 'N' TO ASTERISK-FLAG.
        MOVE ACCOUNT-NUMBER TO PREVIOUS-ACCOUNT-NUMBER.
        PERFORM E010-PROCESS-ACCOUNT-RECORD UNTIL
                ACCOUNT-NUMBER IS NOT EQUAL TO PREVIOUS-ACCOUNT-NUMBER
            OR SELLER-NUMBER IS NOT EQUAL TO PREVIOUS-SELLER-NUMBER
            OR REGION-NUMBER IS NOT EQUAL TO PREVIOUS-REGION-NUMBER
            OR NO-MORE-DATA.
        MOVE SPACES TO DETAIL-LINE.
        MOVE PREVIOUS-ACCOUNT-NUMBER TO ACCOUNT-NUMBER-OUT.
        MOVE ACCOUNT-TOTAL TO ACCOUNT-TOTAL-OUT.
        MOVE NO-OF-TRANSACTIONS TO NO-OF-TRANSACTIONS-OUT.
        IF ASTERISK-FLAG-ON
            MOVE '*' TO ASTERISK-OUT.
        PERFORM X010-LINE-OUT.
        ADD ACCOUNT-TOTAL TO SELLER-TOTAL.


    E010-PROCESS-ACCOUNT-RECORD.
        ADD SALE-AMOUNT TO ACCOUNT-TOTAL.
        ADD 1 TO NO-OF-TRANSACTIONS.
        IF SALE-AMOUNT IS GREATER THAN 1000.00
            MOVE 'Y' TO ASTERISK-FLAG.
        READ ACCOUNT-FILE
                AT END MOVE 'N' TO MORE-DATA-FLAG.
```

```
X010-LINE-OUT.
    ADD 1 TO LINE-NUMBER.
*              SEE IF WE ARE AT THE END OF THE PAGE
*              IF SO, PRINT A NEW PAGE HEADING
    IF LINE-NUMBER IS GREATER THAN 55
        ADD 1 TO PAGE-NUMBER
        MOVE PAGE-NUMBER TO PAGE-NUMBER-OUT
        WRITE REPORT-RECORD FROM HEADING-LINE
                AFTER ADVANCING TO-TOP-OF-PAGE
        MOVE SPACES TO REPORT-RECORD
        WRITE REPORT-RECORD
                AFTER ADVANCING 2 LINES
        MOVE 4 TO LINE-NUMBER.
    WRITE REPORT-RECORD FROM DETAIL-LINE
            AFTER ADVANCING 1 LINE.
```

FIGURE 9.9 A correctly modified program for producing three-level control totals.

ACCOUNT	TOTAL	NUMBER	SALESPERSON	TOTAL	REGION	TOTAL	PAGE	1
20	$17.00	3						
24	$36.00	1						
27	$184.00	5						
			1	$237.00				
17	$26.00	2						
24	$266.90	3						
			2	$292.90				
10	$87.50	1						
16	$54.75	3						
			12	$142.25				
					1	$672.15		
40	$50.12	2						
41	$105.99	1						
			4	$156.11				
44	$1,594.14	6						
			39	$1,594.14				
					2	$1,750.25		
30	$1,180.94	4						
35	$69.26	3						
38	$157.43	2						
49	$45.00	2						
60	$1,234.56	1*						
78	$276.02	12						
			15	$2,963.21				
					3	$2,963.21		
				FINAL TOTAL		$5,385.61		

FIGURE 9.10 A three-level control total report produced by the program of Figure 9.9.

For one last word about this program, it should be obvious that we can now develop control break programs for any number of levels, from one on up. The pattern of the program is clear, and the general structure applies to any number of levels. Of course, there are many different correct ways of expressing program logic, and the structure shown in this example can be modified as necessary to fit different circumstances.

REVIEW QUESTIONS

1. What would the one-level program produce from the following input (in the sequence given)?

Account Number	Amount
15	$1
15	2
17	3
17	2
17	6
16	5
17	3
16	2
19	7
19	8
19	4

2. Suppose the input file for the one-level program were in descending sequence on account number. What would the program do? Would there be any simple way to present the results with the account numbers in ascending sequence?

3. Suppose the client for the program of this chapter were to request that the region numbers and total for the region be printed on a line *before* the salesperson and account totals for the region, and similarly for the salesperson total. How would you respond?

4. Is the following pseudocode logically equivalent to that of Figure 9.3? That is, would a program based on it produce the same results as does the program of Figure 9.4?

```
PRODUCE-SALES-REPORT:
    open files
    get account record; at end set more-data-flag to 'N'
    IF more data remains THEN
        set final total to zero
        set account total to zero
        move current account number to previous account number
        PERFORM-UNTIL no more data
            IF current and previous account numbers are different THEN
                perform account total processing
            ENDIF
            add sale amount to account total, final total
            get account record; at end set more-data-flag to 'N'
        ENDPERFORM
        perform account total processing
        set up final total line
```

```
        print final total line
    ENDIF
    close files

ACCOUNT-TOTAL-PROCESSING:
    set up account total line
    print account total line
    move current account number to previous account number
    move zero to account total
```

5. What would be the result of executing the following program?

```
IDENTIFICATION DIVISION.
PROGRAM-ID.
    CH9RQ05.

ENVIRONMENT DIVISION.
CONFIGURATION SECTION.
SPECIAL-NAMES.
    C01 IS TO-TOP-OF-PAGE.
INPUT-OUTPUT SECTION.
FILE-CONTROL.
    SELECT OUTPUT-FILE ASSIGN TO S-PRINTER.

DATA DIVISION.
FILE SECTION.
FD  OUTPUT-FILE
    LABEL RECORDS ARE OMITTED.
01  PRINT-LINE.
    05  CARRIAGE-CONTROL      PIC X.
    05  BODY                  PIC X(50).

WORKING-STORAGE SECTION.
01  HEADING-LINE              PIC X(14)
    VALUE 'REPORT HEADING'.

PROCEDURE DIVISION.
ONLY-PARAGRAPH.
    OPEN OUTPUT OUTPUT-FILE.

    WRITE PRINT-LINE FROM HEADING-LINE
        AFTER ADVANCING TO-TOP-OF-PAGE.

    CLOSE OUTPUT-FILE.
    STOP RUN.
```

ANSWERS

1. ACCOUNT NUMBER	AMOUNT	FINAL TOTAL
15	$ 3	
17	11	
16	5	
17	3	
16	2	
19	19	
	43	

There would be no error indication, since the program does not check for the sequence of the input. See Exercise 4.

2. The program would produce the same kind of report as shown in the chapter, but with the account total in descending sequence on account number. There would be no simple way to reverse the sequence, since it would not be possible to begin printing the report until the last account group had been computed. One way or another, the results would have to be stored, probably on a temporary file, and then the file would have to be sorted into ascending sequence before printing.

3. You would have to explain that this is impossible without considerable extra effort, since the total for a region is not known until all the salesperson totals within the region have been computed, and the total for a salesperson is not known until all that person's accounts have been added. To do what was asked would require some way to save the subordinate totals in temporary storage. This can be done (although we haven't yet learned the techniques), but it would be costly in time.

4. Yes, with the small difference that if the input file is empty, this version would print no output while the text version would print a final total of zero. This shows that there is seldom just one good way to design a program.

5. The result would be

    EPORT HEADING

    The problem is that when the **ADVANCING** phrase is used on the **WRITE** statement, the first position of the output line is preempted for the carriage control character. The way the program is written, the first **R** in **REPORT** was moved into the carriage control character and then lost.

    One solution is to provide a blank space at the start of the heading for the carriage control character; another is to write

    ```
    MOVE HEADING-LINE TO BODY.
    WRITE PRINT-LINE AFTER ADVANCING TO-TOP-OF-PAGE.
    ```

EXERCISES

*1. Modify Exercise 7 of Chapter 7 so that no more than 45 detail lines are written on a page.

*2. Modify the program of Figure 9.7 so that when an account total is printed, the region and seller number of the account are also printed, and when a salesperson total is printed, the region number of the salesperson is also printed.

3. Modify the program of Figure 9.7 so that it prints, to the left of the final total on the bottom line, the sum of the sales amounts for sales over $1000.00, together with the percentage of the total sales that these large sales represent.

---

* Answers to starred exercises will be found in Appendix IV at the end of the book.

*4. Modify the one-level program of Figure 9.4 to check for a sequence error, which consists of any instance in which the account number of a record is less than that of the previous record. If such a sequence error is found, the program should write a brief error message and stop.

5. Modify the three-level program of Figure 9.7 so that it performs a sequence check similar to that described in the previous exercise. *Hint*: Make a group item of region number, seller number, and account number, so that the sequence check can be made with just one IF. Will this falsely signal an error when the account number is less than the previous account number, but the region number is larger than the previous region number?

6. (This exercise is suitable for a small project.)
The Commercial Real Estate Corporation (CREC) manages office buildings in several cities. Rental data for each office is maintained in records with the following format:

Columns 1-5	building number
Columns 6-9	office number
Columns 10-15	office size in square feet
Columns 16-21	annual rent per square foot
Columns 22-27	monthly surcharges
Columns 28	occupied code (Y or N)
Columns 29-30	rental agent number

Monthly rent for an office is computed as 1/12 the annual rent times the office size, plus monthly surcharges if any.

Prepare a report showing rental income for the current month for all properties managed by CREC. The report is to have the following format:

Columns 3-4	rental agent number
Columns 8-20	total rent for all buildings managed by this agent
Columns 25-29	building number
Columns 33-45	total rent for this building
Columns 49-52	office number
Columns 56-65	monthly rent for this office

The report is to show rent for occupied offices only (those with a value of Y for the occupied code), and should show total rental for each building, for each rental agent, and for the company. Any field containing a dollar amount should begin with a dollar sign, should have leading zeros suppressed, and should have commas in appropriate places. There should be a heading at the top of each page and there should be no more than 50 detail lines per page.

There may be errors in the data and invalid records should be detected and rejected. To be valid, all fields in a record must be numeric, except for the "occupied code" field that must contain either Y or N. If you detect an invalid record, print the record on an error report with an appropriate error message. You may choose any format for the error report you wish, but it should be neat and easily understood by a clerk who is reading the report. In other words, simply printing the record image with a message such as "ERROR FOUND" is not acceptable. Finally, you must assume that a record may contain more than one error; all errors in a record should be detected and reported.

A sample of the monthly rental report is shown below:

```
              MONTHLY RENTAL REPORT                  PAGE 001

   AGENT       TOTAL      BUILDING       TOTAL      OFFICE      TOTAL


                                                     1001     $10,000.00
                                                     2500     $    250.00
                             10     $  10,250.00

                                                     100     $ 2,500.00
                                                     200     $ 2,500.00
                                                     300     $25,000.00
                           12345     $  30,000.00
     10    $   40,250.00

                                                     8888     $99,999.99
                                                     9999     $99,999.99
                           99999     $ 199,999.98
     99    $  199,999.98

   TOTAL   $  240,249.98
```

CHAPTER 10

DATA REPRESENTATION AND RELATED TOPICS

10.1 INTRODUCTION

In this chapter we shall discuss a number of matters related to the representation of information within a computer: the various forms in which data may be stored, choices available in the assignment of items to computer storage, and how to give the same area of computer storage different names with possibly different attributes.

10.2 DATA REPRESENTATION*

The most basic unit of information in any computer is the *bit*, which is an abbreviation for *binary digit*. "Binary" means "having two values," and a binary digit is one that has only the values zero and one. A binary number is one in which the digits are allowed to take on only the values zero and one, and where the digits are multiplied by successive powers of 2, rather than powers of 10 as in decimal. Thus, where the decimal number 2073 means

$$
\begin{aligned}
2 \times 1000 &= 2000 \\
+ 0 \times 100 &= 0 \\
+ 7 \times 10 &= 70 \\
+ 3 \times 1 &= 3
\end{aligned}
$$

the binary number 1101 means

$$
\begin{aligned}
1 \times 8 &= 8 \\
+ 1 \times 4 &= 4 \\
+ 0 \times 2 &= 0 \\
+ 1 \times 1 &= 1
\end{aligned}
$$

---

* The way data is represented varies greatly from one computer to another. The representation here is based on IBM mainframes such as the IBM 370 and the IBM 30XX series. These computers, and those compatible with them, comprise the largest single group of computers on which COBOL is commonly used. A textbook cannot be an encyclopedia. Readers who are serious about programming will need to have reference materials for the computer they use in any event; with the introduction given here, it will not be difficult to get the necessary information from the manual.

Thus the binary number 1101 is the equivalent of the decimal number 13 or, as we might write, $1101_2 = 13_{10}$.

When large binary numbers must be written, it is more convenient to combine the bits into groups of four and write the hexadecimal (base 16) equivalent of each group, according to the following table:

Binary Number	Decimal Equivalent	Hexadecimal Equivalent
0001	1	1
0010	2	2
0011	3	3
0100	4	4
0101	5	5
0110	6	6
0111	7	7
1000	8	8
1001	9	9
1010	10	A
1011	11	B
1100	12	C
1101	13	D
1110	14	E
1111	15	F

For example, the binary number 0010 0010 1101 1000 0001 0000 1111 1011 could be written in hexadecimal as 22D810FB, which is considerably simpler and takes less space.

10.3   BYTES

In the IBM mainframe computers, bits are combined into groups of eight bits called *bytes*. (Each byte has a *parity bit* associated with it for checking the accuracy of machine functioning, but the parity bit is not accessible to the programmer and will not be considered further.)

A computer capable of compiling a **COBOL** program, even a microcomputer, generally has at least 131,000 bytes of internal storage; at the time of this writing microcomputers frequently have about 655,000 bytes of internal storage, and mainframe computers can offer users what appears to the program to be over 16,000,000 bytes of internal storage.* (Mainframe computers frequently use a technique called *virtual memory*, which makes other storage devices appear to be part of internal memory; however, the details of virtual memory are irrelevant to our discussion.) Internal storage, which is also called RAM, for *random access memory*, is most commonly made from integrated circuits. A byte of information can be retrieved from internal storage in a fraction of one microsecond (millionth of a second) in any computer, and in a few nanoseconds (billionths of a second) in many computers.

---

* Computer memory is frequently measured in terms of kilobytes, or *K bytes*, which is actually 1024 bytes. Thus, 128K bytes of memory is 131,072 bytes in decimal, 640K bytes is 655,360, and so on.

Internal storage is distinguished from auxiliary storage, which consists of devices like magnetic disks and tapes, where access times are no faster than milliseconds (thousandths of a second) and can sometimes be measured in seconds or even minutes. We shall consider these latter devices in Chapter 14.

Each byte of internal storage has associated with it an *address*, by which it is identified. Operations on data items are specified, in the object program, in terms of the contents of addressed locations in internal storage. Where we write

    ADD 1 TO RECORD-COUNT

the object program might have an instruction to obtain the contents of location 12536, which the computer had assigned as the location where `RECORD-COUNT` is to be stored for the particular program, add to this the contents of 13044, where the computer has stored the value 1, and place the sum back in 12536.

Bytes may be handled separately or grouped into *fields*. A *halfword* is two consecutive bytes; a *word* is four consecutive bytes; a double word is a field consisting of two words. Because of the way in which some of the earlier IBM mainframe computers operated, IBM compilers still generally require that the address of a halfword be a multiple of two, that the address of a word be a multiple of four, and that the address of a double word be a multiple of eight.

Fields are not required to consist of just these groupings. A field can be of any size from one byte up to some maximum depending on the machine; for IBM mainframes, the limit is 32,767 bytes. When a field consists of more than one byte, the address of the leftmost byte is the address of the entire field.

10.4 FORMS OF DATA REPRESENTATION IN IBM MAINFRAME COMPUTERS

The *byte* is a basic building block. Alone or in combinations, it can hold information in any of four different forms, three of which are of primary importance in `COBOL`. The four forms, together with the `COBOL` terms used to describe them, are:

IBM Form	COBOL Term
Character or Zoned decimal	`DISPLAY`
Binary	`COMPUTATIONAL`
Floating point	`COMPUTATIONAL-1` and `COMPUTATIONAL-2`
Packed decimal	`COMPUTATIONAL-3`

`DISPLAY`, `COMPUTATIONAL`, and `COMPUTATIONAL-3` are much more important in `COBOL` than the others.

10.5 DISPLAY USAGE

The simplest form of representation of information is for one byte to contain one character. Since this is the form in which information must appear when it is to be printed, this is called—in `COBOL`—`DISPLAY` usage. Because of the way numeric digits are represented, which we shall explore briefly, when this form contains numbers it is called—in IBM terminology—*zoned decimal*. When each byte contains an alphanumeric character, whether digit or not, it is simply called a character field in IBM terms.

For alphanumeric information this is the only way that data can be represented; for numeric data, there are other choices, which we discuss below. Each alphanumeric character is assigned an eight-bit code. Figure 10.1 shows some of the most commonly used characters and their EBCDIC and ASCII (see Section 5.8) representations.

Observe that the characters in Figure 10.1 are listed in ascending sequence on the EBCDIC binary representations, which is also their ascending sequence when characters are compared in a relation condition. In other words, the characters in Figure 10.1 are shown in collating sequence, which in fact is determined by the binary representation of the characters. (If your computer uses ASCII characters, the collating sequence should be reordered according to the ASCII representation.)

All 256 of the possible eight-bit combinations can be stored in the computer. Not all 256 eight-bit combinations have printable graphic symbols associated with them, however; if it is necessary to get such information out of the computer, it has to be converted to some other form (such as hexadecimal digits) that is printable. We shall have no occasion to deal with such information in this book, other than to note that if an attempt is made to print a byte containing a nonprinting combination, a blank is usually produced.

The internal representation of numeric data (**PIC 9**) in **DISPLAY** format places one digit in each byte. The digit is placed in the rightmost four bits, which are called the *numeric bits*. The leftmost four bits, called the *zone bits*, hold bit combinations of no interest to us right now except that the zone bits of the rightmost byte contain the sign of the entire number. The origin of the term *zoned decimal* is now clear. Here is how the seven bytes of +4135729 would appear in zoned decimal format:

1111 0100	1111 0001	1111 0011	1111 0101	1111 0111	1111 0010	1100 1001
4	1	3	5	7	2	+ 9

We see that the zone bits are 1111 on all except the last byte, where 1100 represents a plus sign in this format. A minus sign is represented by 1101. The numeric bits of the seven bytes are the binary representations of these digits.

Notice that the full byte—zone bits plus numeric bits—forms the EBCDIC representation of each digit (see Figure 10.1), except for the rightmost byte. This byte, which contains the sign of the number in the zone bits, forms the EBCDIC representation of a character other than the digit stored in the byte; in the example above, the rightmost byte contains the representation of the letter I instead of the digit 9. In fact, the rightmost byte of a numeric field will always contain the representation of some nonnumeric character, providing the **PICTURE** character string of the field contains the sign character (S). If the field is unsigned, then all bytes will contain the EBCDIC representation of the digits contained in them. This characteristic of zoned decimal data affects the way in which numeric fields are printed by the **DISPLAY** and **EXHIBIT** statements. If you have printed any signed numeric data using **DISPLAY** or **EXHIBIT**, you will have noticed that the rightmost character printed is not numeric. To deter-

Graphic symbol	EBCDIC Binary code	ASCII Binary code
space	0100 0000	0010 0000
¢	0100 1010	1001 1011
.	0100 1011	0010 1110
<	0100 1100	0011 1100
(	0100 1101	0010 1000
+	0100 1110	0010 1011
&	0101 0000	0010 0110
$	0101 1011	0010 0100
*	0101 1100	0010 1010
)	0101 1101	0010 1001
;	0101 1110	0011 1011
− (minus)	0110 0000	0010 1101
, (comma)	0110 1011	0010 1100
>	0110 1110	0011 1110
' (quote)	0111 1101	0010 0111
=	0111 1110	0011 1101
A	1100 0001	0100 0001
B	1100 0010	0100 0010
C	1100 0011	0100 0011
D	1100 0100	0100 0100
E	1100 0101	0100 0101
F	1100 0110	0100 0110
G	1100 0111	0100 0111
H	1100 1000	0100 1000
I	1100 1001	0100 1001
J	1101 0001	0100 1010
K	1101 0010	0100 1011
L	1101 0011	0100 1100
M	1101 0100	0100 1101
N	1101 0101	0100 1110
O	1101 0110	0100 1111
P	1101 0111	0101 0000
Q	1101 1000	0101 0001
R	1101 1001	0101 0010
S	1110 0010	0101 0011
T	1110 0011	0101 0100
U	1110 0100	0101 0101
V	1110 0101	0101 0110
W	1110 0110	0101 0111
X	1110 0111	0101 1000
Y	1110 1000	0101 1001
Z	1110 1001	0101 1010
0	1111 0000	0011 0000
1	1111 0001	0011 0001
2	1111 0010	0011 0010
3	1111 0011	0011 0011
4	1111 0100	0011 0100
5	1111 0101	0011 0101
6	1111 0110	0011 0110
7	1111 0111	0011 0111
8	1111 1000	0011 1000
9	1111 1001	0011 1001

FIGURE 10.1 The representation of selected characters in EBCDIC and ASCII.

mine what digit is represented by this character, find the character displayed in the table in Figure 10.1 (or a more complete table in your computer's documentation), ignore the zone bits, and convert the numeric bits into their decimal equivalent. For example, the character I is represented by 1100 1001. The numeric bits are 1001, which are equivalent to decimal 9.

It is possible to specify that an item has display format by writing the word **DISPLAY** in its data description entry in the Data Division. This is rarely done, however, since in the absence of any explicit declaration about usage, the compiler assumes as a default that an item is **DISPLAY**.

10.6 COMPUTATIONAL-3 USAGE

Within the computer, arithmetic cannot be done directly on data in zoned decimal format (that is, **DISPLAY** data). When a **COBOL** program calls for arithmetic on **DISPLAY** items, as we have done in all programs to this point in the book, the object program has to be set up to make a conversion to the format required for arithmetic on decimal data. In this format, called *packed decimal*, the decimal digits are packed two to a byte except for the rightmost four bits of the rightmost byte, which hold the sign for the entire number. Here, for example, is how the number +4135729 would appear in packed decimal format:

0100 0001	0011 0101	0111 0010	1001 1100
4 1	3 5	7 2	9 +

We see that the number has been represented in four bytes, whereas in zoned decimal format it required seven. A number with eight digits would require eight bytes in zoned decimal format and five in packed; the leftmost four bits of the leftmost byte would be filled with zeros in the packed format. In short, the packed format uses just over half as much storage space as the zoned. A packed decimal field in the IBM mainframe computers can contain a maximum of 31 digits, which is more than enough to accommodate the maximum of 18 permitted in a **COBOL** numeric item.

The packed decimal format is specified in a **COBOL** program by entering the clause **COMPUTATIONAL-3** or **COMP-3** in the data description entry for an item. Thus, we might have

```
05  ACCOUNT-TOTAL    PIC S9(5)V99 COMPUTATIONAL-3.
```

or, more commonly,

```
05  ACCOUNT-TOTAL    PIC S9(5)V99 COMP-3.
```

It is also possible to write a more complete entry

```
05  ACCOUNT-TOTAL    PIC S9(5)V99 USAGE IS COMPUTATIONAL-3.
```

This form is seldom used.

The **COMPUTATIONAL-3** (and other computational clauses considered below) may be written at any level. If a group is described as **COMPUTATIONAL-**

3, then every elementary item in the group is defined to be **COMPUTATIONAL-3**. However, we recommend that descriptive characteristics such as this be defined at the elementary level.

The reason **COBOL** provides the **COMPUTATIONAL-3** option, even though arithmetic on display items is permitted, is that the conversion from zoned to packed format that is required in the latter case is rather time-consuming, even though the programmer may never realize it is happening. In the case of addition and subtraction, the conversion takes longer than the arithmetic. Thus any item involved in very many arithmetic operations should be in **COMPUTATIONAL-3** form, to avoid unnecessary conversions. Since data read from keyed input such as a computer terminal is always in **DISPLAY** form, it is sometimes necessary to move items from a field described as **DISPLAY** to one that is described as **COMPUTATIONAL-3**. When this is done, a conversion from zoned format to packed is provided in the object program. If, when the arithmetic operations are completed, it is necessary to print or otherwise display an item that is in **COMPUTATIONAL-3** format, it must be moved to an item that has **DISPLAY** format. This, however, is ordinarily no extra effort in the **COBOL** program since such a move would normally be involved in editing the item for output anyway.

10.7   COMPUTATIONAL USAGE

A halfword or fullword may hold an item in *pure binary* format, rather than decimal; this usage is described in the data description entry by the term **COMPUTATIONAL** or **COMP**. (The omission of the suffix is intentional; **COMPUTATIONAL-1** is something else, as we shall learn shortly.) A halfword contains 16 bits, which in **COMPUTATIONAL** format would be assigned as 15 bits for the number and one for what amounts to a sign bit.*

The largest binary number that can be held in a halfword has the decimal equivalent 32,767. The largest binary number that can be held in a fullword has the decimal equivalent 2,147,483,647. If the **COBOL** item is described as four digits or fewer, the compiler stores it in a halfword; if the item is between five and nine digits, the compiler stores it in a fullword; and if the item is over nine digits the compiler stores it in two fullwords (*not* as a double word).

For fields that are used extensively in arithmetic operations with little or no conversion to **DISPLAY** or **COMPUTATIONAL-3** format during the arithmetic, the **COMPUTATIONAL** format can provide the most efficient form of data storage and arithmetic. Furthermore, **COMPUTATIONAL** fields are frequently used in connection with indexing and subscripting, which we shall consider in Chapter 13. However, the cost of converting data between **DISPLAY** format and **COMPUTATIONAL** format is higher than the cost of converting between **DISPLAY** and **COMPUTATIONAL-3**, so the latter tends to be used more frequently.

---

* Negative numbers are actually represented in two's complement form, but the details are of little concern to most **COBOL** programmers.

10.8 COMPUTATIONAL-1 AND COMPUTATIONAL-2 FORMATS

Most computers provide for *floating point* operations.* In floating point data, a separate part of each number has the function of keeping track of the location of the decimal point. On the IBM computers the point is actually a hexadecimal point, since base-16 numbers are used. There are two forms of floating point numbers. The short form takes up four bytes and is described in the Data Division as **COMPUTATIONAL-1** or **COMP-1**. The long form takes up eight bytes and is described by **COMPUTATIONAL-2** or **COMP-2**.

There is little occasion to use floating point numbers in the kind of work that is typically done with **COBOL**, and we shall not pursue this matter further. Indeed, many **COBOL** compilers do not support floating point arithmetic at all.

The terms **DISPLAY** and **COMPUTATIONAL** are meant to suggest that data items in **DISPLAY** format are suitable for entering data into the computer or sending information out from it, whereas items in **COMPUTATIONAL** format may be used only internally. If we attempt to read a number from a computer terminal into a **COMPUTATIONAL-3** item, for example, or attempt to print a **COMPUTATIONAL** item, the results will be meaningless. (However, the **DISPLAY** and **EXHIBIT** statements automatically convert **COMPUTATIONAL** items to **DISPLAY** format before printing them.) When we move an item in **DISPLAY** form to an item with one of the **COMPUTATIONAL** forms, the compiler arranges an appropriate conversion of format, as it does when we specify arithmetic on a **DISPLAY** item. There is no conversion, however, if we try to read into or write from a **COMPUTATIONAL** item.

Likewise, great confusion results from a group **MOVE** in which the elementary items are not of the same usage. For example, if the elementary items in one group item are all **DISPLAY**, we cannot move the group to another group having elementary items that are **COMPUTATIONAL-3**.

COBOL-85

10.9 DATA REPRESENTATION IN COBOL-85

Data representation in **COBOL-85** is essentially the same as in previous versions of **COBOL**, but some of the names have changed. Standard **COBOL-85** does not include the names **COMPUTATIONAL-1**, **COMPUTATIONAL-2**, or **COMPUTATIONAL-3**. It uses the term **BINARY** to specify binary numeric data, and the term **PACKED-DECIMAL** to specify decimal numeric data that is not in **DISPLAY** format. The term **COMPUTATIONAL** can be used by compiler implementers to specify any type of arithmetic data they choose. For the IBM mainframe compilers available at the time of this writing, **BINARY** is exactly equivalent to **COMPUTATIONAL**, and **PACKED-DECIMAL** is exactly equivalent to **COMPUTATIONAL-3**.

END COBOL-85

---

* Although most computers provide some form of floating point arithmetic, some computers, especially microcomputers, do so by using software to simulate the floating point operations, rather than by actually providing hardware capabilities. Floating point arithmetic implemented with software is very much slower than hardware floating point.

10.10   THE SYNCHRONIZED CLAUSE

At the machine language level in the System/360, predecessor to the current IBM mainframe computers, binary and floating point items were required to be *aligned* on appropriate *boundaries*. Thus, a binary halfword number (COM-PUTATIONAL) was required to begin at a byte with an address that was a multiple of 2; binary fullword or short floating point numbers (COMPUTATIONAL or COMPUTATIONAL-1) began on bytes with addresses that were multiples of four; and double word data (COMPUTATIONAL-2) began with addresses that were multiples of eight. In general, to maintain compatibility with older hardware and to improve efficiency, the current IBM COBOL compilers still support these alignment standards even though the hardware no longer requires it. The COBOL programmer is not required to organize storage so that items have these characteristics, but if they do not, the object program will not be as efficient. This inefficiency can be significant, and could easily erase the time savings of having the data in binary form.

The solution is the SYNCHRONIZED clause, which may also be written SYNC (pronounced "sink"). When this clause is specified for an item, the compiler assigns storage so that the item begins on a proper boundary. If the item would otherwise not have begun on the boundary, *slack bytes* are inserted between the end of the previous item and this one; these slack bytes have no other function and are never used.

For a binary (COMPUTATIONAL) item small enough to fit in a halfword, which means one having a PICTURE character string with no more than four 9s, a SYNCHRONIZED item is aligned on a halfword boundary. Larger binary items are aligned on fullword boundaries. Level 01 items are always aligned on double word boundaries, whether or not the SYNCHRONIZED clause is used, and level 77 items are aligned on fullword boundaries.

The following examples show how slack bytes are inserted:

As written				Slack marked with FILLER		
01	GROUP-A.			01	GROUP-A.	
	05	FLD-1	PIC X.		05 FLD-1	PIC X.
	05	FLD-2	PIC 9(4) COMP SYNC.		05 FILLER	PIC X.
					05 FLD-2	PIC 9(4)
						COMP SYNC.
01	GROUP-B.			01	GROUP-B.	
	05	FLD-3	PIC X.		05 FLD-3	PIC X.
	05	FLD-4	PIC 9(8) COMP SYNC.		05 FILLER	PIC XXX.
	05	FLD-5	PIC X.		05 FLD-4	PIC 9(8)
	05	FLD-6	PIC 9(18) COMP SYNC.			COMP SYNC.
					05 FLD-5	PIC X.
					05 FILLER	PIC XXX.
					05 FLD-6	PIC 9(18)
						COMP SYNC.

10.11   THE JUSTIFIED CLAUSE

Very occasionally it is necessary to override the normal positioning of alphanumeric items that are larger or smaller than the receiving field to which they are being sent. The normal action, we recall, is that if the item is longer than the receiving field, extra characters on the *right* are dropped, and if the item is shorter than the receiving field, the extra positions on the *right* are filled with spaces. When the **JUSTIFIED** (or simply **JUST**) clause is written, the action is switched from right to left: extra characters on the *left* are dropped from long items, and extra positions on the *left* are filled with spaces for short items. The **JUSTIFIED** clause may be used only for elementary items, and may *never* be used for numeric or edited numeric items.

JUSTIFIED and **SYNCHRONIZED** may seem somewhat similar at first glance, but they are quite different. **SYNCHRONIZED** has to do with the assignment of storage to an item, and to the possible insertion of slack bytes. The compiler would carry out its function for a **SYNCHRONIZED** item even if no Procedure Division statement ever sent anything to the item. **JUSTIFIED**, on the other hand, has no connection with the assignment of storage to an item; its action is completely independent of whether or not the item being sent to a receiving field is **SYNCHRONIZED**.

In most commercial applications, **SYNCHRONIZED** will be found useful mostly in connection with **COMPUTATIONAL** items (Chapter 13). **JUSTIFIED** is rarely used.

10.12 THE REDEFINES CLAUSE

It is often useful to allow the same computer storage area to be described by different data description entries. This is the function of the **REDEFINES** clause, which has the general format:

level-number   data-name-**1** **REDEFINES** data-name-2

For a simple example, suppose that a program reads a tax rate figure that may be either dollars per hundred, such as 4.239, or dollars per thousand, such as 42.39. What appears on the input record is just the numeric digits; elsewhere there is a code that specifies which form the digits represent. It would be convenient to describe this field with two **PICTURE** clauses, having the character strings **9V999** and **99V99**, so that the arithmetic would be correct for both. This is precisely what the **REDEFINES** clause permits. We can write

```
05   RATE.
       10   RATE-CODE                      PIC X.
       10   100-RATE                       PIC 9V999.
       10   1000-RATE REDEFINES 100-RATE   PIC 99V99.
```

Here, **1000-RATE** is data-name-1 and **100-RATE** is data-name-2. This entry (including **RATE-CODE**) consists of only five characters, not nine. **100-RATE** and **1000-RATE** are different descriptions of the same storage area. Now, in the Procedure Division, we may write

MULTIPLY ASSESSMENT BY 100-RATE GIVING TAX

and the compiler will set up the arithmetic operations so that the decimal points are handled properly for a four-digit tax rate having three decimal places. Elsewhere, we may write

MULTIPLY ASSESSMENT BY 1000-RATE GIVING TAX

and the compiler will set up the object program to handle a four-digit tax rate having two decimal places. We shall explore other ways to use the **REDEFINES** clause after we consider the rules governing its use.

10.13 RULES FOR THE REDEFINES CLAUSE

Use of the REDEFINES clause is subject to the following rules:

1. When the REDEFINES clause is used it must immediately follow data-name-1. That is, we may *not* write

   ```
   05  A-FIELD           PIC XXX REDEFINES B-FIELD.
   ```

2. The level numbers of data-name-1 and data-name-2 must be identical, but must not be **66** or **88**.

3. The REDEFINES clause must not be used in level **01** entries in the File Section. If multiple descriptions of a File Section record area are given, an automatic redefinition is assumed. In other words, REDEFINES is not needed in this case.

4. No entry having a level number numerically lower than the level number of data-name-2 may occur between the data description entries of data-name-2 and data-name-1. That is, we are *not* permitted to write things like

   ```
   05  NAME-1.
       10  INITIALS        PIC XX.
       10  LAST-NAME-1     PIC X(23).
   05  NAME-2.
       10  INITIAL         PIC X.
       10  LAST-NAME-2 REDEFINES LAST-NAME-1
                           PIC X(24).
   ```

5. Redefinition starts at data-name-1 and ends when a level number less than or equal to that of data-name-1 is encountered. For example, consider this structure:

   ```
   01  INPUT-RECORD.
       05  FIELD-1.
           10  SUB-FIELD-A     PIC XXX.
           10  SUB-FIELD-B     PIC X(4).
       05  FIELD-2 REDEFINES FIELD-1.
           10  SUB-FIELD-C     PIC X.
           10  SUB-FIELD-D     PIC X(6).
       05  FIELD-3             PIC X(20).
   ```

   Redefinition stops before **05 FIELD-3**, since its level number is equal to that of the entry with the REDEFINES.

6. Multiple redefinitions of the same storage area are permitted. The entries giving the new descriptions of the storage area must follow the entries defining the area being redefined, without intervening entries that define new areas. Multiple redefinitions of the same storage area must all use the data-name of the entry that originally defined the area. Thus the following structure is legal.

   ```
   05  A                  PIC 9(4).
   05  B REDEFINES A      PIC 9V999.
   05  C REDEFINES A      PIC 99V99.
   ```

   The following structure is an example of a violation of this rule:

   ```
   05  A                  PIC 9(4).
   05  B REDEFINES A      PIC 9V999.
   05  C REDEFINES B      PIC 99V99.
   ```

7. When the level number of data-name-1 is other than **01**, it must specify the same number of character positions as the data item referenced by

data-name-2 contains. This rule emphasizes that what **REDEFINES** does is to give a different name and (usually) attributes to *one storage area*. The size of the storage area that is redefined does not change.

The reason this restriction does not apply to **01** level data names is that it may occasionally be useful to do in the Working-Storage Section what is done automatically in the File Section, namely, to obtain a redefinition with different length records. When several records are defined on the same storage area, either through implicit redefinition in the File Section or through an explicit **REDEFINES** in **01** level entries in the Working-Storage Section, the longest record controls the amount of storage allocated; all records are aligned on the leftmost character.

8. The entries giving a new description (the entries under dataname-1) must not contain any **VALUE** clauses other than level **88** condition name entries. The area being redefined is permitted to have **VALUE** clauses.

10.14 EXAMPLES OF THE USEFULNESS OF THE REDEFINES CLAUSE

One common situation where the **REDEFINES** is useful has already been suggested in the example at the beginning of Section 10.12. Whenever data has alternative formats, we need to be able to describe all the possibilities, and then to utilize other characteristics of the input to determine which one applies.

For example, suppose that an employee's name may appear with the first name either before or after the last name, depending on the value of **FORMAT-CODE**. In the Data Division we write

```
05  NAME-2.
    10   FIRST-NAME-2        PIC X(10).
    10   LAST-NAME-2         PIC X(15).
05  NAME-1 REDEFINES NAME-2.
    10   LAST-NAME-1         PIC X(15).
    10   FIRST-NAME-1        PIC X(10).
```

Here is the storage layout for the 25 characters of the name:

1 2 3 4 5 6 7 8 9 10	11 12 13 14 15 16 17 18 19 20 21 22 23 24 25
FIRST-NAME-2	LAST-NAME-2
LAST-NAME-1	FIRST-NAME-1

Now we can write statements such as this:

```
IF FORMAT-CODE = '1'
    MOVE LAST-NAME-1 TO LAST-NAME-OUT
ELSE
    IF FORMAT-CODE = '2'
        MOVE LAST-NAME-2 TO LAST-NAME-OUT
    ELSE
        PERFORM D055-CODE-ERROR.
```

It is not necessary that the data items in a redefinition have any logical relationship to each other. Consider this example:

```
05  SIZE-INFO.
    10  FRAME-SIZE            PIC X(4).
    10  HORSEPOWER           PIC 99V99.
    10  SHAFT-LENGTH         PIC 99V9.
05  RATINGS REDEFINES SIZE-INFO.
    10  TEMPERATURE-RISE     PIC 999.
    10  OVERLOAD             PIC 9V99.
    10  INSULATION           PIC XX.
    10  KW                   PIC 99V9.
```

Here is the storage layout for these 11 characters:

1	2	3	4	5	6	7	8	9	10	11
FRAME-SIZE				HORSEPOWER				SHAFT-LENGTH		
TEMPERATURE-RISE			OVERLOAD			INSULATION		KW		

Finally, an item can be redefined simply to assign it different attributes, so that the compiler will treat it differently in different Procedure Division operations. Consider the following situation. An input item contains a price; if the actual input consists of anything but digits, we want to discard the record after printing the bad data so that it can be corrected. This means that the price needs to be defined both as numeric, for normal processing, and as alphanumeric, for handling when it is in error. Here is the solution:

```
10  X-PRICE                  PIC X(7).
10  9-PRICE REDEFINES X-PRICE  PIC 9(5)V99.
```

Now, in any Procedure Division reference to **X-PRICE**, the seven characters will be treated as alphanumeric. In any reference to **9-PRICE** they will be treated as numeric, with two decimal places.

We end this section with a warning: do not use **REDEFINES** in such a way that it obscures the structure of the data, particularly if you use multiple **REDEFINES** in a single structure. For example, the following definition is *legal*, but it is not very readable.

```
01  TRANSACTION-RECORD.
    05  RECORD-TYPE          PIC X.
    05  CUST-NUMBER          PIC X(7).
    05  CODE-FIELD REDEFINES CUST-NUMBER.
        10  INV-CODE         PIC X(6).
        10  FILLER           PIC X.
    05  DATE-AND-CODE.
        10  SALE-DATE        PIC 9(6).
        10  SALE-DATE-X REDEFINES SALE-DATE
                             PIC X(6).
        10  ITEM-CODE        PIC X(5).
    05  ITEM-DESC REDEFINES DATE-AND-CODE
                             PIC X(11).
    05  REORDER-QTY          PIC 9(4).
    05  SALE-QTY REDEFINES REORDER-QTY
                             PIC 9(4).
    05  AMOUNT               PIC 9(5)V99.
    05  QTY-ON-HAND REDEFINES AMOUNT
                             PIC 9(7).
```

The programmer was working with a program that processes both sales and inventory transaction records from the same input file. Noticing that several of the fields on these records seemed to overlap, he then created a single transaction record that contained all the fields. A much better approach, both for readability and ease of maintenance, would be to create two separate records, one of which redefines the other.

```
01   SALES-RECORD.
     05   RECORD-TYPE-S          PIC X.
     05   CUST-NUMBER            PIC X(7).
     05   SALE-DATE              PIC 9(6).
     05   SALE-DATE-X REDEFINES SALE-DATE PIC X(6).
     05   ITEM-CODE              PIC X(5).
     05   SALE-QTY               PIC 9(4).
     05   AMOUNT                 PIC 9(5)V99.
01   INVENTORY-RECORD REDEFINES SALES-RECORD.
     05   RECORD-TYPE-I          PIC X.
     05   INV-CODE               PIC X(6).
     05   ITEM-DESC              PIC X(10).
     05   REORDER-QTY            PIC 9(4).
     05   QTY-ON-HAND            PIC 9(5).
```

Not only are these structures easier to understand, we can now modify either record as needed without worrying about how the format of the other record might be affected. Furthermore, several fields in INVENTORY-RECORD have been shortened or eliminated to reflect the sizes actually needed by the program, rather than what is convenient for redefinition.

10.15   DATA NAME QUALIFICATION

COBOL does not require that all the data names in a program be unique. If a name appears in more than one place, it must be written with enough *qualifiers* to establish which occurrence is meant. This process is called *data name qualification*. The higher-level qualifiers are written after the data name, preceded by OF or IN, which are interchangeable.

Consider an example. Suppose we have these record descriptions:

```
01   IN-REC.
     05   NAME              PIC X(30).
     05   EMP-NO            PIC X(7).
     05   HOURS-WORKED      PIC 99V99.
01   OUT-REC.
     05   NAME              PIC X(30).
     05   FILLER            PIC XXX.
     05   EMP-NO            PIC X(7).
     05   FILLER            PIC X(4).
     05   HOURS-WORKED      PIC Z9.99.
```

It will clearly not do to write things like

```
MOVE NAME TO NAME.
```

The compiler would report back "NAME NOT UNIQUE." We write instead

```
MOVE NAME OF IN-REC TO NAME OF OUT-REC.
```

or

```
MOVE HOURS-WORKED IN IN-REC TO HOURS-WORKED IN OUT-REC.
```

It is permissible to have a hierarchy of levels, with qualification used to whatever extent is necessary to achieve a unique identification. Consider this structure:

```
01  TRANS.
    05  INSURED.
        10  INITIALS        PIC XXX.
        10  LAST-NAME       PIC X(24).
    05  BENEFICIARY.
        10  INITIALS        PIC XXX.
        10  LAST-NAME       PIC X(24).
01  MASTER.
    05  INSURED.
        10  INITIALS        PIC XXX.
        10  LAST-NAME       PIC X(24).
    05  BENEFICIARY.
        10  INITIALS        PIC XXX.
        10  LAST-NAME       PIC X(24).
```

An identifier such as **LAST-NAME** is certainly not unique, since there are four occurrences of it. But **LAST-NAME OF INSURED** is not unique either, since **INSURED** occurs twice. We must write **LAST-NAME OF INSURED OF TRANS**, or **LAST-NAME OF BENEFICIARY OF MASTER**, or whatever is meant. On the other hand, suppose that the record definition for **TRANS** were this:

```
01  TRANS.
    05  INSURED.
        10  INITIALS        PIC XXX.
        10  LAST-NAME       PIC X(24).
```

With the same definition for **MASTER** as before, we have **INITIALS** and **LAST-NAME** appearing three times, but **INSURED** only twice. **LAST-NAME OF INSURED** would not be unique, but since **LAST-NAME** appears only once in **TRANS**, we could get a unique name by writing **LAST-NAME OF TRANS**. It would not be incorrect to write **LAST-NAME OF INSURED OF TRANS**, but it is not necessary to give all the possible qualifications. Likewise, **LAST-NAME OF BENEFICIARY** would be unique. **LAST-NAME OF INSURED OF MASTER** would need the full qualification, since neither **LAST-NAME** nor **INSURED** is unique.

Actually, it is uncommon for data name qualification to extend beyond one level, if it is used at all. When the formats of related records are closely similar, such as an old master record and a new master record for the same file, using the same names for all items and then using data name qualification is an attractive alternative to making up completely different names.

10.16 MOVE CORRESPONDING

When data name qualification is used, it sometimes happens that one wants to move all items having the same name from one group item to another. (We assume that the two groups are not *identical*, because then a group **MOVE** does the job.) Suppose that we have record descriptions like these:

```
01  TRANS.
    05  ACCOUNT         PIC X(9).
    05  AMOUNT          PIC 9(5)V99.
    05  TRANS-CODE      PIC X.
    05  TRANS-DATE      PIC X(5).
```

```
01   TRANS-OUT.
     05   ACCOUNT          PIC X(9).
     05   FILLER           PIC XXX.
     05   NAME             PIC X(30).
     05   FILLER           PIC XXX.
     05   TRANS-DATE       PIC X(5).
     05   FILLER           PIC XXX.
     05   AMOUNT           PIC ZZ,ZZ9.99.
```

Observe that **ACCOUNT**, **AMOUNT**, and **TRANS-DATE** appear in both records, although not in the same order; that **TRANS-CODE** appears in **TRANS** but not in **TRANS-OUT**; that **NAME** appears in **TRANS-OUT** but not in **TRANS**. We assume that **NAME** is to be found in another record named **MASTER**. To move the four items from the input records to **TRANS-OUT** it is possible to write four **MOVE** statements:

```
MOVE ACCOUNT OF TRANS        TO ACCOUNT OF TRANS-OUT.
MOVE NAME OF MASTER          TO NAME OF TRANS-OUT.
MOVE TRANS-DATE OF TRANS     TO TRANS-DATE OF TRANS-OUT.
MOVE AMOUNT OF TRANS         TO AMOUNT OF TRANS-OUT.
```

However, the **MOVE CORRESPONDING** option provides a simpler way:

```
MOVE NAME OF MASTER          TO NAME OF TRANS-OUT.
MOVE CORRESPONDING TRANS     TO TRANS-OUT.
```

The effect is exactly the same as that of the four **MOVE** statements shown previously.

The format of the **MOVE CORRESPONDING** is as follows.

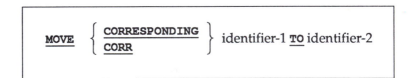

Two rules govern the use of the **MOVE CORRESPONDING** option:

1. Data items are taken to be **CORRESPONDING** when they have the same name and qualification, up to but not including identifier-1 and identifier-2.
2. Any elementary item containing a **REDEFINES** clause is ignored, as is any elementary item containing a **RENAMES**, **OCCURS**, or **USAGE IS INDEX** clause. These latter are considered in Chapters 12 and 13.

MOVE CORRESPONDING is superficially attractive, but it has pitfalls that have caused experienced programmers to minimize its use. The main trouble is that it tends to create problems when a program is changed, as virtually all programs are if they are used for any length of time. One of the things in a program that most generally changes is the format of records, and experience has shown that record format changes very frequently cause a **MOVE COR-RESPONDING** to give undesired results. The effort of writing out the **MOVE** statements explicitly is a rather minor part of the total cost of developing a program successfully, and doing so has the further advantage of providing easier understanding of how the program works. Ease of understanding, reduced chance of error, and ease of maintenance are far more important than the saving of a bit of typing time.

REVIEW QUESTIONS

Many of the following questions and exercises refer specifically to the EBCDIC character set and IBM mainframe computers. If you are using a different computer or character set, you may wish to answer the questions for your computer. However, answers given in this book will be for EBCDIC characters on IBM mainframes.

1. Show the ASCII and EBCDIC representations of the following characters:

   A1,$KR7

2. How many bytes are there in the zoned decimal (**DISPLAY**) and packed decimal (**COMPUTATIONAL-3**) representations of these numbers?

   -173
   -42611329
   +109011365

3. Show the **DISPLAY** and **COMPUTATIONAL-3** representations, at the bit level, of these numbers:

   +123
   -67

4. Show the storage layout, in bytes, of the following records:

   ```
   a.  01  A-REC.
           05  A-1      PIC S999 COMP-3.
           05  A-2      PIC XXX.
           05  A-3      PIC S999.
           05  A-4      PIC S9(4) COMP-3.

   b.  01  B-REC.
           05  B-1      PIC XXX VALUE 'YES'.
           05  B-2      PIC S999 COMP.
           05  B-3      PIC S9(6) COMP.
           05  B-4      PIC S9 COMP-3.
           05  B-5      PIC XXX.

   c.  01  C-REC.
           05  C-1      PIC XXX VALUE 'YES'.
           05  C-2      PIC S999 COMP SYNC.
           05  C-3      PIC S9(6) COMP SYNC.
           05  C-4      PIC S9 COMP-3.
           05  C-5      PIC XXX.
   ```

5. May **SYNCHRONIZED** be used with **COMPUTATIONAL-3**? With **DISPLAY**?

6. How many characters in storage are described by the following?

   ```
   05  A.
       10  A-1      PIC XX.
       10  A-2      PIC 999.
   05  B REDEFINES A.
       10  B-1      PIC 9.
       10  B-2      PIC X.
       10  B-3      PIC XXX.
   05  C REDEFINES A  PIC X(5).
   ```

7. Find errors in the following examples of the use of REDEFINES.

a.
```
FD   A-FILE
     LABEL RECORDS ARE OMITTED.
01   A.
     05   A1          PIC X(20).
     05   A2          PIC X(60).
01   B REDEFINES A.
     05   B1          PIC X(40).
     05   B2          PIC X(40).
```

b.
```
05   CAT.
     10   KITTY-CAT   PIC X(10).
     10   PUSSY-CAT   PIC X(8).
     10   TOM-CAT     PIC X(12).
05   DOG REDEFINES CAT.
     10   PUPPY-DOG   PIC X(8).
     10   FIDO        PIC X(12).
     10   BRANDY      PIC X(12).
```

c.
```
05   CARS.
     10   FORD          PIC X(10).
     10   CHEVY         PIC X(10).
     10   DODGE         PIC X(10).
     10   TRUCKS REDEFINES CARS.
          15   FORD     PIC X(10).
          15   CHEVY    PIC X(10).
          15   DODGE    PIC X(10).
```

d.
```
05   LITTLE-KIDS.
     10   TOM                       PIC XX.
     10   ALIZA                     PIC XX.
     10   RACHEL                    PIC XX.
05   OLDER-KIDS.
     10   CHARLIE REDEFINES TOM     PIC XX.
     10   JUDE REDEFINES ALIZA      PIC XX.
     10   CINDY REDEFINES RACHEL    PIC XX.
```

e.
```
05   GINIS-FRIENDS.
     10   JOHN                      PIC X(12).
     10   PETE REDEFINES JOHN       PIC X(12).
     10   DOUG REDEFINES PETE       PIC X(12).
```

8. REDEFINES is not permitted at the 01 level in the File Section. What can be done when this facility is needed?

9. Given the following Data Division entries:

```
01   TEMPORARY-RECORD.
     05   COLORS.
          10   RED                  PIC X.
          10   BLUE.
               15   SKY             PIC X.
               15   ROBINS-EGG      PIC X.
          10   GREEN.
               15   PEA             PIC X.
               15   GRASS           PIC X.
          10   WHITE                PIC X.
```

```
01  PAINT-RECORD.
    05  COLORS.
        10  WHITE        PIC X.
        10  PINK         PIC X.
        10  BLUE.
            15  SKY      PIC X.
            15  NAVY     PIC X.
        10  RED.
            15  FIRE-ENGINE PIC X.
            15  BARN     PIC X.
```

are the following statements legal?

a. MOVE RED TO PINK.

b. MOVE WHITE TO PINK.

c. MOVE ROBINS-EGG TO BARN.

d. MOVE SKY OF TEMPORARY-RECORD TO SKY OF PAINT-RECORD.

e. MOVE SKY OF BLUE OF COLORS OF TEMPORARY-RECORD TO SKY OF PAINT-RECORD.

f. MOVE GRASS TO WHITE OF PAINT-RECORD.

g. MOVE BLUE OF TEMPORARY-RECORD TO BLUE OF PAINT-RECORD.

h. MOVE COLORS OF TEMPORARY-RECORD TO COLORS OF PAINT-RECORD.

10. Given the following Data Division entries:

```
01  OFFICE.
    05  DESK         PIC XXX.
    05  CHAIR-1      PIC XXX.
    05  CHAIR-2      PIC XXX.
    05  LAMP         PIC XXX.
    05  BOOKCASE     PIC XXX.

01  LIVING-ROOM.
    05  SOFA         PIC XXX.
    05  LAMP-1       PIC XXX.
    05  LAMP-2       PIC XXX.
    05  CHAIR-1      PIC XXX.
    05  CHAIR-2      PIC XXX.
    05  CHAIR-3      PIC XXX.
```

what would this statement do?

```
MOVE CORRESPONDING OFFICE TO LIVING-ROOM.
```

ANSWERS

1. ASCII:

0100 0001	0011 0001	0010 1100	0010 0100	0100 1011	0101 0010	0011 0111
A	1	,	$	K	R	7

EBCDIC:

1100 0001	1111 0001	0110 1011	0101 1011	1101 0010	1101 1001	1111 0111
A	1	,	$	K	R	7

2. The decimal number -173 takes three bytes in zoned decimal; the bit representation is

    1111 0001 1111 0111 1101 0011

    This can also be written in hexadecimal as F1 F7 D3. In packed decimal the same number takes two bytes:

    0001 0111 0011 1101

    This is 173D in hexadecimal.

    The number -42611329 takes eight bytes in zoned decimal (F4 F2 F6 F1 F1 F3 F2 D9) and five in packed (04 26 11 32 9D). The number +109011365 takes nine bytes in zoned decimal (F1 F0 F9 F0 F1 F1 F3 F6 C5) and five in packed (10 90 11 36 5C). If your answers don't agree, review the handling of the sign in each form and also what happens in packed decimal with an even number of digits.

3. **COMPUTATIONAL-3:**

    0001 0010 0011 1100
      1   2   3   +

    0000 0110 0111 1101
      0   6   7   −

    DISPLAY:

    1111 0001 1111 0010 1100 0011
         1   2   +   3

    1111 0110 1101 0111
        6   −   7

4.

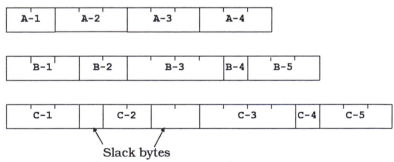

Slack bytes

5. In the IBM mainframe computers, neither **COMPUTATIONAL-3** nor **DISPLAY** items are required to have any prescribed boundary alignment, so the **SYNCHRONIZED** clause has no meaning. If present, it is ignored. In computers where the basic storage unit is a word rather than a byte, **DISPLAY SYNCHRONIZED** would be meaningful.

6. Five characters total. The five characters may be referred to in the Procedure Division as a two-character alphanumeric item and a three-character numeric item (group item **A**); or as a one-character numeric item, a one-character alphanumeric item, and a three-character item (group item **B**); or as a five-character alphanumeric item (item **C**).

7. **a.** Redefinition at level **01** in the File Section is not permitted; redefinition is automatic for multiple record descriptions in an **FD**.

   b. **CAT** and **DOG** do not have the same number of characters.

   c. **TRUCKS**, at level **10**, cannot redefine a level **05** entry.

   d. This violates the rule that no entry having a numerically smaller level number may occur between an item and its redefinition.

   e. Redefinitions may not be "chained" in this way. Make the third entry

   ```
   10    DOUG REDEFINES JOHN     PIC X(12).
   ```

8. Redefinition is achieved automatically; nothing need be done to achieve it. That is, if the **FD** for a file is followed by a number of **01** level entries, they are all considered to be alternative definitions of the same storage space.

9. **a.** Illegal; **RED** is not unique.

   b. Illegal; **WHITE** is not unique.

   c. No problem.

   d. No problem. Note that neither name needs to be qualified by **COLORS** or **BLUE**, although it would be legal to do so.

   e. Legal, although the full qualification of the first name is not required.

   f. No problem.

   g. No problem.

   h. No problem.

10. It would move **CHAIR-1** and **CHAIR-2** of **OFFICE** to the elementary items of the same name in **LIVING-ROOM**.

EXERCISES

*1. Give the binary and hexadecimal equivalents of these decimal numbers.

    7
    8
    19
    23
    34

2. Give the binary and hexadecimal equivalents of these decimal numbers.

    4
    9
    17
    32
    36

* Answers to starred exercises will be found in Appendix IV at the end of the book.

*3. Give the binary and decimal equivalents of these hexadecimal numbers.

4
B
10
14

4. Give the binary and decimal equivalents of these hexadecimal numbers.

1
F
20
2A

*5. Show the packed and zoned representations of these decimal numbers. Use as few bytes as will hold the number.

+123
+1234
-90345
-6

6. Show the packed and zoned representations of these decimal numbers. Use as few bytes as will hold the number.

-400
+1603429
-9876
+42

*7. Show the binary representations of these characters.

2
B
M
W
+
(

8. Show the binary representations of these characters.

7
S
R
A
$
)

*9. Show the storage layout created from the following Data Division entry.

```
01   RECORD-1.
     05   FLD-1            PIC XX.
     05   FLD-2            PIC 9(4).
     05   FLD-3            PIC 9.
     05   FLD-4            PIC XXX.
01   RECORD-2 REDEFINES RECORD-1.
     05   FLD-5            PIC X(5).
     05   FLD-6            PIC 9(5).
```

10. Show the storage layout created from the following Data Division entry.

```
01   SAM.
     04   GEORGE        PIC X.
     04   HARRY         PIC 9(8).
     04   DAVE          PIC X(7).
01   TOM REDEFINES SAM  PIC X(16).
```

CHAPTER 11

COMPOUND CONDITIONALS AND THE SEED CATALOG PROGRAM

11.1 INTRODUCTION

We have reached a point where we need to pull together the concepts we have been learning, to see how they can be used in a program. The program we shall study checks one line of a seed catalog order for validity, a more involved task than it might seem at first.*

The program we are to write is required to process an input file that has one record for each line in a catalog order. (We imagine that this program is part of a larger program that handles other aspects of the order, such as the name and address of the customer and the total amount of the order.) Each record in the input file contains an order number, a record type code, a catalog number, a size code, a quantity, an item description, and a price. We are to perform certain tests on the data to determine whether it has any of eight possible kinds of errors that would make it impossible to process. If it has none of these errors, we are to write it in edited form to a normal handling file. If it contains any one or more of the errors, we are to write it to a different file for special handling.

The validity checks that we are to make are as follows:

1. A catalog number should be entirely numeric.
2. The first digit of the catalog number should not be 0 or 2.
3. If the first digit of the catalog number is 1, 8, or 9, then there should not be a size code.
4. The only permissible size codes are A, D, G, J, K, L, S, T, U, and blank.
5. The quantity must be numeric. Two digits are allowed for the quantity and both of them must be present.
6. The price is five digits with two assumed decimal places. Leading zeros must be present.

* This illustration was inspired by perusal of the W. Atlee Burpee Company seed catalog. The data processing personnel at the Burpee Company have indicated that this example is representative of some of the kinds of things they do, but the details of the program were invented by the authors. Of course, the complete data processing operations of the company are very much more complex than this illustration shows.

7. The price must be exactly divisible by the quantity. (If not, the customer has miscopied something or has made an error in multiplication.)
8. The price must not be greater than $125. (Such a price may be legitimate—and certainly welcome—but since most orders are much smaller than this, it *may* be an error.)

These are by no means the only possible errors. In fact, as we observed before, it is not meaningful to claim to have thought of all possible errors. One obvious possibility is that although the catalog number passes the tests here, there is nevertheless no such number—either because the customer wrote it down incorrectly or because it was keyed incorrectly. Checking this, however, involves access to a master file of all catalog numbers. The techniques involved in matching a transaction file against a master file will concern us in Chapters 12 and 14.

Most of these errors are directed at mistakes the customer might make in writing down the information on the order form. It is difficult to write a program that tries to anticipate the kinds of errors that can be made in keying data into a computer, such as omitting one character and, therefore, having everything else on the rest of the record off by one column. We can only hope that an error of that kind would cause at least one of the validity checks to fail, which is generally true.

11.2 MORE ON COMPOUND CONDITIONALS

It is clear from the specifications of the seed catalog program that it will be necessary to test for a variety of combinations of input data. The most natural way to specify such operations in a COBOL program involves the use of compound conditionals in IF statements, which we now explore briefly.

In Chapter 5, when the IF statement was introduced, it was mentioned that relation conditions can be combined by using the logical operators AND, OR, and NOT. The only examples we have seen thus far have involved only one of these operators in any one relation condition. Actually, they may be combined in any way the programmer pleases, subject to one important rule. Let us summarize the earlier material and then see what happens when the operators are combined.

1. A compound condition consisting of simple conditions connected by ANDs is satisfied if and only if each one of the simple conditions is satisfied. For example, consider this:

```
IF      AGE IS GREATER THAN 60
        AND LENGTH-OF-SERVICE IS GREATER THAN 20
        AND DEPT-NO = '123'
        PERFORM D010-DEPT-123-RETIREMENT.
```

The routine named will be performed only if all three of the simple conditions are true. For example, if age is greater than 60 and length of service is greater than 20 but the department number is not 123, then the compound condition is not true.

2. A compound condition consisting of simple conditions connected by ORs is satisfied if any one or more of the simple conditions is satisfied. Consider this IF statement:

```
IF      DEPT = '6'
   OR DEPT = '12'
   OR DEPT = '17'
   OR DEPT = '39'
   ADD 1 TO SPECIAL-ORDER.
```

The **ADD** statement will be executed if any of the simple conditions is true. In this example it is obvious that not more than one condition can be true at any one time. In the following statement, however, zero, one, two, or three of them could be true depending on the value of the variables:

```
IF      DEPT = '43'
   OR PROD-CODE = 'AG'
   OR PRIORITY-CODE = 'C'
   PERFORM E-155-RUSH-ORDER.
```

3. When a compound condition contains both **AND** and **OR** without parentheses, the *operator precedence rule* says that **AND**s are performed before **OR**s. Consider this example:

```
IF A = 1 OR B = 1 AND C = 1 . . .
```

Without the precedence rule we would not know which of the following correctly describes what is meant by the compound condition:

a. It is true whenever **A** is one, or **B** is one and **C** is one.

b. It is true whenever **A** is one or **B** is one, and **C** is one. (The punctuation in these sentences is crucial.)

The operator precedence rule tells us that the first interpretation is correct.

One way to suggest that the difference is important is to appeal to the analogy in arithmetic, where we know that $1 + (2 \times 3)$ is not the same as $(1 + 2) \times 3$. A more convincing proof is simply to write down all possible true/false combinations of the three variables and compare the results with the two possible interpretations, as follows:

A=1	B=1	C=1	B=1 AND C=1	A=1 OR (B=1 AND C=1)	A=1 OR B=1	(A=1 OR B=1) AND C=1
T	T	T	T	T	T	T
T	T	F	F	T	T	F
T	F	T	F	T	T	T
T	F	F	F	T	T	F
F	T	T	T	T	T	T
F	T	F	F	F	T	F
F	F	T	F	F	F	F
F	F	F	F	F	F	F

The two columns (5 and 7) in which the two results are different prove that they are two different functions.

Here are some additional examples that suggest some of the possibilities in writing compound conditions using **AND** and **OR**:

```
IF      HOURS-WORKED = 40 AND SALARY-CODE = 'W'
   OR HOURS-WORKED = 80 AND SALARY-CODE = 'S'
   PERFORM C030-NORMAL-PAY.

IF      (COL-1 = 'X' OR COL-1 = 'Y' OR COL-1 = 'Z')
   AND COL-2 = '4'
   ADD 1 TO SHEEP.
```

```
IF      (COL-1 = 'A'  OR COL-1 = 'V')
    AND COL-2 = '3'
    OR  (COL-1 = 'A'  OR COL-1 = 'W')
    AND COL-2 = '4'
    ADD 1 TO GOATS.
```

COBOL-85

COBOL-85 has added a feature to the evaluation of compound conditionals that can be quite useful. Consider the following example:*

```
IF A / B  < 1 OR A / B > 10
    MOVE 'Y' TO FLAG.
```

If **B** is equal to zero, this statement will cause an abnormal termination, since division by zero is illegal. We might consider correcting the problem by testing **B** as follows:

```
IF B NOT = 0  AND  (A / B < 1 OR A / B > 10)
    MOVE 'Y' TO FLAG.
```

Unfortunately, on most **COBOL** compilers this still will not work. Although the first condition (**B NOT = 0**) is false if **B** equals zero, compilers prior to **COBOL-85** evaluate the entire condition, causing the abend. **COBOL-85** produces code that stops evaluating a condition as soon as the truth or falsity of the expression can be determined. In the example above, as soon as the program determines that **B** is equal to zero, the first part of the condition is false which means that the entire condition must be false, regardless of the value of the expression within the parentheses. Therefore, evaluation stops immediately and no abend occurs.

In **COBOL-85**, evaluation of a compound condition that uses only **AND**s will stop as soon as one of the subconditions is found to be false; evaluation of a compound condition that uses only **OR**s will stop as soon as one of the subconditions is found to be true. This is called short-circuiting the evaluation of the compound condition. If the compound condition uses both **AND**s and **OR**s, evaluation continues as far as necessary. This addition to **COBOL-85** avoids some common errors and occasionally saves some execution time. However, if necessary you can always test for a critical condition by using a nested **IF** statement, as in the following code:

```
IF B NOT = 0
    IF A / B IS LESS THAN 1 OR A / B IS GREATER THAN 10
        MOVE 'Y' TO FLAG.
```

END COBOL-85

It is possible to describe the desired precedence by the use of parentheses, as we have already seen in the illustrations. Parentheses may also be used to make a **NOT** apply to a compound condition rather than just the first simple condition in it. For an example of how this might be useful, consider this:

---

* Notice that we have a simple arithmetic expression, **A / B**, as part of each relation condition. We will discuss this a bit more in Chapter 12, but defer a complete explanation till Chapter 19. For now, simply accept it as a valid part of the example.

```
IF COL-16 = '7' OR COL-16 = '8'
    NEXT SENTENCE
ELSE
    ADD 1 TO SPECIAL-COUNT.
```

Suppose we wish to reverse the condition so that the statement is written in a more direct form without the **NEXT SENTENCE** phrase. It might be tempting to write

```
IF COL-16 NOT = '7' OR COL-16 NOT = '8'
    ADD 1 TO SPECIAL-COUNT.
```

This is a very common mistake. The problem is that at least one of the simple conditions will always be true; column 16 will always either not contain a 7 or not contain an 8, or not contain either one. Thus the compound condition is always true. If it is desired to write this without parentheses, then the logical operator must be **AND**, not **OR**:

```
IF COL-16 NOT = '7' AND COL-16 NOT = '8'
    ADD 1 TO SPECIAL-COUNT.
```

This formulation may seem artificial and therefore hamper easy understanding. An alternative is to use the **NOT** to reverse the effect of the entire compound condition as originally written.

```
IF NOT (COL-16 = '7' OR COL-16 = '8')
    ADD 1 TO SPECIAL-COUNT.
```

This example demonstrates one of two important rules for compound conditionals. These rules, called *DeMorgan's Laws*, are as follows:

1. **NOT (C1 AND C2)** is equivalent to **NOT C1 OR NOT C2**
2. **NOT (C1 OR C2)** is equivalent to **NOT C1 AND NOT C2**

where **C1** and **C2** are any conditions. The example we showed is an instance of the second law, where **C1** is "**COL-16 = '7'**" and **C2** is "**COL-16 = '8'**".

The review questions at the end of the chapter contain a number of opportunities for practice in interpreting logical expressions using **AND**, **OR**, and **NOT** with parentheses.

11.3 ABBREVIATED COMBINED RELATION CONDITIONS

It is possible to condense combined conditions by omitting elements that are repeated. The omitted elements are then said to be *implied*. In the following discussion recall that we defined a simple condition in terms of a subject, a relation, and an object.

11.4 IMPLIED SUBJECT

When a compound condition has the same subject immediately preceding each relation, then only the first occurrence of the subject need be written, with the omitted subjects being implied.

Thus, instead of

```
IF SERVICE IS GREATER THAN 10 AND SERVICE IS LESS THAN 21
    ADD 1 TO GROUP-3-COUNT.
```

we could write

```
IF SERVICE IS GREATER THAN 10 AND LESS THAN 21
    ADD 1 TO GROUP-3-COUNT.
```

Similarly, instead of

```
IF     CATALOG-FIRST-DIGIT OF ORDER-RECORD = '0'
    OR CATALOG-FIRST-DIGIT OF ORDER-RECORD = '2'
    MOVE 'X' TO FIRST-DIGIT-INVALID.
```

we could write

```
IF CATALOG-FIRST-DIGIT OF ORDER-RECORD = '0' OR = '2'
    MOVE 'X' TO FIRST-DIGIT-INVALID.
```

11.5 IMPLIED SUBJECT AND RELATIONAL OPERATOR

When the simple conditions in a compound condition have the same subject and the same relational operator, then only the first occurrence of the subject and relational operator need be written. Thus the example just stated could also be written

```
IF CATALOG-FIRST-DIGIT OF ORDER-RECORD = '0' OR '2'
    MOVE 'X' TO FIRST-DIGIT-INVALID.
```

This form of abbreviation applies whether or not all logical operators are the same. Thus

```
IF A = B OR A = C AND A = D . . .
```

could be written as

```
IF A = B OR C AND D
```

Note that a complete condition (subject, relational operator, and object) must be expressed first, before anything else is added. Thus the statement

```
IF A > B OR = B . . .
```

cannot be abbreviated

```
IF A > OR = B . . .
```

COBOL-85

Of course, in **COBOL-85** it could be written as

```
IF A >= B . . .
```

or as

```
IF A GREATER THAN OR EQUAL TO B . . .
```

END COBOL-85

Great care should be exercised to be sure that conditions involving **AND**, **OR**, and **NOT** really express what is meant, and that the meaning be *clear* as well as accurate. For example, does

```
    IF A NOT = B AND C . . .
```

mean

```
    IF A NOT = B AND A NOT = C . . .
```

or does it mean

```
    IF A NOT = B AND A = C . . .
```

In fact, the second meaning is the one the compiler would use, although it is not likely that this is what the programmer wanted. Many programmers follow the maxim, "When in doubt, spell it out." A few extra parentheses or a bit more writing are much preferable to the possibility of mistake or misunderstanding.

Very complex and condensed logical expressions can be built up by using the three logical operators in conjunction with implied subjects and relational operators. Care must be exercised, however, that conciseness is not gained at the expense of accuracy or clarity. In fact, these condensed forms should be used only when their usage *improves* understandability.

11.6 DESIGN OF THE SEED CATALOG PROGRAM

Now that we have studied conditional expressions in more depth, we can proceed to the design of the seed catalog program. The basic program structure is relatively simple, and is just a matter of reading and processing all the records in the input file. The logic of the individual validity tests is simple enough that it can be read from the program.

The omission of a complete program design in this case should not be taken as a minimization of the importance of the subject. It is just that in this case, the program is nearly as easy to read as the pseudocode would be, and the hierarchy is quite simple. It is always desirable that a program should be, as much as possible, its own documentation, because then we can be sure that the "documentation" is always up to date. This is a problem, because when programs are changed sometimes the associated pseudocode is not changed, and a program design document that is out of date is worse than useless.

11.7 THE SEED CATALOG ORDER PROGRAM

Looking at the Environment Division of the program shown in Figure 11.1 we see that there are three **SELECT** statements. When **COBOL** first became popular it was not uncommon for a computer installation to have several printers, all of which might be used simultaneously by a single program. Today, even if an installation has several printers it is unlikely that any one program will use more than one printer, since an installation with a mainframe computer will probably be running many programs concurrently. In this case, or if the computer has only one printer available to it, the operating system automatically stores the print files in temporary storage, usually on a disk, until the printer is available. Then all the print files for the program are written to the printer in sequence, so that although all files for a program are together the lines for one file are never intermixed with the lines for another.

In the file description for the order file we see that the catalog number has been made a group item so that the first digit can be processed separately from the remaining four digits.

```
00001          IDENTIFICATION DIVISION.
00002          PROGRAM-ID.
00003             SEEDS.
00004          DATE-WRITTEN.
00005             MARCH 16, 1987.
00006
00007          ENVIRONMENT DIVISION.
00008          INPUT-OUTPUT SECTION.
00009          FILE-CONTROL.
00010             SELECT ORDER-FILE              ASSIGN TO S-ORDERS.
00011             SELECT NORMAL-HANDLING-FILE    ASSIGN TO S-NORMAL.
00012             SELECT SPECIAL-HANDLING-FILE   ASSIGN TO S-SPECIAL.
00013
00014          DATA DIVISION.
00015          FILE SECTION.
00016          FD  ORDER-FILE
00017              LABEL RECORDS ARE OMITTED.
00018          01  ORDER-RECORD.
00019              05   ORDER-NUMBER             PIC X(6).
00020              05   RECORD-TYPE              PIC X.
00021              05   CATALOG-NUMBER.
00022                   10   CATALOG-FIRST-DIGIT PIC X.
00023                   10   CATALOG-REMAINING   PIC X(4).
00024              05   SIZE-CODE                PIC X.
00025              05   QUANTITY                 PIC 99.
00026              05   ITEM-DESCRIPTION         PIC X(40).
00027              05   X-PRICE                  PIC X(5).
00028              05   9-PRICE REDEFINES X-PRICE  PIC 999V99.
00029              05   FILLER                   PIC X(20).
00030
00031          FD  NORMAL-HANDLING-FILE
00032              LABEL RECORDS ARE OMITTED.
00033          01  NORMAL-LINE                   PIC X(133).
00034
00035          FD  SPECIAL-HANDLING-FILE
00036              LABEL RECORDS ARE OMITTED.
00037          01  SPECIAL-LINE                  PIC X(133).
00038          WORKING-STORAGE SECTION.
00039          01  ERROR-FLAGS.
00040              88   RECORD-OK                          VALUE SPACES.
00041              05   CAT-NO-NOT-NUMERIC       PIC X.
00042              05   FIRST-DIGIT-INVALID      PIC X.
00043              05   SIZE-CODE-NOT-PERMITTED  PIC X.
00044              05   NO-SUCH-SIZE-CODE        PIC X.
00045              05   QUANTITY-AND-PRICE-CODES.
00046                   88   QTY-AND-PRICE-OK              VALUE SPACES.
00047                   10   QTY-NOT-NUMERIC     PIC X.
00048                   10   PRICE-NOT-NUMERIC   PIC X.
00049              05   INVALID-PRICE-OR-QTY     PIC X.
00050              05   LARGE-PRICE              PIC X.
00051
```

```
00052                01   ERROR-MESSAGES.
00053                     05   CAT-NO-NOT-NUMERIC-MSG      PIC X(50)
00054                       VALUE ' CATALOG NUMBER CONTAINS AN IMPROPER CHARACTER'.
00055                     05   FIRST-DIGIT-INVALID-MSG     PIC X(50)
00056                          VALUE ' FIRST DIGIT OF CATALOG NUMBER INVALID'.
00057                     05   SIZE-CODE-NOT-PERMITTED-MSG PIC X(50)
00058                          VALUE ' THIS ITEM DOES NOT TAKE A SIZE CODE'.
00059                     05   NO-SUCH-SIZE-CODE-MSG       PIC X(50)
00060                          VALUE ' THERE IS NO SUCH SIZE CODE'.
00061                     05   QTY-NOT-NUMERIC-MSG         PIC X(50)
00062                          VALUE ' QUANTITY CONTAINS AN IMPROPER CHARACTER'.
00063                     05   PRICE-NOT-NUMERIC-MSG       PIC X(50)
00064                          VALUE ' PRICE CONTAINS AN IMPROPER CHARACTER'.
00065                     05   INVALID-PRICE-OR-QTY-MSG    PIC X(50)
00066                          VALUE ' EITHER PRICE OR QUANTITY IS WRONG'.
00067                     05   LARGE-PRICE-MSG             PIC X(50)
00068                          VALUE ' PRICE LARGE - SHOULD BE CHECKED'.
00069
00070                01   MORE-DATA-REMAINS-FLAG           PIC X      VALUE 'Y'.
00071                     88   NO-MORE-DATA-REMAINS                   VALUE 'N'.
00072
00073                01   OUTPUT-LINE.
00074                     05   CARRIAGE-CONTROL            PIC X.
00075                     05   ORDER-NUMBER                PIC Z(5)9.
00076                     05   CATALOG-NUMBER.
00077                          10   CATALOG-FIRST-DIGIT    PIC BBX.
00078                          10   CATALOG-REMAINING      PIC BX(4).
00079                     05   SIZE-CODE                   PIC BX.
00080                     05   QUANTITY                    PIC BBZ9.
00081                     05   OUTPUT-PRICE                PIC BB$$$9.99.
00082                     05   ITEM-DESCRIPTION            PIC BBX(40).
00083                     05   FILLER                      PIC X(59) VALUE SPACES.
00084
00085                01   TEXT-LINE REDEFINES OUTPUT-LINE.
00086                     05   CARRIAGE-CONTROL            PIC X.
00087                     05   UNKNOWN-LINE                PIC X(132).
00088
00089                01   PRICE-LIMIT                      PIC  999V99 VALUE 125.00.
00090                01   TEST-REMAINDER                   PIC S999V99 COMP-3.
00091                01   UNIT-PRICE                       PIC S999V99 COMP-3.
00092
00093           PROCEDURE DIVISION.
00094           A000-VALIDATE-ORDERS.
00095                OPEN INPUT ORDER-FILE
00096                     OUTPUT NORMAL-HANDLING-FILE
00097                            SPECIAL-HANDLING-FILE.
00098                READ ORDER-FILE
00099                     AT END MOVE 'N' TO MORE-DATA-REMAINS-FLAG.
00100                PERFORM B010-VALIDATE-ONE-LINE
00101                     UNTIL NO-MORE-DATA-REMAINS.
00102                CLOSE ORDER-FILE
00103                      NORMAL-HANDLING-FILE
00104                      SPECIAL-HANDLING-FILE.
00105                STOP RUN.
00106
00107           B010-VALIDATE-ONE-LINE.
00108                MOVE SPACES TO ERROR-FLAGS.
00109                PERFORM C010-EDIT-LINE.
00110
```

```
00111              IF QTY-AND-PRICE-OK
00112                  MOVE CORRESPONDING ORDER-RECORD TO OUTPUT-LINE
00113                  MOVE 9-PRICE TO OUTPUT-PRICE
00114                  IF RECORD-OK
00115                      WRITE NORMAL-LINE FROM OUTPUT-LINE
00116                            AFTER ADVANCING 2 LINES
00117                  ELSE
00118                      WRITE SPECIAL-LINE FROM OUTPUT-LINE
00119                            AFTER ADVANCING 2 LINES
00120                      PERFORM C020-WRITE-MESSAGES
00121              ELSE
00122                  MOVE ORDER-RECORD TO UNKNOWN-LINE
00123                  WRITE SPECIAL-LINE FROM OUTPUT-LINE
00124                        AFTER ADVANCING 2 LINES
00125                  PERFORM C020-WRITE-MESSAGES.
00126
00127              READ ORDER-FILE
00128                  AT END MOVE 'N' TO MORE-DATA-REMAINS-FLAG.
00129
00130          C010-EDIT-LINE.
00131              IF CATALOG-NUMBER OF ORDER-RECORD IS NOT NUMERIC
00132                  MOVE 'X' TO CAT-NO-NOT-NUMERIC.
00133
00134              IF CATALOG-FIRST-DIGIT OF ORDER-RECORD = '0' OR '2'
00135                  MOVE 'X' TO FIRST-DIGIT-INVALID.
00136
00137              IF (CATALOG-FIRST-DIGIT OF ORDER-RECORD = '1' OR '8' OR '9')
00138                  AND SIZE-CODE OF ORDER-RECORD IS NOT EQUAL TO SPACES
00139                  MOVE 'X' TO SIZE-CODE-NOT-PERMITTED.
00140
00141              IF SIZE-CODE OF ORDER-RECORD = 'A' OR 'D' OR 'G' OR 'J'
00142                  OR 'K' OR 'L' OR 'S' OR 'T' OR 'U' OR ' '
00143                  NEXT SENTENCE
00144              ELSE
00145                  MOVE 'X' TO NO-SUCH-SIZE-CODE.
00146
00147              IF QUANTITY OF ORDER-RECORD IS NOT NUMERIC
00148                  MOVE 'X' TO QTY-NOT-NUMERIC.
00149
00150              IF X-PRICE NOT NUMERIC
00151                  MOVE 'X' TO PRICE-NOT-NUMERIC.
00152
00153              IF QTY-AND-PRICE-OK
00154                  DIVIDE 9-PRICE BY QUANTITY OF ORDER-RECORD
00155                         GIVING UNIT-PRICE REMAINDER TEST-REMAINDER
00156                      ON SIZE ERROR MOVE 'X' TO INVALID-PRICE-OR-QTY.
00157              IF QTY-AND-PRICE-OK AND TEST-REMAINDER NOT EQUAL TO ZERO
00158                  MOVE 'X' TO INVALID-PRICE-OR-QTY.
00159
00160              IF X-PRICE IS NUMERIC AND 9-PRICE IS GREATER THAN PRICE-LIMIT
00161                  MOVE 'X' TO LARGE-PRICE.
00162
00163          C020-WRITE-MESSAGES.
00164              IF CAT-NO-NOT-NUMERIC = 'X'
00165                  WRITE SPECIAL-LINE FROM CAT-NO-NOT-NUMERIC-MSG
00166                        AFTER ADVANCING 1 LINE.
00167              IF FIRST-DIGIT-INVALID = 'X'
00168                  WRITE SPECIAL-LINE FROM FIRST-DIGIT-INVALID-MSG
00169                        AFTER ADVANCING 1 LINE.
```

```
00170                    IF SIZE-CODE-NOT-PERMITTED = 'X'
00171                        WRITE SPECIAL-LINE FROM SIZE-CODE-NOT-PERMITTED-MSG
00172                            AFTER ADVANCING 1 LINE.
00173                    IF NO-SUCH-SIZE-CODE = 'X'
00174                        WRITE SPECIAL-LINE FROM NO-SUCH-SIZE-CODE-MSG
00175                            AFTER ADVANCING 1 LINE.
00176                    IF QTY-NOT-NUMERIC = 'X'
00177                        WRITE SPECIAL-LINE FROM QTY-NOT-NUMERIC-MSG
00178                            AFTER ADVANCING 1 LINE.
00179                    IF PRICE-NOT-NUMERIC = 'X'
00180                        WRITE SPECIAL-LINE FROM PRICE-NOT-NUMERIC-MSG
00181                            AFTER ADVANCING 1 LINE.
00182                    IF INVALID-PRICE-OR-QTY = 'X'
00183                        WRITE SPECIAL-LINE FROM INVALID-PRICE-OR-QTY-MSG
00184                            AFTER ADVANCING 1 LINE.
00185                    IF LARGE-PRICE = 'X'
00186                        WRITE SPECIAL-LINE FROM LARGE-PRICE-MSG
00187                            AFTER ADVANCING 1 LINE.
00188
00189         *************** END OF PROGRAM *****************************
```

Figure 11.1 A program to perform a number of validity checks on records representing lines in an order from a seed catalog.

We also see here our first example of a **REDEFINES** clause in use. The idea is that the price as read from the record may have nonnumeric characters in it, either through a typing error or because leading zeros have not been keyed. In the Procedure Division we therefore need to be able to deal with the price as an alphanumeric item. But if the price as entered is in fact numeric, then we need to be able to do arithmetic on it. It would, of course, be possible to move the price to a Working-Storage location having the appropriate attributes, but the **REDEFINES** feature makes it unnecessary to do that. What we have, in effect, is two different definitions of the same five characters of the input record. These two descriptions, used in conjunction with different parts of the Procedure Division, make it possible for the compiler to set up dissimilar operations on the contents of those locations. The names **X-PRICE** and **9-PRICE** are meant to suggest alphanumeric and numeric, respectively, corresponding to the characters **X** and **9** in the **PICTURE** clauses. The records for the two output files are simply 133-character items to which the actual output will be moved using **WRITE FROM** statements.

The structures in the Working-Storage Section are, for the most part, in alphabetical sequence to facilitate locating any particular structure. Thus, we begin with eight error flags that may be set depending on what is found in the input. Each flag is set up as one character. In processing each order, as we shall see shortly, spaces are moved to the entire group item **ERROR-FLAGS**, which sets all eight of the flags to the "no error" condition. A level **88** entry is established for the entire group item so that after we have made all the validity checks, we can have a statement that says **IF RECORD-OK** and thus test with one comparison whether any errors have been detected. Similarly, a group item is made of the flags for nonnumeric quantity and price so that these two can be checked with one **IF** statement.

After making all of the required validity checks and setting a flag for each error that is detected, we shall be writing appropriate error messages corresponding to each flag that is found to be set. These messages are established in the eight elementary items of the group item named **ERROR-MESSAGES**. Observe that the **PICTURE** for all eight of these items specifies that the item contains 50 characters, whereas in fact the literals are of variable length and none of them is actually that long. The idea is that since nothing else occurs in the record after these error messages, the exact size is unimportant, and by putting in a uniform size we don't have to count the number of characters in the literals. Any time that the literal contains fewer characters than the number specified in its picture, the literal is left-justified just as on a nonnumeric **MOVE**.

Next, beginning with line 73, we have the definition of the actual output records. The record named **OUTPUT-LINE** will be used in two different circumstances. A line containing no errors will be moved there, and then will be written to the normal handling file. Second, a line that contains errors but where the quantity and price are correct will be edited there, and then will be written to the special handling file. It is assumed that an order line containing any of the other errors is very possibly mistyped, for instance, by omitting a character early in the line. A line containing such an error is harder to read after it has been edited than if it is simply written out exactly as it was entered. Therefore, a separate definition is provided for **OUTPUT-LINE** using a **REDEFINES** clause. This shows another motivation for the use of **REDEFINES**. With slight modifications the program would work if **TEXT-LINE** were simply a separate 133-character Working-Storage record. However, since we never need both **OUTPUT-LINE** and **TEXT-LINE** for any one input record, we may as well use the same storage area for both. There are very few computers where the saving of 133 characters would make much difference in a program like this, but the same principle applies to larger areas where it could be important.

In line 89 we have created a constant item to test whether the price has exceeded the limit of $125. As in earlier examples, we could simply have coded the value 125.00 in the Procedure Division wherever we need it, but using a Working-Storage item with the value of 125.00 simplifies maintenance should this limit ever change—which is *highly* probable.

Observe in lines 90 and 91 that these temporary storage items have been given signs and that their usage has been established in **COMPUTATIONAL-3**. Since these items are involved in arithmetic, rather than just comparison as is **PRICE-LIMIT**, making them signed and **COMPUTATIONAL-3** improves the efficiency of the program. Since they are never used for input or output, there is no need for them to be in **DISPLAY** format. As it happens in this program, the amount of arithmetic involved is trivial, but we should get in the habit of using signed computational items in this way as a matter of course.

The main paragraph of the Procedure Division, **A000-VALIDATE-ORDERS**, contains nothing new except that there are three files to open instead of the two that have been usual up to now. The paragraph named **B010-VALIDATE-ONE-LINE** begins by moving spaces to the error flags to clear out any indications of errors on the previous record, then performs **C010-EDIT-LINE**, which makes the prescribed tests. Of course, we could have executed the editing code in line in **B010-VALIDATE-ONE-LINE**, but moving it to a separate paragraph allows us to focus our attention on the logic of the validation process, while the editing details can be defined elsewhere.

After the editing has been performed, we are ready to write the output. It is only at this point, incidentally, that we can do any writing, since until we have made all of the tests, we don't know whether the order line is to be written to the normal handling file or to the special handling file. We begin by asking if the quantity and price are okay because if they are, we want to edit the output. This is done with a MOVE CORRESPONDING; everything in the order record having the same name as the items in the record named OUTPUT-LINE is moved with whatever editing is called for. Since 9-PRICE does not correspond to anything in the order record, it is moved separately. Now, if the record had no errors, we write the order line to the normal file. If it had errors, we write it to the special file and then use a PERFORM to call for the writing of whatever error messages are required immediately following it. If the quantity and price were not correct, then we move the entire order record to the record named UNKNOWN-LINE, without any editing, write that to the special file, and also write any necessary messages. Study the IF statement in lines 111-125 carefully to be sure you understand the flow of the logic.

In C010-EDIT-LINE we begin by checking the catalog number, taken here as a group item consisting of all five characters, to determine if it is numeric. Observe the use of data name qualification: since CATALOG-NUMBER appears in two different records, qualification must be used to establish which one we mean. Data name qualification will be required for all items in the input record except X-PRICE and 9-PRICE, which are unique.

The next validity check is to determine whether the first digit of the catalog number is zero or two, illustrating the use of an implied subject. The meaning is perfectly clear, and since the subject involves a qualified data name, it can be argued that this form is clearer than if the entire statement were written out.

The third validity test is to determine whether the customer has entered the size code for an item that does not have one. (This could also mean that the catalog number was copied down incorrectly.) This IF statement illustrates the use of the implied subject and implied relational operator together with parentheses to alter what would otherwise be the normal precedence of the logical operators. Without the parentheses, the meaning would be that the record is invalid if the first digit of the catalog number is 1 or 8, or if it is 9 and there is a size code. In other words, since AND takes precedence over OR, the testing of the size code would be combined only with a catalog first digit of 9. Saying it another way, a line in which the first digit of the catalog number is 1 or 8 would be considered erroneous regardless of the value of the size code, which is not what is desired.

Testing of the size code, beginning with line 141, exhibits the use of implied subject and relational operator. It could have been written with the operator NOT preceding the entire compound condition in parentheses to avoid the use of the NEXT SENTENCE feature. It is perhaps a matter of taste whether that would have been easier to understand than the form written here. Combinations of NOT and OR tend to be rather confusing.

The checking of the quantity and price contains nothing new.

Next we want to divide the price by the quantity and check to see if the remainder is zero—which it must be if the multiplication is correct. We do not want to do this, however, unless the price and quantity both have been found to be numeric. Therefore, we put the DIVIDE statement in an IF statement so that the division will be done only if quantity and price have both been found to be legitimate. Failure to do so could result in abnormal termination of the program—which is highly undesirable. One possible way to have an error in quantity is to have left it blank or entered zero. Ideally such a customer mistake should have been caught in a preliminary visual inspection of the order form, but the program must nevertheless make allowance for the possibility of the error. This is especially true since attempted division by zero will either produce a meaningless result or cause abnormal termination. One of the functions of the **ON SIZE ERROR** phrase is to prevent attempted division by zero.

The next thing to be done after the division is to test whether the remainder is zero or not. This, of course, must not be done unless the division was done, which means that we want to make it a part of an **IF** statement, conditional on the quantity and price having been found to be numeric. Since that same condition applies to the preceding statement, it would seem to be reasonably simple to make the testing of the remainder a part of the preceding **IF** statement. However, this is not possible because of the **ON SIZE ERROR** phrase; anything written after the words **ON SIZE ERROR** is considered to be part of that phrase, which is not what is desired here. Therefore, we write a separate statement with a compound condition.

COBOL-85

If you are using **COBOL-85**, you can use the **END-DIVIDE** phrase and write the code as follows:

```
IF QTY-AND-PRICE-OK
    DIVIDE 9-PRICE BY QUANTITY OF ORDER RECORD
            GIVING UNIT-PRICE REMAINDER TEST-REMAINDER
            ON SIZE ERROR MOVE 'X' TO INVALID-PRICE-OR-QTY
    END-DIVIDE
    IF TEST-REMAINDER NOT EQUAL TO ZERO
        MOVE 'X' TO INVALID-PRICE-OR-QUANTITY
    END-IF
END-IF.
```

END COBOL-85

The checking of the price is also part of a compound condition, since the test makes little sense unless the price was found to be numeric. If you are using a version of **COBOL** prior to **COBOL-85**, both parts of the test will be performed, but the condition will not be true unless the price is numeric; if you are using **COBOL-85**, the second test will not be performed at all unless the price is numeric.

The rest of the program contains no new special features. The printing of headings and the counting of lines have been omitted here partly to save space by not repeating familiar material, but also partly on the grounds that in a realistic application the results might very well go onto preprinted forms that do not require the program to produce headings.

11.8   THE RESULTS OF RUNNING THE PROGRAM

This program was run with a small sample of representative data. Figure 11.2 shows the input file, which contains both correct and erroneous entries. Figure

11.3 is the output onto the normal handling file when the program was run with this data. We see that the first five items are as we would expect, but the last one is a bit of a shock: even though the input record has the appearance of random characters designed to determine how the program would react to erroneous data, the record has passed all tests. This is meant to be a caution that strange things are always possible. Figure 11.4 is the output of the program onto the special handling file. We see that the various kinds of errors were properly diagnosed.

```
o     r  c  s q
r     e  a  i u
d     c  t  z a
e     o  a  e n                          Description                    Price
r     r  l    t
      d     o
123456251656A01ALASKA PEAS                                          00045
123456294342 01GARDEN AND TREE SPRAYER                              02095
123456262638U02HONEYCROSS CORN - 1 LB                               00700
222233293188 01EARTHWORMS - PKG OF 2000                             01795
222234293526A01PRAYING MANTIS EGG CASES                             00275
222235233183L02NASTURTIUM - MIXED COLORS - 1 OZ                     00400
222236241939H00PHLOX - GRANIFLORA - 1/8 OZ                          00105
222237233761B02HIBISCUS                                               390
222238269088U01GARLIC SETS - 2 LBS                                  008.80
222239622257T01LITTLE MARVEL PEAS - 1/2 LB                          0120
222240252829I 2HOT PEPPER - LONG RED CAYENNE - 1 OZ                 00550
123456222241SCUCUMBER - WEST INDIAN GHERKIN - 1/4 LB                00275
122345213466 10ABUNDANCE PEAR                                       18650
321321321321321321321321321321321321321321321321321321321321
436543643987698769769876 9JHGF JHGF JHGCHJHGF JGF JHGF JHF JHGF JH5876587658
231231231231A12A12A12A12A12A12A12A12A12A12A01201201201212
```

FIGURE 11.2 Sample input to the program of Figure 11.1.

ORDER NUMBER	CATALOG NUMBER	SZ CD	QTY	PRICE	DESCRIPTION
123456	5 1656	A	1	$0.45	ALASKA PEAS
123456	9 4342		1	$20.95	GARDEN AND TREE SPRAYER
123456	6 2638	U	2	$7.00	HONEYCROSS CORN - 1 LB
222233	9 3188		1	$17.95	EARTHWORMS - PKG OF 2000
222235	3 3183	L	2	$4.00	NASTURTIUM - MIXED COLORS - 1 OZ
231231	3 1231	A	12	$12.12	A12A12A12A12A12A12A12A12A12A12A012012012

FIGURE 11.3 The contents of the **NORMAL-HANDLING-FILE** when the program of Figure 11.1 was run with the sample data of Figure 11.2.

```
222234  9 3526 A   1     $2.75  PRAYING MANTIS EGG CASES
THIS ITEM DOES NOT TAKE A SIZE CODE

222236  4 1939 H   0     $1.05  PHLOX - GRANIFLORA - 1/8 OZ
THERE IS NO SUCH SIZE CODE
EITHER PRICE OR QUANTITY IS WRONG

222237233761B02HIBISCUS                                390
THERE IS NO SUCH SIZE CODE
PRICE CONTAINS AN IMPROPER CHARACTER

222238269088U01GARLIC SETS - 2 LBS            008.80
PRICE CONTAINS AN IMPROPER CHARACTER

22223962257T01LITTLE MARVEL PEAS - 1/2 LB     0120
CATALOG NUMBER CONTAINS AN IMPROPER CHARACTER
FIRST DIGIT OF CATALOG NUMBER INVALID
THERE IS NO SUCH SIZE CODE
QUANTITY CONTAINS AN IMPROPER CHARACTER
PRICE CONTAINS AN IMPROPER CHARACTER

222240252829L 2HOT PEPPER - LONG RED CAYENNE - 1 OZ   00550
QUANTITY CONTAINS AN IMPROPER CHARACTER

123456222241SCUCUMBER - WEST INDIAN GHERKIN - 1/4 LB  00275
FIRST DIGIT OF CATALOG NUMBER INVALID
QUANTITY CONTAINS AN IMPROPER CHARACTER

122345  1 3466    10   $186.50  ABUNDANCE PEAR
PRICE LARGE - SHOULD BE CHECKED

321321  2 1321 3  21   $213.21  321321321321321321321321321321321321213
FIRST DIGIT OF CATALOG NUMBER INVALID
THERE IS NO SUCH SIZE CODE
EITHER PRICE OR QUANTITY IS WRONG
PRICE LARGE - SHOULD BE CHECKED

436543643987698769769876 9JHGFJHGFJHGCHJHGFJGFJHGFJHFJHGFJH5876587658
THERE IS NO SUCH SIZE CODE
PRICE CONTAINS AN IMPROPER CHARACTER
```

FIGURE 11.4 The output of the SPECIAL-HANDLING-FILE when the program of Figure 11.1 was run with the sample data of Figure 11.2.

REVIEW QUESTIONS

1. Shown below are five pairs of skeleton IF statements. Do the two statements in each pair have the same effect?

   a. IF A = 1 AND B = 2 OR C = 2 AND D = 2 . . .

       IF (A = 1 AND B = 2) OR (C = 2 AND D = 2) . . .

b. IF   TRANSFER-CODE NOT = '1'
          OR TRANSACTION-AMOUNT IS NOT NUMERIC . . .

   IF   NOT (TRANSFER-CODE = '1'
       OR   TRANSACTION-AMOUNT IS NUMERIC) . . .

c. IF SAM < 30 AND GEORGE > 40 OR RUTH = 50 . . .

   IF (SAM < 30 AND GEORGE > 40) OR RUTH = 50 . .

d. IF (WEATHER = CLOUDY AND TEMP > 60) AND TEMP < 85
          OR WEATHER = CLEAR AND TEMP < 75 . . .

   IF WEATHER = CLOUDY AND (TEMP > 60 AND TEMP < 85)
       OR WEATHER = CLEAR AND TEMP < 75 . . .

e. IF A = 1 OR A NOT = 1 . . .

   IF NOT (A = 1 AND A = 2) . . .

2. Shown below are three groups of skeleton **IF** statements. Do the statements in each group have the same effect?

a. IF A = 1 OR A = 2 OR A = 4 . . .

   IF A = 1 OR 2 OR 4 . . .

b. IF (A = 1 OR A = 2) AND (B = 6 OR 8) . . .

   IF (A = 1 OR 2) AND (B = 6 OR 8) . . .

   IF A = 1 OR 2 AND B = 6 OR 8 . . .

c. IF A = 1 OR 2 OR 9 AND B = SPACES . . .

   IF (A = 1 OR 2 OR 9) AND B = SPACES . . .

3. In the seed catalog problem, would it not be simpler to write each error message as the corresponding error is detected, rather than setting flags and writing the messages later?

4. In the seed catalog program we have the statement:

```
IF X-PRICE IS NUMERIC AND 9-PRICE IS GREATER THAN
PRICE-LIMIT
    MOVE 'X' TO LARGE-PRICE.
```

What would be the effect if we had written this instead?

```
IF X-PRICE IS NUMERIC AND X-PRICE IS GREATER THAN
PRICE-LIMIT
    MOVE 'X' TO LARGE-PRICE.
```
How about this?

```
IF X-PRICE IS NUMERIC AND X-PRICE IS GREATER THAN '12500'
    MOVE 'X' TO LARGE-PRICE.
```

How about this?

```
IF 9-PRICE IS GREATER THAN PRICE-LIMIT
    MOVE 'X' TO LARGE-PRICE.
```

ANSWERS

1. a. No difference. The parentheses express the effect of the precedence rule.

b. Not the same at all; it is not permissible to "factor out" **NOT** in this way. Change the **OR** in the second statement to **AND**, however, and the two statements are the same. (Work it out with examples.) This is an instance of DeMorgan's Laws.

c. No difference. Again, the parentheses simply express the precedence rule.

d. No difference. The two uses of the parentheses express the idea that the three elements joined by **AND**s may be grouped either way in reducing the evaluation to operations on pairs of values. This is similar to the *associative rule* in arithmetic, which says, for instance, that $(A \times B) \times C = A \times (B \times C)$.

e. Oddly enough, these two *are* equivalent, in the sense that both of them are always true regardless of the value of **A**. **A** must always either equal 1 or not equal 1, so that the first statement is always true. Likewise, **A** can never be equal to both 1 and 2 at the same time, so the expression in parentheses is always false and its negation is always true.

2. a. The two are equivalent.

b. The first two are equivalent to each other, but the third is quite different. In the third form, without the parentheses, the **AND** is a higher ranking operator than the **OR**—the implied subjects have nothing to do with it. The effect of the third form is as if we had written

```
IF A = 1 OR (A = 2 AND B = 6) OR B = 8  . . .
```

c. The two are not equivalent, as discussed in the chapter in connection with the seed catalog order program.

3. So it would seem at first, but there are two problems. First, until checking price and quantity you don't know the format in which the order line is to be printed (with or without editing). More important, you don't know until detecting the first error whether to write the order line to the normal or the special handling file. If you write the order line as soon as you find the first error, then you have to set a flag to tell the program not to write it again if another error is found. The way shown is simpler, on balance.

4. The first alternative would fail in comparing an alphanumeric quantity (**X-PRICE**) with a numeric quantity (**PRICE-LIMIT**). The second version would give correct results, but the meaning is less obvious. The third version would apply the test even if the price had been found to be nonnumeric, making the test meaningless; that is, certain nonnumeric values would be "less" than the value of **PRICE-LIMIT**, but the comparison would be meaningless.

EXERCISES

*1. Write an **IF** statement to place an **X** in **INVALID-CODE-FLAG** if **COLUMN-23-CODE** contains anything except 1, 2, or 3.

2. Write an **IF** statement to do the following: If **COL-29** contains any digit, add 1 to **CLASS-A**; if **COL-29** contains A, B, or R, add 1 to **CLASS-B**; if **COL-29** contains C, F, G, H, S, or W, add 1 to **CLASS-C**; if none of these is true, add 1 to **CLASS-ERROR** and move X to **CLASS-ERROR-FLAG**. Use implied subjects and relational operators to shorten the statement.

*3. Write an **IF** statement that will add 1 to **REGULAR-COUNT** if **SIZE-A** is in the range of 14 to 36 inclusive and **SIZE-B** is less than 50, and add 1 to **SPECIAL-COUNT** otherwise.

4. Write an **IF** statement to place an **X** in **NORMAL-CASE** if **VOLUME** is in any of the ranges 12-19, 27-46, or 83-91 (all ranges inclusive), and place an **X** in **ERROR-CASE** otherwise. If you are using **COBOL-85**, write this once using the >= and <= operators, and once without using them.

*5. Modify the program of Figure 11.1 to produce an appropriate error message if the order number is not numeric.

6. Modify the program in Figure 11.1 so that it produces column headings for the normal output as shown in Figure 11.3. You may use the routine **X010-LINE-OUT** in Figure 9.7. Since this routine counts the lines for only one report, however, it cannot be used with both output files.

7. Continuing with Exercise 6, further modify the program of Figure 11.1 to produce a heading line for each page of the special handling file. The heading need not identify columns, but should simply describe what is being printed. This output routine should be set up to allow a "normal" maximum of 50 lines per page, including headings and blanks, but it should continue printing lines after 50 if necessary to get all of the error comments for any one order on the same page.

8. Modify the program of Figure 11.1 so that if the catalog number is 14100, 78667, 74005, 53512, 15537, or 92528, then that item is included both in the normal handling file and the special handling file. In the special handling file the message should be **CHECK THAT DESCRIPTION MATCHES CATALOG NUMBER**.

The problem here is that these six catalog numbers are used in the sample order form shown in the seed catalog; people fairly frequently miscopy these numbers in writing their orders. In a related situation, manufacturers frequently place an identification card in wallets with a sample Social Security number. People surprisingly often copy these numbers as their own Social Security number. This phenomenon of "pocketbook numbers" is one reason why Social Security numbers are not always unique.

---

* Answers to starred exercises will be found in Appendix IV at the end of the book.

CHAPTER 12

UPDATING
SEQUENTIAL FILES

12.1 INTRODUCTION

This chapter develops one of the most fundamental techniques of data processing: updating a sequential file. The program for this operation is developed in seven stages, in a sequence that is important in its own right. We concentrate first on the highest level control logic and bring in additional details of the required processing only after we have assured ourselves that the high level logic is correct. This process, which is called *top-down development*, will be described as we go along.

File updating refers to any situation in which we have a master file of information about a group of related people or objects that must periodically be modified as a result of changes in the status of the people or things that are described by the file. There are literally thousands of different kinds of file updating applications. For concreteness, we shall talk about one of the most common, that of inventory control. In this example, we assume that some company maintains a record for each item in its warehouse. Each record, at an absolute minimum, must contain some kind of identification of the item, such as a stock number or part number, and a quantity that says how many of that item are in the warehouse. In fact, there would be a good deal of additional information, some of which we shall sketch later after the basic processing logic is clear. For our initial purposes we shall call these two elements of information about each stock item the key and the *quantity*.

The master file, consisting of a record for each item in the inventory, is assumed to be in ascending sequence on the keys of the items. That is, the first record in the file is the one that has the lowest key in the entire file, in terms of the machine's collating sequence (see Section 5.8). The second record is the one having the next higher key, and so on. This sequential nature of the file organization is fundamental to the processing logic that we shall develop.

Besides this master file we have a *transaction file* that gives information about changes in the status of inventory items. The most common changes are *receipts* of new stock from suppliers and *shipments* of stock to customers. It is also necessary, however, to be able to enter adjustments to any of the information in the master file. An example would be when a physical inventory count shows that the actual quantity on hand is different from that shown in the master file, perhaps because of various kinds of errors in the past or because of some kind of fraud. It is also necessary to be able to handle *additions* to the master file, when the company begins to stock new items, and *deletions*, when it drops them from inventory altogether.

The master and transaction files are the two input files to the program. The most important output file is an updated version of the master, which reflects all the changes dictated by the transaction file. There is also a much smaller file listing all of the deletions of items from the inventory, which can be combined with a listing of various kinds of errors. In the final version of the program at the end of this chapter, we shall produce a file of order recommendations for items for which the stock is getting low. The overall relationships of these five files is shown in Figure 12.1. The dotted line connecting the new

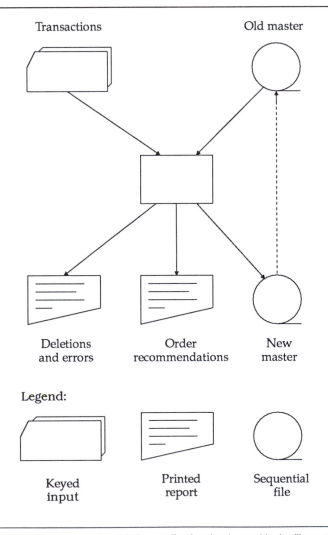

FIGURE 12.1 Run diagram of a file updating application that is used in the illustrative programs of the chapter.

master to the old master is based on the fact that this kind of program is run periodically, perhaps every week. Each time the program is run, what we are calling the old master is the file that was called the new master the previous time the program was run.

There is more to the story, in terms of the processing that is required and the kinds of errors that must be detected. We shall postpone the discussion of these matters, however, until we have worked out the logic of a program that will handle this much.

12.2   A SIMPLE MERGE PROGRAM

We begin with an operation that is the simplest one possible, while still related to the one that we eventually want to produce. We begin with two files named **IN-FILE-1** and **IN-FILE-2**, both in ascending sequence on the keys in their records. The operation of merging consists of producing one output file, here called **OUT-FILE**, that is also in ascending sequence on the keys of its records. A generalized merge permits either file to have records with the same key and permits *matches*, that is, a condition where a record in one file has the same key as a record in the other file. In the file update program these duplicate keys and matched keys have special significance that must be taken into consideration. In a merge, however, we take no account of such situations and simply produce an output file that is in ascending sequence on the keys of its records.

You will notice in the following material that we show no design specifications. Hierarchy charts and pseudocode specifications were written in the development of all of the programs. However, since the emphasis in the programs is specifically on the logic of the programs, there is remarkably little difference between the pseudocode and the programs. This is hardly surprising because the function of the pseudocode is precisely to encourage a close focus on the program logic rather than on the details of processing. All this being true, and since space in a textbook is at a premium, is seems best to omit the pseudocode. We cannot emphasize too strongly, however, that while the pseudocode may not be needed as documentation *after* the program has been written, it is a vital part of the *design* process.

A program for the merge process is shown in Figure 12.2. After reading one record from each input file we enter a **PERFORM...UNTIL** loop that is repeated until both keys are equal to **HIGH-VALUES.*** **HIGH-VALUES** is moved to the keys by the **AT END** phrase of the **READ** statements. The logic of selecting a record from either **IN-FILE-1** or **IN-FILE-2** is based on a comparison of the keys of the two records. If **KEY-1**, the key of the record from **IN-FILE-1**, is less than **KEY-2**, the key of the record from **IN-FILE-2**, then we write the record from **IN-FILE-1** to the output file and read another record from **IN-FILE-1**. If **KEY-1** is not less than **KEY-2**, that is, if they are equal or if **KEY-1** is greater, then we write the record from **IN-FILE-2** to the output file and read another record from **IN-FILE-2**. Assuming only that both input files are in ascending sequence, this logic guarantees that the records on the output file will also be in ascending sequence.

---

* **HIGH-VALUES** is a figurative constant; in its place the compiler supplies the largest data value in the computer's collating sequence. **LOW-VALUES**, in like manner, represents the smallest values in the computer's collating sequence.

The only aspect of the program that is perhaps not entirely familiar is the use of the **READ...INTO** option. The problem is that we want to have access to the key of a record after we have reached the end of the file. In some versions of **COBOL** the record area is not available after the end of file is reached. Therefore, we define a record in the File Section and use the **READ...INTO** to get the information into the Working-Storage Section record area where all processing is done on it.

```
00001              IDENTIFICATION DIVISION.
00002              PROGRAM-ID.
00003                  MERGE1.
00004              DATE-WRITTEN.
00005                  MARCH 18, 1987.
00006          *        SIMPLE MERGE
00007
00008              ENVIRONMENT DIVISION.
00009              INPUT-OUTPUT SECTION.
00010              FILE-CONTROL.
00011                  SELECT IN-FILE-1          ASSIGN TO S-INFILE1.
00012                  SELECT IN-FILE-2          ASSIGN TO S-INFILE2.
00013                  SELECT OUT-FILE           ASSIGN TO S-OUTFILE.
00014
00015              DATA DIVISION.
00016              FILE SECTION.
00017
00018              FD  IN-FILE-1
00019                  LABEL RECORDS ARE OMITTED.
00020              01  IN-RECORD-1-BUFFER        PIC X(80).
00021
00022              FD  IN-FILE-2
00023                  LABEL RECORDS ARE OMITTED.
00024              01  IN-RECORD-2-BUFFER        PIC X(80).
00025
00026              FD  OUT-FILE
00027                  LABEL RECORDS ARE OMITTED.
00028              01  OUT-RECORD.
00029                  05   OUT-KEY              PIC X(5).
00030                  05   REST-OF-RECORD       PIC X(75).
00031
00032              WORKING-STORAGE SECTION.
00033
00034              01  IN-RECORD-1.
00035                  05   KEY-1                PIC X(5).
00036                  05   REST-OF-RECORD-1     PIC X(75).
00037
00038              01  IN-RECORD-2.
00039                  05   KEY-2                PIC X(5).
00040                  05   REST-OF-RECORD-2     PIC X(75).
00041
00042
00043              PROCEDURE DIVISION.
00044              A000-MERGE-TWO-FILES.
00045                  OPEN INPUT IN-FILE-1
00046                             IN-FILE-2
00047                       OUTPUT OUT-FILE.
00048                  PERFORM B020-READ-1.
00049                  PERFORM B030-READ-2.
```

```
00050                 PERFORM B010-MERGE-LOGIC
00051                     UNTIL KEY-1 = HIGH-VALUES  AND  KEY-2 = HIGH-VALUES.
00052                 CLOSE IN-FILE-1
00053                     IN-FILE-2
00054                     OUT-FILE.
00055                 STOP RUN.
00056
00057             B010-MERGE-LOGIC.
00058                 IF KEY-1 IS LESS THAN KEY-2
00059                     WRITE OUT-RECORD FROM IN-RECORD-1
00060                     PERFORM B020-READ-1
00061                 ELSE
00062                     WRITE OUT-RECORD FROM IN-RECORD-2
00063                     PERFORM B030-READ-2.
00064
00065             B020-READ-1.
00066                 READ IN-FILE-1 INTO IN-RECORD-1
00067                     AT END MOVE HIGH-VALUES TO KEY-1.
00068
00069             B030-READ-2.
00070                 READ IN-FILE-2 INTO IN-RECORD-2
00071                     AT END MOVE HIGH-VALUES TO KEY-2.
00072
00073             ******************** END OF PROGRAM ***********************
```

FIGURE 12.2 A program to merge two files.

Here are two sample input files and the resulting output file produced by the execution of this program. Since we are interested primarily in the keys, the main body of the records has been reduced to the letter **A** for **IN-FILE-1** and to the letter **B** for **IN-FILE-2**.

File 1	File 2	Merged File
00001A	00002B	00001A
00003A	00004B	00002B
00007A	00005B	00003A
00010A	00005B	00004B
00010A	00007B	00005B
00012A	00012B	00005B
00015A	00015B	00007B
	00015B	00007A
	00020B	00010A
		00010A
		00012B
		00012A
		00015B
		00015B
		00015A
		00020B

There is no need to try to demonstrate that this program works for all the kinds of special cases that one can think of, but on the next page is a sample showing that the program correctly handles a one-record file and that it operates correctly no matter which file runs out first.

File 1	File 2	Merged File
00019C	00001D	00001D
	00008D	00008D
	00016D	00016D
	00017D	00017D
		00019C

12.3 THE MERGE PROGRAM WITH SEQUENCE CHECKING

Any program written to process files that are supposed to be in ascending sequence will rapidly get into deep trouble if the files are, in fact, *not* in sequence. It is therefore advisable to check the sequence of the incoming records, especially since doing so is quite simple. A modified program is shown in Figure 12.3. The major changes are the introduction of three new items at the end of the Working-Storage Section and changes in the paragraphs named **B020-READ-1** and **B030-READ-2**. Since we are always going to be comparing a record with a previous record, we must have somewhere to save the keys of the previous records, for both files. To prevent the possibility of a false error indication on the very first record of each file, we initialize both of these *save items* to **LOW-VALUES**. A sequence error flag is used to signal the mainline logic if an error occurs. In the mainline paragraph the **UNTIL** phrase of the **PERFORM** is modified to make the loop stop if a sequence error is detected.

```
00001          IDENTIFICATION DIVISION.
00002          PROGRAM-ID.
00003              MERGE2.
00004          DATE-WRITTEN.
00005              MARCH 18, 1987.
00006      *        MERGE WITH SEQUENCE CHECKING
00007
00008          ENVIRONMENT DIVISION.
00009          INPUT-OUTPUT SECTION.
00010          FILE-CONTROL.
00011              SELECT IN-FILE-1          ASSIGN TO S-INFILE1.
00012              SELECT IN-FILE-2          ASSIGN TO S-INFILE2.
00013              SELECT OUT-FILE           ASSIGN TO S-OUTFILE.
00014
00015          DATA DIVISION.
00016          FILE SECTION.
00017
00018      FD  IN-FILE-1
00019              LABEL RECORDS ARE OMITTED.
00020      01  IN-RECORD-1-BUFFER          PIC X(80).
00021
00022      FD  IN-FILE-2
00023              LABEL RECORDS ARE OMITTED.
00024      01  IN-RECORD-2-BUFFER          PIC X(80).
00025      FD  OUT-FILE
00026              LABEL RECORDS ARE OMITTED.
00027      01  OUT-RECORD.
00028          05  OUT-KEY                PIC X(5).
00029          05  REST-OF-RECORD         PIC X(75).
00030
```

```
00031              WORKING-STORAGE SECTION.
00032
00033          01  IN-RECORD-1.
00034              05  KEY-1                     PIC X(5).
00035              05  REST-OF-RECORD-1          PIC X(75).
00036
00037          01  IN-RECORD-2.
00038              05  KEY-2                     PIC X(5).
00039              05  REST-OF-RECORD-2          PIC X(75).
00040
00041          01  PREVIOUS-KEY-1                PIC X(5) VALUE LOW-VALUES.
00042          01  PREVIOUS-KEY-2                PIC X(5) VALUE LOW-VALUES.
00043
00044          01  SEQUENCE-ERROR-FLAG           PIC X    VALUE 'N'.
00045              88  SEQUENCE-ERROR                     VALUE 'Y'.
00046
00047
00048          PROCEDURE DIVISION.
00049          A000-MERGE-TWO-FILES.
00050              OPEN INPUT IN-FILE-1
00051                         IN-FILE-2
00052                  OUTPUT OUT-FILE.
00053              PERFORM B020-READ-1.
00054              PERFORM B030-READ-2.
00055              PERFORM B010-MERGE-LOGIC
00056                  UNTIL (KEY-1 = HIGH-VALUES AND  KEY-2 = HIGH-VALUES)
00057                        OR SEQUENCE-ERROR.
00058              IF SEQUENCE-ERROR
00059                  DISPLAY 'SEQUENCE ERROR - JOB ABORTED'.
00060              CLOSE IN-FILE-1
00061                    IN-FILE-2
00062                    OUT-FILE.
00063              STOP RUN.
00064
00065          B010-MERGE-LOGIC.
00066              IF KEY-1 IS LESS THAN KEY-2
00067                  WRITE OUT-RECORD FROM IN-RECORD-1
00068                  PERFORM B020-READ-1
00069              ELSE
00070                  WRITE OUT-RECORD FROM IN-RECORD-2
00071                  PERFORM B030-READ-2.
00072
00073          B020-READ-1.
00074              READ IN-FILE-1 INTO IN-RECORD-1
00075                  AT END MOVE HIGH-VALUES TO KEY-1.
00076              IF KEY-1 IS LESS THAN PREVIOUS-KEY-1
00077                  MOVE 'Y' TO SEQUENCE-ERROR-FLAG
00078              ELSE
00079                  MOVE KEY-1 TO PREVIOUS-KEY-1.
00080
00081          B030-READ-2.
00082              READ IN-FILE-2 INTO IN-RECORD-2
00083                  AT END MOVE HIGH-VALUES TO KEY-2.
00084              IF KEY-2 IS LESS THAN PREVIOUS-KEY-2
00085                  MOVE 'Y' TO SEQUENCE-ERROR-FLAG
00086              ELSE
00087                  MOVE KEY-2 TO PREVIOUS-KEY-2.
00088
00089          *********************** END OF PROGRAM ***********************
```

FIGURE 12.3   A program to merge two files and stop with an error message if a sequence error is detected.

This program is written on the assumption that if any sequence error is found, the situation is unrecoverable and the job should be stopped. It is hardly acceptable, however, to stop a job in midstream and give no warning that processing was not completed. The approach to this problem taken here is to use the **DISPLAY** statement to print a notification of the situation, which is acceptable for this simple example. Normally, however, this is *not* a satisfactory way of dealing with the problem. In a more complete program we would write an error message on an output file, not only telling what had happened but giving the user enough information to be able to track down the cause of the error. In fact, we might not even want to stop the program after detecting a single sequence error. For example, if the input files were prepared by clerks keying the data into a terminal, errors are not unlikely and, if they are not too damaging, we might wish to continue processing. We would generally keep count of the number of errors and give up only if that number exceeded some reasonable maximum. (This approach is shown later in this chapter.) On the other hand, if both input files were the output of computer programs such that sequence errors ought to be virtually impossible, then we might indeed stop after detecting one error, since such an error would be indicative of some kind of very serious processing problem.

12.4 THE SIMPLEST POSSIBLE UPDATE LOGIC

Recall that our strategy in developing a complete update program is to concentrate first on the top-level logic and to worry about the details of processing later. As we begin, we shall also call on a tactic we have used before, that of starting with a simpler problem.

To be specific, we shall simplify the program by ignoring additions and deletions. Any transaction that matches a master is assumed to contain information to be used in updating the master information. The second simplification is that we shall not do the updating. When a match is discovered, we shall invoke a paragraph that contains nothing but a **DISPLAY** statement, which will prove that we reached it and will show the keys of the records. The final simplification—a major one—is to ignore the possibility of errors in the files.

The basic logic of this most elementary version has a close resemblance to the logic of the simple merge, but with important differences. Similarities exist in that whenever the key of the master record is less than the key of the transaction record, we write the old master to the new master (output) file and read another old master record. Two kinds of differences can be noted. First, since we are assuming no errors, it can never happen that the transaction' key is less than the old master key; this could occur only because of an unmatched transaction, which is an error, or because of an addition record, which we are not considering here. Second, when the old master and the transaction have equal keys, we carry out the updating operation and read another transaction, but *we do not write anything*. It is entirely permissible to have a number of transactions for the same master record, the transactions to be applied in sequence. For instance, there may have been several receipts of stock from suppliers and many shipments of stock to customers since the last updating of the file. As long as transactions come in having the same key as the old master, we simply continue to update that one old master record. Eventually, we get a transaction with a higher key, which will force the writing of the old master record.

12.5   **TOP-DOWN PROGRAM DEVELOPMENT AND PROGRAM STUBS**

The program is shown in Figure 12.4. With the logic clearly understood, and drawing on the similarity of the merge program, there is almost nothing to explain except one matter of terminology. The paragraph named **B040-UPDATE-MASTER**, which does not do any processing but simply signals that it was reached, is called a *stub*. Stubs are used during program development by the top-down approach while we are concentrating on the top-level logic. During this stage all we really want to know is that the program sections represented by the stubs have been reached.

```
00001          IDENTIFICATION DIVISION.
00002          PROGRAM-ID.
00003             UPDATE1.
00004          DATE-WRITTEN.
00005             MARCH 18, 1987.
00006
00007          ENVIRONMENT DIVISION.
00008          INPUT-OUTPUT SECTION.
00009          FILE-CONTROL.
00010             SELECT TRANSACTION-FILE        ASSIGN TO S-TRANS.
00011             SELECT OLD-MASTER-FILE         ASSIGN TO S-OLDMAST.
00012             SELECT NEW-MASTER-FILE         ASSIGN TO S-NEWMAST.
00013
00014          DATA DIVISION.
00015
00016          FILE SECTION.
00017
00018          FD  TRANSACTION-FILE
00019              LABEL RECORDS ARE OMITTED.
00020          01  TRANSACTION-BUFFER            PIC X(80).
00021
00022          FD  OLD-MASTER-FILE
00023              LABEL RECORDS ARE OMITTED.
00024          01  OLD-MASTER-BUFFER             PIC X(80).
00025
00026          FD  NEW-MASTER-FILE
00027              LABEL RECORDS ARE OMITTED.
00028          01  NEW-MASTER.
00029              05   NM-KEY                    PIC X(5).
00030              05   NM-QUANTITY               PIC 9(5).
00031              05   FILLER                    PIC X(70).
00032
00033          WORKING-STORAGE SECTION.
00034
00035          01  OLD-MASTER.
00036              05   OM-KEY                    PIC X(5).
00037              05   OM-QUANTITY               PIC 9(5).
00038              05   FILLER                    PIC X(70).
00039
00040          01  TRANSACTION.
00041              05   TR-KEY                    PIC X(5).
00042              05   TR-QUANTITY               PIC 9(5).
00043              05   FILLER                    PIC X(70).
00044
00045
```

```
00046              PROCEDURE DIVISION.
00047              A000-UPDATE-FILE.
00048                  OPEN INPUT TRANSACTION-FILE
00049                            OLD-MASTER-FILE
00050                       OUTPUT NEW-MASTER-FILE.
00051                  PERFORM B020-READ-TRANSACTION.
00052                  PERFORM B030-READ-MASTER.
00053                  PERFORM B010-UPDATE-LOGIC
00054                      UNTIL OM-KEY = HIGH-VALUES AND TR-KEY = HIGH-VALUES.
00055                  CLOSE TRANSACTION-FILE
00056                        OLD-MASTER-FILE
00057                        NEW-MASTER-FILE.
00058                  STOP RUN.
00059
00060              B010-UPDATE-LOGIC.
00061                  IF OM-KEY IS LESS THAN TR-KEY
00062                      WRITE NEW-MASTER FROM OLD-MASTER
00063                      PERFORM B030-READ-MASTER
00064                  ELSE
00065                      PERFORM B040-UPDATE-MASTER
00066                      PERFORM B020-READ-TRANSACTION.
00067
00068              B020-READ-TRANSACTION.
00069                  READ TRANSACTION-FILE INTO TRANSACTION
00070                      AT END MOVE HIGH-VALUES TO TR-KEY.
00071
00072              B030-READ-MASTER.
00073                  READ OLD-MASTER-FILE INTO OLD-MASTER
00074                      AT END MOVE HIGH-VALUES TO OM-KEY.
00075
00076              B040-UPDATE-MASTER.
00077                  DISPLAY ' OM ', OM-KEY, ' TR ', TR-KEY.
00078
00079              ******************* END OF PROGRAM ************************
```

FIGURE 12.4 A program for the simplest possible file update.

This method of program development is called *top-down development*, since it concentrates first on the high-level logic and postpones the details until later. The approach is followed deliberately, as a matter of policy. The theory is that the top-level logic is the most crucial and the most likely to be wrong; therefore, it should receive the most testing. Writing the first version of the program with almost total concentration on the top logic and almost no concentration on the details of processing has this result.

The alternative approach, called bottom-up development, would have us first write the program sections that do the detailed processing. To test them independently of the complete program, we would have to write small programs called *drivers*. The first testing of the top-level logic would not be possible until all of the lower-level program sections had been developed. While bottom-up development is not used to any great extent, it is occasionally productive to combine top-down and bottom-up development. That is, although the major emphasis is on top-down development, critical bottom level modules may be developed concurrently to be sure they will work. However, we shall generally use only top-down development.

12.6 THE OUTPUT OF THE PROGRAM

This program was run with small sample files, here shown together with the output produced as a result of the **DISPLAY** statement and the new master file.

Old Master	Transaction	Displayed Output		New Master
Key Qty	Key Qty			Key Qty
00002 00111	00008 00050	OM 00008	TR 00008	00002 00111
00008 00123	00021 00100	OM 00021	TR 00021	00008 00123
00011 00200	00024 01000	OM 00024	TR 00024	00011 00200
00021 00210	00037 12300	OM 00037	TR 00037	00021 00210
00024 00099	00051 00000	OM 00051	TR 00051	00024 00099
00036 01234				00036 01234
00037 12345				00037 12345
00051 54321				00051 54321
00059 43210				00059 43210
00061 32109				00061 32109

We see that the paragraph named **B040-UPDATE-MASTER** was reached for each of the transactions, since each transaction matches a master. We also see that the new master is an exact copy of the old master; this is as it should be because we have not yet provided for additions, deletions, or actual updating.

12.7 PROCESSING ADDITIONS AND DELETIONS

Now we consider the two important transaction types of additions and deletions. An addition, we recall, is a record describing some inventory item not previously stocked by the company. An addition record comes in from the transaction file and is to be inserted in the proper place in the new master. Such a transaction should, of course, not match any record in the old master; if it does, either someone was unaware of the existence of that stock number or perhaps the stock number was entered incorrectly. In this version of the program, however, we are still ignoring the possibility of errors.

The other new transaction deals with the deletion process, in which a record in the old master is not to be written to the new master, since the company is no longer stocking that inventory item. A deletion transaction obviously *should* match an old master record, but again we are ignoring the possibility of error. When a deletion match occurs, we are required simply to write the deleted old master record onto a deletion report and carry on.

The program to implement these new features is shown in Figure 12.5. We observe that the record description for the transaction now includes a field to identify which of five different types of transactions is being processed, and that there are level **88** entries associated with each transaction code to make the Procedure Division logic easier to read. We assume that the records for any one transaction key are in sequence on the basis of transaction code. This guarantees, for instance, that receipts are processed before shipments; if this were not true, the processing of shipments first could give a false indication of an out-of-stock condition. Arranging a file so that it is in sequence on two different fields this way is a normal part of sorting operations, one approach to which is considered in Chapter 17.

```
00001              IDENTIFICATION DIVISION.
00002              PROGRAM-ID.
00003                 UPDATE2.
00004              DATE-WRITTEN.
00005                 MARCH 19, 1987.
00006
00007              ENVIRONMENT DIVISION.
00008              INPUT-OUTPUT SECTION.
00009              FILE-CONTROL.
00010                 SELECT TRANSACTION-FILE          ASSIGN TO S-TRANS.
00011                 SELECT OLD-MASTER-FILE           ASSIGN TO S-OLDMAST.
00012                 SELECT NEW-MASTER-FILE           ASSIGN TO S-NEWMAST.
00013                 SELECT DELETION-FILE             ASSIGN TO S-DELETION.
00014
00015              DATA DIVISION.
00016
00017              FILE SECTION.
00018
00019              FD  TRANSACTION-FILE
00020                  LABEL RECORDS ARE OMITTED.
00021              01  TRANSACTION-BUFFER              PIC X(80).
00022
00023              FD  OLD-MASTER-FILE
00024                  LABEL RECORDS ARE OMITTED.
00025              01  OLD-MASTER-BUFFER              PIC X(80).
00026
00027              FD  NEW-MASTER-FILE
00028                  LABEL RECORDS ARE OMITTED.
00029              01  NEW-MASTER.
00030                  05  NM-KEY                     PIC X(5).
00031                  05  NM-QUANTITY                PIC 9(5).
00032                  05  FILLER                     PIC X(70).
00033
00034              FD  DELETION-FILE
00035                  LABEL RECORDS ARE OMITTED.
00036              01  DELETION-REPORT.
00037                  05  CARRIAGE-CONTROL           PIC X.
00038                  05  DELETION-LINE              PIC X(132).
00039
00040              WORKING-STORAGE SECTION.
00041
00042              01  OLD-MASTER.
00043                  05  OM-KEY                     PIC X(5).
00044                  05  OM-QUANTITY                PIC 9(5).
00045                  05  FILLER                     PIC X(70).
00046
00047              01  TRANSACTION.
00048                  05  TR-KEY                     PIC X(5).
00049                  05  TR-QUANTITY                PIC 9(5).
00050                  05  TR-TRANSACTION-CODE        PIC X.
00051                      88  ADDITION                         VALUE '1'.
00052                      88  ADJUSTMENT                       VALUE '2'.
00053                      88  RECEIPT                          VALUE '3'.
00054                      88  SHIPMENT                         VALUE '4'.
00055                      88  DELETION                         VALUE '5'.
00056                  05  FILLER                     PIC X(69).
00057
00058
```

```
00059            PROCEDURE DIVISION.
00060            A000-UPDATE-FILE.
00061                OPEN INPUT TRANSACTION-FILE
00062                           OLD-MASTER-FILE
00063                     OUTPUT NEW-MASTER-FILE
00064                            DELETION-FILE.
00065                PERFORM C010-READ-TRANSACTION.
00066                PERFORM C020-READ-MASTER.
00067                PERFORM B010-UPDATE-LOGIC
00068                    UNTIL OM-KEY = HIGH-VALUES AND TR-KEY = HIGH-VALUES.
00069                CLOSE TRANSACTION-FILE
00070                      OLD-MASTER-FILE
00071                      NEW-MASTER-FILE
00072                      DELETION-FILE.
00073                STOP RUN.
00074
00075            B010-UPDATE-LOGIC.
00076                IF OM-KEY IS LESS THAN TR-KEY
00077                    WRITE NEW-MASTER FROM OLD-MASTER
00078                    PERFORM C020-READ-MASTER
00079                ELSE
00080                    IF OM-KEY = TR-KEY
00081                        IF DELETION
00082                            MOVE OLD-MASTER TO DELETION-LINE
00083                            WRITE DELETION-REPORT AFTER ADVANCING 1 LINE
00084                            PERFORM C010-READ-TRANSACTION
00085                            PERFORM C020-READ-MASTER
00086                        ELSE
00087                            PERFORM C030-UPDATE-MASTER
00088                            PERFORM C010-READ-TRANSACTION
00089                    ELSE
00090                        WRITE NEW-MASTER FROM TRANSACTION
00091                        PERFORM C010-READ-TRANSACTION.
00092
00093            C010-READ-TRANSACTION.
00094                READ TRANSACTION-FILE INTO TRANSACTION
00095                    AT END MOVE HIGH-VALUES TO TR-KEY.
00096
00097            C020-READ-MASTER.
00098                READ OLD-MASTER-FILE INTO OLD-MASTER
00099                    AT END MOVE HIGH-VALUES TO OM-KEY.
00100
00101            C030-UPDATE-MASTER.
00102                DISPLAY ' OM ', OM-KEY, '  TR ', TR-KEY.
00103
00104        ******************** END OF PROGRAM ***********************
```

Figure 12.5 A program for file updating with addition and deletion records but no error checking.

There are two changes in the Procedure Division. First, we have revised the hierarchy slightly, moving the read and update paragraphs down a level to reflect the second change, the increased complexity of B010-UPDATE-LOGIC. The fundamental logic of this paragraph is based on the fact that the old master key and the transaction key can have three relative values:

1. The old master key can be less than the transaction key; this means that there are no more transactions for this master;

2. The old master key can be equal to the transaction key; this means that the transaction should be applied to the master;

3. The old master key can be greater than the transaction key; this means that the transaction represents a new inventory item that should be added to the master file.

When the program decides that there are no further transactions for the old master record (indeed, there may have been none at all) the processing is exactly the same as it was in the previous version of the program. When we find a match, however, we must now check to see whether it is a deletion. If so, it is handled in the manner shown. If not, the transaction must be (assuming no errors) either an adjustment, a receipt, or a shipment; therefore, we perform **C030-UPDATE-MASTER** and read another transaction. Finally, if the old master key is neither less than the transaction key nor equal to it, then the old master key must be greater than the transaction key, and (again assuming no errors) this can only represent an addition. In this case we write the new master record from the transaction and get another transaction.

There is one aspect of the file processing in this program that is not immediately obvious. Notice that when we write **DELETION-REPORT** we use the **ADVANCING** clause, but when we write **NEW-MASTER** we do not. Furthermore, although we have allowed for a carriage control character in **DELETION-REPORT** there is no such provision in **NEW-MASTER**. The difference between the two files is that **DELETION-FILE** is a *print* file and is going to a printer, while **NEW-MASTER-FILE** is a *data* file and is going to some other output medium, probably a disk or tape. The carriage control character is necessary only when you use the **ADVANCING** clause, and the **ADVANCING** clause is used only for print files. If a file is used for data, the **ADVANCING** clause should not be used, and all characters in the file records, including the first character, contain data.

The program was run with the same old master file used to test the first version and a transaction file that included all five types of transactions. They are presented in Figure 12.6, together with the output produced.

We see that **C030-UPDATE-MASTER** was reached for all of the transactions representing adjustments, receipts, or shipments. The two transactions representing deletions are seen to have been handled correctly and the new master file is correct, in that it contains the records in the old master file, plus the addition, minus the deletions. The fact that the transaction code of the addition is included in the new master is a minor detail that will be corrected later.

12.8 PROVISION FOR HANDLING ERRORS

It would be foolish and irresponsible to write a program of this type assuming that all the data is correct. It is essential to build the program so that it checks for various kinds of errors. In the next version of the program we shall check for four possibilities: an addition where there is already an existing master, a transaction other than an addition for which there is no master, a transaction file sequence error, and a master file sequence error. Since unmatched transactions in particular must be expected occasionally, and since they are not disabling, we shall keep an error count and not stop the job unless the number of errors exceeds 10. (If there are a great many errors, it probably indicates some kind of completely disabling mistake, such as using the wrong files for input.)

	Old Master			Transaction	
	Key	Qty	Key	Qty	Code
	00002	00111	00008	00050	4
	00008	00123	00015	00999	1
	00011	00200	00021	00100	3
	00021	00210	00024	01000	3
	00024	00099	00024	00050	4
	00036	01234	00024	00040	4
	00037	12345	00036	00000	5
	00051	54321	00037	12300	2
	00059	43210	00051	00000	5
	00061	32109	00059	01000	3
			00061	01234	4

Displayed Output:

```
        OM    00008    TR    00008
        OM    00021    TR    00021
        OM    00024    TR    00024
        OM    00024    TR    00024
        OM    00024    TR    00024
        OM    00037    TR    00037
        OM    00059    TR    00059
        OM    00061    TR    00061
```

Deletions		New Master	
Key	Qty	Key	Qty
00036	01234	00002	00111
00051	54321	00008	00123
		00011	00200
		00015	009991
		00021	00210
		00024	00099
		00037	12345
		00059	43210
		00061	32109

FIGURE 12.6 Data and output for the program in Figure 12.5.

The revised program is shown in Figure 12.7; it contains a number of changes from the previous version. As we add code to implement the new features we have discussed, the structure of the program becomes more complicated, particularly the nested **IF** statement in **B010-UPDATE-LOGIC**. We have broken out some of the functions into separate paragraphs for clarity, and modified some of the existing code to make the program more realistic (but still rather skeletal) and less like a textbook example.

```
00001          IDENTIFICATION DIVISION.
00002          PROGRAM-ID.
00003              UPDATE3.
00004          DATE-WRITTEN.
00005              MARCH 19, 1987.
00006
00007          ENVIRONMENT DIVISION.
00008          INPUT-OUTPUT SECTION.
00009          FILE-CONTROL.
00010              SELECT LOG-FILE              ASSIGN TO S-LOGFILE.
00011              SELECT NEW-MASTER-FILE       ASSIGN TO S-NEWMAST.
00012              SELECT OLD-MASTER-FILE       ASSIGN TO S-OLDMAST.
00013              SELECT TRANSACTION-FILE      ASSIGN TO S-TRANS.
00014
```

```
00015              DATA DIVISION.
00016
00017              FILE SECTION.
00018
00019         FD   LOG-FILE
00020              LABEL RECORDS ARE OMITTED.
00021         01   LOG-RECORD.
00022              05   CARRIAGE-CONTROL          PIC X.
00023              05   LOG-LINE.
00024                   10   LOG-KEY              PIC X(5).
00025                   10   LOG-QUANTITY         PIC 9(5).
00026                   10   LOG-TRANSACTION-CODE PIC X.
00027                   10   LOG-MESSAGE          PIC X(121).
00028
00029         FD   NEW-MASTER-FILE
00030              LABEL RECORDS ARE OMITTED.
00031         01   NEW-MASTER.
00032              05   NM-KEY                    PIC X(5).
00033              05   NM-QUANTITY               PIC 9(5).
00034              05   FILLER                    PIC X(70).
00035
00036         FD   OLD-MASTER-FILE
00037              LABEL RECORDS ARE OMITTED.
00038         01   OLD-MASTER-BUFFER             PIC X(80).
00039
00040         FD   TRANSACTION-FILE
00041              LABEL RECORDS ARE OMITTED.
00042         01   TRANSACTION-BUFFER            PIC X(80).
00043
00044              WORKING-STORAGE SECTION.
00045
00046         77   ERROR-COUNT                   PIC S999.
00047         77   OM-KEY-PREVIOUS               PIC X(5).
00048         77   SEQUENCE-ERROR-FLAG           PIC X.
00049         77   TR-KEY-PREVIOUS               PIC X(5).
00050
00051         01   ERROR-MESSAGES.
00052              05   BAD-ADDITION-MSG         PIC X(50) VALUE
00053                   '   THIS ADDITION MATCHES AN EXISTING MASTER'.
00054              05   DELETE-MSG               PIC X(50) VALUE
00055                   '   THIS MASTER RECORD HAS BEEN DELETED'.
00056              05   MASTER-SEQUENCE-ERROR-MSG   PIC X(50) VALUE
00057                   '   THIS MASTER IS OUT OF SEQUENCE'.
00058              05   TERMINATION-MSG          PIC X(50) VALUE
00059                   'MORE THAN 10 ERRORS - JOB TERMINATED'.
00060              05   TRANS-SEQUENCE-ERROR-MSG    PIC X(50) VALUE
00061                   '   THIS TRANSACTION IS OUT OF SEQUENCE'.
00062              05   UNMATCHED-TRANS-MSG      PIC X(50) VALUE
00063                   '   THERE IS NO MASTER FOR THIS TRANSACTION'.
00064
00065         01   OLD-MASTER.
00066              05   OM-KEY                    PIC X(5).
00067              05   OM-QUANTITY               PIC 9(5).
00068              05   FILLER                    PIC X(70).
00069
00070         01   TRANSACTION.
00071              05   TR-KEY                    PIC X(5).
00072              05   TR-QUANTITY               PIC 9(5).
00073              05   TR-TRANSACTION-CODE       PIC X.
00074                   88   ADDITION                      VALUE '1'.
00075                   88   ADJUSTMENT                    VALUE '2'.
```

```
00076                    88   RECEIPT                              VALUE '3'.
00077                    88   SHIPMENT                             VALUE '4'.
00078                    88   DELETION                             VALUE '5'.
00079               05   FILLER                    PIC X(69).
00080
00081
00082          PROCEDURE DIVISION.
00083          A000-UPDATE-FILE.
00084     *          INITIALIZE WORK AREAS
00085              MOVE ZERO                        TO ERROR-COUNT.
00086              MOVE LOW-VALUES                  TO OM-KEY-PREVIOUS.
00087              MOVE LOW-VALUES                  TO TR-KEY-PREVIOUS.
00088              OPEN INPUT TRANSACTION-FILE
00089                         OLD-MASTER-FILE
00090                   OUTPUT NEW-MASTER-FILE
00091                          LOG-FILE.
00092     *        GET PRIMING RECORDS
00093              PERFORM X010-GET-VALID-TRANSACTION.
00094              PERFORM X020-GET-VALID-MASTER.
00095     *        PROCESS THE FILES
00096              PERFORM B010-UPDATE-LOGIC
00097                  UNTIL (OM-KEY = HIGH-VALUES  AND  TR-KEY = HIGH-VALUES)
00098                       OR ERROR-COUNT IS GREATER THAN 10.
00099              IF ERROR-COUNT IS GREATER THAN 10
00100                  MOVE TERMINATION-MSG TO LOG-LINE
00101                  WRITE LOG-RECORD AFTER ADVANCING 1 LINE.
00102              CLOSE TRANSACTION-FILE
00103                    OLD-MASTER-FILE
00104                    NEW-MASTER-FILE
00105                    LOG-FILE.
00106              STOP RUN.
00107
00108          B010-UPDATE-LOGIC.
00109              IF OM-KEY IS LESS THAN TR-KEY
00110                  WRITE NEW-MASTER FROM OLD-MASTER
00111                  PERFORM X020-GET-VALID-MASTER
00112              ELSE
00113                  IF OM-KEY = TR-KEY
00114                      PERFORM C010-APPLY-TRANSACTION
00115                      PERFORM X010-GET-VALID-TRANSACTION
00116                  ELSE
00117                      IF ADDITION
00118                          PERFORM C020-ADD-MASTER
00119                          PERFORM X010-GET-VALID-TRANSACTION
00120                      ELSE
00121                          PERFORM C030-INVALID-TRANSACTION
00122                          PERFORM X010-GET-VALID-TRANSACTION.
00123
00124          C010-APPLY-TRANSACTION.
00125              IF DELETION
00126                  PERFORM D010-DELETE-MASTER
00127                  PERFORM X020-GET-VALID-MASTER
00128              ELSE
00129                  IF ADDITION
00130                      PERFORM D030-INVALID-ADDITION
00131                  ELSE
00132                      PERFORM D020-UPDATE-MASTER.
00133
00134          C020-ADD-MASTER.
00135              WRITE NEW-MASTER FROM TRANSACTION.
00136
```

```
00137          C030-INVALID-TRANSACTION.
00138              MOVE TRANSACTION TO LOG-LINE.
00139              MOVE UNMATCHED-TRANS-MSG TO LOG-MESSAGE.
00140              WRITE LOG-RECORD AFTER ADVANCING 1 LINE.
00141              ADD 1 TO ERROR-COUNT.
00142
00143          D010-DELETE-MASTER.
00144              MOVE OLD-MASTER TO LOG-LINE.
00145              MOVE DELETE-MSG TO LOG-MESSAGE.
00146              WRITE LOG-RECORD AFTER ADVANCING 1 LINE.
00147
00148          D020-UPDATE-MASTER.
00149              DISPLAY '  OM ', OM-KEY, '  TR  ', TR-KEY.
00150
00151          D030-INVALID-ADDITION.
00152              MOVE TRANSACTION TO LOG-LINE.
00153              MOVE BAD-ADDITION-MSG TO LOG-MESSAGE.
00154              WRITE LOG-RECORD AFTER ADVANCING 1 LINE.
00155              ADD 1 TO ERROR-COUNT.
00156
00157          X010-GET-VALID-TRANSACTION.
00158              MOVE '?' TO SEQUENCE-ERROR-FLAG.
00159              PERFORM Y010-READ-TRANSACTION
00160                  UNTIL     SEQUENCE-ERROR-FLAG = 'N'
00161                        OR ERROR-COUNT IS GREATER THAN 10.
00162
00163          X020-GET-VALID-MASTER.
00164              MOVE '?' TO SEQUENCE-ERROR-FLAG.
00165              PERFORM Y020-READ-MASTER
00166                  UNTIL     SEQUENCE-ERROR-FLAG = 'N'
00167                        OR ERROR-COUNT IS GREATER THAN 10.
00168
00169          Y010-READ-TRANSACTION.
00170              READ TRANSACTION-FILE INTO TRANSACTION
00171                  AT END MOVE HIGH-VALUES TO TR-KEY.
00172              IF TR-KEY IS LESS THAN TR-KEY-PREVIOUS
00173                  MOVE TRANSACTION TO LOG-LINE
00174                  MOVE TRANS-SEQUENCE-ERROR-MSG TO LOG-MESSAGE
00175                  WRITE LOG-RECORD AFTER ADVANCING 1 LINE
00176                  ADD 1 TO ERROR-COUNT
00177              ELSE
00178                  MOVE 'N' TO SEQUENCE-ERROR-FLAG.
00179              MOVE TR-KEY TO TR-KEY-PREVIOUS.
00180
00181          Y020-READ-MASTER.
00182              READ OLD-MASTER-FILE INTO OLD-MASTER
00183                  AT END MOVE HIGH-VALUES TO OM-KEY.
00184              IF OM-KEY IS LESS THAN OM-KEY-PREVIOUS
00185                  MOVE OLD-MASTER TO LOG-LINE
00186                  MOVE MASTER-SEQUENCE-ERROR-MSG TO LOG-MESSAGE
00187                  WRITE LOG-RECORD AFTER ADVANCING 1 LINE
00188                  ADD 1 TO ERROR-COUNT
00189              ELSE
00190                  MOVE 'N' TO SEQUENCE-ERROR-FLAG.
00191              MOVE OM-KEY TO OM-KEY-PREVIOUS.
00192
00193          ******************** END OF PROGRAM *************************
```

FIGURE 12.7 A fairly complete file update program, with additions, deletions, and basic error checking.

The first changes simply involve the order in which files are defined. Both in the **SELECT** statements in the **FILE-CONTROL** paragraph and in the **FD**s in the **FILE SECTION** we have placed the files in alphabetical order. Although this is certainly not mandatory, it frequently makes it easier to locate a definition when you need to refer to it during program maintenance. We have also changed the name of the print file from **DELETION-FILE** to **LOG-FILE** because this name more accurately reflects the usage of the file. That is, it will not only be used to list deleted records, it will be used to log all changes and errors found during processing. The output from the log file would enable the program user to determine what major activity had occurred during a run. In a real program, of course, the output from the log file would be formatted more extensively and would include column headings, page numbers, and so on; again we have omitted these familiar details to save space and to allow a focus on other matters.

In the Working-Storage Section we have added several level **77** items to count errors, track file keys, and report sequence errors. We have also included several error and diagnostic messages in the structure **ERROR-MESSAGES**. The remainder of Working-Storage is as in the previous program.

The main paragraph of the Procedure Division begins by initializing various Working-Storage items. Although this initialization could have been done in the Working-Storage Section using the **VALUE** phrase, we will generally reserve the **VALUE** clause for data that is not changed during execution, such as constants, headings, messages, and so on. Initializing changeable data in the Procedure Division emphasizes which of these variables must be given initial values. We have also changed the **PERFORM** statement so that it will terminate if we find too many errors, in which case the program will also print an appropriate error message.

Paragraph **B010-UPDATE-LOGIC** has been changed considerably from the version in Figure 12.5. Because the paragraph is controlling much more activity than in the previous example, we have moved almost all the detail to lower level paragraphs and left only the control structure and several **PERFORM** statements. The basic control structure is much the same as in the previous example: if the old master key is less than the transaction key, we are done with the master record so we write a new master record and get the next old master; if the master key is equal to the transaction key we apply the transaction to the master and get the next transaction. If the master key is greater than the transaction key, however, we have a new situation. In the previous version of the program we assumed that this case means that we are adding a new master record. In this current program, we may indeed be adding a new record, but we might also have an erroneous transaction key, one that does not correspond to any master record. If we have an addition, we add the new master record and get the next transaction; if we have any other type of transaction we process the error and get the next transaction. By using **PERFORM** statements to take care of the processing details, we leave a relatively clear and simple structure in **B010-UPDATE-LOGIC**.

The structure of the lower levels of the program has changed completely from the version in Figure 12.5. To begin with, we now have paragraphs to perform the functions of applying a transaction to the master record, adding a new master record, and reporting a transaction with an invalid key.

Paragraph **C010-APPLY-TRANSACTION** is itself a control paragraph and performs no detailed work; as in the previous paragraph, this allows us to concentrate on the structure of the function while leaving the details for lower level paragraphs. At this point in the program a transaction falls into one of three classes: it can be a deletion, causing a record to be removed from the master file; it can be an addition, which is an error since we would be trying to add a master record with the same key as an existing master record; or it can be any other type of transaction, which is used to update the current master record. Although the details of *how* each of these activities is carried out fall to still lower level paragraphs, the logic of *when* the tasks are performed is clear. Notice that applying a transaction does not involve getting the next transaction; that function is performed in **B010-UPDATE-LOGIC**.

The work required to add a new master record is simple and is unchanged from the previous program: we simply write the new master from the transaction. We have placed this in a separate paragraph primarily to keep the structure of **C010-APPLY-TRANSACTION** simple, but also to prepare for future enhancements in which the activity becomes more complex.

Processing an invalid transaction is also quite easy. We simply write an appropriate error message and increment the error count.

The next three paragraphs, at the **D** level of hierarchy, are also clear and should require no explanation. Where these activities match the previous version of the program, they are unchanged.

The remaining paragraphs, which involve getting records from the input files, have changed considerably. To begin with, we have renumbered the paragraphs as "utility" paragraphs at the **X** and **Y** levels. The reason is that they are now called from several levels of hierarchy; **X020-GET-VALID-MASTER**, for instance, is used at levels **A**, **B**, and **C**. Furthermore, the names have been revised to reflect the fact that we are no longer simply reading a record: we are getting the next *valid* record from a file. The higher levels of the program should not be concerned with *how* these valid records are obtained, only that they are made available.

The checking procedure for sequence errors is more complex than it was in the second version of the program. This is because we do not wish to stop when we find a sequence error, unless we have found a total of more than 10 errors. Paragraph **X010-GET-VALID-TRANSACTION** begins by giving a value of "?" to an error flag, because we don't know yet if we have a sequence error or not. Then it says to perform another paragraph until the flag equals "**N**" (no sequence error was found) or the maximum error limit is exceeded. The performed paragraph does the actual reading, checks for a sequence error and handles it if one is found, and moves the transaction key to the previous transaction key. Getting a valid master record is handled in the same way.

The old master and transaction files used to demonstrate the operation of this program have been expanded to include various kinds of errors, as may be seen on the opposite page.

We see that these conditions have been handled in the way the program specifies, although other ways of treating them could be defended. The second transaction, for instance, is not processed even though it has a matching master record. At the expense of considerable extra complication, the program could be written to try to process out-of-sequence transactions, but there do have to be limits on how many abnormal conditions one tries to cope with.

Old Master

Key	Qty
00002	00111
00008	00123
00011	00200
00021	00210
00024	00099
00036	01234
00037	12345
00051	54321
00059	43210
00061	32109
00070	22222
00068	33333
00080	44444

Transaction

Key	Qty	Code
00003	00100	4
00002	00010	2
00008	00050	4
00011	98765	1
00015	00999	1
00021	00100	3
00024	01000	3
00024	00050	4
00024	00040	4
00037	12300	2
00036	00000	5
00051	00000	5
00052	00000	5
00059	01000	3
00061	01234	4

Displayed Output

OM	00008	TR	00008
OM	00021	TR	00021
OM	00024	TR	00024
OM	00024	TR	00024
OM	00024	TR	00024
OM	00037	TR	00037
OM	00059	TR	00059
OM	00061	TR	00061

New Master

Key	Qty
00002	00111
00008	00123
00011	00200
00015	00999
00021	00210
00024	00099
00036	01234
00037	12345
00059	43210
00061	32109
00070	22222
00080	44444

Log File

Transaction

Key	Qty	Code	
00003	00100	4	THERE IS NO MASTER FOR THIS TRANSACTION
00002	00010	2	THIS TRANSACTION IS OUT OF SEQUENCE
00011	98765	1	THIS ADDITION MATCHES AN EXISTING MASTER
00036	00000	5	THIS TRANSACTION IS OUT OF SEQUENCE
00051	54321		THIS MASTER RECORD HAS BEEN DELETED
00052	00000	5	THERE IS NO MASTER FOR THIS TRANSACTION
00068	33333		THIS MASTER IS OUT OF SEQUENCE

Also, note that an out-of-sequence old master is not written to the new master. Likewise, an out-of-sequence deletion record does not result in the deletion of the record when the new master is written. Considering that file sequence errors are ordinarily rather serious matters that usually have to be handled by resequencing the files and running the job again, it is probably reasonable not to try to deal with all these situations, beyond simply detecting them.

12.9 UPDATING THE MASTER ON A MATCH

Now it is time to consider the processing to be done when there is a normal match between the transaction and the master, that is, an adjustment, a receipt, or a shipment. This is, of course, the heart of the whole application, in one sense, but since it is subordinate to the top-level file processing logic of the program we have postponed our consideration of it until this point.

Actually, with the rudimentary record contents that we have specified thus far, the processing is not very difficult. The only possible adjustment is to update the old master quantity with the transaction quantity. For a receipt, we add the transaction quantity to the old master quantity. For a shipment, we basically want to subtract the transaction quantity from the old master quantity, but we must do so only if there is sufficient stock on hand. If there is not, we need to signal this fact, which can be done in the log file report. (In real life one would ordinarily ship as much as there is on hand and back-order the rest, but we shall not concern ourselves with this complication.)

While we are processing the transaction we have an easy opportunity to check that the transaction is valid (in the range 1 through 5); if not, we can print an error message on the log file. We will get to the updating operation if the transaction is anything other than 1 or 5. It would be possible to assume in the updating section that if the transaction code is not 2 or 3 it must be 4, but we would be ill-advised to place this much faith in the correctness of input.

Figure 12.8 shows the program modified to update the master record. The only change required in the Data Division is the addition of two new error messages, one for an invalid transaction code and one for an insufficient-stock condition. In the Procedure Division, we have modified the paragraph named **D020-UPDATE-MASTER** and added three paragraphs at level **E** to carry out the different update operations. The simple operations to be carried out in these three paragraphs could, of course, have been written in **D020-UPDATE-MASTER** as one nested **IF** statement, but the method used results in clearer code and easier maintenance.

```
00001          IDENTIFICATION DIVISION.
00002          PROGRAM-ID.
00003             UPDATE4.
00004          DATE-WRITTEN.
00005             MARCH 20, 1987.
00006
00007          ENVIRONMENT DIVISION.
00008          INPUT-OUTPUT SECTION.
00009          FILE-CONTROL.
00010             SELECT LOG-FILE              ASSIGN TO S-LOGFILE.
00011             SELECT NEW-MASTER-FILE       ASSIGN TO S-NEWMAST.
00012             SELECT OLD-MASTER-FILE       ASSIGN TO S-OLDMAST.
00013             SELECT TRANSACTION-FILE      ASSIGN TO S-TRANS.
00014
00015          DATA DIVISION.
00016
00017          FILE SECTION.
00018
```

```
00019          FD   LOG-FILE
00020               LABEL RECORDS ARE OMITTED.
00021          01   LOG-RECORD.
00022               05   CARRIAGE-CONTROL         PIC X.
00023               05   LOG-LINE.
00024                    10   LOG-KEY             PIC X(5).
00025                    10   LOG-QUANTITY        PIC 9(5).
00026                    10   LOG-TRANSACTION-CODE PIC X.
00027                    10   LOG-MESSAGE         PIC X(121).
00028
00029          FD   NEW-MASTER-FILE
00030               LABEL RECORDS ARE OMITTED.
00031          01   NEW-MASTER.
00032               05   NM-KEY                   PIC X(5).
00033               05   NM-QUANTITY              PIC 9(5).
00034               05   FILLER                   PIC X(70).
00035
00036          FD   OLD-MASTER-FILE
00037               LABEL RECORDS ARE OMITTED.
00038          01   OLD-MASTER-BUFFER             PIC X(80).
00039
00040          FD   TRANSACTION-FILE
00041               LABEL RECORDS ARE OMITTED.
00042          01   TRANSACTION-BUFFER            PIC X(80).
00043
00044          WORKING-STORAGE SECTION.
00045
00046          77   ERROR-COUNT                   PIC S999.
00047          77   OM-KEY-PREVIOUS               PIC X(5).
00048          77   SEQUENCE-ERROR-FLAG           PIC X.
00049          77   TR-KEY-PREVIOUS               PIC X(5).
00050
00051          01   ERROR-MESSAGES.
00052               05   BAD-ADDITION-MSG          PIC X(50) VALUE
00053                    '   THIS ADDITION MATCHES AN EXISTING MASTER'.
00054               05   BAD-TRANS-CODE-MSG        PIC X(50) VALUE
00055                    '   TRANSACTION CODE ILLEGAL'.
00056               05   DELETE-MSG                PIC X(50) VALUE
00057                    '   THIS MASTER RECORD HAS BEEN DELETED'.
00058               05   MASTER-SEQUENCE-ERROR-MSG PIC X(50) VALUE
00059                    '   THIS MASTER IS OUT OF SEQUENCE'.
00060               05   OUT-OF-STOCK-MSG          PIC X(50) VALUE
00061                    '   INSUFFICIENT STOCK TO SHIP AMOUNT SPECIFIED'.
00062               05   TERMINATION-MSG           PIC X(50) VALUE
00063                    'MORE THAN 10 ERRORS - JOB TERMINATED'.
00064               05   TRANS-SEQUENCE-ERROR-MSG  PIC X(50) VALUE
00065                    '   THIS TRANSACTION IS OUT OF SEQUENCE'.
00066               05   UNMATCHED-TRANS-MSG       PIC X(50) VALUE
00067                    '   THERE IS NO MASTER FOR THIS TRANSACTION'.
00068
00069          01   OLD-MASTER.
00070               05   OM-KEY                    PIC X(5).
00071               05   OM-QUANTITY               PIC 9(5).
00072               05   FILLER                    PIC X(70).
00073
00074          01   TRANSACTION.
00075               05   TR-KEY                    PIC X(5).
00076               05   TR-QUANTITY               PIC 9(5).
```

```
00077                 05  TR-TRANSACTION-CODE          PIC X.
00078                     88  ADDITION                             VALUE '1'.
00079                     88  ADJUSTMENT                           VALUE '2'.
00080                     88  RECEIPT                              VALUE '3'.
00081                     88  SHIPMENT                             VALUE '4'.
00082                     88  DELETION                             VALUE '5'.
00083                 05  FILLER                       PIC X(69).
00084
00085
00086             PROCEDURE DIVISION.
00087             A000-UPDATE-FILE.
00088         *          INITIALIZE WORK AREAS
00089                 MOVE ZERO                        TO ERROR-COUNT.
00090                 MOVE LOW-VALUES                  TO OM-KEY-PREVIOUS.
00091                 MOVE LOW-VALUES                  TO TR-KEY-PREVIOUS.
00092                 OPEN INPUT TRANSACTION-FILE
00093                            OLD-MASTER-FILE
00094                      OUTPUT NEW-MASTER-FILE
00095                            LOG-FILE.
00096         *          GET PRIMING RECORDS
00097                 PERFORM X010-GET-VALID-TRANSACTION.
00098                 PERFORM X020-GET-VALID-MASTER.
00099         *          PROCESS THE FILES
00100                 PERFORM B010-UPDATE-LOGIC
00101                     UNTIL (OM-KEY = HIGH-VALUES  AND  TR-KEY = HIGH-VALUES)
00102                         OR ERROR-COUNT IS GREATER THAN 10.
00103                 IF ERROR-COUNT IS GREATER THAN 10
00104                     MOVE TERMINATION-MSG TO LOG-LINE
00105                     WRITE LOG-RECORD AFTER ADVANCING 1 LINE.
00106                 CLOSE TRANSACTION-FILE
00107                       OLD-MASTER-FILE
00108                       NEW-MASTER-FILE
00109                       LOG-FILE.
00110                 STOP RUN.
00111
00112             B010-UPDATE-LOGIC.
00113                 IF OM-KEY IS LESS THAN TR-KEY
00114                     WRITE NEW-MASTER FROM OLD-MASTER
00115                     PERFORM X020-GET-VALID-MASTER
00116                 ELSE
00117                     IF OM-KEY = TR-KEY
00118                         PERFORM C010-APPLY-TRANSACTION
00119                         PERFORM X010-GET-VALID-TRANSACTION
00120                     ELSE
00121                         IF ADDITION
00122                             PERFORM C020-ADD-MASTER
00123                             PERFORM X010-GET-VALID-TRANSACTION
00124                         ELSE
00125                             PERFORM C030-INVALID-TRANSACTION
00126                             PERFORM X010-GET-VALID-TRANSACTION.
00127
00128             C010-APPLY-TRANSACTION.
00129                 IF DELETION
00130                     PERFORM D010-DELETE-MASTER
00131                     PERFORM X020-GET-VALID-MASTER
00132                 ELSE
00133                     IF ADDITION
00134                         PERFORM D030-INVALID-ADDITION
00135                     ELSE
00136                         PERFORM D020-UPDATE-MASTER.
00137
```

```
00138          C020-ADD-MASTER.
00139              WRITE NEW-MASTER FROM TRANSACTION.
00140
00141          C030-INVALID-TRANSACTION.
00142              MOVE TRANSACTION TO LOG-LINE.
00143              MOVE UNMATCHED-TRANS-MSG TO LOG-MESSAGE.
00144              WRITE LOG-RECORD AFTER ADVANCING 1 LINE.
00145              ADD 1 TO ERROR-COUNT.
00146
00147          D010-DELETE-MASTER.
00148              MOVE OLD-MASTER TO LOG-LINE.
00149              MOVE DELETE-MSG TO LOG-MESSAGE.
00150              WRITE LOG-RECORD AFTER ADVANCING 1 LINE.
00151
00152          D020-UPDATE-MASTER.
00153              IF      SHIPMENT
00154                  PERFORM E010-PROCESS-SHIPMENT
00155              ELSE IF RECEIPT
00156                  PERFORM E020-PROCESS-RECEIPT
00157              ELSE IF ADJUSTMENT
00158                  PERFORM E030-PROCESS-ADJUSTMENT
00159              ELSE
00160                  MOVE TRANSACTION TO LOG-LINE
00161                  MOVE BAD-TRANS-CODE-MSG TO LOG-MESSAGE
00162                  WRITE LOG-RECORD AFTER ADVANCING 1 LINE
00163                  ADD 1 TO ERROR-COUNT.
00164
00165          D030-INVALID-ADDITION.
00166              MOVE TRANSACTION TO LOG-LINE.
00167              MOVE BAD-ADDITION-MSG TO LOG-MESSAGE.
00168              WRITE LOG-RECORD AFTER ADVANCING 1 LINE.
00169              ADD 1 TO ERROR-COUNT.
00170
00171          E010-PROCESS-SHIPMENT.
00172              IF OM-QUANTITY IS NOT LESS THAN TR-QUANTITY
00173                  SUBTRACT TR-QUANTITY FROM OM-QUANTITY
00174              ELSE
00175                  MOVE TRANSACTION TO LOG-LINE
00176                  MOVE OUT-OF-STOCK-MSG TO LOG-MESSAGE
00177                  WRITE LOG-RECORD AFTER ADVANCING 1 LINE
00178                  ADD 1 TO ERROR-COUNT.
00179
00180          E020-PROCESS-RECEIPT.
00181              ADD TR-QUANTITY TO OM-QUANTITY.
00182
00183          E030-PROCESS-ADJUSTMENT.
00184              MOVE TR-QUANTITY TO OM-QUANTITY.
00185
00186          X010-GET-VALID-TRANSACTION.
00187              MOVE '?' TO SEQUENCE-ERROR-FLAG.
00188              PERFORM Y010-READ-TRANSACTION
00189                  UNTIL      SEQUENCE-ERROR-FLAG = 'N'
00190                      OR ERROR-COUNT IS GREATER THAN 10.
00191
00192          X020-GET-VALID-MASTER.
00193              MOVE '?' TO SEQUENCE-ERROR-FLAG.
00194              PERFORM Y020-READ-MASTER
00195                  UNTIL      SEQUENCE-ERROR-FLAG = 'N'
00196                      OR ERROR-COUNT IS GREATER THAN 10.
00197
```

```
00198              Y010-READ-TRANSACTION.
00199                  READ TRANSACTION-FILE INTO TRANSACTION
00200                      AT END MOVE HIGH-VALUES TO TR-KEY.
00201                  IF TR-KEY IS LESS THAN TR-KEY-PREVIOUS
00202                      MOVE TRANSACTION TO LOG-LINE
00203                      MOVE TRANS-SEQUENCE-ERROR-MSG TO LOG-MESSAGE
00204                      WRITE LOG-RECORD AFTER ADVANCING 1 LINE
00205                      ADD 1 TO ERROR-COUNT
00206                  ELSE
00207                      MOVE 'N' TO SEQUENCE-ERROR-FLAG.
00208                  MOVE TR-KEY TO TR-KEY-PREVIOUS.
00209
00210              Y020-READ-MASTER.
00211                  READ OLD-MASTER-FILE INTO OLD-MASTER
00212                      AT END MOVE HIGH-VALUES TO OM-KEY.
00213                  IF OM-KEY IS LESS THAN OM-KEY-PREVIOUS
00214                      MOVE OLD-MASTER TO LOG-LINE
00215                      MOVE MASTER-SEQUENCE-ERROR-MSG TO LOG-MESSAGE
00216                      WRITE LOG-RECORD AFTER ADVANCING 1 LINE
00217                      ADD 1 TO ERROR-COUNT
00218                  ELSE
00219                      MOVE 'N' TO SEQUENCE-ERROR-FLAG.
00220                  MOVE OM-KEY TO OM-KEY-PREVIOUS.
00221
00222              ******************** END OF PROGRAM ************************
```

FIGURE 12.8 A file update program containing code that updates the master file.

The program was tested with the same data used with the program **UPDATE3**. The old master and transaction files again, together with the new master and log files produced by this program, are shown on the next page.

Observe that the log messages are the same as those for **UPDATE3**, which is reasonable since **UPDATE3** contained the same error checking features as this program does. The new master, however, is different since now we are actually updating the master. Let us see how the program operated.

The first transaction produced an unmatched-transaction error message. The second produced an out-of-sequence message even though it matches the first master; the master was not updated. The third transaction, the one with the key of 00008, had a quantity of 50 and a transaction code of 4, which is a shipment. We see that where the old master for this item had a quantity of 123, the new master has a quantity of 73. The next transaction (key=00011) was an erroneous addition. The next one was a legitimate addition. For item 0021, we received a shipment of 100; the old master quantity was increased from 210 to 310. The next three transactions are all for item 0024, for which we have a receipt of 1000 and two shipments totaling 90; we see that the old master quantity has been increased by 910. The transaction for item 0037 is an adjustment of the quantity that was done correctly. Item 0052 is an unmatched transaction. The receipt for 0059 was handled correctly, as was the shipment for 0061. The items in the old master for which there were no transactions were copied correctly to the new master.

Old Master Key Qty	Transaction Key Qty Code	New Master Key Qty
0000200111	00003001004	0000200111
0000800123	00002000102	0000800073
0001100200	00008000504	0001100200
0002100210	00011987651	00015009991
0002400099	00015009991	0002100310
0003601234	00021001003	0002401009
0003712345	00024010003	0003601234
0005154321	00024000504	0003712300
0005943210	00024000404	0005944210
0006132109	00037123002	0006130875
0007022222	00036000005	0007022222
0006833333	00051000005	0008044444
0008044444	00052000005	
	00059010003	
	00061012344	

Log File

Transaction Key Qty Code	
00003001004	THERE IS NO MASTER FOR THIS TRANSACTION
00002000102	THIS TRANSACTION IS OUT OF SEQUENCE
00011987651	THIS ADDITION MATCHES AN EXISTING MASTER
00036000005	THIS TRANSACTION IS OUT OF SEQUENCE
0005154321	THIS MASTER RECORD HAS BEEN DELETED
00052000005	THERE IS NO MASTER FOR THIS TRANSACTION
0006833333	THIS MASTER IS OUT OF SEQUENCE

12.10   THE COMPLETE PROGRAM

With all of the important logic apparently working correctly, we may now take the final step of incorporating all the processing that is actually required of the program.

The most important extension from the simplified version that we have considered thus far is the inclusion of more information from the master records. Besides a quantity, which we now rename as quantity on hand, we need a *quantity on order* to show how much stock is on its way from suppliers. We also need a *reorder point*; whenever the amount of stock on hand plus the amount on order falls below this number we will issue an instruction to order more stock. When this is done, it is necessary to have in the master record a reorder quantity. Finally, there must be provision for an alphanumeric description of the stock item.

Here is the record description for the master, as it will appear in the program.

```
01   OLD-MASTER.
     05   OM-KEY                PIC X(5).
     05   OM-QUAN-ON-HAND       PIC 9(5).
     05   OM-QUAN-ON-ORDER      PIC 9(5).
     05   OM-REORDER-POINT      PIC 9(5).
     05   OM-REORDER-QUAN       PIC 9(5).
     05   OM-DESCRIPTION        PIC X(20).
     05   FILLER                PIC X(35).
```

We must emphasize that the 35 characters of filler at the end of the record are needed only because of the requirements of the input device used for the file. When we study the use of disk and tape files in Chapter 14, we will be able to eliminate this filler.

A realistic inventory control file would contain much additional information. It would provide for handling back orders. It might have some information about how long stock has been on order, and would probably have some information about vendors from whom stock can be ordered. It would have information about physical locations of the stock in the warehouse. A complete inventory system can be a very elaborate affair, which we can no more than sketch in a program that is primarily intended to teach other things.

The transaction records in our final version must be expanded to contain everything that is in the old master, since a transaction may be an addition to the master file. Furthermore, there needs to be an adjustment code so that we can specify which of the items in a master record is to be changed. This means, in summary, that a transaction record has everything that a master record has plus a transaction code and an adjustment code that tells which item in the master record is to be adjusted. The complete record description for the transaction can be seen in the program in Figure 12.9.

```
00001              IDENTIFICATION DIVISION.
00002              PROGRAM-ID.
00003                 UPDATE5.
00004              DATE-WRITTEN.
00005                 MARCH 20, 1987.
00006
00007              ENVIRONMENT DIVISION.
00008              INPUT-OUTPUT SECTION.
00009              FILE-CONTROL.
00010                 SELECT LOG-FILE              ASSIGN TO S-LOGFILE.
00011                 SELECT NEW-MASTER-FILE       ASSIGN TO S-NEWMAST.
00012                 SELECT OLD-MASTER-FILE       ASSIGN TO S-OLDMAST.
00013                 SELECT ORDER-FILE            ASSIGN TO S-ORDERS.
00014                 SELECT TRANSACTION-FILE      ASSIGN TO S-TRANS.
00015
00016              DATA DIVISION.
00017
00018              FILE SECTION.
00019
00020              FD  LOG-FILE
00021                  LABEL RECORDS ARE OMITTED.
00022              01  LOG-RECORD.
00023                  05  CARRIAGE-CONTROL        PIC X.
00024                  05  LOG-LINE.
00025                      10  FILLER              PIC X(45).
00026                      10  LOG-MESSAGE         PIC X(87).
00027
00028              FD  NEW-MASTER-FILE
00029                  LABEL RECORDS ARE OMITTED.
00030              01  NEW-MASTER.
00031                  05  NM-KEY                  PIC X(5).
00032                  05  NM-QUANTITY             PIC 9(5).
00033                  05  NM-QUAN-ON-ORDER        PIC 9(5).
00034                  05  NM-REORDER-POINT        PIC 9(5).
00035                  05  NM-REORDER-QUAN         PIC 9(5).
00036                  05  NM-DESCRIPTION          PIC X(20).
00037                  05  NM-NOT-USED             PIC X(35).
00038
```

```
00039             FD   OLD-MASTER-FILE
00040                  LABEL RECORDS ARE OMITTED.
00041             01   OLD-MASTER-BUFFER                PIC X(80).
00042
00043             FD   TRANSACTION-FILE
00044                  LABEL RECORDS ARE OMITTED.
00045             01   TRANSACTION-BUFFER               PIC X(80).
00046
00047             FD   ORDER-FILE
00048                  LABEL RECORDS ARE OMITTED.
00049             01   ORDER-RECORD.
00050                  05   CARRIAGE-CONTROL            PIC X.
00051                  05   OR-KEY                      PIC X(5).
00052                  05   FILLER                      PIC XXX.
00053                  05   OR-QUANTITY                 PIC Z(5)9.
00054                  05   FILLER                      PIC XXX.
00055                  05   OR-DESCRIPTION              PIC X(20).
00056                  05   FILLER                      PIC X(95).
00057
00058             WORKING-STORAGE SECTION.
00059
00060             77   ERROR-COUNT                      PIC S999.
00061             77   OM-KEY-PREVIOUS                  PIC X(5).
00062             77   SEQUENCE-ERROR-FLAG              PIC X.
00063             77   TR-KEY-PREVIOUS                  PIC X(5).
00064
00065             01   ERROR-MESSAGES.
00066                  05   BAD-ADDITION-MSG            PIC X(50) VALUE
00067                       '  THIS ADDITION MATCHES AN EXISTING MASTER'.
00068                  05   BAD-ADJ-CODE-MSG            PIC X(50) VALUE
00069                       '  BAD ADJUSTMENT CODE'.
00070                  05   BAD-TRANS-CODE-MSG          PIC X(50) VALUE
00071                       '  TRANSACTION CODE ILLEGAL'.
00072                  05   DELETE-MSG                  PIC X(50) VALUE
00073                       '  THIS MASTER RECORD HAS BEEN DELETED'.
00074                  05   MASTER-SEQUENCE-ERROR-MSG   PIC X(50) VALUE
00075                       '  THIS MASTER IS OUT OF SEQUENCE'.
00076                  05   OUT-OF-STOCK-MSG            PIC X(50) VALUE
00077                       '  INSUFFICIENT STOCK TO SHIP AMOUNT SPECIFIED'.
00078                  05   TERMINATION-MSG             PIC X(50) VALUE
00079                       'MORE THAN 10 ERRORS - JOB TERMINATED'.
00080                  05   TRANS-SEQUENCE-ERROR-MSG    PIC X(50) VALUE
00081                       '  THIS TRANSACTION IS OUT OF SEQUENCE'.
00082                  05   UNMATCHED-TRANS-MSG         PIC X(50) VALUE
00083                       '  THERE IS NO MASTER FOR THIS TRANSACTION'.
00084
00085             01   OLD-MASTER.
00086                  05   OM-KEY                      PIC X(5).
00087                  05   OM-QUAN-ON-HAND             PIC 9(5).
00088                  05   OM-QUAN-ON-ORDER            PIC 9(5).
00089                  05   OM-REORDER-POINT            PIC 9(5).
00090                  05   OM-REORDER-QUAN             PIC 9(5).
00091                  05   OM-DESCRIPTION              PIC X(20).
00092                  05   FILLER                      PIC X(35).
00093
00094             01   TRANSACTION.
00095                  05   TR-KEY                      PIC X(5).
00096                  05   TR-QUANTITY                 PIC 9(5).
00097                  05   TR-TRANSACTION-CODE         PIC X.
00098                       88   ADDITION                         VALUE '1'.
00099                       88   ADJUSTMENT                       VALUE '2'.
```

```
00100                          88   RECEIPT                              VALUE '3'.
00101                          88   SHIPMENT                             VALUE '4'.
00102                          88   DELETION                             VALUE '5'.
00103                     05   TR-ADJUSTMENT-CODE        PIC 9.
00104                     05   TR-QUAN-ON-ORDER          PIC 9(5).
00105                     05   TR-REORDER-POINT          PIC 9(5).
00106                     05   TR-REORDER-QUAN           PIC 9(5).
00107                     05   TR-DESCRIPTION            PIC X(20).
00108                     05   FILLER                    PIC X(33).
00109
00110
00111           PROCEDURE DIVISION.
00112           A000-UPDATE-FILE.
00113       *          INITIALIZE WORK AREAS
00114             MOVE ZERO                         TO ERROR-COUNT.
00115             MOVE LOW-VALUES                   TO OM-KEY-PREVIOUS.
00116             MOVE LOW-VALUES                   TO TR-KEY-PREVIOUS.
00117             OPEN INPUT TRANSACTION-FILE
00118                        OLD-MASTER-FILE
00119                 OUTPUT NEW-MASTER-FILE
00120                        LOG-FILE
00121                        ORDER-FILE.
00122       *         GET PRIMING RECORDS
00123             PERFORM X010-GET-VALID-TRANSACTION.
00124             PERFORM X020-GET-VALID-MASTER.
00125       *         PROCESS THE FILES
00126             PERFORM B010-UPDATE-LOGIC
00127                 UNTIL (OM-KEY = HIGH-VALUES  AND  TR-KEY = HIGH-VALUES)
00128                       OR ERROR-COUNT IS GREATER THAN 10.
00129             IF ERROR-COUNT IS GREATER THAN 10
00130                 MOVE TERMINATION-MSG TO LOG-LINE
00131                 WRITE LOG-RECORD AFTER ADVANCING 1 LINE.
00132             CLOSE TRANSACTION-FILE
00133                   OLD-MASTER-FILE
00134                   NEW-MASTER-FILE
00135                   LOG-FILE
00136                   ORDER-FILE.
00137             STOP RUN.
00138
00139           B010-UPDATE-LOGIC.
00140             IF OM-KEY IS LESS THAN TR-KEY
00141                 PERFORM C040-CHECK-QUANTITY
00142                 WRITE NEW-MASTER FROM OLD-MASTER
00143                 PERFORM X020-GET-VALID-MASTER
00144             ELSE
00145                 IF OM-KEY = TR-KEY
00146                     PERFORM C010-APPLY-TRANSACTION
00147                     PERFORM X010-GET-VALID-TRANSACTION
00148                 ELSE
00149                     IF ADDITION
00150                         PERFORM C020-ADD-MASTER
00151                         PERFORM X010-GET-VALID-TRANSACTION
00152                     ELSE
00153                         PERFORM C030-INVALID-TRANSACTION
00154                         PERFORM X010-GET-VALID-TRANSACTION.
00155
00156           C010-APPLY-TRANSACTION.
00157             IF DELETION
00158                 PERFORM D010-DELETE-MASTER
00159                 PERFORM X020-GET-VALID-MASTER
00160             ELSE
```

```
00161                     IF ADDITION
00162                         PERFORM D030-INVALID-ADDITION
00163                     ELSE
00164                         PERFORM D020-UPDATE-MASTER.
00165
00166             C020-ADD-MASTER.
00167                 MOVE TR-KEY                     TO NM-KEY.
00168                 MOVE TR-QUANTITY                TO NM-QUANTITY.
00169                 MOVE TR-QUAN-ON-ORDER           TO NM-QUAN-ON-ORDER.
00170                 MOVE TR-REORDER-POINT           TO NM-REORDER-POINT.
00171                 MOVE TR-REORDER-QUAN            TO NM-REORDER-QUAN.
00172                 MOVE TR-DESCRIPTION             TO NM-DESCRIPTION.
00173                 MOVE SPACES                     TO NM-NOT-USED.
00174                 WRITE NEW-MASTER.
00175
00176             C030-INVALID-TRANSACTION.
00177                 MOVE TRANSACTION TO LOG-LINE.
00178                 MOVE UNMATCHED-TRANS-MSG TO LOG-MESSAGE.
00179                 WRITE LOG-RECORD AFTER ADVANCING 1 LINE.
00180                 ADD 1 TO ERROR-COUNT.
00181
00182             C040-CHECK-QUANTITY.
00183                 IF OM-QUAN-ON-ORDER + OM-QUAN-ON-HAND < OM-REORDER-POINT
00184                     MOVE SPACES                 TO ORDER-RECORD
00185                     MOVE OM-KEY                 TO OR-KEY
00186                     MOVE OM-DESCRIPTION         TO OR-DESCRIPTION
00187                     MOVE OM-REORDER-QUAN        TO OR-QUANTITY
00188                     WRITE ORDER-RECORD AFTER ADVANCING 1 LINE
00189                     ADD OM-REORDER-QUAN TO OM-QUAN-ON-ORDER.
00190
00191             D010-DELETE-MASTER.
00192                 MOVE OLD-MASTER TO LOG-LINE.
00193                 MOVE DELETE-MSG TO LOG-MESSAGE.
00194                 WRITE LOG-RECORD AFTER ADVANCING 1 LINE.
00195
00196             D020-UPDATE-MASTER.
00197                 IF      SHIPMENT
00198                     PERFORM E010-PROCESS-SHIPMENT
00199                 ELSE IF RECEIPT
00200                     PERFORM E020-PROCESS-RECEIPT
00201                 ELSE IF ADJUSTMENT
00202                     PERFORM E030-PROCESS-ADJUSTMENT
00203                 ELSE
00204                     MOVE TRANSACTION TO LOG-LINE
00205                     MOVE BAD-TRANS-CODE-MSG TO LOG-MESSAGE
00206                     WRITE LOG-RECORD AFTER ADVANCING 1 LINE
00207                     ADD 1 TO ERROR-COUNT.
00208
00209             D030-INVALID-ADDITION.
00210                 MOVE TRANSACTION TO LOG-LINE.
00211                 MOVE BAD-ADDITION-MSG TO LOG-MESSAGE.
00212                 WRITE LOG-RECORD AFTER ADVANCING 1 LINE.
00213                 ADD 1 TO ERROR-COUNT.
00214
00215             E010-PROCESS-SHIPMENT.
00216                 IF OM-QUAN-ON-HAND IS NOT LESS THAN TR-QUANTITY
00217                     SUBTRACT TR-QUANTITY FROM OM-QUAN-ON-HAND
00218                 ELSE
00219                     MOVE TRANSACTION TO LOG-LINE
00220                     MOVE OUT-OF-STOCK-MSG TO LOG-MESSAGE
00221                     WRITE LOG-RECORD AFTER ADVANCING 1 LINE
00222                     ADD 1 TO ERROR-COUNT.
00223
```

```
00224          E020-PROCESS-RECEIPT.
00225              ADD TR-QUANTITY TO OM-QUAN-ON-HAND.
00226              SUBTRACT TR-QUANTITY FROM OM-QUAN-ON-ORDER.
00227
00228          E030-PROCESS-ADJUSTMENT.
00229              IF        TR-ADJUSTMENT-CODE = 1
00230                  MOVE TR-QUANTITY TO OM-QUAN-ON-HAND
00231              ELSE IF TR-ADJUSTMENT-CODE = 2
00232                  MOVE TR-QUANTITY TO OM-QUAN-ON-ORDER
00233              ELSE IF TR-ADJUSTMENT-CODE = 3
00234                  MOVE TR-QUANTITY TO OM-REORDER-POINT
00235              ELSE IF TR-ADJUSTMENT-CODE = 4
00236                  MOVE TR-QUANTITY TO OM-REORDER-QUAN
00237              ELSE IF TR-ADJUSTMENT-CODE = 5
00238                  MOVE TR-DESCRIPTION TO OM-DESCRIPTION
00239              ELSE
00240                  MOVE TRANSACTION TO LOG-LINE
00241                  MOVE BAD-ADJ-CODE-MSG TO LOG-MESSAGE
00242                  WRITE LOG-RECORD AFTER ADVANCING 1 LINE
00243                  ADD 1 TO ERROR-COUNT.
00244
00245          X010-GET-VALID-TRANSACTION.
00246              MOVE '?' TO SEQUENCE-ERROR-FLAG.
00247              PERFORM Y010-READ-TRANSACTION
00248                  UNTIL     SEQUENCE-ERROR-FLAG = 'N'
00249                        OR ERROR-COUNT IS GREATER THAN 10.
00250
00251          X020-GET-VALID-MASTER.
00252              MOVE '?' TO SEQUENCE-ERROR-FLAG.
00253              PERFORM Y020-READ-MASTER
00254                  UNTIL     SEQUENCE-ERROR-FLAG = 'N'
00255                        OR ERROR-COUNT IS GREATER THAN 10.
00256
00257          Y010-READ-TRANSACTION.
00258              READ TRANSACTION-FILE INTO TRANSACTION
00259                  AT END MOVE HIGH-VALUES TO TR-KEY.
00260              IF TR-KEY IS LESS THAN TR-KEY-PREVIOUS
00261                  MOVE TRANSACTION TO LOG-LINE
00262                  MOVE TRANS-SEQUENCE-ERROR-MSG TO LOG-MESSAGE
00263                  WRITE LOG-RECORD AFTER ADVANCING 1 LINE
00264                  ADD 1 TO ERROR-COUNT
00265              ELSE
00266                  MOVE 'N' TO SEQUENCE-ERROR-FLAG.
00267              MOVE TR-KEY TO TR-KEY-PREVIOUS.
00268
00269          Y020-READ-MASTER.
00270              READ OLD-MASTER-FILE INTO OLD-MASTER
00271                  AT END MOVE HIGH-VALUES TO OM-KEY.
00272              IF OM-KEY IS LESS THAN OM-KEY-PREVIOUS
00273                  MOVE OLD-MASTER TO LOG-LINE
00274                  MOVE MASTER-SEQUENCE-ERROR-MSG TO LOG-MESSAGE
00275                  WRITE LOG-RECORD AFTER ADVANCING 1 LINE
00276                  ADD 1 TO ERROR-COUNT
00277              ELSE
00278                  MOVE 'N' TO SEQUENCE-ERROR-FLAG.
00279              MOVE OM-KEY TO OM-KEY-PREVIOUS.
00280
00281          ******************** END OF PROGRAM ************************
```

FIGURE 12.9 The complete file update program, including more complete files and adjustments for all record fields.

This version of the program contains a number of changes from previous versions. To begin with, we have added a new file, ORDER-FILE, which requires a SELECT statement in the Environment Division and an FD in the Data Division. This file will be used for order recommendations when stock is found to be low. The record description for ORDER-FILE provides for a bit of editing, but in the interests of simplicity and space the program does not show the printing of headings or counting of pages and lines that would normally be provided.

The LOG-RECORD and NEW-MASTER record have both been modified. The change to LOG-RECORD is simple, made primarily to emphasize the more general usage of the record in this version of the program. The revised format of NEW-MASTER reflects the more detailed file definition that we are using. Notice that we have named the last field instead of just calling it FILLER; this allows us to initialize the field when we create a new master record.

In the Working-Storage Section we have added a message to report an invalid adjustment code on a transaction, and the formats of OLD-MASTER and TRANSACTION have been revised to fit our new requirements. In OLD-MASTER the last field is simply called FILLER, since we have no need to refer to it in the program.

In the Procedure Division, the only change in B010-UPDATE-LOGIC is a statement to perform C040-CHECK-QUANTITY before a master record is written to NEW-MASTER-FILE. It is important to understand why this code, which determines whether or not we need to order more merchandise, is placed at this point in the program. It will, of course, be done any time an old master has no activity, that is, no matching transaction. In this case, the execution of the reordering decision will ordinarily not result in the placement of another order. But then again, it may, so it is not wrong to check even in this case. When an old master does have activity, whether that consists of adjustments, receipts, or shipments—or any combination of the three—we do not want to make the reordering decision until all the transactions have been processed. As the program has been written, the old master is modified in its Working-Storage location and is not written until a new transaction is found that has a different key. When this occurs, the modified old master is forced out to the new master file, and it is at precisely this point that we want to make the reordering decision.

The paragraph that makes this decision, C040-CHECK-QUANTITY, contains one new feature that we may note in passing and then shall defer until Chapter 19 for a complete explanation. We see that within a relation condition it is permissible to write an arithmetic expression, using a plus sign. What we want to know is whether the sum of the quantity on order and the quantity on hand is less than the reorder point. The statement shown expresses exactly that. If you wish to use simple arithmetic expressions of this sort without looking ahead to the full story in Chapter 19, just keep the arithmetic *very simple* and always write a space before and a space after the arithmetic operators.

The last thing to be done when it has been determined that more stock is needed is to add the reorder quantity to the quantity on order. This is necessary because otherwise the next time the inventory control program is run it would again order some more stock. This is the main function of the quantity-on-order field.

Aside from the changes needed to build the new master record in C020-ADD-MASTER, the only remaining changes involve modification of the three level E paragraphs. We see now why we did not simply include these paragraphs as in-line code in the nested IF of D020-UPDATE-MASTER, in the previous version of the program. We are able to modify the three update paragraphs as needed, with no change to the code that controls their execution. Of these three paragraphs, the most significant change has to do with the processing of adjustments, since we how have an adjustment code that indicates which of five fields is being changed. The nested **IF** statement that we have used is the code that we developed in Section 5.14 for the case structure. If you are using **COBOL-85**, you may replace this code with an equivalent **EVALUATE** statement. Basically, we are executing one of five different actions depending on the value of **TR-ADJUSTMENT-CODE**, with a sixth action to take care of the error case if **TR-ADJUSTMENT-CODE** has an illegal value.

We note one final feature of this program from an inventory control standpoint. When a receipt is processed, it represents the completion of a cycle that was begun when the stock item was ordered in a previous execution of the program. When the material was ordered, that quantity was added to the quantity on order. Now, when it is received, the quantity must be subtracted from the quantity on order and added to the quantity on hand. Naturally, in real life there would have to be provision for handling partial shipments, incorrect quantities, and various other considerations.

The program was run with sample files. Here is the sample old master.

```
                  Reorder   Reorder
                  point     quantity
         On    On    |        /
Key     hand  order  |       /       Description
000020011100040001200004 BOLT,  3 INCH X 1/2
000080007300000000600004 BOLT,  4 INCH X 1/2
000110020000100003500100 NUT,   1/2 INCH
000210021000100003000100 BUSHING, 2 INCH OD
000240009901000020000500 WASHER, 2 INCH
000360123400000010000100 PIN,   1 INCH
000371234500000100000100 PIN,   1-1/2 INCH
000515432100000100000100 GADGET, BLUE
000594321000000100000100 GADGET, RED
000613210900000100000100 WIDJET, GREEN
000702222200000100000100 WIDJET, PURPLE
000683333300000100000100 MIS-FILE, RED-FACED
000804444400000100000100 SAMPLE
000810010000000000800005 DRILL, 8 SPINDLE
000820100000100012000020 COTTER PINS, 2 IN
000840106200000010000020 COTTER PINS, 3 IN
```

The transaction file that was used appears at the top of the next page. When the program was run the log file report contained the following:

```
000010001021                                   THIS TRANSACTION IS OUT OF SEQUENCE
00011987651 111112222233333ERROR ENTRY         THIS ADDITION MATCHES AN EXISTING MASTER
00024012004                                    INSUFFICIENT STOCK TO SHIP AMOUNT SPECIFIED
00036000005                                    THIS TRANSACTION IS OUT OF SEQUENCE
00051543210000010000010000GADGET, BLUE         THIS MASTER RECORD HAS BEEN DELETED
00052000005                                    THERE IS NO MASTER FOR THIS TRANSACTION
00059001230                                    TRANSACTION CODE ILLEGAL
00068333330000010000010000MIS-FILE, RED-FACED  THIS MASTER IS OUT OF SEQUENCE
000810000029                                   BAD ADJUSTMENT CODE
```

```
                         ┌─ Transaction code
                         │ ┌─ Adjustment code
        Key   Qty        │ │
        00002000010|4|
        00001000102|1|
        00008000050|4|
        00011987651| 111112222233333ERROR ENTRY
        00015009991| 008880077700666A CORRECT ADDITION
        00021001003
        00024005003
        00024000504
        00024000404
        00024012004
        00037123002|1|
        00036000005
        00051000005
        00052000005
        00059010004
        00059001230
        00061012344
        00080000102|1|
        00080000222|2|
        00080000502|3|
```

This is the order report:

```
00008          40     BOLT,  4 INCH X 1/2
00011         100     NUT,  1/2 INCH
00024         500     WASHER,  2 INCH
00080          30     SAMPLE
00082         200     COTTER PINS,  2 IN
00084         200     COTTER PINS,  3 IN
```

Here is the new master that was produced.

```
                      Reorder   Reorder
                       point    quantity
       On    On                   /           Description
Key    hand  order       |      /
00002001010000400012000040BOLT,  3 INCH X 1/2
00008000230000400006000040BOLT,  4 INCH X 1/2
00011002000002000035000100NUT,  1/2 INCH
00015009990088800777006A CORRECT ADDITION
00021003100000000030000100BUSHING,  2 INCH OD
00024005090100002000005000WASHER,  2 INCH
00036012340000001000010000PIN,  1 INCH
00037123000000010000100000PIN,  1-1/2 INCH
00059422100000010000100000GADGET,  RED
00061308750000001000010000WIDJET,  GREEN
00070222220000001000010000WIDJET,  PURPLE
00080000100052000050000030SAMPLE
00081001000000000008000005DRILL,  6 SPINDLE
00082010000030001200000200COTTER PINS,  2 IN
00084008620020001000000200COTTER PINS,  3 IN
```

A careful study of these sample files will be rewarded with a thorough understanding of the logic of this program. The best way to do this is to take the transactions in sequence and satisfy yourself that the outputs are correct for the conditions represented. As one example, consider stock item 24. The old master began with 99 on hand and 1000 on order. The first transaction for this stock item represented a receipt of 500. The next two transactions represented shipments of 50 and 40 giving a quantity on hand of 509. The last transaction attempted to ship 1200. The impossibility of doing this was noted in the log report. With 509 on hand and 500 still on order after subtracting the shipment of 500, the quantity on hand plus the quantity on order was less than the reorder point of 2000, so another order was placed. This left the quantity on order at 1000 again, as we note in the new master.

Inspection of the other transactions will show that all of the various kinds of transactions and the variations of adjustments were handled correctly and that all of the erroneous transactions were reported properly. This is not an exhaustive test to really satisfy ourselves that the program will handle all eventualities for which it was designed, but at least it indicates that there are no glaring errors.

REVIEW QUESTIONS

1. Here is a pseudocode representation of the logic of the merge program without sequence checking. Does it represent the same logic as the program of Figure 12.2? Could the program be written in this fashion without separate paragraphs for the **READ** statements?

   ```
   Open files
   Read a file-1 record; at end move HIGH-VALUES to KEY-1
   Read a file-2 record; at end move HIGH-VALUES to KEY-2
   PERFORM-UNTIL KEY-1 = HIGH-VALUES and KEY-2 = HIGH-VALUES
       IF KEY-1 is less than KEY-2 THEN
           Write output record from file-1 record
           Read a file-1 record; at end move HIGH-VALUES to KEY-1
       ELSE
           Write output record from file-2 record
           Read a file-2 record; at end move HIGH-VALUES to KEY-2
       ENDIF
   ENDPERFORM
   Close files
   Stop
   ```

2. Suppose that in a file updating application, the master file is in ascending sequence but the transaction file is in descending sequence. Could program logic be devised to do the updating? If not, what would have to be done before the transaction could be processed?

3. Suppose that a master file in a file updating application were lost or destroyed. What would have to be done to reconstruct it?

4. Suppose that in the sample old master file shown following **UPDATE1**, the first two records were reversed. What would **UPDATE1** produce, given the same transaction file? What would the program do if the master file were correct but the first two records of the transaction file were reversed?

5. Suppose that the transactions for one stock item consisted of a number of shipments followed by a deletion. Would the logic of the program of Figure 12.5 (**UPDATE2**) handle this situation correctly?

6. What would happen with the program of Figure 12.5 if a deletion record were followed by shipments or receipts for the same stock item?

7. It is generally believed that the use of level 88 entries improves readability. For instance, an **IF** statement that begins

    `IF ADDITION . . .`

is easier to understand without looking at the Data Division than the equivalent statement

    `IF TR-TRANSACTION-CODE = '1' . . .`

Can you think of a circumstance where readability considerations might argue for writing the tests in the second form?

8. The versions of the file update program—from Figure 12.7 (**UPDATE3**) on—all sequence check the transaction file and the old master file but they do not sequence check the new master file. Can you think of reasons why it might be advisable to include such a sequence check of the output?

ANSWERS

1. The logic is identical. The program could be written this way, but using separate paragraphs for input usually makes the code easier to read and modify.

2. Program logic cannot be set up to handle sequential file updating unless the two files are in the same sequence on the same key. Under certain limited circumstances it might be possible to find a way to process the transactions, but the real solution would be to sort the transaction file into the same sequence as the master.

3. The file updating program would have to be run using the previous copies of the master file and the transaction file that was processed against it. It is customary to retain copies of old master and transaction files for just this purpose.

4. The program would process the erroneous master file correctly. It would detect equality of the first master and first transaction, update the master, and get another transaction. This new transaction would force out the first three master records, even though not in correct sequence, and everything else would proceed normally.

    With the first two transaction records reversed, the program would read master records until it found the one with the key 00021, which would be updated correctly. On reading another transaction, the update logic would compare an old master key of 00021 with a transaction key of 00008; since the old master key is not less than the transaction key, it would do the updating and thus create a garbled master record. Subsequent records would be processed correctly.

5. Yes.

6. This should not happen because it was specified that the transactions for any one key will be in sequence on the transaction code. Since this error is possible, however, the sequence checking of the transaction file really ought to include an appropriate test for this error possibility.

    To answer the question as posed, however, the first transaction after the deletion would be treated as an addition, and the new master would be thoroughly garbled. The rudimentary checking of the program in Figure 12.7 would catch this error.

7. During program testing or debugging, whether of the original program or of the program as changed during maintenance, it is necessary to determine that the program acts correctly in response to specific data. At this stage it is, of course, necessary to know the actual values of the data items rather than the more descriptive condition names. It can be argued that since the programmer has to know the actual codes anyway, it is preferable to write the **IF** statements to use the codes and possibly use a comment to indicate what they stand for. The alternative argument, however, is that this type of testing is generally a short-term activity, and that the more common requirement is to be able to determine what *function* the program is supposed to be performing. This requirement is met better by condition names, and one can use the Data Division to prepare test data if necessary.

8. It might seem that there would be no point to sequence checking to output, since the only ways the output could be out of sequence are rather unlikely. One way this could happen would be for the input to be out of sequence but for the program not to catch the error. Another would be undetected computer malfunction. Another would be an error in program logic. It could be argued that undetected computer malfunction is extremely unlikely and that the other two types of errors are very unlikely once the program has been tested thoroughly.

    However, since a sequence error in the new master is indicative of very serious errors that will disable the next cycle of processing completely, it is sometimes felt desirable to make a check of this kind even though the error is very unlikely to occur. This is especially true since sequence checking does not appreciably complicate the program and since it takes very little machine time. Such a check is especially useful during program testing, before it is known with assurance that the logic is correct. (Admittedly, however, this is not done very often in actual programs once testing is finished.)

EXERCISES

*1. There are occasions when files to be merged should not have any matching records. Prepare pseudocode for a merge program that makes two error tests:

    a. It sequence checks both files and stops on finding any error.

    b. It stops if the keys of the records from the two files are the same.

---

* Answers to starred exercises will be found in Appendix IV at the end of the book.

2. Prepare pseudocode and write a program to check for sequence errors in an input file and also check for duplicate records. The program should print an appropriate message and stop if either condition is detected.

*3. Write a program to merge three input files, each of which is in ascending sequence on a key. Include sequence checking.

4. The program in Figure 12.9 (**UPDATE5**) checks the key, the transaction code, and the adjustment code of the transaction file but assumes that the quantity, quantity on order, reorder point, and reorder quantity are all valid. Modify the program so that it will validate these four fields as being numeric before it accepts the transaction as valid. The program should test all fields, not just stop when the first error is found. That is, if more than one field is in error, the transaction record should be printed *once*, but error messages should be printed for *all* fields in error. You should move the editing of the transaction code and the adjustment code to this point in the program so that all editing except sequence checking is done as part of the input process. In other words, once a transaction record is accepted as valid, it should contain no data errors except (possibly) not matching a master record. (No matter how many errors you find in one transaction record, only add 1 to **ERROR-COUNT** for the entire record.)

*5. The program of Figure 12.5 (**UPDATE2**) and the programs following it will not operate correctly if an addition record is followed by other transactions for the same key. Modify the program so that this type of transaction file can be processed correctly. This is much harder than it might sound. Try it first on the relatively simple program in Figure 12.5, then when you have the technique developed, apply it to the program in Figure 12.9 (**UPDATE5**).

*6. Modify the program of Figure 12.9 so that it distinguishes between file sequence errors and errors in the transaction data. Errors in the transaction file other than sequence errors should be allowed up to a maximum of 100; since they are to be expected and do not affect other transactions, they are not too serious. However, since sequence errors are usually disabling and indicative of serious trouble, especially on the master file, report all sequence errors and allow only *ten* sequence errors on the transaction file or *one* sequence error on the old master file before processing is halted.

7. Modify the program of Figure 12.9 so that when there is insufficient stock on hand to process a shipment, as many as are on hand are shipped and the difference is added to the quantity back-ordered, a new field in the master record. Create appropriate test data and test the program.

8. (This exercise is suitable for a project.)
   Assume that a company's employee payroll records have the following format:

Columns 1-5	employee pay number	9(5)
Columns 6-30	employee name	X(25)
Columns 31-39	social security number	9(9)
Columns 40-47	year-to-date gross pay	9(6)V99
Columns 48-55	year-to-date federal tax	9(6)V99
Columns 56-62	year-to-date state tax	9(5)V99

Columns 63-69	year-to-date city tax	9(5)V99
Columns 70-77	year-to-date net pay	9(6)V99
Column 78	pay type; **H** for hourly, **S** for salaried	X
Columns 79-85	weekly salary	9(5)V99
	or hourly pay rate	BBB99V99
Columns 86-87	municipality code	99

This file may be updated by three types of transactions. The functions and formats of these transactions are:

1. add a new employee

Column 1	record type (**A**)
Columns 2-6	employee pay number
Columns 7-31	employee name
Columns 32-40	social security number
Columns 41	pay type; **H** or **S**
Columns 42-48	for salaried employees, weekly salary; for hourly employees, hourly pay rate
Columns 49-50	municipality code

2. delete an employee

Column 1	record type (**B**)
Columns 2-6	employee pay number
Columns 7-50	not used

3. weekly pay record (for hourly employees only)

Columns 1	record type (**C**)
Columns 2-6	employee pay number
Columns 8-12	department number
Columns 13-16	hours worked; numeric, 2 decimals
Columns 17-50	not used

The weekly payroll transaction file is sorted on employee pay number, and on record type within employee. Two reports are produced by the payroll program. The first is the Weekly Payroll Report. For each employee paid during the week, the report shows the following:

Columns 1-5	employee pay number	PIC 9(5)
Columns 8-32	employee name	PIC X(25)
Columns 35-43	gross pay	PIC ZZ,ZZ9.99
Columns 46-54	total deductions	PIC ZZ,ZZ9.99
Columns 57-65	net pay	PIC ZZ,ZZ9.99

At the bottom of the report is a line showing total gross pay, total deductions, and total net pay for the company. At the top of each page is a line containing column headings.

All salaried employees are paid each week. Hourly employees are paid in any given week only if there is a pay record for them. Because an hourly employee can work in more than one department in a week, an hourly employee may have more than one pay record. The employee's pay is based on total hours, regardless of the department(s) in which these hours are accrued. Hourly employees are paid at base rate for the first 37.5 hours worked and at 1.5 times base for hours in excess of 37.5.

Deductions consist of federal tax (25% of gross pay), state tax (5% of gross pay), and city tax. City tax varies depending on where the employee lives; this is coded in the *municipality code* field. Using the municipality code, city tax is calculated as follows:

Municipality	Tax
03	1.50% of gross pay
07	2.00%
15	5.25%
23	3.75%
77	2.50%

The employee's net pay is the gross pay minus the sum of all deductions.

After an employee has been paid, the various year-to-date total fields in his or her master payroll record are updated by adding the current values of gross pay, federal tax, state tax, city tax, and net pay to the old year-to-date totals. The updated record is then written to a new master payroll file. Of course, for hourly employees the payroll record must be written to the new master file regardless of whether or not the employee was actually paid during the week.

The second report produced by the payroll program is the Payroll Activity Log. If an employee is added to the master payroll file, all year-to-date fields in the new record are initialized to zero and a message is written to the Activity Log indicating the employee's pay number, name, social security number, pay type (hourly or salaried), weekly salary or hourly pay rate, and municipality code.

If an employee is deleted from the master payroll file, a message is written to the Activity Log showing all data in the payroll record. (In a real payroll system employee records are not actually removed from the system when an employee leaves the company since for tax purposes records must be maintained at least until the end of the year. However, these records may be transferred to an *inactive* file for the sake of efficiency.)

Design of the actual format of the Payroll Activity Log is left as part of the exercise. However, remember that all reports should be designed to be used by people who are not programmers and who do not have the time or interest to guess what the information on the report means. Design reports to be as useful as possible, not just to minimize the amount of code you have to write.

Optional added feature: Assume that payroll transaction records may contain errors. To be valid, the record type must be **A**, **B**, or **C**. In a type **A** record the pay number, social security number, salary or hourly pay rate, and municipality code must be numeric. The pay type must be **H** or **S**, and for hourly employees the pay rate must not exceed $99.99. For type **B** records, the pay number must be numeric and the remainder of the record must be blank. For type **C** records, the pay number, department number, and hours worked must be numeric; hours worked must not exceed 80.00; and the remainder of the record must be blank. For type **A** records, there *must not* be a record already on the master file with the same pay number; and for type **B** and **C** records there *must* be a match with a record on the master file.

CHAPTER 13

TABLE HANDLING

13.1 INTRODUCTION

In this chapter we shall study the COBOL facilities for handling groups of related items with *subscripting* and *indexing*. These features make it possible to refer to a large number of related items by one name, selecting—by using appropriate subscripts or indices—the one part of the large group that is desired.

13.2 THE BASICS OF SUBSCRIPTING

Suppose that we need to be able to refer to a list of 100 accounts in Working-Storage, each six digits long. It would certainly be possible to give them 100 different names, such as ACCOUNT-1, ACCOUNT-2, etc., up to ACCOUNT-100. The Data Division would have to include an entry for each of the different data names, which may be sketched as follows:

```
01   ACCOUNT-GROUP.
     05   ACCOUNT-1          PIC 9(6).
     05   ACCOUNT-2          PIC 9(6).
     .
     .
     .
     05   ACCOUNT-99         PIC 9(6).
     05   ACCOUNT-100        PIC 9(6).
```

This would be time-consuming both for the programmer and for the compiler, would be highly error prone, and in many cases would lead to hopelessly complicated Procedure Division code.

By using subscripts we can, instead, give the entire list a single name such as ACCOUNT. We inform the compiler that the name ACCOUNT stands for 100 different items—not just one—by writing the clause OCCURS 100 TIMES in the Data Division entry for ACCOUNT. This might be done as follows:

```
01   TABLE-OF-ACCOUNTS.
     05   ACCOUNT              PIC 9(6) OCCURS 100 TIMES.
```

This indicates to the compiler that **ACCOUNT** is the name of a subscripted data item having 100 elements, each element being six digits in length. **ACCOUNT** has been shown as a 05 level name because the **OCCURS** clause may not be written at the **01** or **77** levels. The **01** level name shown in this entry refers to the group containing the table and has no necessary relationship to the name of the subscripted data item. However, as the **01** level name implies, **ACCOUNT** is now generally referred to as a *table* in **COBOL**.

In the Procedure Division, when we want to refer to a particular item out of the 100 items that are described by the general name **ACCOUNT**, we follow the name with parentheses enclosing an integer in the range of 1 to 100. Thus if we want to refer to the first item in the table, we can write

```
ACCOUNT (1)
```

If we want the fourteenth item in the table, we can write

```
ACCOUNT (14)
```

We will commonly leave a space between the data name and the left parenthesis, although this is no longer required in **COBOL**.

If the only way to refer to a particular element of a subscripted data item were to use literals, subscripting would be of limited use. This is not all we can do, however; it is possible to use a variable as a subscript. We might, for instance, write

```
ACCOUNT (ACCOUNT-NUMBER)
```

ACCOUNT-NUMBER must be an integer data item that has been given a value by previous statements. Whatever value **ACCOUNT-NUMBER** has would be used to select the corresponding element from the table named **ACCOUNT**. It is the programmer's responsibility to be sure that the value of a subscript is never less than 1 nor greater than the number of elements in the table. If a subscript outside these limits is used, the result depends on the compiler being used. The IBM **COBOL** compilers, for example, will give no warning of the error and will simply access whatever is in storage adjacent to the table; other compilers may issue a warning at compile time (if the error can be detected then), and will abort the run during execution.

In the example just given, **ACCOUNT-NUMBER** is used as a subscript. It is permitted to be either binary (**COMPUTATIONAL** usage) or decimal (**DISPLAY** or **COMPUTATIONAL-3** usage). In the object program, however, if a subscript is not already in binary, it will usually be converted to that form. Therefore, unless there is good reason not to do so, we prefer subscripts to be binary items. This is achieved by writing **COMPUTATIONAL SYNC** in the Data Division entry for a subscript item. For our example, we could write

```
01   ACCOUNT-NUMBER          PIC 999 COMP SYNC.
```

(Even though the **01** level entry may be aligned on a double word boundary by the compiler, making the **SYNC** unnecessary, it is better to make the intention clear by writing the clauses as shown.)

13.3 A SIMPLE PROGRAM ILLUSTRATING SUBSCRIPTING

In Figure 13.1 we have the Data and Procedure Divisions for a program that employs subscripting to develop a frequency table describing input data. We are given a file whose records each contain a four-digit number identifying a year, together with other data that we will not process. The year identification should be 1985, 1986, 1987, or 1988. The function of the program is to produce a line showing the number of records for each year and a count of the total number of records outside this range.

```
00013          DATA DIVISION.
00014
00015          FILE SECTION.
00016
00017          FD  IN-FILE
00018              LABEL RECORDS ARE OMITTED.
00019          01  IN-RECORD.
00020              05  ACCOUNT-NUMBER         PIC X(6).
00021              05  YEAR                   PIC 9(4).
00022              05  FILLER                 PIC X(70).
00023
00024          FD  REPORT-FILE
00025              LABEL RECORDS ARE OMITTED.
00026          01  REPORT-RECORD.
00027              05  FILLER                 PIC X.
00028              05  YEAR-COUNT-OUT         PIC Z(6)9 OCCURS 4 TIMES.
00029              05  BAD-DATA-COUNT-OUT     PIC Z(6)9.
00030
00031          WORKING-STORAGE SECTION.
00032
00033          01  YEAR-TABLE.
00034              05  YEAR-COUNT             PIC S9(4) COMP SYNC
00035                                         OCCURS 4 TIMES.
00036          01  BAD-DATA-COUNT             PIC S9(4) COMP SYNC.
00037
00038          01  MORE-DATA-REMAINS-FLAG     PIC X VALUE 'Y'.
00039              88  MORE-DATA-REMAINS          VALUE 'Y'.
00040              88  NO-MORE-DATA-REMAINS       VALUE 'N'.
00041
00042          01  YEAR-SUBSCRIPT             PIC S9 COMP SYNC.
00043
00044          PROCEDURE DIVISION.
00045          A000-COUNT-DATA.
00046              MOVE 0 TO YEAR-COUNT (1).
00047              MOVE 0 TO YEAR-COUNT (2).
00048              MOVE 0 TO YEAR-COUNT (3).
00049              MOVE 0 TO YEAR-COUNT (4).
00050              MOVE 0 TO BAD-DATA-COUNT.
00051              OPEN INPUT IN-FILE
00052                   OUTPUT REPORT-FILE.
00053              PERFORM B010-COUNT-YEARS
00054                   UNTIL NO-MORE-DATA-REMAINS.
00055              PERFORM B020-WRITE-TABLE.
00056              CLOSE IN-FILE
00057                    REPORT-FILE.
00058              STOP RUN.
00059
```

```
00060          B010-COUNT-YEARS.
00061              READ IN-FILE
00062                  AT END MOVE 'N' TO MORE-DATA-REMAINS-FLAG.
00063              IF MORE-DATA-REMAINS
00064                  IF YEAR IS LESS THAN 1985 OR IS GREATER THAN 1988
00065                      ADD 1 TO BAD-DATA-COUNT
00066                  ELSE
00067                      SUBTRACT 1984 FROM YEAR GIVING YEAR-SUBSCRIPT
00068                      ADD 1 TO YEAR-COUNT (YEAR-SUBSCRIPT).
00069
00070          B020-WRITE-TABLE.
00071              MOVE YEAR-COUNT (1) TO YEAR-COUNT-OUT (1).
00072              MOVE YEAR-COUNT (2) TO YEAR-COUNT-OUT (2).
00073              MOVE YEAR-COUNT (3) TO YEAR-COUNT-OUT (3).
00074              MOVE YEAR-COUNT (4) TO YEAR-COUNT-OUT (4).
00075              MOVE BAD-DATA-COUNT TO BAD-DATA-COUNT-OUT.
00076              WRITE REPORT-RECORD AFTER ADVANCING 1 LINE.
```

FIGURE 13.1   The Data and Procedure Divisions of a program using subscripting to produce a frequency table.

The program operates with a table (**YEAR-TABLE**) having four locations for recording the four counts. This table is shown in the Working-Storage Section with an **OCCURS** clause specifying that **YEAR-COUNT** has four elements. Since we never do anything with these locations other than use them in arithmetic and as source items in **MOVE** statements, it makes the program slightly more efficient to designate them as **COMPUTATIONAL**. The data item named **YEAR-SUBSCRIPT** is **COMPUTATIONAL** and **SYNCHRONIZED**.

The Procedure Division begins by moving zeros to all elements of the table, and to **BAD-DATA-COUNT**. It is necessary to do something of this sort, since an item that has an **OCCURS** clause is not allowed to have a **VALUE** clause. Although there are other ways of initializing a table (which we will discuss in the following sections), all but one of them are variations on this approach. **COBOL** does not have a statement that says "Move this constant to every element of the table," and trying to move an initial value to the group item **YEAR-TABLE** will frequently give incorrect results.

After we initialize the table, the following code is very similar to previous programs. In the processing paragraph named **B010-COUNT-YEARS** we get the information from a record and then inspect the year to see if it is in the range 1985 to 1988, inclusive. If it is not, we add one to the count of bad data. If the year is valid, we now need to add one to the appropriate element of **YEAR-COUNT**. We must somehow make the correspondence between year 1985 and subscript 1, between year 1986 and subscript 2, etc. An easy way to do this is to subtract 1984 from the year number, giving a result in the range 1 to 4. This value is then used as the subscript.

When all the records have been processed, we need to move the values to the output line and print them. This is done using subscripted variables as well, taking advantage of the fact that the item named **REPORT-RECORD** in the File Section has an **OCCURS** clause on its 05 level entry for **YEAR-COUNT-OUT**.

13.4 ENTERING VALUES INTO A TABLE USING REDEFINES

Even in the previous example, which primarily involved producing table values by execution of a program, it was necessary to give initial values to the elements of the table. If we wish to do the reverse, namely, to select entries from values already in a table, initialization becomes even more important. For a concrete example, suppose that records in an input file contain, among other things, a transaction date represented as a six-digit number. For example, July 4, 1990 might be represented as 900704. We wish to convert the representation of the month, 07 in the example, into its English equivalent and print the text as part of a report. The question is how to arrange the Data Division so that a subscripted value—which must have an OCCURS clause and must not have a VALUE clause—can be associated with 12 VALUE clauses giving the names of the months. Figure 13.2 shows how the REDEFINES clause provides the answer.

```
WORKING-STORAGE SECTION.

01    MONTH-NAME-VALUES.
      05    FILLER              PIC X(9) VALUE 'JANUARY  '.
      05    FILLER              PIC X(9) VALUE 'FEBRUARY '.
      05    FILLER              PIC X(9) VALUE 'MARCH    '.
      05    FILLER              PIC X(9) VALUE 'APRIL    '.
      05    FILLER              PIC X(9) VALUE 'MAY      '.
      05    FILLER              PIC X(9) VALUE 'JUNE     '.
      05    FILLER              PIC X(9) VALUE 'JULY     '.
      05    FILLER              PIC X(9) VALUE 'AUGUST   '.
      05    FILLER              PIC X(9) VALUE 'SEPTEMBER'.
      05    FILLER              PIC X(9) VALUE 'OCTOBER  '.
      05    FILLER              PIC X(9) VALUE 'NOVEMBER '.
      05    FILLER              PIC X(9) VALUE 'DECEMBER '.

01    MONTH-NAME-TABLE REDEFINES MONTH-NAME-VALUES.
      05    MONTH-NAME          PIC X(9) OCCURS 12 TIMES.

01    MONTH-NUMBER             PIC S99 COMP SYNC.

01    MONTH-TEXT              PIC X(9).
```

FIGURE 13.2 An illustration of the use of **REDEFINES** to enter values into a table in Working-Storage.

Given this table, we could then write code such as

```
MOVE MONTH-NAME (MONTH-NUMBER) TO MONTH-TEXT.
```

We see that the 01 level entry named MONTH-NAME-VALUES has 12 filler entries at the 05 level, each containing the name of a month. Each entry is 9 characters long, corresponding to the longest month's name (September); all entries in a table must be of the same length. After the group item consisting of these 12 fillers, another 01 level entry with a REDEFINES clause follows. Subordinate to it at the 05 level is an entry with the clause OCCURS 12 TIMES. It is this last data name, the one that has an OCCURS clause, that is written with a subscript in the Procedure Division.

It is worth pausing to consider the way in which the correspondence between a month name and and a month number is established. **MONTH-NAME-VALUES** and **MONTH-NAME-TABLE** are both group items, and the number of characters in each of them must accordingly be established by counting the number of characters of the elementary items of which they are composed. The compiler determines that **MONTH-NAME-VALUES** consists of 12 entries of nine characters each, which is 108 characters. The compiler then determines that the group item named **MONTH-NAME-TABLE** consists of an elementary item having nine characters, which occurs 12 times, and which also totals 108 characters. The correspondence between a code of 01 and the name January is established by the fact that the name January occurs first in the list of elementary items in **MONTH-NAME-VALUES**. Likewise, July is associated with the code 07 only because that name is the seventh one in the list. If the lines in the source program were to be mixed up so that July appeared as the first **05** level entry under **MONTH-NAME-VALUES** and January as the seventh, the program would, of course, produce results that would be correct in terms of the information supplied to it; and "900704" would become January 04, 1990.

This type of Data Division structure will frequently be seen in programs involving subscripting and indexing and should be understood thoroughly. This structure can be shown in skeleton form as follows:

```
01   NAME-1.
     05   FILLER        ...           PIC ... VALUE ...
     .
     .
     .
01   NAME-2 REDEFINES NAME-1.
     05   SUBSCRIPTED-NAME       PIC ... OCCURS ...
```

SUBSCRIPTED-NAME is the only one that will appear in the Procedure Division; this is the name that is written with a subscript. **NAME-1** and **NAME-2** are required simply to make the **REDEFINES** work. It is good programming style to make these names correspond to the subscripted name that will be used in the Procedure Division, but no information is taken from such correspondence by the compiler. Also, the **PIC** clauses for **NAME-1** and **SUBSCRIPTED-NAME** should be identical.

13.5 ENTERING VALUES INTO A TABLE FROM A FILE

Using **REDEFINES** to initialize a table is a technique that is useful only if the initial table values never change, as was the case in the previous example. In many cases, however, the initial values of the table entries may change from run to run, which would require changing the source code and recompiling the program every time the program was run—which is not an acceptable procedure. In these situations, we generally load the table data from an input file.

For example, consider the seed catalog program presented in Chapter 11. Suppose that in addition to the data validation already in the program, we want to be certain that every catalog number on an order matches a number in a master file. One way to do this is to load all catalog numbers from a master inventory file into a table, then search the table for every order record to be certain that the catalog number in the order record is in the table. We will discuss ways of searching the table shortly; for now, we want to considered how the table might be loaded.

The program segment in Figure 13.3 shows the code that could be used to initialize the table of catalog numbers. To save space we have not shown the complete program, but only the parts that would be added to load the table.

```
        SELECT CATALOG-FILE                   ASSIGN TO S-CATALOG.
        .
        .
        .
FD   CATALOG-FILE
        LABEL RECORDS ARE OMITTED.
01   CATALOG-RECORD.
        05   MASTER-CATALOG-NUMBER            PIC X(5).
        05   REST-OF-RECORD                   PIC X(75).
        .
        .
        .
WORKING-STORAGE SECTION.
01   CATALOG-NUMBER-TABLE.
        05   VALID-NUMBER                      PIC X(5) OCCURS 1000 TIMES.

01   VALID-NUMBER-MAX                          PIC S9(4) COMP SYNC
                                                         VALUE 1000.
01   X-CATALOG                                 PIC S9(4) COMP SYNC.
        .
        .
        .
PROCEDURE DIVISION.
A000-VALIDATE-ORDERS.
     PERFORM B020-LOAD-VALID-NUMBER.
     OPEN INPUT ORDER-FILE
          OUTPUT NORMAL-HANDLING-FILE
                 SPECIAL-HANDLING-FILE.
     MOVE 'Y' TO MORE-DATA-REMAINS-FLAG.
     READ ORDER-FILE
          AT END MOVE 'N' TO MORE-DATA-REMAINS-FLAG.
     PERFORM B010-VALIDATE-ONE-LINE
          UNTIL NO-MORE-DATA-REMAINS.
     CLOSE ORDER-FILE
           NORMAL-HANDLING-FILE
           SPECIAL-HANDLING-FILE.
     STOP RUN.
        .
        .
        .
B020-LOAD-VALID-NUMBER.
     OPEN INPUT CATALOG-FILE.
     MOVE 'Y' TO MORE-DATA-REMAINS-FLAG.
     MOVE ZERO TO X-CATALOG.
     READ CATALOG-FILE
          AT END MOVE 'N' TO MORE-DATA-REMAINS-FLAG.
     PERFORM C030-LOAD-CATALOG-RECORD
          UNTIL NO-MORE-DATA-REMAINS.
     CLOSE CATALOG-FILE.
     MOVE X-CATALOG TO VALID-NUMBER-MAX.
        .
        .
        .
```

```
C030-LOAD-CATALOG-RECORD.
    ADD 1 TO X-CATALOG.
    MOVE MASTER-CATALOG-NUMBER TO VALID-NUMBER (X-CATALOG).
    READ CATALOG-FILE
        AT END MOVE 'N' TO MORE-DATA-REMAINS-FLAG.
```

FIGURE 13.3 **COBOL** code to load a table of valid catalog numbers from a master file.

The first addition needed is, of course, the definition of a new file, **CATALOG-FILE**, which contains the valid catalog numbers. Presumably the file contains data about each catalog item, but we have defined only the one field needed for this program.

In the Working-Storage Section we define the table itself, as well as two additional variables we will need. The table has been defined to have 1000 entries; we will assume for simplicity that **CATALOG-FILE** contains no more than 1000 records, although in a real program we would check to make sure that we do not accidentally try to load more records than the table has room for. Notice that **VALID-NUMBER-MAX** has an initial value of 1000, the maximum table size. This variable serves two functions. First, during the loading process it tells us how large the table actually is if we wish to test for possible overflow (loading too many records into the table). Second, after the table has been loaded **VALID-NUMBER-MAX** tells how many records have *actually* been loaded into the table; we will need this information later when we try to search for specific records in the table.

X-CATALOG is the variable we will use as a subscript for table entries. We will tend to use the prefix **X** in a variable name to indicate that it is being used as an index or subscript for a table.

In the Procedure Division, paragraph **A000-VALIDATE-ORDERS** is exactly the same as it was in Figure 11.1, except that we have added the statement

PERFORM B020-LOAD-VALID-NUMBER.

as the first statement of the paragraph. This statement controls all activity required to load the table, including opening and closing **CATALOG-FILE**, initializing the subscript and end of file flag, and setting the updated value for **VALID-NUMBER-MAX**. These activities are all part of the task of loading the table, and do not belong in the main paragraph.

B020-LOAD-VALID-NUMBER is very much like the driver paragraphs we have seen in examples up to now. It begins by opening the data file, initializing variables, and reading the priming record. It performs a work paragraph (which in this case loads entries in the table) until the data file is empty, then closes the data file and sets the new value for **VALID-NUMBER-MAX**. At this point, the table has been loaded and **VALID-NUMBER-MAX** tells how many entries are actually in use in the table.

C030-LOAD-CATALOG-RECORD is very simple and requires little discussion. The only point of interest is to note that at all times **X-CATALOG** tells how many records are actually contained in the table. An alternative, for example, is to initialize the subscript to one, then add one to it after a record has been loaded so that it points to the next available space. The problem with this approach is that when we reach the end of the input file, the subscript contains a value one *greater* than the number of records in the file, and we have to subtract one from **X-CATALOG** to get the correct value for **VALID-NUMBER-MAX**.

13.6 INITIALIZING A TABLE WITH A VALUE CLAUSE

In **COBOL-85** we are permitted to place a **VALUE** clause on elements of a table. In this case, every element in the table is initialized to the specified value. For example, we could initialize the table in Figure 13.1 as follows instead of using code in the Procedure Division.

```
01   YEAR-TABLE.
     05   YEAR-COUNT              PIC S9(4) COMP SYNC
                                  OCCURS 4 TIMES VALUE ZERO.
```

In the following example, each entry in the table contains a structure, and each occurrence of the structure contains an occurrence of **X-FIELD** and **9-FIELD**. Each occurrence of **X-FIELD** is initialized to spaces, and each occurrence of **9-FIELD** is initialized to zero.

```
01   TABLE-AREA.
     05   WORK-TABLE   OCCURS 100 TIMES.
          10   X-FIELD            PIC X(5)    VALUE SPACES.
          10   9-FIELD            PIC 9(5)V99 VALUE ZERO.
```

END COBOL-85

13.7 SUBSCRIPTED VARIABLES WITH TWO OR MORE SUBSCRIPTS

A subscripted variable in **COBOL** is not restricted to just one subscript, but may have two or three. (In **COBOL-85** a subscripted variable may have up to seven subscripts, which is far more than is likely to be needed in the kinds of problems **COBOL** deals with.) For an example of how this works, suppose that we must process a two-way table showing the enrollment in a school system classified by grade and year. We assume that the school system has grades 1 to 12 and that we are dealing with the years 1985 to 1988. This means that the table will have 48 entries, showing the enrollment for each grade for each year. Written in the form in which it might be displayed in a school system report, the table would be as follows:

	1985	1986	1987	1988
1	240	239	229	205
2	299	280	277	260
3	257	255	238	220
4	230	230	220	215
5	225	220	210	200
6	220	215	218	208
7	210	209	195	205
8	105	200	204	190
9	260	266	270	289
10	270	270	274	270
11	300	301	290	309
12	310	320	315	337

A subscripted variable is established as having two subscripts by writing a group item name having two subordinate **OCCURS** clauses. For this application the Data Division entry could be

```
01  SIZE-TABLE.
    05  SIZE-BY-GRADE                OCCURS 12 TIMES.
        10  SIZE-BY-GRADE-AND-YEAR   PIC 999 OCCURS 4 TIMES.
```

SIZE-TABLE is an 01 level entry made necessary by the fact that an OCCURS clause is not permitted at the 01 level. SIZE-BY-GRADE has an OCCURS clause establishing that the number of occurrences of this level is 12 and that the corresponding subscript can therefore range from 1 to 12. This entry does not have a PICTURE clause. SIZE-BY-GRADE-AND-YEAR is subordinate to SIZE-BY-GRADE and has an OCCURS clause establishing that there are four occurrences of this level and that the corresponding subscript ranges from 1 to 4. It also has a PICTURE clause showing the nature of the elementary items of which the table is composed.

This structure of the Data Division entry for SIZE-TABLE established that when we write

```
SIZE-BY-GRADE-AND-YEAR (1, 2)
```

in the Procedure Division we mean the first grade and the second year. If the Data Division entry had been

```
01  SIZE-TABLE.
    05  SIZE-BY-YEAR                 OCCURS 4 TIMES.
        10  SIZE-BY-GRADE-AND-YEAR   PIC 999 OCCURS 12 TIMES.
```

then the reference

```
SIZE-BY-GRADE-AND-YEAR (1, 2)
```

would be to the first year and the second grade. What is important is not the names used, which the compiler obviously cannot interpret, but the order of the OCCURS clauses.

Looking at paragraph B020-LOAD-TABLE in Figure 13.4, we see that it is similar to B010-COUNT-YEARS in Figure 13.1 except that here we have two subscripts. Observe in the last line in the paragraph that GRADE is a DISPLAY item, since it is part of the input record, whereas YEAR-SUBSCRIPT has been defined as COMPUTATIONAL. This means trivial extra work for the compiler but no real difficulty in keeping such matters straight. If the program involved a good deal of manipulation of these table elements, the constant internal conversion from DISPLAY to COMPUTATIONAL could cause some inefficiencies. The solution would be to do the conversion once by moving GRADE to a COMPUTATIONAL item and always using the latter as a subscript.

```
IDENTIFICATION DIVISION.
PROGRAM-ID.
    ENROLLMENT.
DATE-WRITTEN.
    MARCH 27, 1987.

ENVIRONMENT DIVISION.
INPUT-OUTPUT SECTION.
FILE-CONTROL.
    SELECT ENROLLMENT-FILE          ASSIGN TO S-ENROLL.

DATA DIVISION.

FILE SECTION.
```

```
FD   ENROLLMENT-FILE
     LABEL RECORDS ARE OMITTED.
01   ENROLLMENT-RECORD.
     05   GRADE                        PIC 99.
     05   YEAR                         PIC 9(4).
     05   ENROLLMENT                   PIC 999.


WORKING-STORAGE SECTION.

77   ERROR-COUNT                       PIC S9(4) COMP SYNC.
77   GRADE-SUBSCRIPT                   PIC  99   COMP SYNC.
77   MORE-DATA-REMAINS-FLAG            PIC X.
     88   MORE-DATA-REMAINS                      VALUE 'Y'.
     88   NO-MORE-DATA-REMAINS                   VALUE 'N'.
77   YEAR-SUBSCRIPT                    PIC  9    COMP SYNC.

01   SIZE-TABLE.
     05   SIZE-BY-GRADE                OCCURS 12 TIMES.
          10   SIZE-BY-GRADE-AND-YEAR  PIC 999 OCCURS 4 TIMES.

PROCEDURE DIVISION.
A000-CREATE-ENROLLMENT-TABLE.
     MOVE ZERO TO ERROR-COUNT.
     MOVE 'Y'  TO MORE-DATA-REMAINS-FLAG.
     MOVE 1 TO GRADE-SUBSCRIPT.
     PERFORM B010-INITIALIZE-TABLE
         UNTIL GRADE-SUBSCRIPT > 12.
     OPEN INPUT ENROLLMENT-FILE.
     PERFORM B020-LOAD-TABLE
         UNTIL NO-MORE-DATA-REMAINS.
     DISPLAY SIZE-BY-GRADE-AND-YEAR (1, 1).
     DISPLAY SIZE-BY-GRADE-AND-YEAR (1, 2).
     DISPLAY SIZE-BY-GRADE-AND-YEAR (1, 3).
     DISPLAY SIZE-BY-GRADE-AND-YEAR (1, 4).
     DISPLAY SIZE-BY-GRADE (1).
     DISPLAY SIZE-BY-GRADE-AND-YEAR (2, 3).
     CLOSE ENROLLMENT-FILE.
     STOP RUN.

B010-INITIALIZE-TABLE.
     MOVE ZERO TO SIZE-BY-GRADE-AND-YEAR (GRADE-SUBSCRIPT, 1).
     MOVE ZERO TO SIZE-BY-GRADE-AND-YEAR (GRADE-SUBSCRIPT, 2).
     MOVE ZERO TO SIZE-BY-GRADE-AND-YEAR (GRADE-SUBSCRIPT, 3).
     MOVE ZERO TO SIZE-BY-GRADE-AND-YEAR (GRADE-SUBSCRIPT, 4).
     ADD 1 TO GRADE-SUBSCRIPT.

B020-LOAD-TABLE.
     READ ENROLLMENT-FILE
         AT END MOVE 'N' TO MORE-DATA-REMAINS-FLAG.
     IF MORE-DATA-REMAINS
         IF      YEAR < 1985 OR > 1988
             OR GRADE < 1 OR > 12
             ADD 1 TO ERROR-COUNT
         ELSE
             SUBTRACT 1984 FROM YEAR GIVING YEAR-SUBSCRIPT
             MOVE ENROLLMENT TO
                 SIZE-BY-GRADE-AND-YEAR (GRADE, YEAR-SUBSCRIPT).
```

FIGURE 13.4 A program illustrating operations on a table with two subscripts.

In the main-line routine for this program **DISPLAY** statements are used to print out a few values from this table.* The first four **DISPLAY** statements print the enrollments for grade 1 in all four years. The next **DISPLAY** statement demonstrates another capability of **COBOL** subscripting. If we write only one subscript for a variable that is defined as having two, using the name on the highest-level **OCCURS** clause, then we obtain all of the elements corresponding to that one subscript. In this case we obtain the entries for all four years at grade 1. Another way of looking at this is to say that **SIZE-BY-GRADE** is a one-subscript table, each of whose elements contains 12 characters.

Here are the results that were printed when this program was run with sample data.

```
240
239
229
205
240239229205
277
```

We see in the fifth line what was produced when we called for **SIZE-BY-GRADE (1)**. This shows the enrollments for all four years in the first grade, as may be seen by comparing the fifth line with the first four lines.

Tables with three subscripts are handled in an entirely equivalent manner. That is, the Data Division definition of the table has three **OCCURS** clauses. The Procedure Division references to individual elements of the table are written with three subscripts separated by commas. It is unusual, however, to find commercial application programs that involve more than two subscripts.

13.8 THE PERFORM ... VARYING OPTION

Thus far we have been dealing with the mechanics of subscripting and have not seen an illustration of its real power. The true value of subscripting is found in arranging the program to change subscript values rather than simply writing literals or subscript data items that are given one value. We have seen some simple examples of this type of subscript modification in the code to initialize tables in some of the sample programs, but now we go a step further.

Consider, for instance, an extension of the school enrollment application. Suppose that when the program is given the number of a year, it is to print the total enrollment for that year in all 12 grades, together with the sum of all the entries in the table. (The latter value has no direct meaning in itself, but could be used, for instance, to find the average enrollment for the four years.)

We will assume that some part of the program, not shown, has obtained the year number and stored in a variable called **YEAR-NUMBER**. What we need to do to get the total is to initialize a variable (which we may as well call **TOTAL**) to zero, then add all the enrollment figures for that year to **TOTAL**. This in turn means that we need a way to have a subscript variable take on the values from 1 to 12 in succession. Although we showed one way to do this in Figure 13.4 when we initialized the table, it is done much more easily by using the **VARYING** form of the **PERFORM** verb, which is shown in the general format at the top of the next page.

---

* Bear in mind that **DISPLAY** statements should be used only for simple diagnostic output. In a complete program the table would be printed using **WRITE** statements.

> **PERFORM** procedure-name-1 [**THRU** procedure-name-2]
>
> **VARYING** $\left\{\begin{array}{l}\text{index-name-1}\\\text{identifier-1}\end{array}\right\}$ **FROM** $\left\{\begin{array}{l}\text{index-name-2}\\\text{identifier-2}\\\text{literal-1}\end{array}\right\}$
>
> **BY** $\left\{\begin{array}{l}\text{literal-2}\\\text{identifier-3}\end{array}\right\}$ **UNTIL** condition-1

Figure 13.5 shows how easily the **PERFORM** verb carries out the needed operations. The variable name written after the **VARYING** in the first **PERFORM** statement is given a succession of values. The starting value is established by the **FROM** phrase, and the amount by which the subscript variable is to be changed between repetitions is given in the **BY** phrase. Finally, we indicate the termination condition with an **UNTIL** phrase. This means that the paragraph named **D010-TOTALLER** will be executed first with **GRADE-SUBSCRIPT** equal to 1. **GRADE-SUBSCRIPT** will then be increased by one and **D010-TOTALLER** will be executed again. Eventually **D010-TOTALLER** will have been executed with **GRADE-SUBSCRIPT** equal to 12. Now when **GRADE-SUBSCRIPT** is increased by one, the **UNTIL** condition will be satisfied and the repetitions stop.

This portion of the program could be represented by the following pseudocode:

```
set grade-subscript to 1
PERFORM-UNTIL grade-subscript > 12
    execute the totaller function
    add 1 to grade-subscript
ENDPERFORM
```

```
C010-SUM-EXAMPLES.
    SUBTRACT 1984 FROM YEAR-NUMBER GIVING YEAR-SUBSCRIPT.
    MOVE ZERO TO TOTAL.
    PERFORM D010-TOTALLER
        VARYING GRADE-SUBSCRIPT FROM 1 BY 1
            UNTIL GRADE-SUBSCRIPT > 12.
    DISPLAY YEAR-NUMBER '  ' TOTAL.

    MOVE ZERO TO TOTAL.
    PERFORM D010-TOTALLER
        VARYING GRADE-SUBSCRIPT FROM 1 BY 1
            UNTIL GRADE-SUBSCRIPT > 12
        AFTER YEAR-SUBSCRIPT FROM 1 BY 1
            UNTIL YEAR-SUBSCRIPT > 4.
    DISPLAY TOTAL.

D010-TOTALLER.
    ADD SIZE-BY-GRADE-AND-YEAR (GRADE-SUBSCRIPT, YEAR-SUBSCRIPT)
            TO TOTAL.
```

FIGURE 13.5 An illustration of the use of the **PERFORM** ... **VARYING** statement with subscripting.

More generally, the **PERFORM ... VARYING** is equivalent to this pseudocode:

```
set identifier-1 to the FROM value
PERFORM-UNTIL the condition is true
      execute procedure-1 through procedure-2
      add the BY value to identifier-1
ENDPERFORM
```

There are two points to observe about this structure. First, the **PERFORM** statement allows you to execute a sequence of paragraphs, rather than just a single paragraph; we shall *never* use this option. Second, remember that **PERFORM-UNTIL** (and the **COBOL PERFORM** statement) tests the **UNTIL** condition *before* the loop is executed, and that identifier-1 is changed *inside* the loop *after* the paragraph is executed. These factors determine the value that identifier-1 will have at the end of the loop.

The first **PERFORM...VARYING** in Figure 13.5 is about the simplest possible form of that verb. In general, the **FROM** and **BY** phrases are both permitted to be either literals or identifiers, and we may write any condition whatever in the **UNTIL** phrase. The condition can be compound and in some circumstances will not involve the subscripted variable at all. Suggestions of some of these possibilities may be found in the Review Questions at the end of the chapter.

The **PERFORM ... VARYING** option may be written to run through two or more subscripts in succession, as shown in the following general format:

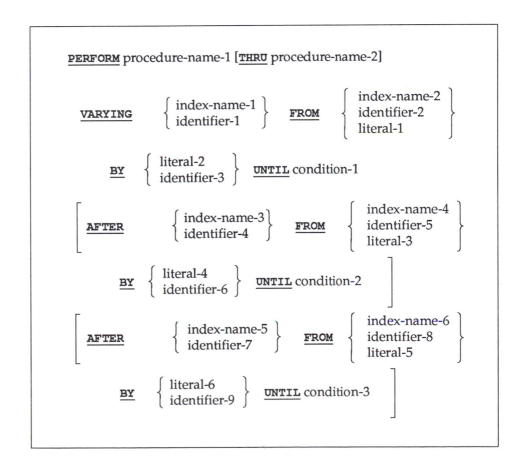

The second **PERFORM** in Figure 13.5 says to set **GRADE-SUBSCRIPT** to 1 and then run **YEAR-SUBSCRIPT** through all the values from 1 to 4. Then **GRADE-SUBSCRIPT** is increased to 2 and **YEAR-SUBSCRIPT** is again run through all the values from 1 to 4. This process continues until **D010-TOTALLER** has been performed for all 48 combinations of the values of the two subscripts.

The pseudocode for this version of the **PERFORM ... VARYING** is

```
set grade-subscript to 1
set year-subscript to 1
PERFORM-UNTIL grade-subscript > 12
    PERFORM-UNTIL year-subscript > 4
        execute the totaller function
        add 1 to year-subscript
    ENDPERFORM
    set year-subscript to 1
    add 1 to grade-subscript
ENDPERFORM
```

and the general **PERFORM ... VARYING** is equivalent to:

```
set identifier-1 to its FROM value
set identifier-4 to its FROM value
set identifier-7 to its FROM value
PERFORM-UNTIL condition-1 is true
    PERFORM-UNTIL condition-2 is true
        PERFORM-UNTIL condition-3 is true
            execute procedure-1 through procedure-2
            increment identifier-7 by its BY value
        END-PERFORM
        set identifier-7 to its FROM value
        increment identifier-4 by its BY value
    ENDPERFORM
    set identifier-4 to its FROM value
    increment identifier-1 by its BY value
ENDPERFORM
```

The **PERFORM...VARYING** form is used heavily in table handling programs, and it is important to be very clear about exactly how it works. Study the pseudocode until you are certain you understand how and when the basic functions of the **PERFORM** loop are executed:

1. Initializing the subscript or index variable (which is generally called the *loop variable*);
2. Testing for the end of the loop;
3. Executing the performed paragraph;
4. Incrementing the loop variable.

It is not required that the loop variable be a subscript or an index. It could be a variable to which we are giving a succession of values for some other purpose, or it could be a simple counter that tells how many times the performed paragraph was executed before the **UNTIL** clause stopped execution.

COBOL-85

Just as **COBOL-85** permits the use of **END-PERFORM** with the **PERFORM ...** **UNTIL** statement, it permits **END-PERFORM** with **PERFORM ... VARYING**. The complete form of the **PERFORM ... VARYING** statement in **COBOL-85** is

$$\text{\underline{PERFORM}} \left[\text{procedure-name-1} \left[\left\{ \begin{array}{l} \text{\underline{THROUGH}} \\ \text{\underline{THRU}} \end{array} \right\} \text{procedure-name-2} \right] \right]$$

$$\text{\underline{VARYING}} \left\{ \begin{array}{l} \text{index-name-1} \\ \text{identifier-1} \end{array} \right\} \text{\underline{FROM}} \left\{ \begin{array}{l} \text{index-name-2} \\ \text{identifier-2} \\ \text{literal-1} \end{array} \right\}$$

$$\text{\underline{BY}} \left\{ \begin{array}{l} \text{literal-2} \\ \text{identifier-3} \end{array} \right\} \text{\underline{UNTIL}} \text{ condition-1}$$

$$\left[\text{\underline{AFTER}} \left\{ \begin{array}{l} \text{index-name-3} \\ \text{identifier-4} \end{array} \right\} \text{\underline{FROM}} \left\{ \begin{array}{l} \text{index-name-4} \\ \text{identifier-5} \\ \text{literal-3} \end{array} \right\} \right.$$

$$\left. \text{\underline{BY}} \left\{ \begin{array}{l} \text{literal-4} \\ \text{identifier-6} \end{array} \right\} \text{\underline{UNTIL}} \text{ condition-2} \right] \dots$$

[imperative-statement-1 **END-PERFORM**]

This usage is as you would expect. That is, you may omit the procedure name(s) and use an in-line imperative statement instead, followed by the END-PERFORM. Note also that since **COBOL-85** allows up to seven levels of subscripting, there may be up to six **AFTER** clauses.

END COBOL-85

13.9 INDEXING

In addition to subscripting, **COBOL** provides a second way of referring to tables of data. Indexing and subscripting are very similar in some respects and quite different in others. From an application programmer's point of view, the main difference is that the object program in many cases can deal with indexed variables more efficiently than it can with subscripted variables, and with indexing we have a powerful new verb, **SEARCH**. Along with these advantages, there are a few new matters of mechanics that we must consider.

We inform the compiler that a variable will be referenced with indexing by setting up its description in the Data Division, just as we would with a subscripted variable, and by adding the clause **INDEXED BY**. This clause specifies that indexing is desired and establishes the name of the index. For example, a variable having one index could be established with this Data Division entry:

```
01   TABLE-OF-ACCOUNTS.
     05  ACCOUNT              PIC 9(6) OCCURS 100 TIMES
                              INDEXED BY ACCOUNT-INDEX.
```

(The **INDEXED BY** clause is written on a separate line only for reasons of clarity and space.) The **OCCURS** clause specifies that the table contains 100 entries. By looking at this, the compiler knows that the variable is either subscripted or indexed; the **INDEXED BY** clause tells it that the variable is indexed and identifies the index variable. As a result, we can write in the Procedure Division statements similar to the following.

```
MOVE ACCOUNT (ACCOUNT-INDEX) TO ACCOUNT-OUT.
```

When we write the name of a variable in an **INDEXED BY** clause, we establish that variable as an index name. No other definition of the index is required; indeed, no other is permitted. Furthermore, the index is associated with the table whose definition contains the **INDEXED BY** clause, and it should not be used with any other table. **COBOL** also requires that any particular reference to a table use indices only or subscripts only; a mixture of the two is not permitted. For example, if we have the following data

```
01   TABLE-AREA.
     05   TABLE-1              OCCURS 10 TIMES INDEXED BY X-1.
          10   TABLE-2         PIC X(5)
                               OCCURS 20 TIMES INDEXED BY X-2.
01   SUB-1                     PIC 99 COMP SYNC.
01   SUB-2                     PIC 99 COMP SYNC.
```

we can write

```
TABLE-2 (X1, X2)   or   TABLE-2 (SUB-1, SUB-2)
```

but not

```
TABLE-2 (X1, SUB-2)   or   TABLE-2 (SUB-1, X2)
```

However, **COBOL-85** *does* permit mixing subscripts and indices in this manner.

An index name is also special in that it may not be used in any sort of arithmetic operation (**ADD, SUBTRACT,** etc.) or in a **MOVE** statement. To carry out these kinds of operations on index names, we have the **SET** statement, which is shown in the general formats below and at the top of the next page.

This is most commonly used to give an initial value to an index name, as in statements like these:

```
SET ACCOUNT-INDEX TO 1.
SET ACCOUNT-INDEX TO RECORD-FIELD-6.
```

Statements of this type have the same function as a **MOVE**, including carrying out any necessary conversions of data representation. In the **SET** statement

---

Format 1
$$\text{\underline{SET}} \left\{ \begin{array}{l} \text{index-1 [index-2]} \ldots \\ \text{identifier-1 [identifier-2]} \ldots \end{array} \right\}$$ $$\text{\underline{TO}} \left\{ \begin{array}{l} \text{index-name-3} \\ \text{identifier-3} \\ \text{literal-1} \end{array} \right\}$$

```
┌─────────────────────────────────────────────────────────────┐
│                         Format 2                            │
├─────────────────────────────────────────────────────────────┤
│                                                             │
│        SET index-name-1 [index-name-2] . . .                │
│                                                             │
│             ⎧ UP BY   ⎫   ⎧ identifier-1 ⎫                   │
│             ⎨         ⎬   ⎨              ⎬                   │
│             ⎩ DOWN BY ⎭   ⎩ literal-1    ⎭                   │
│                                                             │
└─────────────────────────────────────────────────────────────┘
```

the sending item is on the right and the receiving item is on the left; this reversal of the pattern of the **MOVE** statement may not be obvious at first glance. The arithmetic permitted on index names is restricted to addition and subtraction using the **UP BY** and **DOWN BY** variations of **SET** as shown in these examples:

```
SET LIST-INDEX UP BY 8.
SET INDEX-OF-FIELDS UP BY FIELD-2.
SET INDEX-A DOWN BY 1.
SET POINTER-A DOWN BY FIELD-LENGTH.
```

It is permitted to use index names in relation conditions, but doing so involves slightly complex rules since it is necessary to be clear about exactly what an index represents internally. Since we shall have no reason to utilize this feature, the reader should refer to the appropriate **COBOL** reference manual for his or her system.

It is occasionally necessary to be able to store a value of an index name for later retrieval. This can be done using a **SET** statement together with a temporary storage location that is defined with a **USAGE IS INDEX** (or simply **USAGE INDEX**) clause. This feature would be used only in fairly sophisticated programs, and we shall make no further use of it in this book.

COBOL-85

13.10   THE SET STATEMENT AND CONDITION NAMES

In **COBOL-85** there is a use of the **SET** statement that has nothing to do with index variables. Recall that condition names (level 88 items) allow us to test the value of a variable without actually knowing the specific values that the variable may take. For example, we might have

```
01  COLOR                      PIC X.
    88  RED                        VALUE 'A'.
    88  BLUE                       VALUE 'B'.
    88  YELLOW                     VALUE 'C'.
    88  GREEN                      VALUE 'D'.
    88  PURPLE                     VALUE 'E'.
```

and we could write

```
IF GREEN
    MOVE 'GREEN' TO COLOR-TEXT.
```

However, in order to set the color to green, we would have to know the proper code value and write

```
MOVE 'D' TO COLOR.
```

In **COBOL-85** we can use the **SET** statement to write

```
SET GREEN TO TRUE.
```

The result of this statement is exactly the same as the previous **MOVE** statement (that is, we move 'D' to **COLOR**), but the Procedure Division code does not depend on the specific values used by **COLOR**. This presents two advantages. First, using the **SET** statement provides better documentation of the function being performed than simply moving a code to **COLOR**. Secondly (and more importantly), the exact value used for each color code is completely defined in the Data Division; if we wish to change these values we do so in the Data Division and do not need to modify any Procedure Division code.

END COBOL-85

13.11 THE SEARCH VERB

One of the primary motivations for using indexing, in addition to increased speed in some cases, is that it makes possible the use of the **SEARCH** verb. To understand how this verb functions and what its usefulness is, let us look once more at the seed catalog program. In Section 13.5 we showed how a table of valid catalog numbers might be loaded into the program. We will now consider how this table might be used.

The catalog number is a five-digit number, which means that potentially there are 100,000 catalog numbers. However, we have assumed that less than 1000 of these numbers correspond to actual products, and, to determine if the catalog number on an order record is valid, we need to be able to find the record's catalog number in the table.

We could, of course, allow a one-character entry for each possible catalog number and mark this entry as either 'Y' or 'N', depending on whether the corresponding catalog number is valid or not. This would allow us simply to use the catalog number on the order record as a subscript into the table and test the value of the table entry. However, this would require 100,000 bytes of memory, as opposed to the 5000 bytes required by the method we are using; even on large computers this savings in memory is not to be ignored.

The program in Figure 13.6 shows how this can be accomplished.

```
00001          IDENTIFICATION DIVISION.
00002          PROGRAM-ID.
00003             SEEDS.
00004          DATE-WRITTEN.
00005             MARCH 28, 1987.
00006
00007          ENVIRONMENT DIVISION.
00008          INPUT-OUTPUT SECTION.
00009          FILE-CONTROL.
```

```
00010            SELECT CATALOG-FILE              ASSIGN TO S-CATALOG.
00011            SELECT ORDER-FILE                ASSIGN TO S-ORDERS.
00012            SELECT NORMAL-HANDLING-FILE      ASSIGN TO S-NORMAL.
00013            SELECT SPECIAL-HANDLING-FILE     ASSIGN TO S-SPECIAL.
00014
00015       DATA DIVISION.
00016       FILE SECTION.
00017       FD  CATALOG-FILE
00018           LABEL RECORDS ARE OMITTED.
00019       01  CATALOG-RECORD.
00020           05  MASTER-CATALOG-NUMBER        PIC X(5).
00021           05  REST-OF-RECORD               PIC X(75).
00022
00023       FD  ORDER-FILE
00024           LABEL RECORDS ARE OMITTED.
00025       01  ORDER-RECORD.
00026           05  ORDER-NUMBER                 PIC X(6).
00027           05  RECORD-TYPE                  PIC X.
00028           05  CATALOG-NUMBER.
00029               10  CATALOG-FIRST-DIGIT      PIC X.
00030               10  CATALOG-REMAINING        PIC X(4).
00031           05  SIZE-CODE                    PIC X.
00032           05  QUANTITY                     PIC 99.
00033           05  ITEM-DESCRIPTION             PIC X(40).
00034           05  X-PRICE                      PIC X(5).
00035           05  9-PRICE REDEFINES X-PRICE    PIC 999V99.
00036           05  FILLER                       PIC X(20).
00037
00038       FD  NORMAL-HANDLING-FILE
00039           LABEL RECORDS ARE OMITTED.
00040       01  NORMAL-LINE                      PIC X(133).
00041
00042       FD  SPECIAL-HANDLING-FILE
00043           LABEL RECORDS ARE OMITTED.
00044       01  SPECIAL-LINE                     PIC X(133).
00045
00046       WORKING-STORAGE SECTION.
00047       01  CATALOG-NUMBER-TABLE.
00048           05  VALID-NUMBER                 PIC X(5) OCCURS 1000 TIMES
00049                                                INDEXED BY X-CATALOG.
00050
00051       01  ERROR-FLAGS.
00052           88  RECORD-OK                               VALUE SPACES.
00053           05  CAT-NO-NOT-NUMERIC           PIC X.
00054           05  CAT-NO-NOT-VALID             PIC X.
00055           05  FIRST-DIGIT-INVALID          PIC X.
00056           05  SIZE-CODE-NOT-PERMITTED      PIC X.
00057           05  NO-SUCH-SIZE-CODE            PIC X.
00058           05  QUANTITY-AND-PRICE-CODES.
00059               88  QTY-AND-PRICE-OK                    VALUE SPACES.
00060               10  QTY-NOT-NUMERIC          PIC X.
00061               10  PRICE-NOT-NUMERIC        PIC X.
00062           05  INVALID-PRICE-OR-QTY         PIC X.
00063           05  LARGE-PRICE                  PIC X.
00064
00065       01  ERROR-MESSAGES.
00066           05  CAT-NO-NOT-NUMERIC-MSG       PIC X(50)
00067               VALUE ' CATALOG NUMBER CONTAINS AN IMPROPER CHARACTER'.
00068           05  CAT-NO-NOT-VALID-MSG         PIC X(50)
00069               VALUE ' CATALOG NUMBER IS NOT IN THE MASTER FILE'.
```

```
00070          05  FIRST-DIGIT-INVALID-MSG      PIC X(50)
00071              VALUE ' FIRST DIGIT OF CATALOG NUMBER INVALID'.
00072          05  SIZE-CODE-NOT-PERMITTED-MSG PIC X(50)
00073              VALUE ' THIS ITEM DOES NOT TAKE A SIZE CODE'.
00074          05  NO-SUCH-SIZE-CODE-MSG        PIC X(50)
00075              VALUE ' THERE IS NO SUCH SIZE CODE'.
00076          05  QTY-NOT-NUMERIC-MSG          PIC X(50)
00077              VALUE ' QUANTITY CONTAINS AN IMPROPER CHARACTER'.
00078          05  PRICE-NOT-NUMERIC-MSG        PIC X(50)
00079              VALUE ' PRICE CONTAINS AN IMPROPER CHARACTER'.
00080          05  INVALID-PRICE-OR-QTY-MSG     PIC X(50)
00081              VALUE ' EITHER PRICE OR QUANTITY IS WRONG'.
00082          05  LARGE-PRICE-MSG              PIC X(50)
00083              VALUE ' PRICE LARGE - SHOULD BE CHECKED'.
00084
00085      01  MORE-DATA-REMAINS-FLAG           PIC X.
00086          88  NO-MORE-DATA-REMAINS                  VALUE 'N'.
00087
00088      01  OUTPUT-LINE.
00089          05  CARRIAGE-CONTROL             PIC X.
00090          05  ORDER-NUMBER                 PIC Z(5)9.
00091          05  CATALOG-NUMBER.
00092              10  CATALOG-FIRST-DIGIT      PIC BBX.
00093              10  CATALOG-REMAINING        PIC BX(4).
00094          05  SIZE-CODE                    PIC BX.
00095          05  QUANTITY                     PIC BBZ9.
00096          05  OUTPUT-PRICE                 PIC BB$$$$9.99.
00097          05  ITEM-DESCRIPTION             PIC BBX(40).
00098          05  FILLER                       PIC X(59) VALUE SPACES.
00099
00100      01  TEXT-LINE REDEFINES OUTPUT-LINE.
00101          05  CARRIAGE-CONTROL             PIC X.
00102          05  UNKNOWN-LINE                 PIC X(132).
00103
00104      01  PRICE-LIMIT                      PIC   999V99 VALUE 150.00.
00105      01  TEST-REMAINDER                   PIC S999V99 COMP-3.
00106      01  UNIT-PRICE                       PIC S999V99 COMP-3.
00107      01  VALID-NUMBER-MAX                 PIC S9(4) COMP SYNC
00108                                                  VALUE +1000.
00109
00110      PROCEDURE DIVISION.
00111      A000-VALIDATE-ORDERS.
00112          PERFORM B020-LOAD-VALID-NUMBER.
00113          OPEN INPUT ORDER-FILE
00114              OUTPUT NORMAL-HANDLING-FILE
00115                     SPECIAL-HANDLING-FILE.
00116          MOVE 'Y' TO MORE-DATA-REMAINS-FLAG.
00117          READ ORDER-FILE
00118              AT END MOVE 'N' TO MORE-DATA-REMAINS-FLAG.
00119          PERFORM B010-VALIDATE-ONE-LINE
00120              UNTIL NO-MORE-DATA-REMAINS.
00121          CLOSE ORDER-FILE
00122                NORMAL-HANDLING-FILE
00123                SPECIAL-HANDLING-FILE.
00124          STOP RUN.
00125
00126      B010-VALIDATE-ONE-LINE.
00127          MOVE SPACES TO ERROR-FLAGS.
00128          PERFORM C010-EDIT-LINE.
00129
```

```
00130                IF QTY-AND-PRICE-OK
00131                    MOVE CORRESPONDING ORDER-RECORD TO OUTPUT-LINE
00132                    MOVE 9-PRICE TO OUTPUT-PRICE
00133                    IF RECORD-OK
00134                        WRITE NORMAL-LINE FROM OUTPUT-LINE
00135                                AFTER ADVANCING 2 LINES
00136                    ELSE
00137                        WRITE SPECIAL-LINE FROM OUTPUT-LINE
00138                                AFTER ADVANCING 2 LINES
00139                        PERFORM C020-WRITE-MESSAGES
00140                ELSE
00141                    MOVE ORDER-RECORD TO UNKNOWN-LINE
00142                    WRITE SPECIAL-LINE FROM OUTPUT-LINE
00143                            AFTER ADVANCING 2 LINES
00144                    PERFORM C020-WRITE-MESSAGES.
00145
00146            READ ORDER-FILE
00147                AT END MOVE 'N' TO MORE-DATA-REMAINS-FLAG.
00148
00149        B020-LOAD-VALID-NUMBER.
00150            OPEN INPUT CATALOG-FILE.
00151            MOVE 'Y' TO MORE-DATA-REMAINS-FLAG.
00152            READ CATALOG-FILE
00153                AT END MOVE 'N' TO MORE-DATA-REMAINS-FLAG.
00154            PERFORM C030-LOAD-CATALOG-RECORD
00155                VARYING X-CATALOG FROM 1 BY 1
00156                UNTIL NO-MORE-DATA-REMAINS.
00157            CLOSE CATALOG-FILE.
00158            SET X-CATALOG DOWN BY 1.
00159            SET VALID-NUMBER-MAX TO X-CATALOG.
00160
00161        C010-EDIT-LINE.
00162            IF CATALOG-NUMBER OF ORDER-RECORD IS NOT NUMERIC
00163                MOVE 'X' TO CAT-NO-NOT-NUMERIC
00164            ELSE
00165                SET X-CATALOG TO 1
00166                SEARCH VALID-NUMBER
00167                    AT END MOVE 'X' TO CAT-NO-NOT-VALID
00168                    WHEN VALID-NUMBER (X-CATALOG) =
00169                        CATALOG-NUMBER OF ORDER-RECORD
00170                        NEXT SENTENCE.
00171
00172            IF CATALOG-FIRST-DIGIT OF ORDER-RECORD = '0' OR '2'
00173                MOVE 'X' TO FIRST-DIGIT-INVALID.
00174
00175            IF (CATALOG-FIRST-DIGIT OF ORDER-RECORD = '1' OR '8' OR '9')
00176                AND SIZE-CODE OF ORDER-RECORD IS NOT EQUAL TO SPACES
00177                MOVE 'X' TO SIZE-CODE-NOT-PERMITTED.
00178
00179            IF SIZE-CODE OF ORDER-RECORD = 'A' OR 'D' OR 'G' OR 'J'
00180                OR 'K' OR 'L' OR 'S' OR 'T' OR 'U' OR ' '
00181                NEXT SENTENCE
00182            ELSE
00183                MOVE 'X' TO NO-SUCH-SIZE-CODE.
00184
00185            IF QUANTITY OF ORDER-RECORD IS NOT NUMERIC
00186                MOVE 'X' TO QTY-NOT-NUMERIC.
00187
00188            IF X-PRICE NOT NUMERIC
00189                MOVE 'X' TO PRICE-NOT-NUMERIC.
00190
```

```
00191              IF QTY-AND-PRICE-OK
00192                  DIVIDE 9-PRICE BY QUANTITY OF ORDER-RECORD
00193                      GIVING UNIT-PRICE REMAINDER TEST-REMAINDER
00194                  ON SIZE ERROR MOVE 'X' TO INVALID-PRICE-OR-QTY.
00195              IF QTY-AND-PRICE-OK AND TEST-REMAINDER NOT EQUAL TO ZERO
00196                  MOVE 'X' TO INVALID-PRICE-OR-QTY.
00197
00198              IF X-PRICE IS NUMERIC AND 9-PRICE IS GREATER THAN PRICE-LIMIT
00199                  MOVE 'X' TO LARGE-PRICE.
00200
00201          C020-WRITE-MESSAGES.
00202              IF CAT-NO-NOT-NUMERIC = 'X'
00203                  WRITE SPECIAL-LINE FROM CAT-NO-NOT-NUMERIC-MSG
00204                      AFTER ADVANCING 1 LINE.
00205              IF CAT-NO-NOT-VALID = 'X'
00206                  WRITE SPECIAL-LINE FROM CAT-NO-NOT-VALID-MSG
00207                      AFTER ADVANCING 1 LINE.
00208              IF FIRST-DIGIT-INVALID = 'X'
00209                  WRITE SPECIAL-LINE FROM FIRST-DIGIT-INVALID-MSG
00210                      AFTER ADVANCING 1 LINE.
00211              IF SIZE-CODE-NOT-PERMITTED = 'X'
00212                  WRITE SPECIAL-LINE FROM SIZE-CODE-NOT-PERMITTED-MSG
00213                      AFTER ADVANCING 1 LINE.
00214              IF NO-SUCH-SIZE-CODE = 'X'
00215                  WRITE SPECIAL-LINE FROM NO-SUCH-SIZE-CODE-MSG
00216                      AFTER ADVANCING 1 LINE.
00217              IF QTY-NOT-NUMERIC = 'X'
00218                  WRITE SPECIAL-LINE FROM QTY-NOT-NUMERIC-MSG
00219                      AFTER ADVANCING 1 LINE.
00220              IF PRICE-NOT-NUMERIC = 'X'
00221                  WRITE SPECIAL-LINE FROM PRICE-NOT-NUMERIC-MSG
00222                      AFTER ADVANCING 1 LINE.
00223              IF INVALID-PRICE-OR-QTY = 'X'
00224                  WRITE SPECIAL-LINE FROM INVALID-PRICE-OR-QTY-MSG
00225                      AFTER ADVANCING 1 LINE.
00226              IF LARGE-PRICE = 'X'
00227                  WRITE SPECIAL-LINE FROM LARGE-PRICE-MSG
00228                      AFTER ADVANCING 1 LINE.
00229
00230          C030-LOAD-CATALOG-RECORD.
00231              MOVE MASTER-CATALOG-NUMBER TO VALID-NUMBER (X-CATALOG).
00232              READ CATALOG-FILE
00233                  AT END MOVE 'N' TO MORE-DATA-REMAINS-FLAG.
00234
00235          **************** END OF PROGRAM *****************************
```

FIGURE 13.6 A revised version of the seed catalog program, showing the use of index variables and the **SEARCH** verb.

This version of the program contains several changes from Figure 13.3. To begin with, we have changed the definitions in Working-Storage so that **X-CATALOG** is now an index associated with the table **VALID-NUMBER**. We have also changed the way in which paragraph **C030-LOAD-CATALOG-RECORD** is executed, using a **PERFORM . . . VARYING** instead of a simple **PERFORM . . . UNTIL**. There are two reasons for this change. First, use of the **PERFORM . . . VARYING** eliminates the need to initialize and increment **X-CATALOG**. Second, it avoids a problem in initializing **X-CATALOG**. Since the lowest valid index value for the table is 1, statements such as

```
SET X-CATALOG TO ZERO.
SET X-CATALOG TO 0.
```

are illegal. Therefore, we would change the program so that **X-CATALOG** could be initialized to 1, which complicates the table loading process slightly.

Notice that we must decrement **X-CATALOG** by 1 before we store it in **VALID-NUMBER-MAX**. Remember that **PERFORM...VARYING** increments the loop variable *after* the paragraph has been performed. This means that even after the end of file is detected and **MORE-DATA-REMAINS-FLAG** is set to **'N'**, **X-CATALOG** is still incremented once more before it is tested by the condition in the **UNTIL** clause.

The **SEARCH** verb is shown in **C010-EDIT-LINE** (line 166). If the catalog number is numeric, we go on to test whether it is a valid number. (If the number is not numeric, it cannot possibly be valid so we don't bother with the test.) We begin by initializing **X-CATALOG** to one, then execute the **SEARCH** verb, which has the following general format:

$$
\boxed{
\begin{array}{l}
\underline{\text{SEARCH}}\ \text{identifier-1}\ \left[\ \underline{\text{VARYING}}\ \left\{ \begin{array}{l} \text{index-name-1} \\ \text{identifier-2} \end{array} \right\} \right] \\[2em]
\quad [\underline{\text{AT END}}\ \text{imperative-statement-1}] \\[1em]
\quad \underline{\text{WHEN}}\ \text{condition-1}\ \left\{ \begin{array}{l} \text{imperative-statement-2} \\ \underline{\text{NEXT SENTENCE}} \end{array} \right\} \\[2em]
\quad \left[\ \underline{\text{WHEN}}\ \text{condition-2}\ \left\{ \begin{array}{l} \text{imperative-statement-3} \\ \underline{\text{NEXT}}\ \underline{\text{SENTENCE}} \end{array} \right\} \right]\ \ldots
\end{array}
}
$$

Immediately following the word **SEARCH** we write the name of the item that contains the **INDEXED BY** clause; this is the table that will be searched. Next is an optional **AT END** phrase in which we specify what is to be done (other than proceeding to the next statement) if the program goes all the way through the table without ever satisfying the condition in the **WHEN** phrase. In the **WHEN** phrase, we write a condition followed by an imperative statement or **NEXT SENTENCE**. For the **SEARCH** verb to make any sense, the condition in the **WHEN** phrase must involve the indexed variable. Here we have specified that when the input catalog number is equal to a catalog number in the table, we want to proceed to the next sentence, stopping the search. It is permissible to have any number of **WHEN** phrases specifying differing circumstances and differing actions; the search stops when any one of them is satisfied.

After completing this search, either **X-CATALOG** will point to the entry in **VALID-NUMBER** that matches the input catalog number or else **CAT-NO-NOT-VALID** will have been set. Although this program simply looks to see if the catalog number is in the table, it is quite common that a program will use other fields in the table entry containing the target key.

Here is the output when this program was run with the data from Chapter 11 and a sample master file. The first five lines were written to **NORMAL-HAN-DLING-FILE** and the rest to **SPECIAL-HANDLING-FILE**.

```
0123456  5 1656 A   1      $0.45   ALASKA PEAS

0123456  9 4342     1     $20.95   GARDEN AND TREE SPRAYER

0123456  6 2638 U   2      $7.00   HONEYCROSS CORN - 1 LB

0222233  9 3188     1     $17.95   EARTHWORMS - PKG OF 2000

0222235  3 3183 L   2      $4.00   NASTURTIUM - MIXED COLORS - 1 OZ


222234  9 3526 A   1      $2.75   PRAYING MANTIS EGG CASES
THIS ITEM DOES NOT TAKE A SIZE CODE

222236  4 1939 H   0      $1.05   PHLOX - GRANIFLORA - 1/8 OZ
THERE IS NO SUCH SIZE CODE
EITHER PRICE OR QUANTITY IS WRONG

222237233761B02HIBISCUS                         390
CATALOG NUMBER IS NOT IN THE MASTER FILE
THERE IS NO SUCH SIZE CODE
PRICE CONTAINS AN IMPROPER CHARACTER

222238269088U01GARLIC SETS - 2 LBS             008.80
PRICE CONTAINS AN IMPROPER CHARACTER

22223962257T01LITTLE MARVEL PEAS - 1/2 LB      0120
CATALOG NUMBER CONTAINS AN IMPROPER CHARACTER
FIRST DIGIT OF CATALOG NUMBER INVALID
THERE IS NO SUCH SIZE CODE
QUANTITY CONTAINS AN IMPROPER CHARACTER
PRICE CONTAINS AN IMPROPER CHARACTER

222240252829L 2HOT PEPPER - LONG RED CAYENNE - 1 OZ    00550
QUANTITY CONTAINS AN IMPROPER CHARACTER

123456222241SCUCUMBER - WEST INDIAN GHERKIN - 1/4 LB   00275
CATALOG NUMBER IS NOT IN THE MASTER FILE
FIRST DIGIT OF CATALOG NUMBER INVALID
QUANTITY CONTAINS AN IMPROPER CHARACTER

122345  1 3466    10   $186.50   ABUNDANCE PEAR
PRICE LARGE - SHOULD BE CHECKED

321321  2 1321 3   21   $213.21   3213213213213213213213213213213213213213
CATALOG NUMBER IS NOT IN THE MASTER FILE
FIRST DIGIT OF CATALOG NUMBER INVALID
THERE IS NO SUCH SIZE CODE
EITHER PRICE OR QUANTITY IS WRONG
PRICE LARGE - SHOULD BE CHECKED

43654364398769876976987 69JHGFJHGFJHGCHJHGFJGFJHGFJHFJHGFJH5876587658
CATALOG NUMBER IS NOT IN THE MASTER FILE
THERE IS NO SUCH SIZE CODE
PRICE CONTAINS AN IMPROPER CHARACTER

231231  3 1231 A   12   $12.12   A12A12A12A12A12A12A12A12A12A012012012
CATALOG NUMBER IS NOT IN THE MASTER FILE
```

The output is much the same as in Chapter 11, except that several of the special handling records now have the message "CATALOG NUMBER IS NOT IN THE MASTER FILE" in addition to previously marked errors. Furthermore, the record for order number 231231, which was formerly accepted as valid, is now marked as being in error.

13.12   THE SEARCH ALL OPTION

In carrying out the search of a table using the **SEARCH** verb (without the **ALL**), the program simply inspects the table entries starting wherever the index variable currently points (which is why we were careful to reset **X-CATALOG** to 1 in **C010-EDIT-LINE**) and proceeding one entry at a time. If a match is not found until the last entry of the table, the program must have tested all of the previous entries. Assuming a random distribution of the items to be searched for, we expect that the average search will go halfway through the table before finding a match. For a long table this becomes wastefully time consuming. The **SEARCH ALL** form is a much faster alternative, providing that one condition about the table can be met.

If the table entries to be searched can be placed either in ascending or descending sequence, the use of the **SEARCH ALL** form in the program can proceed as follows. The program first compares the item being searched for with the item in the middle of the table. If by lucky chance they match, the search is completed. If not, it has been established whether the item being searched for is in the first half of the table or the second half. Either way, half of the table has been completely eliminated from further consideration. The program next inspects the item at the midway point of the half of the table where the item could be. This process is continued, each time narrowing down the range of possibilities by half, until the match is found or it is established that there is no match. Because of this factor of 2, the process is called a *binary search*; this has no relation to binary representation, and the table being searched certainly does not have to be in binary form. The speed advantage of **SEARCH ALL** becomes greater and greater as the size of the table increases. For example, in a table with 100 entries, **SEARCH** requires an average of 50 comparisons while **SEARCH ALL** requires only 7. This is good but not spectacular; the method becomes more attractive as the table size increases. If the table contains 1000 entries, **SEARCH** requires 500 comparisons while **SEARCH ALL** requires only 10, a dramatic saving.

The format of the **SEARCH ALL** verb is as follows.

```
SEARCH ALL identifier-1 [AT END imperative-statement-1]

                           ⎧ imperative-statement-2 ⎫
    WHEN condition-1       ⎨                        ⎬
                           ⎩ NEXT SENTENCE          ⎭
```

To use the **SEARCH ALL** form, we must specify in the Data Division which item in the table is to be used for the search and whether the table is in ascending or descending sequence on this item. For example, the Data Division entry for the table in Figure 13.6 would become

```
01   CATALOG-NUMBER-TABLE.
     05 VALID-NUMBER          PIC X(5) OCCURS 1000
                              ASCENDING KEY IS VALID-NUMBER
                              INDEXED BY X-CATALOG.
```

Inserting the **ASCENDING KEY** clause here and changing the **SEARCH** to **SEARCH ALL** are the only changes required in the program. Since the **SEARCH ALL** handles all operations with the index, the **SET** statement before the **SEARCH** can be deleted. If it is left in the program, it has no effect, since **SEARCH ALL** ignores the initial value of the index.

The **SEARCH ALL** permits only one **WHEN** phrase, but the condition in that **WHEN** phrase may be compound. This is useful when the search is to be made on several items simultaneously. For example, suppose that only certain size codes are valid with each catalog number. That is, the valid size codes for 33183 might be A, G, and L, the valid size codes for 62638 might be D and U, and so on. We can modify the table in the seed catalog program as follows:

```
01   CATALOG-NUMBER-TABLE.
     05   VALID-ENTRY         OCCURS 1000
                              ASCENDING KEY IS VALID-NUMBER
                              ASCENDING KEY IS VALID-SIZE
                              INDEXED BY X-CATALOG.
          10   VALID-NUMBER   PIC X(5).
          10   VALID-SIZE     PIC X.
```

We assume that the catalog file contains one record for each valid combination of catalog number and size, and the table is loaded accordingly. The match we seek now would be on both catalog number and size. To carry out this search we change the **SEARCH ALL** statement to

```
SEARCH ALL VALID-ENTRY
    AT END MOVE 'X' TO INVALID-CAT-NO-OR-SIZE
    WHEN VALID-NUMBER(X-CATALOG) = CATALOG-NUMBER OF ORDER-RECORD
        AND VALID-SIZE (X-CATALOG) = SIZE-CODE OF ORDER-RECORD
        NEXT SENTENCE.
```

It is important to remember that the order of the **ASCENDING KEY** phrases must be from major to minor. That is, because the phrase for **VALID-NUMBER** comes first, the program knows that **VALID-NUMBER** is the major key and **VALID-SIZE** is the minor key.

13.13   TABLE INITIALIZATION AND THE SEARCH STATEMENTS

It should be clear by now that initialization of data is always important, but when you use either **SEARCH** or **SEARCH ALL**, it is particularly important that *all* entries of the table be initialized correctly, even if they do not contain valid data. For instance, consider the following table definition:

```
01   ACCOUNT-TABLE-AREA.
     05   ACCOUNT-TABLE-MAX      PIC S999 COMP SYNC VALUE 500.
     05   ACCOUNT-TABLE          OCCURS 500 TIMES
                                 ASCENDING KEY IS ACCOUNT-NUMBER
                                 INDEXED BY ACCOUNT-INDEX.
          10   ACCOUNT-NUMBER    PIC 9(5) COMP-3.
          10   ACCOUNT-NAME      PIC X(25).

01   CURRENT-ACCOUNT            PIC 9(5) COMP-3.
01   ACCOUNT-FLAG               PIC X.
```

Suppose that we have loaded ACCOUNT-TABLE from an input file and stored the number of records loaded, 425 for example, in ACCOUNT-TABLE-MAX. We want to search the account table until we find an entry that matches the current value of CURRENT-ACCOUNT. We can do this with the following statements:

```
SET ACCOUNT-INDEX TO 1.
SEARCH ACCOUNT-TABLE
    AT END MOVE 'N' TO ACCOUNT-FLAG
    WHEN CURRENT-ACCOUNT = ACCOUNT-NUMBER (ACCOUNT-INDEX)
        MOVE 'Y' TO ACCOUNT-FLAG.
```

There are two problems with this approach. First, since we are searching even those entries that do not have valid data in them, we will require an average of 250 accesses per search instead of the 213 average that would be required if we looked only at valid entries. Much more important, however, is the fact that on many computers the program will abend the first time CURRENT-ACCOUNT contains a value that is not in the table. The problem is that since we have not initialized entries 426 through 500, we do not know what they contain. In most cases they will not contain valid packed decimal data, causing an abnormal termination when the computer tries to compare CURRENT-ACCOUNT to invalid data.

There are several possible solutions to the problem. In most cases, the simplest is to make use of the fact that ACCOUNT-TABLE-MAX contains the number of valid entries in the table. We can modify the search code to make use of this information as follows:

```
SET ACCOUNT-INDEX TO 1.
SEARCH ACCOUNT-TABLE
    AT END MOVE 'N' TO ACCOUNT-FLAG
    WHEN ACCOUNT-INDEX > ACCOUNT-TABLE-MAX
        MOVE 'N' TO ACCOUNT-FLAG
    WHEN CURRENT-ACCOUNT = ACCOUNT-NUMBER (ACCOUNT-INDEX)
        MOVE 'Y' TO ACCOUNT-FLAG.
```

The order of the two WHEN clauses is important. If the value of CURRENT-ACCOUNT is not in the table, the statement will eventually set ACCOUNT-INDEX to 426. The first WHEN clause will then be true and the statement will terminate (after moving 'N' to ACCOUNT-FLAG) before it tries to compare CURRENT-ACCOUNT to ACCOUNT-NUMBER (426).

An alternative solution is to initialize ACCOUNT-TABLE so that all entries contain a value for ACCOUNT-NUMBER that is a valid packed decimal value but which is not the value of any actual account, such as 00000 or 99999.

If we are using the **SEARCH ALL** option, we *must* initialize the table, since we cannot limit the value of **ACCOUNT-INDEX** to the range defined by **ACCOUNT-TABLE-MAX**. Further, since all values of **ACCOUNT-NUMBER** must be in increasing order (although duplicates are allowed), the only value we could assign for an initial value is something greater than any actual account number, such as 99999. If the key field is nonnumeric, you may wish to use **HIGH-VALUES** as the initial value. Do not use this with numeric data, however, since **HIGH-VALUES** is generally not a valid numeric value.

13.14 A PROGRAM TO PROCESS A TWO-LEVEL TABLE WITH INDEXING

To show how a program might use several tables at once and tables with more than one level, we shall consider the following application. An input file contains one record for each employee of a company. Among other information, an employee record contains one character showing the employee's sex (M for male and F for female), the employee's length of service with the company in years, the employee's age, and a code showing whether the employee is a member of management or not (1 for management, 2 for nonmanagement). We want to produce a tabulation showing the distribution of employees by age and length of service, within each of the four combinations of male/female, and management/nonmanagement. (A glance at Figure 13.7 will make this clearer than any verbal description could.)

The program must be designed to produce the numbers of employees in each of the various categories and then to print these numbers in an easily readable form. Both of these parts of the work of the program can usefully employ indexing. The determination of what age and length of service brackets an employee falls into is most easily done by using the **SEARCH** verb, and appropriate tables must be established for this purpose.

The basic structure of the program involves two major functions: building the table, and printing the results. In addition, because we cannot use a **VALUE** clause or simple **MOVE** statement to initialize the table so that all entries contain zero, we will consider this to be a separate function. A complete hierarchy chart for this program is shown in Figure 13.8.

The program based on this hierarchy chart is shown in Figure 13.9. There is nothing remarkable about the first two divisions of the program or the File Section of the Data Division. The data name **LOS** stands for "length of service." Looking at the Working-Storage Section, we see a table that is established for use by the **SEARCH** verb in determining which age bracket the employee falls into. We shall consider how the values were chosen when we look at the **SEARCH** verb. A similar table defines the values for use in searching for the proper length of service bracket. The table named **STATISTICS-TABLE** holds the tabulations of the numbers of employees in the various categories. The names of the 05 and 10 levels of this table are meant to suggest rows and columns. (**COLUMN** could not be used because it is a reserved word.)

MANAGEMENT PERSONNEL REPORT

MANAGEMENT

	MALE								FEMALE							
SERVICE->	1-4	5-9	10-14	15-19	20-23	24-31	32-39	40-48	1-4	5-9	10-14	15-19	20-23	24-31	32-39	40-48
AGE																
17-20	1	0	0	0	0	0	0	0	0	0	0	0	0	0	0	0
21-27	5	3	0	0	0	0	0	0	1	2	0	0	0	0	0	0
28-32	1	4	7	0	0	0	0	0	0	1	2	0	0	0	0	0
33-39	3	2	3	4	1	0	0	0	2	4	2	1	0	0	0	0
40-44	3	5	4	4	1	1	0	0	0	2	4	6	0	4	0	0
45-51	2	9	5	5	3	3	0	0	0	4	2	6	3	0	0	0
52-57	4	3	2	3	5	5	8	0	3	6	3	3	4	1	2	0
58-62	1	2	0	10	4	5	9	3	1	2	2	3	3	6	3	2
63-65	1	1	0	6	1	3	2	1	0	0	0	4	1	1	1	0
NON-MANAGEMENT																
17-20	3	0	0	0	0	0	0	0	3	0	0	0	0	0	0	0
21-27	1	6	0	0	0	0	0	0	3	1	0	0	0	0	0	0
28-32	2	5	1	0	0	0	0	0	0	4	2	0	0	0	0	0
33-39	6	2	5	3	0	0	0	0	4	7	8	4	1	0	0	0
40-44	5	1	7	2	6	4	0	0	3	2	3	2	4	1	0	0
45-51	3	1	3	3	6	12	2	0	2	6	5	4	5	9	0	0
52-57	3	7	4	6	2	6	7	0	4	2	5	7	2	6	2	0
58-62	3	3	4	4	5	7	6	2	3	6	2	2	2	5	7	4
63-65	1	1	3	1	5	4	2	2	2	1	2	4	3	3	0	4

FIGURE 13.7 A report showing the distribution of employees by four categories. This is the output of the program of Figure 13.9.

```
00001              IDENTIFICATION DIVISION.
00002              PROGRAM-ID.
00003                  NEWSTATS.
00004              DATE-WRITTEN.
00005                  APRIL 3, 1987.
00006
00007              ENVIRONMENT DIVISION.
00008              CONFIGURATION SECTION.
00009              SPECIAL-NAMES.
00010                  C01 IS TO-TOP-OF-PAGE.
00011              INPUT-OUTPUT SECTION.
00012              FILE-CONTROL.
00013                  SELECT EMPLOYEE-MASTER-IN      ASSIGN TO S-MASTER.
00014                  SELECT REPORT-FILE            ASSIGN TO S-REPORT.
00015
00016              DATA DIVISION.
00017              FILE SECTION.
00018
```

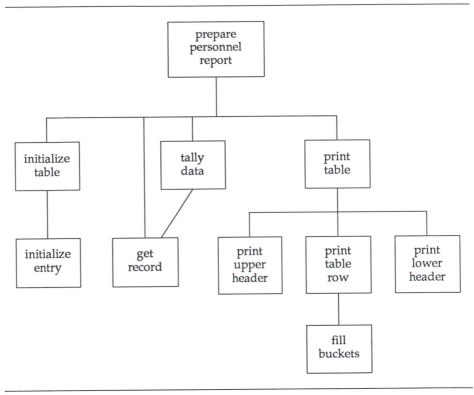

FIGURE 13.8 Hierarchy chart for program to produce report in Figure 13.7.

```
00019          FD   EMPLOYEE-MASTER-IN
00020               LABEL RECORDS ARE OMITTED.
00021          01   EMPLOYEE-MASTER-REC.
00022               05   EMPLOYEE-NUMBER        PIC 9(4).
00023               05   FILLER                 PIC X.
00024               05   SEX                    PIC X.
00025                    88   MALE                   VALUE 'M'.
00026                    88   FEMALE                 VALUE 'F'.
00027               05   FILLER                 PIC XXX.
00028               05   LOS                    PIC 99.
00029               05   FILLER                 PIC XXX.
00030               05   AGE                    PIC 99.
00031               05   FILLER                 PIC XXX.
00032               05   MANAGEMENT-CODE        PIC X.
00033                    88   MANAGEMENT             VALUE '1'.
00034                    88   NON-MANAGEMENT         VALUE '2'.
00035               05   FILLER                 PIC X(60).
00036
00037          FD   REPORT-FILE
00038               LABEL RECORDS ARE OMITTED.
00039          01   REPORT-RECORD.
00040               05   CARRIAGE-CONTROL       PIC X.
00041               05   REPORT-LINE            PIC X(132).
00042
00043          WORKING-STORAGE SECTION.
00044
00045          77   MORE-DATA-REMAINS-FLAG     PIC X.
00046               88   MORE-DATA-REMAINS          VALUE 'Y'.
00047               88   NO-MORE-DATA-REMAINS       VALUE 'N'.
00048
```

```
00049            01  AGE-TABLE-VALUES.
00050                05  FILLER                  PIC X(18)
00051                                            VALUE '212833404552586366'.
00052            01  AGE-TABLE-X REDEFINES AGE-TABLE-VALUES.
00053                05  AGE-TABLE               PIC 99 OCCURS 9 TIMES
00054                                            INDEXED BY AGE-INDEX.
00055
00056            01  LOS-TABLE-VALUES            PIC X(16)
00057                                            VALUE '0510152024324049'.
00058            01  LOS-TABLE-X REDEFINES LOS-TABLE-VALUES.
00059                05  LOS-TABLE               PIC 99 OCCURS 8 TIMES
00060                                            INDEXED BY LOS-INDEX.
00061
00062            01  STATISTICS-TABLE.
00063                05  ROW OCCURS 18 TIMES INDEXED BY ROW-INDEX.
00064                    10  COL OCCURS 16 TIMES INDEXED BY COL-INDEX.
00065                        15  STATISTICS      PIC S9(4) COMP SYNC.
00066
00067            01  ROW-IDENT-VALUES.
00068                05  FILLER                  PIC X(25)
00069                                VALUE '17-2021-2728-3233-3940-44'.
00070                05  FILLER                  PIC X(20)
00071                                VALUE '45-5152-5758-6263-65'.
00072                05  FILLER                  PIC X(25)
00073                                VALUE '17-2021-2728-3233-3940-44'.
00074                05  FILLER                  PIC X(20)
00075                                VALUE '45-5152-5758-6263-65'.
00076            01  ROW-IDENT-X REDEFINES ROW-IDENT-VALUES.
00077                05  ROW-IDENT               PIC X(5) OCCURS 18 TIMES
00078                                            INDEXED BY ROW-IDENT-INDEX.
00079
00080            01  REPORT-LINE-DETAIL.
00081                05  CARRIAGE-CONTROL        PIC X.
00082                05  ROW-IDENT-OUT           PIC X(8).
00083                05  BUCKET                  PIC BBZZZ9 OCCURS 16 TIMES
00084                                            INDEXED BY BUCKET-INDEX.
00085                05  FILLER                  PIC X(28) VALUE SPACES.
00086
00087            01  HEADER-1.
00088                05  FILLER                  PIC X(45) VALUE SPACES.
00089                05  FILLER                  PIC X(87)
00090                            VALUE 'MANAGEMENT PERSONNEL REPORT'.
00091
00092            01  HEADER-2.
00093                05  FILLER                  PIC X(52) VALUE SPACES.
00094                05  FILLER                  PIC X(80) VALUE 'MANAGEMENT'.
00095
00096            01  HEADER-3.
00097                05  FILLER                  PIC X(31) VALUE SPACES.
00098                05  FILLER                  PIC X(49) VALUE 'MALE'.
00099                05  FILLER                  PIC X(52) VALUE 'FEMALE'.
00100
00101            01  HEADER-4.
00102                05  FILLER                  PIC X(9) VALUE 'SERVICE->'.
00103                05  FILLER                  PIC X(48) VALUE
00104                    '  1-4   5-9 10-14 15-19 20-23 24-31 32-39 40-48 '.
00105                05  FILLER                  PIC X(75) VALUE
00106                    '  1-4   5-9 10-14 15-19 20-23 24-31 32-39 40-48 '.
00107
00108            01  HEADER-5.
00109                05  FILLER                  PIC X(50) VALUE SPACES.
00110                05  FILLER                  PIC X(82) VALUE 'NON-MANAGEMENT'.
```

```
00111
00112           PROCEDURE DIVISION.
00113           A000-EMPLOYEE-STATISTICS.
00114               PERFORM B010-INIT-STAT-TABLE.
00115               MOVE 'Y' TO MORE-DATA-REMAINS-FLAG.
00116               OPEN INPUT EMPLOYEE-MASTER-IN
00117                   OUTPUT REPORT-FILE.
00118               PERFORM X010-GET-EMPLOYEE-REC.
00119               PERFORM B020-TALLY-DATA
00120                   UNTIL NO-MORE-DATA-REMAINS.
00121               PERFORM B030-PRINT-TABLE.
00122               CLOSE EMPLOYEE-MASTER-IN
00123                     REPORT-FILE.
00124               STOP RUN.
00125
00126           B010-INIT-STAT-TABLE.
00127               PERFORM C010-INIT-STAT-CELL
00128                   VARYING ROW-INDEX FROM 1 BY 1 UNTIL ROW-INDEX > 18
00129                   AFTER   COL-INDEX FROM 1 BY 1 UNTIL COL-INDEX > 16.
00130
00131           B020-TALLY-DATA.
00132               SET AGE-INDEX ROW-INDEX TO 1.
00133               SEARCH AGE-TABLE VARYING ROW-INDEX
00134                   WHEN AGE < AGE-TABLE (AGE-INDEX) NEXT SENTENCE.
00135               SET LOS-INDEX COL-INDEX TO 1.
00136               SEARCH LOS-TABLE VARYING COL-INDEX
00137                   WHEN LOS < LOS-TABLE (LOS-INDEX) NEXT SENTENCE.
00138               IF FEMALE
00139                   SET COL-INDEX UP BY 8.
00140               IF NON-MANAGEMENT
00141                   SET ROW-INDEX UP BY 9.
00142               ADD 1 TO STATISTICS (ROW-INDEX, COL-INDEX).
00143               PERFORM X010-GET-EMPLOYEE-REC.
00144
00145           B030-PRINT-TABLE.
00146               PERFORM C020-PRINT-UPPER-HEADER.
00147               PERFORM C030-PRINT-TABLE-ROW
00148                   VARYING ROW-INDEX FROM 1 BY 1
00149                   UNTIL ROW-INDEX > 9.
00150               PERFORM C040-PRINT-LOWER-HEADER.
00151               PERFORM C030-PRINT-TABLE-ROW
00152                   VARYING ROW-INDEX FROM 10 BY 1
00153                   UNTIL ROW-INDEX > 18.
00154
00155           C010-INIT-STAT-CELL.
00156               MOVE ZERO TO STATISTICS (ROW-INDEX, COL-INDEX).
00157
00158           C020-PRINT-UPPER-HEADER.
00159               MOVE HEADER-1 TO REPORT-LINE.
00160               WRITE REPORT-RECORD AFTER ADVANCING TO-TOP-OF-PAGE.
00161               MOVE HEADER-2 TO REPORT-LINE.
00162               WRITE REPORT-RECORD AFTER ADVANCING 2 LINES.
00163               MOVE HEADER-3 TO REPORT-LINE.
00164               WRITE REPORT-RECORD AFTER ADVANCING 2 LINES.
00165               MOVE HEADER-4 TO REPORT-LINE.
00166               WRITE REPORT-RECORD AFTER ADVANCING 2 LINES.
00167               MOVE ' AGE' TO REPORT-LINE.
00168               WRITE REPORT-RECORD AFTER ADVANCING 2 LINES.
00169               MOVE SPACES TO REPORT-LINE.
00170               WRITE REPORT-RECORD AFTER ADVANCING 1 LINE.
00171
```

```
00172              C030-PRINT-TABLE-ROW.
00173                  PERFORM D010-FILL-BUCKETS
00174                      VARYING COL-INDEX FROM 1 BY 1
00175                      UNTIL COL-INDEX > 16.
00176                  SET ROW-IDENT-INDEX TO ROW-INDEX.
00177                  MOVE ROW-IDENT (ROW-IDENT-INDEX) TO ROW-IDENT-OUT.
00178                  WRITE REPORT-RECORD FROM REPORT-LINE-DETAIL
00179                          AFTER ADVANCING 1 LINE.
00180
00181              C040-PRINT-LOWER-HEADER.
00182                  MOVE HEADER-5 TO REPORT-LINE.
00183                  WRITE REPORT-RECORD AFTER ADVANCING 2 LINES.
00184                  MOVE SPACES TO REPORT-LINE.
00185                  WRITE REPORT-RECORD AFTER ADVANCING 1 LINE.
00186
00187              D010-FILL-BUCKETS.
00188                  SET BUCKET-INDEX TO COL-INDEX.
00189                  MOVE STATISTICS (ROW-INDEX, COL-INDEX)
00190                          TO BUCKET (BUCKET-INDEX).
00191
00192              X010-GET-EMPLOYEE-REC.
00193                  READ EMPLOYEE-MASTER-IN
00194                      AT END MOVE 'N' TO MORE-DATA-REMAINS-FLAG.
00195
00196     ********************* END OF PROGRAM **************************
```

FIGURE 13.9 A program to produce an employee distribution table like that shown in Figure 13.7.

Next we have a table setting up the row identifications that will be printed on the output report. This is also accomplished with indexing. Then comes a work area that will be used in printing the body of the table; we shall discuss this more in connection with the Procedure Division. Finally, there are values for the five header lines that are printed on the report.

The structure of the Procedure Division clearly reflects the hierarchy chart. After the table is initialized to zeros, the program performs two major functions: tally the data and print the table. Notice the two UNTIL conditions in B010-INIT-STAT-TABLE. The table contains 18 rows and 16 columns, and we continue the loop until ROW-INDEX is *greater than* 18 and COL-INDEX is *greater than* 16. If we had tested for equality instead, the program would not have initialized the last row and column of the table, since the PERFORM loop terminates as soon as the UNTIL condition becomes true. This type of code is used very commonly in processing tables and its use should be understood thoroughly.

The next paragraph, B020-TALLY-DATA, begins by setting AGE-INDEX and ROW-INDEX to 1; it is possible to set any number of index data names using one SET statement in this way, just as any number of ordinary data names can be set to the same value with one MOVE. The SEARCH statement is different in two ways from the examples we studied earlier. First, it has a VARYING phrase, which means simply that as we step through AGE-TABLE with its AGE-INDEX, the index named ROW-INDEX will automatically be incremented at the same time. Accordingly, when we have found our place in AGE-TABLE we shall also know in which row of STATISTICS-TABLE we want to add a 1. Second, this SEARCH statement does not have an AT END phrase. We assume that since the data is coming from a master file and has presumably been subject to extensive editing, it is very likely to be correct. If it is felt that this assumption is not justified, modifying the program accordingly would involve no new concepts.

The condition in this SEARCH tests AGE, which is the employee's age from the input record, against successive entries in AGE-TABLE. Consider how this works. Observe on the report in Figure 13.7 that the first age category is 17 through 20. That means that if the employee is less than 21, he or she is in the first age bracket. That is why the first entry in the age table is 21, not 20. If this comparison does not stop the search, then the employee is evidently older than 20 and is not in the first age bracket. The next test is whether the employee's age is less than 28. If the age was not less than 21 but is less than 28, then the employee's age must be in the range of 21 to 27, which is the second bracket. These comparisons continue until the condition is finally satisfied, at which time we get out of the search. A similar set of search combinations finds the appropriate bracket for length of service.

Now we come to the handling of the male/female and management/nonmanagement factors. Looking at the output in Figure 13.7, we see that the left half of the table is for men and the right half is for women. Since there are eight columns in each half of the table, this means that if the employee is a woman, the column index that has just been determined by the second SEARCH must be increased by 8. A similar analysis shows that if the employee is not a member of management, the row index should be increased by 9. At this stage we have row and column indices pointing to one element in the table of statistics. The ADD statement with its doubly indexed data name increments the proper element.

When all of the input has been processed by the paragraphs we have just studied, it is time to print the report. Looking at B030-PRINT-TABLE, we see that it begins by performing C020-PRINT-UPPER-HEADER, which consists of a number of MOVE and WRITE combinations involving no new concepts. We then have a PERFORM that carries out C030-PRINT-TABLE-ROW with ROW-INDEX running through the values from 1 to 9 in succession; again notice that we test for ROW-INDEX *greater than* 9. With ROW-INDEX having been given a value, C030-PRINT-TABLE-ROW, as its name suggests, prints all of the 16 elements in that row together with the row identification. To do this, it is necessary to move the row identification and the 16 values to temporary locations, both so that they may be edited and so that the values can be gotten into one consecutive string of characters for printing. This moving of elements from the doubly indexed table to the singly indexed work area is accomplished with another PERFORM. This PERFORM runs COL-INDEX through all the values from 1 to 16. For each, it PERFORMS D010-FILL-BUCKETS. D010-FILL-BUCKETS first gives BUCKET-INDEX the same value as COL-INDEX, then moves the proper element of the statistics table to the proper element of BUCKET. After the 16 values have been moved, the index ROW-IDENT-INDEX is given the same value as ROW-INDEX with a SET, and the row identification is moved to the output area for printing.

Finally, referring again to B030-PRINT-TABLE, we see that it carries out the paragraph C040-PRINT-LOWER-HEADER and then prints all the rows of the statistics table from 10 to 18.

You may perhaps wonder whether it is necessary to have a distinct index name for every table. For example, COL-INDEX and BUCKET-INDEX both run through the values from 1 to 18 and both always have the same value at the time they are used. It might therefore appear that BUCKET could just as well be indexed with **COL-INDEX** as with **BUCKET-INDEX**. It turns out, however, because of the way indices relate to the assignment of tables to storage, that this is true only in special circumstances. It is entirely possible to learn what those circumstances are, since they are described in any **COBOL** reference manual. On the other hand, there is very little advantage in doing so and there can be some loss of understandability. As a general rule, it is good practice simply to give every table its own distinct index name(s).

13.15 SYNCHRONIZED DATA IN TABLES

In Chapter 10 we discussed the relationship between **COMPUTATIONAL** data, the **SYNCHRONIZED** phrase, and slack bytes. The same considerations apply if the **COMPUTATIONAL** fields are contained in a table, but with one additional factor. For example, consider the following table, based on an example in Section 10.10:

```
01   TABLE-AREA.
     05   TABLE-B              OCCURS 100 TIMES.
          10   FLD-3           PIC X.
          10   FLD-4           PIC 9(8)   COMP SYNC.
          10   FLD-5           PIC X.
          10   FLD-6           PIC 9(18)  COMP SYNC.
          10   FLD-7           PIC X.
```

From the example in Chapter Ten, we know that there are three bytes of slack inserted between **FLD-3** and **FLD-4**, and three bytes of slack between **FLD-5** and **FLD-6**. We don't need to worry about the alignment of **FLD-7** since character data can be aligned on any byte. However, notice the storage layout shown in the diagram below.

```
       S                   S                           S                   S                                   S
       L                   L                           L                   L                                   L
 F     A     F     F A     F         F F     A     F     F F     A     F         F F     A    ...
 L     C     L     L C     L         L L     C     L     L L     C     L         L L     C
 D     K     D     D K     D         D D     K     D     D D     K     D         D D     K
 3     1     4     5 2     6         7 3     1     4     5 2     6         7 3     1

 |  |  |  |  |  |  |  |  |  |  |  |  |  |  |  |  |  |  |  |  |  |  |  |  |  |  |  |  |  |  |  |
 
 Word                        Word                        Word
  1                           6                          11
```

The first entry of **TABLE-B** begins in the first byte of word 1 and continues through the first byte of word 6. Because of the slack bytes (fields **SLACK1** and **SLACK2**), **FLD-4** and **FLD-6** begin on word boundaries for this entry, as they are required to do by the **SYNC** clauses. However, the second entry of **TABLE-B** begins in the *second* byte of word 6. Since **FLD-3** is followed by three bytes of slack, this means that **FLD-4** also begins in the second byte of a word (word 7) and is not aligned properly. **FLD-6** also begins in the second byte of a word and is misaligned. In other words, when a structure containing binary data is contained in a table, it is not sufficient to align the first entry of the table; slack must be included so that *all* entries of the table are aligned.

The compiler accomplishes this by inserting additional slack at the end of each record so that following records align properly. Thus, the example given above is equivalent to the following.

```
01   TABLE-AREA.
     05   TABLE-B            OCCURS 100 TIMES.
          10  FLD-3          PIC X.
          10  SLACK-1        PIC XXX.
          10  FLD-4          PIC 9(8)   COMP SYNC.
          10  FLD-5          PIC X.
          10  SLACK-2        PIC XXX.
          10  FLD-6          PIC 9(18) COMP SYNC.
          10  FLD-7          PIC X.
          10  SLACK-3        PIC XXX.
```

This gives the alignment shown in the following diagram, which keeps all synchronized binary fields on the proper boundaries.

Word 1   Word 12

TABLE-B(1)   TABLE-B(2)

The exact mechanism for determining where the compiler will insert slack bytes for alignment can become somewhat complicated and will vary from computer to computer. As with many advanced characteristics of **COBOL**, the serious programmer should study the appropriate manual for the computer being used.

13.16 SUMMARY

Subscripting and indexing are very powerful features of **COBOL**. Mastery of their use sufficient for most applications requires only a modest investment of study and practice. To become completely familiar with all of the implications of these features is a serious undertaking, but one that is not required of all **COBOL** programmers. Since this is an elementary text, those who desire to know the full story must refer to other sources, such as the manufacturers' manuals.

REVIEW QUESTIONS

1. Which of the following is *not* an advantage of subscripting (or indexing)?
   a. Saves time and effort in writing the Data Division.
   b. Makes possible shortcuts in writing the Procedure Division.
   c. Simplifies the compilation of the source program.

2. Which of the following best summarizes the subscripting concept?
   a. Subscripting is a way to improve object program efficiency by reducing the number of different data names in a program.
   b. Subscripting is a way to let one data name refer to a whole table of data items, with a particular one (or group) being specified by the value(s) of the subscript(s) written after the data name.
   c. Subscripting is a way to simplify writing of the Data Division, which at the same time makes the Procedure Division easier to write.
   d. Subscripting is a way to write more compact Procedure Division statements.

3. What is the difference between subscripting and indexing?

4. Identify four errors in the following subscripting example. (If you are using **COBOL-85** there are only three errors.)

   ```
   MOVE ZERO TO AMOUNT IN TRANS (2) OF TAPEX(0,1,RATE+1).
   ```

5. What will the following do?
   In the Data Division:

   ```
   01   SUM-TABLE-AREA COMPUTATIONAL.
        05   SUM-TABLE            PIC 9(5) OCCURS 100 TIMES.
   ```

   In the Procedure Division:

   ```
   ADD DOLLARS TO SUM-TABLE (X-ACCOUNT).
   ```

6. Assuming the Data Division entry of Question 5, what will this do?

   ```
   MOVE ZERO TO TOTAL-A.
   MOVE 1 TO SUBSCRIPT.
   PERFORM PARAGRAPH-A
       UNTIL SUBSCRIPT > 100.
           .
           .
           .

   PARAGRAPH-A.
       ADD SUM-TABLE (SUBSCRIPT) TO TOTAL-A.
       ADD 1 TO SUBSCRIPT.
   ```

7. What will the following put into object program storage when the object program is loaded? (There are 50 fillers.)

   ```
   01   NAME-RECORD.
        05   FILLER           PIC X(10) VALUE 'JONES'.
        05   FILLER           PIC X(10) VALUE 'SMITH'.
        05   FILLER           PIC X(10) VALUE 'ANDERSON'.
                 .
                 .
                 .

        05   FILLER           PIC X(10) VALUE 'THOMPSON'.
   01   NAME TABLE REDEFINES NAME-RECORD.
        05   NAME-A           PIC X(10) OCCURS 50 TIMES.
   ```

8. In the program of Figure 13.1 why not change the entries for **REPORT-RECORD** and **YEAR-TABLE** as follows:

```
01   YEAR-TABLE.
     03   YEAR-GROUP.
          05   YEAR-COUNT        PIC S9(4) COMP OCCURS 4 TIMES.

01   REPORT-RECORD.
     03   FILLER                 PIC X.
     03   REPORT-GROUP-OUT.
          05 YEAR-COUNT-OUT      PIC Z(6)9 OCCURS 4 TIMES.
     03   BAD-DATA-COUNT-OUT     PIC X(6)9.
```

and then in the Procedure Division in place of the four **MOVE** statements in the paragraph named **B020-WRITE-TABLE** insert

```
MOVE YEAR-GROUP TO REPORT-GROUP-OUT.
```

9. Why could **COBOL** not have been designed so that the compiler would deduce that a variable is subscripted from the fact that it is written with a subscript in the Procedure Division and thus avoid the need for the **OCCURS** clause in the Data Division?

10. What would happen in the **VARYING** data-name option of the **PERFORM** if the procedure called by the **PERFORM** changed the value of the data-name? Would the original or the changed value determine the number of repetitions?

11. What would be the difference between the results of these two examples?

a.
```
     MOVE ZERO TO TOTAL-A.
     MOVE 1 TO SUBSCRIPT.
     PERFORM ROUTINE-A
          UNTIL SUBSCRIPT > 10.
        .
        .
        .

 ROUTINE-A.
     ADD DATA-B (SUBSCRIPT) TO TOTAL-A.
     ADD 1 TO SUBSCRIPT.
```

b.
```
     MOVE ZERO TO TOTAL-A.
     PERFORM ROUTINE-B
          VARYING SUBSCRIPT FROM 1 BY 1
          UNTIL SUBSCRIPT > 10.
        .
        .
        .

 ROUTINE-B.
     ADD DATA-B (SUBSCRIPT) TO TOTAL-A.
```

12. How many times will the procedure named **ROUTINE-X** be executed by these **PERFORM** statements?

a.
```
PERFORM ROUTINE-X
     VARYING X FROM 1 BY 1 UNTIL X = 10.
```

b. `PERFORM ROUTINE-X`
      `VARYING X FROM 1 BY 1 UNTIL X > 10.`

c. `PERFORM ROUTINE-X`
      `VARYING X FROM 1 BY 1 UNTIL X < 10.`

d. `PERFORM ROUTINE-X`
      `VARYING X FROM 5 BY 1 UNTIL X > 10.`

e. `PERFORM ROUTINE-X`
      `VARYING X FROM 1 BY 1 UNTIL X = NUMBER-A.`

13. Consider the following example:

```
PERFORM ROUTINE-C
    VARYING A FROM 1 BY 1 UNTIL A > 2
    AFTER   B FROM 1 BY 1 UNTIL B > 3.
```

Write out the six pairs of values that would be taken on by **A** and **B** in the order in which they would appear.

14. Given the following Data Division entry:

```
01  TABLE-AREA.
    05  SUB-1       PIC 999 COMP SYNC.
    05  TABLE-A     PIC X(50) OCCURS 100 TIMES
                    INDEXED BY X-1.
```

and an appropriate definition for **INPUT-FILE** and **INPUT-RECORD**, what value would be displayed in each of the following cases if **INPUT-FILE** contained exactly 50 records in each case?

a.
```
    MOVE 'Y' TO MORE-DATA-FLAG.
    PERFORM LOAD-TABLE
        VARYING X-1 FROM 1 BY 1
        UNTIL MORE-DATA-FLAG = 'N'.
    SET SUB-1 TO X-1.
    DISPLAY SUB-1.
        .
        .
        .

LOAD-TABLE.
    READ INPUT-FILE
        AT END MOVE 'N' TO MORE-DATA-FLAG.
    IF MORE-DATA-FLAG = 'Y'
        MOVE INPUT-RECORD TO TABLE-A (X-1).
```

b.
```
    MOVE 'Y' TO MORE-DATA-FLAG.
    READ INPUT-FILE
        AT END MOVE 'N' TO MORE-DATA-FLAG.
    PERFORM LOAD-TABLE
        VARYING X-1 FROM 1 BY 1
        UNTIL MORE-DATA-FLAG = 'N'.
    SET SUB-1 TO X-1.
    DISPLAY SUB-1.
        .
        .
        .

LOAD-TABLE.
    MOVE INPUT-RECORD TO TABLE-A (X-1).
    READ INPUT-FILE
        AT END MOVE 'N' TO MORE-DATA-FLAG.
```

```
c.        MOVE 'Y' TO MORE-DATA-FLAG.
          MOVE ZERO TO SUB-1.
          READ INPUT-FILE
              AT END MOVE 'N' TO MORE-DATA-FLAG.
          PERFORM LOAD-TABLE
              UNTIL MORE-DATA-FLAG = 'N'.
          DISPLAY SUB-1.
              .
              .
              .
      LOAD-TABLE.
          ADD 1 TO SUB-1.
          MOVE INPUT-RECORD TO TABLE-A (SUB-1).
          READ INPUT-FILE
              AT END MOVE 'N' TO MORE-DATA-FLAG.
```

15. Given the following Data Division entries

```
FILE SECTION.
    .
    .
    .
01  OUTPUT-LINE.
    05    SAMPLE-ITEM-OUT      PIC Z(4)9 OCCURS 12 TIMES.
    .
    .
    .
WORKING-STORAGE SECTION.
01  SAMPLE-TABLE.
    05    SAMPLE-ITEM          PIC 9(5) OCCURS 12 TIMES.
```

what would the following Procedure Division statements do?

```
MOVE SPACES TO OUTPUT-LINE.
PERFORM PARAGRAPH-1
    VARYING N FROM 1 BY 1 UNTIL N > 12.
WRITE OUTPUT-LINE.
    .
    .
    .
PARAGRAPH-1.
    MOVE SAMPLE-ITEM (N) TO SAMPLE-ITEM-OUT (N).
```

16. Given the same Data Division entries as in Question 15, what would the following Procedure Division statements do?

```
MOVE SPACES TO OUTPUT-LINE.
PERFORM PARAGRAPH-2
    VARYING N FROM 1 BY 1 UNTIL N > 12.
    .
    .
    .
PARAGRAPH-2.
    MOVE SAMPLE-ITEM (N) TO SAMPLE-ITEM-OUT (1).
    WRITE OUTPUT-LINE.
```

ANSWERS

1. Part (c) might be true in isolated instances but certainly not in general.

2. Part (a) is not true at all in general; (b) is completely true; (c) is true to a certain extent, but the meaning of "easier" is subject to argument; (d) is true in most cases, but not always, and it is not the main point.

3. The major differences have to do with the way tables are stored and accessed in the object program, which can have a bearing on the speed of execution of that program. Since we did not discuss these matters—which are fairly complex—subscripting and indexing will, no doubt, have seemed to be very similar. From a source program standpoint, the differences are that with indexing we use the **INDEXED BY** clause in the Data Division and in the Procedure Division we are able to use the **SET**, **SEARCH**, and **SEARCH ALL** verbs.

4. **a.** A qualifier must not be subscripted.
   b. A subscript must be greater than zero.
   c. There must be a space following the commas separating the subscripts.
   d. In versions of **COBOL** prior to **COBOL-85**, subscripts cannot be arithmetic expressions; only literals and data names are permitted as subscripts. (Indices, however, may be followed by a + or a - and an integer, and in **COBOL-85** a subscript may also be followed by a + or a - and an integer.)
      There should generally be a space between a data name and a left parenthesis, although this is not strictly required; absence of such a space was an error in earlier versions of **COBOL**.

5. Add the dollar amount (defined elsewhere) to the element of **SUM-TABLE** identified by the current value of **X-ACCOUNT** (defined elsewhere).

6. Form the sum of the 100 dollar amounts in **SUM-TABLE**. (This assumes, of course, that **TOTAL-A** and **SUBSCRIPT** have been defined elsewhere.)

7. Establish a table of 50 names available to the program without reading any data records.

8. This would work very nicely except that editing can be performed only on elementary items. If no editing were involved, this would be an excellent way to proceed. If the number of items were larger than four, then we would use the **PERFORM ... VARYING** in a loop rather than write out many **MOVE** statements.

9. Without the **OCCURS** clause, the compiler would not know how much storage to allocate to the data item.

10. The changed value would probably be used. However, this may vary between compilers and the results are not always easily predicted. In any case, code that alters the data-name tends to make the execution of the loop harder to understand and should be avoided.

11. There would be no difference in the results but there might be some difference in the object code produced by the compiler.

12. **a.** 9.
    b. 10.
    c. None.

     d. 6.

     e. One time less than the value of **NUMBER-A**, if **NUMBER-A** is greater than or equal to 1. If **NUMBER-A** is less than 1 the loop will be performed endlessly, since **X** will never be equal to **NUMBER-A**.

13. **A** = 1, **B** = 1; 1, 2; 1, 3; 2, 1; 2, 2; 2, 3.

14. **a.** 52

     b. 51

     c. 50

15. The 12 items in **SAMPLE-TABLE** would be edited and printed on one line.

16. The 12 items in **SAMPLE-TABLE** would be edited and printed on 12 lines.

EXERCISES

*1. Two tables of 50 entries each have already been established in the Data Division; they are named **SET-UP** and **UNIT-TIME**. **JOB-TIME** is a nonsubscripted variable. Write a statement to compute **JOB-TIME** as the sum of the thirteenth entries of the two tables.

2. Continuing with Exercise 1, there is a third table of 50 entries named **NUMBER-OF-UNITS**. Write a statement to compute **JOB-TIME** for the thirteenth entry of these tables, where **JOB-TIME** is the sum of **SET-UP** plus the product of **UNIT-TIME** multiplied by the **NUMBER-OF-UNITS**.

*3. A table named **SALES** has 50 entries corresponding to 50 salespeople whose numbers run from 1 to 50. Write statements to do the following: after reading a record from a file named **SALES-DATA**, values will be available for **SELLER-NUMBER** and **AMOUNT**. Using **SELLER-NUMBER** as a subscript, add **AMOUNT** to the appropriate entry in **SALES**.

4. An electric utility billing operation requires that **KWH** be multiplied by a value from a table named **RATE**, where the appropriate entry in the rate table is given by the value of **SERVICE-TYPE**. Write a statement using subscripting to perform the multiplication and make the result the new value of an item named **BILLING-AMOUNT**.

*5. A table named **A-TIME** contains five entries corresponding to the five working days of a week. Using a **PERFORM** with the **VARYING** option, write a program segment to get the sum of these five items and then divide by 5 to produce **AVERAGE-TIME**.

6. Data is the same as in Exercise 5, except **B-TIME** has seven entries. Write a program segment using a **PERFORM . . . VARYING** statement to form the sum of the seven entries and also to produce in **B-COUNT** the number of those entries that are nonzero. Divide the total by **B-COUNT** to get average time; place this division in an **IF** statement that first checks that **B-COUNT** is nonzero and places zero in **AVERAGE-TIME** if it is.

*7. The table named **SALES** has 50 entries corresponding to 50 salespeople whose numbers run from 1 to 50. Write a program segment that will display the number and the sales amount for the salesperson having the largest sales in the table.

---

* Answers to starred exercises will be found in Appendix IV at the end of the book.

8. Given the same information as in Exercise 7, write a program segment to display the seller number and amount for the salesperson having the smallest sales. Any sales amounts that are zero should be excluded, however, so that the problem statement actually requests the smallest *nonzero* sales amount.

*9. Suppose that the 40 students in a COBOL programming class have been given numbers from 1 to 40. Write the Data Division entries necessary to establish a table of the 40 names corresponding to the 40 numbers.

10. Using the table in Exercise 9, write a program to produce a listing of the names and numbers of all students in the class.

*11. Using the enrollment table in the program of Figure 13.4, write a program to produce a listing of the enrollments for all 12 grades in 1987. The enrollments should be printed on 12 lines and each line should be identified with its grade.

12. Using the enrollment table in the program of Figure 13.4, write a program to produce a table like that shown at the start of Section 13.7.

*13. Using the enrollment table in the program of Figure 13.4, write a program to compute and print, for all 12 grades, the average enrollment over four years. The averages should be rounded to the nearest whole number and should be identified by grade.

14. Using the enrollment table in the program of Figure 13.4, write a program to compute and print the total enrollment for each of the four years. These totals should be identified with the years.

*15. Using the enrollment table in the program of Figure 13.4, write a program that will read a record specifying a year, then locate and print the largest enrollment for that year. The line of output should contain the year, the grade, and the enrollment.

16. Using the enrollment table in the program of Figure 13.4, write a program that will read a record specifying a year, then compute and print the total enrollment for that year.

*17. Modify the table loading procedure of Figure 13.3 to detect overflow (attempting to load more records into the table than there is room for). The program should not terminate immediately but should continue until the end of the input file is reached. However, do not attempt to insert records beyond the actual size of the table; overflow records should simply be discarded. After the end of the input file is reached, print an error message telling how many records were in the input file and how large the table actually is, then terminate the run.

18. Modify the program of Figure 13.9 in the following ways.
   a. The word MANAGEMENT in the second line of the heading is actually misplaced and should be on the same line as the word AGE.
   b. Validate the data by determining that the codes for male/female, management/nonmanagement are correct, that the age is not less than 17 nor greater than 65, and that the length of service is nonzero and less than 49.
   c. Insert a count of the number of input records. If the count exceeds 9999, display a message and terminate execution without printing the table.

19. (This exercise is suitable for a project.)

Modify Exercise 14 of Chapter 5 according to the following specifications.

Instead of coding the municipality codes and tax rates directly into the program, the program should read a municipality tax file, load the data into a table, and search the table to find the entry that matches the municipality code in an employee pay record.

The records in the municipality tax file have the following format:

| Columns 1-2 | municipality code | PIC 99 |
| Columns 3-6 | tax rate | PIC 99V99 |

Design an appropriate table to hold this data. If the table overflows while it is being loaded, count the total number of records in the municipality file, print a message telling the user what happened and how large the table needs to be to hold the entire file, and stop the run. When you are processing the payroll records, if a record contains a municipality code that is not in the table, print an appropriate error message and go on to the next payroll record; as always, the error message should contain enough information in a readable format so that a clerk using the program would be able to locate and correct the invalid record.

CHAPTER 14

FILE STORAGE DEVICES
AND PROGRAMMING

14.1 INTRODUCTION

Most business applications of computers involve processing large files of more or less permanent information. For example, a payroll application requires a payroll file that contains information about each employee; a purchasing application requires a file of data about vendors from whom supplies can be obtained; and an order fulfillment application requires a file of information about the company's own products with which to verify data in customers' orders.

Files differ in characteristics such as the number of records, the amount of information in each record, whether or not the records are in order on some key, and the sequence in which records may be accessed. File storage media differ in characteristics such as cost, the maximum and average time with which an arbitrarily chosen record can be located, and the speed with which a record can be read once it has been located. File processing applications differ in characteristics such as the percentage of the records in a file that are processed in a typical run, whether the records are retrieved sequentially or randomly, whether new records are added to the file, and whether or not existing records may be modified.

All of these considerations, and others, interact to determine how files should be stored and how programs to process them are written. Although a thorough discussion of files is beyond the scope of this book, this chapter presents the highlights of file storage devices and illustrates some of the more important concepts related to file processing.

14.2 MAGNETIC TAPE STORAGE

Magnetic tape can store large quantities of information more cheaply than any other storage medium now available, and it can be written and read very rapidly. There are several characteristics of magnetic tape, however, that make it impractical for use in many data processing applications. To understand when magnetic tape can and cannot be used we need to know more about tape as a storage medium.

Magnetic tapes are typically one-half inch wide and about 2400 feet long. In a byte-oriented machine, information is written in nine channels along the tape. The eight information bits of a byte are stored in eight of these channels, while the ninth channel is used to store a parity, or error checking, bit (see Figure 14.1). Today, data is typically stored on a magnetic tape at a density of either 1600 or 6250 bytes per inch of tape (bpi).

Except for size and quality, the magnetic tape used on a computer is much like the tape used in a home tape recorder. It is used by moving the tape past read/write heads that either encode data on the tape magnetically, or read the data already written on the tape. In order for the read/write heads to process data, the tape must be moving at speeds that typically are about 200 inches per second. Because the tape cannot start and stop instantly, it is necessary to allow time for the tape to be brought up to working speed and time for the tape to come to a stop after it is moving. This means that between blocks of recorded data on the tape there must be gaps, called interblock gaps, that are typically one-half inch long.

The need for interblock gaps has an important bearing on the organization of information on a magnetic tape. Suppose, for example, that we are working with records containing 250 bytes of information, and that we write these records on the tape with one record per data block. If the tape density is 6250 bpi, then only 0.04 inch is needed to record one record. However, we still have one-half inch between every pair of records, which means that about 92 percent of the tape will be used for interblock gaps, with only about 8 percent used for data! This not only wastes tape space; it also wastes processing time. The solution to this problem is record blocking. Suppose that instead of writing our 250-byte records to the tape one at a time, we accumulate them in

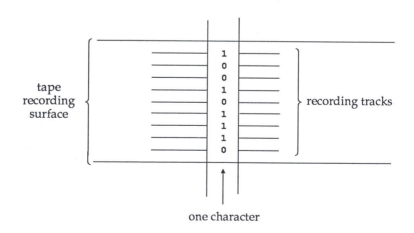

FIGURE 14.1 Data format of a typical magnetic tape. The ninth bit is for parity checking.

memory until we have 25 of them for a total of 6250 bytes. This block of 25 records could be written in one inch of space, so we are now using about 67 percent of the tape for data. The number of records contained in one data block is called the *blocking factor*. In our example, we have a blocking factor of 25. If we increase the blocking factor to 50, we would be utilizing 80 percent of the tape, and so on.

Reading and writing blocked records requires a good deal of additional program code in the object program. Fortunately for the **COBOL** programmer, however, what we need to know about blocking is rather easily stated.

For concreteness, suppose that we are reading a tape that has blocks of ten records. When we carry out an **OPEN** statement for that file, an entire block of 10 records is read from the tape and brought into computer storage. When we execute the first **READ** for that file, the first record in the block is made available to the program. When we execute the second **READ**, the second record is made available, and so on. No data moves from tape to internal storage on the first ten reads after the **OPEN**.

The **COBOL** programmer has no concern with the details of how all this is accomplished. He or she simply provides a record area in the File Section and depends on the fact that whenever a **READ** is executed, the next sequential record in the file will be placed in this record area. When all of the records in the block have been processed and another **READ** is executed, another block of data is actually transferred from the tape to internal storage. For the next nine **READ**s after that, there will be no data transfer. This process continues until the entire file has been read. If the last block does not have 10 records in it, that fact will be handled properly with no attention from the programmer.

A similar process occurs on writing information from internal storage to a tape. Again, assuming 10 records in a block, the first nine **WRITE**s would move information internally, from the File Section record description to another storage area not under the programmer's control. On the tenth **WRITE** all 10 records in the block would be written to tape in one continuous transfer.

All of the above descriptions assume the existence of only one buffer for each file. A *buffer* is an internal storage area where an entire block is held. In the case of a **READ**, the block is read into a buffer and then the records are moved one at a time to the File Section area. (This statement should not be taken 100 percent literally. Much effort is devoted to making buffering schemes as efficient as possible, and records are generally not actually moved from the buffer at all but, instead, record addresses are modified. The details of these matters are beyond the scope of this book and are of little concern to the **COBOL** application programmer.) On a **WRITE**, the records are moved from the File Section to the buffer until the buffer is filled and then the entire block is written. At this point we need to know two additional facts:

1. All modern computers are capable of carrying out internal processing at the same time that data is moving between internal and external storage;
2. The CPU operates *much* faster than even the fastest I/O devices.

The normal procedure, therefore, is to allocate two or more buffers to each file. On the execution of the **OPEN** statement for an input file, a block is read for every buffer assigned to the file. As **READ**s are executed, the records in the first buffer are processed. When the first buffer has been exhausted, the object program switches to processing the records in the second buffer while another data block is brought from tape into the first buffer. Since the process of loading a buffer may take longer than the process of using the data in the buffer, some computers will allocate more than two buffers, which are used in sequence. In all cases, the objective is to insure that it never happens that the program finishes processing the last record in a buffer and then has to wait for the time required to read a new block of data from the tape.

An obvious conclusion from the preceding discussion is that one should make blocks as big as possible to save wasted tape space and reduce program execution time. While this is true in principle, in practice we are limited by the availability of internal storage. In a typical version of one of IBM's operating systems, files are assigned five buffers. If our data blocks are 6K bytes each, and if a program requires ten files, then we are using 300K bytes of storage just for file buffers, which may not be acceptable even on a large computer. We must make a trade-off between the cost of wasted tape and computer time, against the cost of additional internal storage. Details of analyzing this trade-off are beyond the scope of this book and in many instances are not entirely under the control of the applications programmer, but the reader should be aware of the considerations involved.

14.3 RECORD BLOCKING AND COBOL

The COBOL programmer is not required to know how the various actions of record blocking and buffering are carried out, but it is necessary to know how to specify to the compiler what the characteristics of the files are. That is the function of the file description (FD) entry of the File Section of the Data Division. Looking now at the program code shown in Figure 14.2, the FD entries for the files show some of the alternatives available.

```
IDENTIFICATION DIVISION.
PROGRAM-ID.
     FILE-UPDATE.
DATE-WRITTEN.
     APRIL 13, 1987.

ENVIRONMENT DIVISION.
INPUT-OUTPUT SECTION.
FILE-CONTROL.
     SELECT TRANSACTION-FILE     ASSIGN TO S-TRANS.
     SELECT OLD-MASTER-FILE      ASSIGN TO S-OLDMAST.
     SELECT NEW-MASTER-FILE      ASSIGN TO S-NEWMAST.
     SELECT MESSAGE-FILE         ASSIGN TO S-MESSAGES.

DATA DIVISION.

FILE SECTION.

FD   TRANSACTION-FILE
     BLOCK CONTAINS 1 RECORDS
     RECORD CONTAINS 62 CHARACTERS
     LABEL RECORDS ARE STANDARD
     DATA RECORD IS TRANSACTION-REC.
01   TRANSACTION-REC               PIC X(62).
```

```
FD   OLD-MASTER-FILE
     BLOCK CONTAINS 0 RECORDS
     LABEL RECORDS STANDARD.
01   OLD-MASTER-REC              PIC X(135).

FD   NEW-MASTER-FILE
     BLOCK CONTAINS 25 RECORDS
     LABEL RECORDS STANDARD.
01   NEW-MASTER-REC              PIC X(135).

FD   MESSAGE-FILE
     LABEL RECORDS OMITTED.
01   MESSAGE-REC.
     05   FILLER                 PIC X.
     05   MESSAGE-TEXT           PIC X(132).
```

FIGURE 14.2 Representative **FD** entries.

The entry for **TRANSACTION-FILE** contains all the commonly used clauses, even though most of them are optional in this case. The order shown is typical although most compilers accept the **FD** clauses in any order. This example shows that **TRANSACTION-FILE** has a blocking factor of one (that is, one record per block). Normally, the **BLOCK CONTAINS** clause is only used if the blocking factor is something other than one. If the clause is omitted, the compiler assumes that the blocking factor is one; that is, the file is unblocked.

COBOL-85

In **COBOL-85**, omitting the **BLOCK CONTAINS** clause tells the compiler to obtain the block size from the file itself. This is equivalent to writing

BLOCK CONTAINS 0 RECORDS

in older versions of **COBOL**, as discussed in connection with **OLD-MASTER-FILE**, below.

END COBOL-85

The **RECORD CONTAINS** clause tells how many characters are contained in records in the file. This clause is optional since the compiler can determine that information by inspecting the record definition. Similarly, the **DATA RECORD** clause is optional. This clause specifies the name of the data record in the file. However, this information can also be determined by inspecting the data record definitions following the **FD**. If the file has several different record descriptions, then it is possible to write a **DATA RECORDS ARE** clause, but this is also optional.

The **LABEL RECORDS** clause is always required even though the file has no labels. Labels are special records at the beginning and/or end of a tape that contain information about the file. The most common usage of a label is to provide an identification to the program to establish that the proper reel of tape has been mounted. In an installation with a library containing thousands of reels of tape even the most careful operators will make occasional mistakes, picking up the wrong tape, mounting a tape on the wrong tape drive, or getting reels of a multireel file out of sequence. Information in a label record at the beginning of a tape makes it possible for the program to check that it is processing the reel of tape that it expects. To perform this type of checking requires using advanced features of **COBOL** that are used only infrequently and which are beyond the scope of this book. Therefore, we shall pursue this matter no further. The most common use of the **LABEL RECORDS** clause simply specifies **LABEL RECORDS ARE STANDARD**, which tells the compiler to use whatever labelling conventions have been defined as standard for your computer. An alternative that can be used for files that are going to a printer or are coming from a CRT or card reader is to specify that **LABEL RECORDS ARE OMITTED**. Since files from these simple input/output devices have no labels, the **OMITTED** option may be used, as is shown in the **FD** for **MESSAGE-FILE**.

The **FD** entry for **OLD-MASTER-FILE** is typical for files that are not being created in the current program. The **RECORD CONTAINS** and **DATA RECORD** clauses have been omitted since they are optional. The **LABEL RECORDS** clause indicates that standard labels are being used. The **BLOCK CONTAINS** clause, however, is unusual in that it appears to specify that the block contains no records. This is an IBM convention which does not mean what it says but, instead, indicates that the blocking information will be supplied separately, from outside the program, when the program is executed. This is usually done either through the Job Control Language (JCL), or through data contained in the file label. Then, if the program is to be run with files having different blocking factors, the appropriate information can be conveyed to the program without the need of recompiling it.

The **FD** for **NEW-MASTER-FILE** is similar to the one for **OLD-MASTER-FILE** except that we have specified the blocking factor for the new file to be exactly 25 records. This approach has the advantage that we are certain that the new file will have precisely the block size that we want, but it has the disadvantage that we lose a certain degree of flexibility. If the blocking factor is specified within the **FD**, it cannot be changed from outside the program; any change in this blocking factor requires recompiling the program. Any time a nonzero blocking factor is used, be certain to include the word **RECORDS** in the clause. If we write only

```
BLOCK CONTAINS 25
```

the compiler assumes that we want blocks to contain 25 *characters*, which is certainly not what is intended.

14.4 MAGNETIC TAPE PROCESSING

Because of the physical nature of magnetic tape, records on a tape must be accessed in sequential order. This requires that, for all practical purposes, both the file and the transactions being processed against it must be in either ascending or descending sequence on some key in the records. The alternative, allowing transactions to arrive in random order, would lead to hopelessly inefficient programs in which almost all the time would be wasted spinning tape reels. Since most of the time transactions arrive for processing in a random sequence, this means that they must be sorted into the correct sequence before processing.

Another consequence of the sequential nature of tape storage is that some reasonable number of transactions must be accumulated before they are processed. Even though the transactions are sorted, if there is only one transaction for every thousand master records, say, the computer will be spending most of its time dealing unproductively with all the master file records for which there is no activity. Since this consideration is so prominent in the discussion of file processing, the term *activity ratio* was devised to designate the fraction of the records in a file for which there is activity. Thus an activity ratio of 10 percent means that in a given run there are matching transactions for 10 percent of the records in the master file. Although it is hazardous to generalize, it is usually not economical to process tape applications with activity ratios of less than about 5 percent, and most are considerably higher.

There is one other characteristic of magnetic tapes that severely limits their use, and that is the fact that tape drives are relatively expensive to use. Not only are the drives themselves expensive (typically from $5000 to $40,000) but they require considerable attention by human operators. Every time a new tape is needed, an operator must remove the tape from a library and mount it on the proper tape drive, after first removing any tape already mounted on that drive. After the computer is finished with the tape, it must be removed from the drive and returned to the library. In a typical computing center with a large mainframe computer, there may be dozens of programs using the computer simultaneously, each of which requires several files to run. The impossibility of providing enough tape drives and enough operators to deal with this volume of activity means that some alternative must be found for all but relatively few files.

14.5 DISK STORAGE

Even though the files used by programs you have written for this course have been sequential files, they were probably not stored on magnetic tapes. Instead, they were stored on a disk storage unit. A disk storage unit consists of a number (typically 10 to 20) of rotating circular disks mounted on a vertical spindle, not unlike a number of phonograph records mounted on a record player. Since each disk has two recording surfaces (top and bottom), there are typically 20 or more recording surfaces available for each unit. These units are called disk packs. Each recording surface records data in a series of concentric circles called *tracks*. Typical disk packs contain over 500 tracks per surface, and each track holds from 19,000 to 50,000 bytes of data, depending on the design of the disk unit. Figure 14.3 shows the layout of a typical disk pack.

Some disk drives (the physical unit in which a disk pack is mounted) have a magnetic read/write head for each track of each recording surface, but it is more common that the drive has only one head per surface, with the heads mounted on a comblike set of arms that move in or out to the correct track. If there is one head for every track on the pack, the drive is called a *fixed head* drive. Drives with only one head per surface are called *movable head* drives. For a fixed-head drive, the maximum time to retrieve any record on the disk is the time required for one complete revolution of the disk, typically between 15 and 20 milliseconds, while the average retrieval time is half that. For a movable head drive, we must add to this retrieval time the time needed to move from the head's current position to the track containing the required data. This

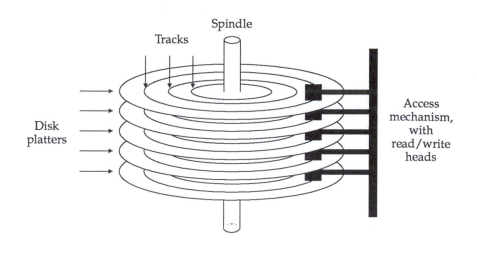

FIGURE 14.3 Schematic representation of a disk pack.

time typically has a maximum value of about 50 milliseconds, and an average value of about 30 milliseconds. In any case, once the disk drive has located the correct data on the disk, the data is transferred into main storage at a rate that varies from about 800,000 to 3,000,000 bytes per second, depending on the disk drive.

Although the cost of a magnetic tape is much less that the cost of a disk pack, the greater flexibility of a disk more than compensates for this cost difference for most applications. To begin with, a disk pack can hold many files and can access all these files in what is essentially a concurrent manner. For example, if five programs, each of which requires two files, are executing concurrently in the computer, then we would need ten tape drives to run these jobs even if each file contained only a few records. On the other hand, for all but the largest jobs the ten data files could all reside on a single disk pack that could be used concurrently by all five programs.

There are also types of applications that are not feasible to run with magnetic tapes because of the inherent limitations of tape processing. One such type of application is any in which the transactions must be processed when they are received, so that it is unacceptable to save up transactions until a sizable batch has been accumulated. An example of this type of application would be an airline reservation system. Since the master records must be accessed and action taken while the customer waits for a response, it is impossible to batch the transactions.

Another important type of disk application is one that requires master records to be accessed in a random sequence. In the the airline reservation application, the fact that the transactions must be processed immediately also means that the master records on the file will be accessed randomly, since clearly we cannot sort the transactions into a convenient order. We will examine ways of dealing with this type of application later in this chapter.

14.6 A PROGRAM USING DISK STORAGE SEQUENTIALLY

Our first disk example program uses a disk for temporary storage of groups of records from an input file. It uses the disk as a sequential storage medium and involves a technique, which we have not discussed previously, in which a file is opened and closed many times in the course of executing one program.

The application can be thought of as an extension of the order processing program for a seed company that was considered in previous chapters. The input file consists of records representing lines from customers' orders. Each line is shown in skeleton form for this example program so that we can concentrate on the new disk storage concepts and techniques; a record consists only of an order number and 74 characters of unspecified transaction data. For our purposes here we assume that the transaction data should be entirely numeric; this can be thought of as an indication of all of the kinds of data validation that were done in Chapter 11.

The records are in ascending sequence on order number. A complete customer order may consist of any number of order lines, from one to dozens. Our task is to inspect all the lines of any one customer order and to determine whether any of the lines contain an error. If any one or more lines of the order does contain an error, we are to write the entire order to a special handling file. If the order is completely error-free, we are to write the entire order to a normal handling file. This requirement makes it impossible to print the lines as they are read from the input, since we do not know until we have read all the lines from an order where the output should go. We must accordingly store the entire order temporarily until we know where it goes, and then must read it back and direct it to the appropriate output file. Either disk or tape could be used for this intermediate storage, but disk is much faster. With tape, it would be necessary to wait for the tape to rewind before the order records could be read back in, to say nothing of the fact that we would be tying up an entire tape drive for the sake of a few hundred records.

This will be the first program in which we have a file that is used as both input and output in the same program. We will open it for output before writing the order lines onto it. When the program logic detects the end of the order group, the file will be closed and immediately opened as input so that we can get the records back into the computer and write them to the appropriate output file. The disk is being used here as a sequential storage medium, in that we write the records to it in the sequence in which they appear and read them back in the same sequence.

The design of the program contains no surprises. The **SELECT** and **FD** statements look just as they would if we had used tape storage instead of disk, and indeed, there is nothing in the program that specifically indicates that the program will be using disk files. The assignment of files to a storage medium is made by the Job Control Language outside the program. In the Working-Storage Section, we have one flag to indicate the end of the input file of order records that we are processing, and a separate one to indicate the end of the temporary disk file. Another flag indicates whether any errors were found in an order, and a save area contains the order number of the current record.

The program begins with code that should be quite familiar by now. In **B010-VALIDATE-ONE-ORDER** we save the current order number, make sure that the error flag is off, then open the temporary disk file for output. **C010-EDIT-**

LINE writes all of the records for one order onto that file, checking each one to determine if it contains an error and setting the error flag if so. When a control break is detected, the temporary disk file is closed and then immediately reopened as input. Then, depending on the setting of the error flag, all of the records in the temporary disk storage are written either to the special handling file or the normal handling file.

```
00001              IDENTIFICATION DIVISION.
00002              PROGRAM-ID.
00003                  SEED3.
00004              DATE-WRITTEN.
00005                  APRIL 13, 1987.
00006
00007              ENVIRONMENT DIVISION.
00008              INPUT-OUTPUT SECTION.
00009              FILE-CONTROL.
00010                  SELECT WORK-FILE                ASSIGN TO S-WORK
00011                      ACCESS IS SEQUENTIAL.
00012                  SELECT ORDER-FILE               ASSIGN TO S-ORDERS.
00013                  SELECT NORMAL-HANDLING-FILE     ASSIGN TO S-NORMAL.
00014                  SELECT SPECIAL-HANDLING-FILE    ASSIGN TO S-SPECIAL.
00015
00016              DATA DIVISION.
00017
00018              FILE SECTION.
00019
00020              FD  WORK-FILE
00021                  BLOCK CONTAINS 10 RECORDS
00022                  LABEL RECORDS ARE STANDARD.
00023              01  WORK-RECORD                 PIC X(80).
00024
00025              FD  ORDER-FILE
00026                  LABEL RECORDS ARE OMITTED.
00027              01  ORDER-RECORD.
00028                  05  ORDER-NUMBER            PIC X(6).
00029                  05  ORDER-DATA              PIC X(74).
00030
00031              FD  NORMAL-HANDLING-FILE
00032                  LABEL RECORDS ARE OMITTED.
00033              01  NORMAL-LINE                 PIC X(80).
00034
00035              FD  SPECIAL-HANDLING-FILE
00036                  LABEL RECORDS ARE OMITTED.
00037              01  SPECIAL-LINE                PIC X(80).
00038
00039              WORKING-STORAGE SECTION.
00040
00041              01  MORE-DATA-REMAINS-FLAG      PIC X.
00042                  88  MORE-DATA-REMAINS           VALUE 'Y'.
00043                  88  NO-MORE-DATA-REMAINS        VALUE 'N'.
00044
00045              01  MORE-WORK-REMAINS-FLAG      PIC X.
00046                  88  MORE-WORK-REMAINS           VALUE 'Y'.
00047                  88  NO-MORE-WORK-REMAINS        VALUE 'N'.
00048
00049              01  ERRORS-FOUND-FLAG           PIC X.
00050                  88  ERRORS-FOUND                VALUE 'Y'.
00051
```

```
00052          01  PREVIOUS-ORDER-NUMBER              PIC X(6).
00053
00054
00055          PROCEDURE DIVISION.
00056          A000-VALIDATE-ORDERS.
00057              OPEN INPUT ORDER-FILE
00058                  OUTPUT NORMAL-HANDLING-FILE
00059                         SPECIAL-HANDLING-FILE.
00060              MOVE 'Y' TO MORE-DATA-REMAINS-FLAG.
00061              READ ORDER-FILE
00062                  AT END MOVE 'N' TO MORE-DATA-REMAINS-FLAG.
00063              PERFORM B010-VALIDATE-ONE-ORDER
00064                  UNTIL NO-MORE-DATA-REMAINS.
00065              CLOSE ORDER-FILE
00066                    NORMAL-HANDLING-FILE
00067                    SPECIAL-HANDLING-FILE.
00068              STOP RUN.
00069
00070          B010-VALIDATE-ONE-ORDER.
00071              MOVE ORDER-NUMBER TO PREVIOUS-ORDER-NUMBER.
00072              MOVE 'N' TO ERRORS-FOUND-FLAG.
00073              OPEN OUTPUT WORK-FILE.
00074              PERFORM C010-EDIT-LINE
00075                  UNTIL ORDER-NUMBER IS NOT EQUAL TO PREVIOUS-ORDER-NUMBER
00076                        OR NO-MORE-DATA-REMAINS.
00077              CLOSE WORK-FILE.
00078
00079              OPEN INPUT WORK-FILE.
00080              MOVE 'Y' TO MORE-WORK-REMAINS-FLAG.
00081              IF ERRORS-FOUND
00082                  PERFORM C020-WRITE-TO-SPECIAL-HANDLING
00083                      UNTIL NO-MORE-WORK-REMAINS
00084              ELSE
00085                  PERFORM C030-WRITE-TO-NORMAL-HANDLING
00086                      UNTIL NO-MORE-WORK-REMAINS.
00087              CLOSE WORK-FILE.
00088
00089          C010-EDIT-LINE.
00090              IF ORDER-DATA IS NOT NUMERIC
00091                  MOVE 'Y' TO ERRORS-FOUND-FLAG.
00092              WRITE WORK-RECORD FROM ORDER-RECORD.
00093              READ ORDER-FILE
00094                  AT END MOVE 'N' TO MORE-DATA-REMAINS-FLAG.
00095
00096          C020-WRITE-TO-SPECIAL-HANDLING.
00097              READ WORK-FILE
00098                  AT END MOVE 'N' TO MORE-WORK-REMAINS-FLAG.
00099              IF MORE-WORK-REMAINS
00100                  WRITE SPECIAL-LINE FROM WORK-RECORD.
00101
00102          C030-WRITE-TO-NORMAL-HANDLING.
00103              READ WORK-FILE
00104                  AT END MOVE 'N' TO MORE-WORK-REMAINS-FLAG.
00105              IF MORE-WORK-REMAINS
00106                  WRITE NORMAL-LINE FROM WORK-RECORD.
00107
00108     ***************** END OF PROGRAM ******************************
```

FIGURE 14.4 A program using temporary disk storage.

We should take a moment to consider why we bothered to block the disk file **WORK-FILE**. After all, when we introduced the concept of blocking it was because of the interrecord gap that is required for magnetic tapes. However, since disks keep rotating at a constant speed, an interrecord gap is not necessary. Why, then, do we still use blocks? The answer lies in the amount of time required to locate a data record on the disk. Remember that a disk record cannot be read until its physical spot on the disk reaches the read/write heads. If we read the records one at a time, by the time the disk has read record #1 and received a signal from the computer to read record #2, record #2 has already gone past the read/write head and the unit must wait almost a full rotation to read it. However, if we group records into blocks, we can read all records in the block as they pass under the heads with no additional rotational delay between records. The total time required to read the block, therefore, is the time for the first record in the block to reach the read/write head plus the time to transfer the block into memory. On the other hand, we did not block **ORDER-FILE** or either of the output files since **ORDER-FILE** is assumed to be coming from a device such as a CRT, and the output files are both going to a printer.

Another factor affecting file blocking on disks is the number of bytes that can be stored on one track. Since computers do not split records or blocks over tracks, a certain amount of space on a track will be unused if the block size does not divide exactly into the track size. The amount of unused space on a track can be varied by choosing different blocking factors for a file, thus changing the efficiency of the data storage. However, determining disk utilization precisely depends on the details of how files are stored on disks, which is beyond the scope of this book. Therefore, we shall not discuss the subject further, although we do recommend that you investigate disk utilization more thoroughly in appropriate sources.

14.7   INDEXED FILES

Disk storage, as we have just learned, can be used sequentially and is commonly used in this way. However, more importantly, it can also be used as a random access device, which means that we can retrieve records in any sequence we wish without any significant penalty for "skipping around" in the file. If the nature of the application makes random access an essential part of the approach, then we turn to the file organization and programming techniques that use random processing. There are several such methods of accessing disk storage, the most common being *indexed* and *relative record*. We shall discuss the indexed method first. Indexed files are frequently called "indexed sequential" files, since they can be used both sequentially and randomly.

Although an indexed file appears to the **COBOL** programmer to be a single file, it actually consists of two parts: a *data storage* area, which contains the data records stored in the file; and an *index* area, which contains an index used to find records in the data area.* When an indexed file is created it is created sequentially, with all records sorted on a key field. As the file is built, the

---

* In some implementations there are actually three parts, the third area being used to store records that do not fit into the data area. However, we will not be concerned with these implementation details.

record keys are used to build an index that can be used to find individual records very rapidly. When we wish to access records in the file, we can do so in two different ways. First, we can use the indexed file as an ordinary sequential file. If we use this method, the file is used exactly like any other sequential file. The second approach, however, allows us to access selected records randomly, in any order we wish. If we use this method, we specify the key of the record we wish to use, and the index uses this key to find the desired record and retrieve it without passing over intervening records in the file.

An indexed file is different from an ordinary sequential file in another regard: it is possible to insert new records into the file after it has been created and delete records from the file without rewriting the entire file.

This is a highly condensed version of how indexed files actually work. One of the topics in the further study of programming is a more thorough consideration of how some of these operations are carried out and their various implications for programming and for data management. What has been presented here is adequate for an introductory study of the subject, but it should be understood that this is hardly a complete explanation.

14.8 A PROGRAM TO CREATE AN INDEXED SEQUENTIAL FILE

Continuing with our use of the seed catalog order system for illustrative purposes, we now consider how an indexed file of the company's products could be created. As before, this will be a skeleton version with regard to the actual record contents so that we can concentrate on the new file processing techniques. Specifically, we assume that we are given a file consisting of one record for each product that the company sells. Each record contains a five-character catalog number, three size codes and corresponding prices, and a forty-character description. The entire file is to be written onto an indexed sequential file, with a certain amount of compression of the data to save disk space.

The program shown in Figure 14.5 demonstrates the **SELECT** statement required to create an indexed file. This statement contains three new clauses: **ORGANIZATION**, **ACCESS**, and **RECORD KEY**. The **ORGANIZATION** clause tells the compiler that the file will be an indexed file. Since an indexed file can be accessed either sequentially or randomly, the **COBOL** compiler must know which is to be used for this particular file. Therefore we specify that **ACCESS IS SEQUENTIAL**. As it happens, sequential access is the default and the **ACCESS** clause could have been omitted from the statement. However, with random access files it is generally a good idea to specify the access method for documentation purposes, even if the compiler does not require it. With the **RECORD KEY** clause, we specify what field in the output record should be used to index the file as it is created on disk; this clause is always required when an indexed file is used, and always specifies a field in the record of the indexed file. The fact that data name qualification is used here is entirely unrelated to indexed file considerations.

In addition to the new clauses in the **SELECT** statement for **IS-PRODUCT-FILE**, there is a change in the **ASSIGN** clause. We use **I** as a prefix to the file name instead of **S**, to indicate that this is an indexed file rather than a sequential one. On IBM mainframe computers the **I** prefix is ignored, but we will use it in any case for documentation.

```
1      IDENTIFICATION DIVISION.
2      PROGRAM-ID.
3          BUILD-ISAM.
4      DATE-WRITTEN.
5          APRIL 14, 1987.
6
7      ENVIRONMENT DIVISION.
8      INPUT-OUTPUT SECTION.
9      FILE-CONTROL.
10         SELECT PRODUCT-FILE            ASSIGN TO S-PRODUCTS.
11         SELECT IS-PRODUCT-FILE         ASSIGN TO I-ISPROD
12                ORGANIZATION IS INDEXED
13                ACCESS IS SEQUENTIAL
14                RECORD KEY IS CATALOG-NUMBER OF IS-PRODUCT-RECORD.
15
16     DATA DIVISION.
17
18     FILE SECTION.
19
20     FD  PRODUCT-FILE
21         LABEL RECORDS ARE STANDARD.
22     01  PRODUCT-RECORD.
23         05  CATALOG-NUMBER            PIC X(5).
24         05  SIZE-1                    PIC X.
25         05  PRICE-1                   PIC 99V99.
26         05  SIZE-2                    PIC X.
27         05  PRICE-2                   PIC 99V99.
28         05  SIZE-3                    PIC X.
29         05  PRICE-3                   PIC 99V99.
30         05  DESCRIPTION               PIC X(40).
31
32     FD  IS-PRODUCT-FILE
33         LABEL RECORDS ARE STANDARD.
34     01  IS-PRODUCT-RECORD.
35         05  CATALOG-NUMBER            PIC X(5).
36         05  SIZE-1                    PIC X.
37         05  PRICE-1                   PIC S99V99  COMP-3.
38         05  SIZE-2                    PIC X.
39         05  PRICE-2                   PIC S99V99  COMP-3.
40         05  SIZE-3                    PIC X.
41         05  PRICE-3                   PIC S99V99  COMP-3.
42         05  DESCRIPTION               PIC X(40).
43
44     WORKING-STORAGE SECTION.
45
46     01  INVALID-KEY-FLAG              PIC X VALUE 'N'.
47         88  INVALID-KEY-FOUND               VALUE 'Y'.
48
49     01  MORE-DATA-REMAINS-FLAG        PIC X VALUE 'Y'.
50         88  MORE-DATA-REMAINS               VALUE 'Y'.
51         88  NO-MORE-DATA-REMAINS            VALUE 'N'.
52
53
54     PROCEDURE DIVISION.
55     A000-CREATE-INDEXED-PROD-FILE.
56         OPEN  INPUT PRODUCT-FILE
57               OUTPUT IS-PRODUCT-FILE.
```

```
58              PERFORM B010-TRANSFER-ONE-RECORD
59                  UNTIL NO-MORE-DATA-REMAINS   OR   INVALID-KEY-FOUND.
60              IF INVALID-KEY-FOUND
61                  DISPLAY 'DUPLICATE OR SEQ ERROR - JOB ABORTED'.
62              CLOSE PRODUCT-FILE
63                    IS-PRODUCT-FILE.
64              STOP RUN.
65
66          B010-TRANSFER-ONE-RECORD.
67              READ PRODUCT-FILE
68                      AT END MOVE 'N' TO MORE-DATA-REMAINS-FLAG.
69              IF MORE-DATA-REMAINS
70                  MOVE CORRESPONDING PRODUCT-RECORD TO IS-PRODUCT-RECORD
71                  WRITE IS-PRODUCT-RECORD
72                      INVALID KEY MOVE 'Y' TO INVALID-KEY-FLAG.
73
74          ********************* END OF PROGRAM **************************
```

FIGURE 14.5   A program for creating an indexed sequential file.

Notice that the **FD** for the indexed file contains no **BLOCK CONTAINS** clause, indicating that the file is unblocked. In general, indexed files may also be blocked, although this is less valuable than it is for sequential files since random processing rarely requires accessing two records in the same block in sequence. That is, since a program tends to jump from record to record throughout the file, there is usually little advantage in having more than one record in a block.

In previous chapters we emphasized the idea that information coming into or going out of the computer must be in **DISPLAY** format. Actually that statement is too strong, since it applies only to information coming from input or going to output that must be read by people, such as CRT input and printed output. Information that is going to file storage, whether tape or disk, may be in any format that is convenient. The binary format (**COMPUTATIONAL**) is not generally used for data that involves dollars and cents, but the packed format (**COMPUTATIONAL-3**) frequently is. For purposes of illustration, we have shown the four-byte prices being compressed into three bytes by placing them in **COMPUTATIONAL-3** fields.

The Procedure Division involves just one new feature. The basic idea is simply to read each record and immediately write it to the indexed file. However, two kinds of errors could be encountered in the input: there could be two or more records with the same key, or the records could be out of sequence. When a **COBOL** program is creating a new indexed file, it requires that every record in the file have a unique key and that the records be sorted in strictly ascending sequence on that key. If an attempt is made to write to the indexed file a record whose key is not strictly greater than the key of the preceding record, an error condition is raised. To detect that error condition and allow the program to respond to it, we have added the **INVALID KEY** clause to the **WRITE** statement for the indexed file. Just as the **AT END** clause is executed only when a special condition (end of file) is encountered during a read, so the **INVALID KEY** clause is executed only when a special condition (duplicate or out of sequence key) is encountered during a write.

A listing of a ten-record file that was used to test this program appears at the top of the next page.

Catalog number	Size Price	Size Price	Size Price	Description
33597	A0050	G0250	0000	STOCKS - TRYSOMIC 7 WEEKS MIXED COLORS
36574	A0050	G0150	0000	STOCKS - GIANT COLUMN MIXED COLORS
37515	A0035	H0100	0000	SWEET WILLIAM PINK BEAUTY
39156	A0035	H0100	0000	SWEET WILLIAM PURE WHITE
43125	A0035	H0105	K0325	ZINNIAS - GIANTS OF CALIFORNIA MIXED
50013	A0045	K0100	L0185	CABBAGE, BURPEES DANISH ROUNDHEAD
51904	A0075	J0450	0000	CRENSHAH MELON, BURPEES EARLY HYBRID
62471	A0075	T0185	U0250	HYBRID CORN, HONEY AND CREAM
62547	A0050	L0110	S0275	CUCUMBER, BURPEE PICKLER
96461	1595	0000	0000	COMPOST KIT

Observe that there are no size codes for the last item because it is one that does not require a size code. Further, several of the items have only two size codes. Items that have fewer than three prices have zeros for the missing prices, since if these fields are left blank the attempt to convert the blanks to packed decimal creates a data exception.

14.9 A PROGRAM TO PRINT AN INDEXED SEQUENTIAL FILE

On many computers it is not possible simply to list the indexed file that was produced by the previous program because it can be accessed meaningfully only by programs using indexed sequential software. Also, since the records contain packed decimal data, we would not be able to print that information without appropriate conversions anyway. Although the program shown in Figure 14.6 only prints the indexed file, it is shown because it demonstrates how indexed files can be accessed sequentially after they have been created.

The program is similar to that of Figure 14.5, since both programs access the indexed file sequentially. Again we include the **ACCESS IS SEQUENTIAL** clause for documentation in the **SELECT** statement even though it could have been omitted (since sequential access is the default). Note that although the **SELECT** statement identifies **IS-PRODUCT-FILE** as an indexed file, the remainder of the program looks just like any other program reading an ordinary sequential file.

```
1     IDENTIFICATION DIVISION.
2     PROGRAM-ID.
3        PRINT-PRODUCT.
4     DATE-WRITTEN.
5        APRIL 14, 1987.
6
7     ENVIRONMENT DIVISION.
8     INPUT-OUTPUT SECTION.
9     FILE-CONTROL.
10        SELECT IS-PRODUCT-FILE           ASSIGN TO I-ISPROD
11               ORGANIZATION IS INDEXED
12               ACCESS IS SEQUENTIAL
13               RECORD KEY IS CATALOG-NUMBER OF IS-PRODUCT-RECORD.
14        SELECT REPORT-FILE               ASSIGN TO S-REPORT.
15
```

```
16     DATA DIVISION.
17
18     FILE SECTION.
19
20     FD   IS-PRODUCT-FILE
21          LABEL RECORDS ARE STANDARD.
22     01   IS-PRODUCT-RECORD.
23          05   CATALOG-NUMBER            PIC X(5).
24          05   SIZE-1                    PIC X.
25          05   PRICE-1                   PIC S99V99  COMP-3.
26          05   SIZE-2                    PIC X.
27          05   PRICE-2                   PIC S99V99  COMP-3.
28          05   SIZE-3                    PIC X.
29          05   PRICE-3                   PIC S99V99  COMP-3.
30          05   DESCRIPTION               PIC X(40).
31
32     FD   REPORT-FILE
33          LABEL RECORDS ARE OMITTED.
34     01   REPORT-LINE.
35          05   FILLER                    PIC X.
36          05   CATALOG-NUMBER            PIC X(5).
37          05   SIZE-1                    PIC BBX.
38          05   PRICE-1                   PIC ZZ9.99.
39          05   SIZE-2                    PIC BBX.
40          05   PRICE-2                   PIC ZZ9.99.
41          05   SIZE-3                    PIC BBX.
42          05   PRICE-3                   PIC ZZ9.99.
43          05   DESCRIPTION               PIC BBX(40).
44
45     WORKING-STORAGE SECTION.
46
47     01   MORE-DATA-REMAINS-FLAG        PIC X VALUE 'Y'.
48          88   MORE-DATA-REMAINS             VALUE 'Y'.
49          88   NO-MORE-DATA-REMAINS          VALUE 'N'.
50
51     PROCEDURE DIVISION.
52     A000-PRINT-PRODUCTS.
53         OPEN   INPUT IS-PRODUCT-FILE
54                OUTPUT REPORT-FILE.
55         PERFORM B010-PRINT-RECORD
56             UNTIL NO-MORE-DATA-REMAINS.
57         CLOSE IS-PRODUCT-FILE
58               REPORT-FILE.
59         STOP RUN.
60
61     B010-PRINT-RECORD.
62         READ IS-PRODUCT-FILE
63                 AT END MOVE 'N' TO MORE-DATA-REMAINS-FLAG.
64         IF MORE-DATA-REMAINS
65             MOVE SPACES TO REPORT-LINE
66             MOVE CORRESPONDING IS-PRODUCT-RECORD TO REPORT-LINE
67             WRITE REPORT-LINE AFTER ADVANCING 1.
68
69     ************************ END OF PROGRAM ************************
```

FIGURE 14.6   A program to print the contents of an indexed file.

Here is the output produced when this program was run, taking as its input the file produced by the program in Figure 14.5.

```
33597  A  0.50  G  2.50      0.00  STOCKS - TRYSOMIC 7 WEEKS MIXED COLORS
36574  A  0.50  G  1.50      0.00  STOCKS - GIANT COLUMN MIXED COLORS
37515  A  0.35  H  1.00      0.00  SWEET WILLIAM  PINK BEAUTY
39156  A  0.35  H  1.00      0.00  SWEET WILLIAM  PURE WHITE
43125  A  0.35  H  1.05  K  3.25  ZINNIAS - GIANTS OF CALIFORNIA MIXED
50013  A  0.45  K  1.00  L  1.85  CABBAGE, BURPEES DANISH ROUNDHEAD
51904  A  0.75  J  4.50      0.00  CRENSHAH MELON, BURPEES EARLY HYBRID
62471  A  0.75  T  1.85  U  2.50  HYBRID CORN, HONEY AND CREAM
62547  A  0.50  L  1.10  S  2.75  CUCUMBER, BURPEE PICKLER
96461    15.95      0.00      0.00  COMPOST KIT
```

14.10 AN ORDER VALIDATION PROGRAM

We will now see how an indexed file can be accessed in the random mode. To do this we will consider a program that is a modification of the program in Figure 14.4, which printed messages on one of two files depending on whether or not an order contained any errors. The idea now is that a complete customer order consists of a header record that gives the customer's name and address, as many body records as there are separate items in the customer's order, and a trailer record giving the order total, handling charge, and tax as computed by the customer. Every record, of whatever type, contains an order number in the first six characters. Every record type has as its next character either a 1, 2, or 3 that identifies it as a header, body, or trailer record, respectively. The program is required not only to validate each line of the customer order, as we did in Figure 14.4, but also to determine that the complete order group does consist of one header record followed by one or more body records followed by one trailer record. No validation of the header record is required other than to establish that exactly one is present, but for the trailer record it would ordinarily be necessary to check that the customer's computation of the total matches the sum of all the prices on the body records. We shall not actually do the validation of either the body records or the trailer records, but shall leave these operations as stubs that may be completed by the student as exercises. The program is shown in Figure 14.7.

```
1     IDENTIFICATION DIVISION.
2     PROGRAM-ID.
3         VALIDATE-ORDERS.
4     DATE-WRITTEN.
5         APRIL 14, 1987.
6
7     ENVIRONMENT DIVISION.
8     INPUT-OUTPUT SECTION.
9     FILE-CONTROL.
10        SELECT ORDER-FILE              ASSIGN TO S-ORDERS.
11        SELECT IS-PRODUCT-FILE         ASSIGN TO I-ISPROD
12               ORGANIZATION IS INDEXED
13               ACCESS IS RANDOM
14               RECORD KEY IS CATALOG-NUMBER OF IS-PRODUCT-RECORD.
```

```
15              SELECT TEMP-DISK-FILE              ASSIGN TO S-TEMPDISK.
16              SELECT NORMAL-HANDLING-FILE        ASSIGN TO S-NORMAL.
17              SELECT SPECIAL-HANDLING-FILE       ASSIGN TO S-SPECIAL.
18
19         DATA DIVISION.
20
21         FILE SECTION.
22
23         FD   ORDER-FILE
24              LABEL RECORDS ARE OMITTED.
25         01   ORDER-RECORD.
26              05   ORDER-NUMBER              PIC X(6).
27              05   RECORD-TYPE               PIC X.
28                   88   HEADER                   VALUE '1'.
29                   88   BODY                     VALUE '2'.
30                   88   TRAILER                  VALUE '3'.
31              05   FILLER                    PIC X(73).
32
33         01   HEADER-RECORD.
34              05   ORDER-NUMBER              PIC X(6).
35              05   RECORD-TYPE               PIC X.
36              05   NAME-AND-ADDRESS          PIC X(73).
37
38         01   BODY-RECORD.
39              05   ORDER-NUMBER              PIC X(6).
40              05   RECORD-TYPE               PIC X.
41              05   CATALOG-NUMBER.
42                   10   CATALOG-FIRST-DIGIT  PIC X.
43                   10   CATALOG-REMAINING    PIC X(4).
44              05   SIZE-CODE                 PIC X.
45              05   QUANTITY                  PIC 99.
46              05   ITEM-DESCRIPTION          PIC X(40).
47              05   X-PRICE                   PIC X(5).
48              05   9-PRICE REDEFINES X-PRICE PIC 9(3)V99.
49              05   FILLER                    PIC X(20).
50
51         01   TRAILER-RECORD.
52              05   ORDER-NUMBER              PIC X(6).
53              05   RECORD-TYPE               PIC X.
54              05   SUB-TOTAL                 PIC 9(3)V99.
55              05   HANDLING-CHARGE           PIC 9V99.
56              05   TAX                       PIC 99V99.
57              05   GRAND-TOTAL               PIC 9(3)V99.
58              05   FILLER                    PIC X(56).
59
60         FD   IS-PRODUCT-FILE
61              LABEL RECORDS ARE STANDARD.
62         01   IS-PRODUCT-RECORD.
63              05   CATALOG-NUMBER            PIC X(5).
64              05   SIZE-1                    PIC X.
65              05   PRICE-1                   PIC S99V99   COMP-3.
66              05   SIZE-2                    PIC X.
67              05   PRICE-2                   PIC S99V99   COMP-3.
68              05   SIZE-3                    PIC X.
69              05   PRICE-3                   PIC S99V99   COMP-3.
70              05   DESCRIPTION               PIC X(40).
71
```

```
 72    FD  TEMP-DISK-FILE
 73        BLOCK CONTAINS 10 RECORDS
 74        LABEL RECORDS ARE STANDARD.
 75    01  TEMP-DISK-RECORD.
 76        05  ORDER-NUMBER              PIC X(6).
 77        05  FILLER                    PIC X(74).
 78
 79    FD  NORMAL-HANDLING-FILE
 80        LABEL RECORDS ARE OMITTED.
 81    01  NORMAL-HANDLING-RECORD.
 82        05  FILLER                    PIC X.
 83        05  NORMAL-HANDLING-LINE      PIC X(132).
 84
 85
 86    FD  SPECIAL-HANDLING-FILE
 87        LABEL RECORDS ARE OMITTED.
 88    01  SPECIAL-HANDLING-RECORD.
 89        05  FILLER                    PIC X.
 90        05  SPECIAL-HANDLING-LINE     PIC X(132).
 91
 92    WORKING-STORAGE SECTION.
 93
 94    01  CURRENT-ORDER-NUMBER          PIC X(6).
 95
 96    01  ERROR-FLAGS.
 97        88  RECORD-OK                              VALUE SPACES.
 98        05  CAT-NO-NOT-NUMERIC        PIC X.
 99        05  FIRST-DIGIT-INVALID       PIC X.
100        05  INVALID-SIZE-CODE         PIC X.
101        05  NO-SUCH-SIZE-CODE         PIC X.
102        05  QTY-NOT-NUMERIC           PIC X.
103        05  PRICE-NOT-NUMERIC         PIC X.
104        05  INVALID-PRICE-OR-QTY      PIC X.
105        05  LARGE-PRICE               PIC X.
106        05  MISSING-HEADER            PIC X.
107        05  MISSING-TRAILER           PIC X.
108        05  INVALID-CATALOG-NUMBER    PIC X.
109        05  INVALID-RECORD-TYPE       PIC X.
110
111    01  ERRORS-FOUND-FLAG             PIC X.
112        88  ERRORS-FOUND                           VALUE 'Y'.
113
114    01  MORE-ORDERS-FLAG             PIC X VALUE 'Y'.
115        88  MORE-ORDERS                            VALUE 'Y'.
116        88  NO-MORE-ORDERS                         VALUE 'N'.
117
118    01  MORE-TEMP-RECORDS-FLAG        PIC X.
119        88  MORE-TEMP-RECORDS                      VALUE 'Y'.
120        88  NO-MORE-TEMP-RECORDS                   VALUE 'N'.
121
122
123    PROCEDURE DIVISION.
124    A000-VALIDATE-CATALOG-ORDERS.
125        OPEN   INPUT ORDER-FILE
126                     IS-PRODUCT-FILE
127              OUTPUT NORMAL-HANDLING-FILE
128                     SPECIAL-HANDLING-FILE.
129        READ ORDER-FILE
130              AT END MOVE 'N' TO MORE-ORDERS-FLAG.
131        PERFORM B010-PROCESS-ONE-ORDER
132           UNTIL NO-MORE-ORDERS.
```

```
133        CLOSE ORDER-FILE
134              IS-PRODUCT-FILE
135              NORMAL-HANDLING-FILE
136              SPECIAL-HANDLING-FILE.
137        STOP RUN.
138
139    B010-PROCESS-ONE-ORDER.
140        MOVE 'N' TO ERRORS-FOUND-FLAG.
141        MOVE SPACES TO ERROR-FLAGS.
142        MOVE ORDER-NUMBER OF ORDER-RECORD TO CURRENT-ORDER-NUMBER.
143        OPEN OUTPUT TEMP-DISK-FILE.
144        IF HEADER
145            PERFORM C010-VALIDATE-HEADER-RECORD;
146            WRITE TEMP-DISK-RECORD FROM ORDER-RECORD;
147            READ ORDER-FILE
148                    AT END MOVE 'N' TO MORE-ORDERS-FLAG
149        ELSE
150            MOVE 'Y' TO ERRORS-FOUND-FLAG
151            MOVE 'X' TO MISSING-HEADER.
152        PERFORM C020-PROCESS-BODY-RECORD
153                UNTIL ORDER-NUMBER OF ORDER-RECORD
154                        IS NOT EQUAL TO CURRENT-ORDER-NUMBER  OR
155                        NO-MORE-ORDERS  OR
156                        NOT BODY.
157        IF ORDER-NUMBER OF ORDER-RECORD = CURRENT-ORDER-NUMBER  AND
158                TRAILER
159            PERFORM C030-VALIDATE-TRAILER-RECORD;
160            WRITE TEMP-DISK-RECORD FROM ORDER-RECORD;
161            READ ORDER-FILE
162                    AT END MOVE 'N' TO MORE-ORDERS-FLAG
163        ELSE
164            MOVE 'Y' TO ERRORS-FOUND-FLAG
165            MOVE 'X' TO MISSING-TRAILER.
166        IF NOT HEADER  AND  NOT BODY  AND  NOT TRAILER
167            MOVE 'Y' TO ERRORS-FOUND-FLAG
168            MOVE 'X' TO INVALID-RECORD-TYPE
169            WRITE TEMP-DISK-RECORD FROM ORDER-RECORD
170            READ ORDER-FILE
171                    AT END MOVE 'N' TO MORE-ORDERS-FLAG.
172        CLOSE TEMP-DISK-FILE.
173        OPEN INPUT TEMP-DISK-FILE.
174        MOVE 'Y' TO MORE-TEMP-RECORDS-FLAG.
175        IF ERRORS-FOUND
176            PERFORM C040-WRITE-TO-SPECIAL-HANDLING
177                    UNTIL NO-MORE-TEMP-RECORDS
178        ELSE
179            PERFORM C050-WRITE-TO-NORMAL-HANDLING
180                    UNTIL NO-MORE-TEMP-RECORDS.
181        CLOSE TEMP-DISK-FILE.
182
183    C010-VALIDATE-HEADER-RECORD.
184        DISPLAY 'HEADER VALIDATION REACHED '
185            ORDER-NUMBER OF ORDER-RECORD.
186
187    C020-PROCESS-BODY-RECORD.
188        PERFORM D010-VALIDATE-BODY-RECORD.
189        WRITE TEMP-DISK-RECORD FROM ORDER-RECORD.
190        READ ORDER-FILE
191                AT END MOVE 'N' TO MORE-ORDERS-FLAG.
192
```

```
193      C030-VALIDATE-TRAILER-RECORD.
194          DISPLAY 'TRAILER VALIDATION REACHED '
195                  ORDER-NUMBER OF ORDER-RECORD.
196
197      C040-WRITE-TO-SPECIAL-HANDLING.
198          READ TEMP-DISK-FILE
199                  AT END MOVE 'N' TO MORE-TEMP-RECORDS-FLAG.
200          IF MORE-TEMP-RECORDS
201              MOVE TEMP-DISK-RECORD TO SPECIAL-HANDLING-LINE
202              WRITE SPECIAL-HANDLING-RECORD AFTER ADVANCING 1 LINES.
203
204      C050-WRITE-TO-NORMAL-HANDLING.
205          READ TEMP-DISK-FILE
206                  AT END MOVE 'N' TO MORE-TEMP-RECORDS-FLAG.
207          IF MORE-TEMP-RECORDS
208              MOVE TEMP-DISK-RECORD TO NORMAL-HANDLING-LINE
209              WRITE NORMAL-HANDLING-RECORD AFTER ADVANCING 1 LINES.
210
211      D010-VALIDATE-BODY-RECORD.
212          MOVE CATALOG-NUMBER OF BODY-RECORD TO
213                  CATALOG-NUMBER OF IS-PRODUCT-RECORD.
214          READ IS-PRODUCT-FILE
215                  KEY IS CATALOG-NUMBER OF IS-PRODUCT-RECORD
216                  INVALID KEY MOVE 'Y' TO ERRORS-FOUND-FLAG
217                          MOVE 'X' TO INVALID-CATALOG-NUMBER.
218          DISPLAY 'BODY VALIDATION REACHED '
219                  ORDER-NUMBER OF BODY-RECORD    '  '
220                  CATALOG-NUMBER OF BODY-RECORD    '  '
221                  DESCRIPTION OF IS-PRODUCT-RECORD.
222
223
224      ************************* END OF PROGRAM ***********************
```

FIGURE 14.7 A program to validate orders from a seed catalog, using an indexed file to obtain product information and a sequential file for intermediate storage.

The program shown in Figure 14.7 contains some new features in the **SELECT** statement for **IS-PRODUCT-FILE**. As before, the **ORGANIZATION** clause specifies that the organization of the file is indexed. However, the **ACCESS** clause specifies that **ACCESS IS RANDOM**, which allows us to access records in the file randomly. To perform a random access we must specify where the key can be found in the record being searched for; this requirement is met by the **RECORD KEY** clause. The record key always refers to a field in the records of the indexed file; it tells where to find the key that uniquely identifies each record.

14.11 THE DEFINITION OF MULTIPLE RECORD TYPES

As we read the file of customer orders, we don't know until after we have a record in the computer whether it is a header, a body, or a trailer record. That can be determined only by reading the record and then inspecting the record type field in it. The record-type field must always be in the same place in all records of the file for us to know where to look for it, but the three types of records can otherwise be entirely different. As it happens here, they all have an order number as their first six bytes and they are otherwise altogether different. In a different application they might not even have the order number in the same place in each record. We are able to specify in the File Section what the formats of the different types of record codes are, by using the implicit redefinition that applies to **01** level entries in the File Section. This, we recall, means that all **01** level entries in any one **FD** are considered to be alternative definitions of the same record area. What we have done here is to set up a first record definition that is used only to define the three values of the record type code that always appears as the seventh byte of every record, then follow this with definitions of the records for the header, body, and trailer.

The rest of the Data Division contains nothing new. The definition of the records in the indexed file is identical to that of the program that created them. The Working-Storage Section contains the definition of several end-of-file flags and numerous error flags. Even though most of these error flags are not used in this example, they are listed here as a reminder that a complete version of the program would do all of this error checking.

14.12 THE PROCEDURE DIVISION

The structure of the Procedure Division reflects the logical structure of the order file. The order file contains a series of one or more orders. Each order consists of one header record, one or more body records, and one trailer record, assuming there are no errors. The main line logic in the first paragraph reads the first record on the order file to start things off, then executes **B010-PROCESS-ONE-ORDER** repeatedly until the program runs out of data.

As its name implies, paragraph **B010-PROCESS-ONE-ORDER** is required to process one complete order. It begins by resetting all error flags to indicate that no errors have been found yet, saving the order number of the current order record as the current order number, and opening the temporary disk file for output so that we can save the records for this order. Since an order is supposed to begin with a header record, the program checks to make sure that we have, in fact, read a header. If the record is a header record, we validate the header, write it to the temporary storage file, and read the next order record. If the record is not a header, we mark the appropriate error flags and continue until we find a match on record type.

At this point in the program, we are ready to start processing body records for the current order. The program continues to do so until one of three conditions occurs:

1. An order record is read whose order number is not the same as the current order;
2. The program runs out of order records;
3. A record other than a body record is read.

If the order number of the order record is the same as the current order number and if the record is a trailer, then we have read the trailer for the current order. In this case the program validates the trailer record, writes it to the temporary disk file, and reads the first record of the next order. If the record is not a trailer for the current order or if we have run out of order records, then the program simply marks error flags and continues.

We have now finished processing the data for an order and have written all records for that order to the temporary disk file. The remainder of this paragraph is essentially the same as the corresponding code in Figure 14.4.

C010-VALIDATE-HEADER-RECORD and **C030-VALIDATE-TRAILER-RECORD** use **DISPLAY** statements; in a complete program these stubs would perform appropriate error checking for the header and trailer records, respectively. **C020-PROCESS-BODY-RECORD** validates a body record, then reads the next order record.

The paragraph named **D010-VALIDATE-BODY-RECORD** is the one that involves reading the indexed file. The basic idea is that we want to determine whether there is such a catalog number as the one the customer has written and, if there is, to determine whether the customer's information is consistent with the nature of the product as it is described in the product file. We begin by moving the catalog number from the body record to the location in the indexed record that has been defined in the **SELECT** statement to be the record key for the product file. The **READ** statement that follows looks for the record specified by the key and executes the **INVALID KEY** clause only if the record is not on the file; in that case, the appropriate error flags are set. Notice the **KEY IS** clause. Since **COBOL** actually allows you to define more than one key for an indexed file, this clause tells the **READ** statement which key you are using for this particular **READ**. Our example, however, will use only one key. Normally the **READ** statement would be followed by code that would do a thorough job of validating a body record, including various tests based on information available in the product record. For this stub paragraph we simply **DISPLAY** the order number of the body record and other useful information.

The assumption in organizing the program this way is that when errors are detected in a seed order, they must be corrected manually after output from the program has been inspected by a human being. Naturally, if there are errors that can be corrected by the program—incorrect totals might be one such error—this should be done to reduce the amount of human effort required.

Here is an illustrative file used to test this program and to demonstrate its operation. It contains three order groups that pass all the validation tests, those with the order numbers of 111111, 444444, and 666666. All of the other groups contain errors of one type or another that cause the validation routines here to reject the order. Many of them contain other errors, some of which would be caught by a full-scale validation program and others of which are simple data input errors that would go through the system.

```
1111111J H GRIESMER  INNINGWOOD ROAD  OSSINING, NY 10562
11111250013A01CABBAGE                              00045
111111262471T01CORN, HYBRID                        00185
111111237515H02WHITE SWEET WILLIAM                 00200
1111113003200500016003 86
222222296461 01COMPOST KIT                         01495
2222230149505001200160 15
3333331S I GOODMAN  4 ICHTHYIC LANE STATEN ISLAND, NY 10312
333333239156A01PINK BEAUTY SWEET WILLIAM           00035
333333237515A01PURE WHITE SWEET WILLIAM            00035
4444441JAMES SCALZO  2 DONALD LANE OSSINING, NY 10562
444444262471U02CORN                                00370
444444262547L01PICKLES                             00110
4444443004800500024005 54
```

```
5555551M P BARNHARD  43 DONALD LANE  OSSINING, NY 10562
555555243125K05GIANT ZINNIAS                            01625
555555233597G02TRYSOMIC STOCKS                          00500
555555239156A01PLAIN WHITE SWEET WILLIAM                00035
5555553021700100011302373
5555554
666666250013K01CABBAGE                                  00100
6666661S J GOODMAN  4 RUE POISSON  BROOKLYN, NY 10452
666663001000050000000150
777777300045050000000095
777777250031A01CABBAGE                                  00045
7777771S K GOODMAN  4 FISCHLICHE STRASSE  BRONX, NY 11220
8888881S L GOODMAN  4 DAGISH AVE.  FLUSHING, NY 11361
888888252159L01COLLARDS                                 00080
888888250211K01CHICKORY, WITLOOF                        00095
888888300175005000000225
999999251904J01CRENSHAH MELNO                           00450
```

When the program was executed with this input, it produced the following output on the DISPLAY file.

```
HEADER VALIDATION REACHED 111111
BODY VALIDATION REACHED 111111   50013   CABBAGE, BURPEES DANISH ROUNDHEAD
BODY VALIDATION REACHED 111111   62471   HYBRID CORN, HONEY AND CREAM
BODY VALIDATION REACHED 111111   37515   SWEET WILLIAM  PINK BEAUTY
TRAILER VALIDATION REACHED 111111
BODY VALIDATION REACHED 222222   96461   COMPOST KIT
TRAILER VALIDATION REACHED 222222
HEADER VALIDATION REACHED 333333
BODY VALIDATION REACHED 333333   39156   SWEET WILLIAM  PURE WHITE
BODY VALIDATION REACHED 333333   37515   SWEET WILLIAM  PINK BEAUTY
HEADER VALIDATION REACHED 444444
BODY VALIDATION REACHED 444444   62471   HYBRID CORN, HONEY AND CREAM
BODY VALIDATION REACHED 444444   62547   CUCUMBER, BURPEE PICKLER
TRAILER VALIDATION REACHED 444444
HEADER VALIDATION REACHED 555555
BODY VALIDATION REACHED 555555   43125   ZINNIAS - GIANTS OF CALIFORNIA MIXED
BODY VALIDATION REACHED 555555   33597   STOCKS - TRYSOMIC 7 WEEKS MIXED COLORS
BODY VALIDATION REACHED 555555   39156   SWEET WILLIAM  PURE WHITE
TRAILER VALIDATION REACHED 555555
BODY VALIDATION REACHED 666666   50013   CABBAGE, BURPEES DANISH ROUNDHEAD
HEADER VALIDATION REACHED 666666
TRAILER VALIDATION REACHED 666666
TRAILER VALIDATION REACHED 777777
BODY VALIDATION REACHED 777777   50031   CABBAGE, BURPEES DANISH ROUNDHEAD
HEADER VALIDATION REACHED 777777
HEADER VALIDATION REACHED 888888
BODY VALIDATION REACHED 888888   52159   CABBAGE, BURPEES DANISH ROUNDHEAD
BODY VALIDATION REACHED 888888   50211   CABBAGE, BURPEES DANISH ROUNDHEAD
TRAILER VALIDATION REACHED 888888
BODY VALIDATION REACHED 999999   51904   CRENSHAH MELON, BURPEES EARLY HYBRID
```

This listing demonstrates that the appropriate routines were reached for validation of body and trailer records, but it also reveals some ways in which the program output is not as helpful as it might be. Look, for instance, at the three successive entries for cabbage near the end of the listing. Actually, all three of these entries represent catalog numbers for which there was no master record, and the description is simply a carryover from the last valid catalog number of the previous order.

Here is the content of the normal handling file with its two good orders.

```
1111111J H GRIESMER  INNINGWOOD ROAD  OSSINING, NY 10562
111111250013A01CABBAGE                                  00045
111111262471T01CORN, HYBRID                             00185
111111237515H02WHITE SWEET WILLIAM                      00200
111111300320050001600386
4444441JAMES SCALZO  2 DONALD LANE OSSINING, NY 10562
444444262471U02CORN                                     00370
444444262547L01PICKLES                                  00110
444444300480050002400554
6666661S J GOODMAN  4 RUE POISSON  BROOKLYN, NY 10452
666666300100005000000150
```

The special handling file is as follows.

```
222222296461 01COMPOST KIT                              01495
222222301495050012001601S
3333331S I GOODMAN  4 ICHTHYIC LANE STATEN ISLAND, NY 10312
333333239156A01PINK BEAUTY SWEET WILLIAM                00035
333333237515A01PURE WHITE SWEET WILLIAM                 00035
5555551M P BARNHARD  43 DONALD LANE  OSSINING, NY 10562
555555243125K05GIANT ZINNIAS                            01625
555555233597G02TRYSOMIC STOCKS                          00500
555555239156A01PLAIN WHITE SWEET WILLIAM                00035
555555302170010001130237S
5555554
666666250013K01CABBAGE                                  00100
777777300045050000000095
777777250031A01CABBAGE                                  00045
7777771S K GOODMAN  4 FISCHLICHE STRASSE  BRONX, NY 11220
8888881S L GOODMAN  4 DAGISH AVE.  FLUSHING, NY 11361
888888252159L01COLLARDS                                 00080
888888250211K01CHICKORY, WITLOOF                        00095
888888300175005000000225
999999251904J01CRENSHAH MELNO                           00450
```

We said before that the group with order number 666666 is a valid group and, indeed, it does appear on the normal handling file. Notice, however, that one record from this group also appears on the special handling file. What happened was that the first record of the group, a body record, was treated as a group with no header and marked for special handling. However, the next record, a header for order 666666, was treated as the start of a new group, one that had a header and a trailer but no body records. Since the program does not check for this condition, the group was accepted as valid. We leave it to the reader to study each of the remaining order groups and note the various kinds of errors that cause these orders to be rejected.

14.13 A PROGRAM TO UPDATE AN INDEXED SEQUENTIAL FILE

An indexed sequential file, like any other, must ordinarily be updated from time to time. New records must be added to the file, old records must be deleted, and changes must be made to existing records. These operations are especially easy with an indexed file since the access method handles all the problems associated with finding space for the addition records and also maintains the index so that records can still be accessed either randomly or sequentially.

A program that updates the seed company product file is shown in Figure 14.8. Observe the **ACCESS IS RANDOM** clause. Notice also that the transaction record for this application has been modified to include an update code that designates the type of update that is to be performed.

```
1     IDENTIFICATION DIVISION.
2     PROGRAM-ID.
3         UPDATE-PRODUCT.
4     DATE-WRITTEN.
5         APRIL 14, 1987.
6
7     ENVIRONMENT DIVISION.
8     INPUT-OUTPUT SECTION.
9     FILE-CONTROL.
10        SELECT UPDATE-FILE              ASSIGN TO S-UPDATE.
11        SELECT IS-PRODUCT-FILE          ASSIGN TO I-ISPROD
12                ORGANIZATION IS INDEXED
13                ACCESS IS RANDOM
14                RECORD KEY IS CATALOG-NUMBER OF IS-PRODUCT-RECORD.
15
16    DATA DIVISION.
17
18    FILE SECTION.
19
20    FD  UPDATE-FILE
21        LABEL RECORDS ARE OMITTED.
22    01  UPDATE-RECORD.
23        05  CATALOG-NUMBER              PIC X(5).
24        05  SIZE-1                      PIC X.
25        05  PRICE-1                     PIC 99V99.
26        05  SIZE-2                      PIC X.
27        05  PRICE-2                     PIC 99V99.
28        05  SIZE-3                      PIC X.
29        05  PRICE-3                     PIC 99V99.
30        05  DESCRIPTION                 PIC X(40).
31        05  UPDATE-CODE                 PIC X.
32            88  ADDITION                    VALUE '1'.
33            88  DELETION                    VALUE '2'.
34            88  CORRECTION                  VALUE '3'.
35
36    FD  IS-PRODUCT-FILE
37        LABEL RECORDS ARE STANDARD.
38    01  IS-PRODUCT-RECORD.
39        05  CATALOG-NUMBER              PIC X(5).
40        05  SIZE-1                      PIC X.
41        05  PRICE-1                     PIC 99V99   COMP-3.
42        05  SIZE-2                      PIC X.
43        05  PRICE-2                     PIC 99V99   COMP-3.
44        05  SIZE-3                      PIC X.
45        05  PRICE-3                     PIC 99V99   COMP-3.
46        05  DESCRIPTION                 PIC X(40).
47
48    WORKING-STORAGE SECTION.
49
50    01  INVALID-KEY-FLAG               PIC X.
51        88  INVALID-KEY                     VALUE 'Y'.
52
```

```
53     01  MORE-DATA-REMAINS-FLAG          PIC X VALUE 'Y'.
54         88  MORE-DATA-REMAINS                 VALUE 'Y'.
55         88  NO-MORE-DATA-REMAINS              VALUE 'N'.
56
57     PROCEDURE DIVISION.
58     A000-UPDATE-PRODUCT-FILE.
59         OPEN INPUT UPDATE-FILE
60              I-O   IS-PRODUCT-FILE.
61         PERFORM B010-PROCESS-ONE-UPDATE
62              UNTIL NO-MORE-DATA-REMAINS.
63         CLOSE UPDATE-FILE
64               IS-PRODUCT-FILE.
65         STOP RUN.
66
67     B010-PROCESS-ONE-UPDATE.
68         READ UPDATE-FILE
69              AT END MOVE 'N' TO MORE-DATA-REMAINS-FLAG.
70         IF MORE-DATA-REMAINS
71             IF      ADDITION
72                 PERFORM C010-ADDITION
73             ELSE IF DELETION
74                 PERFORM C020-DELETION
75             ELSE IF CORRECTION
76                 PERFORM C030-CORRECTION
77             ELSE
78                 PERFORM C040-INVALID-TYPE.
79
80     C010-ADDITION.
81         MOVE CATALOG-NUMBER OF UPDATE-RECORD TO
82                 CATALOG-NUMBER OF IS-PRODUCT-RECORD.
83         MOVE CORRESPONDING UPDATE-RECORD TO IS-PRODUCT-RECORD.
84         WRITE IS-PRODUCT-RECORD
85               INVALID KEY DISPLAY 'BAD ADDITION; RECORD ALREADY '
86                       'EXISTS FOR '
87                       CATALOG-NUMBER OF IS-PRODUCT-RECORD.
88
89     C020-DELETION.
90         MOVE CATALOG-NUMBER OF UPDATE-RECORD TO
91                 CATALOG-NUMBER OF IS-PRODUCT-RECORD.
92         MOVE 'N' TO INVALID-KEY-FLAG.
93         READ IS-PRODUCT-FILE
94               KEY IS CATALOG-NUMBER OF IS-PRODUCT-RECORD
95               INVALID KEY MOVE 'Y' TO INVALID-KEY-FLAG.
96         IF INVALID-KEY
97             DISPLAY 'BAD DELETION; NO RECORD IN FILE FOR '
98                     CATALOG-NUMBER OF IS-PRODUCT-RECORD
99         ELSE
100            DELETE IS-PRODUCT-FILE
101                  INVALID KEY DISPLAY 'BIG TROUBLES AT '
102                          CATALOG-NUMBER OF IS-PRODUCT-RECORD.
103
104    C030-CORRECTION.
105        MOVE CATALOG-NUMBER OF UPDATE-RECORD TO
106                CATALOG-NUMBER OF IS-PRODUCT-RECORD.
107        MOVE 'N' TO INVALID-KEY-FLAG.
108        READ IS-PRODUCT-FILE
109              KEY IS CATALOG-NUMBER OF IS-PRODUCT-RECORD
110              INVALID KEY MOVE 'Y' TO INVALID-KEY-FLAG.
```

```
111        IF INVALID-KEY
112            DISPLAY 'BAD CORRECTION; NO RECORD IN FILE FOR '
113                    CATALOG-NUMBER OF IS-PRODUCT-RECORD
114        ELSE
115            MOVE CORRESPONDING UPDATE-RECORD TO IS-PRODUCT-RECORD
116            REWRITE IS-PRODUCT-RECORD
117                    INVALID KEY DISPLAY 'BIG TROUBLES AT '
118                        CATALOG-NUMBER OF IS-PRODUCT-RECORD.
119
120    C040-INVALID-TYPE.
121        DISPLAY 'THE FOLLOWING RECORD IS NEITHER AN UPDATE NOR '
122            'A DELETION NOR A CORRECTION:  '.
123        DISPLAY '      "' UPDATE-RECORD '"'.
124
125
126    *********************** END OF PROGRAM ***********************
```

FIGURE 14.8 A program to update an indexed sequential file.

In the OPEN statement for the indexed file we find a new feature: the file is opened for both input and output. Since we must read the records to be sure that they exist before we make deletions and corrections, the file is input; since records must be written for all three types of transactions, the file is also output.

Paragraph B010-PROCESS-ONE-UPDATE is executed once for each update until the input file of updates is exhausted. So long as data remains, it simply determines what type of update is involved and performs an appropriate routine.

For additions, we must set the record key equal to the key of the update record to permit checking for the possibility that a record with this key already exists in the file. In the operation of adding a record where there should not be a matching record in the file, the INVALID KEY clause is activated if a matching record is found. That is, the program will not write a new record if its key matches the key of a record already on the file; an attempt to do so raises the invalid key condition.

To delete a record from the file, we first get the record, thus guaranteeing that a record with the specified key does exist in the file. The INVALID KEY clause on this READ is activated if there is no such record; in this case we DISPLAY an appropriate message. If the record does exist in the file, we delete the record from the file with a new verb that exists for this purpose, DELETE. Observe that DELETE specifies the file name, not the record name; the value of the record key determines which record will be deleted.

Since we have already checked to make certain that the record exists, there is no way to get an invalid key without a serious failure of either the hardware or the access routines. In this example, we simply display a message indicating that something is very seriously wrong if the invalid key condition is raised. Actually, one would ordinarily terminate program execution if this happened. If we wished, we could omit the READ step and simply DELETE the record, using the INVALID KEY clause to notify us if the record is not actually on the file. The choice between the two approaches is mostly a matter of style.

To carry out a correction, we obtain the existing record, which in this example is needed primarily to establish that the record does indeed exist on the file. The record is modified to contain the new data, then we use another new verb, **REWRITE**, to replace the record on the file. Notice the difference between **WRITE** and **REWRITE**. **WRITE** is used to insert a new record on the file; an invalid key condition exists if the new record duplicates an existing record. **REWRITE** is used to modify an existing record, and an invalid key condition indicates that the record does not exist, which is generally a serious error.

The following data shows a file of updates to be applied to the master file that was shown in previous examples.

```
31658A0100P0400 0000SNAPDRAGON, BRIGHT BUTTERFLIES, MIXED      1
36160A0050K0150L0175ROYAL SWEET PEAS, MIXED                    1
50013                                                          2
15131 0550 0000 0000APPLE TREE, JONATHAN                       1
43125A0035H0105K0325ZINNIAS, GIANTS OF CALIFORNIA, MIXED       3
36574A0050G0150 0000STOCKS - GIANT COLUMN MIXED COLORS         1
62471A0075T0185U0350HYBRID CORN, HONEY AND CREAM               3
61218A0035L0060S0125TURNIPS, PURPLE-TOP WHITE GLOBE         1
62547                                                          2
51094A0075J0450 0000CRENSHAW MELON, BURPEES EARLY HYBRID       3
50260A0075J0450 0000EGGPLANT, EARLY BEAUTY HYBRID              1
51367A0050T0145U0275DECORATIVE CORN, RAINBOW                   1
12345                                                          2
31773A0075G0225 0000VERBENA, RUFFLED WHITE                     1
```

When the program was executed, the following **DISPLAY** messages were produced.

```
BAD ADDITION; RECORD ALREADY EXISTS FOR 36574
THE FOLLOWING RECORD IS NEITHER AN UPDATE NOR A DELETION NOR A CORRECTION:
    "61218A0035L0060S0125TURNIPS, PURPLE-TOP WHITE GLOBE         1  "
BAD CORRECTION; NO RECORD IN FILE FOR 51094
BAD DELETION; NO RECORD IN FILE FOR 12345
```

We can now use the program in Figure 14.6 to print the updated file, giving the following output.

```
15131       5.50        0.00        0.00  APPLE TREE, JONATHAN
31658   A   1.00   P    4.00        0.00  SNAPDRAGON, BRIGHT BUTTERFLIES, MIXED
31773   A   0.75   G    2.25        0.00  VERBENA, RUFFLED WHITE
33597   A   0.50   G    2.50        0.00  STOCKS - TRYSOMIC 7 WEEKS MIXED COLORS
36160   A   0.50   K    1.50   L    1.75  ROYAL SWEET PEAS, MIXED
36574   A   0.50   G    1.50        0.00  STOCKS - GIANT COLUMN MIXED COLORS
37515   A   0.35   H    1.00        0.00  SWEET WILLIAM   PINK BEAUTY
39156   A   0.35   H    1.00        0.00  SWEET WILLIAM   PURE WHITE
43125   A   0.35   H    1.05   K    3.25  ZINNIAS, GIANTS OF CALIFORNIA, MIXED
50260   A   0.75   J    4.50        0.00  EGGPLANT, EARLY BEAUTY HYBRID
51367   A   0.50   T    1.45   U    2.75  DECORATIVE CORN, RAINBOW
51904   A   0.75   J    4.50        0.00  CRENSHAH MELON, BURPEES EARLY HYBRID
62471   A   0.75   T    1.85   U    3.50  HYBRID CORN, HONEY AND CREAM
96461      15.95        0.00        0.00  COMPOST KIT
```

Notice that the various updates have been carried out correctly. The addition records are all present, other than the one that was a duplication. The two valid deletion updates have resulted in the removal of records from the file. The two valid corrections have modified the corresponding records properly. The most important thing to notice about this output is that the records are in sequence on the key even though the updating inserted new records at various places in the file, including three records before the first record in the file as originally created. This ability to access and update a file randomly and still to retrieve records sequentially when convenient is the essence of indexed file processing.

We must emphasize that the examples we have shown, while presenting some of the most common uses of indexed files, do not begin to cover the full range of this topic. We strongly urge the serious COBOL programmer to study the use of indexed files more fully in an advanced text or in a COBOL manual.

14.14   RELATIVE RECORD FILES

Although indexed files are useful in many applications, they are not the only random access technique available to the COBOL programmer. One of the basic requirements of an indexed file is that the file must be sorted on a key field, and that this field be unique for every record. Furthermore, although some implementations of indexed files permit more than one key for the file, there are versions of COBOL that permit only one key per indexed file. However, there are applications in which a record may have no obvious key, or may have more than one key, or in which the key may not be unique. In any of these cases, the indexed sequential method cannot be used. In cases such as these, relative files are commonly used.

A relative file is one in which records are retrieved by specifying their relative record number, that is, how far they are from the start of the file. This is analogous to the way in which records are accessed in a table, where you simply provide the subscript number of a particular record to be able to refer to it. In many ways, a relative file may be thought of as a very large table stored on a disk. You should be careful not to carry this analogy too far, however! There are very important differences between tables stored in memory and relative files stored on a disk. The details of how you refer to a record in a file looks nothing like the details of how you refer to a record in a table. However, just as in a table, records in a relative file are referred to by record number, not by key. Furthermore, once the file has been created, it is not possible to insert new records between existing records. However, just as we do with a table, it is possible to move existing records around to make room for new data, or to write new records into "empty" entries, called *dummy* records.

14.15   A PROGRAM TO CREATE A RELATIVE RECORD FILE

We now will use the seed catalog product file to demonstrate how a relative record file might be built. The following example (Figure 14.9) is analogous to the program in Figure 14.5 that showed the construction of an indexed file. Again, this will be a skeleton program so that we can concentrate on the file processing techniques.

```
 1      IDENTIFICATION DIVISION.
 2      PROGRAM-ID.
 3          BUILD-RELATIVE.
 4      DATE-WRITTEN.
 5          APRIL 14, 1987.
 6
 7      ENVIRONMENT DIVISION.
 8      INPUT-OUTPUT SECTION.
 9      FILE-CONTROL.
10          SELECT PRODUCT-FILE          ASSIGN TO S-PRODUCTS.
11          SELECT REL-PRODUCT-FILE      ASSIGN TO R-RELPROD
12              ORGANIZATION IS RELATIVE
13              ACCESS IS SEQUENTIAL
14              RELATIVE KEY IS PRODUCT-KEY.
15
16      DATA DIVISION.
17
18      FILE SECTION.
19
20      FD  PRODUCT-FILE
21          LABEL RECORDS ARE STANDARD.
22      01  PRODUCT-RECORD.
23          05  CATALOG-NUMBER      PIC X(5).
24          05  SIZE-1              PIC X.
25          05  PRICE-1             PIC 99V99.
26          05  SIZE-2              PIC X.
27          05  PRICE-2             PIC 99V99.
28          05  SIZE-3              PIC X.
29          05  PRICE-3             PIC 99V99.
30          05  DESCRIPTION         PIC X(40).
31
32      FD  REL-PRODUCT-FILE
33          LABEL RECORDS ARE STANDARD.
34      01  REL-PRODUCT-RECORD.
35          05  CATALOG-NUMBER      PIC X(5).
36          05  SIZE-1              PIC X.
37          05  PRICE-1             PIC 99V99 COMP-3.
38          05  SIZE-2              PIC X.
39          05  PRICE-2             PIC 99V99 COMP-3.
40          05  SIZE-3              PIC X.
41          05  PRICE-3             PIC 99V99 COMP-3.
42          05  DESCRIPTION         PIC X(40).
43
44      WORKING-STORAGE SECTION.
45
46      01  MORE-DATA-REMAINS-FLAG        PIC X VALUE 'Y'.
47          88  MORE-DATA-REMAINS                    VALUE 'Y'.
48          88  NO-MORE-DATA-REMAINS                 VALUE 'N'.
49
50      01  PRODUCT-KEY                   PIC 9(8) COMP SYNC.
51
52
53      PROCEDURE DIVISION.
54      A000-CREATE-RELATIVE-PROD-FILE.
55          OPEN  INPUT PRODUCT-FILE
56                OUTPUT REL-PRODUCT-FILE.
57          MOVE 1 TO PRODUCT-KEY.
58          PERFORM B010-TRANSFER-ONE-RECORD
59              UNTIL NO-MORE-DATA-REMAINS.
```

```
60            CLOSE PRODUCT-FILE
61                  REL-PRODUCT-FILE.
62            STOP RUN.
63
64       B010-TRANSFER-ONE-RECORD.
65            READ PRODUCT-FILE
66                  AT END MOVE 'N' TO MORE-DATA-REMAINS-FLAG.
67            IF MORE-DATA-REMAINS
68                MOVE CORRESPONDING PRODUCT-RECORD TO REL-PRODUCT-RECORD
69                WRITE REL-PRODUCT-RECORD
70                      INVALID KEY DISPLAY 'FILE CAPACITY EXCEEDED; '
71                                  'CANNOT WRITE ' CATALOG-NUMBER OF
72                                  REL-PRODUCT-RECORD.
73
74
75       *********************** END OF PROGRAM ***********************
```

FIGURE 14.9   A program for creating a relative record file.

There are several points to notice about the **SELECT** statement for the relative file. First, the name of the file to which **REL-PRODUCT-FILE** is assigned begins with "**R-**". As with indexed files, this is ignored by the compiler, but we use the **R** to indicate that this is a relative record file. The **ORGANIZATION IS RELATIVE** clause specifies the file's organization, and as we did with the indexed files, we have specified that **ACCESS IS SEQUENTIAL** even though this is the default and not really required. Finally, we have included a **RELATIVE KEY** clause instead of a **RECORD KEY** clause. In relative record files a record is identified by its position in the file (its relative record number), just as an entry in a table is identified by its position in the table (its subscript number). Instead of a subscript we use the relative key to specify the relative record number. Since the key for a relative record file specifies a record number, it may be any integer field whose value does not exceed the physical size of the file. We have shown **PRODUCT-KEY** to be a fullword binary field, but this is not required.

The File Section holds nothing that is new. Notice, however, that we have omitted the **BLOCK CONTAINS** clause from the **FD** for **REL-PRODUCT-FILE**. This is not optional! Relative files are always unblocked. In some **COBOL** compilers the **BLOCK CONTAINS** clause will be ignored, if present, but other compilers may flag it as an error.

The Procedure Division in Figure 14.9 is very much like the one in Figure 14.5, although there are a few differences. We have initialized **PRODUCT-KEY** to one, and from then on the value of **PRODUCT-KEY** is automatically incremented by one every time a record is written to **REL-PRODUCT-FILE**. Actually, this initialization is shown more for documentation than anything else. When creating a relative file we can omit the **RELATIVE KEY** clause entirely and the program will do just as it does in our example.

As with indexed files, the **WRITE** statement for a relative file has an **INVALID KEY** clause. However, with relative files the only situation that can cause an invalid key condition is if the value of the relative key exceeds the physical capacity of the file. If this happens, we simply display an error message and continue, although a more complete program would have more sophisticated error handling code.

14.16 A PROGRAM TO UPDATE A RELATIVE RECORD FILE

The program to print a relative record file is almost identical to that shown in Figure 14.5 to print an indexed file, and we leave the actual construction of such a program to the student; the output should look much like that for the corresponding indexed file, although you might wish to include the relative record number as part of the output. Instead, let us focus on the problems involved in updating a relative record file. The first problem we have is finding the record we wish to update. When we were working with indexed files we simply used the catalog number as the record key and proceeded from there. With relative files this won't work. In the first place, one of the reasons that one wishes to use relative files is often that there is no field that can be used as a record key. Even if there is such a field, it is not always numeric and so cannot be used as the relative key, and even if it is numeric, it is not always suitable for use as the relative key. For example, the catalog number in the seed catalog example is a five-digit number, which means that we can have 100,000 different catalog numbers. However, it is highly unlikely that the seed company actually has anywhere near this many products. If we try to use the catalog number directly as the relative key, we will have a huge file that is 95 percent empty. We will defer the solution to this problem for a bit, and for now we will simply assume that the relative key is somehow known to us and is presented to the program as part of UPDATE-RECORD , shown in Figure 14.10.

```
1      IDENTIFICATION DIVISION.
2      PROGRAM-ID.
3          UPDATE-RELATIVE.
4      DATE-WRITTEN.
5          APRIL 14, 1987.
6
7      ENVIRONMENT DIVISION.
8      INPUT-OUTPUT SECTION.
9      FILE-CONTROL.
10         SELECT UPDATE-FILE              ASSIGN TO S-UPDATE.
11         SELECT REL-PRODUCT-FILE         ASSIGN TO R-RELPROD
12             ORGANIZATION IS RELATIVE
13             ACCESS IS RANDOM
14             RELATIVE KEY IS PRODUCT-NUMBER.
15
16     DATA DIVISION.
17
18     FILE SECTION.
19     FD  UPDATE-FILE
20         LABEL RECORDS ARE OMITTED.
21     01  UPDATE-RECORD.
22         05  CATALOG-NUMBER             PIC X(5).
23         05  PRODUCT-NUMBER             PIC 9(5).
24         05  SIZE-1                     PIC X.
25         05  PRICE-1                    PIC 99V99.
26         05  SIZE-2                     PIC X.
27         05  PRICE-2                    PIC 99V99.
28         05  SIZE-3                     PIC X.
29         05  PRICE-3                    PIC 99V99.
30         05  DESCRIPTION                PIC X(40).
```

```
31           05   UPDATE-CODE                 PIC X.
32                88   ADDITION                      VALUE '1'.
33                88   DELETION                      VALUE '2'.
34                88   CORRECTION                    VALUE '3'.
35
36     FD   REL-PRODUCT-FILE
37          LABEL RECORDS ARE STANDARD.
38     01   REL-PRODUCT-RECORD.
39           05   CATALOG-NUMBER              PIC X(5).
40           05   SIZE-1                      PIC X.
41           05   PRICE-1                     PIC 99V99   COMP-3.
42           05   SIZE-2                      PIC X.
43           05   PRICE-2                     PIC 99V99   COMP-3.
44           05   SIZE-3                      PIC X.
45           05   PRICE-3                     PIC 99V99   COMP-3.
46           05   DESCRIPTION                 PIC X(40).
47
48     WORKING-STORAGE SECTION.
49
50     01   MORE-DATA-REMAINS-FLAG       PIC X VALUE 'Y'.
51           88   MORE-DATA-REMAINS             VALUE 'Y'.
52           88   NO-MORE-DATA-REMAINS          VALUE 'N'.
53
54     01   REC-FOUND-FLAG               PIC X.
55           88   REC-FOUND                     VALUE 'Y'.
56           88   REC-NOT-FOUND                 VALUE 'N'.
57
58     PROCEDURE DIVISION.
59
60     A000-UPDATE-PRODUCT-FILE.
61          OPEN INPUT UPDATE-FILE
62               I-O   REL-PRODUCT-FILE.
63          PERFORM B010-PROCESS-ONE-UPDATE
64                  UNTIL NO-MORE-DATA-REMAINS.
65          CLOSE UPDATE-FILE
66                  REL-PRODUCT-FILE.
67          STOP RUN.
68
69     B010-PROCESS-ONE-UPDATE.
70          READ UPDATE-FILE
71                  AT END MOVE 'N' TO MORE-DATA-REMAINS-FLAG.
72          IF MORE-DATA-REMAINS
73             IF      ADDITION
74                 PERFORM C010-ADDITION
75             ELSE IF DELETION
76                 PERFORM C020-DELETION
77             ELSE IF CORRECTION
78                 PERFORM C030-CORRECTION
79             ELSE
80                 PERFORM C040-INVALID-TYPE.
81
82     C010-ADDITION.
83          MOVE CORRESPONDING UPDATE-RECORD TO REL-PRODUCT-RECORD
84          WRITE REL-PRODUCT-RECORD
85                  INVALID KEY
86                      DISPLAY 'BAD ADDITION FOR '
87                              CATALOG-NUMBER OF UPDATE-RECORD
88                              '; RECORD ALREADY EXISTS AT '
89                              PRODUCT-NUMBER.
90
```

```
91     C020-DELETION.
92         DELETE REL-PRODUCT-FILE
93                 INVALID KEY
94                         DISPLAY 'BAD DELETION FOR '
95                         CATALOG-NUMBER OF UPDATE-RECORD
96                         '; NO RECORD IN FILE AT '
97                         PRODUCT-NUMBER.
98
99     C030-CORRECTION.
100        MOVE 'Y' TO REC-FOUND-FLAG.
101        READ REL-PRODUCT-FILE
102                INVALID KEY MOVE 'N' TO REC-FOUND-FLAG.
103        IF REC-NOT-FOUND
104            DISPLAY 'BAD CORRECTION FOR '
105                    CATALOG-NUMBER OF UPDATE-RECORD
106                    '; NO RECORD IN FILE AT ' PRODUCT-NUMBER
107        ELSE
108            MOVE CORRESPONDING UPDATE-RECORD TO REL-PRODUCT-RECORD
109            REWRITE REL-PRODUCT-RECORD
110                    INVALID KEY DISPLAY 'BIG TROUBLES AT '
111                                        PRODUCT-NUMBER.
112
113    C040-INVALID-TYPE.
114        DISPLAY 'THE FOLLOWING RECORD IS NEITHER AN UPDATE NOR '
115                'A DELETION NOR A CORRECTION:  '.
116        DISPLAY '     "' UPDATE-RECORD '"'.
117
118
119    ************************* END OF PROGRAM *************************
```

FIGURE 14.10 A program to update a relative record file.

The Procedure Division of the program in Figure 14.10 very similar to that of the indexed file update program in Figure 14.8. The major difference is that we do not need to move any value to a key field since we have declared **PRODUCT-NUMBER**, located in **UPDATE-RECORD**, to be the relative key. The relative key may be located anywhere in the Data Division *except* in a record that is part of the **FD** entry for the relative file. Compare the remainder of the code in the two programs of Figures 14.8 and 14.10. Although there are differences between the programs, they are primarily differences of style intended to demonstrate alternative approaches to performing various tasks.

If we print the updated file, using the same test data as we used to build and update an indexed file in Sections 14.8 - 14.13, we get this output.

```
33597   A   0.50   G   2.50          0.00   STOCKS - TRYSOMIC 7 WEEKS MIXED COLORS
36574   A   0.50   G   1.50          0.00   STOCKS - GIANT COLUMN MIXED COLORS
37515   A   0.35   H   1.00          0.00   SWEET WILLIAM  PINK BEAUTY
39156   A   0.35   H   1.00          0.00   SWEET WILLIAM  PURE WHITE
43125   A   0.35   H   1.05   K   3.25   ZINNIAS, GIANTS OF CALIFORNIA, MIXED
51904   A   0.75   J   4.50          0.00   CRENSHAH MELON, BURPEES EARLY HYBRID
62471   A   0.75   T   1.85   U   3.50   HYBRID CORN, HONEY AND CREAM
96461       15.95          0.00          0.00   COMPOST KIT
31658   A   1.00   P   4.00          0.00   SNAPDRAGON, BRIGHT BUTTERFLIES, MIXED
36160   A   0.50   K   1.50   L   1.75   ROYAL SWEET PEAS, MIXED
15131       5.50          0.00          0.00   APPLE TREE, JONATHAN
50260   A   0.75   J   4.50          0.00   EGGPLANT, EARLY BEAUTY HYBRID
51367   A   0.50   T   1.45   U   2.75   DECORATIVE CORN, RAINBOW
31773   A   0.75   G   2.25          0.00   VERBENA, RUFFLED WHITE
```

Notice that although all the records are the same as we had in the indexed file, these records are not in numeric order. The reason is that new records are simply inserted wherever we specify in the update record, and there is no attempt made by the file access software to keep records in any order.

14.17   A TECHNIQUE FOR COMPUTING RELATIVE RECORD NUMBERS

In most cases the records in a relative record file do not contain fields that can be used directly as record keys. There are numerous techniques for converting data fields into values that can be used as records keys, and a thorough discussion of these techniques is beyond the scope of this text. However, we will present a brief discussion of a common technique called *hash coding* and will show some simple examples of its use.

Hash coding involves performing a simple calculation on a numeric field and using the result of this calculation as the key for the record being processed. For example, if our record contains a telephone number and we wish to use this as the basis for our key, we can extract selected digits from the number to form the relative key. Specifically, suppose that we have the telephone number 555-1234, and we wish to use the second, third, fourth, and fifth digits as the key. We could simply define the following fields in Working-Storage:

```
01   PHONE-NUMBER                 PIC X(7).
01   KEY-FIELDS   REDEFINES PHONE-NUMBER.
     02   FILLER                  PIC X.
     02   PHONE-KEY               PIC 9(4).
     02   FILLER                  PIC XX.
```

then use **PHONE-KEY** as the relative key to access the record. In this example, the relative key would contain "5512".

A common technique for hashing a number to produce a key is used when we wish to produce keys in a specific range; this is what is required if we wish to allow for a specific number of records on a file. For example, if we want to allow for 3000 records on a relative record file, we need to have a key in the range 1-3000. We can produce this by dividing the numeric field by 3000 (which gives a remainder in the range of 0-2999), adding 1 to the remainder, and using the result as the key. Other calculations are possible, but this division-remainder technique is very common.

One problem that occurs in hash coding is that two or more records may hash to the same value. For example, using the division-remainder example described above, both 3100 and 6100 produce a key value of 101. This condition is called a collision, since we are trying to assign two records to the same file location. The solution is to assign the first record to location 101, then assign any colliding records to other locations in the file. We will demonstrate how this technique works in the following examples.

14.18   USING A HASH KEY TO CREATE A RELATIVE FILE

The following program (Figure 14.11) is similar to the one shown in Figure 14.9, except that we will use a simple division-remainder hash coding algorithm to determine where records are located in the file. Since the catalog number is numeric, we will use this as the basis of our hashing process. We assume that the seed company has about 4000 products. To allow for future growth, we would normally allow for 5000 records on the file, and the keys we calculate would be in the range 1-5000. However, to save file space during testing we will use a file size of 50.

```
 1     IDENTIFICATION DIVISION.
 2     PROGRAM-ID.
 3         BUILD-HASHED.
 4     DATE-WRITTEN.
 5         APRIL 14, 1987.
 6
 7     ENVIRONMENT DIVISION.
 8     INPUT-OUTPUT SECTION.
 9     FILE-CONTROL.
10         SELECT PRODUCT-FILE              ASSIGN TO S-PRODUCTS.
11         SELECT REL-PRODUCT-FILE          ASSIGN TO R-RELPROD
12                 ORGANIZATION IS RELATIVE
13                 ACCESS IS RANDOM
14                 RELATIVE KEY IS PRODUCT-KEY.
15
16     DATA DIVISION.
17
18     FILE SECTION.
19
20     FD  PRODUCT-FILE
21         LABEL RECORDS ARE STANDARD.
22     01  PRODUCT-RECORD.
23         05  CATALOG-NUMBER              PIC 9(5).
24         05  SIZE-1                      PIC X.
25         05  PRICE-1                     PIC 99V99.
26         05  SIZE-2                      PIC X.
27         05  PRICE-2                     PIC 99V99.
28         05  SIZE-3                      PIC X.
29         05  PRICE-3                     PIC 99V99.
30         05  DESCRIPTION                 PIC X(40).
31
32     FD  REL-PRODUCT-FILE
33         LABEL RECORDS ARE STANDARD.
34     01  REL-PRODUCT-RECORD.
35         05  CATALOG-NUMBER              PIC 9(5).
36         05  SIZE-1                      PIC X.
37         05  PRICE-1                     PIC 99V99   COMP-3.
38         05  SIZE-2                      PIC X.
39         05  PRICE-2                     PIC 99V99   COMP-3.
40         05  SIZE-3                      PIC X.
41         05  PRICE-3                     PIC 99V99   COMP-3.
42         05  DESCRIPTION                 PIC X(40).
43
44     WORKING-STORAGE SECTION.
45
46     01  FILE-FULL-FLAG                  PIC X.
47         88  FILE-FULL                        VALUE 'Y'.
48
49     01  FILE-SIZE                       PIC 9(5) COMP SYNC VALUE 50.
50
51     01  KEY-QUOTIENT                    PIC 9(5) COMP SYNC.
52
53     01  MORE-DATA-REMAINS-FLAG          PIC X VALUE 'Y'.
```

```
54            88   MORE-DATA-REMAINS                    VALUE 'Y'.
55            88   NO-MORE-DATA-REMAINS                 VALUE 'N'.
56
57       01   PRODUCT-KEY                     PIC 9(5) COMP SYNC.
58
59       01   RECORD-INSERTED-FLAG            PIC X.
60            88   RECORD-INSERTED                      VALUE 'Y'.
61
62       01   START-KEY                       PIC S9(5) COMP SYNC.
63
64
65       PROCEDURE DIVISION.
66       A000-CREATE-RELATIVE-PROD-FILE.
67           OPEN   INPUT PRODUCT-FILE
68                  OUTPUT REL-PRODUCT-FILE.
69           PERFORM B010-TRANSFER-ONE-RECORD
70                  UNTIL NO-MORE-DATA-REMAINS.
71           CLOSE PRODUCT-FILE
72                 REL-PRODUCT-FILE.
73           STOP RUN.
74
75       B010-TRANSFER-ONE-RECORD.
76           READ PRODUCT-FILE
77                   AT END MOVE 'N' TO MORE-DATA-REMAINS-FLAG.
78           IF MORE-DATA-REMAINS
79              MOVE CORRESPONDING PRODUCT-RECORD TO
80                      REL-PRODUCT-RECORD
81              PERFORM C010-INSERT-REL-RECORD
82              IF FILE-FULL
83                  DISPLAY 'FILE CAPACITY EXCEEDED; CANNOT WRITE '
84                      CATALOG-NUMBER OF PRODUCT-RECORD.
85
86       C010-INSERT-REL-RECORD.
87           DIVIDE CATALOG-NUMBER OF PRODUCT-RECORD BY FILE-SIZE
88                   GIVING KEY-QUOTIENT
89                   REMAINDER PRODUCT-KEY.
90           ADD 1 TO PRODUCT-KEY.
91           MOVE 'N' TO FILE-FULL-FLAG.
92           MOVE 'N' TO RECORD-INSERTED-FLAG.
93           MOVE PRODUCT-KEY TO START-KEY.
94           PERFORM D010-PROBE
95                   UNTIL RECORD-INSERTED  OR  FILE-FULL.
96
97       D010-PROBE.
98           MOVE 'Y' TO RECORD-INSERTED-FLAG.
99           WRITE REL-PRODUCT-RECORD
100                  INVALID KEY MOVE 'N' TO RECORD-INSERTED-FLAG.
101          IF NOT RECORD-INSERTED
102             PERFORM E100-INCREMENT-KEY
103             IF PRODUCT-KEY = START-KEY
104                 MOVE 'Y' TO FILE-FULL-FLAG.
105
106      E100-INCREMENT-KEY.
107          ADD 1 TO PRODUCT-KEY.
108          IF PRODUCT-KEY > FILE-SIZE
109             MOVE 1 TO PRODUCT-KEY.
110
111      *********************** END OF PROGRAM *************************
```

FIGURE 14.11   A program to create a relative file using hashing.

The first paragraph is standard. The next paragraph, **B010-TRANSFER-ONE-RECORD**, is also straightforward. We read a record from **PRODUCT-FILE**, move the update data to the file record, then use **C010-INSERT-REL-RECORD** to insert the new record in the file. If the file is full and there is no room to insert the new record, we display a simple error message.

The algorithm for computing the relative key begins by dividing the catalog number of the input product record by the file size, adding 1 to the remainder, and storing the sum as the relative key. However, we may have a collision condition in which two or more records generate the same initial key value. Therefore, we may have to try several locations on the file before we find one available for the new record. This testing is done in **D010-PROBE**. Here we begin the probing by trying to write the record at the location initially calculated for the relative key. We assume that the insertion will work, then use the **INVALID KEY** clause to tell if we failed; the invalid key condition occurs if we attempt to write a record into a location that already contains a record. In this case we must increment the key and try again. If incrementing the key has brought us back to the starting point, the file is full and we set **FILE-FULL-FLAG**. Notice that we cannot simply add 1 to **PRODUCT-KEY** when it is incremented; we must test to see if we have reached the end of the file. If so, then **PRODUCT-KEY** is reset to one and the search continues beginning at the start of the file.

The result of this key calculation algorithm is that the division-remainder step is used merely to find the starting point for record insertion. In case of a collision, successive records are simply placed in the first empty space in the file, treating the file as a large circular list of records. Although there are more sophisticated and efficient ways of dealing with the collision problem, this technique has the advantage of being simple to implement.

We used the program of Figure 14.11 and the data used to build the previous files, then printed the resulting file. The print program was modified to show the relative record number as well as the record, and produced the following results. Notice that the file records are not in any particular sequence, nor is every location in the file in use. This is the result of the hashing algorithm, which scatters the records throughout the file.

```
(00005)   51904  A  0.75  J  4.50       0.00  CRENSHAH MELON, BURPEES EARLY HYBRID
(00007)   39156  A  0.35  H  1.00       0.00  SWEET WILLIAM  PURE WHITE
(00012)   96461     15.95        0.00       0.00  COMPOST KIT
(00014)   50013  A  0.45  K  1.00  L  1.85  CABBAGE, BURPEES DANISH ROUNDHEAD
(00016)   37515  A  0.35  H  1.00       0.00  SWEET WILLIAM  PINK BEAUTY
(00022)   62471  A  0.75  T  1.85  U  2.50  HYBRID CORN, HONEY AND CREAM
(00025)   36574  A  0.50  G  1.50       0.00  STOCKS - GIANT COLUMN MIXED COLORS
(00026)   43125  A  0.35  H  1.05  K  3.25  ZINNIAS - GIANTS OF CALIFORNIA MIXED
(00048)   33597  A  0.50  G  2.50       0.00  STOCKS - TRYSOMIC 7 WEEKS MIXED COLORS
(00049)   62547  A  0.50  L  1.10  S  2.75  CUCUMBER, BURPEE PICKLER
```

14.19 USING A HASH KEY TO UPDATE A RELATIVE FILE

Let us now examine a program (Figure 14.12) to update the hashed file created by the program in Figure 14.11.

```
 1      IDENTIFICATION DIVISION.
 2      PROGRAM-ID.
 3          UPDATE-HASHED.
 4      DATE-WRITTEN.
 5          APRIL 14, 1987.
 6
 7      ENVIRONMENT DIVISION.
 8      INPUT-OUTPUT SECTION.
 9      FILE-CONTROL.
10          SELECT UPDATE-FILE              ASSIGN TO S-UPDATE.
11          SELECT REL-PRODUCT-FILE         ASSIGN TO R-RELPROD
12                  FILE STATUS IS REL-STATUS
13                  ORGANIZATION IS RELATIVE
14                  ACCESS IS RANDOM
15                  RELATIVE KEY IS PRODUCT-KEY.
16
17      DATA DIVISION.
18
19      FILE SECTION.
20
21      FD  UPDATE-FILE
22          LABEL RECORDS ARE OMITTED.
23      01  UPDATE-RECORD.
24          05  CATALOG-NUMBER             PIC 9(5).
25          05  SIZE-1                     PIC X.
26          05  PRICE-1                    PIC 99V99.
27          05  SIZE-2                     PIC X.
28          05  PRICE-2                    PIC 99V99.
29          05  SIZE-3                     PIC X.
30          05  PRICE-3                    PIC 99V99.
31          05  DESCRIPTION                PIC X(40).
32          05  UPDATE-CODE                PIC X.
33              88  ADDITION                   VALUE '1'.
34              88  DELETION                   VALUE '2'.
35              88  CORRECTION                 VALUE '3'.
36
37      FD  REL-PRODUCT-FILE
38          LABEL RECORDS ARE STANDARD.
39      01  REL-PRODUCT-RECORD.
40          05  CATALOG-NUMBER             PIC X(5).
41          05  SIZE-1                     PIC X.
42          05  PRICE-1                    PIC 99V99  COMP-3.
43          05  SIZE-2                     PIC X.
44          05  PRICE-2                    PIC 99V99  COMP-3.
45          05  SIZE-3                     PIC X.
46          05  PRICE-3                    PIC 99V99  COMP-3.
47          05  DESCRIPTION                PIC X(40).
48
49      WORKING-STORAGE SECTION.
50
51      01  FILE-FULL-FLAG                 PIC X VALUE 'N'.
52          88  FILE-FULL                     VALUE 'Y'.
53
54      01  FILE-SIZE                     PIC 9(5) COMP SYNC VALUE 50.
55
56      01  KEY-QUOTIENT                  PIC 9(5) COMP SYNC.
57
58      01  MORE-DATA-REMAINS-FLAG        PIC X VALUE 'Y'.
59          88  MORE-DATA-REMAINS             VALUE 'Y'.
60          88  NO-MORE-DATA-REMAINS          VALUE 'N'.
61
```

```
62     01   PRODUCT-KEY                        PIC 9(5) COMP SYNC.
63
64     01   RECORD-FOUND-FLAG                  PIC X.
65          88   RECORD-FOUND                       VALUE 'Y'.
66          88   RECORD-NOT-FOUND                   VALUE 'N'.
67
68     01   REL-STATUS                         PIC XX VALUE 'XX'.
69
70     01   START-KEY                          PIC S9(5) COMP SYNC.
71
72
73     PROCEDURE DIVISION.
74     A000-UPDATE-PRODUCT-FILE.
75         OPEN INPUT UPDATE-FILE
76             I-O   REL-PRODUCT-FILE.
77         PERFORM B010-PROCESS-ONE-UPDATE
78             UNTIL NO-MORE-DATA-REMAINS.
79         CLOSE UPDATE-FILE
80             REL-PRODUCT-FILE.
81         STOP RUN.
82
83     B010-PROCESS-ONE-UPDATE.
84         READ UPDATE-FILE
85             AT END MOVE 'N' TO MORE-DATA-REMAINS-FLAG.
86         IF MORE-DATA-REMAINS
87             IF      ADDITION
88                 PERFORM C010-ADDITION
89             ELSE IF DELETION
90                 PERFORM C020-DELETION
91             ELSE IF CORRECTION
92                 PERFORM C030-CORRECTION
93             ELSE
94                 PERFORM C040-INVALID-TYPE.
95
96     C010-ADDITION.
97         PERFORM X010-COMPUTE-KEY.
98         IF FILE-FULL
99             DISPLAY 'BAD ADDITION; FILE IS FULL; CANNOT ADD '
100                    CATALOG-NUMBER OF UPDATE-RECORD
101        ELSE
102            IF RECORD-FOUND
103                DISPLAY 'BAD ADDITION; RECORD ALREADY EXISTS FOR '
104                        CATALOG-NUMBER OF UPDATE-RECORD
105            ELSE
106                MOVE CORRESPONDING UPDATE-RECORD TO
107                        REL-PRODUCT-RECORD
108                WRITE REL-PRODUCT-RECORD
109                    INVALID KEY DISPLAY 'BIG TROUBLES AT '
110                                        PRODUCT-KEY.
111
112    C020-DELETION.
113        PERFORM X010-COMPUTE-KEY.
114        IF RECORD-NOT-FOUND
115            DISPLAY 'BAD DELETION; NO RECORD IN FILE FOR '
116                    CATALOG-NUMBER OF UPDATE-RECORD
117        ELSE
118            DELETE REL-PRODUCT-FILE
119                    INVALID KEY DISPLAY 'BIG TROUBLES AT '
120                                        PRODUCT-KEY.
121
```

```
122      C030-CORRECTION.
123          PERFORM X010-COMPUTE-KEY.
124          IF RECORD-NOT-FOUND
125              DISPLAY 'BAD CORRECTION; NO RECORD IN FILE FOR '
126                      CATALOG-NUMBER OF UPDATE-RECORD
127          ELSE
128              MOVE CORRESPONDING UPDATE-RECORD TO REL-PRODUCT-RECORD
129              REWRITE REL-PRODUCT-RECORD
130                      INVALID KEY DISPLAY 'BIG TROUBLES AT '
131                                  PRODUCT-KEY.
132
133      C040-INVALID-TYPE.
134          DISPLAY 'THE FOLLOWING RECORD IS NEITHER AN UPDATE NOR '
135                  'A DELETION NOR A CORRECTION:  '.
136          DISPLAY '    "' UPDATE-RECORD '"'.
137
138      X010-COMPUTE-KEY.
139          DIVIDE CATALOG-NUMBER OF UPDATE-RECORD BY FILE-SIZE
140                  GIVING KEY-QUOTIENT
141                  REMAINDER PRODUCT-KEY.
142          ADD 1 TO PRODUCT-KEY.
143          MOVE 'X' TO RECORD-FOUND-FLAG.
144          MOVE PRODUCT-KEY TO START-KEY.
145          PERFORM X020-PROBE
146                  UNTIL RECORD-FOUND  OR  RECORD-NOT-FOUND OR
147                      FILE-FULL.
148
149      X020-PROBE.
150          READ REL-PRODUCT-FILE
151                  INVALID KEY MOVE 'N' TO RECORD-FOUND-FLAG.
152          IF RECORD-FOUND-FLAG = 'X'
153              IF CATALOG-NUMBER OF REL-PRODUCT-RECORD =
154              CATALOG-NUMBER OF UPDATE-RECORD
155                  MOVE 'Y' TO RECORD-FOUND-FLAG
156          ELSE
157              PERFORM X030-INCREMENT-KEY
158              IF PRODUCT-KEY = START-KEY
159                  MOVE 'Y' TO FILE-FULL-FLAG.
160
161      X030-INCREMENT-KEY.
162          ADD 1 TO PRODUCT-KEY.
163          IF PRODUCT-KEY > FILE-SIZE
164              MOVE 1 TO PRODUCT-KEY.
165
166
167      ********************** END OF PROGRAM **************************
```

FIGURE 14.12 A program to update a hash-coded relative record file.

The general organization of this program is very similar to that of pre-
vious update examples. The **SELECT** statement for **REL-PRODUCT-FILE** and the
FD for the file should be familiar by now, and paragraphs preceding **X010-
COMPUTE-KEY** in the Procedure Division are similar to those in Figure 14.10.

The work required to locate the proper record in the file is contained in the
three paragraphs beginning with **X010-COMPUTE-KEY**. While the code in these
paragraphs is similar to that used in the program that created the hash-coded

version of **REL-PRODUCT-FILE**, there are a few important differences. First, notice that we initialize **RECORD-FOUND-FLAG** to "**X**", which is neither **RECORD-FOUND** nor **RECORD-NOT-FOUND**. The reason for this is indicated by the **UNTIL** condition in the following **PERFORM** statement. Since this program is going to be modifying records that already exist on the relative file we want to search the file until one of three conditions is satisfied:

1. The record we want to update has been found;
2. A dummy record has been found, which indicates that the record we are looking for is not in the file;
3. We have gone all the way through the file and have arrived back at our starting point, which indicates that the file is full.

Since we don't know which of these conditions will terminate the **PERFORM**, **RECORD-FOUND-FLAG** is initialized to a neutral value. Paragraph **X020-PROBE** sets the flag to "**N**" if a dummy record is found or to "**Y**" if a record is found whose catalog number matches the catalog number of the update record. If the file is full, **FILE-FULL-FLAG** is set to "**Y**".

The resulting file, using the updates from previous examples, is shown below. Again notice that although the updates have been made correctly, the new records are scattered randomly through the file by the hashing algorithm.

```
(00005)   51904   A   0.75   J   4.50       0.00   CRENSHAH MELON, BURPEES EARLY HYBRID
(00007)   39156   A   0.35   H   1.00       0.00   SWEET WILLIAM  PURE WHITE
(00009)   31658   A   1.00   P   4.00       0.00   SNAPDRAGON, BRIGHT BUTTERFLIES, MIXED
(00011)   36160   A   0.50   K   1.50   L   1.75   ROYAL SWEET PEAS, MIXED
(00012)   96461      15.95          0.00       0.00   COMPOST KIT
(00013)   50260   A   0.75   J   4.50       0.00   EGGPLANT, EARLY BEAUTY HYBRID
(00016)   37515   A   0.35   H   1.00       0.00   SWEET WILLIAM  PINK BEAUTY
(00018)   51367   A   0.50   T   1.45   U   2.75   DECORATIVE CORN, RAINBOW
(00022)   62471   A   0.75   T   1.85   U   3.50   HYBRID CORN, HONEY AND CREAM
(00024)   31773   A   0.75   G   2.25       0.00   VERBENA, RUFFLED WHITE
(00025)   36574   A   0.50   G   1.50       0.00   STOCKS - GIANT COLUMN MIXED COLORS
(00026)   43125   A   0.35   H   1.05   K   3.25   ZINNIAS, GIANTS OF CALIFORNIA, MIXED
(00032)   15131       5.50          0.00       0.00   APPLE TREE, JONATHAN
(00048)   33597   A   0.50   G   2.50       0.00   STOCKS - TRYSOMIC 7 WEEKS MIXED COLORS
```

The examples and discussion that we have presented to demonstrate the use of hash coding and relative files should give you a general idea of what these files look like and how they can be used. However, the power and flexibility of direct access files goes far beyond what we can cover in this book. A more complete study of these topics is recommended for further study.

REVIEW QUESTIONS

1. What is the major advantage of organizing records in a magnetic tape file into blocks?
2. How does the **COBOL** compiler know that a file contains blocked records?
3. What would be involved in trying to access a tape file randomly?
4. Assume a magnetic tape with a recording density of 2000 characters per inch and a half-inch gap between blocks. Compare the amount of tape required to record 10,000 records of 200 characters each, under each of the following conditions:

    a. Records are unblocked; that is, each block contains one record.

    b. Each block contains 10 records.

    c. Each block contains 100 records.

5. In the program of Figure 14.4, how many times will the paragraph names **B010-VALIDATE-ONE-ORDER** be executed? The question actually has to do with the **PERFORM ... UNTIL** in the main paragraph, which is of the same form as that in programs that have carried out a performed paragraph once for each record in a file.

6. What would the program in Figure 14.4 do with a jumbled input file, where the records for any one order were not properly grouped together?

7. In the program of Figure 14.5 what would the occurrence of an invalid key indicate?

8. In the program of Figure 14.5 there is no priming **READ** in the main paragraph. Instead, the performed paragraph begins with a **READ** and if that **READ** does not detect the end of the file, there is a **WRITE**. Would it have been possible to use the program skeleton that has appeared in most of the other programs in the book, where there is a priming **READ** and where the performed paragraph begins with a **WRITE** followed by a **READ**?

9. Can you suggest a situation where it might be advantageous to sort the transactions in an indexed file updating applications even though the index file will have **ACCESS MODE IS RANDOM**?

10. In the program of Figure 14.7, what will happen if an order has two header records? How about two trailer records?

11. In the program of Figure 14.9, suppose we initialized **PRODUCT-KEY** to 100 instead of 1. Would we then start writing at record 100 instead of record 1?

12. Compare the program of Figure 14.9 to the program of Figure 14.5. How does the invalid key condition differ in the two programs?

13. We discussed the use of hash coding to locate a record in a relative file if there was no field that could be used directly as the relative key. Can you suggest other methods of locating records in a relative file besides hash coding?

ANSWERS

1. Except in unusual cases where records are already very large (thousands of bytes), record blocking saves both space on tape and time in reading the tape information.

2. The **FD** for that file has a **BLOCK CONTAINS** clause. This clause may specify either the number of records or the number of characters; in the latter case the compiler can deduce from the number of characters in the block and in the record how many records there are in the block.

3. For each transaction record it would be necessary to search the tape file, looking for a match between the key of the transaction record and the

keys of the tape records. If the search were begun from the beginning of the tape each time, one would expect to have to search halfway through the tape before finding a match. This could be accelerated somewhat by keeping track of the key of the most recent tape record and not rewinding the tape if the transaction key is after the current tape key, but even so the process would be hopelessly inefficient.

4. **a.** Each record requires a separate block containing 200 characters, which would take 0.1 inch, and a half-inch gap, for a total of 0.6 inches per record. This would require 6000 inches of tape, or 500 feet.

   b. There would be 1000 blocks, each containing 10 records. Each record thus contains 2000 characters, which is one inch. A thousand such blocks and a thousand gaps is 1500 inches, or 125 feet.

   c. There would be 100 blocks each 10 inches long plus 100 gaps, which is 1050 inches or 87.5 feet.

   The point is that although there is a big saving in tape in blocking records, the curve of improvement flattens out as the blocks become vary large. Once blocks have been made moderately large, any further gains would be canceled out by the requirements for very large tape buffers in main storage.

5. The paragraph will be carried out as many times as there are *orders* in the file. In the extreme case of a file consisting of one order having many records, the paragraph would be carried out once. The point is that control stays in the paragraph until the **PERFORM** logic in the main paragraph determines either that the beginning of a new group has been detected or that the end of the file has been reached.

6. The results would essentially be meaningless, but the program would run without error indication, processing whatever groups it might find. The answer to this unacceptable state of affairs is to include sequence checking in the program.

7. In the creation of an indexed file, the records are required to be in ascending sequence and there must be no duplicate keys. The **INVALID KEY** phrase checks for the occurrence of either of these errors in the input.

8. Certainly. The program was written as it was partly to demonstrate that we usually do have this choice, but mostly because this way fits in better with the requirements of the program of Figure 14.7.

9. Transactions can be processed against an indexed file somewhat more rapidly if they are in sequence than if they are not. However, it would be unusual for the time savings to be large enough to justify the time required to sort the transactions.

10. If the order has two headers, the first header will be treated as an order without a trailer record and will be reported accordingly, while the second header will be treated as the start of a new order. If there are two trailer records, the second trailer will be treated as an order without a header record.

11. No. In current versions of **COBOL**, if the file is defined with **ACCESS IS SE-QUENTIAL** and is opened for output, the relative key is ignored in determining where records are to be written. If present, the relative key is

assigned the record number as the record is written but that is its only use. In earlier versions of COBOL, prior to COBOL-74, the relative key could be used to set the location of the record being written.

12. In a relative file (Figure 14.9), the invalid key condition indicated that you are trying to write a record beyond the physical bounds of the file. In an indexed file (Figure 14.5), the invalid key condition indicates a duplicate key or a record out of sequence, both having to do with errors in the input data.

13. There are several other ways of locating records in a relative record file. One of the most common is to use a secondary file, such as an indexed file, as a *key* file. Records in the indexed file would use some key field as the record key of the file, then would contain the relative key of the actual data record as data in the indexed records. To find a record in the relative file, you would use its key to find a record in the indexed file, then use the data in the indexed record as the relative key to find the record in the relative file.

EXERCISES

1. Modify the program in Figure 14.4 so that it sequence checks the transaction file.

2. Modify the program in Figure 14.7 to include sequence checking. This should check both the order number and the record type, to be sure that records for each order are in proper sequence. (This does not greatly complicate the test.)

3. Modify the program in Figure 14.7 to include validation of the trailer record. This will require totaling the amounts on the body records.

4. Add checking to the program of Figure 14.7 so that it labels as erroneous any order that does not contain exactly one header record, at least one body record, and exactly one trailer record, in that order.

5. Modify the program of Figure 14.7 so that the catalog file is a relative record file instead of an indexed file. Use hash coding to find records.

6. Combine the program of Figure 14.7 with an appropriately modified version of the program in Figure 11.1 to produce a complete validation program for the seed catalog orders.

7. (This exercise is suitable for a project.)

   The product file for the National Widget Corporation has the following format:

Columns 1-5	product code	PIC AA999
Columns 6-30	product description	PIC X(25)
Columns 31-35	sales for three weeks ago	PIC 9(5)
Columns 36-40	sales for two weeks ago	PIC 9(5)
Columns 41-45	sales for last week	PIC 9(5)
Columns 46-50	inventory level	PIC 9(5)
Columns 51-57	selling price in dollars and cents	PIC 9(5)V99

   When merchandise is received from a supplier, a record with the following format is prepared:

Column 1	record type ("A")	PIC X
Columns 2-6	product code	PIC AA999
Columns 7-12	quantity received	PIC 9(6)
Columns 13-19	supplier code	PIC 99A9(4)
Columns 20-25	purchase order number	PIC 9(6)
Columns 26-31	date received (YYMMDD)	PIC 9(6)
Columns 32-47	not used	

When merchandise is sold, a sales record is prepared, in the following format:

Column 1	record type ("B")	PIC X
Columns 2-6	product code	PIC AA999
Columns 7-14	transaction number	PIC 9(8)
Columns 15-21	customer number	PIC 9(7)
Columns 22-25	quantity sold	PIC 9(4)
Columns 26-33	amount of sale	PIC 9(6)V99
Columns 34-39	date of sale (YYMMDD)	PIC 9(6)
Columns 40-47	not used	

If merchandise is returned by a customer, a record describing the return is prepared with the following format:

Column 1	record type ("C")	PIC X
Columns 2-6	product code	PIC AA999
Columns 7-14	reference number	PIC 9(8)
Columns 15-22	credit number	PIC 9(8)
Columns 23-29	customer number	PIC 9(7)
Columns 30-33	quantity returned	PIC 9(4)
Columns 34-41	credit amount	PIC 9(6)V99
Columns 42-47	date of return (YYMMDD)	PIC 9(6)

An inventory maintenance program uses the transaction records (receipt, sales, and return) to maintain the current inventory level of all products. At the end of each working day, all transactions for the day are processed against the master file. The records are not sorted; they are simply in chronological order, i.e., the order in which the various activities occurred. When a merchandise receipt is processed, the quantity received is added to the current inventory level. For sales records the quantity sold is subtracted from the current inventory level, and for returns the quantity returned is added to the inventory level.

To prevent data entry errors from causing errors in the inventory processing, the transactions are edited before they are processed. The record type must be A, B, or C. The product code must correspond to a record in the product file, and the merchandise quantity must be numeric. Dates must be valid. That is, the month must be in the range 1-12, the day must be valid for the month (February 30, for example, is not valid), and the date must be less than or equal to the date on which the data is being processed. Finally, if the inventory level ever goes below zero this should be reported as an error.

The product file is maintained as a relative file, keyed to product code. Keys are computed using a hashing algorithm based on product code, with linear probing being used to resolve collisions. The hashing algorithm is the following:

1. Convert the first letter of the product code to its numeric equivalent; that is, A = 1, B = 2, ..., Z = 26;
2. Multiply the result of step 1 by 1000;
3. Add the numeric portion of the product code to the result of step 2;
4. Divide the result of step 3 by 7500 and add 1 to the remainder;
5. The result of step 4 is the relative key.

For example, suppose we have a product code of KB152. The numeric equivalent of K is 11. Multiplying this by 1000 gives 11000. To this we add 152, giving 11152. Dividing 11152 by 7500 gives a quotient of 1 (which we ignore) and a remainder of 3652. Adding 1 to the remainder gives the relative key of 3653.

Assume you have a sequential product master file, sorted on product key. Write a program to convert this to a relative file using a technique similar to that shown in Figure 14.11. Write a second program to print the relative file. Finally, write a program that takes a file of transaction records in the formats given above and applies these transactions to the master file to update the inventory level. Be sure that your update program makes the edit tests required, reports any errors detected, and rejects invalid transaction records. Print the relative file both before and after the update program is run.

8. The same as Exercise 7, except create an indexed file for the product file instead of a relative file.

CHAPTER 15

CHARACTER MANIPULATION

15.1 INTRODUCTION

A considerable amount of the work that is performed in a typical COBOL program involves manipulating character data. We have seen examples of this when we move numeric data into a numeric edited field, or simply MOVE one character field to another. However, these examples all involve moving one complete field to another, and there are times when we need to perform manipulation of the characters within a single field. We may need to count the number of times a particular character occurs in a field, we may need to replace all occurrences of one character with another (such as replacing blanks by zeros or zeros by blanks), or we may need to extract selected portions of a field (such as separating house number and street name in a field keyed simply as "address"). COBOL has three statements for character manipulation: INSPECT, STRING, and UNSTRING. We shall discuss each of these statements and show how each might be used. In the following discussion, the term "string" will be used to represent a sequence of characters, generally a single field.

15.2 THE INSPECT STATEMENT

Consider the following record:

```
01   PAY-RECORD.
     05   EMPLOYEE-ID        PIC X(6).
     05   DEPARTMENT         PIC XX.
     05   ACCOUNT-NUMBER     PIC X(5).
     05   REGULAR-HOURS      PIC 99V99.
     05   OVERTIME-HOURS     PIC 99V99.
```

Suppose we discover that leading zeros in **REGULAR-HOURS** and **OVER-TIME-HOURS** have been entered as spaces. Further, we find that if the value of either field is zero, it has been left entirely blank. This creates several serious processing problems. If we try to perform arithmetic on a field containing all blanks we will probably get an error, possibly even an abend. Furthermore, if we test these fields to see if they are numeric, leading blanks will not be numeric. Up to now we have no good way of dealing with this problem. Although we could test to see if a field is equal to spaces, this complicates the program and still does not deal with the problem of *leading* spaces in a field that is not entirely blank. Some computers may treat leading spaces as zero, but we should not count on all computer hardware conveniently giving the right result. We could require that the data be rekeyed in the input file, but for large files this would not be practical, and there is a much better solution in any case.

A simple solution to the problem lies with the **INSPECT** statement. Before we process the data in the record, we execute the following statements:

```
INSPECT REGULAR-HOURS   REPLACING LEADING SPACES BY ZERO.
INSPECT OVERTIME-HOURS  REPLACING LEADING SPACES BY ZERO.
```

These statements scan **REGULAR-HOURS** and **OVERTIME-HOURS** and substitute a zero for each leading space. We could also write

```
INSPECT REGULAR-HOURS   REPLACING ALL SPACES BY ZERO.
INSPECT OVERTIME-HOURS  REPLACING ALL SPACES BY ZERO.
```

However, this would change *all* blanks to zeros, including spaces that were erroneously keyed in the middle of a field or at the right end of the field, which we do not want.

The basic functions of the **INSPECT** statement are the following:

1. Count the number of times a specified sequence of characters occurs in a string;
2. Replace specified characters with other characters;
3. Do both counting and replacing.

The actual format of the **INSPECT** statement is quite complex and we will not attempt to show it here or discuss all its possible uses. We will, however, show a few examples of what can be done with the **INSPECT**.

The first option is to count occurrences of characters in any of several possible contexts:

1. All occurrences of a character in a string;
2. All *leading* occurrences of a character; that is, before any other character occurs in the string;
3. All occurrences of a character *before* the *first* occurrence of some other specified character;
4. All occurrences of a character *after* the *first* occurrence of some other specified character;
5. All characters occurring *before* some *specified* character;
6. All characters occurring *after* some *specified* character.

For example, we might have statements such as the following:

INSPECT Statement	Sample	Resulting value of COUNTER
INSPECT SAMPLE TALLYING COUNTER FOR ALL '0'.	102030	3
INSPECT SAMPLE TALLYING COUNTER FOR ALL LEADING '0'.	102030	0
INSPECT SAMPLE TALLYING COUNTER FOR ALL LEADING '0'.	002030	2
INSPECT SAMPLE TALLYING COUNTER FOR ALL '0' BEFORE '3'.	002030	3
INSPECT SAMPLE TALLYING COUNTER FOR ALL '0' AFTER '3'.	003030	2
INSPECT SAMPLE TALLYING COUNTER FOR CHARACTERS BEFORE 'C'.	AABACA	4
INSPECT SAMPLE TALLYING COUNTER FOR CHARACTERS AFTER 'B'.	AABABA	3

For this version of the **INSPECT** statement we specify the identifier to be examined, then specify the variable used to tally the number of character occurrences found, and finally define the characters to be counted and the context in which they occur. It is important to note that the **TALLYING** option does not *store* the character count in the tallying variable (**COUNTER** in the examples), it *adds* the count to the current value of the variable. Thus in the preceding examples, we assume that **COUNTER** has a value of zero prior to the execution of each **INSPECT** statement.

We have already seen one example of the second **INSPECT** option, replacing leading blanks with zeros. Just as tallying can be done in several different contexts, so can replacing. In fact, the replacing option can also be limited to replacing just the first occurrence of a character. The following examples will demonstrate some of the replacing options. We will use the underscore character (_) to denote blanks.

INSPECT Statement	SAMPLE Before	SAMPLE After
INSPECT SAMPLE REPLACING ALL SPACES BY ZERO.	__2_3_	002030
INSPECT SAMPLE REPLACING LEADING SPACES BY ZERO.	__2_3_	002_3_
INSPECT SAMPLE REPLACING ALL 'A' BY 'B' BEFORE 'X'.	AABXAA	BBBXAA
INSPECT SAMPLE REPLACING CHARACTERS BY 'Z' AFTER 'X'.	AAXXBC	AAXZZZ
INSPECT SAMPLE REPLACING ALL 'A' BY 'X', 'B' BY 'Y', 'C' BY 'Z' AFTER SPACE.	ABC_ABC	XYC_XYZ
INSPECT SAMPLE REPLACING ALL 'ABC' BY 'XYZ' AFTER SPACE.	ABC_ABC	ABC_XYZ
INSPECT SAMPLE REPLACING FIRST 'X' AFTER 'Y' BY 'Z'.	XYXYXX	XYZYXX

Finally, we can perform both tallying and replacing in the same operation. As with the previous examples of the **TALLYING** option, we assume that **COUNTER** is set to zero prior to the execution of each **INSPECT** statement.

		SAMPLE		
INSPECT Statement		Before	After	COUNTER

INSPECT SAMPLE TALLYING COUNTER
    FOR ALL '0'
    REPLACING '0' BY SPACE.
		0016047	__16_47	3

INSPECT SAMPLE TALLYING COUNTER
    FOR LEADING '0'
    REPLACING FIRST '0' BY 'X'.
		0016047	X016047	2

INSPECT SAMPLE TALLYING COUNTER
    FOR LEADING '*'
    REPLACING ALL '.' BY ',',
    FIRST '*' BY '$'.
		****.123.456	$***,123,456	4

As we indicated at the start of this section, these examples merely scratch the surface of what can be done with the **INSPECT** statement. For instance, the **INSPECT** statement can be used in combination with the **UNSTRING** statement (see Section 15.4) to extract data from strings. The serious **COBOL** programmer should study the appropriate **COBOL** manual for further details.

15.3 THE STRING STATEMENT

The **STRING** statement permits us to assemble fields from various locations into one combined string. In its simplest form it is no different from a series of **MOVE**s, but features are available to do things that can be accomplished only with much greater effort otherwise.

For example, suppose that we have these entries in the Working-Storage Section of a program.

```
WORKING-STORAGE SECTION.

01  CREDIT-MASTER-RECORD.
    05   CUSTOMER-NUMBER          PIC X(5).
    05   CUSTOMER-NAME            PIC X(20).
    05   CUSTOMER-ADDRESS         PIC X(60).
    05   OLD-BALANCE              PIC $$,$$9.99.

01  MONTHLY-SUMMARY-RECORD.
    05   CURRENT-PURCHASES        PIC $$,$$9.99.
    05   CREDIT-AVAILABLE         PIC $$,$$9.99.
    05   BALANCE-DUE              PIC $$,$$9.99.

01  INITIAL-POSITION             PIC 99.
```

We wish to prepare a line containing, in sequence, **CUSTOMER-NAME**, **CUSTOMER-NUMBER**, **OLD-BALANCE**, **CURRENT-PURCHASES**, **BALANCE-DUE**, and **CREDIT-AVAILABLE**. For simplicity, we shall assume that only a single space is required between fields, although providing any number of spaces would not be difficult. All of the items except **CREDIT-AVAILABLE** are to be moved to the combined output line in their entirety. **CREDIT-AVAILABLE**, however, is to have its decimal point and the cents position deleted. Finally, we want to be able to make the starting position of the first field in the line variable. We can imagine that certain classes of accounts might need to be indented differently from others, for instance.

All of this can be done with the statements shown on the next page.

```
MOVE SPACES TO BILLING-RECORD.
MOVE 14 TO INITIAL-POSITION.

STRING
    CUSTOMER-NAME DELIMITED BY SIZE
    SPACE
    CUSTOMER-NUMBER DELIMITED BY SIZE
    SPACE
    OLD-BALANCE DELIMITED BY SIZE
    SPACE
    CURRENT-PURCHASES DELIMITED BY SIZE
    SPACE
    BALANCE-DUE DELIMITED BY SIZE
    SPACE
    CREDIT-AVAILABLE DELIMITED BY '.'
        INTO BILLING-RECORD
        WITH POINTER INITIAL-POSITION.

WRITE BILLING-RECORD.
```

We begin by moving spaces to the output line, which is called **BILLING-RECORD**, to remove any contents that might be in positions of the record in which we shall place no data. We then place 14 in the item that will be used as a pointer to determine where the first field is placed in the line. Now comes the **STRING** statement. In this we list all of the items that are to be combined into one string. For each, we indicate whether it is delimited by size, which means simply that the entire item is to be moved, or whether it is delimited by some character in the field. For **CREDIT-AVAILABLE** we indicate that it is delimited by a period, which means that only the characters before the decimal point will be moved. We then indicate the name of the item (**BILLING-RECORD**) that will hold the combined string and designate the pointer.

When the **WITH POINTER** clause is used, the **STRING** statement automatically updates the value of the pointer so that after the statement has been executed, the pointer points to the first byte following the end of the string. For example, if the pointer initially contains the value 1 and we insert strings with a total of 15 bytes, the pointer will contain the value 16 after execution of the **STRING** statement.

Here is a line produced when these statements were executed with illustrative data in the records:

```
J. B. HUGHES         12609 $1,058.40    $126.27 $1,184.67    $815
```

The general format for the **STRING** statement is as follows:

$$
\textbf{STRING} \quad \left\{ \left\{ \begin{array}{l} \text{identifier-1} \\ \text{literal-1} \end{array} \right\} \ldots \textbf{DELIMITED BY} \left\{ \begin{array}{l} \text{identifier-2} \\ \text{literal-2} \\ \textbf{SIZE} \end{array} \right\} \right\} \ldots
$$

$\underline{\textbf{INTO}}$ identifier-3

[**WITH** **POINTER** identifier-4]

[**ON** **OVERFLOW** imperative-statement]

COBOL-85

In **COBOL-85**, the **STRING** statement may be terminated with an optional **END-STRING** phrase.

END COBOL-85

Observe that we are able to intermix data items and literals at will. Providing more than one space between fields in the example above would be a simple matter of using nonnumeric literals. Delimiters can also be identifiers, which means that we can use the value of some other problem data to terminate transmission of fields. An **ON OVERFLOW** option is available to specify what should be done if there is insufficient space in the receiving item for all the items being sent to it. Although we have shown only a simple example, it should be obvious that the **STRING** statement can be used to perform tasks like removing blanks from the ends of fields in name and address lines, producing customized form letters, and so on.

15.4 THE UNSTRING STATEMENT

The **UNSTRING** statement is the opposite of the **STRING** statement in that it permits us to distribute fields within one combined item into any number of separate elementary items. The sending field must contain delimiters that can be used to determine the lengths of the fields that are to be distributed. We shall consider one simple but useful example and then shall sketch the other features that are available.

We are given a file of records each consisting of a person's name and address. A legitimate address in this application is allowed to have from two to five lines. The information for the lines of an address is keyed in a record with equal signs for delimiters. For example, here are the sample input records to be used with the program that we shall study shortly:

```
D G GOLDEN=CLEVELAND STATE UNIVERSITY=CLEVELAND, OHIO 44115=
MR. ASHLEY H. WOODSON=223 MAPLE PLACE=APT. 3D=ANYTOWN, USA 12345=
MS. J. D. APPLETON=ENGINEERING DEPT.=ACME MFG. CO.=1200 YORK=ARKVILLE, GA 36000=
MR. T.H.JONES=MAIL DROP 23K=BLDG. 239=GENERAL ELECTRONICS=ROSETOWN, PA 18900=
JAMES B. THOMPSON, ESQ.=SMALLTOWN, NY 14200=
JAMES B. THOMPSON, ESQ.==SMALLTOWN, NY 14200=
ROGER MILLS=
MR. ROGER B. SHILLITO 23 ELM STREET GEORGETOWN, PA 15200
J C CLARK=DATA PROC=MAIL CODE 45=NORTH PLANT BLDG. 6=ACME CO.=ACKLEY, NJ 03800=
```

We wish to produce mailing labels for each address. Each label is to consist of six lines, the sixth line always being blank. If the input record contains only one line, it is assumed to be mistyped and we shall replace it with an error message. (In real life other measures would probably need to be taken, but this is sufficient to indicate the possibilities.) Likewise, if an address contains more than five lines, it will be considered to be erroneous.

A program to read such records and print the labels is shown in Figure 15.1. Everything is familiar until we come to the paragraph named **B010-PRODUCE-ONE-LABEL**. We begin by clearing the storage space for all six lines and resetting the flag that will tell us if there are more than five lines. We then move zero to the item that will count the number of fields filled, with which we can determine if there was only one line. The **UNSTRING** statement is fairly straightforward. We indicate what the delimiter is; name the items that are to receive the fields separated by this delimiter; specify the item that is to receive the tally of fields filled; and specify what to do if information remains in the sending item after all receiving items have been filled. The rest of the program is routine.

There is one subtle point to be careful of, however. **UNSTRING** scans the sending item to the end of the item, not just to the last delimiter. Any spaces to the right of the last delimiter are treated as a blank field and the end of the sending item is treated as an implied delimiter. Thus, for example, the first record produces *four* lines, the last of which consists of 20 blanks.

```
00001          IDENTIFICATION DIVISION.
00002          PROGRAM-ID.
00003              UNSTRING-DEMO.
00004          DATE-WRITTEN.
00005              MAY 15, 1987.
00006
00007          ENVIRONMENT DIVISION.
00008          INPUT-OUTPUT SECTION.
00009          FILE-CONTROL.
00010              SELECT ADDRESS-FILE         ASSIGN TO S-ADDRESS.
00011              SELECT LABEL-FILE           ASSIGN TO S-LABELS.
00012
00013          DATA DIVISION.
00014
00015          FILE SECTION.
00016
00017          FD  ADDRESS-FILE
00018              LABEL RECORDS ARE OMITTED.
00019          01  ADDRESS-RECORD              PIC X(80).
00020
00021          FD LABEL-FILE
00022              LABEL RECORDS ARE OMITTED.
00023          01  LABEL-RECORD                PIC X(132).
00024
00025          WORKING-STORAGE SECTION.
00026
00027          01  ADDRESS-WORK-AREA.
00028              05  ADDRESS-LINE-1          PIC X(132).
00029              05  ADDRESS-LINE-2          PIC X(132).
00030              05  ADDRESS-LINE-3          PIC X(132).
00031              05  ADDRESS-LINE-4          PIC X(132).
00032              05  ADDRESS-LINE-5          PIC X(132).
00033              05  ADDRESS-LINE-6          PIC X(132).
00034
00035          01  FIELDS-FILLED               PIC 99.
00036
00037          01  FIELD-OVERFLOW-FLAG         PIC X.
00038              88  FIELD-OVERFLOW                  VALUE 'Y'.
00039
00040          01  MORE-DATA-REMAINS-FLAG      PIC X VALUE 'Y'.
00041              88  NO-MORE-DATA-REMAINS            VALUE 'N'.
00042
00043
```

```
00044              PROCEDURE DIVISION.
00045              A000-PRODUCE-LABELS.
00046                  OPEN INPUT ADDRESS-FILE
00047                      OUTPUT LABEL-FILE.
00048                  READ ADDRESS-FILE
00049                      AT END MOVE 'N' TO MORE-DATA-REMAINS-FLAG.
00050                  PERFORM B010-PRODUCE-ONE-LABEL
00051                      UNTIL NO-MORE-DATA-REMAINS.
00052                  CLOSE ADDRESS-FILE
00053                        LABEL-FILE.
00054                  STOP RUN.
00055
00056              B010-PRODUCE-ONE-LABEL.
00057                  MOVE SPACES TO             ADDRESS-WORK-AREA.
00058                  MOVE 'N' TO               FIELD-OVERFLOW-FLAG.
00059                  MOVE ZERO TO              FIELDS-FILLED.
00060                  UNSTRING ADDRESS-RECORD DELIMITED BY '='
00061                      INTO ADDRESS-LINE-1
00062                           ADDRESS-LINE-2
00063                           ADDRESS-LINE-3
00064                           ADDRESS-LINE-4
00065                           ADDRESS-LINE-5
00066                           ADDRESS-LINE-6
00067                      TALLYING IN FIELDS-FILLED
00068                      ON OVERFLOW MOVE 'Y' TO FIELD-OVERFLOW-FLAG.
00069                  IF FIELDS-FILLED IS LESS THAN 3  OR  FIELD-OVERFLOW
00070                      MOVE 'BAD ADDRESS' TO ADDRESS-WORK-AREA.
00071                  WRITE LABEL-RECORD FROM ADDRESS-LINE-1.
00072                  WRITE LABEL-RECORD FROM ADDRESS-LINE-2.
00073                  WRITE LABEL-RECORD FROM ADDRESS-LINE-3.
00074                  WRITE LABEL-RECORD FROM ADDRESS-LINE-4.
00075                  WRITE LABEL-RECORD FROM ADDRESS-LINE-5.
00076                  WRITE LABEL-RECORD FROM ADDRESS-LINE-6.
00077                  READ ADDRESS-FILE
00078                      AT END MOVE 'N' TO MORE-DATA-REMAINS-FLAG.
00079
00080     ******************** END OF PROGRAM ************************
```

FIGURE 15.1 A program using the **UNSTRING** statement to distribute variable length fields of an input record to separate lines for printing.

Here is the output produced when the input records shown earlier were processed by this program.

```
D G GOLDEN
CLEVELAND STATE UNIVERSITY
CLEVELAND, OHIO 44115


MR. ASHLEY H. WOODSON
223 MAPLE PLACE
APT. 3D
ANYTOWN, USA 12345


MS. J. D. APPLETON
ENGINEERING DEPT.
ACME MFG. CO.
1200 YORK
ARKVILLE, GA 36000
```

```
MR. T.H.JONES
MAIL DROP 23K
BLDG. 239
GENERAL ELECTRONICS
ROSETOWN, PA 18900

JAMES B. THOMPSON, ESQ.
SMALLTOWN, NY 14200




JAMES B. THOMPSON, ESQ.

SMALLTOWN, NY 14200



BAD ADDRESS



BAD ADDRESS



BAD ADDRESS
```

The **UNSTRING** statement provides a number of other capabilities that are not illustrated in this program, as we see by considering the following general format:

UNSTRING identifier-1

$$\left[\text{\underline{DELIMITED} BY [\underline{ALL}]} \left\{ \begin{array}{l} \text{identifier-2} \\ \text{literal-1} \end{array} \right\} \left[\text{OR [\underline{ALL}]} \left\{ \begin{array}{l} \text{identifier-3} \\ \text{literal-2} \end{array} \right\} \right] \dots \right]$$

[**INTO** identifier-4 [**DELIMITER IN** identifier-5] [**COUNT IN** identifier-6] . . .

[**WITH POINTER** identifier-7] [**TALLYING IN** identifier-8]

[**ON OVERFLOW** imperative-statement]

COBOL-85

In **COBOL-85**, the **UNSTRING** statement may be terminated with an optional **ENDSTRING** phrase.

END COBOL-85

We see that delimiters may be either identifiers or literals and that there may be any number of them. We could, for instance, have an **UNSTRING** statement with this phrase in it

UNSTRING RECORD-A DELIMITED BY ALL SPACES OR '/' OR FIELD-A

This would mean that any one or more blanks is a delimiter, or that a slash is a delimiter, or that the contents of **FIELD-A** is a delimiter. In all cases, delimiters may be one or more characters.

It is possible to specify, for any field moved, that a count of the number of characters in the field should be placed in a specified location. The pointer option allows us to begin unstringing the sending item at other than the first character in it.

The **STRING** and **UNSTRING** statements are very powerful features of the **COBOL** language. They permit us to do in a simple way things that in some instances would otherwise be extremely difficult to do and much less easy to understand, and in some installations they are used quite frequently.

REVIEW QUESTIONS

1. Show what the contents of **SAMPLE** and **COUNTER** would be after the execution of each of the following **INSPECT** statements with the initial values of the eleven-character **SAMPLE** that are shown, and an initial value of zero for **COUNTER**.

	SAMPLE
INSPECT SAMPLE TALLYING COUNTER FOR CHARACTERS BEFORE ','.	$128,064.32
INSPECT SAMPLE REPLACING ALL '*' BY SPACE.	$*****12.69
INSPECT SAMPLE TALLYING COUNTER FOR ALL '-' REPLACING ALL '-' BY SPACE.	535-22-1583
INSPECT SAMPLE REPLACING FIRST '.' BY 'X'.	9A6.77X.,XX
INSPECT SAMPLE TALLYING COUNTER FOR ALL SPACES.	JOHN SMITH
INSPECT SAMPLE TALLYING COUNTER FOR ALL '.' REPLACING ALL '.' BY SPACE.	T.F.X.JONES
INSPECT SAMPLE TALLYING COUNTER FOR ALL LEADING SPACES.	1.23

2. What is the difference between the **STRING** and **UNSTRING** statements?

3. What is the function of the **DELIMITED** clause in the **STRING** statement? The **POINTER** clause?

4. What happens in the **UNSTRING** statement if there are too many substrings in the sending field to fit into the receiving fields? What if there are too few substrings to fill the receiving fields?

ANSWERS

1.

SAMPLE	COUNTER
No Change	4
$ 12.69	No Change
535 22 1583	2
9A6X77X.,XX	No Change
No Change	2
T F X JONES	3
No Change	7

2. The **STRING** statement takes strings from several elementary fields and connects them together to form one long string in a new field. The **UNSTRING** statement extracts strings from one elementary field and distributes them into several separate elementary fields.

3. The **DELIMITED** clause tells the program how to detect the end of a string in a sending field. The string might consist of the entire sending field, or just the portion terminated by a specified character. The **POINTER** clause tells the program where to start building the new string in the receiving field.

4. If there is not sufficient space in the receiving fields in an **UNSTRING** statement, the overflow condition is raised and the action specified in the **ON OVERFLOW** clause is executed. Any space in the receiving fields not filled by substrings from the sending field is left unchanged.

EXERCISES

*1. Write **INSPECT** statements to do the following.

   a. Change all the blank characters in **ITEM-A** to zeros.

   b. Change the first A in **ITEM-B** to 2.

   c. Place in **STRING-TALLY** a count of the number of leading asterisks in **ITEM-C**.

   d. Convert all leading asterisks in **ITEM-D** to zeros and place in **COUNTER** a count of the number of leading asterisks.

   e. Change all characters in **ITEM-E** that precede the first X to 9s.

2. Write **INSPECT** statements to do the following.

   a. Count the number of commas in **GRAND-TOTAL** and place that number in **COMMAS**.

   b. Replace the first blank in **LAST-NAME** with a period.

   c. Change all the characters in **ERROR-FIELD** up to the first hyphen to blanks, and place a count of the number of characters replaced in **COUNTER**.

---

* Answers to starred exercises will be found in Appendix IV at the end of the book.

*3. Assume that a customer record has the following format:

```
01  CUSTOMER-RECORD.
    05  CUSTOMER-NAME.
        10  LAST-NAME          PIC X(15).
        10  FIRST-NAME         PIC X(15).
        10  TITLE              PIC X(5).
    05  CUSTOMER-ADDRESS.
        10  HOUSE-NUMBER       PIC X(5).
        10  STREET-NAME        PIC X(15).
        10  CITY               PIC X(15).
        10  STATE              PIC X(15).
        10  ZIP                PIC X(5).
    05  REST-OF-RECORD         PIC X(110).
```

TITLE contains the customer's title such as Mr., Mrs., Ms., Dr., etc. Using the customer record as input, write a program segment that will produce the heading and salutation for a form letter. There should be no extra blanks anywhere in the text. The output should resemble the following:

Ms. Mary Smith
123 Main St.
Anytown, Ohio 44999

Dear Ms. Smith:

4. Suppose you are given a file of records containing heading lines like the example shown in Exercise 3. The records have the format **PIC X(50)**, and there are three records for each customer; assume there are no errors in the data. Write a program that will read this file as input and create a file of customer records having the format shown at the start of Exercise 3; set **REST-OF-RECORD** to spaces.

CHAPTER 16

THE REPORT WRITER

16.1 INTRODUCTION

All the programs we have examined so far have required some form of printed output. Although we tended to make this output as simple as possible to save space and avoid complication, in actual programs preparing the formatted output for reports can require as much work as calculating the results to be reported. This is particularly true if the report involves control breaks, as we saw in Chapter 9; you may wish to review Chapter 9 before proceeding.

In this chapter we will present some features of COBOL that can simplify the work of producing reports. We will begin with some options available for sequential print files, then go on to discuss the COBOL Report Writer.

16.2 PRINT FILE ENHANCEMENTS

A task common to most reports is producing a heading at the top of each page. Using only the material we have presented so far, this requires defining a variable to be used as a line counter. The counter is initialized at the start of the program, incremented each time a line is printed or skipped over, tested to see if we are at the bottom of the page, then reset at the start of the next page. However, we can let COBOL do most of this work by using the LINAGE clause. To demonstrate how this works we have modified the payroll program of Figure 8.5 to allow the program to print the report on more than one page, with column headings at the top of each page. We have omitted those parts of the program that do not relate to producing the report, as seen in Figure 16.1.

```
00001          IDENTIFICATION DIVISION.
00002          PROGRAM-ID.
00003             PAYROLL5.
00004          DATE-WRITTEN.
00005             APRIL 22, 1987.
00006
```

```
00007              ENVIRONMENT DIVISION.
00008              INPUT-OUTPUT SECTION.
00009              FILE-CONTROL.
00010                  SELECT PAYROLL-FILE      ASSIGN TO S-PAYROLL.
00011                  SELECT REPORT-FILE       ASSIGN TO S-REPORT.
00012
00013              DATA DIVISION.
00014              FILE SECTION.
00015              FD  PAYROLL-FILE
00016                  LABEL RECORDS ARE OMITTED.
00017              01  PAYROLL-RECORD.
00018                  05  I-PAYROLL-NUMBER     PIC X(5).
00019                  05  I-NAME               PIC X(20).
00020                  05  I-HOURS-WORKED       PIC 99V9.
00021                  05  FILLER               PIC X(3).
00022                  05  I-PAYRATE            PIC 99V999.
00023                  05  I-DEPENDENTS         PIC 99.
00024                  05  FILLER               PIC X(42).
00025
00026              FD  REPORT-FILE
00027                  LABEL RECORDS ARE OMITTED
00028                  LINAGE IS 15 LINES
00029                      WITH FOOTING AT 15
00030                      LINES AT TOP 3
00031                      LINES AT BOTTOM 3.
00032              01  REPORT-RECORD            PIC X(76).
00033
00034              WORKING-STORAGE SECTION.
                     .
                     .
                     .
00040              77  W-OUT-OF-RECORDS-FLAG    PIC X           VALUE 'N'.
00041                  88  OUT-OF-RECORDS                       VALUE 'Y'.
                     .
                     .
                     .
00051              01  HEADING-LINE-1.
00052                  05  FILLER               PIC X.
00053                  05  FILLER               PIC X(26)
00054                      VALUE 'PAYROLL CALCULATION REPORT'.
00055                  05  FILLER               PIC X(41)       VALUE SPACES.
00056                  05  REPORT-DATE.
00057                  10  MM                   PIC Z9/.
00058                  10  DD                   PIC 99/.
00059                  10  YY                   PIC 99.
00060
00061              01  HEADING-LINE-2.
00062                  05  FILLER               PIC X.
00063                  05  FILLER               PIC X(42)
00064                      VALUE 'NUMBER         NAME             HOURS  RATE  '.
00065                  05  FILLER               PIC X(29)
00066                      VALUE ' DEP  GROSS     TAX     NET'.
00067
00068              01  NORMAL-OUTPUT-LINE.
00069                  05  FILLER               PIC X.
00070                  05  O-PAYROLL-NUMBER     PIC X(5).
00071                  05  O-NAME               PIC BBX(20).
00072                  05  O-HOURS-WORKED       PIC BBZ9.9.
00073                  05  O-PAYRATE            PIC BBZ9.999.
00074                  05  O-DEPENDENTS         PIC BBZ9.
```

```
00075              05   O-GROSS-PAY          PIC BB$$$9.99.
00076              05   O-TAX                PIC BB$$$9.99.
00077              05   O-NET-PAY            PIC BB$$$9.99.
00078
00079         01   ERROR-RECORD.
00080              05   FILLER               PIC X.
00081              05   BAD-DATA             PIC X(38).
00082              05   FILLER               PIC X(4)         VALUE SPACES.
00083              05   ERROR-MESSAGE        PIC X(30).
00084
00085         01   MESSAGE-1                 PIC X(30)
00086              VALUE 'INVALID DATA IN THIS RECORD'.
00087         01   MESSAGE-2                 PIC X(30)
00088              VALUE 'GROSS PAY SUSPICIOUSLY LARGE'.
00089
00090         01   W-TODAYS-DATE.
00091              05   YY                   PIC 99.
00092              05   MM                   PIC 99.
00093              05   DD                   PIC 99.
00094
00095
00096         PROCEDURE DIVISION.
00097         A000-PRODUCE-PAYROLL-CALC.
00098              OPEN   INPUT PAYROLL-FILE
00099                     OUTPUT REPORT-FILE.
00100              ACCEPT W-TODAYS-DATE FROM DATE.
00101              MOVE CORRESPONDING W-TODAYS-DATE TO REPORT-DATE.
00102              PERFORM X010-PRINT-COLUMN-HEADINGS.
00103              PERFORM C010-GET-VALID-PAY-REC.
00104              PERFORM B010-CALC-EMP-PAYROLL
00105                  UNTIL OUT-OF-RECORDS.
00106              CLOSE PAYROLL-FILE
00107                     REPORT-FILE.
00108              STOP RUN.
00109
00110         B010-CALC-EMP-PAYROLL.
00111              PERFORM C020-COMPUTE-GROSS-PAY.
00112              IF NO-SIZE-ERROR
00113                  PERFORM C030-COMPUTE-EXEMPTIONS
00114                  PERFORM C040-COMPUTE-TAX
00115                  PERFORM C050-COMPUTE-NET-PAY
00116                  PERFORM C060-PRINT-NORMAL-OUTPUT
00117              ELSE
00118                  PERFORM C070-PRINT-ERROR-OUTPUT.
00119              PERFORM C010-GET-VALID-PAY-REC.
                 .
                 .
                 .
00157         C060-PRINT-NORMAL-OUTPUT.
00158              MOVE I-PAYROLL-NUMBER     TO O-PAYROLL-NUMBER.
00159              MOVE I-NAME               TO O-NAME.
00160              MOVE I-HOURS-WORKED       TO O-HOURS-WORKED.
00161              MOVE I-PAYRATE            TO O-PAYRATE.
00162              MOVE I-DEPENDENTS         TO O-DEPENDENTS.
00163              MOVE W-TAX                TO O-TAX.
00164              MOVE W-GROSS-PAY          TO O-GROSS-PAY.
00165              MOVE W-NET-PAY            TO O-NET-PAY.
00166              WRITE REPORT-RECORD FROM NORMAL-OUTPUT-LINE
00167                      AFTER ADVANCING 1 LINE
00168                      AT END-OF-PAGE
00169                          PERFORM X010-PRINT-COLUMN-HEADINGS.
00170
```

```
00171              C070-PRINT-ERROR-OUTPUT.
00172                  MOVE PAYROLL-RECORD TO BAD-DATA.
00173                  MOVE MESSAGE-2 TO ERROR-MESSAGE.
00174                  WRITE REPORT-RECORD FROM ERROR-RECORD
00175                          AFTER ADVANCING 1 LINE
00176                          AT EOP PERFORM X010-PRINT-COLUMN-HEADINGS.
                       .
                       .
                       .
00187              E020-EDIT-PAYROLL-RECORD.
00188                  IF     I-PAYROLL-NUMBER IS NOT NUMERIC
00189                     OR  I-HOURS-WORKED   IS NOT NUMERIC
00190                     OR  I-PAYRATE        IS NOT NUMERIC
00191                     OR  I-DEPENDENTS     IS NOT NUMERIC
00192                      MOVE PAYROLL-RECORD TO BAD-DATA
00193                      MOVE MESSAGE-1 TO ERROR-MESSAGE
00194                      WRITE REPORT-RECORD FROM ERROR-RECORD
00195                              AFTER ADVANCING 1 LINE
00196                              AT EOP PERFORM X010-PRINT-COLUMN-HEADINGS
00197                  ELSE
00198                      MOVE 'Y' TO W-VALID-RECORD-FLAG.
00199
00200              X010-PRINT-COLUMN-HEADINGS.
00201                  WRITE REPORT-RECORD FROM HEADING-LINE-1
00202                          AFTER ADVANCING PAGE.
00203                  WRITE REPORT-RECORD FROM HEADING-LINE-2
00204                          AFTER ADVANCING 2 LINES.
00205                  MOVE SPACES TO REPORT-RECORD.
00206                  WRITE REPORT-RECORD AFTER ADVANCING 2 LINES.
```

FIGURE 16.1   A report program using the **LINAGE** clause and **WRITE** statement enhancements.

The **SELECT** statements and the **FD** entry for **PAYROLL-FILE** are the same as they were in Figure 8.5, but the **FD** for **REPORT-FILE** has a new clause, the **LINAGE** clause. The **LINAGE** clause divides the report page into three sections: blank space at the top of the page (**LINES AT TOP**), blank space at the bottom of the page (**LINES AT BOTTOM**), and the body of the report (**LINAGE**) which contains *all* text printed by the **COBOL** program, including column headings. In the program above, for example, there will be 3 blank lines at the top of each page, 3 blank lines at the bottom of each page, and 15 lines in the report body, including the 5 lines used by the column headings; this gives a total page length of 21 lines. Normally a page is much longer than this, typically 66 lines, and we have used a shorter page only for this example. If we were printing the report on standard paper, the **LINAGE** clause might look like the following:

```
LINAGE IS 60 LINES
    WITH FOOTING AT 60
    LINES AT TOP 3
    LINES AT BOTTOM 3.
```

The **FOOTING** clause is used in connection with the **WRITE** statement, and we will discuss this shortly.

In the Procedure Division, the first paragraph is much as it was in Figure 8.5, with a few minor changes. First, we have moved the code that initializes the date field in the heading into the main paragraph. The heading will now be printed repeatedly, but we want to carry out the initialization only once. We also use **MOVE CORRESPONDING** to rearrange the fields in **REPORT-DATE** to a more familiar sequence. The second change in this paragraph simply involves renumbering the **CALC-EMP-PAYROLL** paragraph, since there is now only one paragraph at the **B** level.

In **B010-CALC-EMP-PAYROLL** the only change is that we have taken the code that prints erroneous data and moved it to a separate paragraph.

Paragraphs **C010-GET-VALID-PAY-REC** through **C050-COMPUTE-NET-PAY** are unchanged, which brings us to **C060-PRINT-NORMAL-OUTPUT** and the **END-OF-PAGE** clause in the **WRITE** statement. This new clause makes use of the **LINAGE** information in the **FD** entry to tell when it is time to skip to a new page. Whenever you specify a **LINAGE** clause for a file, **COBOL** automatically creates a special reserved variable for that file called **LINAGE-COUNTER**. When you open the file for output or when you start a new page, **LINAGE-COUNTER** is automatically set to one. Whenever you write to the file, **LINAGE-COUNTER** is incremented by the number of lines specified in the **ADVANCING** clause so that it always points to the line being written on the page. When a **WRITE** statement causes **LINAGE-COUNTER** to become greater than or equal to the value in the **FOOTING** clause, the **END-OF-PAGE** condition becomes true and the statement in the **AT END-OF-PAGE** clause is executed.

The order in which some of these actions takes place is critical. When **LINAGE-COUNTER** becomes greater than or equal to the **FOOTING** value, the **WRITE** statement prints the current line, and only then is the **END-OF-PAGE** action executed. Consider what this means in the current example. We begin the program by printing a heading at the top of a page, which takes five lines including the two blanks printed after the second line of text. **LINAGE-COUNTER** is now set to 5. When we print the first line of output, the **ADVANCING** clause specifies

```
AFTER ADVANCING 1 LINE
```

so **LINAGE-COUNTER** is now set to 6. This continues for the next eight records. When we are ready to print the tenth record (on line 15), the following actions occur:

1. **LINAGE-COUNTER** is incremented to 15;
2. The program detects that **LINAGE-COUNTER** is equal to the **FOOTING** value and prepares the **END-OF-PAGE** condition;
3. The **WRITE** statement prints the current line;
4. The **END-OF-PAGE** action is executed;
5. Because the **END-OF-PAGE** action causes the printer to skip to the top of a new page, **LINAGE-COUNTER** is reset to 1.

The **WRITE** statement in **C070-PRINT-ERROR-OUTPUT** is almost identical to that of the previous paragraph, except that we use **EOP** instead of **END-OF-PAGE**. **EOP** is an acceptable abbreviation for **END-OF-PAGE** and the meanings are identical. We have used both formats only to demonstrate the alternatives.

Paragraph **X010-PRINT-COLUMN-HEADINGS** introduces a new feature, the **AFTER ADVANCING PAGE** clause in the first **WRITE** statement. This is almost the same as defining a mnemonic name for **C01** in the **SPECIAL-NAMES** paragraph as we have done in previous programs. There are two important differences, however. First, the **PAGE** option is standard for all current **COBOL** implementations, but the **C01** notation is used only by IBM mainframes. Second, the **C01** convention will not work correctly with a **LINAGE** clause in the **FD** entry.

We can now show the complete **WRITE** statement for sequential files.

WRITE record-name [FROM identifier-1]

$$
\left[
\left\{ \begin{array}{l} \underline{\text{BEFORE}} \\ \underline{\text{AFTER}} \end{array} \right\}
\text{ADVANCING}
\left\{ \begin{array}{l} \left\{ \begin{array}{l} \text{identifier-2} \\ \text{integer} \end{array} \right\} \left[\begin{array}{l} \text{LINE} \\ \text{LINES} \end{array} \right] \\ \left\{ \begin{array}{l} \text{mnemonic-name-1} \\ \text{PAGE} \end{array} \right\} \end{array} \right\}
\right]
$$

$$
\left[\text{AT} \left\{ \begin{array}{l} \underline{\text{END-OF-PAGE}} \\ \underline{\text{EOP}} \end{array} \right\} \text{imperative-statement} \right]
$$

The output from the program is shown in Figure 16.2 and is much the same as in Chapter 8. There are three blank lines at the top of each page and three at the bottom. Dashed lines show where the page margins would be.

We conclude this section by mentioning that the **LINAGE-COUNTER** can be referred to (but not changed) in the Procedure Division. For example, if we wanted to allow several lines at the bottom of the page so that certain text was not split over two pages, we might write

```
IF LINAGE-COUNTER IS GREATER THAN 55
    PERFORM X010-PRINT-COLUMN-HEADINGS.
```

If more than one file has a **LINAGE** clause, its use can be qualified by the file name. For example,

```
IF LINAGE-COUNTER OF ERROR-REPORT-FILE > 55 . . .
```

16.3 REPORT WRITER CONCEPTS

Although the **LINAGE** and **END-OF-PAGE** clauses simplify some of the work of producing reports, a considerable amount still remains for the programmer to do. However, many of the tasks needed to produce a report are repeated from report to report and follow much the same pattern in many types of reports. The function of the Report Writer is to let the computer do the routine work for you. In particular, the Report Writer performs the following types of activities:

1. Detects control breaks;
2. Computes subtotals for control groups, as well as a grand total for the entire report;
3. Prints headings and footings before and after control groups;
4. Controls the page format, including producing headings and footings on each page.

The statements used to control the Report Writer are found in three places in the program. First, in the File Section we put a clause in the **FD** entry for the report file that tells the program that this report will be generated by the Report Writer. Second, in a new section of the Data Division called the Report

----

```
PAYROLL CALCULATION REPORT                                    4/22/87

NUMBER        NAME              HOURS  RATE    DEP  GROSS     TAX      NET


12345   THOS H. KELLY          20.0   5.350   0   $107.00   $22.47   $84.53
12401   HENRY JENSEN           40.0   7.500   1   $300.00   $52.50   $247.50
12511   NANCY KAHN             40.0   7.500   3   $300.00   $31.50   $268.50
UILKMB. R. BROOKS        400   0575002     INVALID DATA IN THIS RECORD
26017   JANE MILANO            10.0   6.875   3   $68.75    $0.00    $68.75
12  4KAY DELUCCIA         400   0600004     INVALID DATA IN THIS RECORD
26109   PETER W. SHERWOOD      40.0  10.000   5   $400.00   $31.50   $368.50
26222   GEORGE M. MULVANEY     41.0  10.000   5   $415.00   $34.65   $380.35
26500A. W. ENWRIGHT       40    0545001     INVALID DATA IN THIS RECORD
27511   RUTH GARRISON          50.0  10.000   4   $550.00   $73.50   $476.50
```

```
PAYROLL CALCULATION REPORT                                    4/22/87

NUMBER        NAME              HOURS  RATE    DEP  GROSS     TAX      NET


28819   LEO X. BUTLER          40.1  10.000   2   $401.50   $63.32   $338.18
28820D. X. IANNUZZI       450   4.50003     INVALID DATA IN THIS RECORD
28821K. L. NG, JR.        350   450003      INVALID DATA IN THIS RECORD
28822DANIEL REINER        350   045000C     INVALID DATA IN THIS RECORD
28822L. E. SIMON          388   06000 3     INVALID DATA IN THIS RECORD
28839QA. REAL BAD-ONE     3 8   4.5KJXX     INVALID DATA IN THIS RECORD
7HGV6GARBAGE-CASE-1            ..M.,M.,M.,M.   INVALID DATA IN THIS RECORD
 NJI9GARBAGE-CASE-2            GV 6 46  8  H    INVALID DATA IN THIS RECORD
       GARBAGE-CASE-3  ----------++++++,M    INVALID DATA IN THIS RECORD
29000   ANNE HENDERSON         40.2  10.000   3   $403.00   $53.13   $349.87
```

```
PAYROLL CALCULATION REPORT                                    4/22/87

NUMBER        NAME              HOURS  RATE    DEP  GROSS     TAX      NET


29001   JULIA KIPP             40.3  10.000   1   $404.50   $74.45   $330.05
99999IMA TESTCASE         999   9999999     GROSS PAY SUSPICIOUSLY LARGE
```

FIGURE 16.2 Output from the program in Figure 16.1.

Section we define what the report is to look like. This includes describing the format of the report pages, telling what headings and footings look like, defining control groups and control variables, and generally specifying what various lines on a page will look like and where report data will come from. Finally, in the Procedure Division we have a few simple statements that start a report, tell what data will be used in producing the report, and terminate the report. The bulk of these specifications will fall in the Report Section of the Data Division. In most cases, if you can define the format of the report you have done the hardest part of using the Report Writer.

To demonstrate how the Report Writer works, we will revise the three-level control program presented in Figure 9.9.

16.4 THE THREE-LEVEL CONTROL PROGRAM

Recall that the three-level control program is based on a simple sales accounting system. A company has divided its sales territory into several regions, each of which is identified by a five-character code. In addition, each salesperson and each customer account is identified by other five-character codes. As input to the program we are given a file of account records, each of which specifies a sales region, a salesperson, an account, and the amount of the sale. The file is sorted by region, salesperson, and account, in that order. The purpose of the program is to produce a report that shows the total sales for each region, the total sales for each salesperson within the region, and the total sales for each of the salesperson's customers. Figure 9.1, which shows a sample of the output from this program, is reproduced below as Figure 16.3 for ease of reference.

REGION	TOTAL	SALESPERSON	TOTAL	ACCOUNT	TOTAL	FINAL TOTAL	PAGE	1
				20	$17.00			
				24	$36.00			
				27	$184.00			
		1	$237.00					
				17	$26.00			
				24	$266.90			
		2	$292.90					
				10	$87.50			
				16	$54.75			
		12	$142.25					
1	$672.15							
				40	$50.12			
				41	$105.99			
		4	$156.11					
				44	$1,594.14			
		39	$1,594.14					
2	$1,750.25							
				30	$1,180.94			
				35	$69.26			
				38	$157.43			
				49	$45.00			
				60	$1,234.56			
				78	$276.02			
		15	$2,963.21					
3	$2,963.21							
						$5,385.61		

FIGURE 16.3 Example of a report using three-level control totals. (This is the same as Figure 9.1.)

The report shown in Figure 16.3 is unusual in that the individual sales records, the detail records that contain the basic data, do not appear in the report. The report is actually a summary, showing only totals for each of the control variables. We shall begin, therefore, with a program that produces a slight variation of this report to show the sales records as well as the totals. The program is shown in Figure 16.4.

```
00001            IDENTIFICATION DIVISION.
00002            PROGRAM-ID.
00003                3LEVEL3A.
00004            AUTHOR.
00005                D. GOLDEN.
00006            DATE-WRITTEN.
00007                APRIL 27, 1987.
00008        *
00009        *    THIS PROGRAM PRODUCES A SIMPLE THREE-LEVEL SUMMARY REPORT FOR
00010        *    A SALES ACCOUNTING SYSTEM, USING THE COBOL REPORT WRITER
00011        *
00012
00013            ENVIRONMENT DIVISION.
00014            INPUT-OUTPUT SECTION.
00015            FILE-CONTROL.
00016                SELECT ACCOUNT-FILE          ASSIGN TO S-ACCOUNT.
00017                SELECT REPORT-FILE           ASSIGN TO S-REPORT.
00018
00019            DATA DIVISION.
00020            FILE SECTION.
00021
00022            FD  ACCOUNT-FILE
00023                LABEL RECORDS ARE OMITTED.
00024            01  ACCOUNT-RECORD.
00025                05   REGION-NUMBER          PIC X(5).
00026                05   SELLER-NUMBER          PIC X(5).
00027                05   ACCOUNT-NUMBER         PIC X(5).
00028                05   SALE-AMOUNT            PIC 9(5)V99.
00029                05   FILLER                 PIC X(58).
00030
00031            FD  REPORT-FILE
00032                REPORT IS SALES-REPORT
00033                RECORD CONTAINS 133 CHARACTERS
00034                LABEL RECORDS ARE OMITTED.
00035
00036            WORKING-STORAGE SECTION.
00037
00038            77  MORE-DATA-FLAG             PIC X.
00039                88  NO-MORE-DATA                        VALUE 'N'.
00040
00041            REPORT SECTION.
00042            RD  SALES-REPORT
00043                CONTROLS ARE FINAL
00044                            REGION-NUMBER
00045                            SELLER-NUMBER
00046                            ACCOUNT-NUMBER
```

```
00047                 PAGE LIMIT IS 63 LINES
00048                     HEADING       4
00049                     FIRST DETAIL 7
00050                     LAST DETAIL  59
00051                     FOOTING        63.
00052            01  TYPE IS PAGE HEADING LINE IS 4.
00053                 05  COLUMN 1              PIC X(40)
00054                           VALUE 'REGION      TOTAL      SALESPERSON    TOTAL'.
00055                 05  COLUMN 48             PIC X(46)
00056                           VALUE 'ACCOUNT      TOTAL                FINAL TOTAL'.
00057                 05  COLUMN 93             PIC X(10)  VALUE 'PAGE'.
00058                 05  COLUMN 103            PIC Z(6)9
00059                           SOURCE IS PAGE-COUNTER.
00060            01  CUSTOMER-SALE TYPE DETAIL LINE PLUS 1
00061                     COLUMN 61  PIC $$$$,$$9.99 SOURCE IS SALE-AMOUNT.
00062            01  TYPE CONTROL FOOTING ACCOUNT-NUMBER LINE PLUS 1.
00063                 05  COLUMN 49
00064                           PIC Z(4)9 SOURCE IS ACCOUNT-NUMBER.
00065                 05  ACCOUNT-TOTAL-OUT  COLUMN 57
00066                           PIC $$$$,$$9.99 SUM SALE-AMOUNT.
00067            01  TYPE CONTROL FOOTING SELLER-NUMBER LINE PLUS 1.
00068                 05  COLUMN 25
00069                           PIC Z(4)9 SOURCE IS SELLER-NUMBER.
00070                 05  SELLER-TOTAL-OUT COLUMN 33
00071                           PIC $$$$,$$9.99 SUM ACCOUNT-TOTAL-OUT.
00072            01  TYPE CONTROL FOOTING REGION-NUMBER LINE PLUS 1.
00073                 05  COLUMN 1
00074                           PIC Z(4)9     SOURCE IS REGION-NUMBER.
00075                 05  REGION-TOTAL-OUT COLUMN 9
00076                           PIC $$$$,$$9.99 SUM SELLER-TOTAL-OUT.
00077            01  TYPE CONTROL FOOTING FINAL LINE PLUS 1.
00078                 05  COLUMN 76
00079                           PIC $$$$,$$9.99 SUM REGION-TOTAL-OUT.
00080
00081
00082       PROCEDURE DIVISION.
00083       A000-PREPARE-SALES-REPORT.
00084           OPEN  INPUT ACCOUNT-FILE
00085                OUTPUT REPORT-FILE.
00086           MOVE 'Y'  TO MORE-DATA-FLAG.
00087           INITIATE SALES-REPORT.
00088           READ ACCOUNT-FILE
00089                 AT END MOVE 'N' TO MORE-DATA-FLAG.
00090           PERFORM B010-PRODUCE-SALES-REPORT
00091               UNTIL NO-MORE-DATA.
00092           TERMINATE SALES-REPORT.
00093           CLOSE ACCOUNT-FILE
00094                 REPORT-FILE.
00095           STOP RUN.
00096
00097       B010-PRODUCE-SALES-REPORT.
00098           GENERATE CUSTOMER-SALE.
00099           READ ACCOUNT-FILE
00100                 AT END MOVE 'N' TO MORE-DATA-FLAG.
00101
00102       ********************** END OF PROGRAM **************************
```

FIGURE 16.4 A program that produces a three-level control break report using the **COBOL** Report Writer.

The first change from the program used in Chapter 9 occurs in the **FD** entry for **REPORT-FILE**. We have two new clauses, **REPORT IS** and **RECORD CONTAINS**, but more unusual is the fact that there is no record description for this file! The clause

    REPORT IS SALES-REPORT

tells the **COBOL** compiler that all output to **REPORT-FILE** will be produced by a report named **SALES-REPORT** that will be defined in a later part of the Data Division. Therefore, we do not define any file records in the **FD** entry. However, we do want to tell the compiler how long each record is to be, and this is accomplished by the clause

    REPORT CONTAINS 133 CHARACTERS

This specifies enough space for a 132-character line of text, plus one extra position for the carriage control character.

The next change is in the Working-Storage Section, and it is a striking one. All Working-Storage data except for the end-of-file flag has been deleted. None of this data is needed any longer since all the work that it performed in the original program is now performed in a new section of the Data Division called the *Report Section*.

The Report Section comes at the end of the Data Division and specifies the format of all headings and report lines, as well as telling how the report is to be computed. We shall skip over this section for the moment and look at the remainder of the program, returning to the Report Section after we have seen the output from the program.

The main paragraph of the Procedure Division looks fairly familiar in format, although there are some new statements. The most obvious change from Chapter 9 is that the paragraph is much shorter than in the original program. We begin by opening the two files that the program uses, including **REPORT-FILE**. Even though the output to this file is controlled by the Report Writer, we must still open and close it just as we would any other file.

After initializing the end-of-file flag for the input file, we execute a new statement, **INITIATE SALES-REPORT**. **SALES-REPORT** is the name of the report defined in the Report Section, and the **INITIATE** statement prepares this report for execution. Various counters, totals, and flags, including a line counter and a page counter, all internal to the Report Writer and mostly invisible to the programmer, are given their initial values. At this point the Report Writer is ready to produce the first line of output, but nothing has been written yet.

The next two statements of the driver paragraph read the first input record and perform the paragraph that controls the report output. Both of these statements are much as they were in previous programs.

After the program has read all the data in **ACCOUNT-FILE**, we exit from the **PERFORM** statement and go on to another new statement, **TERMINATE SALES-REPORT**. As you might guess, this statement ends the report. Any outstanding totals are printed, including the grand total for company sales, and the report is concluded. Any attempt to write additional data to **SALES-REPORT** will produce an error.

The work paragraph, **B010-PRODUCE-SALES-REPORT**, consists of only two statements, a **GENERATE** statement and a **READ** statement. The **GENERATE** statement tells the Report Writer to produce one more line of detail on the report. In this example, the Report Writer takes the data in the current **ACCOUNT-RECORD** and prepares to write it to **SALES-REPORT**. However, it first checks to see if a control break has occurred. If so, any appropriate subtotals are printed and internal variables are reset before the detail record is printed.

It is clear that the Report Writer saves you a considerable amount of work. The Procedure Division in Figure 9.7 requires six paragraphs and about 70 lines of code, while the one in Figure 16.4 requires only two paragraphs and fewer than 20 lines of code. You should understand, however, that we have not reduced the amount of work that the *computer* has to do during execution. The amount of code in the object program is at least as great when you use the Report Writer as when you write the code yourself.

The report produced by this program is shown in Figure 16.5. The dashed line at the top of the report represents the page margin, and was inserted to emphasize the fact that there are three blank lines at the top of the page preceding the page heading. Although we have provided several detail records for each of the first three accounts, to save space the remaining accounts have only one record each. In a real program, of course, there would likely be many sales records for each account. Also, although the dollar amounts for the sales records have been offset to distinguish them from various totals, we have not bothered to modify the column headings, since we will soon eliminate the detail lines when we return to the original report format.

16.5   THE REPORT SECTION

Now that we have a sample report to look at, we will return to the Report Section of the program in Figure 16.4. Just as the File Section defines files with an **FD** entry, the Report Section defines reports with **RD** entries, each of which defines one report. Although our examples will use only one report, we can have as many reports as we wish, each defined by a separate **RD** entry.

The **RD** entry itself performs two functions: it defines the data names to be used as control variables in the report, and it defines the page format. The control variables are defined in the **CONTROLS ARE** clause; in this example the control variables are **FINAL**, **REGION-NUMBER**, **SELLER-NUMBER**, and **ACCOUNT-NUMBER**. **FINAL** is a reserved word that represents the highest level of control. In this program, for instance, it represents a grand total for the entire company. The use of **FINAL** is optional, but if we omit it we cannot produce a total for the company. In any case, control variables must always be listed in order from major to minor. They are usually fields of the input record and may not contain any editing characters in their **PICTURE** clauses.

The **PAGE** clause describes the overall format of the report page. It begins with **PAGE LIMIT IS**, which tells how many lines there are on one page of the report, from the first line of heading (including any blank lines) to the last line at the bottom. In our example we have specified a total of 63 lines.

The **HEADING** phrase indicates where the first line of heading will begin. We have specified that headings will begin on line 4, so lines 1-3 of each page will be blank.

The heading on our report consists of three lines, one line of text followed by two blank lines. Therefore, we want the first line of data to be printed on line 7. This is specified by the **FIRST DETAIL** phrase. In addition, this phrase controls the location of any subtotals, so that if the report requires more than one page no total line will be printed before line 7.

REGION	TOTAL	SALESPERSON	TOTAL	ACCOUNT	TOTAL	FINAL TOTAL	PAGE	1
					$11.50			
					$5.50			
				20	$17.00			
					$10.25			
					$10.00			
					$15.75			
				24	$36.00			
					$9.00			
					$101.00			
					$22.00			
					$42.60			
					$9.40			
				27	$184.00			
		1	$237.00					
					$26.00			
				17	$26.00			
					$266.90			
				24	$266.90			
		2	$292.90					
					$87.50			
				10	$87.50			
					$54.75			
				16	$54.75			
		12	$142.25					
1	$672.15							
					$50.12			
				40	$50.12			
					$105.99			
				41	$105.99			
		4	$156.11					
					$1,594.14			
				44	$1,594.14			
		39	$1,594.14					
2	$1,750.25							
					$1,180.94			
				30	$1,180.94			
					$69.26			
				35	$69.26			
					$157.43			
				38	$157.43			
					$45.00			
				49	$45.00			
					$1,234.56			
				60	$1,234.56			
					$276.02			
				78	$276.02			
		15	$2,963.21					
3	$2,963.21							
						$5,385.61		

FIGURE 16.5 Output produced by the program in Figure 16.4.

To determine where the last line of detail on a page will be printed (the sales amounts in this example) we use the **LAST DETAIL** phrase. Thus, no sales record will be printed after line 59. This leaves us lines 60-63 to print the subtotals for a group. The **FOOTING** phrase specifies that the last line of footing is line 63, which in this example is also the last line on the page. This means that we will allow subtotals to run to the bottom of the page. In other reports we might wish to allow some space at the bottom of the page for *page footings* just as we have *page headings* at the top of the page. In this case, the **FOOTING** clause would contain a value that is less than the value in the **PAGE LIMIT** phrase; later in this chapter we will show an example of how page footings are used.

The remainder of the **RD** entry consists of a number of **01** level entries, each of which defines a *report group*. Basically, a report group is a series of one or more lines on a report that print as a group. Report groups fall into one of seven different categories:

REPORT HEADING—the report heading appears once, at the start of a report; there may be at most one report heading per report.

PAGE HEADING—the page heading appears at the top of each page; there may be at most one page heading per report, which means that all pages in the report will have the same heading.

CONTROL HEADING—there may be one control heading given for each control variable listed in the **CONTROLS ARE** clause; the control heading is printed whenever a control break is detected for its associated variable, *before* the detail line containing the new value of the variable is printed.

DETAIL—a detail group is printed whenever a **GENERATE** statement is executed; there may be as many different detail groups as you wish, and the name specified in the **GENERATE** statement determines which detail group is to be printed.

CONTROL FOOTING—there may be one control footing associated with each control variable; the control footing is printed whenever a control break is detected for its associated variable, *after* the last detail line containing old value of the variable has been printed.

PAGE FOOTING—the page footing appears at the bottom of each page; just as with the page heading, there may be at most one page footing per report.

REPORT FOOTING—the report footing appears once, at the end of the report; there may be at most one report footing per report.

We will discuss each of these types of report groups in more detail, including where they appear on the report, as we go through various examples.

The first report group definition for **SALES-REPORT** is a page heading group, and many of the features of this definition are typical of all report group definitions. To begin with, notice that neither the **01** level entry nor any of its subordinate entries has a data name. This is quite common in the Report Section. Although data names may be used (as you can see by the following definition), they are not required except for fields that you wish to refer to elsewhere in the program. Since page headings are produced automatically by the Report Writer, you need never refer to them explicitly so we don't bother with data names.

The first clause in the definition of the page heading group is the **TYPE** clause, which tells the compiler which of the seven report group types we are defining. This is followed by a **LINE** clause which specifies that the page heading will begin on line 4. As we will see in other group definitions, the **LINE** clause has several options; its complete format is

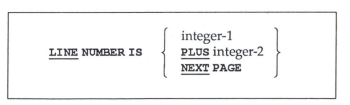

If we specify an integer, as in the current definition, the line is printed on the line specified; this is called an *absolute line number*. If we specify the **PLUS** option, the indicated number of lines is added to the current line position to determine where the output will be printed; this type of line number is called a *relative line number*. The **NEXT PAGE** option causes the printer to skip to the top of the next page before printing the line.

COBOL-85

The format for the **LINE** clause shown above is for the IBM version of **COBOL-74**. The format for **COBOL-85** is slightly different.

The only real difference that this format makes is that you can specify that the line should print on the next page starting on a line other than the first line of the page.

END COBOL-85

The first subordinate entry in the page heading group represents one field on the line and begins with a **COLUMN** clause. This tells in which column of the line the field begins. The column numbers must always be integer constants, and must appear in ascending order for all fields. Notice that we need not specify fillers for blank fields between fields; any unspecified column positions are automatically filled with blanks. In addition, although the **RECORD CONTAINS** clause of the file's **FD** entry specifies that the output record is 133 characters long, the carriage control position is automatically set by the Report Writer. As far as we are concerned in defining the report each line consists of 132 characters, and the first position in each line is in column 1.

With one exception, the rest of this group definition is quite familiar. The **PICTURE** clause in a report group definition is used in exactly the same way as in any other part of the Data Division, as is the **VALUE** clause. The last new feature of this group definition is, of course, the **SOURCE** clause on line 59. This clause is analogous to a **MOVE** statement in the Procedure Division. It specifies that the value of the identifier named in the clause is to be moved into the current field whenever the report group is printed. In this case we have said that the identifier to be used as the source in the field is a **COBOL**-defined variable called **PAGE-COUNTER**. **PAGE-COUNTER** is used by the Report Writer to keep track of the current page number. It is set to 1 by the **INITIATE** statement, and is incremented by 1 every time the top of a new page is reached. In addition to **PAGE-COUNTER**, the identifier used in a **SOURCE** clause may be any data name defined outside the Report Section, or a special type of Report Section variable called a **SUM** counter; we shall discuss **SUM** counters shortly.

The next report group is a detail group (specified by the **TYPE DETAIL** clause), and has been given a data name, **CUSTOMER-SALE**, so that it can be referred to in the **GENERATE** statement in the Procedure Division. Notice that the **LINE** clause of this group uses the **PLUS** option; this is equivalent to using **AFTER ADVANCING 1 LINE** in a **WRITE** statement.

Although, as the page heading group demonstrated, we can use subordinate entries to define a report, we need not do so. For **CUSTOMER-SALE** we simply need to define one field of one line, which can be done quite easily in a single entry.

The third report group is a control footing group. Control footings are always associated with specific control variables, and the variable name must follow immediately after the **TYPE** clause; in this case we are defining the control footing associated with **ACCOUNT-NUMBER**. When a control break occurs for **ACCOUNT-NUMBER** or any control variable higher than **ACCOUNT-NUMBER** in the control hierarchy, the control footing for **ACCOUNT-NUMBER** is printed. The footing is printed after any control footings for subordinate control variables, and before any control footings for higher level control variables. All control footings being printed are printed before the detail line that triggered the control break is printed.

The control footing group introduces a new clause, the **SUM** clause, shown on line 66. Unlike most other clauses, the **SUM** clause may be used only in a control footing group. Whenever a **SUM** clause is used the Report Writer creates a **SUM** counter. This counter is used to keep a total for a specified variable, **SALE-AMOUNT** in this case. Notice that **SALE-AMOUNT** is the same variable that was used in the **SOURCE** clause in the preceding detail group. The **SUM** counter is set to zero by the **INITIATE** statement, and is incremented by the current value of **SALE-AMOUNT** each time a **GENERATE** statement is executed for **CUSTOMER-SALE**. After the control footing has been printed, the **SUM** counter is reset to zero and the process repeats. It is important to remember that if the variable being summed is not defined within the Report Section, it must be used as a **SOURCE** variable in a detail group. This is the only way that the Report Writer knows when to update the value of the **SUM** counter.

The next report group is also a control footing group, this time for **SELLER-NUMBER**. The format of this group is much the same as for the previous group, except for one difference in the **SUM** clause. The identifier named in the **SUM** clause on line 71 is the data name associated with the **SUM** clause in the control footing for **ACCOUNT-NUMBER**. Every time the control footing for **ACCOUNT-NUMBER** is printed, the value of its **SUM** counter is added to the **SUM** counter on line 71. In other words, instead of using a variable named in a **SOURCE** clause as the object of a summation, you can also use the **SUM** counter of any lower level control footing. Thus the reason we gave a data name to the entry defined on lines 65-66 is so that the **SUM** counter could be referenced on line 71.

The remaining control groups are also control footings and are much the same as the footing for **SELLER-NUMBER**. For the final control footing we have used a subordinate entry (**05** level) even though we are only defining one field on one line. Either approach may be used and the choice is largely a matter of personal taste.

16.6 A REPORT WITH NO DETAIL LINES

The program presented in the previous section uses many of the features of the **COBOL** Report Writer, but there are still others to be presented. Furthermore, the report shown in Figure 16.5 was not quite what we wanted to produce since the report in Figure 16.3 did not include the sales amounts. The change needed to produce the proper report is quite simple. We need only modify the detail group **CUSTOMER-SALE** as follows:

```
01   CUSTOMER-SALE TYPE DETAIL
                      PIC 9(6)V99 SOURCE IS SALE-AMOUNT.
```

We have made three changes from what was shown in Figure 16.4:

1. The **LINE** clause has been deleted;
2. The **COLUMN** clause has been deleted;
3. The **PICTURE** has been changed.

Omitting the **LINE** and **COLUMN** clauses suppresses printing of the report group. If a report group has several fields in a line, omitting the **COLUMN** clause for one or more of the fields will suppress printing of those fields. In other words, you will get blank space where the field would have printed. However, if we had only removed the **COLUMN** clause for this report group, we would still have had a blank line printed. To suppress printing the entire line, we delete the **LINE** clause. Changing the **PICTURE** for the group was not really necessary; it was done primarily to emphasize that the field will no longer be printed.

We could not simply have deleted the entire report group, for two reasons. First, in order for the **SUM** clause on line 66 to work, **SALE-AMOUNT** must be used in a **SOURCE** clause in a detail group. It is not necessary for **SALE-AMOUNT** to be printed, but it must appear in a **SOURCE** clause somewhere. Second, and more important, is the fact that in order for any output to be produced there must be at least one detail group used by a **GENERATE** statement in the Procedure Division. Again, it is not necessary that this detail group be printed, but it must appear as part of the report.

After this change was made to the program of Figure 16.4, the program was rerun and produced the same output as appears in Figure 16.3.

16.7 ADDITIONAL REPORT WRITER FEATURES

Suppose we decide that we want to make a few simple changes to the report we have been producing. To begin with, we would like to start the output for each region at the top of a new page. In addition, we want to put two blank lines between the last region total and the final total. Both of these changes are accomplished quite easily.

To start each region at the top of a new page, we modify the control footing group for **REGION-NUMBER** as follows:

```
01   TYPE CONTROL FOOTING REGION-NUMBER LINE PLUS 1
                      NEXT GROUP NEXT PAGE.
     05  ...
```

In other words, we simply add the clause

```
NEXT GROUP NEXT PAGE
```

The **NEXT GROUP** clause acts very much like the **LINE** clause, but instead of affecting the printing of the *current* report group, it affects the printing of the *next* report group to be printed. The options for this clause are the same as for the **LINE** clause; we could print the next group on an absolute line number, on a relative line number, or at the top of the next page. The **NEXT GROUP** option does not actually override the **LINE** clause of the following group. Rather, it specifies what line spacing is to take place after the current group has been printed. For example, if we had specified

        NEXT GROUP PLUS 2

the program would print two blank lines following the control footing for **REGION-NUMBER**, then print whatever group came next using that group's standard line spacing.

To insert blank lines before the final line, we simply change the **LINE** clause in the control footing group for **FINAL** to **LINE PLUS 3**. The resulting output is shown in Figure 16.6. As in previous examples, the dashed lines represent page margins. To save space, we do not show the blank space at the bottom of each page.

16.8   A COMPREHENSIVE EXAMPLE

To conclude this chapter we present a version of the sales accounting program that uses all the features of the Report Writer that we have presented. The Report Section for this example is shown in Figure 16.7, and the output is shown in Figure 16.8. So that the line spacing produced by the report is very clear, we have added markers and line numbers to the left of each line.

We have set the **PAGE LIMIT** to 35 lines, with **LAST DETAIL** and **FOOTING** modified accordingly, to demonstrate some of the line spacing that will occur. Following the **RD** entry we have the first new report group, a report heading group. This group simply prints the company name at the start of the report. You can see in Figure 16.8 that the report heading appears at the top of the first page but not on any of the other pages. However, in order to allow room for the report heading on line 4 of page 1 we must start the page heading on line 6, which is where it prints on all pages regardless of whether or not the report heading is also printed.

The page heading has been modified slightly so that it uses two lines. This is the first example we have of a report group that uses more than one line. To accomplish this we simply define each line as a **05** level group under the **01** level group, and define individual fields on a line as 10 level entries under a 05 level entry. Since each 05 level entry defines a separate line, we place a **LINE** clause on each entry to specify its line number.

After the page heading we have a control heading for **REGION-NUMBER**. The control heading is similar to the control footing in that we must specify the control variable with which the heading is associated. However, control headings do not contain **SUM** clauses since they are printed at the start of a control group, before any summation for the group has been done. In this example we simply print the number of the region about to be processed.

```
----------------------------------------------------------------------------------------------------

REGION    TOTAL    SALESPERSON    TOTAL    ACCOUNT    TOTAL        FINAL TOTAL    PAGE        1

                                             20       $17.00
                                             24       $36.00
                                             27      $184.00
                       1       $237.00
                                             17       $26.00
                                             24      $266.90
                       2       $292.90
                                             10       $87.50
                                             16       $54.75
                      12       $142.25
   1     $672.15
   .
   .
   .

----------------------------------------------------------------------------------------------------

REGION    TOTAL    SALESPERSON    TOTAL    ACCOUNT    TOTAL        FINAL TOTAL    PAGE        2

                                             40       $50.12
                                             41      $105.99
                       4       $156.11
                                             44    $1,594.14
                      39     $1,594.14
   2    $1,750.25
   .
   .
   .

----------------------------------------------------------------------------------------------------

REGION    TOTAL    SALESPERSON    TOTAL    ACCOUNT    TOTAL        FINAL TOTAL    PAGE        3

                                             30    $1,180.94
                                             35       $69.26
                                             38      $157.43
                                             49       $45.00
                                             60    $1,234.56
                                             78      $276.02
                      15     $2,963.21
   3    $2,963.21

                                                                   $5,385.61
   .
   .
   .
```

FIGURE 16.6 Output demonstrating the use of the NEXT GROUP clause.

```
00041                  REPORT SECTION.
00042              RD  SALES-REPORT
00043                  CONTROLS ARE FINAL
00044                              REGION-NUMBER
00045                              SELLER-NUMBER
00046                              ACCOUNT-NUMBER
00047                 PAGE LIMIT IS 35 LINES
00048                     HEADING        4
00049                     FIRST DETAIL 10
00050                     LAST DETAIL   29
00051                     FOOTING        33.
00052             01   TYPE IS REPORT HEADING LINE 4
00053                     COLUMN 39      PIC X(15)
00054                         VALUE 'ABC CORPORATION'.
00055             01   TYPE IS PAGE HEADING.
00056                 05   LINE IS 6.
00057                     10   COLUMN 40        PIC X(12)
00058                         VALUE 'SALES REPORT'.
00059                 05   LINE IS 7.
00060                     10   COLUMN 1         PIC X(40)
00061                         VALUE 'REGION     TOTAL     SALESPERSON     TOTAL'.
00062                     10   COLUMN 48        PIC X(46)
00063                         VALUE 'ACCOUNT       TOTAL            FINAL TOTAL'.
00064             01   TYPE CONTROL HEADING REGION-NUMBER LINE PLUS 2.
00065                 05   COLUMN 1
00066                         PIC X(20) VALUE '-----  BEGIN REGION '.
00067                 05   COLUMN 21
00068                         PIC Z(4)9 SOURCE REGION-NUMBER.
00069             01   CUSTOMER-SALE TYPE DETAIL LINE PLUS 1.
00070                 05   COLUMN 49
00071                         PIC Z(4)9 SOURCE IS ACCOUNT-NUMBER
00072                         GROUP INDICATE.
00073                 05   COLUMN 61
00074                         PIC $$$$,$$9.99 SOURCE IS SALE-AMOUNT.
00075             01   TYPE CONTROL FOOTING ACCOUNT-NUMBER LINE PLUS 1.
00076                 05   COLUMN 49
00077                         PIC Z(4)9 SOURCE IS ACCOUNT-NUMBER.
00078                 05   ACCOUNT-TOTAL-OUT   COLUMN 57
00079                         PIC $$$$,$$9.99 SUM SALE-AMOUNT.
00080             01   TYPE CONTROL FOOTING SELLER-NUMBER LINE PLUS 1.
00081                 05   COLUMN 25
00082                         PIC Z(4)9 SOURCE IS SELLER-NUMBER.
00083                 05   SELLER-TOTAL-OUT COLUMN 35
00084                         PIC $$$$,$$9.99 SUM ACCOUNT-TOTAL-OUT.
00085             01   TYPE CONTROL FOOTING REGION-NUMBER LINE PLUS 1
00086                         NEXT GROUP PLUS 5.
00087                 05   COLUMN 1
00088                         PIC Z(4)9      SOURCE IS REGION-NUMBER.
00089                 05   REGION-TOTAL-OUT COLUMN 9
00090                         PIC $$$$,$$9.99 SUM SELLER-TOTAL-OUT.
00091             01   TYPE CONTROL FOOTING FINAL LINE PLUS 3.
00092                 05   COLUMN 76
00093                         PIC $$$$,$$9.99 SUM REGION-TOTAL-OUT.
00094             01   TYPE PAGE FOOTING LINE 34.
00095                 05   COLUMN 40           PIC X(4) VALUE 'PAGE'.
00096                 05   COLUMN 45           PIC Z(6)9
00097                         SOURCE IS PAGE-COUNTER.
00098             01   TYPE REPORT FOOTING LINE PLUS 5
00099                     COLUMN 35
```

FIGURE 16.7 The Report Section for a comprehensive Report Writer example.

Notice the control break at the start of region 2 on page 2 of the output (see next page). The control break is generated when the Report Writer realizes that the region number on the sales record for account 40 is not the same as the region number on the previous sales record for account 16. At this point a control break is generated for **REGION-NUMBER** and all subordinate control variables, **SELLER-NUMBER** and **ACCOUNT-NUMBER** in this case. It would make no difference whether either **SELLER-NUMBER** or **ACCOUNT-NUMBER** had changed value, although both did in this example. Whenever a control break is generated for a control variable it is also generated for all lower level control variables. The control footings are then printed in order from lowest level to highest, followed by the control headings for the new control groups. If we had defined more than one control heading they would print from highest to lowest. Observe also that the Report Writer prints the region number of the *old* control group on the control footing, and prints the region number of the *new* group on the control heading.

The next report group definition is for the detail group **CUSTOMER-SALE**. There have been several changes to this group, beginning with the fact that we have restored the **LINE** and **COLUMN** clauses so that the individual sales records will be printed. We have also added a field to print the account number as well as the sale amount. If we had many sales records for each account, the account number field would simply be repeated on each line. To make it easier to spot the start of a new account, we wish to print the account number only for the first record of an account and leave the field blank for all following records of the account. We accomplish this with the **GROUP INDICATE** clause. The **GROUP INDICATE** clause may only be used in an elementary item of a **TYPE DETAIL** report group. It tells the Report Writer that the field is to be printed only the first time the group is printed after a control or page break.

The next four report groups are the control footings that we have seen in previous examples. The only change here is that we have modified the **NEXT GROUP** clause of the **REGION-NUMBER** footing to advance 5 lines instead of skipping to a new page. This was done simply to make it easier to observe the line spacing action of the **NEXT GROUP** clause. In Figure 16.8 we see that the footing group for region 1 is printed on line 15 of page 2, and that the heading group for region 2 is printed on line 22. This comes about because of the combination of the **NEXT GROUP** clause in the footing group and the **LINE** clause of the heading group. The **NEXT GROUP** clause increments the line counter by 5 after the footing group has been printed, bringing the counter to 20. The **LINE** clause of the heading group then increments the counter by 2, so the next output is printed on line 22. However, observe the line spacing following the footing group for region 3 on page 3. The output for this group appears on line 24, while the output for the next group, the **FINAL** control footing, appears on line 27. The reason for this is that the **NEXT GROUP** clause takes effect only if the next group is for a control variable at the same level or lower than the variable controlling the **NEXT GROUP**. In other words, when the next group to be printed is at the same level as or lower than **REGION-NUMBER**, the **NEXT GROUP** clause affects the spacing; but when the control variable for the next group is **FINAL**, which is higher than **REGION-NUMBER**, the **NEXT GROUP** clause is ignored.

```
----------------------------------------------------------------------------------------------
.
.
.
.                                ABC CORPORATION
v
.                                 SALES REPORT
.REGION      TOTAL    SALESPERSON    TOTAL      ACCOUNT      TOTAL          FINAL TOTAL
.
.
1-----  BEGIN REGION     1
.                                                  20          $11.50
.                                                               $5.50
.                                                  20       $17.00
.                                                  24          $10.25
v                                                             $10.00
.                                                             $15.75
.                                                  24       $36.00
.                                                  27           $9.00
.                                                            $101.00
2                                                            $22.00
.                                                            $42.60
.                                                             $9.40
.                                                  27       $184.00
.                          1       $237.00
.                                                  17          $26.00
v                                                  17       $26.00
.                                                  24         $266.90
.                                                  24       $266.90
.                          2       $292.90
3
.
.
.
.                                    PAGE       1
v
----------------------------------------------------------------------------------------------
.
.
.
.
v
.                                 SALES REPORT
.REGION      TOTAL    SALESPERSON    TOTAL      ACCOUNT      TOTAL          FINAL TOTAL
.
.
1                                                  10          $87.50
.                                                  10       $87.50
.                                                  16          $54.75
.                                                  16       $54.75
.                         12       $142.25
v    1     $672.15
.
.
.
.
2
.
.-----  BEGIN REGION     2
.                                                  40          $50.12
.                                                  40       $50.12
v                                                  41         $105.99
.                                                  41       $105.99
.                          4       $156.11
.                                                  44       $1,594.14
.                                                  44     $1,594.14
3                         39     $1,594.14
.    2    $1,750.25
.
.
.                                    PAGE       2
v
```

```
--------------------------------------------------------------------------------
    .
    .
    .
    .
    v
    .                                  SALES REPORT
    .REGION      TOTAL    SALESPERSON    TOTAL      ACCOUNT      TOTAL            FINAL TOTAL
    .
    .
    1-----  BEGIN REGION     3
    .                                                30        $1,180.94
    .                                                30    $1,180.94
    .                                                35            $69.26
    .                                                35    $69.26
    v                                                38           $157.43
    .                                                38    $157.43
    .                                                49            $45.00
    .                                                49    $45.00
    .                                                60         $1,234.56
    2                                                60    $1,234.56
    .                                                78           $276.02
    .                                                78    $276.02
    .                               15    $2,963.21
    .    3    $2,963.21
    v
    .
    .                                                                             $5,385.61
    .
    .
    .
    3
    .
    .
    .
    .                                    PAGE      3
    v
    --------------------------------------------------------------------------------
    .
    .
    .
    5                              -----  END OF REPORT  -----
    .           .
    .           .
    .           .
    --------------------------------------------------------------------------------
```

FIGURE 16.8 Output from the program in Figure 16.7. This output is comprehensive in that it shows an example of every type of report group.

Following the control footings is a page footing. We have simply taken the page number and moved it from the page heading to a page footing so that it prints at the bottom of the page. Notice that the footing prints on line 34, and that the **FOOTING** phrase of the **PAGE LIMIT** clause specifies **FOOTING 33**. The **FOOTING** phrase tells where the last line of *control* footing can be printed; *page* footings are printed in the space between the **FOOTING** limit and the end of the page. In this example, that means that page footings can be printed on lines 34 and 35.

The last control group is for the report footing. Observe that the report footing happens to print on a page by itself, at the top of the page, and that there is no page number on that page. The last line of output (other than the page footing) is the grand total on line 27 of page 3. If we simply add 5 to the line counter at this point, as indicated by the **LINE** clause of the report footing, the report footing would print on line 32 and would be followed by the page footing on line 34. However, a report footing is *always* the last text printed on a report (which is why there is no page footing on page 4), so this spacing is not allowed. To avoid this conflict, the Report Writer ejects a page if the report footing would be printed in the page footing area, sets the line counter to the start of the heading area (line 4), then treats the relative line number as **LINE PLUS 1**. Thus, the report footing is printed on line 5 of page 4 of the output.

16.9 SUMMARY

The Report Writer features presented in this chapter are sufficient to produce most of the reports shown in this book, and to print much more detail than has been used in many of the reports. However, there are several features of the Report Writer that are beyond the scope of the present discussion and that should be studied by the serious **COBOL** programmer in a **COBOL** manual or an advanced textbook. In any case, while the Report Writer is a very powerful tool and can save you a considerable amount of work, there are times when the only way to produce exactly the output format you want is to use standard Procedure Division code.

REVIEW QUESTIONS

1. What is the general function of the **LINAGE** clause? What are the components of the clause and what is the function of each component?

2. What event in a program creates an end-of-page condition?

3. When an end-of-page condition occurs, what actions are performed by the **EOP** clause?

4. What is the difference between using the **PAGE** option in a **WRITE** statement, and using a mnemonic name defined in the **SPECIAL-NAMES** paragraph (such as **C01 IS TO-TOP-OF-PAGE**)?

5. How does the **COBOL** compiler know to which file the output of a report should be directed?

6. What are the Report Writer statements that appear in the Procedure Division? What is the function of each?

7. List the seven report groups; what is the function of each group?

8. Suppose you have the following report groups:

   a. `01    TYPE CONTROL FOOTING FINAL LINE PLUS 3`
       `      PIC Z(5)9.99 SUM DETAIL-AMOUNT.`

   b. `01    TYPE REPORT FOOTING LINE PLUS 3`
       `      PIC Z(5)9.99 SUM DETAIL-AMOUNT.`

   What would be the difference between using one group or the other?

9. Give the format of the **PAGE** clause of the Report Writer, and tell the function of each part of the clause.

10. Suppose that a report contains several control heading groups and several control footing groups. In what order will the output be printed when a control break occurs?

11. What is the difference in function between the **LINE** clause and the **NEXT GROUP** clause?

12. Assume that the following code is part of a report program.

```
FD   INPUT-FILE
     LABEL RECORDS ARE OMITTED.
01   INPUT-RECORD.
     05   ACCOUNT-NUMBER       PIC X(5).
     05   JAN-SALES            PIC 9(5)V99.
     05   FEB-SALES            PIC 9(5)V99.
     05   MAR-SALES            PIC 9(5)V99.
     .
     .
     .

REPORT SECTION.
RD   SALES-REPORT
     CONTROL IS FINAL
     .
     .
     .

01   SALES-LINE TYPE DETAIL LINE PLUS 1.
     05   COLUMN 11            PIC X(5)       SOURCE ACCOUNT-NUMBER.
     05   COLUMN 19            PIC ZZ,ZZ9.99 SOURCE JAN-SALES.
     05   COLUMN 34            PIC ZZ,ZZ9.99 SOURCE FEB-SALES.
     05   COLUMN 49            PIC ZZ,ZZ9.99 SOURCE MAR-SALES.
01   TYPE CONTROL FOOTING FINAL LINE PLUS 3
     05   COLUMN 1             PIC X(14) VALUE '1ST QTR TOTALS'.
     05   JAN-TOTAL COLUMN 16 PIC Z,ZZZ,ZZ9.99 SUM JAN-SALES.
     05   FEB-TOTAL COLUMN 31 PIC Z,ZZZ,ZZ9.99 SUM FEB-SALES.
     05   MAR-TOTAL COLUMN 46 PIC Z,ZZZ,ZZ9.99 SUM MAR-SALES.
     05   QTR-TOTAL COLUMN 61 PIC Z,ZZZ,ZZ9.99
                              SUM JAN-TOTAL FEB-TOTAL MAR-TOTAL.
```

What do you think will be printed for the **FINAL** control footing group?

ANSWERS

1. The **LINAGE** clause is used in the **FD** entry of a sequential file that is going to a printer, and it controls the general format of a page of output. The **LINAGE** phrase tells how many lines of text, including any headings, can be written on a page. The **FOOTING** phrase specifies where the last line of nonfooting output can be printed; any lines between the line given in the **FOOTING** phrase and the end of the page are reserved for footing text. The **LINES AT TOP** phrase tells how many blank lines will appear at the top of the page; it is not possible to write in this area, and the lines are not part of the **LINAGE** value. Finally, the **LINES AT BOTTOM** phrase tells how many blank lines will appear at the bottom of the page; it is not possible to write in this area, and the lines are not part of the **LINAGE** value.

2. An end-of-page condition occurs when the **ADVANCING** clause of a **WRITE** statement increments **LINAGE-COUNTER** so that its value is greater than or equal to the value in the **FOOTING** phrase. For example, suppose we are writing to a file with the following **LINAGE** clause:

```
LINAGE IS 54 LINES
    WITH FOOTING AT 50
    LINES AT TOP 6
    LINES AT BOTTOM 6
```

As soon as the **ADVANCING** clause increments **LINAGE-COUNTER** so that it has a value greater than or equal to 50, the end-of-page condition occurs.

3. The **WRITE** statement prints the current output record; the statements in the **EOP** clause are executed; if any of the **EOP** statements cause the printer to eject to a new page, **LINAGE-COUNTER** is reset to 1.

4. As far as the output is concerned, there will be no difference in most cases. However, the **PAGE** option is standard for all **COBOL** compilers while the **C01** notation is not, and the **C01** convention will not work correctly with a **LINAGE** clause.

5. The **REPORT IS** clause in the **FD** entry tells the compiler that output for the current file will come from a particular report defined in the Report Section.

6. There are three Report Writer statements in the Procedure Division.

    INITIATE—This statement prepares the report for execution. It sets all summation counters to zero and resets all internal data, including the page and line counters. Also, the report heading group, if present, is printed.

    GENERATE—The **GENERATE** statement instructs the Report Writer to print one detail group. If a control break is detected, appropriate control footings and control headings are automatically generated. If a page break is detected, page footings and headings are printed if they have been defined.

    TERMINATE—This statement ends the report. The **FINAL** control break is triggered and any **FINAL** control footings are printed. If a report footing has been defined it is also printed. It is not possible to write any more output to the report without reinitiating the report.

    None of these statements opens or closes the report file. This must be done explicitly with **OPEN** and **CLOSE** statements.

7. **REPORT HEADING**—prints a heading at the start of the report.

    PAGE HEADING—prints a heading at the top of each page.

    CONTROL HEADING—there can be one control heading for each control variable; when a control break occurs for a variable, its control heading is printed before the new control group begins.

    DETAIL—prints detail information when a **GENERATE** statement is executed.

    CONTROL FOOTING—there can be one control footing for each control variable; when a control break occurs for a variable, its control footing is printed at the end of the old control group; control footings frequently contain **SUM** clauses to sum data within the control group.

    PAGE FOOTING—prints a footing at the bottom of each page.

    REPORT FOOTING—prints a footing at the end of the report.

8. If you tried using option (b), you would get a compilation error. The **SUM** clause can only be used in a *control footing* group. This is why we need to use **FINAL** as a control variable.

9. The general format of the **PAGE** clause is

```
PAGE LIMIT IS integer-1 LINES
     HEADING        integer-2
     FIRST DETAIL   integer-3
     LAST DETAIL    integer-4
     FOOTING        integer-5
```

The **PAGE LIMIT** phrase tells how many lines there are on a page, including any blank lines at the top or bottom of the page. The **HEADING** phrase tells where the first line of heading may be printed. The **FIRST DETAIL** phrase tells where the first line of detail may be printed, while **LAST DETAIL** tells where the last line of detail may be printed. The **FOOTING** phrase tells where the last line of control footing may be printed. Report headings and footings may be printed anywhere between integer-2 and integer-1. Page headings may be printed anywhere between integer-2 and integer-3. Detail and control heading groups may be printed anywhere between integer-3 and integer-4. Control footings may be printed anywhere between integer-3 and integer-5, and page footings may be printed between integer-5 and integer-1.

10. Control footings will be printed in order from minor control variable to major, followed by the detail line, followed by control headings in order from major to minor.

11. The **LINE** clause affects the spacing of the current line, while the **NEXT GROUP** clause affects the spacing of the next report group to be printed, providing that the next group is at the same or lower level of hierarchy than the current group.

12. **JAN-TOTAL** will contain the total January sales for all input records, **FEB-TOTAL** will contain the total February sales for all input records, and **MAR-TOTAL** will contain the total March sales for all input records. **QTR-TOTAL** will contain the total of **JAN-TOTAL**, **FEB-TOTAL**, and **MAR-TOTAL**, the total sales for the first quarter of the year. This is an example of *cross-footing*, in which the total of several columns is added across the line to produce a new total for all columns.

EXERCISES

1. Using the Report Writer, revise the payroll program in Figure 8.5 to print headings at the top of every page of output. Assume that a page is 66 lines from top to bottom, that there are 6 blank lines at the top and 6 blank lines at the bottom, and that there are 54 lines in the body of the page.

*2. Modify the one-level control break program in Figure 9.4 to use the Report Writer for output.

3. Revise the seed catalog program in Figure 11.1 to use the **LINAGE** and **END-OF-PAGE** clauses. Print headings for the normal output as shown in Figure 11.3. Print the special output as shown in Figure 11.4; do not split the error messages for an order over two pages.

* Answers to starred exercises will be found in Appendix IV at the end of the book.

4. Assume that the input to the payroll program in Figure 8.5 has been revised to include a project number and department, as shown below.

```
FD   PAYROLL-FILE
     LABEL RECORDS ARE OMITTED.
01   PAYROLL-RECORD.
     05   I-PAYROLL-NUMBER    PIC X(5).
     05   I-NAME              PIC X(20).
     05   I-HOURS-WORKED      PIC 99V9.
     05   FILLER              PIC X(3).
     05   I-PAYRATE           PIC 99V999.
     05   I-DEPENDENTS        PIC 99.
     05   I-PROJECT           PIC X(5).
     05   I-DEPARTMENT        PIC 999.
     05   FILLER              PIC X(34).
```

The records in this file have been sorted by department, project number, and payroll number. Modify the program as follows:

a. Create two output files, one for valid data and one for data with errors;

b. Start the output for each department on a new page; print the department number at the top of the page, after the page heading;

c. Show the total pay charged to each project;

d. Leave two blank lines between projects;

e. For each department, show the total gross pay for all employees in the department, the total tax for the department, and the total net pay for the department;

f. For the company, show the total gross pay, the total tax, and the total net pay; skip 5 lines before printing the company total.

Use the Report Writer to produce the modified report.

CHAPTER 17

THE COBOL SORT

17.1 INTRODUCTION

We have referred several times in this book to the necessity for sorting files, that is, placing records into ascending or descending sequence on a key in the records. COBOL provides a way to specify this sorting operation using the SORT verb. The SORT verb has several levels of complexity, although in principle all variations perform the same three steps:

1. Read all records from an input file into a sort work area;
2. Sort the records in the work area;
3. Pass the sorted records from the work area to an output file.

We will begin by examining a very simple sort, then move on to look at the more sophisticated sort options. In the following examples, notice that the programs must all provide the same basic information:

1. Define the formats of the records to be sorted;
2. Define the sort keys;
3. Produce the records that are input to the sort;
4. Sort these records;
5. Process the sorted output records.

17.2 A BASIC SORT EXAMPLE

For our first example, we will assume that the data needed for the three-level control break program studied in Chapters 9 and 16 initially is not sorted. We will sort the records on the first three fields (REGION-NUMBER, SELLER-NUMBER, and ACCOUNT-NUMBER) and write the sorted data to a new file which could be used as input to the control break program. The program needed to perform the sort is shown in Figure 17.1.

```
00001              IDENTIFICATION DIVISION.
00002              PROGRAM-ID.
00003                  SORT1.
00004              AUTHOR.
00005                  D. GOLDEN.
00006              DATE-WRITTEN.
00007                  MAY 6, 1987.
00008              *
00009              *    THIS PROGRAM SORTS DATA RECORDS FROM AN INPUT FILE AND
00010              *    WRITES THE SORTED RECORDS TO AN OUTPUT FILE
00011              *
00012
00013              ENVIRONMENT DIVISION.
00014              INPUT-OUTPUT SECTION.
00015              FILE-CONTROL.
00016                  SELECT ACCOUNT-FILE        ASSIGN TO S-ACCOUNT.
00017                  SELECT SORTED-ACCOUNTS     ASSIGN TO S-SORTED.
00018                  SELECT SORT-FILE           ASSIGN TO S-SORTWK01.
00019
00020              DATA DIVISION.
00021              FILE SECTION.
00022
00023              FD  ACCOUNT-FILE
00024                  LABEL RECORDS ARE OMITTED.
00025              01  ACCOUNT-RECORD.
00026                  05   REGION-NUMBER         PIC X(5).
00027                  05   SELLER-NUMBER         PIC X(5).
00028                  05   ACCOUNT-NUMBER        PIC X(5).
00029                  05   SALE-AMOUNT           PIC 9(5)V99.
00030                  05   FILLER                PIC X(58).
00031
00032              FD  SORTED-ACCOUNTS
00033                  LABEL RECORDS ARE STANDARD.
00034              01  SORTED-ACCOUNT-RECORD      PIC X(80).
00035
00036              SD  SORT-FILE.
00037              01  SORT-RECORD.
00038                  05   SORT-KEY              PIC X(15).
00039                  05   FILLER                PIC X(65).
00040
00041
00042              PROCEDURE DIVISION.
00043              A000-PREPARE-SALES-REPORT.
00044                  SORT SORT-FILE
00045                      ON ASCENDING KEY SORT-KEY
00046                      USING ACCOUNT-FILE
00047                      GIVING SORTED-ACCOUNTS.
00048                  STOP RUN.
00049
00050              ********************** END OF PROGRAM **********************
```

FIGURE 17.1   A simple sort program. Records from **ACCOUNT-FILE** are sorted on the first 15 characters and written to **SORTED-ACCOUNTS**.

We begin our study of this program by looking at the **FILE-CONTROL** paragraph. In addition to having **SELECT** statements for **ACCOUNT-FILE** and **SORTED-ACCOUNTS**, the input and output files, we have a **SELECT** statement for a file called **SORT-FILE**. **SORT-FILE** is a work file used in sorting the data. The exact mechanism by which the sort is executed is irrelevant. However, from the point of view of the application programmer, the sort work file is the file which is sorted; the input and output files exist only to provide the data for the sort and to take up the sorted results. The sort file defines the records being sorted; in the operating system instructions to run the program you must define **SORTWK01** to be a sequential file large enough to hold the sort work area. The details of this definition will vary depending on the operating system being used, and you should consult the appropriate manual for details.

In the File Section we have a new type of entry to define **SORT-FILE**. Just as a normal file has a file description (**FD**) to define its structure, a sort file has a sort description (**SD**) to define it. In the **SD** clause itself, we have only specified the file name; there is no **LABEL RECORDS** clause or **BLOCK CONTAINS** clause. Not only are these clauses not required, they are either illegal or ignored, depending on the compiler; in any case, they should not be used.

In **SORT-RECORD** we have only defined the fifteen characters that will be used as the sort key and then padded the remainder of the record with filler. We determined that the sort key is the first fifteen characters of the record by looking at **ACCOUNT-RECORD**. We wish to sort these records by **REGION-NUMBER**, **SELLER-NUMBER**, and **ACCOUNT-NUMBER**, which appear as the first fifteen characters of the record. In a more complex example we could make the format of **SORT-RECORD** as detailed as we wished.

The Procedure Division is quite simple, consisting only of a **SORT** statement and **STOP RUN**. The **SORT** statement says that we want to sort the file **SORT-FILE**, that we will use **SORT-KEY** as the field on which to sort the records, and that the records will be sorted in ascending sequence. If we wished, we could choose a *descending* sort, in which case the output would have the records arranged from largest key to smallest. The **USING** clause tells us that the input to the sort is coming from **ACCOUNT-FILE**, and the **GIVING** clause tells us that the sorted data will be written to **SORTED-ACCOUNTS**. Notice that we do not open or close any of the files used by the sort. Not only is it not required, it is not permitted to use **OPEN** or **CLOSE** statements for any file controlled directly by the sort. This includes the **USING** and **GIVING** files, and the sort file itself.

The input to the sort is shown in Figure 17.2, and the sorted output in Figure 17.3.

17.3 THE OUTPUT PROCEDURE

The example in the previous section demonstrates the simplest possible version of the **SORT** statement. There is only one sort key, the input comes directly from a file, and the output goes directly to another file. If this were the only version of the sort it would be of little value, since sort utility programs can accomplish the same result with much less coding than is needed for a **COBOL** program. The main advantage of using the **SORT** verb is that it allows you to sort data within a program, then immediately use the sorted output for additional processing. As an example of how this is done we will again use the three-level control break program and will assume that the input data is not

```
000010001200010008750
00001000010002000000550
00001000010002400001000
00003000150003001180941
00001000010002400001575
00001000010002700000900
00001000010002400001025
00001000010002700010100
00001000010002700002200
00003000150007800276021
00001000010002700000940
00001000020001700002600
00001000020002400026690
00003000150004900004500
00001000120001600005475
00002000040004000005012
00001000010002700004260
00002000040004100105991
00001000010002000001150
00002000390004401594141
00003000150003800157431
00003000150003500069261
00003000150006001234561
```

FIGURE 17.2 Input to the sort program in Figure 17.1.

```
00001000010002000000550
00001000010002000001150
00001000010002400001025
00001000010002400001575
00001000010002400001000
00001000010002700000900
00001000010002700010100
00001000010002700002200
00001000010002700004260
00001000010002700000940
00001000020001700002600
00001000020002400026690
000010001200010008750
00001000120001600005475
00002000040004000005012
00002000040004100105991
00002000390004401594141
00003000150003001180941
00003000150003500069261
00003000150003800157431
00003000150004900004500
00003000150006001234561
00003000150007800276021
```

FIGURE 17.3 Output from the sort.

sorted, a fairly common situation. We will use the **SORT** verb to sort the input data, then, instead of writing it to a file, we will pass the sorted data to code much like the three-level control break program of Chapter 9. The program to accomplish this is shown in Figure 17.4.

```
00001            IDENTIFICATION DIVISION.
00002            PROGRAM-ID.
00003               SORT2.
00004            AUTHOR.
00005               D. GOLDEN.
00006            DATE-WRITTEN.
00007               MAY 7, 1987.
00008        *
00009        *    THIS PROGRAM SORTS DATA FROM AN INPUT FILE, THEN USES THE
00010        *    SORTED DATA TO PRODUCE A SIMPLE THREE-LEVEL SUMMARY REPORT
00011        *    FOR A SALES ACCOUNTING SYSTEM
00012        *
00013
00014            ENVIRONMENT DIVISION.
00015            CONFIGURATION SECTION.
00016            SPECIAL-NAMES.
00017               C01 IS TO-TOP-OF-PAGE.
00018            INPUT-OUTPUT SECTION.
00019            FILE-CONTROL.
00020               SELECT ACCOUNT-FILE      ASSIGN TO S-ACCOUNT.
00021               SELECT REPORT-FILE       ASSIGN TO S-REPORT.
00022               SELECT SORT-FILE         ASSIGN TO S-SORTWK01.
00023
00024            DATA DIVISION.
00025            FILE SECTION.
00026
00027        FD  ACCOUNT-FILE
00028            LABEL RECORDS ARE OMITTED.
00029        01  ACCOUNT-RECORD           PIC X(80).
00030
00031        FD  REPORT-FILE
00032            LABEL RECORDS ARE OMITTED.
00033        01  REPORT-RECORD            PIC X(133).
00034
00035        SD  SORT-FILE.
00036        01  SORT-REC.
00037            05   REGION-NUMBER       PIC X(5).
00038            05   SELLER-NUMBER       PIC X(5).
00039            05   ACCOUNT-NUMBER      PIC X(5).
00040            05   SALE-AMOUNT         PIC 9(5)V99.
00041            05   FILLER              PIC X(58).
00042
00043
00044            WORKING-STORAGE SECTION.
00045
00046        77  ASTERISK-FLAG           PIC X.
00047            88  ASTERISK-FLAG-ON                 VALUE 'Y'.
00048        77  LINE-NUMBER             PIC S99.
00049        77  MORE-DATA-FLAG          PIC X.
00050            88  NO-MORE-DATA                     VALUE 'N'.
00051        77  PAGE-NUMBER             PIC S999.
00052        77  PREVIOUS-ACCOUNT-NUMBER PIC X(5).
00053        77  PREVIOUS-REGION-NUMBER  PIC X(5).
00054        77  PREVIOUS-SELLER-NUMBER  PIC X(5).
```

```
00055
00056          01   DETAIL-LINE.
00057               05   CARRIAGE-CONTROL        PIC X.
00058               05   ACCOUNT-NUMBER-OUT      PIC Z(4)9.
00059               05   ACCOUNT-TOTAL-OUT       PIC BB$$$$,$$9.99.
00060               05   NO-OF-TRANSACTIONS-OUT  PIC BBZZ9.
00061               05   ASTERISK-OUT            PIC X.
00062               05   SELLER-NUMBER-OUT       PIC B(5)Z(4)9.
00063               05   SELLER-TOTAL-OUT        PIC BBB$$$$,$$9.99.
00064               05   REGION-NUMBER-OUT       PIC B(5)Z(5)9.
00065               05   REGION-TOTAL-OUT        PIC BBB$$$$,$$9.99.
00066
00067          01   FINAL-TOTAL-LINE.
00068               05   CARRIAGE-CONTROL        PIC X.
00069               05   FILLER                  PIC X(44) VALUE SPACES.
00070               05   FILLER                  PIC X(11) VALUE 'FINAL TOTAL'.
00071               05   FINAL-TOTAL-OUT         PIC B(7)$$$$,$$9.99.
00072
00073          01   HEADING-LINE.
00074               05   CARRIAGE-CONTROL        PIC X.
00075               05   FILLER                  PIC X(41)
00076                    VALUE 'ACCOUNT     TOTAL     NUMBER   SALESPERSON '.
00077               05   FILLER                  PIC X(39)
00078                    VALUE 'TOTAL          REGION     TOTAL         PAGE'.
00079               05   PAGE-NUMBER-OUT         PIC Z(6)9.
00080
00081          01   TOTALS.
00082               05   ACCOUNT-TOTAL           PIC S9(6)V99.
00083               05   SELLER-TOTAL            PIC S9(6)V99.
00084               05   REGION-TOTAL            PIC S9(6)V99.
00085               05   FINAL-TOTAL             PIC S9(6)V99.
00086               05   NO-OF-TRANSACTIONS      PIC S999.
00087
00088
00089          PROCEDURE DIVISION.
00090          A000-PREPARE-SALES-REPORT.
00091              SORT SORT-FILE
00092                  ON ASCENDING KEY REGION-NUMBER
00093                                   SELLER-NUMBER
00094                                   ACCOUNT-NUMBER
00095                  USING ACCOUNT-FILE
00096                  OUTPUT PROCEDURE IS B001-GENERATE-REPORT.
00097              STOP RUN.
00098
00099          B001-GENERATE-REPORT SECTION.
00100              OPEN OUTPUT REPORT-FILE.
00101              MOVE ZERO                TO FINAL-TOTAL.
00102              MOVE 'Y'                 TO MORE-DATA-FLAG.
00103              MOVE 55                  TO LINE-NUMBER.
00104              MOVE ZERO                TO PAGE-NUMBER.
00105              RETURN SORT-FILE
00106                  AT END MOVE 'N' TO MORE-DATA-FLAG.
00107              PERFORM B010-PROCESS-REGION-GROUP
00108                  UNTIL NO-MORE-DATA.
00109              MOVE FINAL-TOTAL TO FINAL-TOTAL-OUT.
00110              WRITE REPORT-RECORD FROM FINAL-TOTAL-LINE
00111                  AFTER ADVANCING 3 LINES.
00112              CLOSE REPORT-FILE.
00113
```

```
00114              B009-PERFORMED-PROCEDURES SECTION.
00115              B010-PROCESS-REGION-GROUP.
00116                  MOVE ZERO TO REGION-TOTAL.
00117                  MOVE REGION-NUMBER TO PREVIOUS-REGION-NUMBER.
00118                  PERFORM C010-PROCESS-SELLER-GROUP UNTIL
00119                      REGION-NUMBER IS NOT EQUAL TO PREVIOUS-REGION-NUMBER
00120                    OR NO-MORE-DATA.
00121                  MOVE SPACES TO DETAIL-LINE.
00122                  MOVE PREVIOUS-REGION-NUMBER TO REGION-NUMBER-OUT.
00123                  MOVE REGION-TOTAL TO REGION-TOTAL-OUT.
00124                  PERFORM X010-LINE-OUT.
00125                  ADD REGION-TOTAL TO FINAL-TOTAL.
00126
00127              C010-PROCESS-SELLER-GROUP.
00128                  MOVE ZERO TO SELLER-TOTAL.
00129                  MOVE SELLER-NUMBER TO PREVIOUS-SELLER-NUMBER
00130                  PERFORM D010-PROCESS-ACCOUNT-GROUP UNTIL
00131                      SELLER-NUMBER IS NOT EQUAL TO PREVIOUS-SELLER-NUMBER
00132                    OR REGION-NUMBER IS NOT EQUAL TO PREVIOUS-REGION-NUMBER
00133                    OR NO-MORE-DATA.
00134                  MOVE SPACES TO DETAIL-LINE.
00135                  MOVE PREVIOUS-SELLER-NUMBER TO SELLER-NUMBER-OUT.
00136                  MOVE SELLER-TOTAL TO SELLER-TOTAL-OUT.
00137                  PERFORM X010-LINE-OUT.
00138                  ADD SELLER-TOTAL TO REGION-TOTAL.
00139
00140              D010-PROCESS-ACCOUNT-GROUP.
00141                  MOVE ZERO TO ACCOUNT-TOTAL.
00142                  MOVE ZERO TO NO-OF-TRANSACTIONS.
00143                  MOVE 'N' TO ASTERISK-FLAG.
00144                  MOVE ACCOUNT-NUMBER TO PREVIOUS-ACCOUNT-NUMBER.
00145                  PERFORM E010-PROCESS-ACCOUNT-RECORD UNTIL
00146                       ACCOUNT-NUMBER IS NOT EQUAL TO PREVIOUS-ACCOUNT-NUMBER
00147                    OR SELLER-NUMBER  IS NOT EQUAL TO PREVIOUS-SELLER-NUMBER
00148                    OR REGION-NUMBER  IS NOT EQUAL TO PREVIOUS-REGION-NUMBER
00149                    OR NO-MORE-DATA.
00150                  MOVE SPACES TO DETAIL-LINE.
00151                  MOVE PREVIOUS-ACCOUNT-NUMBER TO ACCOUNT-NUMBER-OUT.
00152                  MOVE ACCOUNT-TOTAL TO ACCOUNT-TOTAL-OUT.
00153                  MOVE NO-OF-TRANSACTIONS TO NO-OF-TRANSACTIONS-OUT.
00154                  IF ASTERISK-FLAG-ON
00155                      MOVE '*' TO ASTERISK-OUT.
00156                  PERFORM X010-LINE-OUT.
00157                  ADD ACCOUNT-TOTAL TO SELLER-TOTAL.
00158
00159              E010-PROCESS-ACCOUNT-RECORD.
00160                  ADD SALE-AMOUNT TO ACCOUNT-TOTAL.
00161                  ADD 1 TO NO-OF-TRANSACTIONS.
00162                  IF SALE-AMOUNT IS GREATER THAN 1000.00
00163                      MOVE 'Y' TO ASTERISK-FLAG.
00164                  RETURN SORT-FILE
00165                      AT END MOVE 'N' TO MORE-DATA-FLAG.
00166
00167              X010-LINE-OUT.
00168                  ADD 1 TO LINE-NUMBER.
00169                  IF LINE-NUMBER IS GREATER THAN 55
00170                      ADD 1 TO PAGE-NUMBER
00171                      MOVE PAGE-NUMBER TO PAGE-NUMBER-OUT
00172                      WRITE REPORT-RECORD FROM HEADING-LINE
00173                          AFTER ADVANCING TO-TOP-OF-PAGE
```

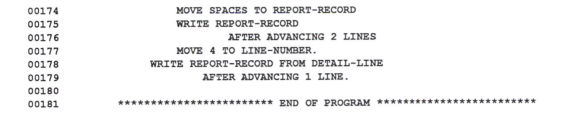

```
00174                    MOVE SPACES TO REPORT-RECORD
00175                    WRITE REPORT-RECORD
00176                           AFTER ADVANCING 2 LINES
00177                    MOVE 4 TO LINE-NUMBER.
00178              WRITE REPORT-RECORD FROM DETAIL-LINE
00179                    AFTER ADVANCING 1 LINE.
00180
00181        *********************** END OF PROGRAM ***********************
```

FIGURE 17.4 A program that sorts data from an input file, then uses the sorted data to produce a report.

The program in Figure 17.4 looks like a cross between the sort program in Figure 17.1 and the three-level control break program of Figure 9.9. We have created an **SD** entry for **SORT-FILE**, and, in contrast to the previous example, **ACCOUNT-RECORD** only has a **PICTURE** of **X(80)** while **SORT-RECORD** contains the complete definition of an account record. We have made this change because we do not really use any of the data in **ACCOUNT-FILE** except to feed it into the sort process. However, we will need to refer to the data fields of the sorted data in order to use them in the output procedure. The remainder of the Data Division is exactly as it was in Chapter 9. In the current program, of course, we now refer to fields in the sort file instead of the input file.

The main paragraph of the Procedure Division still contains only a **SORT** statement and a **STOP RUN** statement, but the **SORT** statement is a bit more complicated than before. For one thing, we are now using three sort keys instead of just one. We have declared **REGION-NUMBER** to be the major key, **SELLER-NUMBER** to be the intermediate key, and **ACCOUNT-NUMBER** to be the minor key. Also, rather than sending the sorted output to **SORTED-ACCOUNTS** we are going to process it in an *output procedure* called **B001-GENERATE-REPORT**.

The first thing to observe about **B001-GENERATE-REPORT** is that it is a *section*, not an ordinary paragraph. The output procedure of a **SORT** statement must be a section.

COBOL-85

In standard **COBOL-85** the output procedure may be an ordinary paragraph. However, this flexibility is not necessarily implemented in all compilers; be sure to check the appropriate manual for the compiler you are using.

END COBOL-85

Just as a paragraph consists of one or more statements, a section consists of one or more paragraphs. It begins with a section header consisting of the section name (just like a paragraph name) followed by the word **SECTION**, and continues until the start of the next section or until the end of the program. Although the first paragraph in a section may have a paragraph name it is not required; notice the difference between sections **B001-GENERATE-REPORT** and **B009-PERFORMED-PROCEDURES**. We also emphasize the reason that **B009-PER-FORMED-PROCEDURES** has been included at all, which is to terminate section **B001-GENERATE-REPORT**. If we did not precede **B010-PROCESS-REGION-GROUP** with a section, after the program had executed the **CLOSE** statement in **B001-**

GENERATE-REPORT it would continue on to B010-PROCESS-REGION-GROUP and try to execute the paragraph again, causing an error.

B001-GENERATE-REPORT looks much like the driver paragraph in the program of Figure 9.9, except that we do not open or close the input file. Since this section is the output procedure of the SORT statement, the input file for the report is SORT-FILE; since this has been defined as a sort file (SD), it may never be opened or closed explicitly.

The only other new feature in this paragraph is that the READ statement has been replaced by a RETURN statement. The RETURN statement is almost identical to a sequential READ statement, except that the file must be a sort file. We RETURN from a file, just as we READ from a file; we could include an optional INTO clause, just as we do in a READ statement; and we have an AT END clause to indicate when we have reached the end of the sort data. The only restriction on the use of a RETURN statement is that it must be used under control of a SORT verb. Notice that in E010-PROCESS-ACCOUNT-RECORD the READ statement has also been replaced by a RETURN statement.

The program was run with the sample data shown in Chapter 9 and produced the same output.

17.4 THE INPUT PROCEDURE

Just as we use the output procedure to process output from a sort, we can use the *input procedure* to process input before it reaches the sort. To demonstrate the use of an input procedure, we shall revise the previous example to edit the account records for nonnumeric fields before passing them to the sort. If a record contains any nonnumeric data, it will be rejected and printed with a simple error message; otherwise, it will be passed to SORT-FILE for sorting. The program to accomplish this is shown in Figure 17.5.

```
00001          IDENTIFICATION DIVISION.
00002          PROGRAM-ID.
00003              SORT3.
00004          AUTHOR.
00005              D. GOLDEN.
00006          DATE-WRITTEN.
00007              MAY 7, 1987.
00008          *
00009          *    THIS PROGRAM SORTS EDITED DATA FROM AN INPUT FILE, THEN USES
00010          *    THE SORTED DATA TO PRODUCE A SIMPLE THREE-LEVEL SUMMARY
00011          *    REPORT FOR A SALES ACCOUNTING SYSTEM
00012
00013          ENVIRONMENT DIVISION.
00014          CONFIGURATION SECTION.
00015          SPECIAL-NAMES.
00016              C01 IS TO-TOP-OF-PAGE.
00017          INPUT-OUTPUT SECTION.
00018          FILE-CONTROL.
00019              SELECT ACCOUNT-FILE        ASSIGN TO S-ACCOUNT.
00020              SELECT LOG-FILE            ASSIGN TO S-LOGFILE.
00021              SELECT REPORT-FILE         ASSIGN TO S-REPORT.
00022              SELECT SORT-FILE           ASSIGN TO S-SORTWK01.
00023
```

```
00024          DATA DIVISION.
00025          FILE SECTION.
00026
00027     FD   ACCOUNT-FILE
00028               LABEL RECORDS ARE OMITTED.
00029     01   ACCOUNT-RECORD.
00030          05   REGION-NUMBER-IN          PIC X(5).
00031          05   SELLER-NUMBER-IN          PIC X(5).
00032          05   ACCOUNT-NUMBER-IN         PIC X(5).
00033          05   SALE-AMOUNT-IN            PIC X(7).
00034          05   FILLER                    PIC X(58).
00035
00036     FD   LOG-FILE
00037               LABEL RECORDS ARE OMITTED.
00038     01   LOG-RECORD.
00039          05   FILLER                    PIC X.
00040          05   LOG-MESSAGE               PIC X(32).
00041          05   BAD-RECORD                PIC X(80).
00042          05   FILLER                    PIC X(20).
00043
00044     FD   REPORT-FILE
00045               LABEL RECORDS ARE OMITTED.
00046     01   REPORT-RECORD                  PIC X(133).
00047
00048     SD   SORT-FILE.
00049     01   SORT-RECORD.
00050          05   REGION-NUMBER             PIC X(5).
00051          05   SELLER-NUMBER             PIC X(5).
00052          05   ACCOUNT-NUMBER            PIC X(5).
00053          05   SALE-AMOUNT               PIC 9(5)V99.
00054          05   FILLER                    PIC X(58).
00055
00056
00057          WORKING-STORAGE SECTION.
00058
00059     77   ASTERISK-FLAG                  PIC X.
00060          88   ASTERISK-FLAG-ON                      VALUE 'Y'.
00061     77   LINE-NUMBER                    PIC S99.
00062     77   MORE-DATA-FLAG                 PIC X.
00063          88   NO-MORE-DATA                          VALUE 'N'.
00064     77   PAGE-NUMBER                    PIC S999.
00065     77   PREVIOUS-ACCOUNT-NUMBER        PIC X(5).
00066     77   PREVIOUS-REGION-NUMBER         PIC X(5).
00067     77   PREVIOUS-SELLER-NUMBER         PIC X(5).
00068
00069     01   DETAIL-LINE.
00070          05   CARRIAGE-CONTROL          PIC X.
00071          05   ACCOUNT-NUMBER-OUT        PIC Z(4)9.
00072          05   ACCOUNT-TOTAL-OUT         PIC BB$$$$,$$9.99.
00073          05   NO-OF-TRANSACTIONS-OUT    PIC BBZZ9.
00074          05   ASTERISK-OUT              PIC X.
00075          05   SELLER-NUMBER-OUT         PIC B(5)Z(4)9.
00076          05   SELLER-TOTAL-OUT          PIC BBB$$$$,$$9.99.
00077          05   REGION-NUMBER-OUT         PIC B(5)Z(5)9.
00078          05   REGION-TOTAL-OUT          PIC BBB$$$$,$$9.99.
00079
00080     01   FINAL-TOTAL-LINE.
00081          05   CARRIAGE-CONTROL          PIC X.
00082          05   FILLER                    PIC X(44) VALUE SPACES.
00083          05   FILLER                    PIC X(11) VALUE 'FINAL TOTAL'.
00084          05   FINAL-TOTAL-OUT           PIC B(7)$$$$,$$9.99.
00085
```

```
00086               01   HEADING-LINE.
00087                    05   CARRIAGE-CONTROL      PIC X.
00088                    05   FILLER               PIC X(41)
00089                         VALUE 'ACCOUNT      TOTAL      NUMBER   SALESPERSON '.
00090                    05   FILLER               PIC X(39)
00091                         VALUE 'TOTAL        REGION      TOTAL        PAGE'.
00092                    05   PAGE-NUMBER-OUT        PIC Z(6)9.
00093
00094               01   TOTALS.
00095                    05   ACCOUNT-TOTAL        PIC S9(6)V99.
00096                    05   SELLER-TOTAL         PIC S9(6)V99.
00097                    05   REGION-TOTAL         PIC S9(6)V99.
00098                    05   FINAL-TOTAL          PIC S9(6)V99.
00099                    05   NO-OF-TRANSACTIONS   PIC S999.
00100
00101
00102               PROCEDURE DIVISION.
00103               A000-PREPARE-SALES-REPORT.
00104                   SORT SORT-FILE
00105                       ON ASCENDING KEY REGION-NUMBER
00106                                         SELLER-NUMBER
00107                                         ACCOUNT-NUMBER
00108                       INPUT  PROCEDURE IS B001-EDIT-INPUT
00109                       OUTPUT PROCEDURE IS B002-GENERATE-REPORT.
00110                   STOP RUN.
00111
00112               B001-EDIT-INPUT SECTION.
00113                   OPEN INPUT ACCOUNT-FILE
00114                        OUTPUT LOG-FILE.
00115                   MOVE 'Y' TO MORE-DATA-FLAG.
00116                   READ ACCOUNT-FILE
00117                       AT END MOVE 'N' TO MORE-DATA-FLAG.
00118                   PERFORM B010-EDIT-ACCOUNTS
00119                       UNTIL NO-MORE-DATA.
00120                   CLOSE ACCOUNT-FILE
00121                         LOG-FILE.
00122
00123               B002-GENERATE-REPORT SECTION.
00124                   OPEN OUTPUT REPORT-FILE.
00125                   MOVE ZERO               TO FINAL-TOTAL.
00126                   MOVE 'Y'                TO MORE-DATA-FLAG.
00127                   MOVE 55                 TO LINE-NUMBER.
00128                   MOVE ZERO               TO PAGE-NUMBER.
00129                   RETURN SORT-FILE
00130                           AT END MOVE 'N' TO MORE-DATA-FLAG.
00131                   PERFORM B020-PROCESS-REGION-GROUP
00132                       UNTIL NO-MORE-DATA.
00133                   MOVE FINAL-TOTAL TO FINAL-TOTAL-OUT.
00134                   WRITE REPORT-RECORD FROM FINAL-TOTAL-LINE
00135                           AFTER ADVANCING 3 LINES.
00136                   CLOSE REPORT-FILE.
00137
00138               B009-PERFORMED-PROCEDURES SECTION.
00139               B010-EDIT-ACCOUNTS.
00140                   IF     REGION-NUMBER-IN IS NOT NUMERIC
00141                       OR SELLER-NUMBER-IN IS NOT NUMERIC
00142                       OR ACCOUNT-NUMBER-IN IS NOT NUMERIC
00143                       OR SALE-AMOUNT-IN IS NOT NUMERIC
```

```
00144                    MOVE SPACES TO LOG-RECORD
00145                    MOVE 'A FIELD CONTAINS INVALID DATA:  ' TO LOG-MESSAGE
00146                    MOVE ACCOUNT-RECORD TO BAD-RECORD
00147                    WRITE LOG-RECORD AFTER ADVANCING 1 LINE
00148                ELSE
00149                    RELEASE SORT-RECORD FROM ACCOUNT-RECORD.
00150                READ ACCOUNT-FILE
00151                    AT END MOVE 'N' TO MORE-DATA-FLAG.
00152
00153        B020-PROCESS-REGION-GROUP.
00154            MOVE ZERO TO REGION-TOTAL.
00155            MOVE REGION-NUMBER TO PREVIOUS-REGION-NUMBER.
00156            PERFORM C010-PROCESS-SELLER-GROUP UNTIL
00157                    REGION-NUMBER IS NOT EQUAL TO PREVIOUS-REGION-NUMBER
00158                OR NO-MORE-DATA.
00159            MOVE SPACES TO DETAIL-LINE.
00160            MOVE PREVIOUS-REGION-NUMBER TO REGION-NUMBER-OUT.
00161            MOVE REGION-TOTAL TO REGION-TOTAL-OUT.
00162            PERFORM X010-LINE-OUT.
00163            ADD REGION-TOTAL TO FINAL-TOTAL.
00164
00165        C010-PROCESS-SELLER-GROUP.
00166            MOVE ZERO TO SELLER-TOTAL.
00167            MOVE SELLER-NUMBER TO PREVIOUS-SELLER-NUMBER
00168            PERFORM D010-PROCESS-ACCOUNT-GROUP UNTIL
00169                    SELLER-NUMBER IS NOT EQUAL TO PREVIOUS-SELLER-NUMBER
00170                OR REGION-NUMBER IS NOT EQUAL TO PREVIOUS-REGION-NUMBER
00171                OR NO-MORE-DATA.
00172            MOVE SPACES TO DETAIL-LINE.
00173            MOVE PREVIOUS-SELLER-NUMBER TO SELLER-NUMBER-OUT.
00174            MOVE SELLER-TOTAL TO SELLER-TOTAL-OUT.
00175            PERFORM X010-LINE-OUT.
00176            ADD SELLER-TOTAL TO REGION-TOTAL.
00177
00178        D010-PROCESS-ACCOUNT-GROUP.
00179            MOVE ZERO TO ACCOUNT-TOTAL.
00180            MOVE ZERO TO NO-OF-TRANSACTIONS.
00181            MOVE 'N' TO ASTERISK-FLAG.
00182            MOVE ACCOUNT-NUMBER TO PREVIOUS-ACCOUNT-NUMBER.
00183            PERFORM E010-PROCESS-ACCOUNT-RECORD UNTIL
00184                    ACCOUNT-NUMBER IS NOT EQUAL TO PREVIOUS-ACCOUNT-NUMBER
00185                OR SELLER-NUMBER  IS NOT EQUAL TO PREVIOUS-SELLER-NUMBER
00186                OR REGION-NUMBER  IS NOT EQUAL TO PREVIOUS-REGION-NUMBER
00187                OR NO-MORE-DATA.
00188            MOVE SPACES TO DETAIL-LINE.
00189            MOVE PREVIOUS-ACCOUNT-NUMBER TO ACCOUNT-NUMBER-OUT.
00190            MOVE ACCOUNT-TOTAL TO ACCOUNT-TOTAL-OUT.
00191            MOVE NO-OF-TRANSACTIONS TO NO-OF-TRANSACTIONS-OUT.
00192            IF ASTERISK-FLAG-ON
00193                MOVE '*' TO ASTERISK-OUT.
00194            PERFORM X010-LINE-OUT.
00195            ADD ACCOUNT-TOTAL TO SELLER-TOTAL.
00196
00197        E010-PROCESS-ACCOUNT-RECORD.
00198            ADD SALE-AMOUNT TO ACCOUNT-TOTAL.
00199            ADD 1 TO NO-OF-TRANSACTIONS.
00200            IF SALE-AMOUNT IS GREATER THAN 1000.00
00201                MOVE 'Y' TO ASTERISK-FLAG.
00202            RETURN SORT-FILE
00203                AT END MOVE 'N' TO MORE-DATA-FLAG.
00204
```

```
00205              X010-LINE-OUT.
00206                  ADD 1 TO LINE-NUMBER.
00207                  IF LINE-NUMBER IS GREATER THAN 55
00208                      ADD 1 TO PAGE-NUMBER
00209                      MOVE PAGE-NUMBER TO PAGE-NUMBER-OUT
00210                      WRITE REPORT-RECORD FROM HEADING-LINE
00211                          AFTER ADVANCING TO-TOP-OF-PAGE
00212                      MOVE SPACES TO REPORT-RECORD
00213                      WRITE REPORT-RECORD
00214                          AFTER ADVANCING 2 LINES
00215                      MOVE 4 TO LINE-NUMBER.
00216                  WRITE REPORT-RECORD FROM DETAIL-LINE
00217                          AFTER ADVANCING 1 LINE.
00218
00219              *********************** END OF PROGRAM *************************
```

FIGURE 17.5   A sort program using both input and output procedures.

We have added a file called **LOG-FILE** to the program. This file will be used to write error messages for invalid input records. Other than the code needed to declare **LOG-FILE**, the Environment and **DATA** Divisions are the same as in the previous example.

In the driver paragraph of the Procedure Division the **SORT** statement has been changed to take the input to the sort from the input procedure **B001-EDIT-INPUT** instead of directly from **ACCOUNT-FILE**. We have also modified the prefix of **GENERATE-REPORT** to keep the paragraphs and sections in prefix sequence. Given this example, we can now show the complete format of the **SORT** statement.

$$
\underline{\text{SORT}} \text{ file-name-1}
$$

$$
\text{ON} \left\{ \begin{array}{l} \underline{\text{ASCENDING}} \\ \underline{\text{DESCENDING}} \end{array} \right\} \underline{\text{KEY}} \text{ data-name-1 } \ldots
$$

$$
\left[\text{ON} \left\{ \begin{array}{l} \underline{\text{ASCENDING}} \\ \underline{\text{DESCENDING}} \end{array} \right\} \underline{\text{KEY}} \text{ data-name-2 } \ldots \right]
$$

$$
\left\{ \begin{array}{l} \underline{\text{USING}} \text{ file-name-2 } \ldots \\ \underline{\text{INPUT}} \ \underline{\text{PROCEDURE}} \ \underline{\text{IS}} \text{ section-name-1 } \left[\left\{ \begin{array}{l} \underline{\text{THRU}} \\ \underline{\text{THROUGH}} \end{array} \right\} \text{ section-name-2} \right] \end{array} \right\}
$$

$$
\left\{ \begin{array}{l} \underline{\text{GIVING}} \text{ file-name-3 } \ldots \\ \underline{\text{OUTPUT}} \ \underline{\text{PROCEDURE}} \ \underline{\text{IS}} \qquad \left[\left\{ \begin{array}{l} \underline{\text{THRU}} \\ \underline{\text{THROUGH}} \end{array} \right\} \text{ section-name-4} \right] \end{array} \right\}
$$

When the **SORT** statement is executed the program first executes **B001-EDIT-INPUT**, which generates the records that are written onto **SORT-FILE**. When we get to the end of **B001-EDIT-INPUT** the records on **SORT-FILE** are sorted on the specified keys, after which **B002-GENERATE-REPORT** is executed. This section takes the sorted records from **SORT-FILE** and uses them to produce the report.

B001-EDIT-INPUT looks much like the driver paragraph of a program whose function is to produce an edited data file, and **B010-EDIT-ACCOUNTS** is similar to edit paragraphs we have seen in previous chapters. It takes the current input record and tests to see if any of its fields are nonnumeric. If so, an error message is written to **LOG-FILE**. If all fields are numeric, the record is sent to the sort file. However, instead of using **WRITE** we use **RELEASE** to put the records in the file. Just as **RETURN** is analogous to the sequential **READ**, so **RELEASE** is analogous to the sequential **WRITE**. Since **RELEASE** always writes to a file, not a printer, it must not have an **ADVANCING** clause; and, like the **RETURN** statement, it must always be executed under control of a **SORT** statement.

Notice that it makes no difference that both **B001-EDIT-INPUT** and **B002-GENERATE-REPORT** perform paragraphs that are located in **B009-PERFORMED-PROCEDURES**. There is no problem in performing paragraphs across section boundaries. In early versions of **COBOL**, where memory management was more of a problem than it is today, sections played a more important roll in **COBOL** programs. Today, however, they are a relatively minor feature of **COBOL**.

The program in Figure 17.5 was tested using the data file of previous examples, with a few erroneous records added. It produced correct results.

17.5   THE SORT-MESSAGE SPECIAL REGISTER

The IBM version of **COBOL** has one feature which frequently causes problems for the programmer. Although we have not shown the job control language for our examples, one of the files that was needed for the sort programs is called **SYSOUT**. This file is used by the **SORT** statement to write record counts and other diagnostic information. If you use **DISPLAY** or **EXHIBIT** in a program, the IBM **COBOL** compiler also sends the output from these verbs to **SYSOUT**. Unfortunately, **SORT** and **DISPLAY** use different formats for the output file. The result of all this is that if you try to use **DISPLAY** or **EXHIBIT** inside an input or output procedure, you will cause an abend.

Fortunately, there is a simple solution for the problem. IBM **COBOL** provides a *special register* called **SORT-MESSAGE**, which can be used to determine the file to which diagnostic messages from the sort will be sent. A special register is essentially nothing more than a predefined variable. **SORT-MESSAGE** acts as though it had been defined as

```
01  SORT-MESSAGE            PIC X(8) VALUE 'SYSOUT'.
```

Understand, however, that this variable is defined by the compiler. You *do not* define it explicitly in your program. To change the file used for diagnostic messages by the **SORT** verb, simply assign a new value to **SORT-MESSAGE** using a **MOVE** statement. For example, Figure 17.6 shows how the previous example might be modified to use **DISPLAY** statements instead of **LOG-FILE** for error messages.

```
IDENTIFICATION DIVISION.
PROGRAM-ID.
    SORT4.
AUTHOR.
    D. GOLDEN.
DATE-WRITTEN.
    MAY 7, 1987.
*
*    THIS PROGRAM SORTS EDITED DATA FROM AN INPUT FILE, THEN USES
*    THE SORTED DATA TO PRODUCE A SIMPLE THREE-LEVEL SUMMARY
*    REPORT FOR A SALES ACCOUNTING SYSTEM

ENVIRONMENT DIVISION.
CONFIGURATION SECTION.
SPECIAL-NAMES.
    C01 IS TO-TOP-OF-PAGE.
INPUT-OUTPUT SECTION.
FILE-CONTROL.
    SELECT ACCOUNT-FILE        ASSIGN TO S-ACCOUNT.
    SELECT REPORT-FILE         ASSIGN TO S-REPORT.
    SELECT SORT-FILE           ASSIGN TO S-SORTWK01.
    .
    .

PROCEDURE DIVISION.
A000-PREPARE-SALES-REPORT.
    MOVE 'SORTMSG' TO SORT-MESSAGE.
    SORT SORT-FILE
        ON ASCENDING KEY REGION-NUMBER
                         SELLER-NUMBER
                         ACCOUNT-NUMBER
        INPUT PROCEDURE IS B001-EDIT-INPUT
        OUTPUT PROCEDURE IS B002-GENERATE-REPORT.
    STOP RUN.

B001-EDIT-INPUT SECTION.
    OPEN INPUT ACCOUNT-FILE.
    MOVE 'Y' TO MORE-DATA-FLAG.
    READ ACCOUNT-FILE
        AT END MOVE 'N' TO MORE-DATA-FLAG.
    PERFORM B010-EDIT-ACCOUNTS
        UNTIL NO-MORE-DATA.
    CLOSE ACCOUNT-FILE.
    .
    .

B009-PERFORMED-PROCEDURES SECTION.
B010-EDIT-ACCOUNTS.
    IF    REGION-NUMBER-IN IS NOT NUMERIC
       OR SELLER-NUMBER-IN IS NOT NUMERIC
       OR ACCOUNT-NUMBER-IN IS NOT NUMERIC
       OR SALE-AMOUNT-IN IS NOT NUMERIC
        DISPLAY 'A FIELD CONTAINS INVALID DATA:  '
                ACCOUNT-RECORD.
    ELSE
        RELEASE SORT-RECORD FROM ACCOUNT-RECORD.
    READ ACCOUNT-FILE
        AT END MOVE 'N' TO MORE-DATA-FLAG.
    .
    .

*********************** END OF PROGRAM **************************
```

FIGURE 17.6 This program demonstrates the use of **SORT-MESSAGE** and **DISPLAY** in a sort program.

There are two points to emphasize about this example. First, the MOVE statement that initializes SORT-MESSAGE must be executed *before* the SORT verb. It cannot be contained within the input or output procedures. Second, the whole problem relating to SYSOUT and SORT-MESSAGE is unique to the IBM mainframe COBOL compiler. Other compilers generally do not have this problem.

REVIEW QUESTIONS

1. Describe the function of each of the following:
   a. the SELECT statement for the sort file
   b. the SD entry
   c. the KEY clause in the SORT statement
   d. the input procedure
   e. the output procedure

2. Write a SORT statement for the sales report program that will read the records from ACCOUNT-FILE, write them to SORTED-ACCOUNTS, and sort the records in the following order:

   ascending on region;
   descending on seller number;
   descending on account number;
   ascending on sale amount

3. Assume that SORT-FILE is defined in an SD entry, SORT-RECORD is a record of SORT-FILE, and SORT-KEY is a field in SORT-RECORD. What is wrong with the following code?

```
PROCEDURE DIVISION.
A000-MAIN.
    SORT SORT-FILE ON ASCENDING KEY SORT-KEY
        INPUT PROCEDURE B001-INPUT
        OUTPUT PROCEDURE B002-OUTPUT.
    STOP RUN.

B001-INPUT.
    OPEN INPUT IN-FILE
        OUTPUT SORT-FILE.
    MOVE 'Y' TO MORE-RECORDS-FLAG.
    READ IN-FILE AT END MOVE 'N' TO MORE-RECORDS-FLAG.
    PERFORM C010-COPY-TO-SORT UNTIL NO-MORE-RECORDS.
    CLOSE IN-FILE SORT-FILE.

B002-OUTPUT.
    OPEN INPUT SORT-FILE
        OUTPUT OUT-FILE.
    MOVE 'Y' TO MORE-RECORDS-FLAG.
    READ SORT-FILE AT END MOVE 'N' TO MORE-RECORDS-FLAG.
    PERFORM C020-COPY-FROM-SORT UNTIL NO-MORE-RECORDS.
    CLOSE OUT-FILE SORT-FILE.
```

```
C010-COPY-TO-SORT.
    WRITE SORT-RECORD FROM IN-RECORD.
    READ IN-FILE AT END MOVE 'N' TO MORE-RECORDS-FLAG.

C020-COPY-FROM-SORT.
    WRITE OUT-RECORD FROM SORT-RECORD.
    READ SORT-FILE AT END MOVE 'N' TO MORE-RECORDS-FLAG.
```

4. Assuming the same conditions as in Question 3, what is wrong with the following code?

```
PROCEDURE DIVISION.
A000-MAIN.
    OPEN INPUT IN-FILE
        OUTPUT OUT-FILE.
    SORT SORT-FILE ON DESCENDING KEY SORT-KEY
        USING IN-FILE
        GIVING OUT-FILE.
    CLOSE IN-FILE OUT-FILE.
    STOP RUN.
```

ANSWERS

1. **a.** The **SELECT** statement for the sort file tells the program which file is to be used as a work area for the data during the sort.

   b. The **SD** entry defines the sort file and the format(s) of the records to be sorted.

   c. The **KEY** clause tells which fields are to be used as sort keys, the hierarchy of the keys from major to minor, and whether a particular key field is to be sorted in ascending or descending sequence.

   d. The input procedure produces the records to be sorted. These records may be the result of selecting certain records from an input file, or may be generated as the result of a calculation, or both.

   e. The output procedure processes the sorted records on the sort file.

2.
```
SORT SORT-FILE
    ON ASCENDING KEY REGION-NUMBER
    ON DESCENDING KEY SELLER-NUMBER
                      ACCOUNT-NUMBER
    ON ASCENDING KEY SALE-AMOUNT.
```

3. There are several errors in the code:

   a. neither **B001-INPUT** nor **B002-OUTPUT** has been defined to be a section (this is acceptable, however, in **COBOL-85**);

   b. the sort file may not be opened or closed explicitly by the program;

   c. you may not use a sort file in a **READ** or **WRITE** statement; you must use **RETURN** or **RELEASE**.

4. You may not open files used in **USING** or **GIVING** clauses before executing a **SORT** statement, and after the **SORT** has executed the files are already closed. However, *after* the **SORT** statement has been executed you may use **IN-FILE** and **OUT-FILE** as ordinary files, opening and closing them as necessary.

EXERCISES

1. Consider the payroll program in Figure 7.4. Write a program which will read records from **PAYROLL-FILE**, sort them in ascending order on **I-PAYROLL-NUMBER**, and write the sorted records to **SORTED-PAYROLL-FILE**.

2. Same as Exercise 1, except that instead of writing the sorted records to **SORTED-PAYROLL-FILE** you should perform the payroll calculations shown in Figure 7.4 as output procedure of the sort.

3. Using the version of the seed catalog program shown in Figure 11.1, assume that the records in **ORDER-FILE** are in random sequence. Perform the edits shown in Figure 11.1 as the input procedure to a sort. Write invalid orders to **SPECIAL-HANDLING-FILE** as shown in the program, but sort valid order records into ascending order on **ORDER-NUMBER** before writing them to **NORMAL-HANDLING-FILE**.

4. (This exercise is suitable for a project.)

   Write a program to produce the payroll reports described in Exercise 8 of Chapter 12. Transaction records are unsorted and must be sorted on employee pay number as the major key and record type as the minor key. Assume that there are errors in the transaction records and that all records must be edited as described in the optional part of Exercise 12.8. Use an Input Procedure to edit the transactions and reject any transaction containing an error. In other words, only valid transactions are to be sorted. After sorting the transactions, use an Output Procedure to produce the main payroll report and the payroll activity log.

CHAPTER 18

SUBPROGRAMS

18.1 INTRODUCTION

Throughout this book we have emphasized the concept of functional modularity, dividing the task that a program must perform into smaller, more manageable tasks, each of which is treated as a module. To build the program, we simply write code that executes the modules in the appropriate sequence. The advantage of this approach, of course, is that modularity allows us to break a problem that is too large to deal with easily into several smaller problems, each of which can be solved without being distracted by the others.

Up to now, we have used paragraphs of the program to implement modules and, in the relatively small problems we have been dealing with so far, this presents little problem. However, as programs become larger and larger they become more and more difficult to deal with even using modular design. One of the problems is simply that the sheer volume of code in a program with 10,000 or 100,000 lines or more strains the capacity of much system software. Many source code editors cannot deal with files this size easily, the work space required by a compiler to compile a large program becomes very large, and the cost of compiling 100,000 lines of code in order to change the one or two characters necessary to fix a bug becomes exorbitant.

The solution to these problems is to use *subprograms* to implement modules. A subprogram is a COBOL program, compiled separately from the main program or other subprograms, which is executed under control of the main program or another subprogram. The complete program consists of the main program, plus all subprograms. The subprogram being executed is designated the *called* program, and the one that controls its execution is designated the *calling* program. The calling program may be either the main program or another subprogram.

Using subprograms to implement modules has several advantages over using only paragraphs. We have implied one advantage already; it is frequently much more efficient to implement a program as a set of subprograms, each of which is only a few thousand lines, than to implement it as a single program consisting of many tens of thousands of lines. If the change required for a program only involves a few lines of code, one need only recompile the affected subprogram, then reconnect all subprograms to create the complete program.* Another advantage is that subprograms can be stored in special files called *libraries*, then reused in other programs. This can reduce significantly the amount of work needed to write new programs. Last but not least, subprograms give much better control over the way in which data is passed between modules than paragraphs do. This is very important in program design, but is more properly part of a book on program design techniques.

18.2 USING SUBPROGRAMS

A **COBOL** subprogram has all the characteristics of a **COBOL** program as we have learned them, including all four divisions and all the sections of the Environment and Data Divisions that have been presented to date. For the idea of a subprogram to make any sense, however, it is almost always necessary that there be some way for the calling program and the subprogram to communicate with each other. The calling program needs to be able to specify what data is to be operated on and the names of the variables that the subprogram is to use in sending information back to the calling program. The answer to this need is as follows.

When we are ready to bring a subprogram into action under control of a calling program, we write the verb **CALL**, follow it with the name of the subprogram written in quotes, then the word **USING**, and finally the names of the variables that the calling program is communicating to the subprogram. Within the subprogram, the Procedure Division header is modified to include the word **USING** and the names of the items being communicated. Within the Data Division of the subprogram there must be a new section, called the *Linkage Section*, in which the items named in the subprogram's Procedure Division header are described.

For example, suppose that in a calling program we wrote

```
CALL 'SUBPROG' USING DATA-REC.
```

The subprogram should have **SUBPROG** as its **PROGRAM-ID**.[†] In its Procedure Division header there should be a **USING** phrase, and its Data Division should have a Linkage Section. It is entirely permissible for the subprogram to use the same name for the information being communicated as the calling program used. In this case its Procedure Division header would be

```
PROCEDURE DIVISION USING DATA-REC.
```

In the Linkage Section there would be an entry for **DATA-REC** describing it.

---

* The task of connecting a main program and its subprograms to form a complete program is called *linking*, and is performed by a program called a *linker*, or *linkage-editor*. The details of how linking is performed varies from computer to computer and is beyond the scope of this book. Your instructor can give you the few details needed to be able to run sample problems.

† Many compilers put a limit on how long a subprogram name can be. The IBM compiler, for example, allows the subprogram name to be any valid **COBOL** identifier, but only the first eight characters are used to identify the subprogram. Check the appropriate manual for the compiler you are using to find out what, if any, restrictions apply.

However, it is not necessary for the information named in the two **USING** phrases to have the same names. They must be of the same length and the same structure, but they can certainly have different names. We mentioned before that one of the motivations for using subprograms is that they can be used by many different calling programs. This is because the data names used in the **USING** phrase in the subprogram (called parameters) need not be the same as the names of the parameters used in the calling program. For example, we could call a subprogram with the heading shown above with any of these statements

```
CALL 'SUBPROG' USING NEW-REC.
CALL 'SUBPROG' USING MASTER-REC.
CALL 'SUBPROG' USING WORK-DATA.
```

The only requirement is that the length and structure of all the records be the same. In this case, the subprogram will work correctly with no changes to it whatever.

In the example above, the list of parameters in the **USING** clauses contains only one data name. However, there is really no practical limit to the number of parameters in a parameter list, other than the fact that a list that is too long may be difficult to understand or to use accurately. In the example we shall be using shortly, the parameter list will contain three parameters. There are only two restrictions that apply to parameters. First, they must always be data names; they can be defined anywhere in the Data Division except the Report Section, but they cannot be file names, paragraph names, or literals. Second, they should always be defined at the **77** or **01** levels.

18.3 THE SEQUENTIAL FILE UPDATE PROGRAM WITH SUBPROGRAMS

To demonstrate the use of subprograms, we will use the sequential file update program from Chapter 12. Specifically, we will take the program **UPDATE5** in Figure 12.9 and modify it to invoke a subprogram that processes transactions other than additions and deletions. The revised program, **UPDATE6**, is shown in Figure 18.1. You may wish to review the program in Chapter 12 before continuing.

```
00001          IDENTIFICATION DIVISION.
00002          PROGRAM-ID.
00003             UPDATE6.
00004          DATE-WRITTEN.
00005             MAY 13, 1987.
00006
00007          ENVIRONMENT DIVISION.
00008          INPUT-OUTPUT SECTION.
00009          FILE-CONTROL.
00010             SELECT LOG-FILE              ASSIGN TO S-LOGFILE.
00011             SELECT NEW-MASTER-FILE       ASSIGN TO S-NEWMAST.
00012             SELECT OLD-MASTER-FILE       ASSIGN TO S-OLDMAST.
00013             SELECT ORDER-FILE            ASSIGN TO S-ORDERS.
00014             SELECT TRANSACTION-FILE      ASSIGN TO S-TRANS.
00015
```

```
00016          DATA DIVISION.
00017
00018          FILE SECTION.
00019
00020          FD  LOG-FILE
00021              LABEL RECORDS ARE OMITTED.
00022          01  LOG-RECORD.
00023              05  CARRIAGE-CONTROL          PIC X.
00024              05  LOG-LINE.
00025                  10  FILLER                PIC X(45).
00026                  10  LOG-MESSAGE           PIC X(87).
00027
00028          FD  NEW-MASTER-FILE
00029              LABEL RECORDS ARE OMITTED.
00030          01  NEW-MASTER.
00031              05  NM-KEY                    PIC X(5).
00032              05  NM-QUANTITY               PIC 9(5).
00033              05  NM-QUAN-ON-ORDER          PIC 9(5).
00034              05  NM-REORDER-POINT          PIC 9(5).
00035              05  NM-REORDER-QUAN           PIC 9(5).
00036              05  NM-DESCRIPTION            PIC X(20).
00037              05  NM-NOT-USED               PIC X(35).
00038
00039          FD  OLD-MASTER-FILE
00040              LABEL RECORDS ARE OMITTED.
00041          01  OLD-MASTER-BUFFER             PIC X(80).
00042
00043          FD  TRANSACTION-FILE
00044              LABEL RECORDS ARE OMITTED.
00045          01  TRANSACTION-BUFFER            PIC X(80).
00046
00047          FD  ORDER-FILE
00048              LABEL RECORDS ARE OMITTED.
00049          01  ORDER-RECORD.
00050              05  CARRIAGE-CONTROL          PIC X.
00051              05  OR-KEY                    PIC X(5).
00052              05  FILLER                    PIC XXX.
00053              05  OR-QUANTITY               PIC Z(5)9.
00054              05  FILLER                    PIC XXX.
00055              05  OR-DESCRIPTION            PIC X(20).
00056              05  FILLER                    PIC X(95).
00057
00058          WORKING-STORAGE SECTION.
00059
00060          77  ERROR-COUNT                   PIC S999.
00061          77  OM-KEY-PREVIOUS               PIC X(5).
00062          77  SEQUENCE-ERROR-FLAG           PIC X.
00063          77  TR-KEY-PREVIOUS               PIC X(5).
00064
00065          01  ERROR-MESSAGES.
00066              05  BAD-ADDITION-MSG          PIC X(50) VALUE
00067                  '  THIS ADDITION MATCHES AN EXISTING MASTER'.
00068              05  BAD-ADJ-CODE-MSG          PIC X(50) VALUE
00069                  '  BAD ADJUSTMENT CODE'.
00070              05  BAD-TRANS-CODE-MSG        PIC X(50) VALUE
00071                  '  TRANSACTION CODE ILLEGAL'.
00072              05  DELETE-MSG                PIC X(50) VALUE
00073                  '  THIS MASTER RECORD HAS BEEN DELETED'.
```

```
00074              05  MASTER-SEQUENCE-ERROR-MSG    PIC X(50) VALUE
00075              '   THIS MASTER IS OUT OF SEQUENCE'.
00076              05  OUT-OF-STOCK-MSG             PIC X(50) VALUE
00077              '   INSUFFICIENT STOCK TO SHIP AMOUNT SPECIFIED'.
00078              05  TERMINATION-MSG             PIC X(50) VALUE
00079              'MORE THAN 10 ERRORS - JOB TERMINATED'.
00080              05  TRANS-SEQUENCE-ERROR-MSG    PIC X(50) VALUE
00081              '   THIS TRANSACTION IS OUT OF SEQUENCE'.
00082              05  UNMATCHED-TRANS-MSG         PIC X(50) VALUE
00083              '   THERE IS NO MASTER FOR THIS TRANSACTION'.
00084
00085          01  OLD-MASTER.
00086              05  OM-KEY                      PIC X(5).
00087              05  OM-QUAN-ON-HAND             PIC 9(5).
00088              05  OM-QUAN-ON-ORDER            PIC 9(5).
00089              05  OM-REORDER-POINT            PIC 9(5).
00090              05  OM-REORDER-QUAN             PIC 9(5).
00091              05  OM-DESCRIPTION              PIC X(20).
00092              05  FILLER                      PIC X(35).
00093
00094          01  TRANSACTION.
00095              05  TR-KEY                      PIC X(5).
00096              05  TR-QUANTITY                 PIC 9(5).
00097              05  TR-TRANSACTION-CODE         PIC X.
00098                  88  ADDITION                        VALUE '1'.
00099                  88  ADJUSTMENT                      VALUE '2'.
00100                  88  RECEIPT                         VALUE '3'.
00101                  88  SHIPMENT                        VALUE '4'.
00102                  88  DELETION                        VALUE '5'.
00103              05  TR-ADJUSTMENT-CODE          PIC 9.
00104              05  TR-QUAN-ON-ORDER            PIC 9(5).
00105              05  TR-REORDER-POINT            PIC 9(5).
00106              05  TR-REORDER-QUAN             PIC 9(5).
00107              05  TR-DESCRIPTION              PIC X(20).
00108              05  FILLER                      PIC X(33).
00109
00110          01  UPDATE-ERROR-FLAGS.
00111              05  BAD-TRANS-CODE              PIC X.
00112              05  OUT-OF-STOCK                PIC X.
00113              05  BAD-ADJ-CODE                PIC X.
00114
00115
00116          PROCEDURE DIVISION.
00117          A000-UPDATE-FILE.
00118      *        INITIALIZE WORK AREAS
00119              MOVE ZERO                   TO ERROR-COUNT.
00120              MOVE LOW-VALUES             TO OM-KEY-PREVIOUS.
00121              MOVE LOW-VALUES             TO TR-KEY-PREVIOUS.
00122              OPEN INPUT TRANSACTION-FILE
00123                         OLD-MASTER-FILE
00124                   OUTPUT NEW-MASTER-FILE
00125                          LOG-FILE
00126                          ORDER-FILE.
00127      *        GET PRIMING RECORDS
00128              PERFORM X010-GET-VALID-TRANSACTION.
00129              PERFORM X020-GET-VALID-MASTER.
```

```
00130        *         PROCESS THE FILES
00131               PERFORM B010-UPDATE-LOGIC
00132                   UNTIL (OM-KEY = HIGH-VALUES  AND  TR-KEY = HIGH-VALUES)
00133                         OR ERROR-COUNT IS GREATER THAN 10.
00134               IF ERROR-COUNT IS GREATER THAN 10
00135                   MOVE TERMINATION-MSG TO LOG-LINE
00136                   WRITE LOG-RECORD AFTER ADVANCING 1 LINES.
00137               CLOSE TRANSACTION-FILE
00138                     OLD-MASTER-FILE
00139                     NEW-MASTER-FILE
00140                     LOG-FILE
00141                     ORDER-FILE.
00142               STOP RUN.
00143
00144           B010-UPDATE-LOGIC.
00145               IF OM-KEY IS LESS THAN TR-KEY
00146                   PERFORM C040-CHECK-QUANTITY
00147                   WRITE NEW-MASTER FROM OLD-MASTER
00148                   PERFORM X020-GET-VALID-MASTER
00149               ELSE
00150                   IF OM-KEY = TR-KEY
00151                       PERFORM C010-APPLY-TRANSACTION
00152                       PERFORM X010-GET-VALID-TRANSACTION
00153                   ELSE
00154                       IF ADDITION
00155                           PERFORM C020-ADD-MASTER
00156                           PERFORM X010-GET-VALID-TRANSACTION
00157                       ELSE
00158                           PERFORM C030-INVALID-TRANSACTION
00159                           PERFORM X010-GET-VALID-TRANSACTION.
00160
00161           C010-APPLY-TRANSACTION.
00162               IF DELETION
00163                   PERFORM D010-DELETE-MASTER
00164                   PERFORM X020-GET-VALID-MASTER
00165               ELSE
00166                   IF ADDITION
00167                       PERFORM D030-INVALID-ADDITION
00168                   ELSE
00169                       MOVE SPACES TO UPDATE-ERROR-FLAGS
00170                       CALL 'UPDATE-MASTER' USING OLD-MASTER
00171                                                  TRANSACTION
00172                                                  UPDATE-ERROR-FLAGS
00173                       IF UPDATE-ERROR-FLAGS NOT = SPACES
00174                           PERFORM D020-UPDATE-ERRORS.
00175
00176           C020-ADD-MASTER.
00177               MOVE TR-KEY              TO NM-KEY.
00178               MOVE TR-QUANTITY         TO NM-QUANTITY.
00179               MOVE TR-QUAN-ON-ORDER    TO NM-QUAN-ON-ORDER.
00180               MOVE TR-REORDER-POINT    TO NM-REORDER-POINT.
00181               MOVE TR-REORDER-QUAN     TO NM-REORDER-QUAN.
00182               MOVE TR-DESCRIPTION      TO NM-DESCRIPTION.
00183               MOVE SPACES             TO NM-NOT-USED.
00184               WRITE NEW-MASTER.
00185
```

```
00186              C030-INVALID-TRANSACTION.
00187                  MOVE TRANSACTION TO LOG-LINE.
00188                  MOVE UNMATCHED-TRANS-MSG TO LOG-MESSAGE.
00189                  WRITE LOG-RECORD AFTER ADVANCING 1 LINE.
00190                  ADD 1 TO ERROR-COUNT.
00191
00192              C040-CHECK-QUANTITY.
00193                  IF OM-QUAN-ON-ORDER + OM-QUAN-ON-HAND < OM-REORDER-POINT
00194                      MOVE SPACES                 TO ORDER-RECORD
00195                      MOVE OM-KEY                 TO OR-KEY
00196                      MOVE OM-DESCRIPTION         TO OR-DESCRIPTION
00197                      MOVE OM-REORDER-QUAN        TO OR-QUANTITY
00198                      WRITE ORDER-RECORD AFTER ADVANCING 1 LINES
00199                      ADD OM-REORDER-QUAN TO OM-QUAN-ON-ORDER.
00200
00201              D010-DELETE-MASTER.
00202                  MOVE OLD-MASTER TO LOG-LINE.
00203                  MOVE DELETE-MSG TO LOG-MESSAGE.
00204                  WRITE LOG-RECORD AFTER ADVANCING 1 LINES.
00205
00206              ***********************************
00207              *D020-UPDATE-MASTER HAS BEEN CHANGED TO A SUBPROGRAM
00208              ***********************************
00209
00210              D020-UPDATE-ERRORS.
00211                  IF BAD-TRANS-CODE = 'X'
00212                      MOVE TRANSACTION TO LOG-LINE
00213                      MOVE BAD-TRANS-CODE-MSG TO LOG-MESSAGE
00214                      WRITE LOG-RECORD AFTER ADVANCING 1 LINE
00215                      ADD 1 TO ERROR-COUNT.
00216                  IF OUT-OF-STOCK = 'X'
00217                      MOVE TRANSACTION TO LOG-LINE
00218                      MOVE OUT-OF-STOCK-MSG TO LOG-MESSAGE
00219                      WRITE LOG-RECORD AFTER ADVANCING 1 LINE
00220                      ADD 1 TO ERROR-COUNT.
00221                  IF BAD-ADJ-CODE = 'X'
00222                      MOVE TRANSACTION TO LOG-LINE
00223                      MOVE BAD-ADJ-CODE-MSG TO LOG-MESSAGE
00224                      WRITE LOG-RECORD AFTER ADVANCING 1 LINE
00225                      ADD 1 TO ERROR-COUNT.
00226
00227              D030-INVALID-ADDITION.
00228                  MOVE TRANSACTION TO LOG-LINE.
00229                  MOVE BAD-ADDITION-MSG TO LOG-MESSAGE.
00230                  WRITE LOG-RECORD AFTER ADVANCING 1 LINES.
00231                  ADD 1 TO ERROR-COUNT.
00232
00233              X010-GET-VALID-TRANSACTION.
00234                  MOVE '?' TO SEQUENCE-ERROR-FLAG.
00235                  PERFORM Y010-READ-TRANSACTION
00236                      UNTIL     SEQUENCE-ERROR-FLAG = 'N'
00237                             OR ERROR-COUNT IS GREATER THAN 10.
00238
00239              X020-GET-VALID-MASTER.
00240                  MOVE '?' TO SEQUENCE-ERROR-FLAG.
00241                  PERFORM Y020-READ-MASTER
00242                      UNTIL     SEQUENCE-ERROR-FLAG = 'N'
00243                             OR ERROR-COUNT IS GREATER THAN 10.
00244
```

```
00245           Y010-READ-TRANSACTION.
00246               READ TRANSACTION-FILE INTO TRANSACTION
00247                   AT END MOVE HIGH-VALUES TO TR-KEY.
00248               IF TR-KEY IS LESS THAN TR-KEY-PREVIOUS
00249                   MOVE TRANSACTION TO LOG-LINE
00250                   MOVE TRANS-SEQUENCE-ERROR-MSG TO LOG-MESSAGE
00251                   WRITE LOG-RECORD AFTER ADVANCING 1 LINES
00252                   ADD 1 TO ERROR-COUNT
00253               ELSE
00254                   MOVE 'N' TO SEQUENCE-ERROR-FLAG.
00255               MOVE TR-KEY TO TR-KEY-PREVIOUS.
00256
00257           Y020-READ-MASTER.
00258               READ OLD-MASTER-FILE INTO OLD-MASTER
00259                   AT END MOVE HIGH-VALUES TO OM-KEY.
00260               IF OM-KEY IS LESS THAN OM-KEY-PREVIOUS
00261                   MOVE OLD-MASTER TO LOG-LINE
00262                   MOVE MASTER-SEQUENCE-ERROR-MSG TO LOG-MESSAGE
00263                   WRITE LOG-RECORD AFTER ADVANCING 1 LINES
00264                   ADD 1 TO ERROR-COUNT
00265               ELSE
00266                   MOVE 'N' TO SEQUENCE-ERROR-FLAG.
00267               MOVE OM-KEY TO OM-KEY-PREVIOUS.
00268
00269           ******************** END OF PROGRAM ****************************
```

FIGURE 18.1 A main program to update a sequential file, which calls the subroutine of Figure 18.2 to do part of the actual file update processing.

The changes actually are rather minor. In the Data Division we have added a structure containing three error flags. In the Procedure Division, we have removed **D020-UPDATE-MASTER** (the paragraph that updated master records) and the subordinate paragraphs that it performed, and added a new paragraph to print some error messages. In **C010-APPLY-TRANSACTION**, the paragraph that is used to perform **D020-UPDATE-MASTER**, we have removed the **PERFORM** statement and replaced it with a **CALL** and a few additional statements. The basic strategy is this. For reasons we will discuss shortly, we cannot print error messages from within the subprogram. Therefore, if any errors are found, we will set an appropriate flag within the subprogram, then test the flag in the main program and, if necessary, print error messages in the main program. The function of each error flag is reasonably self-explanatory, as is the code to print the error messages.

Part of the reason we do not print the error messages in the subprogram is that to do so would complicate the subprogram and the parameter list; we would need to identify the file on which the messages are to be written, the format and text of the messages, the error count, and so on. However, if necessary these problems could be overcome. A more serious problem, however, is that a file can only be used in the program or subprogram that contains the **FD** defining the file. If we try to write the same **FD** in two or more subprograms, **COBOL** will treat the **FD**s as different files, each of which happens to have the same name as another file. The result would be chaos. Putting it another way, file names may not be used as parameters in the **USING** phrase, and a file may not be declared in more than one unit of the program.

18.4 THE SUBPROGRAM

The subprogram is shown in Figure 18.2. We observe that although it has an Environment Division header, nothing is in the division. This reflects the fact that this subprogram does not deal with any files as such. In the Data Division there is no File Section and no Working-Storage Section. This is an accident of the processing to be done here; subprograms certainly may have these sections.

```
00001          IDENTIFICATION DIVISION.
00002          PROGRAM-ID.
00003              UPDATE-MASTER.
00004          DATE-WRITTEN.
00005              MAY 13, 1987.
00006
00007          ENVIRONMENT DIVISION.
00008
00009          DATA DIVISION.
00010
00011          LINKAGE SECTION.
00012
00013          01   OLD-MASTER.
00014               05   OM-KEY                    PIC X(5).
00015               05   OM-QUAN-ON-HAND           PIC 9(5).
00016               05   OM-QUAN-ON-ORDER          PIC 9(5).
00017               05   OM-REORDER-POINT          PIC 9(5).
00018               05   OM-REORDER-QUAN           PIC 9(5).
00019               05   OM-DESCRIPTION            PIC X(20).
00020               05   FILLER                    PIC X(35).
00021
00022          01   TRANSACTION.
00023               05   TR-KEY                    PIC X(5).
00024               05   TR-QUANTITY               PIC 9(5).
00025               05   TR-TRANSACTION-CODE        PIC X.
00026                    88   ADDITION                        VALUE '1'.
00027                    88   ADJUSTMENT                      VALUE '2'.
00028                    88   RECEIPT                         VALUE '3'.
00029                    88   SHIPMENT                        VALUE '4'.
00030                    88   DELETION                        VALUE '5'.
00031               05   TR-ADJUSTMENT-CODE        PIC 9.
00032               05   TR-QUAN-ON-ORDER          PIC 9(5).
00033               05   TR-REORDER-POINT          PIC 9(5).
00034               05   TR-REORDER-QUAN           PIC 9(5).
00035               05   TR-DESCRIPTION            PIC X(20).
00036               05   FILLER                    PIC X(33).
00037
00038          01   UPDATE-ERROR-FLAGS.
00039               05   BAD-TRANS-CODE            PIC X.
00040               05   OUT-OF-STOCK              PIC X.
00041               05   BAD-ADJ-CODE              PIC X.
00042
00043
00044          PROCEDURE DIVISION USING OLD-MASTER
00045                                   TRANSACTION
00046                                   UPDATE-ERROR-FLAGS.
```

```
00047          A000-UPDATE-MASTER.
00048              IF       SHIPMENT
00049                  PERFORM B010-PROCESS-SHIPMENT
00050              ELSE IF RECEIPT
00051                  PERFORM B020-PROCESS-RECEIPT
00052              ELSE IF ADJUSTMENT
00053                  PERFORM B030-PROCESS-ADJUSTMENT
00054              ELSE
00055                  MOVE 'X' TO BAD-TRANS-CODE.
00056
00057          A999-EXIT.
00058              EXIT PROGRAM.
00059
00060          B010-PROCESS-SHIPMENT.
00061              IF OM-QUAN-ON-HAND IS NOT LESS THAN TR-QUANTITY
00062                  SUBTRACT TR-QUANTITY FROM OM-QUAN-ON-HAND
00063              ELSE
00064                  MOVE 'X' TO OUT-OF-STOCK.
00065
00066          B020-PROCESS-RECEIPT.
00067              ADD TR-QUANTITY TO OM-QUAN-ON-HAND.
00068              SUBTRACT TR-QUANTITY FROM OM-QUAN-ON-ORDER.
00069
00070          B030-PROCESS-ADJUSTMENT.
00071              IF       TR-ADJUSTMENT-CODE = 1
00072                  MOVE TR-QUANTITY TO OM-QUAN-ON-HAND
00073              ELSE IF TR-ADJUSTMENT-CODE = 2
00074                  MOVE TR-QUANTITY TO OM-QUAN-ON-ORDER
00075              ELSE IF TR-ADJUSTMENT-CODE = 3
00076                  MOVE TR-QUANTITY TO OM-REORDER-POINT
00077              ELSE IF TR-ADJUSTMENT-CODE = 4
00078                  MOVE TR-QUANTITY TO OM-REORDER-QUAN
00079              ELSE IF TR-ADJUSTMENT-CODE = 5
00080                  MOVE TR-DESCRIPTION TO OM-DESCRIPTION
00081              ELSE
00082                  MOVE 'X' TO BAD-ADJ-CODE.
```

FIGURE 18.2 A subprogram called by the program of Figure 18.1 to perform file update processing.

The main paragraph of this subprogram has a somewhat unusual appearance, since it does not have an **OPEN** or **CLOSE** statement. Furthermore, instead of a **STOP RUN** statement, it has a new statement called **EXIT PROGRAM**, which must appear in a paragraph by itself. When this statement is encountered, execution simply returns to the calling program at the point immediately following the **CALL** statement.

As with **STOP RUN**, you may have any number of **EXIT PROGRAM** statements in the subprogram. The logic of the subprogram is much easier to understand, however, if we make a policy of never having more than one **STOP RUN** or **EXIT PROGRAM** in a program unit.

The code in the subprogram is essentially the same as in the corresponding paragraphs of **UPDATE5** in Figure 12.9. We have changed the prefix codes of the paragraphs to reflect the structure of the subprogram and we have set error flags instead of writing messages; the remaining code is unchanged.

There is one feature of the subprogram that is not at all apparent from looking at the code, but which is very important to the execution of subprograms in general. There is no data storage contained within the Linkage Section of the subprogram! In spite of the fact that the Linkage Section looks very much like the Working-Storage Section of the main program, they are distinctly different in terms of data storage. In the Working-Storage Section of a program unit, whether in a main program or a subprogram, any data declaration causes the compiler to allocate space within the program unit to store the data. In the Linkage Section, the compiler simply uses the data definitions to determine what the parameters to the subprogram will look like. The data that is manipulated by the subprogram is actually located within the calling program. When the subprogram is called, a connection is made between the data described in the Linkage Section and the parameters used in the **CALL** statement to determine what data is being used by the subprogram. If we have several **CALL** statements with different parameters, the subprogram could be working with different data each time it is executed. This gives us tremendous flexibility and is a great advantage over using a paragraph, which must always work with the same data. However, because the data in the Linkage Section is actually located in another program unit, you may never use the **VALUE** clause in the Linkage Section except in level 88 entries.

The connection between a variable in the **USING** phrase of a **CALL** statement and a variable in the **USING** phrase of the Procedure Division header in the subprogram is made on the basis of position, not name. The first parameter in the **CALL** statement is matched to the first parameter in the subprogram, the second parameter in the **CALL** is matched to the second parameter in the subprogram, and so on. **COBOL** has no way of knowing whether the two parameter lists are actually in the same order. For example, if the subprogram had the parameter list in the order shown in Figure 18.2 but the **CALL** statement were written as

```
CALL 'UPDATE-MASTER' USING TRANSACTION
                           UPDATE-ERROR-FLAGS
                           OLD-MASTER
```

the main program and the subprogram would both compile correctly, they would link together correctly, but the results of execution would be totally incorrect and might even cause an abend.

We should make one final comment about this subprogram. IBM **COBOL**, which was used to execute the program, ignores all characters in the **PROGRAM-ID** past the first eight. In this particular example, the name used by the computer to identify the subprogram was "**UPDATEOM**" (the compiler substitutes "0" for "–"). However, for all practical purposes this is invisible to the application programmer and can be ignored.

18.5 EXECUTION RESULTS

When the program was compiled and run, the results were identical to those produced by **UPDATE5** in Chapter 12, shown in Figure 18.3 for easy reference.

NEW MASTER

```
000020010100040001200004OBOLT, 3 INCH X 1/2
000080002300040000600040BOLT, 4 INCH X 1/2
00011002000020000350000100NUT, 1/2 INCH
00015009990088800777700666A CORRECT ADDITION
00021003100000000300000100BUSHING, 2 INCH OD
00024005090100002000000500WASHER, 2 INCH
00036012340000001000001000PIN, 1 INCH
00037123000000001000001000PIN, 1-1/2 INCH
00059422100000001000001000GADGET, RED
00061308750000001000001000WIDJET, GREEN
00070222220000001000001000WIDJET, PURPLE
00080000100005200050000030SAMPLE
000810010000000000008000005DRILL, 6 SPINDLE
00082010000030001200000200COTTER PINS, 2 IN
00084008620020001000000200COTTER PINS, 3 IN
```

LOG REPORT

```
000010001021                                THIS TRANSACTION IS OUT OF SEQUENCE
00011987651 111112222233333ERROR ENTRY      THIS ADDITION MATCHES AN EXISTING MASTER
00024012004                                 INSUFFICIENT STOCK TO SHIP AMOUNT SPECIFIED
00036000005                                 THIS TRANSACTION IS OUT OF SEQUENCE
00051543210000010000001000GADGET, BLUE      THIS MASTER RECORD HAS BEEN DELETED
00052000005                                 THERE IS NO MASTER FOR THIS TRANSACTION
00059001230                                 TRANSACTION CODE ILLEGAL
00068333330000010000001000MIS-FILE, RED-FACED  THIS MASTER IS OUT OF SEQUENCE
000810000029                                BAD ADJUSTMENT CODE
```

ORDER REPORT

```
00008      40    BOLT, 4 INCH X 1/2
00011     100    NUT, 1/2 INCH
00024     500    WASHER, 2 INCH
00080      30    SAMPLE
00082     200    COTTER PINS, 2 IN
00084     200    COTTER PINS, 3 IN
```

FIGURE 18.3 Output from the program in Figures 18.1 and 18.2.

18.6 COBOL-85 SUBPROGRAMS

One of the most significant areas of change in **COBOL-85** is in the way it deals with subprograms. Some of these changes, such as the use of internal subprograms (subprograms that lie within the bounds of the main program or another subprogram), offer the possibility of bringing **COBOL** much closer to the state of the art in software design. Changes this extensive, however, are just becoming available as this book is being written and will take some time to evaluate in actual use. In any case, since these capabilities involve relatively sophisticated concepts, they are beyond the scope of our present discussion.

Two of the changes in the subprogram used are more limited in scope and are worth mentioning here. The first of these changes involves the addition of the **EXTERNAL** phrase for file definition. We said before that a file cannot be defined in more than one program unit because **COBOL** will simply treat this as defining two separate files that happen to have the same name. In **COBOL-85**, however, you can define a file as follows:

```
FD  MASTER-FILE
    IS EXTERNAL
    LABEL RECORDS ARE STANDARD.
```

The **EXTERNAL** phrase tells **COBOL** that **MASTER-FILE** may be defined in more than one program unit; that is, in the main program and a subprogram, or in several subprograms. In this case all of these definitions refer to the same file, which allows you, for example, to open and close the file in one program unit and read from it or write to it in another program unit.

The second feature of **COBOL-85** subprograms of interest to us relates to the way in which program units are compiled. In earlier versions of **COBOL** subprograms were required to be compiled separately from the main program, and no two subprograms could be compiled together. **COBOL-85** includes a feature called the *end program header*, which allows you to chain a main program and its subprograms together as a single stream of code and compile them all at once. The format of the end program header is

```
END PROGRAM program-name
```

For example, the program shown in Figures 18.1 and 18.2 normally would be compiled as two separate units. However, in **COBOL-85** we could write

```
IDENTIFICATION DIVISION.
PROGRAM-ID.
    UPDATE6.
    .
    .
    .

END PROGRAM UPDATE6.
IDENTIFICATION DIVISION.
PROGRAM-ID.
    UPDATE-MASTER.
    .
    .
    .

END PROGRAM UPDATE-MASTER.
```

This file of code could then be submitted to the **COBOL** compiler and both program units would be compiled. In effect, the end program header simply serves to mark the end of one program unit and the start of another. Aside from the fact that both program units are compiled at once, the result is essentially the same as separate compilation.

END COBOL-85

18.7 CONCLUSION

Subprograms offer flexibility, efficiency, and design sophistication far beyond what can be accomplished using only paragraphs. However, using subprograms effectively requires study and practice. What we have presented in this chapter is sufficient to enable you to begin using subprograms but, as with many aspects of **COBOL**, we recommend continued study of advanced subprogram concepts.

REVIEW QUESTIONS

1. Give several reasons for using subprograms.

2. What is the function of the Linkage Section?

3. Is it possible to place the **OPEN** and **CLOSE** statements for a file in a calling program and the **READ** or **WRITE** statements for it in a subprogram?

4. How many bytes of data are allocated within **SUBPROG** by the following code?

```
IDENTIFICATION DIVISION.
PROGRAM-ID.  SUBPROG.

ENVIRONMENT DIVISION.

DATA DIVISION.
LINKAGE SECTION.
77   ERROR-FLAG          PIC X.
01   DATA-REC.
     05   FLD-1           PIC S9(5).
     05   FLD-2           PIC X(10).
     05   FLD-3           PIC S9(8) COMP SYNC.

PROCEDURE DIVISION USING ERROR-FLAG, DATA-REC.
     .
     .
     .
```

5. Suppose you are given the following subprogram:

```
IDENTIFICATION DIVISION.
PROGRAM-ID.  SIMPLE.
ENVIRONMENT DIVISION.
DATA DIVISION.
LINKAGE SECTION.
77  XYZ                          PIC 9 VALUE 0.
PROCEDURE DIVISION USING XYZ.
    MOVE 9 TO XYZ.
EXIT-PARAGRAPH.
    EXIT PROGRAM.
```

What would happen if the program were called by the following statement?

```
CALL 'SIMPLE' USING 7.
```

ANSWERS

1. If a processing function is needed at several points in a program, it saves space to specify that function once in a subprogram and then call the subprogram into action whenever the function is needed. Another reason is that subprograms provide one good way to divide the effort of a project that is too large for one programmer to do in the available time. A third reason is that subprograms provide a way to separate the details of processing functions from the logic that controls them, which can often clarify program relations and improve understandability. Finally, subprograms provide a way to separate use of data between program modules so that one module cannot accidentally alter some data being used by another module.

2. It provides a subprogram with a description of the data from the calling program that the subprogram is to process.

3. No.

4. Zero. There is never any data allocated within the Linkage Section. The definitions in the Linkage Section describe the format of parameters located within the calling program.

5. Nothing, since the program would not compile. The subprogram SIMPLE contains an error in that data in the Linkage Section may not have a VALUE clause. The calling program contains an error in that parameters in a USING clause must always be data names, not literals.

EXERCISES

1. Modify the seed catalog program in Figure 11.1 so that the functions of C010-EDIT-LINE are implemented in a subprogram instead of in the main program.

2. Modify the program in Figure 18.1 so that the functions of **X010-GET-VALID-TRANSACTION** and **X020-GET-VALID-MASTER** are implemented in separate subprograms instead of in the main program. There are several points to remember in carrying out this change. First, the **SELECT** and **FD** statements for each file must be contained within the appropriate subprogram and removed from the main program. Second, the subprograms must open and close the files at the proper time and at no other time. Third, in addition to having a data record as a parameter, each subprogram must return various flags and counts to the calling program. Finally, instead of printing error messages within the subprograms, you must pass a flag to the calling program that prints the error messages.

3. (This exercise is suitable for use as a small project.)

   Make the following changes to the program described in Exercise 4 of Chapter 17. Instead of coding the municipality codes and tax rates directly into the program, the program should read a municipality tax file, load the data into a table, and search the table to find the entry that matches the municipality code in an employee pay record.

   The records in the municipality tax file have the following format:

   | Columns 1-2 | municipality code | `PIC 99` |
   | Columns 3-6 | tax rate | `PIC 99V99` |

   Design an appropriate table to hold this data. If the table overflows when it is being loaded, count the total number of records in the municipality file, print a message telling the user what happened and how large the table needs to be to hold the entire file, and stop the run. When you are processing the payroll records, if a record contains a municipality code that is not in the table print an appropriate error message and go on the the next payroll record.

   The table loading process and the searching process should be performed in two separately compiled subprograms. The table itself must be defined in the main program (so that it can be used in both subprograms), but the file containing the municipality tax data must be defined in the loading subprogram. The call for the first subprogram should look something like the following:

   ```
   CALL 'LOADTAX' USING TAX-TABLE-AREA, RECORD-COUNT,
                        OVERFLOW-FLAG.
   ```

   RECORD-COUNT contains the number of records in the input file. If no overflow occurs this is equal to the number of records loaded into the table. **OVERFLOW-FLAG** indicates whether or not table overflow occurred during the loading process. In a well-designed system the subprogram should not report any errors, nor should its operation depend on any knowledge of how the table will be used or what the main program will do if overflow occurs. The function of the subprogram is to load records into the table, and to return to the calling program a count of the number of records in the input file and an indication of whether or not overflow occurred. The calling program is to determine whether the flag indicates that an error has occurred, and what should be done if it has.

The call for the second subprogram should look like the following:

```
CALL 'FINDTAX' USING TAX-TABLE-AREA, MUNICIPALITY-CODE,
                     TAX-RATE, NOT-FOUND-FLAG.
```

MUNICIPALITY-CODE contains the code for the municipality to be found in the table, **TAX-RATE** contains the tax rate for the specified municipality, and **NOT-FOUND-FLAG** contains a flag indicating whether or not the desired entry actually was found. Inside the subprogram use **SEARCH ALL** to locate the appropriate entry in the table. Note, however, that the method used to search the table is not visible from the main program.

CHAPTER 19

ADDITIONAL COBOL TOPICS

19.1 INTRODUCTION

In this chapter we discuss a number of COBOL features that remain to be considered. Some of them are widely used, but could not be studied appropriately until now. Others are infrequently or even rarely used in current programming practice, but should be discussed for the benefit of readers who will be maintaining programs that use them.

19.2 THE GO TO STATEMENT

The GO TO statement transfers control to the start of a named paragraph. It differs from the PERFORM statement in that the PERFORM executes a paragraph, then returns to the current location in the program, while the GO TO simply jumps to some new point in the program, then continues execution from this location. Current programming practice strongly discourages the use of GO TO statements. A detailed discussion of why GO TO statements add complexity to programs is beyond the scope of our present discussion, but most studies of software design techniques made since the late 1960s agree that GO TO statements tend to detract from the quality of a program. However, they do exist in some programs and can even prove useful in a few specific circumstances.

The GO TO statement has the form

GO TO paragraph-name

The paragraph name may be the same one in which the GO TO appears, a paragraph that appears earlier in the program, or a paragraph that appears later in the program. Generally, however, we recommend that GO TO statements refer to paragraphs that appear later in the program.

One of the situations in which a **GO TO** can simplify code is when execution of a task depends on a set of complex conditions all being true. For example, you might have a function which is performed on a data record only if the record can pass all of a number of edits. If the ability to perform one of these edits requires all previous edits to be successful, the code can look something like the following:

```
IF condition-1
    IF condition-2
        IF condition-3
            .
            .
            .
            IF condition-n
                process data
            ELSE
                process error-n
            .
            .
            .
        ELSE
            process error-3
    ELSE
        process error-2
ELSE
    process error-1.
```

Clearly, we would like to avoid all these nested **IF** statements. We can do this with the **GO TO** statement:

```
IF NOT condition-1
    process error-1
    GO TO PROCESS-EXIT.
IF NOT condition-2
    process error-2
    GO TO PROCESS-EXIT.
IF NOT condition-3
    process error-3
    GO TO PROCESS-EXIT.
    .
    .
    .
IF NOT condition-n
    process error-n
    GO TO PROCESS-EXIT.
*   AT THIS POINT THE DATA MUST BE VALID
    process data.
PROCESS-EXIT.
    EXIT.
```

The last two lines of this example demonstrate the use of a new **COBOL** statement called **EXIT**. **EXIT** must be the only statement in its paragraph, and it does not do anything but mark a location in a program. Execution will continue with the paragraph immediately following the **EXIT** paragraph. However, notice what we have accomplished. We test the conditions one at a time. Although we have only shown simple conditions in this example, each condition could be determined by extensive data analysis and calculation. If the condition is not valid, we process the error, then skip around all the remaining processing. However, if all conditions are true, that is, if no errors are found, we eventually reach the point where we process the data. In spite of the fact that we are using **GO TO** statements, this simple structure is easier to follow than if we had used the corresponding nested **IF** statements.

Note that it is permissible under **COBOL** syntax to complete the actions of one paragraph and the "fall through" to the beginning of the next paragraph; this is the way that execution reaches **PROCESS-EXIT** when the data is valid, and this is the way that execution reaches the paragraph following **PROCESS-EXIT**. Under the guidelines of structured programming used for this book, this never happens in any other circumstance. All paragraphs in this book—other than in this example—are entered through **PERFORM** statements, with the very rare exception of a paragraph entered through a **GO TO**.

There is a variation on the **GO TO** statement which can be used to implement the case structure, again as an alternative to the nested **IF**. This format of the **GO TO** is

---

<u>GO</u> **TO** paragraph-name-1 . . . paragraph-name-n **DEPENDING ON** identifier

---

The paragraph names may be any paragraph names in the program, while the identifier must be an elementary numeric item. To demonstrate the use of the **GO TO** . . . **DEPENDING ON** in the case structure, we will use the sequential file update program. Recall that the transaction record has the following format:

```
01  TRANSACTION.
    05  TR-KEY                  PIC X(5).
    05  TR-QUANTITY             PIC 9(5).
    05  TR-TRANSACTION-CODE     PIC X.
        88  ADDITION                VALUE '1'.
        88  ADJUSTMENT              VALUE '2'.
        88  RECEIPT                 VALUE '3'.
        88  SHIPMENT                VALUE '4'.
        88  DELETION                VALUE '5'.
    05  TR-ADJUSTMENT-CODE      PIC X.
    05  TR-QUAN-ON-ORDER        PIC 9(5).
    05  TR-REORDER-POINT        PIC 9(5).
    05  TR-REORDER-QUAN         PIC 9(5).
    05  TR-DESCRIPTION          PIC X(20).
    05  FILLER                  PIC X(33).
```

If the transaction is an adjustment, the data in the transaction is used to update one of five fields in the master record, depending on the value of **TR-ADJUSTMENT-CODE**. In previous versions of the program we used a nested **IF** statement to implement the case statement that controlled which of the five fields was updated. However, with the **GO TO** . . . **DEPENDING ON** we can use the following code:

```
        IF ADJUSTMENT
            PERFORM E030-PROCESS-ADJUSTMENT
                THRU E039-PROCESS-ADJUSTMENT-EXIT.
        .
        .
        .
    E030-PROCESS-ADJUSTMENT.
        GO TO
            E031-ADJUST-QUAN-ON-HAND
            E032-ADJUST-QUAN-ON-ORDER
            E033-ADJUST-REORDER-POINT
            E034-ADJUST-REORDER-QUAN
            E035-ADJUST-DESCRIPTION
                DEPENDING ON TR-ADJUSTMENT-CODE.
        MOVE 'X' TO BAD-ADJ-CODE.
        GO TO E039-PROCESS-ADJUSTMENT-EXIT.

    E031-ADJUST-QUAN-ON-HAND.
        MOVE TR-QUANTITY TO OM-QUAN-ON-HAND.
        GO TO E039-PROCESS-ADJUSTMENT-EXIT.

    E032-ADJUST-QUAN-ON-ORDER.
        MOVE TR-QUANTITY TO OM-QUAN-ON-ORDER.
        GO TO E039-PROCESS-ADJUSTMENT-EXIT.

    E033-ADJUST-REORDER-POINT.
        MOVE TR-QUANTITY TO OM-REORDER-POINT.
        GO TO E039-PROCESS-ADJUSTMENT-EXIT.

    E034-ADJUST-REORDER-QUAN.
        MOVE TR-QUANTITY TO OM-REORDER-QUAN.
        GO TO E039-PROCESS-ADJUSTMENT-EXIT.

    E035-ADJUST-DESCRIPTION.
        MOVE TR-DESCRIPTION TO OM-DESCRIPTION.
        GO TO E039-PROCESS-ADJUSTMENT-EXIT.

    E039-PROCESS-ADJUSTMENT-EXIT.
        EXIT.
```

The **PERFORM** statement in the **IF** statement uses **THRU** to specify a range of paragraphs to be performed. Complete rules governing the use of the **PERFORM** ... **THRU** option may be found in **COBOL** reference manuals. Since we shall only use the feature to simulate the case statement, we need not be concerned with these matters.

The **GO TO** at the start of the example uses the **DEPENDING ON** option. As the format preceding the examples indicates, we list a number of paragraph names, five in this example. The variable named in the **DEPENDING ON** phrase must be a positive or unsigned integer, and its value should be in the range of one to the number of paragraph names. The execution of the statement results in a transfer to the first-named paragraph if the value of the **DEPENDING ON** variable is one, to the second-named paragraph if the value of the **DEPENDING ON** variable is two, and so on. If the value of the **DEPENDING ON** variable is less than one or greater than the number of paragraph names, there is no transfer and, instead, the statement after the **GO TO** ... **DEPENDING ON** is executed. In our example, if **TR-ADJUSTMENT-CODE** is out of range, we set an error flag, then transfer control to the **EXIT** paragraph.

It is only accidental that the paragraphs named in the `GO TO` ... `DEPEND-ING ON` appear in the same order as their names are written within the range of the case structure. In fact, it is not even necessary that the names in the `GO TO` all be distinct. To see how this could be useful, suppose that we had inherited the adjustment code from a previous file design that we were not permitted to change. Assume that adjustment codes of 1 or 3 specified an adjustment of the quantity on hand, a code of 2 or 5 specified an adjustment of a quantity on order, a code of 4 specified a description change, a code of 6 a reorder point change, and a code of 7 a reorder quantity change. Anything else is an error as before. The desired processing could be carried out with the following `GO TO` statement.

```
GO TO
    E031-ADJUST-QUAN-ON-HAND
    E032-ADJUST-QUAN-ON-ORDER
    E031-ADJUST-QUAN-ON-HAND
    E035-ADJUST-DESCRIPTION
    E032-ADJUST-QUAN-ON-ORDER
    E033-ADJUST-REORDER-POINT
    E034-ADJUST-REORDER-QUAN
        DEPENDING ON TR-ADJUSTMENT-CODE.
```

Nothing else in the case structure need be changed.

Since there are only five cases to be considered in this example, the case structure can be implemented just as effectively with a nested `IF` statement as with the structure shown above. The `GO TO` ... `DEPENDING ON` implementation is really needed, however, when the number of cases becomes large. It is not uncommon in some applications to have a two-digit code, with most or all of the 100 combinations having to be handled by separated routines. In such a situation a nested `IF` is not practical (many compilers will not accept an `IF` nesting this deeply), and writing 100 separate `IF` statements to test all of the possibilities is terribly inefficient. Of course, if you are using **COBOL-85** the **EVALUATE** statement should be used.

19.3 THE COPY STATEMENT

It often happens that there are program segments that are needed in many different programs. An example would be a paragraph that prints a line of text to a report file and, when appropriate, prints a heading at the top of the page. Another very common situation is that many programs in a system process the same files or produce the same output records; all such programs will require identical record descriptions in their Data Divisions. It is time-consuming and error prone for all the programmers needing such program segments to write them out in a program, and for Data Division entries we are likely to wind up with many different descriptions for the same records. A much better solution is available through use of the **COBOL** **COPY** statement.

To use the **COPY** statement it is necessary to place the program segment that is to be copied into a library that can be accessed by the **COBOL** compiler. Precisely how entries are made in such a library differs from one operating system and installation to the next, but it is generally quite easy to do. With this library available we are able to write programs in which we simply specify that sections of code are to be retrieved from the library and inserted at specified points in the program. This insertion is done before compilation, and compilation then proceeds just as through we had written out everything that was obtained from the library. In the program listing we are given the copy statement as we wrote it plus all the lines that were obtained from the library; these lines are generally marked as being copied lines, typically with a **c** in the left margin.

A simple example from programs used in previous chapters appears in Chapter 18, in the discussion of subprograms. In both the main program and the subprogram we need a definition of the old master record and the transaction record. It is easy to imagine that in an actual data processing installation, particularly one which uses subprograms frequently, there would be many other programs processing the same files that would also need the same record descriptions. After preparing the library entries for the two records under the names of **OMLIB** and **TRLIB**, we can simplify the writing of either of the programs using **COPY** statements. Figure 19.1 contains the first portion of the subprogram from Figure 18.2, written in this way.

The source program listing that was produced when this program was compiled is shown in Figure 19.2. As far as the compiler is concerned, this program is identical to the one shown in Figure 18.2.

There are two points to notice about the code in Figures 19.1 and 19.2. First, although it may seem strange to see what looks like procedural code in the Data Division, the **COPY** statement is indeed a *statement*, not just a clause in the record description. The record name is followed by a period and, in keeping with our convention never to put two statements on the same line, we begin the **COPY** statement on the next line. The second point is that the

---

```
IDENTIFICATION DIVISION.
PROGRAM-ID.
    UPDATE-MASTER.
DATE-WRITTEN.
    MAY 13, 1987.

ENVIRONMENT DIVISION.

DATA DIVISION.

LINKAGE SECTION.

01   OLD-MASTER.
     COPY OMLIB.

01   TRANSACTION.
     COPY TRLIB.

01   UPDATE-ERROR-FLAGS.
     05   BAD-TRANS-CODE                PIC X.
     05   OUT-OF-STOCK                  PIC X.
     05   BAD-ADJ-CODE                  PIC X.
```

FIGURE 19.1 An example of source code using the **COPY** statement to copy standard record definition.

```
00001           IDENTIFICATION DIVISION.
00002           PROGRAM-ID.
00003              UPDATE-MASTER.
00004           DATE-WRITTEN.
00005              MAY 13, 1987.
00006
00007           ENVIRONMENT DIVISION.
00008
00009           DATA DIVISION.
00010
00011           LINKAGE SECTION.
00012
00013           01   OLD-MASTER.
00014                COPY OMLIB.
00015 C              05   OM-KEY                  PIC X(5).
00016 C              05   OM-QUAN-ON-HAND         PIC 9(5).
00017 C              05   OM-QUAN-ON-ORDER        PIC 9(5).
00018 C              05   OM-REORDER-POINT        PIC 9(5).
00019 C              05   OM-REORDER-QUAN         PIC 9(5).
00020 C              05   OM-DESCRIPTION          PIC X(20).
00021 C              05   FILLER                  PIC X(35).
00022
00023           01   TRANSACTION.
00024                COPY TRLIB.
00025 C              05   TR-KEY                  PIC X(5).
00026 C              05   TR-QUANTITY             PIC 9(5).
00027 C              05   TR-TRANSACTION-CODE     PIC X.
00028 C                   88   ADDITION                    VALUE '1'.
00029 C                   88   ADJUSTMENT                  VALUE '2'.
00030 C                   88   RECEIPT                     VALUE '3'.
00031 C                   88   SHIPMENT                    VALUE '4'.
00032 C                   88   DELETION                    VALUE '5'.
00033 C              05   TR-ADJUSTMENT-CODE      PIC 9.
00034 C              05   TR-QUAN-ON-ORDER        PIC 9(5).
00035 C              05   TR-REORDER-POINT        PIC 9(5).
00036 C              05   TR-REORDER-QUAN         PIC 9(5).
00037 C              05   TR-DESCRIPTION          PIC X(20).
00038 C              05   FILLER                  PIC X(33).
00039
00040           01   UPDATE-ERROR-FLAGS.
00041                05   BAD-TRANS-CODE          PIC X.
00042                05   OUT-OF-STOCK            PIC X.
00043                05   BAD-ADJ-CODE            PIC X.
```

FIGURE 19.2 A section of a program illustrating the appearance of the compiler source program when the **COPY** feature is used. All lines having a **C** to the right of the line number were obtained from the program library as a result of the **COPY**s in lines 14 and 24.

included code does not contain a **01** level entry. The copied code replaces the **COPY** statement exactly and must make sense in that context. If we had started the library entries with **01** level lines of text, the code in Figure 19.2 would have had two sequential **01** level lines, the first of which has no **PICTURE** clause and no subordinate entries; this is, of course, an error in **COBOL**.

A useful option of the **COPY** statement is the replacing phrase. For example, if we wanted the record key fields to be called **MASTER-KEY** and **XACT-KEY**, we could write the **COPY** statements as follows.

```
IDENTIFICATION DIVISION.
PROGRAM-ID.
    UPDATE-MASTER.
DATE-WRITTEN.
    MAY 13, 1987.

ENVIRONMENT DIVISION.

DATA DIVISION.

LINKAGE SECTION.

01  OLD-MASTER.
    COPY OMLIB
        REPLACING OM-KEY BY MASTER-KEY.

01  TRANSACTION.
    COPY TRLIB
        REPLACING TR-KEY BY XACT-KEY.

01  UPDATE-ERROR-FLAGS.
    05  BAD-TRANS-CODE          PIC X.
    05  OUT-OF-STOCK            PIC X.
    05  BAD-ADJ-CODE            PIC X.
```

The result would be as shown in Figure 19.3.

```
00001           IDENTIFICATION DIVISION.
00002           PROGRAM-ID.
00003               UPDATE-MASTER.
00004           DATE-WRITTEN.
00005               MAY 13, 1987.
00006
00007           ENVIRONMENT DIVISION.
00008
00009           DATA DIVISION.
00010
00011           LINKAGE SECTION.
00012
00013           01  OLD-MASTER.
00014               COPY OMLIB
00015                   REPLACING OM-KEY BY MASTER-KEY.
00016 C             05  MASTER-KEY                PIC X(5).
00017 C             05  OM-QUAN-ON-HAND       PIC 9(5).
00018 C             05  OM-QUAN-ON-ORDER      PIC 9(5).
00019 C             05  OM-REORDER-POINT      PIC 9(5).
00020 C             05  OM-REORDER-QUAN       PIC 9(5).
00021 C             05  OM-DESCRIPTION        PIC X(20).
00022 C             05  FILLER                PIC X(35).
00023
00024           01  TRANSACTION.
00025               COPY TRLIB
00026                   REPLACING TR-KEY BY XACT-KEY.
00027 C             05  XACT-KEY              PIC X(5).
```

```
00028 C              05    TR-QUANTITY                PIC 9(5).
00029 C              05    TR-TRANSACTION-CODE        PIC X.
00030 C                    88   ADDITION                         VALUE '1'.
00031 C                    88   ADJUSTMENT                       VALUE '2'.
00032 C                    88   RECEIPT                          VALUE '3'.
00033 C                    88   SHIPMENT                         VALUE '4'.
00034 C                    88   DELETION                         VALUE '5'.
00035 C              05    TR-ADJUSTMENT-CODE         PIC 9.
00036 C              05    TR-QUAN-ON-ORDER           PIC 9(5).
00037 C              05    TR-REORDER-POINT           PIC 9(5).
00038 C              05    TR-REORDER-QUAN            PIC 9(5).
00039 C              05    TR-DESCRIPTION             PIC X(20).
00040 C              05    FILLER                     PIC X(33).
00041
00042          01    UPDATE-ERROR-FLAGS.
00043                05    BAD-TRANS-CODE             PIC X.
00044                05    OUT-OF-STOCK               PIC X.
00045                05    BAD-ADJ-CODE               PIC X.
```

FIGURE 19.3 A section of a program illustrating the result of using the **COPY** statement with the **REPLACING** option.

The **REPLACING** phrase of the **COPY** statement has several other options, which can be found in the appropriate **COBOL** manual. We should mention that although the **COPY** statement is still used in many **COBOL** installations, the source code processors available on many computers provide their own built-in equivalent of the **COPY** statement, making the **COPY** statement unnecessary for these installations. Nonetheless, whether the result is obtained from the **COPY** statement or a source code processor, most data processing installations keep copies of common data records and other frequently used code in libraries and simply copy them into **COBOL** programs.

19.4   THE COMPUTE STATEMENT

The **COMPUTE** statement provides a way to specify operations that are sometimes more cumbersome or even impossible to express otherwise. The general format is

$$
\text{\underline{COMPUTE} identifier-1 [\underline{ROUNDED}]} = \left\{ \begin{array}{l} \text{identifier-2} \\ \text{literal-1} \\ \text{arithmetic-expression} \end{array} \right\}
$$

$$
\text{[ON \underline{SIZE} \underline{ERROR}] imperative-statement}
$$

COBOL-85

As with other verbs, **COBOL-85** allows an optional **END-COMPUTE** phrase at the end of the statement.

END COBOL-85

Literal-1 must be numeric; identifier-2 must be an elementary numeric item; identifier-1 must be an elementary numeric item, which may or may not specify editing, as the circumstances require. The identifier-2 and literal-1 combinations provide an alternative to using the **MOVE** statement to assign identifier-1 a value; this is seldom done.

The arithmetic-expression option permits one to write formulas, from very simple to quite complex, for expressing operations, rather than writing sequences of arithmetic statements. It also permits the use of exponentiation (raising to a power) that cannot be done any other way in **COBOL**.

19.5   ARITHMETIC EXPRESSIONS

An arithmetic expression is made up of combinations of identifiers and literals, separated by arithmetic operators and parentheses. Although the simplest arithmetic expression consists of a single literal or identifier such as the following

```
COMPUTE TOTAL = 0.00.
COMPUTE TOTAL = FIRST-VALUE.
```

the most common arithmetic expression consists of literals and/or identifiers combined by the following arithmetic operators:

Operator	Meaning
+	add
–	subtract
*	multiply
/	divide
**	exponentiate

Each arithmetic operator must be preceded and followed by a space. Here are examples of the use of the four basic arithmetic operators, followed in each case by a statement expressing the same meaning using arithmetic verbs.

```
COMPUTE C = A + B.
ADD A, B GIVING C.

COMPUTE D = A + B + C + D.
ADD A B C TO D.

COMPUTE D = C - A - B.
SUBTRACT A B FROM C GIVING D.

COMPUTE B = B - A.
SUBTRACT A FROM B.

COMPUTE C = B / A.
DIVIDE B BY A GIVING C.

COMPUTE B = B / A.
DIVIDE A INTO B.

COMPUTE C = A * B.
MULTIPLY A BY B GIVING C.

COMPUTE B = A * B.
MULTIPLY A BY B.
```

Here are some examples of the use of arithmetic expressions in COMPUTE statements to carry out familiar data processing operations.

```
COMPUTE NET-PAY = GROSS-PAY - DEDUCTIONS.
COMPUTE MONTH-AVERAGE = YEAR-TOTAL / 12.
COMPUTE MARGIN = QTY-ON-HAND + QTY-ON-ORDER - QTY-RESERVED.
COMPUTE GROSS-PAY = HOURS-WORKED * PAY-RATE.
```

Exponentiation can be used to raise a quantity to a power like this:

```
COMPUTE B = A ** 4.
```

Most commonly, however, exponentiation is used to get roots, which cannot be done any other way in COBOL. For example, we could used the following to compute a square root:

```
COMPUTE B = A ** 0.5.
```

When there are a number of arithmetic operators in an expression, it is necessary to know the order in which they are carried out. The answer to this question is given by the following *operator hierarchy rule*:

> In the absence of parentheses, all exponentiations are evaluated first, then all multiplications and divisions (from left to right), then all additions and subtractions (from left to right).

Thus, in the following example the division is carried out first, then the multiplication. The result of the division is added to A and the result of the multiplication is subtracted from the result of the addition.

```
A + B / C - D * E
```

In the next example, we take the square root of B, divide it by the square of C, and subtract the result of the division from A.

```
A - B ** 0.5 / C ** 2
```

If there is any doubt about what a given expression means, it can always be made explicit by the use of parentheses. Subexpressions within parentheses are always evaluated first, regardless of what the operator hierarchy rule would otherwise dictate. There should not be a space following a left parenthesis or preceding a right parenthesis, and left and right parentheses must be matched in meaningful pairs. Consider a few examples.

```
A * (B + C)
```

Parentheses are used to force the addition to be done before the multiplication.

```
(A * B / C) ** 0.5
```

Without the parentheses we would have A times B, divided by the square root of C, instead of taking the square root of the entire expression.

```
A / (B * C)
```

The parentheses here force A to be divided by the product of B and C. Without them, A would be divided by B and the result of the division would be multiplied by C. Similarly, in the following example the parentheses cause C to be subtracted from B, then the result subtracted from A. This gives E the value 2, while D has the value 0.

```
MOVE 3 TO A.
MOVE 2 TO B.
MOVE 1 TO C.
COMPUTE D = A - B - C.
COMPUTE E = A - (B - C).
```

A special arithmetic operator, which will find only specialized use, is the *unary minus sign*. The "unary" means that it applies to a single operand, rather than combining two operands as the binary minus does. As you would expect, the unary minus reverses the sign of the expression it precedes.

19.6 EXAMPLES OF THE USE OF THE COMPUTE STATEMENT

In the payroll programs in Chapters 6 and 7 we computed an employee's total exemptions and then, if the gross pay exceeded the exemptions, found the tax (See Figure 6.3). This can be done a bit more directly with a **COMPUTE** statement:

```
IF W-GROSS-PAY IS GREATER THAN W-EXEMPTION-TOTAL
     COMPUTE W-TAX ROUNDED =
               (W-GROSS-PAY - W-EXEMPTIONS-TOTAL) * C-TAXRATE
ELSE
     MOVE ZERO TO W-TAX.
```

Using the **COMPUTE** statement, we can also condense the computation of a worker's gross pay, including overtime, with this statement:

```
IF HOURS-WORKED NOT > 40
     COMPUTE W-GROSS-PAY ROUNDED = I-HOURS-WORKED * I-PAYRATE
ELSE
     COMPUTE W-GROSS-PAY ROUNDED =
            40 * I-PAYRATE
          + 1.5 * (I-HOURS-WORKED - 40) * I-PAYRATE.
```

This arranges the computation differently from the way it was done in the programs given earlier in the book. Since it is a simple matter to put the entire computation into one **IF** statement, we make entirely separate computations of the two cases, with and without overtime. As always, there are many other ways the calculations could be arranged, and the choice between them should be based on simplicity and clarity.

Both of the examples above could have been done using ordinary arithmetic verbs (and indeed were, in earlier chapters). Here is one example that cannot be done that way. In an inventory control application we wish to compute the *economic order quantity*, which is defined to be the number of units of an item that a firm should order at one time to minimize the sum of the cost of ordering and the cost of storing the item. In its simplest form, this is given by

$$\sqrt{2RS/CI}$$

where:

R = number of units used annually
S = cost of placing one order
C = cost of one unit
I = inventory carrying cost, expressed as a fraction of the value of the average inventory.

Since a square root is involved, this computation must be done with the **COMPUTE** statement, which could be as follows:

```
COMPUTE ECONOMIC-ORDER-QUANTITY =
(2 * ANNUAL-UNITS * ORDER-COST / (UNIT-COST * INV-COST)) ** 0.5.
```

19.7 LIMITATIONS ON THE USE OF THE COMPUTE STATEMENT

As in other arithmetic in **COBOL**, no numeric quantity may exceed 18 digits.

The **ON SIZE ERROR** clause may be used, but the test applies only to the final result. This gets us into what can be a serious problem with the free use of the **COMPUTE** statement: the programmer has no control over—or knowledge of—the intermediate results that are developed during the course of a computation. Although some **COBOL** manuals define how the **PICTURE**s of intermediate results are determined, some do not, and even when the information is available many programmers don't use it. As a result, a program that works correctly for most data values may, on rare occasions, give a totally wrong result *with no warning whatsoever*.

In view of these problems and because of the relative unfamiliarity of many **COBOL** programmers with the mathematical rules involved, some installations make minimum use of the **COMPUTE** statement. Some, in fact, prohibit its use for anything except exponentiation. To balance the picture, however, it should be noted that some installations strongly encourage the free use of **COMPUTE** for all arithmetic.

19.8 ARITHMETIC EXPRESSIONS IN RELATION CONDITIONS

Arithmetic expressions may be used in relation conditions anywhere that an identifier or literal is permitted, letting us write statements such as

```
IF (JAN-USE + FEB-USE + MAR-USE) / 3 > PREV-AVERAGE-USE
    ADD 1 TO GROWTH-QUARTER-COUNT.

IF B ** 2 - 4 * A * C < ZERO
    PERFORM IMAGINARY-ROOTS-ROUTINE
ELSE
    PERFORM REAL-ROOTS-ROUTINE.
```

We have seen in earlier chapters how this type of expression can be useful.

Arithmetic expressions used in this way are subject to the same warnings about the lack of control over intermediate results that apply to the **COMPUTE** statement. Arithmetic expressions are not heavily used in this way.

19.9 THE RENAMES CLAUSE

The **RENAMES** clause, which must have the level 66 and which must follow the record description to which it applies, associates a new name with a prior grouping of data. Although this sounds something like **REDEFINES** clauses, there are important differences. As an example let us consider once more the **OLD-MASTER** and **TRANSACTION** records from the file update program in Chapter 12; this record, along with two **RENAMES** entries, is shown in Figure 19.4.

```
01    OLD-MASTER.
      05    OM-KEY                  PIC X(5).
      05    OM-QUAN-ON-HAND         PIC 9(5).
      05    OM-QUAN-ON-ORDER        PIC 9(5).
      05    OM-REORDER-POINT        PIC 9(5).
      05    OM-REORDER-QUAN         PIC 9(5).
      05    OM-DESCRIPTION          PIC X(20).
      05    FILLER                  PIC X(35).

01    TRANSACTION.
      05    TR-KEY                  PIC X(5).
      05    TR-QUANTITY             PIC 9(5).
      05    TR-TRANSACTION-CODE     PIC X.
            88    ADDITION                    VALUE '1'.
            88    ADJUSTMENT                  VALUE '2'.
            88    RECEIPT                     VALUE '3'.
            88    SHIPMENT                    VALUE '4'.
            88    DELETION                    VALUE '5'.
      05    TR-ADJUSTMENT-CODE      PIC 9.
      05    TR-QUAN-ON-ORDER        PIC 9(5).
      05    TR-REORDER-POINT        PIC 9(5).
      05    TR-REORDER-QUAN         PIC 9(5).
      05    TR-DESCRIPTION          PIC X(20).
      05    FILLER                  PIC X(33).
66    TR-GROUP-1 RENAMES TR-KEY THRU TR-QUANTITY.
66    TR-GROUP-2 RENAMES TR-QUAN-ON-ORDER THRU TR-DESCRIPTION.
```

FIGURE 19.4 An example of record definitions using the **RENAMES** clause.

The first **RENAMES** clause in this example makes **TR-GROUP-1** the name of an item consisting of **TR-KEY** and **TR-QUANTITY**. The second one makes **TR-GROUP-2** the name of an item consisting of everything from **TR-QUAN-ON-ORDER** through **TR-DESCRIPTION**. Suppose that instead of defining **NEW-MASTER** using the same structure we have used for **OLD-MASTER**, we define it as follows:

```
01    NEW-MASTER.
      05    NM-GROUP-1              PIC X(10).
      05    NM-GROUP-2              PIC X(35).
      05    FILLER                  PIC X(35).
```

Then in the Procedure Division we could write, for example,

```
MOVE TR-GROUP-1 TO NM-GROUP-1.
MOVE TR-GROUP-2 TO NM-GROUP-2.
```

and get the two elementary items at the start of the transaction record and the four elementary items at the end of the transaction record moved to the new master record, thus eliminating the two codes from the middle of an addition record.

How does **RENAMES** differ from **REDEFINES**? The key to answering that question is the word **THRU** in the **RENAMES** clause. Using the **RENAMES**, we can make a name apply to a whole set of items rather than just one elementary or group item, which is all **REDEFINES** can do. Furthermore, there can be as many

RENAMES clauses as are useful, and there are no restrictions concerning how the groupings they define may or may not overlap. It would be perfectly legal for us to have a third **RENAMES** like this:

```
66   TR-GROUP-3 RENAMES TR-QUANTITY THRU TR-REORDER-POINT.
```

The fact that **TR-GROUP-3** would overlap parts of the other two would make no difference at all.

In the simple example above we could have handled the problem by making the two groupings into ordinary group items. The **RENAMES** clause, however, can handle situations that could not be dealt with in this way. For example, suppose we had the following record description:

```
01   SAMPLE.
     05  A.
         10  B             PIC X.
         10  C             PIC X.
     05  D.
         10  E             PIC X.
         10  F.
             15  G         PIC X.
             15  H         PIC X.
         10  I.
             15  J         PIC X.
             15  K         PIC X.
```

The following **RENAMES** clause would be legal and meaningful, and what it accomplishes could not be done with group items except by restructuring the entire record

```
66   CG-GROUP RENAMES C THRU G.
```

Using the same record description, we could also write things like

```
66   BH   RENAMES A THRU F.
```

The letter **A** is a group item; **RENAMES** begins with the first elementary item in it. The letter **F** is also a group item, and renaming ends with the last elementary item in it.

Having shown some of what the **RENAMES** clause can do, we must ask why one would want to use it. One of the fundamental concepts of structured software design is that data, as well as procedural code, has an intrinsic hierarchy. The **RENAMES** clause completely ignores this hierarchy and the logical structure of the data. In almost all cases, you will find that the only motive for using the **RENAMES** clause is to save a few lines of code in the Procedure Division; this is almost always done at the expense of program clarity.

We have shown the **RENAMES** clause not because we recommend its use, but because maintenance programmers may encounter it in old programs. We strongly urge that the **RENAMES** clause be avoided, and in fact many installations forbid programmers to use it.

19.10   THE ALTER STATEMENT AND WHY IT SHOULD NEVER BE USED

The **ALTER** statement makes it possible to change the transfer point specified in a **GO TO** statement. The general format is shown on the next page.

> ALTER procedure-name-1 TO [PROCEED TO] procedure-name-2
>
> [procedure-name-3 TO [PROCEED TO] procedure-name-4] . . .

Procedure-name-1, Procedure-name-3, etc., must be the names of paragraphs that contain only one sentence: a GO TO statement without the DEPENDING ON option. Procedure-name-2, Procedure-name-4, etc., must be the names of paragraphs or sections in the Procedure Division. The effect is to change the GO TOs so that, instead of whatever they said before, they now specify a transfer to the paragraphs named in the ALTER statement. A GO TO can be ALTERed many times during the course of a program execution.

For an illustration of what the ALTER statement does, consider the program in Figure 19.5. Its purpose is to read a file of records, form the sum of the numbers found in the first three bytes of each record, and produce a count of the number of records. The program is written to take an alternative approach to getting the loop started, other than using VALUE clauses in the definitions of RECORD-COUNT and TOTAL-A. The scheme is that there is a paragraph named FIRST-TIME-PARAGRAPH that puts a 1 in RECORD-COUNT and moves the contents of bytes 1 to 3 on the first record to the total. An ALTER statement within that paragraph is used to assure that it is executed only once. The paragraph must end with a GO TO statement to skip around the paragraph named AFTER-FIRST-PARAGRAPH. (We have avoided using the normal prefix conventions on the paragraph names, because any program that contains code like this one does is not likely to have any meaningful hierarchy or paragraph sequence.)

```
00001           IDENTIFICATION DIVISION.
00002           PROGRAM-ID.
00003               ALTER-DEMO.
00004           DATE-WRITTEN.
00005               MAY 18, 1987.
00006
00007      *    THIS PROGRAM, WHICH USES THE ALTER STATEMENT, IS PRESENTED
00008      *    ONLY TO SHOW FUTURE MAINTENANCE PROGRAMMERS WHAT THE
00009      *    STATEMENT DOES, SINCE SOME EXISTING PROGRAMS DO USE IT.
00010      *    USE OF THE ALTER STATEMENT IS TO BE STRONGLY DISCOURAGED.
00011      *    --- -- --- ----- --------- -- -- -- ------- ----------
00012
00013           ENVIRONMENT DIVISION.
00014           INPUT-OUTPUT SECTION.
00015           FILE-CONTROL.
00016               SELECT INPUT-FILE          ASSIGN TO S-INPUT.
00017               SELECT OUTPUT-FILE         ASSIGN TO S-OUTPUT.
00018
00019           DATA DIVISION.
00020           FILE SECTION.
00021
00022      FD   INPUT-FILE
00023           LABEL RECORDS ARE OMITTED.
00024      01   INPUT-RECORD.
00025           05   FIELD-A               PIC 999.
00026           05   FILLER                PIC X(77).
00027
```

```
00028            FD   OUTPUT-FILE
00029                 LABEL RECORDS ARE OMITTED.
00030            01   OUTPUT-RECORD.
00031                 05   RECORD-COUNT          PIC 9(4).
00032                 05   TOTAL-A               PIC 9(6).
00033
00034            WORKING-STORAGE SECTION.
00035
00036            01   MORE-DATA-REMAINS-FLAG     PIC X VALUE 'Y'.
00037                 88   NO-MORE-DATA-REMAINS         VALUE 'N'.
00038
00039
00040            PROCEDURE DIVISION.
00041            MAIN-LINE-ROUTINE.
00042                OPEN INPUT INPUT-FILE
00043                    OUTPUT OUTPUT-FILE.
00044                PERFORM READ-ROUTINE.
00045                PERFORM PROCESS-ONE-RECORD THRU PROCESS-ONE-RECORD-EXIT
00046                    UNTIL NO-MORE-DATA-REMAINS.
00047                WRITE OUTPUT-RECORD.
00048                CLOSE INPUT-FILE
00049                    OUTPUT-FILE.
00050                STOP RUN.
00051
00052            PROCESS-ONE-RECORD.
00053            *
00054            * THIS GO TO IS ALTERED IN FIRST-TIME-PARAGRAPH
00055            *
00056                GO TO FIRST-TIME-PARAGRAPH.
00057
00058            FIRST-TIME-PARAGRAPH.
00059                MOVE 1 TO RECORD-COUNT.
00060                MOVE FIELD-A TO TOTAL-A.
00061                ALTER PROCESS-ONE-RECORD TO PROCEED TO AFTER-FIRST-PARAGRAPH.
00062                GO TO READ-ROUTINE.
00063
00064            AFTER-FIRST-PARAGRAPH.
00065                ADD 1 TO RECORD-COUNT.
00066                ADD FIELD-A TO TOTAL-A.
00067
00068            READ-ROUTINE.
00069                READ INPUT-FILE
00070                    AT END MOVE 'N' TO MORE-DATA-REMAINS-FLAG.
00071
00072            PROCESS-ONE-RECORD-EXIT.
00073                EXIT.
00074
00075            ********************* END OF PROGRAM *************************
```

FIGURE 19.5   A program using the **ALTER** statement to modify the effect of a **GO TO** statement.

Observe that the **PERFORM...UNTIL** in the main line routine is written with the **THRU** option. Because of the **GO TO**s involved here, there is no way to get all of the actions into one paragraph. Observe also, that the paragraph named **READ-ROUTINE** is entered in *three* different ways. It is executed first by a **PERFORM** in the main line routine, then there is a transfer to it with the **GO TO** in the paragraph executed for the first record, and in all other cases control falls through from the end of the previous paragraph.

This program does work, but even in something this elementary we readily see how much more complex the program is and how much more difficult it is to understand than if it were written in the style that is employed elsewhere in the book. The difficulty in understanding programs that have **ALTER** statements and many **GO TO**s is that to understand how a statement works, we have to know the complete sequence of prior program execution. The characteristic we have striven for throughout has been that to understand how a statement works, we need to know only a few other statements—all physically close by. Sometimes we have come closer to reaching that goal than others, but that has always been the goal. The **GO TO** and especially the **ALTER** statement destroy this "locality of context."

In programs of realistic size the extensive use of **GO TO**s and **ALTER**s can make a program extremely difficult to understand. This is especially true in the maintenance situation, where someone who has never seen the program before must become familiar with it as quickly as possible, sometimes under critical time pressure because the program has failed. In such a circumstance the sight of a **GO TO** statement in a paragraph by itself, signaling as it does the existence of an unknown number of **ALTER** statements at unknown locations throughout the program, strikes fear in the heart of the bravest programmer.

It is recommended most strongly that the **ALTER** statement never be used. (In fact, the **COBOL-85** standard promises that the **ALTER** statement will be removed from the *next* **COBOL** revision.) Nothing that it does cannot be done in other ways, very much more understandably. The subject is presented here solely for the benefit of those who may at some time be involved with existing programs that have **ALTER** statements in them. The maintenance of such programs can be materially simplified by adding comments to them (as in Figure 19.5) showing, for each altered **GO TO** statement, the location of all the **ALTER** statements that refer to it. This in no way converts use of the **ALTER** statement into acceptable programming practice, but it may help a bad situation a little. A better solution, if the use of the **ALTER** is not too extensive, is to recode parts of the program so that the **ALTER** is removed from the program entirely.

CHAPTER 20

INTERACTIVE COBOL

20.1 INTRODUCTION

When computerized data processing began in the late 1950s and early 1960s, all programs were run in *batch* mode. Records were punched onto cards, collected into batches, and run as a batch, frequently at night. It would take at least several hours (if not a full day) for the results to become available. Even if batches were run more frequently than once a day, the key characteristic of the processing was that once processing of a batch of data was begun, it was not possible to interact with that processing until the program finished execution. Even today, although records are usually keyed into a terminal or some similar data entry device, much of data processing goes on in batch mode. However, with the growing use of computers having *interactive* capabilities, such as minicomputers and microcomputers (or even mainframe computers using systems such as IBM's CICS), more and more programs are run in *interactive* mode; that is, a mode in which it is possible to interact with the program as it is executing.

There are advantages and disadvantages to both modes of execution, and we do not propose to discuss the pros and cons of each approach here. However, as interactive processing becomes increasingly common, it is appropriate to discuss some of the ways in which a program written for interactive processing differs from a program written for batch processing.

We present two variations on the basic seed program shown in Chapter 11, to demonstrate how an interactive program can allow the user to correct errors as data is keyed. We follow this with a program to demonstrate how *menus* can be used to guide the program user through execution of the program. All programs in this chapter were written using the Realia COBOL 2.00 compiler, and were run on an IBM PC-compatible AT&T PC6300 computer. We must emphasize that although the *principles* we will discuss in the remainder of this chapter are valid for any interactive COBOL compiler, the *details* of how interactive I/O works varies from computer to computer and compiler to compiler. For example, some compilers have optional phrases for the **DISPLAY** statement which allow you to specify line and column positions directly, while others provide library subroutines which can be used for cursor control. Similar techniques are used to produce various graphic effects, such as blinking displays, reverse video, and special colors.

20.2 AN INTERACTIVE VERSION OF THE SEED CATALOG PROGRAM

One of the basic characteristics of interactive processing is that errors can be reported and usually corrected while the program is running. We will demonstrate how this may be done using the seed catalog program of Figure 11.1. Recall that this program reads a file of order records and edits the records; valid records are written to one output file, while those containing errors are written to a different file. A revised version of this program is shown in Figure 20.1.

```
 1        IDENTIFICATION DIVISION.
 2        PROGRAM-ID.
 3            INTER1.
 4        DATE-WRITTEN.
 5            MAY 28, 1987.
 6
 7     *
 8     *    THIS IS AN INTERACTIVE VERSION OF THE BASIC SEED CATALOG
 9     *    PROGRAM.
10     *
11
12        ENVIRONMENT DIVISION.
13        INPUT-OUTPUT SECTION.
14        FILE-CONTROL.
15            SELECT NORMAL-HANDLING-FILE      ASSIGN TO S-NORMAL.
16
17        DATA DIVISION.
18        FILE SECTION.
19     FD  NORMAL-HANDLING-FILE
20            LABEL RECORDS ARE STANDARD.
21     01  NORMAL-HANDLING-RECORD           PIC X(60).
22
23        WORKING-STORAGE SECTION.
24
25     01  CONTINUE-COMMAND                  PIC X.
26
27     01  CURSOR-CONTROL-FIELDS.
28            05  CLEAR-SCREEN               PIC XX      VALUE '2J'.
29            05  SKIP-3-LINES               PIC XX      VALUE '3B'.
30
31     01  ELB.
32            05  FILLER                     PIC 9(4) COMP VALUE 7003.
33
34     01  ERROR-FLAGS.
35            88  RECORD-OK                              VALUE SPACES.
36            05  CAT-NO-NOT-NUMERIC         PIC X.
37            05  FIRST-DIGIT-INVALID        PIC X.
38            05  SIZE-CODE-NOT-PERMITTED    PIC X.
39            05  NO-SUCH-SIZE-CODE          PIC X.
```

```
40              05  QUANTITY-AND-PRICE-CODES.
41                  88  QTY-AND-PRICE-OK                       VALUE SPACES.
42                  10  QTY-NOT-NUMERIC         PIC X.
43                  10  PRICE-NOT-NUMERIC       PIC X.
44              05  INVALID-PRICE-OR-QTY        PIC X.
45              05  LARGE-PRICE                 PIC X.
46
47      01  ERROR-MESSAGES.
48              05  CAT-NO-NOT-NUMERIC-MSG      PIC X(50)
49                  VALUE 'CATALOG NUMBER CONTAINS AN IMPROPER CHARACTER'.
50              05  FIRST-DIGIT-INVALID-MSG     PIC X(50)
51                  VALUE 'FIRST DIGIT OF CATALOG NUMBER INVALID'.
52              05  SIZE-CODE-NOT-PERMITTED-MSG PIC X(50)
53                  VALUE 'THIS ITEM DOES NOT TAKE A SIZE CODE'.
54              05  NO-SUCH-SIZE-CODE-MSG       PIC X(50)
55                  VALUE 'THERE IS NO SUCH SIZE CODE'.
56              05  QTY-NOT-NUMERIC-MSG         PIC X(50)
57                  VALUE 'QUANTITY CONTAINS AN IMPROPER CHARACTER'.
58              05  PRICE-NOT-NUMERIC-MSG       PIC X(50)
59                  VALUE 'PRICE CONTAINS AN IMPROPER CHARACTER'.
60              05  INVALID-PRICE-OR-QTY-MSG    PIC X(50)
61                  VALUE 'EITHER PRICE OR QUANTITY IS WRONG'.
62              05  LARGE-PRICE-MSG             PIC X(50)
63                  VALUE 'PRICE LARGE - SHOULD BE CHECKED'.
64
65      01  ERROR-MESSAGE-HEADER-1.
66              05  FILLER                      PIC X(15) VALUE SPACES.
67              05  FILLER                      PIC X(14) VALUE
68                  'ERROR MESSAGES'.
69
70      01  ERROR-MESSAGE-HEADER-2.
71              05  FILLER                      PIC X(15) VALUE SPACES.
72              05  FILLER                      PIC X(31) VALUE
73                  'ORDER REJECTED DUE TO ERRORS.  '.
74              05  FILLER                      PIC X(25) VALUE
75                  'PRESS RETURN TO CONTINUE.'.
76
77      01  MORE-DATA-REMAINS-FLAG             PIC X     VALUE 'Y'.
78              88  NO-MORE-DATA-REMAINS                 VALUE 'N'.
79
80      01  NUMBER-OF-CHARACTERS              PIC 99 COMP-4.
81
82      01  ORDER-RECORD.
83              05  ORDER-NUMBER                PIC X(6).
84              05  RECORD-TYPE                 PIC X.
85              05  CATALOG-NUMBER.
86                  10  CATALOG-FIRST-DIGIT     PIC X.
87                  10  CATALOG-REMAINING       PIC X(4).
88              05  SIZE-CODE                   PIC X.
89              05  QUANTITY                    PIC 99.
90              05  ITEM-DESCRIPTION            PIC X(40).
91              05  X-PRICE                     PIC X(5).
92              05  9-PRICE REDEFINES X-PRICE   PIC 999V99.
93
94      01  PRICE-LIMIT                        PIC  999V99 VALUE 125.00.
95      01  TEST-REMAINDER                     PIC S999V99 COMP-3.
96      01  UNIT-PRICE                         PIC S999V99 COMP-3.
97
```

```
 98        PROCEDURE DIVISION.
 99        A000-VALIDATE-ORDERS.
100           OPEN OUTPUT NORMAL-HANDLING-FILE.
101           PERFORM X010-GET-ORDER-RECORD.
102           PERFORM B010-VALIDATE-ONE-ORDER
103              UNTIL NO-MORE-DATA-REMAINS.
104           CLOSE NORMAL-HANDLING-FILE.
105           STOP RUN.
106
107        B010-VALIDATE-ONE-ORDER.
108           MOVE SPACES TO ERROR-FLAGS.
109           PERFORM C010-EDIT-ORDER.
110
111           IF QTY-AND-PRICE-OK
112              IF RECORD-OK
113                 WRITE NORMAL-HANDLING-RECORD FROM ORDER-RECORD
114              ELSE
115                 PERFORM C020-WRITE-MESSAGES
116           ELSE
117              PERFORM C020-WRITE-MESSAGES.
118
119           PERFORM X010-GET-ORDER-RECORD.
120
121        C010-EDIT-ORDER.
122           IF CATALOG-NUMBER OF ORDER-RECORD IS NOT NUMERIC
123              MOVE 'X' TO CAT-NO-NOT-NUMERIC.
124
125           IF CATALOG-FIRST-DIGIT OF ORDER-RECORD = '0' OR '2'
126              MOVE 'X' TO FIRST-DIGIT-INVALID.
127
128           IF (CATALOG-FIRST-DIGIT OF ORDER-RECORD = '1' OR '8' OR '9')
129              AND SIZE-CODE OF ORDER-RECORD IS NOT EQUAL TO SPACES
130              MOVE 'X' TO SIZE-CODE-NOT-PERMITTED.
131
132           IF SIZE-CODE OF ORDER-RECORD = 'A' OR 'D' OR 'G' OR 'J'
133              OR 'K' OR 'L' OR 'S' OR 'T' OR 'U' OR ' '
134              NEXT SENTENCE
135           ELSE
136              MOVE 'X' TO NO-SUCH-SIZE-CODE.
137
138           IF QUANTITY OF ORDER-RECORD IS NOT NUMERIC
139              MOVE 'X' TO QTY-NOT-NUMERIC.
140
141           IF X-PRICE NOT NUMERIC
142              MOVE 'X' TO PRICE-NOT-NUMERIC.
143
144           IF QTY-AND-PRICE-OK
145              DIVIDE 9-PRICE BY QUANTITY OF ORDER-RECORD
146                    GIVING UNIT-PRICE REMAINDER TEST-REMAINDER
147                 ON SIZE ERROR MOVE 'X' TO INVALID-PRICE-OR-QTY.
148           IF QTY-AND-PRICE-OK AND TEST-REMAINDER NOT EQUAL TO ZERO
149              MOVE 'X' TO INVALID-PRICE-OR-QTY.
150
151           IF X-PRICE IS NUMERIC AND 9-PRICE IS GREATER THAN PRICE-LIMIT
152              MOVE 'X' TO LARGE-PRICE.
153
154        C020-WRITE-MESSAGES.
155           DISPLAY ELB SKIP-3-LINES.
156           DISPLAY ERROR-MESSAGE-HEADER-1.
157           DISPLAY SPACES.
158
```

```
159         IF CAT-NO-NOT-NUMERIC = 'X'
160             DISPLAY CAT-NO-NOT-NUMERIC-MSG.
161         IF FIRST-DIGIT-INVALID = 'X'
162             DISPLAY FIRST-DIGIT-INVALID-MSG.
163         IF SIZE-CODE-NOT-PERMITTED = 'X'
164             DISPLAY SIZE-CODE-NOT-PERMITTED-MSG.
165         IF NO-SUCH-SIZE-CODE = 'X'
166             DISPLAY NO-SUCH-SIZE-CODE-MSG.
167         IF QTY-NOT-NUMERIC = 'X'
168             DISPLAY QTY-NOT-NUMERIC-MSG.
169         IF PRICE-NOT-NUMERIC = 'X'
170             DISPLAY PRICE-NOT-NUMERIC-MSG.
171         IF INVALID-PRICE-OR-QTY = 'X'
172             DISPLAY INVALID-PRICE-OR-QTY-MSG.
173         IF LARGE-PRICE = 'X'
174             DISPLAY LARGE-PRICE-MSG.
175
176         DISPLAY ELB SKIP-3-LINES.
177         DISPLAY ERROR-MESSAGE-HEADER-2 WITH NO ADVANCING.
178         ACCEPT CONTINUE-COMMAND.
179
180     X010-GET-ORDER-RECORD.
181     *       CLEAR THE SCREEN
182         DISPLAY ELB CLEAR-SCREEN WITH NO ADVANCING.
183     *       ACCEPT THE FIELDS ONE AT A TIME.
184     *       FOR EACH FIELD, INITIALIZE THE FIELD, DISPLAY A PROMPT
185     *           MESSAGE, THEN ACCEPT THE DATA.
186     *       IF THE ORDER NUMBER IS EMPTY, SET THE EOF FLAG.
187         MOVE LOW-VALUES TO ORDER-NUMBER.
188         MOVE ZERO TO NUMBER-OF-CHARACTERS.
189         DISPLAY 'Enter order number: ' WITH NO ADVANCING.
190         ACCEPT ORDER-NUMBER.
191         INSPECT ORDER-NUMBER TALLYING NUMBER-OF-CHARACTERS
192             FOR CHARACTERS BEFORE LOW-VALUES.
193         IF NUMBER-OF-CHARACTERS IS EQUAL TO ZERO
194             MOVE 'N' TO MORE-DATA-REMAINS-FLAG
195         ELSE
196             PERFORM Y010-GET-REST-OF-ORDER.
197
198     Y010-GET-REST-OF-ORDER.
199         MOVE SPACES TO RECORD-TYPE.
200         DISPLAY 'Enter record type:  ' WITH NO ADVANCING.
201         ACCEPT RECORD-TYPE.
202         MOVE SPACES TO CATALOG-NUMBER.
203         DISPLAY 'Enter catalog number: ' WITH NO ADVANCING.
204         ACCEPT CATALOG-NUMBER.
205         MOVE SPACES TO SIZE-CODE.
206         DISPLAY 'Enter size code:  ' WITH NO ADVANCING.
207         ACCEPT SIZE-CODE.
208         MOVE ZERO TO QUANTITY.
209         DISPLAY 'Enter quantity:  ' WITH NO ADVANCING.
210         ACCEPT QUANTITY.
211         MOVE SPACES TO ITEM-DESCRIPTION.
212         DISPLAY 'Enter item description:  ' WITH NO ADVANCING.
213         ACCEPT ITEM-DESCRIPTION.
214         MOVE SPACES TO X-PRICE.
215         DISPLAY 'Enter item price:  ' WITH NO ADVANCING.
216         ACCEPT X-PRICE.
217
218     ***************** END OF PROGRAM *********************************
```

FIGURE 20.1 A basic interactive version of the seed catalog program.

In spite of some obvious differences in detail, the basic structure of this program is the same as that of the equivalent batch program. After opening files, we get a priming record, then repeat execution of the processing paragraph until we run out of records. When this happens, we close files and stop the run. The main processing paragraph in both programs has the same structure: edit the current record, write some output depending on the results of the editing, then get the next record. Editing is identical in both versions, and there are obvious similarities in the paragraphs that print the error messages.

The differences between the two programs begin in the Environment Division, and are caused by the differences in the way the programs perform I/O. In the batch version, order records are keyed into a file, the file is read by the program, and the results are written to other files for later use by the people who deal with the orders. In the interactive version, orders are read by the program as they are keyed and each order is processed completely before the next order is entered; valid orders go to a new file and errors are reported to the terminal screen. Since errors can be corrected immediately, there is no need to write bad records to any output file.

Because input is read from the keyboard using the **ACCEPT** statement there is no need for an input file. Likewise, there is no need for an output file for invalid records. Therefore, the **FILE-CONTROL** paragraph only contains a **SELECT** statement for the normal handling file. As you can see in the File Section, this file has been modified so that valid orders can be written to a disk for further processing by some other program.

The Working-Storage Section contains some new fields which we will discuss shortly, and we have removed **OUTPUT-LINE** and **TEXT-LINE** since they are no longer needed. The remainder of Working-Storage is essentially the same in both the batch and interactive programs.

One of the most significant differences between the two programs lies in the way in which order records are obtained. In the batch program, we simply read **ORDER-RECORD** from the input file. In the interactive program, **ORDER-RECORD** (which is now in the Working-Storage Section instead of the File Section) is obtained field by field in **X010-GET-ORDER-RECORD**.

We digress for a moment from the discussion of the program to describe how interactive I/O is performed in the **COBOL** system we are using. Output to the CRT is done with the **DISPLAY** statement, which has the following format.

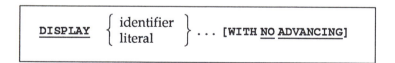

In its simplest form, the **DISPLAY** is used as it is in batch programs. The variables or literals listed are displayed on the computer screen, just as they would be printed on paper in a batch program. After the list has been displayed the cursor moves to the start of the next line unless the **WITH NO ADVANCING** clause is used; this leaves the cursor at the end of the **DISPLAY** list.

A basic difference between a CRT and printed paper is that it is possible to move the cursor to any desired location on the CRT. Furthermore, you may wish to blank the entire screen or selected lines, or use various graphic effects while producing output. In the compiler used to develop programs for this book, these effects are controlled by displaying special strings of characters.

The computer distinguishes screen control strings from data to be displayed by requiring the sequence "**ESC** [" (where **ESC** represents the escape key) at the start of all control strings. This is the function of the variable **ELB** (Escape-Left-Bracket) in the Working-Storage Section. The value 7003 is 256*27 + 91; 27 is the computer's internal representation of **ESC**, multiplying by 256 shifts this value left one byte, and 91 is the internal representation of [. The values used for **CLEAR-SCREEN** and **SKIP-3-LINES** are the codes used by our computer to accomplish the indicated tasks. We must emphasize that these are "magic" values, in that they are appropriate for one particular computer and may be different on other computers. When you write programs to manipulate the CRT on your computer, you must know the control codes that are used for that machine.

To move the cursor or otherwise control the CRT, we only need to write the proper control string to the screen using the **DISPLAY** statement. For example, the statement

```
DISPLAY ELB '2J'.
```

clears the screen and moves the cursor to the first column of the first row. As we have done with special constants in other programs, we use identifiers rather than literals in the Procedure Division to simplify program maintenance should we have to change the value of the "constant."

Returning now to the program, we can look at paragraph **X010-GET-ORDER-RECORD**. The first statement in the paragraph clears the screen and leaves the cursor at the first column of row 1. We are now ready to read a new order. Since we are not reading from a file, there is no end of file indicator to be detected. Instead, we have decided that if the user enters a carriage return with no data instead of typing an order number, this will be interpreted as an end of file; no more data will be requested for the order, and the end of file flag will be set accordingly. This end of file signal was chosen rather arbitrarily; there are many other possibilities.

To determine whether any data was entered for the order number, we initialize **ORDER-NUMBER** to **LOW-VALUES**, which is easily identified and cannot be entered from the keyboard. We also set a counter field to zero. The next **DISPLAY** statement displays a message on the screen, then waits at the end of the text until the user enters the order number and presses the return key. We use the **INSPECT** statement (see Section 15.2) to determine whether any data was actually entered. If not, we simply set the end of file flag to '**N**'; otherwise, we get the remainder of the order.

The statements in paragraph **Y010-GET-REST-OF-ORDER** all follow the same pattern. We initialize a field in **ORDER-RECORD**, **DISPLAY** a message requesting a value for the field, then **ACCEPT** the value from the keyboard.

After all fields have been obtained for the order, the order is edited. If no errors were found, it is written to **NORMAL-HANDLING-FILE**. Otherwise, we skip three lines and display a header on the CRT. Depending on which error flags have been set, we follow the header with one or more error messages. If we did nothing more than print the message, the computer would immediately go on to the next order and the user would not have time to read the messages before they disappeared from the screen. Therefore, we skip three more lines, display a short message, and wait until the user presses the return key before continuing.

20.3 PROGRAM RESULTS

The program was run using the data shown for the batch program in Figure 11.2. The screen image for a typical order is shown in Figure 20.2.

The error messages shown in this example are almost exactly the same as those shown for the same record in Figure 11.4, the output from the batch version of the program. The only difference is that in Figure 11.4, there is a message regarding an improper character in the quantity field. This message was caused by starting to enter the item description one column too far to the left. In the interactive program, when we attempted to enter the same data the computer refused to accept a nonnumeric character as input to a numeric field, so the error was detected and corrected immediately. This characteristic of interactive processing is one of the most useful features of that mode of execution: in many cases the computer will not even accept invalid data.

20.4 IMPROVING THE INTERACTIVE PROGRAM

In spite of the advantages that the previous program has over its batch equivalent, there is considerable room for improvement. The screen format is very crude, and it is necessary to enter the entire record before any errors are reported. Furthermore, if errors are detected, it is necessary to retype the entire record rather than simply correcting the field(s) in error.

```
Enter order number:  222239
Enter record type:  6
Enter catalog number:  2257T
Enter size code:  0
Enter quantity:  1
Enter item description:  LITTLE MARVEL PEAS - 1/2 LB
Enter item price:  0120




        ERROR MESSAGES

CATALOG NUMBER CONTAINS AN IMPROPER CHARACTER
FIRST DIGIT OF CATALOG NUMBER INVALID
THERE IS NO SUCH SIZE CODE
PRICE CONTAINS AN IMPROPER CHARACTER




        ORDER REJECTED DUE TO ERRORS.  PRESS RETURN TO CONTINUE.
```

FIGURE 20.2 Sample output from the program shown in Figure 20.1.

The program shown in Figure 20.3 addresses these weaknesses. The screen format is more attractive, and errors are reported immediately. This gives the user an opportunity to correct errors at once, and merely requires retyping the field in error.

```
1       IDENTIFICATION DIVISION.
2       PROGRAM-ID.
3           INTER2.
4       DATE-WRITTEN.
5           MAY 29, 1987.
6
7       *
8       *    THIS IS AN IMPROVED INTERACTIVE VERSION OF THE BASIC SEED
9       *    CATALOG PROGRAM.
10      *
11
12      ENVIRONMENT DIVISION.
13      INPUT-OUTPUT SECTION.
14      FILE-CONTROL.
15          SELECT NORMAL-HANDLING-FILE      ASSIGN TO S-NORMAL.
16
17      DATA DIVISION.
18      FILE SECTION.
19      FD  NORMAL-HANDLING-FILE
20          LABEL RECORDS ARE STANDARD.
21      01  NORMAL-HANDLING-RECORD           PIC X(60).
22
23      WORKING-STORAGE SECTION.
24
25      01  CONTINUE-COMMAND                 PIC X.
26
27      01  CURSOR-CONTROL-FIELDS.
28          05  CLEAR-LINE                   PIC X      VALUE 'K'.
29          05  CLEAR-SCREEN                 PIC XX     VALUE '2J'.
30          05  NORMAL-SCREEN                PIC X      VALUE '0'.
31          05  REVERSE-VIDEO                PIC X      VALUE '7'.
32          05  SET-GRAPHICS                 PIC X      VALUE 'm'.
33
34      01  CURSOR-MOVES.
35          05  MOVE-TO-HEADING              PIC X(5)   VALUE '6;29H'.
36          05  MOVE-TO-ORDER                PIC X(4)   VALUE '9;1H'.
37          05  MOVE-TO-ORDER-DATA           PIC X(5)   VALUE '9;16H'.
38          05  MOVE-TO-REC-TYPE             PIC X(5)   VALUE '9;27H'.
39          05  MOVE-TO-CAT-NBR              PIC X(5)   VALUE '9;47H'.
40          05  MOVE-TO-CAT-NBR-DATA         PIC X(5)   VALUE '9;64H'.
41          05  MOVE-TO-SIZE                 PIC X(5)   VALUE '10;1H'.
42          05  MOVE-TO-SIZE-DATA            PIC X(6)   VALUE '10;13H'.
43          05  MOVE-TO-QTY                  PIC X(6)   VALUE '10;27H'.
44          05  MOVE-TO-QTY-DATA             PIC X(6)   VALUE '10;38H'.
45          05  MOVE-TO-PRICE                PIC X(6)   VALUE '10;47H'.
46          05  MOVE-TO-PRICE-DATA           PIC X(6)   VALUE '10;56H'.
47          05  MOVE-TO-DESC                 PIC X(5)   VALUE '11;1H'.
48          05  MOVE-TO-ERR-MSG              PIC X(6)   VALUE '14;16H'.
49
50      01  ELB.
51          05  FILLER                       PIC 9(4) COMP-4 VALUE 7003.
52
```

```
 53        01   ERROR-MESSAGES.
 54             05   CAT-NO-NOT-NUMERIC-MSG      PIC X(50)
 55                  VALUE 'CATALOG NUMBER CONTAINS AN IMPROPER CHARACTER'.
 56             05   FIRST-DIGIT-INVALID-MSG     PIC X(50)
 57                  VALUE 'FIRST DIGIT OF CATALOG NUMBER INVALID'.
 58             05   SIZE-CODE-NOT-PERMITTED-MSG  PIC X(50)
 59                  VALUE 'THIS ITEM DOES NOT TAKE A SIZE CODE'.
 60             05   NO-SUCH-SIZE-CODE-MSG       PIC X(50)
 61                  VALUE 'THERE IS NO SUCH SIZE CODE'.
 62             05   QUANTITY-ZERO-MSG           PIC X(50)
 63                  VALUE 'QUANTITY MUST BE GREATER THAN ZERO'.
 64             05   INVALID-PRICE-OR-QTY-MSG    PIC X(50)
 65                  VALUE 'EITHER PRICE OR QUANTITY IS WRONG'.
 66             05   LARGE-PRICE-MSG.
 67                  10   FILLER                 PIC X(49) VALUE
 68                       'PRICE LARGE - TYPE Y TO ACCEPT, ANY OTHER KEY TO '.
 69                  10   FILLER                 PIC X(9)  VALUE 'RE-ENTER '.
 70
 71        01   FIELD-VALID-FLAG                 PIC X.
 72             88   FIELD-VALID                           VALUE 'Y'.
 73
 74        01   MORE-DATA-REMAINS-FLAG           PIC X    VALUE 'Y'.
 75             88   NO-MORE-DATA-REMAINS                  VALUE 'N'.
 76
 77        01   NUMBER-OF-CHARACTERS            PIC 99 COMP-4.
 78
 79        01   ORDER-RECORD.
 80             05   ORDER-NUMBER               PIC X(6).
 81             05   RECORD-TYPE                PIC X.
 82             05   CATALOG-NUMBER.
 83                  10   CATALOG-FIRST-DIGIT   PIC X.
 84                  10   CATALOG-REMAINING     PIC X(4).
 85             05   SIZE-CODE                  PIC X.
 86             05   QUANTITY                   PIC 99.
 87             05   ITEM-DESCRIPTION           PIC X(40).
 88             05   PRICE                      PIC 999V99.
 89
 90        01   PRICE-DISPLAY                   PIC ZZ9.99.
 91
 92        01   PRICE-LIMIT                     PIC  999V99 VALUE 125.00.
 93
 94        01   SCREEN-HEADING                  PIC X(24) VALUE
 95                  'SEED CATALOG ORDER ENTRY'.
 96
 97        01   TEST-REMAINDER                  PIC S999V99 COMP-3.
 98
 99        01   UNIT-PRICE                      PIC S999V99 COMP-3.
100
101        PROCEDURE DIVISION.
102        A000-VALIDATE-ORDERS.
103            OPEN OUTPUT NORMAL-HANDLING-FILE
104            PERFORM B010-VALIDATE-ONE-ORDER THRU
105                 B019-VALIDATE-EXIT
106                UNTIL NO-MORE-DATA-REMAINS.
107            CLOSE NORMAL-HANDLING-FILE.
108            STOP RUN.
109
```

```
110        B010-VALIDATE-ONE-ORDER.
111    *          CLEAR THE SCREEN
112        DISPLAY ELB CLEAR-SCREEN WITH NO ADVANCING.
113    *          DISPLAY THE HEADING
114        DISPLAY ELB MOVE-TO-HEADING SCREEN-HEADING.
115
116    *          IF THE ORDER NUMBER IS EMPTY, SET THE EOF FLAG.
117        MOVE LOW-VALUES TO ORDER-NUMBER.
118        MOVE ZERO TO NUMBER-OF-CHARACTERS.
119        DISPLAY ELB MOVE-TO-ORDER
120               'order number:  ' WITH NO ADVANCING.
121        ACCEPT ORDER-NUMBER.
122        INSPECT ORDER-NUMBER TALLYING NUMBER-OF-CHARACTERS
123               FOR CHARACTERS BEFORE LOW-VALUES.
124        IF NUMBER-OF-CHARACTERS IS EQUAL TO ZERO
125            MOVE 'N' TO MORE-DATA-REMAINS-FLAG
126            GO TO B019-VALIDATE-EXIT.
127
128    *          GET THE RECORD TYPE
129        MOVE SPACES TO RECORD-TYPE.
130        DISPLAY ELB MOVE-TO-REC-TYPE
131               'record type:  ' WITH NO ADVANCING.
132        ACCEPT RECORD-TYPE.
133
134    *          GET THE CATALOG-NUMBER
135        MOVE SPACES TO CATALOG-NUMBER.
136        DISPLAY ELB MOVE-TO-CAT-NBR
137               'catalog number:  ' WITH NO ADVANCING.
138        MOVE 'N' TO FIELD-VALID-FLAG.
139        PERFORM C010-GET-VALID-CATALOG-NUMBER
140            UNTIL FIELD-VALID.
141
142    *          GET THE SIZE CODE
143        MOVE SPACES TO SIZE-CODE.
144        DISPLAY ELB MOVE-TO-SIZE
145               'size code:  ' WITH NO ADVANCING.
146        MOVE 'N' TO FIELD-VALID-FLAG.
147        PERFORM C020-GET-VALID-SIZE-CODE
148            UNTIL FIELD-VALID.
149
150    *          GET THE QUANTITY
151        MOVE ZERO TO QUANTITY.
152        DISPLAY ELB MOVE-TO-QTY
153               'quantity:  ' WITH NO ADVANCING.
154        MOVE 'N' TO FIELD-VALID-FLAG.
155        PERFORM C030-GET-VALID-QUANTITY
156            UNTIL FIELD-VALID.
157
158    *          GET THE PRICE
159        MOVE ZERO TO PRICE.
160        DISPLAY ELB MOVE-TO-PRICE
161               'price: $' WITH NO ADVANCING.
162        MOVE 'N' TO FIELD-VALID-FLAG.
163        PERFORM C040-GET-VALID-PRICE
164            UNTIL FIELD-VALID.
165
```

```
166     *         GET THE DESCRIPTION
167           MOVE SPACES TO ITEM-DESCRIPTION.
168           DISPLAY ELB MOVE-TO-DESC
169                   'description: ' WITH NO ADVANCING.
170           ACCEPT ITEM-DESCRIPTION.
171
172     *         AT THIS POINT THE RECORD MUST BE VALID
173           WRITE NORMAL-HANDLING-RECORD FROM ORDER-RECORD.
174
175       B019-VALIDATE-EXIT.
176           EXIT.
177
178       C010-GET-VALID-CATALOG-NUMBER.
179           ACCEPT CATALOG-NUMBER.
180           DISPLAY ELB MOVE-TO-ERR-MSG ELB CLEAR-LINE.
181           IF CATALOG-NUMBER IS NOT NUMERIC
182               DISPLAY ELB MOVE-TO-CAT-NBR-DATA
183                       ELB REVERSE-VIDEO SET-GRAPHICS
184                       CATALOG-NUMBER
185               DISPLAY ELB MOVE-TO-ERR-MSG
186                       ELB NORMAL-SCREEN SET-GRAPHICS
187                       CAT-NO-NOT-NUMERIC-MSG
188                       ELB MOVE-TO-CAT-NBR-DATA WITH NO ADVANCING
189           ELSE IF CATALOG-FIRST-DIGIT = '0' OR '2'
190               DISPLAY ELB MOVE-TO-CAT-NBR-DATA
191                       ELB REVERSE-VIDEO SET-GRAPHICS
192                       CATALOG-NUMBER
193               DISPLAY ELB MOVE-TO-ERR-MSG
194                       ELB NORMAL-SCREEN SET-GRAPHICS
195                       FIRST-DIGIT-INVALID-MSG
196                       ELB MOVE-TO-CAT-NBR-DATA WITH NO ADVANCING
197           ELSE
198               MOVE 'Y' TO FIELD-VALID-FLAG.
199
200       C020-GET-VALID-SIZE-CODE.
201           ACCEPT SIZE-CODE.
202           DISPLAY ELB MOVE-TO-ERR-MSG ELB CLEAR-LINE.
203           IF (CATALOG-FIRST-DIGIT = '1' OR '8' OR '9')
204               AND SIZE-CODE IS NOT EQUAL TO SPACES
205               DISPLAY ELB MOVE-TO-SIZE-DATA
206                       ELB REVERSE-VIDEO SET-GRAPHICS
207                       SIZE-CODE
208               DISPLAY ELB MOVE-TO-ERR-MSG
209                       ELB NORMAL-SCREEN SET-GRAPHICS
210                       SIZE-CODE-NOT-PERMITTED-MSG
211                       ELB MOVE-TO-SIZE-DATA WITH NO ADVANCING
212           ELSE IF SIZE-CODE = 'A' OR 'D' OR 'G' OR 'J' OR 'K' OR
213                               'L' OR 'S' OR 'T' OR 'U' OR ' '
214               MOVE 'Y' TO FIELD-VALID-FLAG
215               ELSE
216                   DISPLAY ELB MOVE-TO-SIZE-DATA
217                           ELB REVERSE-VIDEO SET-GRAPHICS
218                           SIZE-CODE
219                   DISPLAY ELB MOVE-TO-ERR-MSG
220                           ELB NORMAL-SCREEN SET-GRAPHICS
221                           NO-SUCH-SIZE-CODE-MSG
222                           ELB MOVE-TO-SIZE-DATA WITH NO ADVANCING.
223
```

```
224          C030-GET-VALID-QUANTITY.
225              ACCEPT QUANTITY.
226              DISPLAY ELB MOVE-TO-ERR-MSG ELB CLEAR-LINE.
227              IF QUANTITY IS EQUAL TO ZERO
228                  DISPLAY ELB MOVE-TO-QTY-DATA
229                          ELB REVERSE-VIDEO SET-GRAPHICS
230                          QUANTITY
231                  DISPLAY ELB MOVE-TO-ERR-MSG
232                          ELB NORMAL-SCREEN SET-GRAPHICS
233                          QUANTITY-ZERO-MSG
234                          ELB MOVE-TO-QTY-DATA WITH NO ADVANCING
235              ELSE
236                  MOVE 'Y' TO FIELD-VALID-FLAG.
237
238          C040-GET-VALID-PRICE.
239              ACCEPT PRICE.
240              DISPLAY ELB MOVE-TO-ERR-MSG ELB CLEAR-LINE.
241              DIVIDE PRICE BY QUANTITY
242                      GIVING UNIT-PRICE REMAINDER TEST-REMAINDER.
243              IF TEST-REMAINDER NOT EQUAL TO ZERO
244                  DISPLAY ELB MOVE-TO-QTY-DATA
245                          ELB REVERSE-VIDEO SET-GRAPHICS
246                          QUANTITY
247                  MOVE PRICE TO PRICE-DISPLAY
248                  DISPLAY ELB MOVE-TO-PRICE-DATA
249                          PRICE-DISPLAY
250                  DISPLAY ELB MOVE-TO-ERR-MSG
251                          ELB NORMAL-SCREEN SET-GRAPHICS
252                          INVALID-PRICE-OR-QTY-MSG
253                  DISPLAY ELB MOVE-TO-QTY-DATA WITH NO ADVANCING
254                  ACCEPT QUANTITY
255                  DISPLAY ELB MOVE-TO-PRICE-DATA WITH NO ADVANCING
256              ELSE IF PRICE IS GREATER THAN PRICE-LIMIT
257                  DISPLAY ELB MOVE-TO-ERR-MSG
258                          LARGE-PRICE-MSG WITH NO ADVANCING
259                  MOVE SPACES TO CONTINUE-COMMAND
260                  ACCEPT CONTINUE-COMMAND
261                  IF CONTINUE-COMMAND = 'Y'
262                      DISPLAY ELB MOVE-TO-ERR-MSG ELB CLEAR-LINE
263                      MOVE 'Y' TO FIELD-VALID-FLAG
264                  ELSE
265                      MOVE PRICE TO PRICE-DISPLAY
266                      DISPLAY ELB MOVE-TO-PRICE-DATA
267                              ELB REVERSE-VIDEO SET-GRAPHICS
268                              PRICE-DISPLAY
269                              ELB MOVE-TO-PRICE-DATA WITH NO ADVANCING
270                      DISPLAY ELB NORMAL-SCREEN SET-GRAPHICS
271                                              WITH NO ADVANCING
272              ELSE
273                  MOVE 'Y' TO FIELD-VALID-FLAG.
274
275     ***************** END OF PROGRAM ********************************
```

FIGURE 20.3 An improved version of the interactive seed catalog program. Errors are reported as soon as each field is keyed and can be corrected immediately.

The structure of this program is considerably different from previous versions. Functionally, the tasks of reading a record, editing data, and reporting errors have all been combined into one module, **B010-VALIDATE-ONE-ORDER**. (The activities of obtaining the individual fields in the order record have been included in one paragraph, separated by comments. If you prefer, each field could be processed by a separate paragraph performed from **B010-VALIDATE-ONE-ORDER**. The choice is largely a matter of personal preference.) The first effect of this change is seen in the main driver paragraph. Instead of reading a priming record, we simply perform the processing paragraph until we run out of data. Notice that the **PERFORM** statement that controls this loop uses the **THRU** option. In the first interactive program we read the order number, tested to see if it was empty, and performed another paragraph to get the remainder of the record if the order did contain valid data. In this program we use a **GO TO** to skip to an **EXIT** paragraph if the order number is empty (see Section 19.2). There is no significant difference between the two approaches, and we use the **GO TO** simply to demonstrate an alternative technique.

One of the major changes in this program is the use of cursor and screen control options with the **DISPLAY** statement; we see the first example of how these options work at the start of **B010-VALIDATE-ONE-ORDER**. As in the previous program, we begin by writing control strings that clear the screen and move the cursor to the upper left-hand corner. However, instead of just displaying text, the next statement moves the cursor to the location where we wish to start the screen heading, then displays the heading. You can see from the definition of **MOVE-TO-HEADING** in the Working-Storage Section that the heading will start on line 6 at column 29.

The statements that process the order number are similar to the equivalent statements in Figure 20.1, except for the **DISPLAY** statement that asks for the order number. In this program we move the cursor to the location at which we want the text to begin, then display the field name. This leaves the cursor positioned to accept the order number entered by the user. If the user simply types return, the program branches to the exit paragraph and the loop terminates.

Except for the control strings that position the cursor to the start of the text field, the code to obtain the record type (and later the description) is the same in this program as it was in the previous version. This is because these fields require no editing. The remaining fields, however, do not simply **ACCEPT** the data entered by the user. Consider, for example, paragraph **C010-GET-VALID-CATALOG-NUMBER**. The **ACCEPT** statement on line 179 obtains the catalog number from the keyboard. In case the previously entered field was in error, the **DISPLAY** statement on the next line erases the error message line on the screen.

At this point the program is ready to edit the field. The two tests that begin on line 181 are the same as in previous versions of the program. However, if the data does not pass the error test, instead of setting a flag an error message is displayed on the screen. To display an error, we rewrite the data field in reverse video (black on white, instead of white on black), display the appropriate error message on the screen in normal graphics, and reposition the cursor at the start of the data field. Since **FIELD-VALID-FLAG** has not been set, the **PERFORM** statement on line 139 will cause **C010-GET-VALID-CATALOG-NUMBER** to be executed again. Now, the **ACCEPT** statement allows the user to retype the correct data over the invalid field. When the data has been entered correctly, **FIELD-VALID-FLAG** is set to "Y" on line 198 and the loop terminates.

The code in the remaining paragraphs is essentially the same as in **C010-GET-VALID-CATALOG-NUMBER**, except of course that the edit tests are different. **C040-GET-VALID-PRICE** has two minor differences from the other paragraphs. First, if the price is not a multiple of the quantity, the program requires both the quantity and the price to be reentered, since either one could have been the cause of the error. Second, if the price is greater than the price limit, the user has the option of accepting the price as correct without making any changes.

The program was run using the same data as previous examples; sample screen images are shown in Figures 20.4 and 20.5. When data errors were corrected, an output file was produced which contained correctly formatted order records.

Although the output of this program has a more professional look and feel to it than does the output from the first interactive program, there is still room for improvement. For example, there should probably be a way of rejecting the entire record rather than requiring that all errors be corrected immediately. In addition, you might wish to use more sophisticated graphics in presenting the record on the screen. We leave these and other possible improvements as an exercise for the student. Remember that the details of displaying graphics on a CRT may vary from system to system, and the commands shown in these examples are not necessarily what you need to use on your computer. Find out from your instructor what changes are necessary, or read the appropriate vendor manual.

```
                    SEED CATALOG ORDER ENTRY


order number:  222237      record type:  2      catalog number:  33761
size code:                 quantity:  02        price:  $  3.99



        EITHER PRICE OR QUANTITY IS WRONG
```

FIGURE 20.4 Sample output from the program in Figure 20.3, showing a typical error message.

```
                         SEED CATALOG ORDER ENTRY


    order number:   222237      record type:  2      catalog number:   33761
    size code:                  quantity:  2         price:   $3.90
    description:   HIBISCUS
```

FIGURE 20.5 A correct version of the record shown in Figure 20.4. This record is complete and is ready to be written to the output file.

20.5 MENU-DRIVEN PROGRAMS

The programs presented in the preceding sections both perform one simple task: they edit the seven fields of a record and write a valid output record. Clearly, a clerk using this program would not need much instruction to be able to use the program correctly. One of the advantages of interactive processing, however, is that it can provide guidance to users when the task to be performed is more complex, or when the program is capable of performing several tasks.

Consider, for example, the more complete version of the seed catalog program presented in Chapter 14. In addition to the input file of order records, this program uses a product file to be certain that the catalog number in the order record actually represents a valid product. Furthermore, since the input file contains three types of order records (header, body, and trailer), we might wish to take the customer's name and address from the header record and add them to a mailing file used for advertising the company's products. We might also wish to change records on the product file, or correct data that had been stored temporarily on the special handling file so that the order can be filled. Finally, we would probably like to process the records in the normal handling file so that the warehouse gets instructions to fill the order and the accounting department gets data needed for billing or other financial records. In other words, when we extend the seed catalog program to include realistic requirements, we have an order entry system which would need to perform tasks such as the following:

* Add, change, or delete records on the product file;
* Add the names of new customers to the mailing file;
* Modify data already on the mailing file;
* Correct records on the special handling file and move them to the normal handing file;
* Produce shipping and accounting files from data on the normal handling file;
* Produce sales and other management reports;
* Validate data on the order records.

In batch systems it is likely that each of these tasks would be performed by a separate program, and indeed this might be the case with interactive systems as well. However, it is possible—and in some cases desirable—to perform all these tasks in a single program. If we do so, it is necessary to provide the user with a *menu* to guide him or her through the steps needed to perform any specific activity.

The hierarchy chart in Figure 20.6 shows part of a program to perform these functions.

The basic operation of this system is as follows. When the program begins, the main menu is displayed on the screen. The user is asked to select one of six options from the menu, each of which corresponds to a major task performed by the program. (To save space, not all of these tasks are shown on the hierarchy chart.) The program then executes a subsection to perform the requested task. If, for example, the user selects task number 6, the program executes code that looks very much like the Procedure Division of the program in Figure 20.3. The only major difference is that when the user elects to terminate the task, control returns to the main menu so that other tasks can be requested.

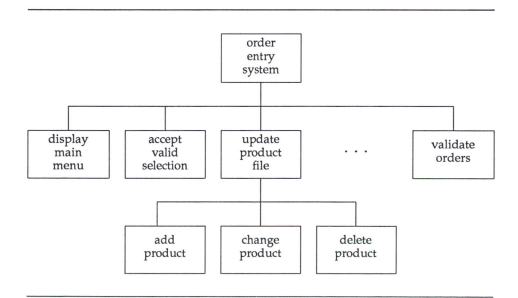

FIGURE 20.6 A partial hierarchy chart for an interactive program for an order entry system.

Depending on the complexity of the task selected, second level menus may be necessary. For example, if the user is updating the product file, different displays are used depending on whether a record is being added, changed, or removed. Figure 20.7 shows what the required program might look like. Since we are interested only in how the menus are used, lower level modules are shown as stubs.

```
1       IDENTIFICATION DIVISION.
2       PROGRAM-ID.
3           ORDER-ENTRY.
4
5       ENVIRONMENT DIVISION.
6   *       FILE SPECIFICATIONS HAVE BEEN OMITTED TO SIMPLIFY
7   *       THE PROGRAM.
8
9       DATA DIVISION.
10
11      WORKING-STORAGE SECTION.
12
13      01   CLEAR-SCREEN              PIC XX      VALUE '2J'.
14      01   CONTINUE-FLAG            PIC X.
15      01   ELB.
16           05   FILLER              PIC 9(4) COMP-4 VALUE 7003.
17      01   END-PRODUCT-UPDATE-FLAG  PIC X.
18      01   S-1                      PIC 99.
19      01   SELECTION               PIC X.
20      01   TERMINATE-FLAG          PIC X.
21      01   VALID-SELECTION-FLAG    PIC X.
22           88   VALID-SELECTION                VALUE 'Y'.
23
24  *       MAIN MENU DISPLAY TABLES
25      01   MAIN-MENU-MOVE-VALUES.
26           05   FILLER              PIC X(6)    VALUE '02;33H'.
27           05   FILLER              PIC X(6)    VALUE '04;32H'.
28           05   FILLER              PIC X(6)    VALUE '08;28H'.
29           05   FILLER              PIC X(6)    VALUE '09;28H'.
30           05   FILLER              PIC X(6)    VALUE '10;28H'.
31           05   FILLER              PIC X(6)    VALUE '11;28H'.
32           05   FILLER              PIC X(6)    VALUE '12;28H'.
33           05   FILLER              PIC X(6)    VALUE '13;28H'.
34           05   FILLER              PIC X(6)    VALUE '14;28H'.
35           05   FILLER              PIC X(6)    VALUE '15;28H'.
36           05   FILLER              PIC X(6)    VALUE '16;28H'.
37           05   FILLER              PIC X(6)    VALUE '17;28H'.
38           05   FILLER              PIC X(6)    VALUE '18;28H'.
39           05   FILLER              PIC X(6)    VALUE '21;28H'.
40      01   MAIN-MENU-MOVE-TABLE REDEFINES MAIN-MENU-MOVE-VALUES.
41           05   MOVE-MAIN-MENU      PIC X(6) OCCURS 14 TIMES.
42
```

```
 43            01   MAIN-MENU-TEXT-VALUES.
 44                 05   FILLER  PIC X(26)  VALUE 'ABC CORPORATION'.
 45                 05   FILLER  PIC X(26)  VALUE 'ORDER ENTRY SYSTEM'.
 46                 05   FILLER  PIC X(26)  VALUE '+-----------------------+'.
 47                 05   FILLER  PIC X(26)  VALUE '| ORDER ENTRY MAIN MENU |'.
 48                 05   FILLER  PIC X(26)  VALUE '+-----------------------+'.
 49                 05   FILLER  PIC X(26)  VALUE '| 1  UPDATE PRODUCT FILE |'.
 50                 05   FILLER  PIC X(26)  VALUE '| 2  UPDATE MAILING FILE |'.
 51                 05   FILLER  PIC X(26)  VALUE '| 3  SPECIAL HANDLING   |'.
 52                 05   FILLER  PIC X(26)  VALUE '| 4  SHIP ORDERS        |'.
 53                 05   FILLER  PIC X(26)  VALUE '| 5  PRODUCE REPORTS    |'.
 54                 05   FILLER  PIC X(26)  VALUE '| 6  VALIDATE ORDERS    |'.
 55                 05   FILLER  PIC X(26)  VALUE '| Q  QUIT ORDER ENTRY   |'.
 56                 05   FILLER  PIC X(26)  VALUE '+-----------------------+'.
 57                 05   FILLER  PIC X(26)  VALUE 'SELECT ONE OPTION:  '.
 58            01   MAIN-MENU-TEXT-TABLE REDEFINES MAIN-MENU-TEXT-VALUES.
 59                 05   MAIN-MENU-TEXT            PIC X(26) OCCURS 14 TIMES.
 60
 61            01   MOVE-TO-MAIN-SELECTION-ERROR PIC X(6) VALUE '23;28H'.
 62            01   MOVE-TO-MAIN-SELECTION       PIC X(6) VALUE '21;48H'.
 63            01   MAIN-SELECTION-ERR-MSG       PIC X(26) VALUE
 64                 'SELECTION MUST BE 1-6 OR Q'.
 65
 66            *         UPDATE-PRODUCT MENU TABLES
 67            01   UPDATE-PRODUCT-MOVE-VALUES.
 68                 05   FILLER                   PIC X(6)   VALUE '02;33H'.
 69                 05   FILLER                   PIC X(6)   VALUE '04;32H'.
 70                 05   FILLER                   PIC X(6)   VALUE '08;28H'.
 71                 05   FILLER                   PIC X(6)   VALUE '09;28H'.
 72                 05   FILLER                   PIC X(6)   VALUE '10;28H'.
 73                 05   FILLER                   PIC X(6)   VALUE '11;28H'.
 74                 05   FILLER                   PIC X(6)   VALUE '12;28H'.
 75                 05   FILLER                   PIC X(6)   VALUE '13;28H'.
 76                 05   FILLER                   PIC X(6)   VALUE '14;28H'.
 77                 05   FILLER                   PIC X(6)   VALUE '15;28H'.
 78                 05   FILLER                   PIC X(6)   VALUE '18;28H'.
 79            01   UPDATE-PRODUCT-MOVE-TABLE
 80                       REDEFINES UPDATE-PRODUCT-MOVE-VALUES.
 81                 05   MOVE-UPDATE-PRODUCT      PIC X(6) OCCURS 11 TIMES.
 82
 83            01   UPDATE-PRODUCT-TEXT-VALUES.
 84                 05   FILLER  PIC X(26)  VALUE 'ABC CORPORATION'.
 85                 05   FILLER  PIC X(26)  VALUE 'ORDER ENTRY SYSTEM'.
 86                 05   FILLER  PIC X(26)  VALUE '+-----------------------+'.
 87                 05   FILLER  PIC X(26)  VALUE '|   UPDATE PRODUCT MENU  |'.
 88                 05   FILLER  PIC X(26)  VALUE '+-----------------------+'.
 89                 05   FILLER  PIC X(26)  VALUE '| 1  ADD     RECORD     |'.
 90                 05   FILLER  PIC X(26)  VALUE '| 2  CHANGE RECORD      |'.
 91                 05   FILLER  PIC X(26)  VALUE '| 3  DELETE RECORD      |'.
 92                 05   FILLER  PIC X(26)  VALUE '| Q  RETURN TO MAIN MENU |'.
 93                 05   FILLER  PIC X(26)  VALUE '+-----------------------+'.
 94                 05   FILLER  PIC X(26)  VALUE 'SELECT ONE OPTION:  '.
 95            01   UPDATE-PRODUCT-TEXT-TABLE
 96                       REDEFINES UPDATE-PRODUCT-TEXT-VALUES.
 97                 05   UPDATE-PRODUCT-TEXT      PIC X(26) OCCURS 11 TIMES.
 98
 99            01   MOVE-TO-UPDATE-PRODUCT-ERR  PIC X(6) VALUE '20;28H'.
100            01   MOVE-TO-PRODUCT-SELECTION   PIC X(6) VALUE '18;48H'.
101            01   PRODUCT-SELECTION-ERR-MSG   PIC X(26) VALUE
102                 'SELECTION MUST BE 1-3 OR Q'.
103
104
```

```
105      PROCEDURE DIVISION.
106      A000-ORDER-ENTRY-CONTROL.
107          MOVE 'N' TO TERMINATE-FLAG.
108          PERFORM B010-MAIN-MENU-DRIVER
109              UNTIL TERMINATE-FLAG = 'Y'.
110          DISPLAY ELB CLEAR-SCREEN WITH NO ADVANCING.
111          STOP RUN.
112
113      B010-MAIN-MENU-DRIVER.
114      *        DISPLAY THE MAIN MENU SCREEN
115          DISPLAY ELB CLEAR-SCREEN WITH NO ADVANCING.
116          PERFORM VARYING S-1 FROM 1 BY 1 UNTIL S-1 > 14
117              DISPLAY ELB MOVE-MAIN-MENU (S-1) MAIN-MENU-TEXT (S-1)
118                  WITH NO ADVANCING
119          END-PERFORM.
120          DISPLAY ELB MOVE-TO-MAIN-SELECTION WITH NO ADVANCING.
121      *        GET THE SELECTION VARIABLE
122          MOVE 'N' TO VALID-SELECTION-FLAG.
123          PERFORM UNTIL VALID-SELECTION
124              ACCEPT SELECTION
125              IF SELECTION = '1' OR '2' OR '3' OR '4' OR '5' OR '6' OR
126                          'Q' THEN
127                  MOVE 'Y' TO VALID-SELECTION-FLAG
128              ELSE
129                  DISPLAY ELB MOVE-TO-MAIN-SELECTION-ERROR
130                          MAIN-SELECTION-ERR-MSG WITH NO ADVANCING
131                  DISPLAY ELB MOVE-TO-MAIN-SELECTION WITH NO ADVANCING
132              END-IF
133          END-PERFORM.
134      *        EXECUTE THE SELECTED TASK
135          IF       SELECTION = '1'
136              MOVE 'N' TO END-PRODUCT-UPDATE-FLAG
137              PERFORM C010-UPDATE-PRODUCT-FILE
138                  UNTIL END-PRODUCT-UPDATE-FLAG = 'Y'
139          ELSE IF SELECTION = '2'
140              PERFORM C020-UPDATE-MAILING-FILE
141          ELSE IF SELECTION = '3'
142              PERFORM C030-SPECIAL-HANDLING
143          ELSE IF SELECTION = '4'
144              PERFORM C040-SHIP-ORDERS
145          ELSE IF SELECTION = '5'
146              PERFORM C050-PRODUCE-REPORTS
147          ELSE IF SELECTION = '6'
148              PERFORM C060-VALIDATE-ORDERS
149          ELSE IF SELECTION = 'Q'
150              MOVE 'Y' TO TERMINATE-FLAG
151          END-IF.
152
153      C010-UPDATE-PRODUCT-FILE.
154          DISPLAY ELB CLEAR-SCREEN WITH NO ADVANCING.
155          PERFORM VARYING S-1 FROM 1 BY 1 UNTIL S-1 > 11
156              DISPLAY ELB MOVE-UPDATE-PRODUCT (S-1)
157                  UPDATE-PRODUCT-TEXT (S-1) WITH NO ADVANCING
158          END-PERFORM.
159          DISPLAY ELB MOVE-TO-PRODUCT-SELECTION WITH NO ADVANCING.
160          MOVE 'N' TO VALID-SELECTION-FLAG.
```

```
161              PERFORM UNTIL VALID-SELECTION
162                  ACCEPT SELECTION
163                  IF SELECTION = '1' OR '2' OR '3' OR 'Q' THEN
164                      MOVE 'Y' TO VALID-SELECTION-FLAG
165                  ELSE
166                      DISPLAY ELB MOVE-TO-UPDATE-PRODUCT-ERR
167                              PRODUCT-SELECTION-ERR-MSG WITH NO ADVANCING
168                      DISPLAY ELB MOVE-TO-PRODUCT-SELECTION
169                              WITH NO ADVANCING
170                  END-IF
171              END-PERFORM.
172              IF      SELECTION = '1' THEN
173                  PERFORM D010-ADD-PRODUCT-RECORD
174              ELSE IF SELECTION = '2' THEN
175                  PERFORM D020-CHANGE-PRODUCT-RECORD
176              ELSE IF SELECTION = '3' THEN
177                  PERFORM D030-DELETE-PRODUCT-RECORD
178              ELSE
179                  MOVE 'Y' TO END-PRODUCT-UPDATE-FLAG.
180
181          C020-UPDATE-MAILING-FILE.
182              DISPLAY ELB CLEAR-SCREEN
183                      'UPDATE-MAILING-FILE MODULE REACHED'.
184              DISPLAY 'PRESS RETURN TO CONTINUE' WITH NO ADVANCING.
185              ACCEPT CONTINUE-FLAG.
186
187          C030-SPECIAL-HANDLING.
188              DISPLAY ELB CLEAR-SCREEN
189                      'SPECIAL-HANDLING MODULE REACHED'.
190              DISPLAY 'PRESS RETURN TO CONTINUE' WITH NO ADVANCING.
191              ACCEPT CONTINUE-FLAG.
192
193          C040-SHIP-ORDERS.
194              DISPLAY ELB CLEAR-SCREEN
195                      'SHIP-ORDERS MODULE REACHED'.
196              DISPLAY 'PRESS RETURN TO CONTINUE' WITH NO ADVANCING.
197              ACCEPT CONTINUE-FLAG.
198
199          C050-PRODUCE-REPORTS.
200              DISPLAY ELB CLEAR-SCREEN
201                      'PRODUCE-REPORTS MODULE REACHED'.
202              DISPLAY 'PRESS RETURN TO CONTINUE' WITH NO ADVANCING.
203              ACCEPT CONTINUE-FLAG.
204
205          C060-VALIDATE-ORDERS.
206              DISPLAY ELB CLEAR-SCREEN
207                      'VALIDATE-ORDERS MODULE REACHED'.
208              DISPLAY 'PRESS RETURN TO CONTINUE' WITH NO ADVANCING.
209              ACCEPT CONTINUE-FLAG.
210
211          D010-ADD-PRODUCT-RECORD.
212              DISPLAY ELB CLEAR-SCREEN
213                      'ADD-PRODUCT-RECORD MODULE REACHED'.
214              DISPLAY 'PRESS RETURN TO CONTINUE' WITH NO ADVANCING.
215              ACCEPT CONTINUE-FLAG.
216
```

```
217         D020-CHANGE-PRODUCT-RECORD.
218             DISPLAY ELB CLEAR-SCREEN
219                     'CHANGE-PRODUCT-RECORD MODULE REACHED'.
220             DISPLAY 'PRESS RETURN TO CONTINUE' WITH NO ADVANCING.
221             ACCEPT CONTINUE-FLAG.
222
223         D030-DELETE-PRODUCT-RECORD.
224             DISPLAY ELB CLEAR-SCREEN
225                     'DELETE-PRODUCT-RECORD MODULE REACHED'.
226             DISPLAY 'PRESS RETURN TO CONTINUE' WITH NO ADVANCING.
227             ACCEPT CONTINUE-FLAG.
```

FIGURE 20.7 An interactive program demonstrating the use of menus in the seed catalog order entry system.

Although the complete program would require the use of several files, this skeleton version uses only **ACCEPT** and **DISPLAY** statements for I/O, so the Environment Division is empty and the File Section has been omitted.

The Working-Storage Section begins with data that is similar to what we saw in the previous example: variables to clear the screen and begin control strings. However, most of the screen control strings and the menu text to be display are stored in tables, initialized using the techniques presented in Section 13.4. As you can see on lines 116 and 155 in the Procedure Division, using tables to store the data allows us to produce the menu displays using **PERFORM** statements instead of dozens of in-line **DISPLAY** statements. For example, **MOVE-MAIN-MENU** contains the control strings that move the pointer to the correct location for each line of the main menu, while **MAIN-MENU-TEXT** contains the text that is printed on each line. You can see approximately what the menu will look like from the **VALUE** clauses in **MAIN-MENU-TEXT-VALUES**, although the heading lines are centered over the menu when the text is actually displayed on the screen. Similarly, the control strings and text needed to display one of the subordinate menus are contained in the tables beginning with **UPDATE-PRODUCT-MOVE-VALUES**.

The first paragraph is very simple. The main menu driver is executed repeatedly until the termination command is received, at which time the screen is erased and the program stops.

The main menu driver paragraph uses the **PERFORM** statement on lines 116-119 to display the main menu on the screen. (Notice that this **PERFORM** statement, as well as several other statements in the program, is in **COBOL-85** format. This was done simply to demonstrate the use of **COBOL-85** and there should be no trouble converting the program to the older format if you wish.) Since all entries in **MAIN-MENU-TEXT** are 26 characters long, and since the non-blank text of the last line is actually only 20 characters long, we follow the **PERFORM** statement with a **DISPLAY** statement that moves the cursor to the proper position to **ACCEPT** the user's menu selection. The selection variable is edited to insure that it contains a valid value, then it is used to **PERFORM** one of the function paragraphs.

Most of the function paragraphs are just stubs; they display a simple message, then return to the calling routine. The function paragraph to update the product file, however, generates a second-level menu using much the same technique as was used to generate the main menu. Although these function

```
                        ABC CORPORATION

                       ORDER ENTRY SYSTEM



                +-----------------------+
                | ORDER ENTRY MAIN MENU |
                +-----------------------+
                | 1   UPDATE PRODUCT FILE |
                | 2   UPDATE MAILING FILE |
                | 3   SPECIAL HANDLING    |
                | 4   SHIP ORDERS         |
                | 5   PRODUCE REPORTS     |
                | 6   VALIDATE ORDERS     |
                | Q   QUIT ORDER ENTRY    |
                +-----------------------+



           SELECT ONE OPTION:   7

           SELECTION MUST BE 1-6 OR Q
```

FIGURE 20.8 The main menu produced by the order entry program. The error message at the bottom of the screen image was triggered when the user entered an invalid selection.

modules are implemented as paragraphs in this example, in a real program it might be more appropriate to implement each function as a separately compiled subprogram and use **CALL** statements instead of **PERFORM**s. The menus produced by the program are shown in Figures 20.8 and 20.9.

20.6 SUMMARY

Although the examples we have shown in this chapter demonstrate some of the techniques of programming with interactive **COBOL**, by no means do they represent a comprehensive study of interactive systems. This is, after all, more properly a topic for systems design than for **COBOL** programming. None the less, you should remember the principles involved. One of the major advantages of interactive programs over batch programs is that they allow the user to correct mistakes immediately, rather than having to wait for hours or days to find out that there is a problem. This applies not only to entering data but to all phases of program execution. The user can be informed of problems that are detected while the program is running, and can be given a choice of alternatives (such as selecting which reports should be produced) depending on preliminary calculation results.

```
                    ABC  CORPORATION

                  ORDER  ENTRY  SYSTEM



          +------------------------+
          |  UPDATE  PRODUCT  MENU   |
          +------------------------+
          | 1   ADD      RECORD      |
          | 2   CHANGE  RECORD       |
          | 3   DELETE  RECORD       |
          | Q   RETURN  TO  MAIN  MENU |
          +------------------------+


          SELECT  ONE  OPTION:   Q
```

FIGURE 20.9 The "update product" subordinate menu produced by the order entry program.

To take full advantage of the flexibility of the interactive capabilities of this type of program, the user should be presented with menus that guide him or her in the use of the program. In addition to the type of menu shown in this chapter, this might include "help" menus or tutorial discussions that explain the functions the program can perform and how they are used.

In **COBOL**, the basic technique for writing interactive programs is to use **ACCEPT** statements for data input and **DISPLAY** statements to write on the computer's screen (or equivalent subprograms from the **COBOL** library). Although the details vary from system to system, compilers for interactive **COBOL** generally provide some mechanism for manipulating the cursor and the computer's graphic capabilities, and a programmer who does much **COBOL** programming for interactive systems will need to become familiar with the necessary techniques.

Above all, remember that the program is being written for the *user*, not the programmer. Programs should be implemented so as to simplify the job of the user as much as possible, even if this requires more time and effort to write the program.

APPENDIX I

COBOL RESERVED WORDS

The following list is based on the 1985 American National Standard. It is thus probably not identical to the list for any existing compiler—but no such list as this can ever *exactly* match more than one compiler, since all implementations differ slightly. This is not a practical problem. For those very rare cases where a word is reserved in your system but is not listed here, the compiler will almost always diagnose the problem.

Words unique to **COBOL-85** are underlined.

ACCEPT	BEFORE	COMMUNICATION
ACCESS	BINARY	COMP
ADD	BLANK	COMPUTATIONAL
ADVANCING	BLOCK	COMPUTE
AFTER	BOTTOM	CONFIGURATION
ALL	BY	CONTAINS
ALPHABET		CONTENT
ALPHABETIC	CALL	CONTINUE
ALPHABETIC-LOWER	CANCEL	CONTROL
ALPHABETIC-UPPER	CD	CONTROLS
ALPHANUMERIC	CF	CONVERTING
ALPHANUMERIC-EDITED	CH	COPY
ALSO	CHARACTER	CORR
ALTER	CHARACTERS	CORRESPONDING
ALTERNATE	CLASS	COUNT
AND	CLOCK-UNITS	CURRENCY
ANY	CLOSE	
ARE	COBOL	DATA
AREA	CODE	DATE
AREAS	CODE-SET	DATE-COMPILED
ASCENDING	COLLATING	DATE-WRITTEN
ASSIGN	COLUMN	DAY
AT	COMMA	DAY-OF-WEEK
AUTHOR	COMMON	DE

DEBUG–CONTENTS	EQUAL	KEY
DEBUG–ITEM	ERROR	
DEBUG–LINE	ESI	LABEL
DEBUG–NAME	EVALUATE	LAST
DEBUG–SUB–1	EVERY	LEADING
DEBUG–SUB–2	EXCEPTION	LEFT
DEBUG–SUB–3	EXIT	LENGTH
DEBUGGING	EXTEND	LESS
DECIMAL–POINT	EXTERNAL	LIMIT
DECLARATIVES		LIMITS
DELETE	FALSE	LINAGE
DELIMITED	FD	LINAGE–COUNTER
DELIMITER	FILE	LINE
DEPENDING	FILE–CONTROL	LINE–COUNTER
DESCENDING	FILLER	LINES
DESTINATION	FINAL	LINKAGE
DETAIL	FIRST	LOCK
DISABLE	FOOTING	LOW–VALUE
DISPLAY	FOR	LOW–VALUES
DIVIDE	FROM	
DIVISION		MEMORY
DOWN	GENERATE	MERGE
DUPLICATES	GIVING	MESSAGE
DYNAMIC	GLOBAL	MODE
	GO	MODULES
EGI	GREATER	MOVE
ELSE	GROUP	MULTIPLE
EMI		MULTIPLY
ENABLE	HEADING	
END	HIGH–VALUE	NATIVE
END–ADD	HIGH–VALUES	NEGATIVE
END–CALL		NEXT
END–COMPUTE	I–O	NO
END–DELETE	I–O–CONTROL	NOT
END–DIVIDE	IDENTIFICATION	NUMBER
END–EVALUATE	IF	NUMERIC
END–IF	IN	NUMERIC–EDITED
END–MULTIPLY	INDEX	
END–OF–PAGE	INDEXED	OBJECT–COMPUTER
END–PERFORM	INDICATE	OCCURS
END–READ	INITIAL	OF
END–RECEIVE	INITIALIZE	OFF
END–RETURN	INITIATE	OMITTED
END–REWRITE	INPUT	ON
END–SEARCH	INPUT–OUTPUT	OPEN
END–START	INSPECT	OPTIONAL
END–STRING	INSTALLATION	OR
END–SUBTRACT	INTO	ORDER
END–UNSTRING	INVALID	ORGANIZATION
END–WRITE	IS	OTHER
ENTER		OUTPUT
ENVIRONMENT	JUST	OVERFLOW
EOP	JUSTIFIED	

PACKED-DECIMAL	RF	TEXT
PADDING	RH	THAN
PAGE	RIGHT	THEN
PAGE-COUNTER	ROUNDED	THROUGH
PERFORM	RUN	THRU
PF		TIME
PH	SAME	TIMES
PIC	SD	TO
PICTURE	SEARCH	TOP
PLUS	SECTION	TRAILING
POINTER	SECURITY	TRUE
POSITION	SEGMENT	TYPE
POSITIVE	SEGMENT-LIMIT	
PRINTING	SELECT	UNIT
PROCEDURE	SEND	UNSTRING
PROCEDURES	SENTENCE	UNTIL
PROCEED	SEPARATE	UP
PROGRAM	SEQUENCE	UPON
PROGRAM-ID	SEQUENTIAL	USAGE
PURGE	SET	USE
	SIGN	USING
QUEUE	SIZE	
QUOTE	SORT	VALUE
QUOTES	SORT-MERGE	VALUES
	SOURCE	VARYING
RANDOM	SOURCE-COMPUTER	
RD	SPACE	WHEN
READ	SPACES	WITH
RECEIVE	SPECIAL-NAMES	WORDS
RECORD	STANDARD	WORKING-STORAGE
RECORDS	STANDARD-1	WRITE
REDEFINES	STANDARD-2	
REEL	START	ZERO
REFERENCE	STATUS	ZEROES
REFERENCES	STOP	ZEROS
RELATIVE	STRING	
RELEASE	SUB-QUEUE-1	+
REMAINDER	SUB-QUEUE-2	–
REMOVAL	SUB-QUEUE-3	*
RENAMES	SUBTRACT	/
REPLACE	SUM	**
REPLACING	SUPPRESS	>
REPORT	SYMBOLIC	<
REPORTING	SYNC	=
REPORTS	SYNCHRONIZED	>=
RERUN		<=
RESERVE	TABLE	
RESET	TALLYING	
RETURN	TAPE	
REVERSED	TERMINAL	
REWIND	TERMINATE	
REWRITE	TEST	

APPENDIX II

COMPOSITE LANGUAGE SKELETON

This appendix shows the general formats for all **COBOL** language elements, in the form of the general formats introduced in Section 3.14.

For ease of use in varying circumstances, both **COBOL-74** and **COBOL-85** formats are shown. See the running heads on the left hand pages to know which you are reading.

The main typographical conventions used may be found on pages 33 and 34. Two other conventions are employed in the **COBOL-85** formats:

- The combination of braces and vertical bars means to select one or more of the options so enclosed.
- The appearance of the italic letter *S, R, I,* or *W* to the left of the format for the verbs **OPEN, CLOSE, READ,** and **WRITE** verbs in the **COBOL-85** formats indicates that the Sequential I-O module, the Relative I-O module, the Indexed I-O module, or the Report Writer I-O module in which that general format is used.

Commas and semicolons, which are always optional, are not shown. The rules are simple: a comma may be used to separate members of a series, and a semicolon may be used after any clause. Each must be followed by a space.

The **COBOL-74** standard (which can no longer be obtained from ANSI) made less extensive use of the series ellipsis than does **COBOL-85**; we have elected to show most of the **COBOL-74** formats using the more condensed form. The rule is: to determine what element the ellipsis applies to, find the brace or bracket that matches the brace or bracket immediately preceding the ellipsis; the enclosed material may be repeated, generally as many times as desired although in some cases there are limits.

Local variations are always possible. For serious programming you need access to the reference manual for the particular compiler you are using.

GENERAL FORMAT FOR IDENTIFICATION DIVISION

IDENTIFICATION DIVISION.

PROGRAM-ID. program-name.

[AUTHOR. [comment-entry] ...]

[INSTALLATION. [comment-entry] ...]

[DATE-WRITTEN. [comment-entry] ...]

[DATE-COMPILED. [comment-entry] ...]

[SECURITY. [comment-entry] ...]

GENERAL FORMAT FOR ENVIRONMENT DIVISION

ENVIRONMENT DIVISION.

CONFIGURATION SECTION.

SOURCE-COMPUTER. computer-name [WITH DEBUGGING MODE].

OBJECT-COMPUTER. computer-name

$$
\left[\text{MEMORY SIZE integer-1} \left\{ \begin{array}{l} \text{WORDS} \\ \text{CHARACTERS} \\ \text{MODULES} \end{array} \right\} \right]
$$

[PROGRAM COLLATING SEQUENCE IS alphabet-name]

[SEGMENT-LIMIT IS segment-number].

[SPECIAL-NAMES. [implementor-name

$$
\left\{
\begin{array}{l}
\underline{IS}\ \text{mnemonic-name-1}\ [\underline{ON}\ \text{STATUS}\ \underline{IS}\ \text{condition-name-1} \\
\qquad\qquad\qquad [\underline{OFF}\ \text{STATUS}\ \underline{IS}\ \text{condition-name-2}]] \\
\underline{IS}\ \text{mnemonic-name-2}\ [\underline{OFF}\ \text{STATUS}\ \underline{IS}\ \text{condition-name-2} \\
\qquad\qquad\qquad [\underline{ON}\ \text{STATUS}\ \underline{IS}\ \text{condition-name-1}]] \\
\underline{ON}\ \text{STATUS}\ \underline{IS}\ \text{condition-name-1}\ [\underline{OFF}\ \text{STATUS}\ \underline{IS}\ \text{condition-name-2}] \\
\underline{OFF}\ \text{STATUS}\ \underline{IS}\ \text{condition-name-2}\ [\underline{ON}\ \text{STATUS}\ \underline{IS}\ \text{condition-name-1}]
\end{array}
\right\} \quad] \quad \ldots
$$

[ALPHABET alphabet-name IS

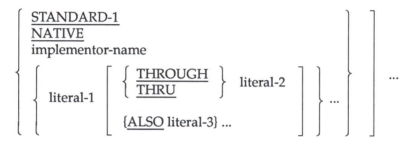

[CURRENCY SIGN IS literal-4]
[DECIMAL-POINT IS COMMA].]

[INPUT-OUTPUT SECTION.

FILE-CONTROL.

{file-control-entry} ...

[I-O-CONTROL.

$$
\left[
\underline{RERUN}\ \left[\underline{ON}\ \left\{\begin{array}{l}\text{file-name-1}\\ \text{implementor-name}\end{array}\right\}\right]
\right.
$$

$$
\underline{EVERY}\ \left\{
\begin{array}{l}
\left\{\begin{array}{l}[\underline{END}\ OF]\ \left\{\begin{array}{l}\underline{REEL}\\ \underline{UNIT}\end{array}\right\}\\ \text{integer-1}\ \underline{RECORDS}\end{array}\right\}\ OF\ \text{file-name-2}\\
\text{integer-2}\ \underline{CLOCK\text{-}UNITS}\\
\text{condition-name}
\end{array}
\right\} \quad \ldots
$$

$$
\left[
\underline{SAME}\ \left[\begin{array}{l}\underline{RECORD}\\ \underline{SORT}\\ \underline{SORT\text{-}MERGE}\end{array}\right]\ AREA\ FOR\ \text{file-name-3}\ \{\text{file-name-4}\}\ \ldots
\right] \quad \ldots
$$

[MULTIPLE FILE TAPE CONTAINS file-name-5 [POSITION integer-3] ...] ... .]

GENERAL FORMAT FOR FILE CONTROL ENTRY

FORMAT 1:

SELECT [OPTIONAL] file-name

    ASSIGN TO implementor-name-1 [implementor-name-2] ...

$$\left[\text{RESERVE integer-1} \left[\begin{array}{l} \text{AREA} \\ \text{AREAS} \end{array} \right] \right]$$

    [ORGANIZATION IS SEQUENTIAL]

    [ACCESS MODE IS SEQUENTIAL]

    [FILE STATUS IS data-name-1].

FORMAT 2:

SELECT file-name

    ASSIGN TO implementor-name-1 [implementor-name-2] ...

$$\left[\text{RESERVE integer-1} \left[\begin{array}{l} \text{AREA} \\ \text{AREAS} \end{array} \right] \right]$$

    [ORGANIZATION IS] RELATIVE

$$\left[\text{ACCESS MODE IS} \left\{ \begin{array}{l} \text{SEQUENTIAL [RELATIVE KEY IS data-name-1]} \\ \left\{ \begin{array}{l} \text{RANDOM} \\ \text{DYNAMIC} \end{array} \right\} \text{RELATIVE KEY IS data-name-1} \end{array} \right\} \right]$$

    [FILE STATUS IS data-name-2].

FORMAT 3:

<u>SELECT</u> file-name

  <u>ASSIGN</u> TO implementor-name-1 [implementor-name-2] ...

  $\left[\ \underline{\text{RESERVE}}\ \text{integer-1}\ \left[\begin{array}{c}\text{AREA}\\\text{AREAS}\end{array}\right]\ \right]$

  [<u>ORGANIZATION</u> IS] <u>INDEXED</u>

  $\left[\ \underline{\text{ACCESS}}\ \text{MODE IS}\ \left\{\begin{array}{c}\underline{\text{SEQUENTIAL}}\\\underline{\text{RANDOM}}\\\underline{\text{DYNAMIC}}\end{array}\right\}\ \right]$

  <u>RECORD</u> KEY IS data-name-1

  [<u>ALTERNATE</u> <u>RECORD</u> KEY IS data-name-2 [WITH <u>DUPLICATES</u>]] ...

  [FILE <u>STATUS</u> IS data-name-3].

FORMAT 4:

<u>SELECT</u> file-name-1 <u>ASSIGN</u> TO implementor-name-1 [implementor-name-2] ...

GENERAL FORMAT FOR DATA DIVISION

<u>DATA</u> <u>DIVISION</u>.

[<u>FILE</u> <u>SECTION</u>.

[<u>FD</u> file-name-1

$$\left[\underline{BLOCK} \text{ CONTAINS [integer-1 } \underline{TO}] \text{ integer-2} \left\{ \begin{array}{l} \underline{RECORDS} \\ \underline{CHARACTERS} \end{array} \right\} \right]$$

[<u>RECORD</u> CONTAINS [integer-3 <u>TO</u>] integer-4 CHARACTERS]

$$\underline{LABEL} \left\{ \begin{array}{l} \underline{RECORD} \text{ IS} \\ \underline{RECORDS} \text{ ARE} \end{array} \right\} \left\{ \begin{array}{l} \underline{STANDARD} \\ \underline{OMITTED} \end{array} \right\}$$

$$\left[\underline{VALUE} \underline{OF} \left\{ \text{implementor-name-1 IS} \left\{ \begin{array}{l} \text{data-name-1} \\ \text{literal-1} \end{array} \right\} \right\} \cdots \right]$$

$$\left[\underline{DATA} \left\{ \begin{array}{l} \underline{RECORD} \text{ IS} \\ \underline{RECORDS} \text{ ARE} \end{array} \right\} \{ \text{data-name-2} \} \cdots \right]$$

$$\left[\underline{LINAGE} \text{ IS} \left\{ \begin{array}{l} \text{data-name-3} \\ \text{integer-5} \end{array} \right\} \text{ LINES} \right.$$

$$\left[\text{ WITH } \underline{FOOTING} \text{ AT} \left\{ \begin{array}{l} \text{data-name-4} \\ \text{integer-6} \end{array} \right\} \right]$$

$$\left[\text{ LINES AT } \underline{TOP} \left\{ \begin{array}{l} \text{data-name-5} \\ \text{integer-7} \end{array} \right\} \right]$$

$$\left. \left[\text{ LINES AT } \underline{BOTTOM} \left\{ \begin{array}{l} \text{data-name-6} \\ \text{integer-8} \end{array} \right\} \right] \right]$$

[<u>CODE-SET</u> IS alphabet-name-1].

$$\left[\left\{ \begin{array}{l} \underline{REPORT} \text{ IS} \\ \underline{REPORTS} \text{ ARE} \end{array} \right\} \text{ report-name } \cdots \right] .$$

[record-description-entry]...] ...

[<u>SD</u> file-name

    [<u>RECORD</u> CONTAINS [integer-1 <u>TO</u>] integer-2 CHARACTERS]

$$
\left[\ \underline{DATA} \ \left\{ \begin{array}{l} \underline{RECORD} \ IS \\ \underline{RECORDS} \ ARE \end{array} \right\} \ \{data\text{-}name\text{-}2\} \ \ldots \ \right]
$$

    [record-description-entry] ...] ...

[<u>WORKING-STORAGE</u> <u>SECTION</u>.

$$
\left[\begin{array}{l} 77\text{-level-description-entry} \\ record\text{-description-entry} \end{array} \right] \quad \cdots \quad \Big]
$$

[<u>LINKAGE</u> <u>SECTION</u>.

$$
\left[\begin{array}{l} 77\text{-level-description-entry} \\ record\text{-description-entry} \end{array} \right] \quad \cdots \quad \Big]
$$

[<u>COMMUNICATION</u> <u>SECTION</u>.

[communications-description-entry

[record-description-entry] ...] ...]

[<u>REPORT</u> <u>SECTION</u>.

[<u>RD</u> report-name

    [<u>CODE</u> literal-1]

$$
\left[\ \left\{ \begin{array}{l} \underline{CONTROL} \ IS \\ \underline{CONTROLS} \ ARE \end{array} \right\} \quad \left\{ \begin{array}{l} \{data\text{-}name\text{-}1\} \ \ldots \\ \underline{FINAL} \ [data\text{-}name\text{-}1] \ \ldots \end{array} \right\} \ \right]
$$

$$
\left[\ \underline{PAGE} \ \left[\begin{array}{l} LIMIT \ IS \\ LIMITS \ ARE \end{array} \right] \ integer\text{-}1 \ \left[\begin{array}{l} LINE \\ LINES \end{array} \right] \ [\underline{HEADING} \ integer\text{-}2]
$$

    [<u>FIRST</u> <u>DETAIL</u> integer-3] [<u>LAST</u> <u>DETAIL</u> integer-4]

$$
[\underline{FOOTING} \ integer\text{-}5] \ \ldots \ \Big] \quad \cdot
$$

    {report-group-description-entry} ...] ...]

GENERAL FORMAT FOR DATA DESCRIPTION ENTRY

FORMAT 1:

level-number $\left[\begin{array}{l} \text{data-name-1} \\ \underline{\text{FILLER}} \end{array}\right]$

[REDEFINES data-name-2]

$\left[\ \left\{\begin{array}{l} \underline{\text{PICTURE}} \\ \underline{\text{PIC}} \end{array}\right\}\ \text{IS character-string}\ \right]$

$\left[\ [\underline{\text{USAGE}}\ \text{IS}]\ \left\{\begin{array}{l} \underline{\text{COMPUTATIONAL}} \\ \underline{\text{COMP}} \\ \underline{\text{DISPLAY}} \\ \underline{\text{INDEX}} \end{array}\right\}\ \right]$

$\left[\ [\underline{\text{SIGN}}\ \text{IS}]\ \left\{\begin{array}{l} \underline{\text{LEADING}} \\ \underline{\text{TRAILING}} \end{array}\right\}\ [\underline{\text{SEPARATE}}\ \text{CHARACTER}]\ \right]$

$\left[\begin{array}{l} \underline{\text{OCCURS}}\ \text{integer-2 TIMES} \\ \qquad \left[\ \left\{\begin{array}{l} \underline{\text{ASCENDING}} \\ \underline{\text{DESCENDING}} \end{array}\right\}\ \text{KEY IS \{data-name-3\}} \ldots \right]\ \ldots \\ \qquad [\underline{\text{INDEXED}}\ \text{BY \{index-name-1\}} \ldots] \\ \underline{\text{OCCURS}}\ \text{integer-1}\ \underline{\text{TO}}\ \text{integer-2 TIMES}\ \underline{\text{DEPENDING}}\ \text{ON data-name-4} \\ \qquad \left[\ \left\{\begin{array}{l} \underline{\text{ASCENDING}} \\ \underline{\text{DESCENDING}} \end{array}\right\}\ \text{KEY IS \{data-name-3\}} \ldots \right]\ \ldots \\ \qquad [\underline{\text{INDEXED}}\ \text{BY \{index-name-1\}} \ldots] \end{array}\right]$

$\left[\ \left\{\begin{array}{l} \underline{\text{SYNCHRONIZED}} \\ \underline{\text{SYNC}} \end{array}\right\}\ \left[\begin{array}{l} \underline{\text{LEFT}} \\ \underline{\text{RIGHT}} \end{array}\right]\ \right]$

$\left[\ \left\{\begin{array}{l} \underline{\text{JUSTIFIED}} \\ \underline{\text{JUST}} \end{array}\right\}\ \text{RIGHT}\ \right]$

[BLANK WHEN ZERO]

[VALUE IS literal-1] .

FORMAT 2:

66 data-name-1 <u>RENAMES</u> data-name-2 $\left[\left\{ \begin{array}{l} \underline{THROUGH} \\ \underline{THRU} \end{array} \right\} \text{data-name-3} \right]$.

FORMAT 3:

88 condition-name-1 $\left\{ \begin{array}{l} \underline{VALUE} \text{ IS} \\ \underline{VALUES} \text{ ARE} \end{array} \right\}$ $\left\{ \text{literal-1} \left[\left\{ \begin{array}{l} \underline{THROUGH} \\ \underline{THRU} \end{array} \right\} \text{literal-2} \right] \right\} \ldots$.

GENERAL FORMAT FOR COMMUNICATION DESCRIPTION ENTRY

FORMAT 1:

<u>CD</u> cd-name-1

FOR [<u>INITIAL</u>] <u>INPUT</u> $\left[\begin{array}{l} \text{[[SYMBOLIC } \underline{QUEUE} \text{ IS data-name-1]} \\ \text{[SYMBOLIC } \underline{SUB\text{-}QUEUE\text{-}1} \text{ IS data-name-2]} \\ \text{[SYMBOLIC } \underline{SUB\text{-}QUEUE\text{-}2} \text{ IS data-name-3]} \\ \text{[SYMBOLIC } \underline{SUB\text{-}QUEUE\text{-}3} \text{ IS data-name-4]} \\ \text{[} \underline{MESSAGE} \ \underline{DATE} \text{ IS data-name-5]} \\ \text{[} \underline{MESSAGE} \ \underline{TIME} \text{ IS data-name-6]} \\ \text{[SYMBOLIC } \underline{SOURCE} \text{ IS data-name-7]} \\ \text{[} \underline{TEXT} \ \underline{LENGTH} \text{ IS data-name-8]} \\ \text{[} \underline{END} \ \underline{KEY} \text{ IS data-name-9]} \\ \text{[} \underline{STATUS} \ \underline{KEY} \text{ IS data-name-10]} \\ \text{[MESSAGE } \underline{COUNT} \text{ IS data-name-11]]} \\ \text{[data-name-1, data-name-2, data-name-3,} \\ \quad \text{data-name-4, data-name-5, data-name-6,} \\ \quad \text{data-name-7, data-name-8, data-name-9,} \\ \quad \text{data-name-10, data-name-11]} \end{array} \right]$

FORMAT 2:

CD cd-name-1 FOR OUTPUT

[DESTINATION COUNT IS data-name-1]

[TEXT LENGTH IS data-name-2]

[STATUS KEY IS data-name-3]

[DESTINATION TABLE OCCURS integer-1 TIMES

[INDEXED BY {index-name-1} ...]]

[ERROR KEY IS data-name-4]

[SYMBOLIC DESTINATION IS data-name-5].

GENERAL FORMAT FOR REPORT GROUP DESCRIPTION ENTRY

FORMAT 1:

01 [data-name-1]

$$
\left[\text{LINE NUMBER IS} \left\{ \begin{array}{l} \text{integer-1 [ON NEXT PAGE]} \\ \text{PLUS integer-2} \end{array} \right\} \right]
$$

$$
\left[\text{NEXT GROUP IS} \left\{ \begin{array}{l} \text{integer-3} \\ \text{PLUS integer-4} \\ \text{NEXT PAGE} \end{array} \right\} \right]
$$

$$
\text{TYPE IS} \left[\begin{array}{l} \left\{ \begin{array}{l} \text{REPORT HEADING} \\ \text{RH} \end{array} \right\} \\ \left\{ \begin{array}{l} \text{PAGE HEADING} \\ \text{PH} \end{array} \right\} \\ \left\{ \begin{array}{l} \text{CONTROL HEADING} \\ \text{CH} \end{array} \right\} \left\{ \begin{array}{l} \text{data-name-2} \\ \text{FINAL} \end{array} \right\} \\ \left\{ \begin{array}{l} \text{DETAIL} \\ \text{DE} \end{array} \right\} \\ \left\{ \begin{array}{l} \text{CONTROL FOOTING} \\ \text{CF} \end{array} \right\} \left\{ \begin{array}{l} \text{data-name-3} \\ \text{FINAL} \end{array} \right\} \\ \left\{ \begin{array}{l} \text{PAGE FOOTING} \\ \text{PF} \end{array} \right\} \\ \left\{ \begin{array}{l} \text{REPORT FOOTING} \\ \text{RF} \end{array} \right\} \end{array} \right]
$$

[[USAGE IS] DISPLAY].

FORMAT 2:

level-number [data-name-1]

$$\left[\text{ \underline{LINE} NUMBER IS } \left\{ \begin{array}{l} \text{integer-1 [ON \underline{NEXT} \underline{PAGE}]} \\ \text{\underline{PLUS} Integer-2} \end{array} \right\} \right]$$

[[\underline{USAGE} IS] \underline{DISPLAY}].

FORMAT 3:

level-number [data-name-1]

$$\left\{ \begin{array}{l} \underline{\text{PICTURE}} \\ \underline{\text{PIC}} \end{array} \right\} \text{ IS character-string}$$

[[\underline{USAGE} IS] \underline{DISPLAY}]

$$\left[\left\{ \begin{array}{l} \underline{\text{JUSTIFIED}} \\ \underline{\text{JUST}} \end{array} \right\} \text{ RIGHT} \right]$$

[\underline{BLANK} WHEN \underline{ZERO}]

$$\left[\text{ \underline{LINE} NUMBER IS } \left\{ \begin{array}{l} \text{integer-1 [ON \underline{NEXT} \underline{PAGE}]} \\ \text{\underline{PLUS} integer-2} \end{array} \right\} \right]$$

[\underline{COLUMN} NUMBER IS integer-3]

$$\left\{ \begin{array}{l} \underline{\text{SOURCE}} \text{ IS identifier-1} \\ \\ \underline{\text{VALUE}} \text{ IS literal-1} \\ \\ \{\underline{\text{SUM}} \text{ \{identifier-2\} } \dots \text{ [\underline{UPON} \{data-name-2\} } \dots \text{]\} } \dots \\ \quad \left[\underline{\text{RESET}} \text{ ON } \left\{ \begin{array}{l} \text{data-name-3} \\ \underline{\text{FINAL}} \end{array} \right\} \right] \end{array} \right\}$$

[\underline{GROUP} INDICATE].

GENERAL FORMAT FOR PROCEDURE DIVISION

FORMAT 1:

[PROCEDURE DIVISION [USING {data-name-1} ...].

[DECLARATIVES.

{section-name SECTION [segment-number].   declarative-sentence

[paragraph-name.

    [sentence] ...] ...} ...

END DECLARATIVES.]

{section-name SECTION [segment-number].

[paragraph-name.

    [sentence] ...] ... } ...]

FORMAT 2:

PROCEDURE DIVISION [USING {data-name-1} ...].

{paragraph-name.

    [sentence] ... } ...

GENERAL FORMAT FOR COBOL VERBS

<u>ACCEPT</u> identifier [<u>FROM</u> mnemonic-name]

<u>ACCEPT</u> identifier <u>FROM</u> $\left\{ \begin{array}{l} \underline{DATE} \\ \underline{DAY} \\ \underline{TIME} \end{array} \right\}$

<u>ACCEPT</u> cd-name MESSAGE <u>COUNT</u>

<u>ADD</u> $\left\{ \begin{array}{l} \text{identifier-1} \\ \text{literal-1} \end{array} \right\}$ ... <u>TO</u> {identifier-2 [<u>ROUNDED</u>]} ...

    [ON <u>SIZE</u> <u>ERROR</u> imperative-statement]

<u>ADD</u> $\left\{ \begin{array}{l} \text{identifier-1} \\ \text{literal-1} \end{array} \right\}$ ...

    <u>GIVING</u> {identifier-2 [<u>ROUNDED</u>]} ...

    [ON <u>SIZE</u> <u>ERROR</u> imperative-statement]

<u>ADD</u> $\left\{ \begin{array}{l} \underline{CORRESPONDING} \\ \underline{CORR} \end{array} \right\}$ identifier-1 <u>TO</u> identifier-2 [<u>ROUNDED</u>]

    [ON <u>SIZE</u> <u>ERROR</u> imperative-statement]

<u>ALTER</u> {procedure-name-1 <u>TO</u> [<u>PROCEED</u> <u>TO</u>] procedure-name-2} ...

<u>CALL</u> $\left\{ \begin{array}{l} \text{identifier-1} \\ \text{literal-1} \end{array} \right\}$ [<u>USING</u> data-name-1 [data-name-2] ...]

    [ON <u>OVERFLOW</u> imperative-statement]

<u>CANCEL</u> $\left\{ \begin{array}{l} \text{identifier-1} \\ \text{literal-1} \end{array} \right\}$ ...

<u>CLOSE</u> $\left\{ \text{file-name-1} \left[\begin{array}{l} \left\{ \begin{array}{l} \underline{REEL} \\ \underline{UNIT} \end{array} \right\} \left\{ \begin{array}{l} \text{WITH } \underline{NO} \underline{REWIND} \\ \text{FOR } \underline{REMOVAL} \end{array} \right\} \\ \text{WITH} \left\{ \begin{array}{l} \underline{NO} \underline{REWIND} \\ \underline{LOCK} \end{array} \right\} \end{array} \right] \right\}$ ...

<u>CLOSE</u> file-name-1 [WITH <u>LOCK</u>]} ...

COMPUTE {identifier-1 [ROUNDED]} ... = arithmetic-expression

    [ON SIZE ERROR imperative-statement]

DELETE file-name RECORD

    [INVALID KEY imperative-statement]

DISABLE $\left\{ \begin{array}{l} \text{INPUT [TERMINAL]} \\ \text{OUTPUT} \end{array} \right\}$ cd-name WITH KEY $\left\{ \begin{array}{l} \text{identifier-1} \\ \text{literal-1} \end{array} \right\}$

DISPLAY $\left\{ \begin{array}{l} \text{identifier-1} \\ \text{literal-1} \end{array} \right\}$ ... [UPON mnemonic-name]

DIVIDE $\left\{ \begin{array}{l} \text{identifier-1} \\ \text{literal-1} \end{array} \right\}$ INTO {identifier-2 [ROUNDED]} ...

    [ON SIZE ERROR imperative-statement]

DIVIDE $\left\{ \begin{array}{l} \text{identifier-1} \\ \text{literal-1} \end{array} \right\}$ INTO $\left\{ \begin{array}{l} \text{identifier-2} \\ \text{literal-2} \end{array} \right\}$

    GIVING {identifier-3 [ROUNDED]} ...

    [ON SIZE ERROR imperative-statement]

DIVIDE $\left\{ \begin{array}{l} \text{identifier-1} \\ \text{literal-1} \end{array} \right\}$ BY $\left\{ \begin{array}{l} \text{identifier-2} \\ \text{literal-2} \end{array} \right\}$

    GIVING {identifier-3 [ROUNDED]} ...

    [ON SIZE ERROR imperative-statement]

DIVIDE $\left\{ \begin{array}{l} \text{identifier-1} \\ \text{literal-1} \end{array} \right\}$ INTO $\left\{ \begin{array}{l} \text{identifier-2} \\ \text{literal-2} \end{array} \right\}$ GIVING identifier-3 [ROUNDED]

    REMAINDER identifier-4

    [ON SIZE ERROR imperative-statement-1]

DIVIDE $\left\{ \begin{array}{l} \text{identifier-1} \\ \text{literal-1} \end{array} \right\}$ BY $\left\{ \begin{array}{l} \text{identifier-2} \\ \text{literal-2} \end{array} \right\}$ GIVING identifier-3 [ROUNDED]

    REMAINDER identifier-4

    [ON SIZE ERROR imperative-statement]

ENABLE $\left\{ \begin{array}{l} \underline{\text{INPUT}} \text{ [TERMINAL]} \\ \underline{\text{OUTPUT}} \end{array} \right\}$ cd-name $\left[\text{ WITH } \underline{\text{KEY}} \left\{ \begin{array}{l} \text{identifier-1} \\ \text{literal-1} \end{array} \right\} \right]$

ENTER language-name-1 [routine-name].

EXIT [PROGRAM]

GENERATE $\left\{ \begin{array}{l} \text{data-name} \\ \text{report-name} \end{array} \right\}$

GO TO [procedure-name-1]

GO TO {procedure-name-1} ... procedure-name-n DEPENDING ON identifier

IF condition $\left\{ \begin{array}{l} \text{statement-1} \\ \underline{\text{NEXT}} \text{ } \underline{\text{SENTENCE}} \end{array} \right\} \left\{ \begin{array}{l} \underline{\text{ELSE}} \text{ statement-2} \\ \underline{\text{ELSE}} \text{ } \underline{\text{NEXT}} \text{ } \underline{\text{SENTENCE}} \end{array} \right\}$

INITIATE {report-name-1} ...

INSPECT identifier-1 TALLYING

$$\left\{ \text{identifier-2 } \underline{\text{FOR}} \left\{ \left\{ \begin{array}{l} \underline{\text{ALL}} \\ \underline{\text{LEADING}} \\ \underline{\text{CHARACTERS}} \end{array} \right\} \left\{ \begin{array}{l} \text{identifier-3} \\ \text{literal-1} \end{array} \right\} \left[\left\{ \begin{array}{l} \underline{\text{BEFORE}} \\ \underline{\text{AFTER}} \end{array} \right\} \text{INITIAL} \left\{ \begin{array}{l} \text{identifier-4} \\ \text{literal-2} \end{array} \right\} \right] \right\} ... \right\}$$

INSPECT identifier-1 REPLACING

$$\left\{ \begin{array}{l} \underline{\text{CHARACTERS}} \text{ } \underline{\text{BY}} \left\{ \begin{array}{l} \text{identifier-5} \\ \text{literal-3} \end{array} \right\} \left[\left\{ \begin{array}{l} \underline{\text{BEFORE}} \\ \underline{\text{AFTER}} \end{array} \right\} \text{INITIAL} \left\{ \begin{array}{l} \text{identifier-4} \\ \text{literal-2} \end{array} \right\} \right] ... \\ \left\{ \begin{array}{l} \underline{\text{ALL}} \\ \underline{\text{LEADING}} \\ \underline{\text{FIRST}} \end{array} \right\} \left\{ \begin{array}{l} \text{identifier-3} \\ \text{literal-1} \end{array} \right\} \underline{\text{BY}} \left\{ \begin{array}{l} \text{identifier-5} \\ \text{literal-3} \end{array} \right\} \left[\left\{ \begin{array}{l} \underline{\text{BEFORE}} \\ \underline{\text{AFTER}} \end{array} \right\} \text{INITIAL} \left\{ \begin{array}{l} \text{identifier-4} \\ \text{literal-2} \end{array} \right\} \right] ... \end{array} \right\} ...$$

INSPECT identifier-1 TALLYING

$$\left\{ \text{identifier-2 } \underline{\text{FOR}} \left\{ \left[\left\{ \begin{matrix} \underline{\text{ALL}} \\ \underline{\text{LEADING}} \end{matrix} \right\} \left\{ \begin{matrix} \text{identifier-3} \\ \text{literal-1} \end{matrix} \right\} \right] \left[\left\{ \begin{matrix} \underline{\text{BEFORE}} \\ \underline{\text{AFTER}} \end{matrix} \right\} \text{ INITIAL } \left\{ \begin{matrix} \text{identifier-4} \\ \text{literal-2} \end{matrix} \right\} \right] \right\} \dots \right\}$$

REPLACING

$$\left\{ \begin{matrix} \underline{\text{CHARACTERS}} \underline{\text{BY}} \left\{ \begin{matrix} \text{identifier-5} \\ \text{literal-3} \end{matrix} \right\} \left[\left\{ \begin{matrix} \underline{\text{BEFORE}} \\ \underline{\text{AFTER}} \end{matrix} \right\} \text{INITIAL } \left\{ \begin{matrix} \text{identifier-4} \\ \text{literal-2} \end{matrix} \right\} \right] \\ \left\{ \begin{matrix} \underline{\text{ALL}} \\ \underline{\text{LEADING}} \\ \underline{\text{FIRST}} \end{matrix} \right\} \left\{ \left\{ \begin{matrix} \text{identifier-3} \\ \text{literal-1} \end{matrix} \right\} \underline{\text{BY}} \left\{ \begin{matrix} \text{identifier-5} \\ \text{literal-3} \end{matrix} \right\} \left[\left\{ \begin{matrix} \underline{\text{BEFORE}} \\ \underline{\text{AFTER}} \end{matrix} \right\} \text{INITIAL} \left\{ \begin{matrix} \text{identifier-4} \\ \text{literal-2} \end{matrix} \right\} \right] \right\} \dots \right\} \dots \right\}$$

$$\underline{\text{MERGE}} \text{ file-name-1} \left\{ \text{ON} \left\{ \begin{matrix} \underline{\text{ASCENDING}} \\ \underline{\text{DESCENDING}} \end{matrix} \right\} \text{KEY \{data-name-1\} } \dots \right\} \dots$$

[COLLATING SEQUENCE IS alphabet-name-1]

USING file-name-2 {file-name-3} ...

$$\left\{ \begin{matrix} \underline{\text{OUTPUT}} \underline{\text{PROCEDURE}} \text{ IS procedure-name-1} \left[\left\{ \begin{matrix} \underline{\text{THROUGH}} \\ \underline{\text{THRU}} \end{matrix} \right\} \text{procedure-name-2} \right] \\ \underline{\text{GIVING}} \text{ file-name-4} \end{matrix} \right\}$$

$$\underline{\text{MOVE}} \left\{ \begin{matrix} \text{identifier-1} \\ \text{literal-1} \end{matrix} \right\} \underline{\text{TO}} \text{ \{identifier-2\} } \dots$$

$$\underline{\text{MOVE}} \left\{ \begin{matrix} \underline{\text{CORRESPONDING}} \\ \underline{\text{CORR}} \end{matrix} \right\} \text{ identifier-1 } \underline{\text{TO}} \text{ identifier-2}$$

$$\underline{\text{MULTIPLY}} \left\{ \begin{matrix} \text{identifier-1} \\ \text{literal-1} \end{matrix} \right\} \underline{\text{BY}} \text{ \{identifier-2 [\underline{ROUNDED}]\} } \dots$$

[ON SIZE ERROR imperative-statement]

$$\underline{\text{MULTIPLY}} \left\{ \begin{array}{l} \text{identifier-1} \\ \text{literal-1} \end{array} \right\} \underline{\text{BY}} \left\{ \begin{array}{l} \text{identifier-2} \\ \text{literal-2} \end{array} \right\}$$

$$\underline{\text{GIVING}} \; \{\text{identifier-3} \; [\underline{\text{ROUNDED}}]\} \; \ldots$$

$$[\text{ON} \; \underline{\text{SIZE}} \; \underline{\text{ERROR}} \; \text{imperative-statement}]]$$

$$\underline{\text{OPEN}} \left\{ \begin{array}{l} \underline{\text{INPUT}} \left\{ \text{file-name-1} \left[\begin{array}{l} \underline{\text{REVERSED}} \\ \text{WITH} \; \underline{\text{NO}} \; \underline{\text{REWIND}} \end{array} \right] \right\} \ldots \\ \underline{\text{OUTPUT}} \; \{\text{file-name-2} \; [\text{WITH} \; \underline{\text{NO}} \; \underline{\text{REWIND}}]\} \; \ldots \\ \underline{\text{I-O}} \; \{\text{file-name-3}\} \; \ldots \\ \underline{\text{EXTEND}} \; \{\text{file-name-4}\} \; \ldots \end{array} \right\} \quad \ldots$$

$$\underline{\text{OPEN}} \left\{ \begin{array}{l} \underline{\text{INPUT}} \; \{\text{file-name-1}\} \; \ldots \\ \underline{\text{OUTPUT}} \; \{\text{file-name-2}\} \; \ldots \\ \underline{\text{I-O}} \; \{\text{file-name-3}\} \; \ldots \end{array} \right\} \quad \ldots$$

$$\underline{\text{PERFORM}} \left[\text{procedure-name-1} \left[\left\{ \begin{array}{l} \underline{\text{THROUGH}} \\ \underline{\text{THRU}} \end{array} \right\} \text{procedure-name-2} \right] \right]$$

$$\underline{\text{PERFORM}} \left[\text{procedure-name-1} \left[\left\{ \begin{array}{l} \underline{\text{THROUGH}} \\ \underline{\text{THRU}} \end{array} \right\} \text{procedure-name-2} \right] \right]$$

$$\left\{ \begin{array}{l} \text{identifier-1} \\ \text{integer-1} \end{array} \right\} \underline{\text{TIMES}}$$

$$\underline{\text{PERFORM}} \left[\text{procedure-name-1} \left[\left\{ \begin{array}{l} \underline{\text{THROUGH}} \\ \underline{\text{THRU}} \end{array} \right\} \text{procedure-name-2} \right] \right]$$

$$\underline{\text{UNTIL}} \; \text{condition-1}$$

PERFORM $\left[\text{procedure-name-1} \left[\left\{ \begin{array}{l} \underline{\text{THROUGH}} \\ \underline{\text{THRU}} \end{array} \right\} \text{procedure-name-2} \right] \right]$

$\underline{\text{VARYING}} \left\{ \begin{array}{l} \text{identifier-2} \\ \text{index-name-1} \end{array} \right\} \underline{\text{FROM}} \left\{ \begin{array}{l} \text{identifier-3} \\ \text{index-name-2} \\ \text{literal-1} \end{array} \right\}$

$\underline{\text{BY}} \left\{ \begin{array}{l} \text{identifier-4} \\ \text{literal-2} \end{array} \right\} \underline{\text{UNTIL}} \text{ condition-1}$

$\left[\underline{\text{AFTER}} \left\{ \begin{array}{l} \text{identifier-5} \\ \text{literal-3} \end{array} \right\} \underline{\text{FROM}} \left\{ \begin{array}{l} \text{identifier-6} \\ \text{index-name-3} \\ \text{literal-4} \end{array} \right\} \right.$

$\left. \underline{\text{BY}} \left\{ \begin{array}{l} \text{identifier-7} \\ \text{literal-5} \end{array} \right\} \underline{\text{UNTIL}} \text{ condition-2} \right]$

$\left[\underline{\text{AFTER}} \left\{ \begin{array}{l} \text{identifier-8} \\ \text{literal-6} \end{array} \right\} \underline{\text{FROM}} \left\{ \begin{array}{l} \text{identifier-9} \\ \text{index-name-4} \\ \text{literal-7} \end{array} \right\} \right.$

$\left. \underline{\text{BY}} \left\{ \begin{array}{l} \text{identifier-10} \\ \text{literal-8} \end{array} \right\} \underline{\text{UNTIL}} \text{ condition-3} \right]$

READ file-name RECORD [INTO identifier]

[AT END imperative-statement]

READ file-name [NEXT] RECORD [INTO identifier]

[AT END imperative-statement]

READ file-name RECORD [INTO identifier]

[INVALID KEY imperative-statement]

READ file-name RECORD [INTO identifier-1]

[KEY IS data-name]

[INVALID KEY imperative-statement]

RECEIVE cd-name $\left\{ \begin{array}{l} \underline{\text{MESSAGE}} \\ \underline{\text{SEGMENT}} \end{array} \right\}$ INTO identifier

[NO DATA imperative-statement]

RELEASE record-name [FROM identifier]

RETURN file-name RECORD [INTO identifier]   AT END imperative-statement

REWRITE record-name [FROM identifier]

REWRITE record-name [FROM identifier] [INVALID KEY imperative-statement]

SEARCH identifier-1 $\left[\text{VARYING} \left\{ \begin{array}{l} \text{identifier-2} \\ \text{index-name-1} \end{array} \right\} \right]$

    [AT END imperative-statement-1]

    $\left\{ \text{WHEN condition-1} \left\{ \begin{array}{l} \text{imperative-statement-2} \\ \text{NEXT SENTENCE} \end{array} \right\} \right\}$ ...

SEARCH ALL identifier-1 [AT END imperative-statement-1]

    WHEN $\left\{ \begin{array}{l} \text{data-name-1} \left\{ \begin{array}{l} \text{IS EQUAL TO} \\ \text{IS =} \end{array} \right\} \left\{ \begin{array}{l} \text{identifier-3} \\ \text{literal-1} \\ \text{arithmetic-expression-1} \end{array} \right\} \\ \text{condition-name-1} \end{array} \right\}$

    $\left[\text{AND} \left\{ \begin{array}{l} \text{data-name-2} \left\{ \begin{array}{l} \text{IS EQUAL TO} \\ \text{IS =} \end{array} \right\} \left\{ \begin{array}{l} \text{identifier-4} \\ \text{literal-2} \\ \text{arithmetic-expression-2} \end{array} \right\} \\ \text{condition-name-2} \end{array} \right\} \right]$ ...

    $\left\{ \begin{array}{l} \text{imperative-statement-2} \\ \text{NEXT SENTENCE} \end{array} \right\}$

SEND cd-name FROM identifier-1

SEND cd-name [FROM identifier-1 $\left\{ \begin{array}{l} \text{WITH identifier-2} \\ \text{WITH ESI} \\ \text{WITH EMI} \\ \text{WITH EGI} \end{array} \right\}$

    $\left[\left\{ \begin{array}{l} \text{BEFORE} \\ \text{AFTER} \end{array} \right\} \text{ADVANCING} \left\{ \begin{array}{l} \left\{ \begin{array}{l} \text{identifier-3} \\ \text{integer-1} \end{array} \right\} \left[\begin{array}{l} \text{LINE} \\ \text{LINES} \end{array} \right] \\ \left\{ \begin{array}{l} \text{mnemonic-name-1} \\ \text{PAGE} \end{array} \right\} \end{array} \right\} \right]$

$$\underline{\text{SET}} \quad \left\{ \begin{array}{l} \text{index-name-1} \\ \text{identifier-1} \end{array} \right\} \quad \dots \quad \underline{\text{TO}} \quad \left\{ \begin{array}{l} \text{index-name-2} \\ \text{identifier-2} \\ \text{integer-1} \end{array} \right\}$$

$$\underline{\text{SET}} \quad \{\text{index-name-3}\} \quad \dots \quad \left\{ \begin{array}{l} \underline{\text{UP}} \ \underline{\text{BY}} \\ \underline{\text{DOWN}} \ \underline{\text{BY}} \end{array} \right\} \quad \left\{ \begin{array}{l} \text{identifier-3} \\ \text{integer-2} \end{array} \right\}$$

$$\underline{\text{SORT}} \ \text{file-name-1} \left\{ \text{ON} \ \left\{ \begin{array}{l} \underline{\text{ASCENDING}} \\ \underline{\text{DESCENDING}} \end{array} \right\} \text{KEY} \ \{\text{data-name-1}\} \ \dots \right\} \dots$$

[COLLATING $\underline{\text{SEQUENCE}}$ IS alphabet-name-1]

$$\left\{ \begin{array}{l} \underline{\text{INPUT}} \ \underline{\text{PROCEDURE}} \ \text{IS section-name-1} \quad \left[\left\{ \begin{array}{l} \underline{\text{THROUGH}} \\ \underline{\text{THRU}} \end{array} \right\} \text{section-name-2} \right] \\ \underline{\text{USING}} \quad \{\text{file-name-2}\} \ \dots \end{array} \right\}$$

$$\left\{ \begin{array}{l} \underline{\text{OUTPUT}} \ \underline{\text{PROCEDURE}} \ \text{IS section-name-3} \quad \left[\left\{ \begin{array}{l} \underline{\text{THROUGH}} \\ \underline{\text{THRU}} \end{array} \right\} \text{section-name-4} \right] \\ \underline{\text{GIVING}} \quad \{\text{file-name-3}\} \ \dots \end{array} \right\}$$

$$\underline{\text{START}} \ \text{file-name} \left[\underline{\text{KEY}} \left\{ \begin{array}{l} \text{IS} \ \underline{\text{EQUAL}} \ \text{TO} \\ \text{IS} = \\ \text{IS} \ \underline{\text{GREATER}} \ \text{THAN} \\ \text{IS} > \\ \text{IS} \ \underline{\text{NOT}} \ \underline{\text{LESS}} \ \text{THAN} \\ \text{IS} \ \underline{\text{NOT}} \ < \end{array} \right\} \text{data-name} \right]$$

[$\underline{\text{INVALID}}$ KEY imperative-statement]

$$\underline{\text{STOP}} \ \left\{ \begin{array}{l} \underline{\text{RUN}} \\ \text{literal} \end{array} \right\}$$

$$\underline{\text{STRING}} \quad \left\{ \left\{ \begin{array}{l} \text{identifier-1} \\ \text{literal-1} \end{array} \right\} \dots \underline{\text{DELIMITED}} \ \text{BY} \left\{ \begin{array}{l} \text{identifier-2} \\ \text{literal-2} \\ \underline{\text{SIZE}} \end{array} \right\} \right\} \dots$$

$\underline{\text{INTO}}$ identifier-3

[WITH $\underline{\text{POINTER}}$ identifier-4]

[ON $\underline{\text{OVERFLOW}}$ imperative-statement]

SUBTRACT $\left\{ \begin{array}{l} \text{identifier-1} \\ \text{literal-1} \end{array} \right\}$ ... FROM {identifier-3 [ROUNDED]} ...

[ON SIZE ERROR imperative-statement]

SUBTRACT $\left\{ \begin{array}{l} \text{identifier-1} \\ \text{literal-1} \end{array} \right\}$ .... FROM $\left\{ \begin{array}{l} \text{identifier-2} \\ \text{literal-2} \end{array} \right\}$

GIVING {identifier-3 [ROUNDED]} ...

[ON SIZE ERROR imperative-statement]

SUBTRACT $\left\{ \begin{array}{l} \text{CORRESPONDING} \\ \text{CORR} \end{array} \right\}$ identifier-1 FROM identifier-2 [ROUNDED]

[ON SIZE ERROR imperative-statement]

SUPPRESS PRINTING

TERMINATE {report-name-1} ...

UNSTRING identifier-1

$\left[\text{DELIMITED BY [ALL]} \left\{ \begin{array}{l} \text{identifier-2} \\ \text{literal-1} \end{array} \right\} \left[\text{OR [ALL]} \left\{ \begin{array}{l} \text{identifier-3} \\ \text{literal-2} \end{array} \right\} \right] ... \right]$

INTO {identifier-4 [DELIMITER IN identifier-5] [COUNT IN identifier-6]} ...

[WITH POINTER identifier-7]

[TALLYING IN identifier-8]

[ON OVERFLOW imperative-statement]

USE AFTER STANDARD $\left\{ \begin{array}{l} \text{EXCEPTION} \\ \text{ERROR} \end{array} \right\}$ PROCEDURE ON $\left\{ \begin{array}{l} \text{\{file-name-1\} ...} \\ \text{INPUT} \\ \text{OUTPUT} \\ \text{I-O} \\ \text{EXTEND} \end{array} \right\}$

USE AFTER STANDARD $\left\{ \begin{array}{l} \text{EXCEPTION} \\ \text{ERROR} \end{array} \right\}$ PROCEDURE ON $\left\{ \begin{array}{l} \text{\{file-name-1\} ...} \\ \text{INPUT} \\ \text{OUTPUT} \\ \text{I-O} \end{array} \right\}$

USE <u>BEFORE</u> <u>REPORTING</u> identifier-1

<u>USE</u> FOR <u>DEBUGGING</u> ON $\left\{ \begin{array}{l} \text{cd-name-1} \\ \text{[\underline{ALL} REFERENCES OF] identifier-1} \\ \text{file-name-1} \\ \text{procedure-name-1} \\ \underline{\text{ALL}} \ \underline{\text{PROCEDURES}} \end{array} \right\}$ ...

<u>WRITE</u> record-name   [<u>FROM</u> identifier-1]

$$\left[\ \left\{ \begin{array}{l} \underline{\text{BEFORE}} \\ \underline{\text{AFTER}} \end{array} \right\} \ \text{ADVANCING} \ \left\{ \begin{array}{l} \left\{ \begin{array}{l} \text{identifier-2} \\ \text{integer-1} \end{array} \right\} \left\{ \begin{array}{l} \text{LINE} \\ \text{LINES} \end{array} \right\} \\ \left\{ \begin{array}{l} \text{mnemonic-name-1} \\ \underline{\text{PAGE}} \end{array} \right\} \end{array} \right\} \ \right]$$

$$\left[\ \text{AT} \ \left\{ \begin{array}{l} \underline{\text{END-OF-PAGE}} \\ \underline{\text{EOP}} \end{array} \right\} \ \text{imperative-statement} \ \right]$$

<u>WRITE</u> record-name-1   [<u>FROM</u> identifier-1]

   [<u>INVALID</u> KEY imperative-statement]

GENERAL FORMAT FOR CONDITIONS

RELATION CONDITION:

$$
\left\{ \begin{array}{l} \text{identifier-1} \\ \text{literal-1} \\ \text{arithmetic-expression-1} \\ \text{index-name-1} \end{array} \right\}
\left\{ \begin{array}{l} \text{IS [NOT] \underline{GREATER} THAN} \\ \text{IS [NOT] >} \\ \text{IS [NOT] \underline{LESS} THAN} \\ \text{IS [NOT] <} \\ \text{IS [NOT] \underline{EQUAL} TO} \\ \text{IS [NOT] =} \end{array} \right\}
\left\{ \begin{array}{l} \text{identifier-2} \\ \text{literal-2} \\ \text{arithmetic-expression-2} \\ \text{index-name-2} \end{array} \right\}
$$

CLASS CONDITION:

$$
\text{identifier IS [NOT]} \left\{ \begin{array}{l} \underline{\text{NUMERIC}} \\ \underline{\text{ALPHABETIC}} \end{array} \right\}
$$

CONDITION-NAME CONDITION:

condition-name

SWITCH-STATUS CONDITION:

condition-name

SIGN CONDITION:

$$
\text{arithmetic-expression IS [NOT]} \left\{ \begin{array}{l} \underline{\text{POSITIVE}} \\ \underline{\text{NEGATIVE}} \\ \underline{\text{ZERO}} \end{array} \right\}
$$

NEGATED CONDITION:

NOT condition

COMBINED CONDITION:

$$
\text{condition} \left\{ \left\{ \begin{array}{l} \underline{\text{AND}} \\ \underline{\text{OR}} \end{array} \right\} \text{condition-name} \right\} \ ...
$$

ABBREVIATED COMBINED RELATION CONDITION:

$$
\text{relation-condition} \left\{ \left\{ \begin{array}{l} \underline{\text{AND}} \\ \underline{\text{OR}} \end{array} \right\} \text{[NOT] [relational-operator] object} \right\} \ ...
$$

MISCELLANEOUS FORMATS

QUALIFICATION:

$$\begin{Bmatrix} \text{data-name-1} \\ \text{condition-name-1} \end{Bmatrix} \left[\begin{Bmatrix} \underline{\text{IN}} \\ \underline{\text{OF}} \end{Bmatrix} \text{data-name-2} \right] \dots$$

$$\text{paragraph-name} \left[\begin{Bmatrix} \underline{\text{IN}} \\ \underline{\text{OF}} \end{Bmatrix} \text{section-name} \right]$$

$$\text{text-name} \left[\begin{Bmatrix} \underline{\text{IN}} \\ \underline{\text{OF}} \end{Bmatrix} \text{library-name} \right]$$

SUBSCRIPTING:

$$\begin{Bmatrix} \text{data-name} \\ \text{condition-name} \end{Bmatrix} \quad (\text{subscript-1 [subscript-2 [subscript-3]])}$$

INDEXING:

$$\begin{Bmatrix} \text{data-name} \\ \text{condition-name} \end{Bmatrix} \left(\begin{Bmatrix} \text{index-name-1 [\{ } \pm \text{ \} literal-1]} \\ \text{literal-2} \end{Bmatrix} \dots \right)$$

IDENTIFIER, FORMAT 1:

$$\text{data-name-1} \left[\begin{Bmatrix} \underline{\text{IN}} \\ \underline{\text{OF}} \end{Bmatrix} \text{data-name-2} \right] \dots \quad \text{(subscript-1 [, subscript-2 [, subscript-3]])}$$

IDENTIFIER, FORMAT 2:

$$\text{data-name-1} \left[\begin{Bmatrix} \underline{\text{IN}} \\ \underline{\text{OF}} \end{Bmatrix} \text{data-name-2} \right] \dots \left[\left(\begin{Bmatrix} \text{index-name-1 [\{ } \pm \text{ \} literal-1]} \\ \text{literal-2} \end{Bmatrix} \right. \right.$$

$$\left[\begin{Bmatrix} \text{index-name-2 [\{ } \pm \text{ \} literal-3]} \\ \text{literal-4} \end{Bmatrix} \right] \left[\begin{Bmatrix} \text{index-name-3 [\{ } \pm \text{ \} literal-5]} \\ \text{literal-6} \end{Bmatrix} \right] \left. \left. \right) \right]$$

GENERAL FORMAT FOR COPY STATEMENT

$$\underline{\text{COPY}} \text{ text-name-1} \left[\begin{Bmatrix} \underline{\text{OF}} \\ \underline{\text{IN}} \end{Bmatrix} \text{library-name} \right]$$

$$\left[\underline{\text{REPLACING}} \begin{Bmatrix} \begin{Bmatrix} \text{==pseudo-text-1==} \\ \text{identifier-1} \\ \text{literal-1} \\ \text{word-1} \end{Bmatrix} \underline{\text{BY}} \begin{Bmatrix} \text{==pseudo-text-2==} \\ \text{identifier-2} \\ \text{literal-2} \\ \text{word-2} \end{Bmatrix} \end{Bmatrix} \dots \right]$$

GENERAL FORMAT FOR IDENTIFICATION DIVISION

IDENTIFICATION DIVISION.

PROGRAM-ID. program-name $\left[\text{IS} \left\{ \begin{array}{|c|} \text{COMMON} \\ \hline \text{INITIAL} \end{array} \right\} \text{PROGRAM} \right]$.

[AUTHOR. [comment-entry] ...]

[INSTALLATION. [comment-entry] ...]

[DATE-WRITTEN. [comment-entry] ...]

[DATE-COMPILED. [comment-entry] ...]

[SECURITY. [comment-entry] ...]

GENERAL FORMAT FOR ENVIRONMENT DIVISION

[ENVIRONMENT DIVISION.

[CONFIGURATION SECTION.

[SOURCE-COMPUTER. [computer-name [WITH DEBUGGING MODE].]]

[OBJECT-COMPUTER. [computer-name

$\left[\text{MEMORY SIZE integer-1} \left\{ \begin{array}{l} \text{WORDS} \\ \text{CHARACTERS} \\ \text{MODULES} \end{array} \right\} \right]$

[PROGRAM COLLATING SEQUENCE IS alphabet-name-1]

[SEGMENT-LIMIT IS segment-number].]]

[SPECIAL-NAMES. [[implementor-name-1

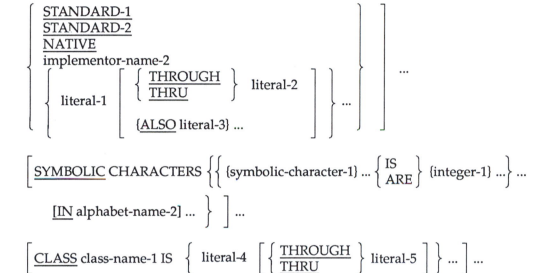

$$
\begin{Bmatrix}
\text{IS mnemonic-name-1 } [\underline{\text{ON}} \text{ STATUS IS condition-name-1} \\
\qquad\qquad [\underline{\text{OFF}} \text{ STATUS IS condition-name-2}]] \\
\text{IS mnemonic-name-2 } [\underline{\text{OFF}} \text{ STATUS IS condition-name-2} \\
\qquad\qquad [\underline{\text{ON}} \text{ STATUS IS condition-name-1}]] \\
\underline{\text{ON}} \text{ STATUS IS condition-name-1 } [\underline{\text{OFF}} \text{ STATUS IS condition-name-2}] \\
\underline{\text{OFF}} \text{ STATUS IS condition-name-2 } [\underline{\text{ON}} \text{ STATUS IS condition-name-1}]
\end{Bmatrix} \; \Big] \;\; \cdots
$$

[ALPHABET alphabet-name-1 IS

$$
\begin{Bmatrix}
\underline{\text{STANDARD-1}} \\
\underline{\text{STANDARD-2}} \\
\underline{\text{NATIVE}} \\
\text{implementor-name-2} \\
\begin{Bmatrix}
\text{literal-1} \begin{bmatrix} \begin{Bmatrix} \underline{\text{THROUGH}} \\ \underline{\text{THRU}} \end{Bmatrix} \text{literal-2} \\ \{\underline{\text{ALSO}} \text{ literal-3}\} \cdots \end{bmatrix}
\end{Bmatrix} \cdots
\end{Bmatrix} \;\; \cdots
$$

$$
\left[\underline{\text{SYMBOLIC}} \text{ CHARACTERS} \begin{Bmatrix} \{\text{symbolic-character-1}\} \cdots \begin{Bmatrix} \text{IS} \\ \underline{\text{ARE}} \end{Bmatrix} \{\text{integer-1}\} \cdots \end{Bmatrix} \cdots \right.
$$

$$
\left. [\underline{\text{IN}} \text{ alphabet-name-2}] \cdots \right] \cdots
$$

$$
\left[\underline{\text{CLASS}} \text{ class-name-1 IS} \begin{Bmatrix} \text{literal-4} \begin{bmatrix} \begin{Bmatrix} \underline{\text{THROUGH}} \\ \underline{\text{THRU}} \end{Bmatrix} \text{literal-5} \end{bmatrix} \end{Bmatrix} \cdots \right] \cdots
$$

[CURRENCY SIGN IS literal-6]
[DECIMAL-POINT IS COMMA].]]]

[INPUT-OUTPUT SECTION.

FILE-CONTROL.

    {file-control-entry} ...

[I-O-CONTROL.

$$
\left[\left[\left[\underline{\text{RERUN}} \left[\underline{\text{ON}} \left\{ \begin{array}{l} \text{file-name-1} \\ \text{implementor-name-1} \end{array} \right\} \right] \right. \right. \right.
$$

$$
\left. \left. \underline{\text{EVERY}} \left\{ \begin{array}{l} \left\{ \begin{array}{l} [\underline{\text{END}} \text{ OF}] \left\{ \begin{array}{l} \underline{\text{REEL}} \\ \underline{\text{UNIT}} \end{array} \right\} \\ \text{integer-1} \ \underline{\text{RECORDS}} \end{array} \right\} \text{OF file-name-2} \\ \text{integer-2} \ \underline{\text{CLOCK-UNITS}} \\ \text{condition-name-1} \end{array} \right\} \right] \right] \ ...
$$

$$
\left[\underline{\text{SAME}} \left[\begin{array}{l} \underline{\text{RECORD}} \\ \underline{\text{SORT}} \\ \underline{\text{SORT-MERGE}} \end{array} \right] \text{AREA FOR file-name-3 \{file-name-4\} ...} \right] \ ...
$$

    [MULTIPLE FILE TAPE CONTAINS {file-name-5 [POSITION integer-3]} ...] ... .]]]]

GENERAL FORMAT FOR FILE CONTROL ENTRY

SEQUENTIAL FILE:

SELECT [OPTIONAL] file-name-1

    ASSIGN TO $\left\{ \begin{array}{l} \text{implementor-name-1} \\ \text{literal-1} \end{array} \right\}$ ...

    $\left[\text{RESERVE integer-1} \left[\begin{array}{l} \text{AREA} \\ \text{AREAS} \end{array} \right] \right]$

    [[ORGANIZATION IS] SEQUENTIAL]

    $\left[\text{PADDING CHARACTER IS} \left\{ \begin{array}{l} \text{data-name-1} \\ \text{literal-2} \end{array} \right\} \right]$

    $\left[\text{RECORD DELIMITER IS} \left\{ \begin{array}{l} \text{STANDARD-1} \\ \text{implementor-name-2} \end{array} \right\} \right]$

    [ACCESS MODE IS SEQUENTIAL]

    [FILE STATUS IS data-name-2].

RELATIVE FILE:

SELECT [OPTIONAL] file-name-1

    ASSIGN TO $\left\{ \begin{array}{l} \text{implementor-name-1} \\ \text{literal-1} \end{array} \right\}$ ...

    $\left[\text{RESERVE integer-1} \left[\begin{array}{l} \text{AREA} \\ \text{AREAS} \end{array} \right] \right]$

    [ORGANIZATION IS] RELATIVE

    $\left[\text{ACCESS MODE IS} \left\{ \begin{array}{l} \text{SEQUENTIAL [RELATIVE KEY IS data-name-1]} \\ \left\{ \begin{array}{l} \text{RANDOM} \\ \text{DYNAMIC} \end{array} \right\} \text{RELATIVE KEY IS data-name-1} \end{array} \right\} \right]$

    [FILE STATUS IS data-name-2].

INDEXED FILE:

<u>SELECT</u> [OPTIONAL] file-name-1

$$\underline{ASSIGN} \text{ TO } \left\{ \begin{array}{l} \text{implementor-name-1} \\ \text{literal-1} \end{array} \right\} \dots$$

$$\left[\underline{RESERVE} \text{ integer-1} \left[\begin{array}{l} \text{AREA} \\ \text{AREAS} \end{array} \right] \right]$$

[<u>ORGANIZATION</u> IS] <u>INDEXED</u>

$$\left[\underline{ACCESS} \text{ MODE IS } \left\{ \begin{array}{l} \underline{SEQUENTIAL} \\ \underline{RANDOM} \\ \underline{DYNAMIC} \end{array} \right\} \right]$$

<u>RECORD</u> KEY IS data-name-1

[<u>ALTERNATE</u> <u>RECORD</u> KEY IS data-name-2 [WITH <u>DUPLICATES</u>]] . . .

[FILE <u>STATUS</u> IS data-name-3].

SORT OR MERGE FILE:

$$\underline{SELECT} \text{ file-name-1 } \underline{ASSIGN} \text{ TO } \left\{ \begin{array}{l} \text{implementor-name-1} \\ \text{literal-1} \end{array} \right\} \dots$$

REPORT FILE:

<u>SELECT</u> [OPTIONAL] file-name-1

$$\underline{ASSIGN} \text{ TO } \left\{ \begin{array}{l} \text{implementor-name-1} \\ \text{literal-1} \end{array} \right\} \dots$$

$$\left[\underline{RESERVE} \text{ integer-1} \left\{ \begin{array}{l} \text{AREA} \\ \text{AREAS} \end{array} \right\} \right]$$

[[<u>ORGANIZATION</u> IS] <u>SEQUENTIAL</u>]

$$\left[\underline{PADDING} \text{ CHARACTER IS } \left\{ \begin{array}{l} \text{data-name-1} \\ \text{literal-2} \end{array} \right\} \right]$$

$$\left[\underline{RECORD} \underline{DELIMITER} \text{ IS } \left\{ \begin{array}{l} \underline{STANDARD-1} \\ \text{implementor-name-2} \end{array} \right\} \right]$$

[<u>ACCESS</u> MODE IS <u>SEQUENTIAL</u>]

[FILE <u>STATUS</u> IS data-name-2].

GENERAL FORMAT FOR DATA DIVISION

[DATA DIVISION.

[FILE SECTION.

$$
\left[\begin{array}{l}
\text{file-description-entry \{record-description-entry\} } \ldots \\
\text{sort-merge-file-description-entry \{record-description-entry\} } \ldots \\
\text{report-file-description-entry}
\end{array}\right] \ldots \Bigg]
$$

[WORKING-STORAGE SECTION.

$$
\left[\begin{array}{l}
\text{77-level-description-entry} \\
\text{record-description-entry}
\end{array}\right] \ldots \Bigg]
$$

[LINKAGE SECTION.

$$
\left[\begin{array}{l}
\text{77-level-description-entry} \\
\text{record-description-entry}
\end{array}\right] \ldots \Bigg]
$$

[COMMUNICATION SECTION.

[communication-description-entry [record-description-entry] ...] ...]

[REPORT SECTION.

[report-description-entry {report-group-description-entry} ...] ...]]

GENERAL FORMAT FOR FILE DESCRIPTION ENTRY

SEQUENTIAL FILE:

FD file-name-1

[IS EXTERNAL]

[IS GLOBAL]

$$\left[\text{BLOCK CONTAINS [integer-1 TO] integer-2} \left\{ \begin{array}{l} \text{RECORDS} \\ \text{CHARACTERS} \end{array} \right\} \right]$$

$$\left[\text{RECORD} \left\{ \begin{array}{l} \text{CONTAINS integer-3 CHARACTERS} \\ \text{IS VARYING IN SIZE [[FROM integer-4] [TO integer-5]} \\ \text{CHARACTERS] [DEPENDING ON data-name-1]} \\ \text{CONTAINS integer-6 TO integer-7 CHARACTERS} \end{array} \right\} \right]$$

$$\left[\text{LABEL} \left\{ \begin{array}{l} \text{RECORD IS} \\ \text{RECORDS ARE} \end{array} \right\} \left\{ \begin{array}{l} \text{STANDARD} \\ \text{OMITTED} \end{array} \right\} \right]$$

$$\left[\text{VALUE OF} \left\{ \text{implementor-name-1 IS} \left\{ \begin{array}{l} \text{data-name-2} \\ \text{literal-1} \end{array} \right\} \right\} \ldots \right]$$

$$\left[\text{DATA} \left\{ \begin{array}{l} \text{RECORD IS} \\ \text{RECORDS ARE} \end{array} \right\} \{\text{data-name-3}\} \ldots \right]$$

$$\left[\text{LINAGE IS} \left\{ \begin{array}{l} \text{data-name-4} \\ \text{integer-8} \end{array} \right\} \text{LINES} \right.$$

$$\left[\text{WITH FOOTING AT} \left\{ \begin{array}{l} \text{data-name-5} \\ \text{integer-9} \end{array} \right\} \right]$$

$$\left[\text{LINES AT TOP} \left\{ \begin{array}{l} \text{data-name-6} \\ \text{integer-10} \end{array} \right\} \right]$$

$$\left. \left[\text{LINES AT BOTTOM} \left\{ \begin{array}{l} \text{data-name-7} \\ \text{integer-11} \end{array} \right\} \right] \right]$$

[CODE-SET IS alphabet-name-1].

RELATIVE FILE:

<u>FD</u> file-name-1

   [IS <u>EXTERNAL</u>]

   [IS <u>GLOBAL</u>]

$$\left[\underline{\text{BLOCK}} \text{ CONTAINS } [\text{integer-1 } \underline{\text{TO}}] \text{ integer-2} \quad \left\{ \begin{array}{l} \text{RECORDS} \\ \text{CHARACTERS} \end{array} \right\} \right]$$

$$\left[\underline{\text{RECORD}} \left\{ \begin{array}{l} \text{CONTAINS integer-3 CHARACTERS} \\ \text{IS } \underline{\text{VARYING}} \text{ IN SIZE [[FROM integer-4] } [\underline{\text{TO}} \text{ integer-5]} \\ \quad \text{CHARACTERS] } [\underline{\text{DEPENDING}} \text{ ON data-name-1]} \\ \text{CONTAINS integer-6 } \underline{\text{TO}} \text{ integer-7 CHARACTERS} \end{array} \right\} \right]$$

$$\left[\underline{\text{LABEL}} \left\{ \begin{array}{l} \underline{\text{RECORD}} \text{ IS} \\ \underline{\text{RECORDS}} \text{ ARE} \end{array} \right\} \left\{ \begin{array}{l} \underline{\text{STANDARD}} \\ \underline{\text{OMITTED}} \end{array} \right\} \right]$$

$$\left[\underline{\text{VALUE}} \underline{\text{OF}} \quad \left\{ \text{implementor-name-1 IS} \quad \left\{ \begin{array}{l} \text{data-name-2} \\ \text{literal-1} \end{array} \right\} \right\} \ldots \right]$$

$$\left[\underline{\text{DATA}} \left\{ \begin{array}{l} \underline{\text{RECORD}} \text{ IS} \\ \underline{\text{RECORDS}} \text{ ARE} \end{array} \right\} \{\text{data-name-3}\} \ldots \right] .$$

INDEXED FILE:

<u>FD</u> file-name-1

   [IS <u>EXTERNAL</u>]

   [IS <u>GLOBAL</u>]

$$\left[\underline{\text{BLOCK}} \text{ CONTAINS } [\text{integer-1 } \underline{\text{TO}}] \text{ integer-2} \quad \left\{ \begin{array}{l} \text{RECORDS} \\ \text{CHARACTERS} \end{array} \right\} \right]$$

$$\left[\underline{\text{RECORD}} \left\{ \begin{array}{l} \text{CONTAINS integer-3 CHARACTERS} \\ \text{IS } \underline{\text{VARYING}} \text{ IN SIZE [[FROM integer-4] } [\underline{\text{TO}} \text{ integer-5]} \\ \quad \text{CHARACTERS] } [\underline{\text{DEPENDING}} \text{ ON data-name-1]} \\ \text{CONTAINS integer-6 } \underline{\text{TO}} \text{ integer-7 CHARACTERS} \end{array} \right\} \right]$$

$$\left[\underline{\text{LABEL}} \left\{ \begin{array}{l} \underline{\text{RECORD}} \text{ IS} \\ \underline{\text{RECORDS}} \text{ ARE} \end{array} \right\} \left\{ \begin{array}{l} \underline{\text{STANDARD}} \\ \underline{\text{OMITTED}} \end{array} \right\} \right]$$

$$\left[\underline{\text{VALUE}} \underline{\text{OF}} \quad \left\{ \text{implementor-name-1 IS} \quad \left\{ \begin{array}{l} \text{data-name-2} \\ \text{literal-1} \end{array} \right\} \right\} \ldots \right]$$

$$\left[\underline{\text{DATA}} \left\{ \begin{array}{l} \underline{\text{RECORD}} \text{ IS} \\ \underline{\text{RECORDS}} \text{ ARE} \end{array} \right\} \{\text{data-name-3}\} \ldots \right] .$$

SORT-MERGE FILE:

<u>SD</u> file-name-1

$$
\left[\ \underline{\text{RECORD}}\ \left\{ \begin{array}{l} \text{CONTAINS integer-1 CHARACTERS} \\ \text{IS } \underline{\text{VARYING}} \text{ IN SIZE [[FROM integer-2] } [\underline{\text{TO}} \text{ integer-3]} \\ \qquad \text{CHARACTERS]} \ \ [\underline{\text{DEPENDING}} \text{ ON data-name-1]} \\ \text{CONTAINS integer-4 } \underline{\text{TO}} \text{ integer-5 CHARACTERS} \end{array} \right\}\ \right]
$$

$$
\left[\ \underline{\text{DATA}}\ \left\{ \begin{array}{l} \underline{\text{RECORD}} \text{ IS} \\ \underline{\text{RECORDS}} \text{ ARE} \end{array} \right\}\ \{\text{data-name-2}\} \ldots\ \right]\ .
$$

REPORT FILE:

<u>FD</u> file-name-1

    [IS <u>EXTERNAL</u>]

    [IS <u>GLOBAL</u>]

$$
\left[\ \underline{\text{BLOCK}} \text{ CONTAINS } [\text{integer-1 } \underline{\text{TO}}]\ \text{integer-2}\ \left\{ \begin{array}{l} \underline{\text{RECORDS}} \\ \text{CHARACTERS} \end{array} \right\}\ \right]
$$

$$
\left[\ \underline{\text{RECORD}}\ \left\{ \begin{array}{l} \text{CONTAINS integer-3 CHARACTERS} \\ \text{CONTAINS integer-4 } \underline{\text{TO}} \text{ integer-5 CHARACTERS} \end{array} \right\}\ \right]
$$

$$
\left[\ \underline{\text{LABEL}}\ \left\{ \begin{array}{l} \underline{\text{RECORD}} \text{ IS} \\ \underline{\text{RECORDS}} \text{ ARE} \end{array} \right\}\ \left\{ \begin{array}{l} \underline{\text{STANDARD}} \\ \underline{\text{OMITTED}} \end{array} \right\}\ \right]
$$

$$
\left[\ \underline{\text{VALUE}}\ \underline{\text{OF}}\ \left\{ \text{implementor-name-1 IS}\ \left\{ \begin{array}{l} \text{data-name-1} \\ \text{literal-1} \end{array} \right\} \right\} \ldots\ \right]
$$

    [<u>CODE-SET</u> IS alphabet-name-1]

$$
\left\{ \begin{array}{l} \underline{\text{REPORT}} \text{ IS} \\ \underline{\text{REPORTS}} \text{ ARE} \end{array} \right\}\ \{\text{report-name-1}\} \ldots\ \ .
$$

GENERAL DESCRIPTION FOR DATA DESCRIPTION ENTRY

FORMAT 1:

level-number $\begin{bmatrix} \text{data-name-1} \\ \text{FILLER} \end{bmatrix}$

[REDEFINES data-name-2]

[IS EXTERNAL]

[IS GLOBAL]

$\left[\left\{ \begin{array}{l} \text{PICTURE} \\ \text{PIC} \end{array} \right\} \text{IS character-string} \right]$

$\left[\text{[USAGE IS]} \left\{ \begin{array}{l} \text{BINARY} \\ \text{COMPUTATIONAL} \\ \text{COMP} \\ \text{DISPLAY} \\ \text{INDEX} \\ \text{PACKED-DECIMAL} \end{array} \right\} \right]$

$\left[\text{[SIGN IS]} \left\{ \begin{array}{l} \text{LEADING} \\ \text{TRAILING} \end{array} \right\} \text{[SEPARATE CHARACTER]} \right]$

$\left[\begin{array}{l} \text{OCCURS integer-2 TIMES} \\[4pt] \qquad \left[\left\{ \begin{array}{l} \text{ASCENDING} \\ \text{DESCENDING} \end{array} \right\} \text{KEY IS \{data-name-3\} ...} \right] \text{...} \\[8pt] \qquad \text{[INDEXED BY \{index-name-1\} ...]} \\[4pt] \text{OCCURS integer-1 TO integer-2 TIMES DEPENDING ON data-name-4} \\[4pt] \qquad \left[\left\{ \begin{array}{l} \text{ASCENDING} \\ \text{DESCENDING} \end{array} \right\} \text{KEY IS \{data-name-3\} ...} \right] \text{...} \\[8pt] \qquad \text{[INDEXED BY \{index-name-1\} ...]} \end{array} \right]$

$\left[\left\{ \begin{array}{l} \text{SYNCHRONIZED} \\ \text{SYNC} \end{array} \right\} \left[\begin{array}{l} \text{LEFT} \\ \text{RIGHT} \end{array} \right] \right]$

$\left[\left\{ \begin{array}{l} \text{JUSTIFIED} \\ \text{JUST} \end{array} \right\} \text{RIGHT} \right]$

[BLANK WHEN ZERO]

[VALUE IS literal-1] .

FORMAT 2:

66 data-name-1 <u>RENAMES</u> data-name-2 $\left[\left\{ \begin{array}{l} \underline{THROUGH} \\ \underline{THRU} \end{array} \right\} \text{data-name-3} \right]$.

FORMAT 3:

88 condition-name-1 $\left\{ \begin{array}{l} \underline{VALUE} \text{ IS} \\ \underline{VALUES} \text{ ARE} \end{array} \right\} \left\{ \text{literal-1} \left[\left\{ \begin{array}{l} \underline{THROUGH} \\ \underline{THRU} \end{array} \right\} \text{literal-2} \right] \right\} \ldots$.

GENERAL FORMAT FOR COMMUNICATION DESCRIPTION ENTRY

FORMAT 1:

<u>CD</u> cd-name-1

FOR [<u>INITIAL</u>] <u>INPUT</u>

$$\begin{bmatrix} \text{[[SYMBOLIC } \underline{QUEUE} \text{ IS data-name-1]} \\[6pt] \text{[SYMBOLIC } \underline{SUB\text{-}QUEUE\text{-}1} \text{ IS data-name-2]} \\[6pt] \text{[SYMBOLIC } \underline{SUB\text{-}QUEUE\text{-}2} \text{ IS data-name-3]} \\[6pt] \text{[SYMBOLIC } \underline{SUB\text{-}QUEUE\text{-}3} \text{ IS data-name-4]} \\[6pt] \text{[}\underline{MESSAGE} \underline{DATE} \text{ IS data-name-5]} \\[6pt] \text{[}\underline{MESSAGE} \underline{TIME} \text{ IS data-name-6]} \\[6pt] \text{[SYMBOLIC } \underline{SOURCE} \text{ IS data-name-7]} \\[6pt] \text{[}\underline{TEXT} \underline{LENGTH} \text{ IS data-name-8]} \\[6pt] \text{[}\underline{END} \underline{KEY} \text{ IS data-name-9]} \\[6pt] \text{[}\underline{STATUS} \underline{KEY} \text{ IS data-name-10]} \\[6pt] \text{[}\underline{MESSAGE} \underline{COUNT} \text{ IS data-name-11]]} \\[6pt] \text{[data-name-1, data-name-2, data-name-3,} \\ \text{data-name-4, data-name-5, data-name-6,} \\ \text{data-name-7, data-name-8, data-name-9,} \\ \text{data-name-10, data-name-11]} \end{bmatrix}$$

FORMAT 2:

CD cd-name-1 FOR OUTPUT

    [DESTINATION COUNT IS data-name-1]

    [TEXT LENGTH IS data-name-2]

    [STATUS KEY IS data-name-3]

    [DESTINATION TABLE OCCURS integer-1 TIMES

        [INDEXED BY {index-name-1} . . .]]

    [ERROR KEY IS data-name-4]

    [SYMBOLIC DESTINATION IS data-name-5].

FORMAT 3:

CD cd-name-1

$$
\text{FOR [INITIAL] I-0}
\begin{bmatrix}
\begin{bmatrix}
[\text{MESSAGE DATE IS data-name-1}] \\
[\text{MESSAGE TIME IS data-name-2}] \\
[\text{SYMBOLIC TERMINAL IS data-name-3}] \\
[\text{TEXT LENGTH IS data-name-4}] \\
[\text{END KEY IS data-name-5}] \\
[\text{STATUS KEY IS data-name-6}]
\end{bmatrix} \\
[\text{data-name-1, data-name-2, data-name-3,} \\
\text{data-name-4, data-name-5, data-name-6}]
\end{bmatrix}
$$

GENERAL FORMAT FOR REPORT DESCRIPTION ENTRY

RD report-name-1

    [IS GLOBAL]

    [CODE literal-1]

$$\left[\left\{ \begin{array}{l} \underline{CONTROL} \text{ IS} \\ \underline{CONTROLS} \text{ ARE} \end{array} \right\} \quad \left\{ \begin{array}{l} \{\text{data-name-1}\} \ldots \\ \underline{FINAL} \text{ [data-name-1]} \ldots \end{array} \right\} \right]$$

$$\left[\underline{PAGE} \left\{ \begin{array}{l} \text{LIMIT IS} \\ \text{LIMITS ARE} \end{array} \right\} \text{ integer-1} \left[\begin{array}{l} \text{LINE} \\ \text{LINES} \end{array} \right] \quad [\underline{HEADING} \text{ integer-2}] \right.$$

      [FIRST DETAIL integer-3] [LAST DETAIL integer-4]

$$\left. [\underline{FOOTING} \text{ integer-5}] \right] \quad .$$

GENERAL FORMAT FOR REPORT GROUP DESCRIPTION ENTRY

FORMAT 1:

01 [data-name-1]

$$\left[\underline{LINE} \text{ NUMBER IS} \left\{ \begin{array}{l} \text{integer-1 [ON } \underline{NEXT} \text{ PAGE]} \\ \underline{PLUS} \text{ integer-2} \end{array} \right\} \right]$$

$$\left[\underline{NEXT} \text{ GROUP IS} \left\{ \begin{array}{l} \text{integer-3} \\ \underline{PLUS} \text{ integer-4} \\ \underline{NEXT} \text{ PAGE} \end{array} \right\} \right]$$

$$\underline{TYPE} \text{ IS} \left[\begin{array}{l} \left\{ \begin{array}{l} \underline{REPORT} \underline{HEADING} \\ \underline{RH} \end{array} \right\} \\ \left\{ \begin{array}{l} \underline{PAGE} \underline{HEADING} \\ \underline{PH} \end{array} \right\} \\ \left\{ \begin{array}{l} \underline{CONTROL} \underline{HEADING} \\ \underline{CH} \end{array} \right\} \left\{ \begin{array}{l} \text{data-name-2} \\ \underline{FINAL} \end{array} \right\} \\ \left\{ \begin{array}{l} \underline{DETAIL} \\ \underline{DE} \end{array} \right\} \\ \left\{ \begin{array}{l} \underline{CONTROL} \underline{FOOTING} \\ \underline{CF} \end{array} \right\} \left\{ \begin{array}{l} \text{data-name-3} \\ \underline{FINAL} \end{array} \right\} \\ \left\{ \begin{array}{l} \underline{PAGE} \underline{FOOTING} \\ \underline{PF} \end{array} \right\} \\ \left\{ \begin{array}{l} \underline{REPORT} \underline{FOOTING} \\ \underline{RF} \end{array} \right\} \end{array} \right]$$

[[USAGE IS] DISPLAY].

FORMAT 2:

level-number [data-name-1]

$$\left[\underline{\text{LINE}} \text{ NUMBER IS} \quad \left\{ \begin{array}{l} \text{integer-1} \quad [\text{ON } \underline{\text{NEXT}} \underline{\text{PAGE}}] \\ \underline{\text{PLUS}} \text{ Integer-2} \end{array} \right\} \right]$$

[[<u>USAGE</u> IS] <u>DISPLAY</u>].

FORMAT 3:

level-number [data-name-1]

$$\left\{ \begin{array}{l} \underline{\text{PICTURE}} \\ \underline{\text{PIC}} \end{array} \right\} \text{ IS character-string}$$

[[<u>USAGE</u> IS] <u>DISPLAY</u>]

$$\left[[\underline{\text{SIGN}} \text{ IS}] \quad \left\{ \begin{array}{l} \underline{\text{LEADING}} \\ \underline{\text{TRAILING}} \end{array} \right\} \quad \underline{\text{SEPARATE}} \text{ CHARACTER} \right]$$

$$\left[\left\{ \begin{array}{l} \underline{\text{JUSTIFIED}} \\ \underline{\text{JUST}} \end{array} \right\} \text{ RIGHT} \right]$$

[<u>BLANK</u> WHEN <u>ZERO</u>]

$$\left[\underline{\text{LINE}} \text{ NUMBER IS} \quad \left\{ \begin{array}{l} \text{integer-1} \quad [\text{ON } \underline{\text{NEXT}} \underline{\text{PAGE}}] \\ \underline{\text{PLUS}} \text{ integer-2} \end{array} \right\} \right]$$

[<u>COLUMN</u> NUMBER IS integer-3]

$$\left\{ \begin{array}{l} \underline{\text{SOURCE}} \text{ IS identifier-1} \\[2ex] \underline{\text{VALUE}} \text{ IS literal-1} \\[2ex] \{\underline{\text{SUM}} \text{ \{identifier-2\}} \ldots [\underline{\text{UPON}} \text{ \{data-name-2\}} \ldots]\} \ldots \\ \qquad \left[\underline{\text{RESET}} \text{ ON} \quad \left\{ \begin{array}{l} \text{data-name-3} \\ \underline{\text{FINAL}} \end{array} \right\} \right] \end{array} \right\}$$

[<u>GROUP</u> INDICATE].

GENERAL FORMAT FOR PROCEDURE DIVSION

FORMAT 1:

[PROCEDURE DIVISION [USING {data-name-1} ...].

[DECLARATIVES.

{section-name SECTION [segment-number].

    USE statement.

[paragraph-name.

    [sentence] ...] ...} ...

END DECLARATIVES.]

{section-name SECTION [segment-number].

[paragraph-name.

    [sentence] ...] ... } ...]

FORMAT 2:

[PROCEDURE DIVISION [USING {data-name-1} ...].

{paragraph-name.

    [sentence] ... } ...]

GENERAL FORMAT FOR COBOL VERBS

ACCEPT identifier-1 [FROM mnemonic-name-1]

ACCEPT identifier-2 FROM $\begin{Bmatrix} \text{DATE} \\ \text{DAY} \\ \text{DAY-OF-WEEK} \\ \text{TIME} \end{Bmatrix}$

ACCEPT cd-name-1 MESSAGE COUNT

ADD $\begin{Bmatrix} \text{identifier-1} \\ \text{literal-1} \end{Bmatrix}$ ... TO {identifier-2 [ROUNDED]} ...

    [ON SIZE ERROR imperative-statement-1]

    [NOT ON SIZE ERROR imperative-statement-2]

    [END-ADD]

ADD $\begin{Bmatrix} \text{identifier-1} \\ \text{literal-1} \end{Bmatrix}$ ... TO $\begin{Bmatrix} \text{identifier-2} \\ \text{literal-2} \end{Bmatrix}$

    GIVING {identifier-3 [ROUNDED]} ...

    [ON SIZE ERROR imperative-statement-1]

    [NOT ON SIZE ERROR imperative-statement-2]

    [END-ADD]

ADD $\begin{Bmatrix} \text{CORRESPONDING} \\ \text{CORR} \end{Bmatrix}$ identifier-1 TO identifier-2 [ROUNDED]

    [ON SIZE ERROR imperative-statement-1]

    [NOT ON SIZE ERROR imperative-statement-2]

    [END-ADD]

ALTER {procedure-name-1 TO [PROCEED TO] procedure-name-2} ...

CALL $\left\{ \begin{array}{l} \text{identifier-1} \\ \text{literal-1} \end{array} \right\}$ $\left[\text{USING} \left\{ \begin{array}{l} \text{[BY REFERENCE] \{identifier-2\} ...} \\ \text{BY CONTENT \{identifier-2\} ...} \end{array} \right\} ... \right]$

    [ON OVERFLOW imperative-statement-1]

    [END-CALL]

CALL $\left\{ \begin{array}{l} \text{identifier-1} \\ \text{literal-1} \end{array} \right\}$ $\left[\text{USING} \left\{ \begin{array}{l} \text{[BY REFERENCE] \{identifier-2\} ...} \\ \text{BY CONTENT \{identifier-2\} ...} \end{array} \right\} ... \right]$

    [[ON EXCEPTION imperative-statement-1]

    [NOT ON EXCEPTION imperative-statement-2]

    [END-CALL]

CANCEL $\left\{ \begin{array}{l} \text{identifier-1} \\ \text{literal-1} \end{array} \right\}$

SW CLOSE $\left\{ \text{file-name-1} \left[\begin{array}{l} \left\{ \begin{array}{l} \underline{\text{REEL}} \\ \underline{\text{UNIT}} \end{array} \right\} \text{[FOR REMOVAL]} \\ \text{WITH} \left\{ \begin{array}{l} \underline{\text{NO REWIND}} \\ \underline{\text{LOCK}} \end{array} \right\} \end{array} \right] \right\} ...$

RI CLOSE file-name-1 [WITH LOCK]} ...

COMPUTE {identifier-1 [ROUNDED]} ... = arithmetic-expression-1

    [ON SIZE ERROR imperative-statement-1]

    [NOT ON SIZE ERROR imperative-statement-2]

    [END-COMPUTE]

CONTINUE

DELETE file-name-1 RECORD

    [INVALID KEY imperative-statement-1]

    [NOT INVALID KEY imperative-statement-2]

    [END-DELETE]

DISABLE $\left\{ \begin{array}{l} \text{INPUT [TERMINAL]} \\ \text{I-O TERMINAL} \\ \text{OUTPUT} \end{array} \right\}$ cd-name-1 $\left[\text{WITH KEY} \left\{ \begin{array}{l} \text{identifier-1} \\ \text{literal-1} \end{array} \right\} \right]$

DISPLAY $\left\{ \begin{array}{l} \text{identifier-1} \\ \text{literal-1} \end{array} \right\}$ ... [UPON mnemonic-name-1] [WITH NO ADVANCING]

DIVIDE $\left\{ \begin{array}{l} \text{identifier-1} \\ \text{literal-1} \end{array} \right\}$ INTO {identifier-2 [ROUNDED]} ...

    [ON SIZE ERROR imperative-statement-1]

    [NOT ON SIZE ERROR imperative-statement-2]

    [END-DIVIDE]

DIVIDE $\left\{ \begin{array}{l} \text{identifier-1} \\ \text{literal-1} \end{array} \right\}$ INTO $\left\{ \begin{array}{l} \text{identifier-2} \\ \text{literal-2} \end{array} \right\}$

    GIVING {identifier-3 [ROUNDED]} ...

    [ON SIZE ERROR imperative-statement-1]

    [NOT ON SIZE ERROR imperative-statement-2]

    [END-DIVIDE]

DIVIDE $\left\{ \begin{array}{l} \text{identifier-1} \\ \text{literal-1} \end{array} \right\}$ BY $\left\{ \begin{array}{l} \text{identifier-2} \\ \text{literal-2} \end{array} \right\}$

    GIVING {identifier-3 [ROUNDED]} ...

    [ON SIZE ERROR imperative-statement-1]

    [NOT ON SIZE ERROR imperative-statement-2]

    [END-DIVIDE]

DIVIDE $\left\{ \begin{array}{l} \text{identifier-1} \\ \text{literal-1} \end{array} \right\}$ INTO $\left\{ \begin{array}{l} \text{identifier-2} \\ \text{literal-2} \end{array} \right\}$ GIVING identifier-3 [ROUNDED]

    REMAINDER identifier-4

    [ON SIZE ERROR imperative-statement-1]

    [NOT ON SIZE ERROR imperative-statement-2]

    [END-DIVIDE]

DIVIDE $\left\{ \begin{array}{l} \text{identifier-1} \\ \text{literal-1} \end{array} \right\}$ BY $\left\{ \begin{array}{l} \text{identifier-2} \\ \text{literal-2} \end{array} \right\}$ GIVING identifier-3 [ROUNDED]

    REMAINDER identifier-4

    [ON SIZE ERROR imperative-statement-1]

    [NOT ON SIZE ERROR imperative-statement-2]

    [END-DIVIDE]

ENABLE $\left\{ \begin{array}{l} \text{INPUT [TERMINAL]} \\ \text{I-O TERMINAL} \\ \text{OUTPUT} \end{array} \right\}$ cd-name-1 $\left[\text{WITH KEY} \left\{ \begin{array}{l} \text{identifier-1} \\ \text{literal-1} \end{array} \right\} \right]$

ENTER language-name-1 [routine-name-1].

$$\text{EVALUATE} \begin{Bmatrix} \text{identifier-1} \\ \text{literal-1} \\ \text{expression-1} \\ \underline{\text{TRUE}} \\ \underline{\text{FALSE}} \end{Bmatrix} \begin{bmatrix} \underline{\text{ALSO}} \begin{Bmatrix} \text{identifier-2} \\ \text{literal-2} \\ \text{expression-2} \\ \underline{\text{TRUE}} \\ \underline{\text{FALSE}} \end{Bmatrix} \end{bmatrix} \dots$$

$\{\{\underline{\text{WHEN}}$

$$\begin{Bmatrix} \underline{\text{ANY}} \\ \text{condition-1} \\ \underline{\text{TRUE}} \\ \underline{\text{FALSE}} \\ [\underline{\text{NOT}}] \begin{Bmatrix} \text{identifier-3} \\ \text{literal-3} \\ \text{arithmetic-expression-1} \end{Bmatrix} \begin{bmatrix} \begin{Bmatrix} \underline{\text{THROUGH}} \\ \underline{\text{THRU}} \end{Bmatrix} \begin{Bmatrix} \text{identifier-4} \\ \text{literal-4} \\ \text{arithmetic-expression-2} \end{Bmatrix} \end{bmatrix} \end{Bmatrix}$$

$[\underline{\text{ALSO}}$

$$\begin{Bmatrix} \underline{\text{ANY}} \\ \text{condition-2} \\ \underline{\text{TRUE}} \\ \underline{\text{FALSE}} \\ [\underline{\text{NOT}}] \begin{Bmatrix} \text{identifier-5} \\ \text{literal-5} \\ \text{arithmetic-expression-3} \end{Bmatrix} \begin{bmatrix} \begin{Bmatrix} \underline{\text{THROUGH}} \\ \underline{\text{THRU}} \end{Bmatrix} \begin{Bmatrix} \text{identifier-6} \\ \text{literal-6} \\ \text{arithmetic-expression-4} \end{Bmatrix} \end{bmatrix} \end{Bmatrix} \dots \} \dots$$

imperative-statement-1

[WHEN OTHER imperative-statement-2]

[END-EVALUATE]

EXIT

EXIT PROGRAM

$$\underline{\text{GENERATE}} \begin{Bmatrix} \text{data-name-1} \\ \text{report-name-1} \end{Bmatrix}$$

GO TO [procedure-name-1]

GO TO {procedure-name-1} ... DEPENDING ON identifier-1

IF condition-1 THEN $\left\{ \begin{array}{l} \{\text{statement-1}\} \ ... \\ \underline{\text{NEXT}} \ \underline{\text{SENTENCE}} \end{array} \right\}$ $\left\{ \begin{array}{l} \underline{\text{ELSE}} \ \{\text{statement-2}\} \ ... \ [\underline{\text{END-IF}}] \\ \underline{\text{ELSE}} \ \underline{\text{NEXT}} \ \underline{\text{SENTENCE}} \\ \underline{\text{END-IF}} \end{array} \right\}$

$\underline{\text{INITIALIZE}}$ {identifier-1} ...

$$\left[\underline{\text{REPLACING}} \left\{ \left\{ \begin{array}{l} \underline{\text{ALPHABETIC}} \\ \underline{\text{ALPHANUMERIC}} \\ \underline{\text{NUMERIC}} \\ \underline{\text{ALPHANUMERIC-EDITED}} \\ \underline{\text{NUMERIC-EDITED}} \end{array} \right\} \text{DATA} \ \underline{\text{BY}} \ \left\{ \begin{array}{l} \text{identifier-2} \\ \text{literal-1} \end{array} \right\} \right\} ... \right]$$

$\underline{\text{INITIATE}}$ {report-name-1} ...

$\underline{\text{INSPECT}}$ identifier-1 $\underline{\text{TALLYING}}$

$$\left\{ \left\{ \text{identifier-2} \ \underline{\text{FOR}} \left\{ \begin{array}{l} \underline{\text{CHARACTERS}} \left[\left\{ \begin{array}{l} \underline{\text{BEFORE}} \\ \underline{\text{AFTER}} \end{array} \right\} \text{INITIAL} \left\{ \begin{array}{l} \text{identifier-4} \\ \text{literal-2} \end{array} \right\} \right] ... \\ \left\{ \begin{array}{l} \underline{\text{ALL}} \\ \underline{\text{LEADING}} \end{array} \right\} \left\{ \left\{ \begin{array}{l} \text{identifier-3} \\ \text{literal-1} \end{array} \right\} \left[\left\{ \begin{array}{l} \underline{\text{BEFORE}} \\ \underline{\text{AFTER}} \end{array} \right\} \text{INITIAL} \left\{ \begin{array}{l} \text{identifier-4} \\ \text{literal-2} \end{array} \right\} \right] ... \right\} ... \end{array} \right\} ... \right\} ... \right\}$$

$\underline{\text{INSPECT}}$ identifier-1 $\underline{\text{REPLACING}}$

$$\left\{ \begin{array}{l} \underline{\text{CHARACTERS}} \ \underline{\text{BY}} \left\{ \begin{array}{l} \text{identifier-5} \\ \text{literal-3} \end{array} \right\} \left[\left\{ \begin{array}{l} \underline{\text{BEFORE}} \\ \underline{\text{AFTER}} \end{array} \right\} \text{INITIAL} \left\{ \begin{array}{l} \text{identifier-4} \\ \text{literal-2} \end{array} \right\} \right] ... \\ \left\{ \begin{array}{l} \underline{\text{ALL}} \\ \underline{\text{LEADING}} \\ \underline{\text{FIRST}} \end{array} \right\} \left\{ \left\{ \begin{array}{l} \text{identifier-3} \\ \text{literal-1} \end{array} \right\} \underline{\text{BY}} \left\{ \begin{array}{l} \text{identifier-5} \\ \text{literal-3} \end{array} \right\} \left[\left\{ \begin{array}{l} \underline{\text{BEFORE}} \\ \underline{\text{AFTER}} \end{array} \right\} \text{INITIAL} \left\{ \begin{array}{l} \text{identifier-4} \\ \text{literal-2} \end{array} \right\} \right] ... \right\} ... \end{array} \right\} ...$$

INSPECT identifier-1 TALLYING

$$
\left\{ \begin{array}{l} \text{identifier-2 } \underline{\text{FOR}} \left\{ \begin{array}{l} \underline{\text{CHARACTERS}} \left[\left\{ \begin{array}{l} \underline{\text{BEFORE}} \\ \underline{\text{AFTER}} \end{array} \right\} \text{INITIAL} \left\{ \begin{array}{l} \text{identifier-4} \\ \text{literal-2} \end{array} \right\} \right] \ldots \\ \left\{ \begin{array}{l} \underline{\text{ALL}} \\ \underline{\text{LEADING}} \end{array} \right\} \left\{ \left\{ \begin{array}{l} \text{identifier-3} \\ \text{literal-1} \end{array} \right\} \left[\left\{ \begin{array}{l} \underline{\text{BEFORE}} \\ \underline{\text{AFTER}} \end{array} \right\} \text{INITIAL} \left\{ \begin{array}{l} \text{identifier-4} \\ \text{literal-2} \end{array} \right\} \right] \ldots \right\} \ldots \end{array} \right\} \ldots \right\} \ldots
$$

REPLACING

$$
\left\{ \begin{array}{l} \underline{\text{CHARACTERS}} \; \underline{\text{BY}} \left\{ \begin{array}{l} \text{identifier-5} \\ \text{literal-3} \end{array} \right\} \left[\left\{ \begin{array}{l} \underline{\text{BEFORE}} \\ \underline{\text{AFTER}} \end{array} \right\} \text{INITIAL} \left\{ \begin{array}{l} \text{identifier-4} \\ \text{literal-2} \end{array} \right\} \right] \ldots \\ \left\{ \begin{array}{l} \underline{\text{ALL}} \\ \underline{\text{LEADING}} \\ \underline{\text{FIRST}} \end{array} \right\} \left\{ \left\{ \begin{array}{l} \text{identifier-3} \\ \text{literal-1} \end{array} \right\} \underline{\text{BY}} \left\{ \begin{array}{l} \text{identifier-5} \\ \text{literal-3} \end{array} \right\} \left[\left\{ \begin{array}{l} \underline{\text{BEFORE}} \\ \underline{\text{AFTER}} \end{array} \right\} \text{INITIAL} \left\{ \begin{array}{l} \text{identifier-4} \\ \text{literal-2} \end{array} \right\} \right] \ldots \right\} \ldots \end{array} \right\} \ldots
$$

INSPECT identifier-1 $\underline{\text{CONVERTING}}$ $\left\{ \begin{array}{l} \text{identifier-6} \\ \text{literal-4} \end{array} \right\}$ $\underline{\text{TO}}$ $\left\{ \begin{array}{l} \text{identifier-7} \\ \text{literal-5} \end{array} \right\}$

$$
\left[\left\{ \begin{array}{l} \underline{\text{BEFORE}} \\ \underline{\text{AFTER}} \end{array} \right\} \text{INITIAL} \left\{ \begin{array}{l} \text{identifier-4} \\ \text{literal-2} \end{array} \right\} \right] \ldots
$$

$\underline{\text{MERGE}}$ file-name-1 $\left\{ \text{ON} \left\{ \begin{array}{l} \underline{\text{ASCENDING}} \\ \underline{\text{DESCENDING}} \end{array} \right\} \text{KEY \{data-name-1\}} \ldots \right\} \ldots$

[COLLATING $\underline{\text{SEQUENCE}}$ IS alphabet-name-1]

$\underline{\text{USING}}$ file-name-2 {file-name-3} ...

$$
\left\{ \begin{array}{l} \underline{\text{OUTPUT}} \; \underline{\text{PROCEDURE}} \text{ IS procedure-name-1} \left[\left\{ \begin{array}{l} \underline{\text{THROUGH}} \\ \underline{\text{THRU}} \end{array} \right\} \text{procedure-name-2} \right] \\ \underline{\text{GIVING}} \; \{\text{file-name-4}\} \ldots \end{array} \right\}
$$

$\underline{\text{MOVE}}$ $\left\{ \begin{array}{l} \text{identifier-1} \\ \text{literal-1} \end{array} \right\}$ $\underline{\text{TO}}$ {identifier-2} ...

$\underline{\text{MOVE}}$ $\left\{ \begin{array}{l} \underline{\text{CORRESPONDING}} \\ \underline{\text{CORR}} \end{array} \right\}$ identifier-1 $\underline{\text{TO}}$ identifier-2

$\underline{\text{MULTIPLY}} \left\{ \begin{array}{l} \text{identifier-1} \\ \text{literal-1} \end{array} \right\} \underline{\text{BY}} \text{ \{identifier-2 [\underline{ROUNDED}]\} } \dots$

    [ON $\underline{\text{SIZE}}$ $\underline{\text{ERROR}}$ imperative-statement-1]

    [$\underline{\text{NOT}}$ ON $\underline{\text{SIZE}}$ $\underline{\text{ERROR}}$ imperative-statement-2]

    [$\underline{\text{END-MULTIPLY}}$]

$\underline{\text{MULTIPLY}} \left\{ \begin{array}{l} \text{identifier-1} \\ \text{literal-1} \end{array} \right\} \underline{\text{BY}} \left\{ \begin{array}{l} \text{identifier-2} \\ \text{literal-2} \end{array} \right\}$

    $\underline{\text{GIVING}}$ \{identifier-3 [$\underline{\text{ROUNDED}}$]\} $\dots$

    [ON $\underline{\text{SIZE}}$ $\underline{\text{ERROR}}$ imperative-statement-1]

    [$\underline{\text{NOT}}$ ON $\underline{\text{SIZE}}$ $\underline{\text{ERROR}}$ imperative-statement-2]

    [$\underline{\text{END-MULTIPLY}}$]

$S \underline{\text{OPEN}} \left\{ \begin{array}{l} \underline{\text{INPUT}} \left\{ \text{file-name-1} \left[\begin{array}{l} \underline{\text{REVERSED}} \\ \text{WITH } \underline{\text{NO}} \text{ } \underline{\text{REWIND}} \end{array} \right] \right\} \dots \\ \underline{\text{OUTPUT}} \text{ \{file-name-2 [WITH } \underline{\text{NO}} \text{ } \underline{\text{REWIND}}\text{]\} } \dots \\ \underline{\text{I-O}} \text{ \{file-name-3\} } \dots \\ \underline{\text{EXTEND}} \text{ \{file-name-4\} } \dots \end{array} \right\} \dots$

$RI \underline{\text{OPEN}} \left\{ \begin{array}{l} \underline{\text{INPUT}} \text{ \{file-name-1\} } \dots \\ \underline{\text{OUTPUT}} \text{ \{file-name-2\} } \dots \\ \underline{\text{I-O}} \text{ \{file-name-3\} } \dots \\ \underline{\text{EXTEND}} \text{ \{file-name-4\} } \dots \end{array} \right\} \dots$

$W \underline{\text{OPEN}} \left\{ \begin{array}{l} \underline{\text{OUTPUT}} \text{ \{file-name-1 [WITH } \underline{\text{NO}} \text{ } \underline{\text{REWIND}}\text{]\} } \dots \\ \underline{\text{EXTEND}} \text{ \{file-name-2\} } \dots \end{array} \right\} \dots$

PERFORM $\left[\text{procedure-name-1} \left[\left\{ \begin{array}{c} \underline{\text{THROUGH}} \\ \underline{\text{THRU}} \end{array} \right\} \text{procedure-name-2} \right] \right]$

   [imperative-statement-1 <u>END-PERFORM</u>]

PERFORM $\left[\text{procedure-name-1} \left[\left\{ \begin{array}{c} \underline{\text{THROUGH}} \\ \underline{\text{THRU}} \end{array} \right\} \text{procedure-name-2} \right] \right]$

$\left\{ \begin{array}{c} \text{identifier-1} \\ \text{integer-1} \end{array} \right\}$ <u>TIMES</u> [imperative-statement-1 <u>END-PERFORM</u>]

PERFORM $\left[\text{procedure-name-1} \left[\left\{ \begin{array}{c} \underline{\text{THROUGH}} \\ \underline{\text{THRU}} \end{array} \right\} \text{procedure-name-2} \right] \right]$

$\left[\text{WITH} \underline{\text{TEST}} \left\{ \begin{array}{c} \underline{\text{BEFORE}} \\ \underline{\text{AFTER}} \end{array} \right\} \right]$ <u>UNTIL</u> condition-1

   [imperative-statement-1 <u>END-PERFORM</u>]

PERFORM $\left[\text{procedure-name-1} \left[\left\{ \begin{array}{c} \underline{\text{THROUGH}} \\ \underline{\text{THRU}} \end{array} \right\} \text{procedure-name-2} \right] \right]$

$\left[\text{WITH} \underline{\text{TEST}} \left\{ \begin{array}{c} \underline{\text{BEFORE}} \\ \underline{\text{AFTER}} \end{array} \right\} \right]$

   <u>VARYING</u> $\left\{ \begin{array}{c} \text{identifier-2} \\ \text{index-name-1} \end{array} \right\}$ <u>FROM</u> $\left\{ \begin{array}{c} \text{identifier-3} \\ \text{index-name-2} \\ \text{literal-1} \end{array} \right\}$

   <u>BY</u> $\left\{ \begin{array}{c} \text{identifier-4} \\ \text{literal-2} \end{array} \right\}$ <u>UNTIL</u> condition-1

$\left[\underline{\text{AFTER}} \left\{ \begin{array}{c} \text{identifier-5} \\ \text{literal-3} \end{array} \right\} \underline{\text{FROM}} \left\{ \begin{array}{c} \text{identifier-6} \\ \text{index-name-3} \\ \text{literal-3} \end{array} \right\} \right.$

   $\left. \underline{\text{BY}} \left\{ \begin{array}{c} \text{identifier-7} \\ \text{literal-4} \end{array} \right\} \underline{\text{UNTIL}} \text{ condition-2} \right]$ ...

   [imperative-statement-1 <u>END-PERFORM</u>]

<u>PURGE</u> cd-name-1

SRI <u>READ</u> file-name-1 [<u>NEXT</u>] RECORD [<u>INTO</u> identifier-1]

    [AT <u>END</u> imperative-statement-1]

    [<u>NOT</u> AT <u>END</u> imperative-statement-2]

    [<u>END-READ</u>]

R <u>READ</u> file-name-1 RECORD [<u>INTO</u> identifier-1]

    [<u>INVALID</u> KEY imperative-statement-3]

    [<u>NOT</u> <u>INVALID</u> KEY imperative-statement-4]

    [<u>END-READ</u>]

I <u>READ</u> file-name-1 RECORD [<u>INTO</u> identifier-1]

    [<u>KEY</u> IS data-name-1]

    [<u>INVALID</u> KEY imperative-statement-3]

    [<u>NOT</u> <u>INVALID</u> KEY imperative-statement-4]

    [<u>END-READ</u>]

<u>RECEIVE</u> cd-name-1 $\left\{ \begin{array}{c} \underline{\text{MESSAGE}} \\ \underline{\text{SEGMENT}} \end{array} \right\}$ <u>INTO</u> identifier-1

    [<u>NO</u> <u>DATA</u> imperative-statement-1]

    [WITH <u>DATA</u> imperative-statement-2]

    [<u>END-RECEIVE</u>]

<u>RELEASE</u> record-name-1 [<u>FROM</u> identifier-1]

<u>RETURN</u> file-name-1 RECORD [<u>INTO</u> identifier-1]

    AT <u>END</u> imperative-statement-1

    [<u>NOT</u> AT <u>END</u> imperative-statement-2]

    [<u>END-RETURN</u>]

S <u>REWRITE</u> record-name-1 [<u>FROM</u> identifier-1]

RI <u>REWRITE</u> record-name-1 [<u>FROM</u> identifier-1]

    [<u>INVALID</u> KEY imperative-statement-1]

    [<u>NOT</u> <u>INVALID</u> KEY imperative-statement-2]

    [<u>END-REWRITE</u>]

$$\underline{\text{SEARCH}} \ \text{identifier-1} \ \left[\ \underline{\text{VARYING}} \ \left\{ \begin{array}{l} \text{identifier-2} \\ \text{index-name-1} \end{array} \right\} \right]$$

    [AT <u>END</u> imperative-statement-1]

$$\left\{ \ \underline{\text{WHEN}} \ \text{condition-1} \ \left\{ \begin{array}{l} \text{imperative-statement-2} \\ \underline{\text{NEXT}} \ \underline{\text{SENTENCE}} \end{array} \right\} \right\} \ \cdots$$

    [<u>END-SEARCH</u>]

<u>SEARCH</u> <u>ALL</u> identifier-1 [AT <u>END</u> imperative-statement-1]

$$\underline{\text{WHEN}} \left\{ \begin{array}{l} \text{data-name-1} \left\{ \begin{array}{l} \text{IS} \ \underline{\text{EQUAL}} \ \text{TO} \\ \text{IS} = \end{array} \right\} \left\{ \begin{array}{l} \text{identifier-3} \\ \text{literal-1} \\ \text{arithmetic-expression-1} \end{array} \right\} \\ \text{condition-name-1} \end{array} \right\}$$

$$\left[\ \underline{\text{AND}} \left\{ \begin{array}{l} \text{data-name-2} \left\{ \begin{array}{l} \text{IS} \ \underline{\text{EQUAL}} \ \text{TO} \\ \text{IS} = \end{array} \right\} \left\{ \begin{array}{l} \text{identifier-4} \\ \text{literal-2} \\ \text{arithmetic-expression-2} \end{array} \right\} \\ \text{condition-name-2} \end{array} \right\} \right] \ \cdots$$

$$\left\{ \begin{array}{l} \text{imperative-statement-2} \\ \underline{\text{NEXT}} \ \underline{\text{SENTENCE}} \end{array} \right\}$$

    [<u>END-SEARCH</u>]

<u>SEND</u> cd-name-1 <u>FROM</u> identifier-1

$$
\underline{\text{SEND}} \text{ cd-name-1 } [\underline{\text{FROM}} \text{ identifier-1}]
\left\{
\begin{array}{l}
\text{WITH identifier-2} \\
\text{WITH } \underline{\text{ESI}} \\
\text{WITH } \underline{\text{EMI}} \\
\text{WITH } \underline{\text{EGI}}
\end{array}
\right\}
$$

$$
\left[
\left\{
\begin{array}{l}
\underline{\text{BEFORE}} \\
\underline{\text{AFTER}}
\end{array}
\right\}
\text{ ADVANCING }
\left\{
\begin{array}{l}
\left\{
\begin{array}{l}
\text{identifier-3} \\
\text{integer-1}
\end{array}
\right\}
\left[
\begin{array}{l}
\text{LINE} \\
\text{LINES}
\end{array}
\right] \\
\left\{
\begin{array}{l}
\text{mnemonic-name-1} \\
\underline{\text{PAGE}}
\end{array}
\right\}
\end{array}
\right\}
\right]
$$

[REPLACING LINE]

$$
\underline{\text{SET}}
\left\{
\begin{array}{l}
\text{index-name-1} \\
\text{identifier-1}
\end{array}
\right\}
\cdots
\underline{\text{TO}}
\left\{
\begin{array}{l}
\text{index-name-2} \\
\text{identifier-2} \\
\text{integer-1}
\end{array}
\right\}
$$

$$
\underline{\text{SET}} \text{ \{index-name-3\} } \cdots
\left\{
\begin{array}{l}
\underline{\text{UP}} \text{ BY} \\
\underline{\text{DOWN}} \text{ BY}
\end{array}
\right\}
\left\{
\begin{array}{l}
\text{identifier-3} \\
\text{integer-2}
\end{array}
\right\}
$$

$$
\underline{\text{SET}}
\left\{
\text{\{mnemonic-name-1\} } \cdots \underline{\text{TO}}
\left\{
\begin{array}{l}
\underline{\text{ON}} \\
\underline{\text{OFF}}
\end{array}
\right\}
\right\}
\cdots
$$

$$
\underline{\text{SET}} \text{ \{condition-name-1\} } \cdots \quad \underline{\text{TO}} \underline{\text{TRUE}}
$$

$$
\underline{\text{SORT}} \text{ file-name-1 }
\left\{
\underline{\text{ON}}
\left\{
\begin{array}{l}
\underline{\text{ASCENDING}} \\
\underline{\text{DESCENDING}}
\end{array}
\right\}
\text{ KEY \{data-name-1\} } \cdots
\right\}
\cdots
$$

[WITH DUPLICATES IN ORDER]

[COLLATING SEQUENCE IS alphabet-name-1]

$$
\left\{
\begin{array}{l}
\underline{\text{INPUT}} \text{ PROCEDURE IS procedure-name-1}
\left[
\left\{
\begin{array}{l}
\underline{\text{THROUGH}} \\
\underline{\text{THRU}}
\end{array}
\right\}
\text{procedure-name-2}
\right] \\
\underline{\text{USING}} \text{ \{file-name-2\} } \cdots
\end{array}
\right\}
$$

$$
\left\{
\begin{array}{l}
\underline{\text{OUTPUT}} \text{ PROCEDURE IS procedure-name-3}
\left[
\left\{
\begin{array}{l}
\underline{\text{THROUGH}} \\
\underline{\text{THRU}}
\end{array}
\right\}
\text{procedure-name-4}
\right] \\
\underline{\text{GIVING}} \text{ \{file-name-3\} } \cdots
\end{array}
\right\}
$$

$$
\underline{\text{START}} \text{ file-name-1} \left[\underline{\text{KEY}} \left\{ \begin{array}{l} \text{IS } \underline{\text{EQUAL}} \text{ TO} \\ \text{IS } = \\ \text{IS } \underline{\text{GREATER}} \text{ THAN} \\ \text{IS } > \\ \text{IS } \underline{\text{NOT}} \text{ } \underline{\text{LESS}} \text{ THAN} \\ \text{IS } \underline{\text{NOT}} \text{ } < \\ \text{IS } \underline{\text{GREATER}} \text{ THAN } \underline{\text{OR}} \text{ } \underline{\text{EQUAL}} \text{ TO} \\ \text{IS } >= \end{array} \right\} \text{data-name-1} \right]
$$

[INVALID KEY imperative-statement-1]

[NOT INVALID KEY imperative-statement-2]

[END-START]

$$
\underline{\text{STOP}} \left\{ \begin{array}{l} \underline{\text{RUN}} \\ \text{literal-1} \end{array} \right\}
$$

$$
\underline{\text{STRING}} \quad \left\{ \left\{ \begin{array}{l} \text{identifier-1} \\ \text{literal-1} \end{array} \right\} \cdots \underline{\text{DELIMITED}} \text{ BY} \left\{ \begin{array}{l} \text{identifier-2} \\ \text{literal-2} \\ \underline{\text{SIZE}} \end{array} \right\} \right\} \cdots
$$

INTO identifier-3

[WITH POINTER identifier-4]

[ON OVERFLOW imperative-statement-1]

[NOT ON OVERFLOW imperative-statement-2]

[END-STRING]

$$
\underline{\text{SUBTRACT}} \quad \left\{ \begin{array}{l} \text{identifier-1} \\ \text{literal-1} \end{array} \right\} \cdots \underline{\text{FROM}} \quad \{\text{identifier-3 } [\underline{\text{ROUNDED}}]\} \cdots
$$

[ON SIZE ERROR imperative-statement-1]

[NOT ON SIZE ERROR imperative-statement-2]

[END-SUBTRACT]

SUBTRACT $\left\{ \begin{array}{l} \text{identifier-1} \\ \text{literal-1} \end{array} \right\}$ .... <u>FROM</u> $\left\{ \begin{array}{l} \text{identifier-2} \\ \text{literal-2} \end{array} \right\}$

    <u>GIVING</u> {identifier-3 [<u>ROUNDED</u>]} ...

    [ON <u>SIZE</u> <u>ERROR</u> imperative-statement-1]

    [<u>NOT</u> ON <u>SIZE</u> <u>ERROR</u> imperative-statement-2]

    [<u>END-SUBTRACT</u>]

SUBTRACT $\left\{ \begin{array}{l} \underline{\text{CORRESPONDING}} \\ \underline{\text{CORR}} \end{array} \right\}$ identifier-1 <u>FROM</u> identifier-2 [<u>ROUNDED</u>]

    [<u>ON</u> <u>SIZE</u> <u>ERROR</u> imperative-statement-1]

    [<u>NOT</u> ON <u>SIZE</u> <u>ERROR</u> imperative-statement-2]

    [<u>END-SUBTRACT</u>]

<u>SUPPRESS</u> PRINTING

<u>TERMINATE</u> {report-name-1} ...

<u>UNSTRING</u> identifier-1

    $\left[\underline{\text{DELIMITED}} \text{ BY } [\underline{\text{ALL}}] \left\{ \begin{array}{l} \text{identifier-2} \\ \text{literal-1} \end{array} \right\} \left[\underline{\text{OR}} \ [\underline{\text{ALL}}] \left\{ \begin{array}{l} \text{identifier-3} \\ \text{literal-2} \end{array} \right\} \right] \right]$ ...

    <u>INTO</u> {identifier-4 [<u>DELIMITER</u> IN identifier-5] [<u>COUNT</u> IN identifier-6]} ...

    [WITH <u>POINTER</u> identifier-7]

    [<u>TALLYING</u> IN identifier-8]

    [ON <u>OVERFLOW</u> imperative-statement-1]

    [<u>NOT</u> ON <u>OVERFLOW</u> imperative-statement-2]

    [<u>END-UNSTRING</u>]

SRI <u>USE</u> [<u>GLOBAL</u>] <u>AFTER</u> STANDARD

$$
\left\{ \begin{array}{l} \underline{\text{EXCEPTION}} \\ \underline{\text{ERROR}} \end{array} \right\} \underline{\text{PROCEDURE}} \text{ ON} \left\{ \begin{array}{l} \{\text{file-name-1}\} \ \dots \\ \underline{\text{INPUT}} \\ \underline{\text{OUTPUT}} \\ \underline{\text{I-O}} \\ \underline{\text{EXTEND}} \end{array} \right\}
$$

W <u>USE</u> <u>AFTER</u> STANDARD $\left\{ \begin{array}{l} \underline{\text{EXCEPTION}} \\ \underline{\text{ERROR}} \end{array} \right\}$ <u>PROCEDURE</u> ON $\left\{ \begin{array}{l} \{\text{file-name-1}\} \ \dots \\ \underline{\text{OUTPUT}} \\ \underline{\text{EXTEND}} \end{array} \right\}$

<u>USE</u> [<u>GLOBAL</u>] <u>BEFORE</u> <u>REPORTING</u> identifier-1

$$
\underline{\text{USE}} \text{ FOR } \underline{\text{DEBUGGING}} \text{ ON} \left\{ \begin{array}{l} \text{cd-name-1} \\ [\underline{\text{ALL}} \ \text{REFERENCES OF}] \ \text{identifier-1} \\ \text{file-name-1} \\ \text{procedure-name-1} \\ \underline{\text{ALL}} \ \underline{\text{PROCEDURES}} \end{array} \right\} \quad \dots
$$

S <u>WRITE</u> record-name-1 [<u>FROM</u> identifier-1]

$$
\left[\left\{ \begin{array}{l} \underline{\text{BEFORE}} \\ \underline{\text{AFTER}} \end{array} \right\} \text{ ADVANCING} \left\{ \begin{array}{l} \left\{ \begin{array}{l} \text{identifier-2} \\ \text{integer-1} \end{array} \right\} \left\{ \begin{array}{l} \text{LINE} \\ \text{LINES} \end{array} \right\} \\ \left\{ \begin{array}{l} \text{mnemonic-name-1} \\ \underline{\text{PAGE}} \end{array} \right\} \end{array} \right\} \right]
$$

$$
\left[\text{ AT } \left\{ \begin{array}{l} \underline{\text{END-OF-PAGE}} \\ \underline{\text{EOP}} \end{array} \right\} \text{ imperative-statement-1} \right]
$$

$$
\left[\underline{\text{NOT}} \text{ AT } \left\{ \begin{array}{l} \underline{\text{END-OF-PAGE}} \\ \underline{\text{EOP}} \end{array} \right\} \text{ imperative-statement-2} \right]
$$

[<u>END-WRITE</u>]

RI <u>WRITE</u> record-name-1 [<u>FROM</u> identifier-1]

[<u>INVALID</u> KEY imperative-statement-1]

[<u>NOT</u> <u>INVALID</u> KEY imperative-statement-2]

[<u>END-WRITE</u>]

GENERAL FORMAT FOR COPY AND REPLACE STATEMENTS

$$\underline{\text{COPY}} \text{ text-name-1} \left[\left\{ \begin{array}{c} \underline{\text{OF}} \\ \underline{\text{IN}} \end{array} \right\} \text{library-name-1} \right]$$

$$\left[\underline{\text{REPLACING}} \left\{ \left\{ \begin{array}{l} \text{==pseudo-text-1==} \\ \text{identifier-1} \\ \text{literal-1} \\ \text{word-1} \end{array} \right\} \underline{\text{BY}} \left\{ \begin{array}{l} \text{==pseudo-text-2==} \\ \text{identifier-2} \\ \text{literal-2} \\ \text{word-2} \end{array} \right\} \right\} \dots \right]$$

$$\underline{\text{REPLACE}} \; \{\text{==pseudo-text-1==} \; \underline{\text{BY}} \; \text{==pseudo-text-2==}\} \; \dots$$

$$\underline{\text{REPLACE}} \; \underline{\text{OFF}}$$

GENERAL FORMAT FOR CONDITIONS

RELATION CONDITION:

$$\left\{ \begin{array}{l} \text{identifier-1} \\ \text{literal-1} \\ \text{arithmetic-expression-1} \\ \text{index-name-1} \end{array} \right\} \left\{ \begin{array}{l} \text{IS [\underline{NOT}] \underline{GREATER} THAN} \\ \text{IS [\underline{NOT}] >} \\ \text{IS [\underline{NOT}] \underline{LESS} THAN} \\ \text{IS [\underline{NOT}] <} \\ \text{IS [\underline{NOT}] \underline{EQUAL} TO} \\ \text{IS [\underline{NOT}] =} \\ \text{IS \underline{GREATER} THAN \underline{OR} \underline{EQUAL} TO} \\ \text{IS >=} \\ \text{IS \underline{LESS} THAN \underline{OR} \underline{EQUAL} TO} \\ \text{IS <=} \end{array} \right\} \left\{ \begin{array}{l} \text{identifier-2} \\ \text{literal-2} \\ \text{arithmetic-expression-2} \\ \text{index-name-2} \end{array} \right\}$$

CLASS CONDITION:

$$\text{identifier-1 IS [\underline{NOT}]} \left\{ \begin{array}{l} \underline{\text{NUMERIC}} \\ \underline{\text{ALPHABETIC}} \\ \underline{\text{ALPHABETIC-LOWER}} \\ \underline{\text{ALPHABETIC-UPPER}} \\ \text{class-name-1} \end{array} \right\}$$

CONDITION-NAME CONDITION:

condition-name-1

SWITCH-STATUS CONDITION:

condition-name-1

SIGN CONDITION:

$$\text{arithmetic-expression-1 IS [\underline{NOT}]} \left\{ \begin{array}{l} \underline{POSITIVE} \\ \underline{NEGATIVE} \\ \underline{ZERO} \end{array} \right\}$$

NEGATED CONDITION:

<u>NOT</u> condition-1

COMBINED CONDITION:

$$\text{condition-1} \left\{ \left\{ \begin{array}{l} \underline{AND} \\ \underline{OR} \end{array} \right\} \text{condition-name-2} \right\} \ldots$$

ABBREVIATED COMBINED RELATION CONDITION:

$$\text{relation-condition} \left\{ \left\{ \begin{array}{l} \underline{AND} \\ \underline{OR} \end{array} \right\} \text{[\underline{NOT}] [relational-operator] object} \right\} \ldots$$

GENERAL FORMAT FOR QUALIFICATION

FORMAT 1:

$$\left\{ \begin{array}{l} \text{data-name-1} \\ \text{condition-name-1} \end{array} \right\} \left\{ \begin{array}{l} \left\{ \left\{ \begin{array}{l} \underline{IN} \\ \underline{OF} \end{array} \right\} \text{data-name-2} \right\} \cdots \left[\left\{ \begin{array}{l} \underline{IN} \\ \underline{OF} \end{array} \right\} \left\{ \begin{array}{l} \text{file-name-1} \\ \text{cd-name-1} \end{array} \right\} \right] \\ \left\{ \begin{array}{l} \underline{IN} \\ \underline{OF} \end{array} \right\} \left\{ \begin{array}{l} \underline{\text{file-name-1}} \\ \underline{\text{cd-name-1}} \end{array} \right\} \end{array} \right\}$$

FORMAT 2:

$$\text{paragraph-name-1} \left\{ \begin{array}{l} \underline{IN} \\ \underline{OF} \end{array} \right\} \text{section-name-1}$$

FORMAT 3:

$$\text{text-name-1} \left\{ \begin{array}{l} \underline{IN} \\ \underline{OF} \end{array} \right\} \text{library-name-1}$$

FORMAT 4:

$$\underline{\text{LINAGE-COUNTER}} \left\{ \begin{array}{l} \underline{IN} \\ \underline{OF} \end{array} \right\} \text{file-name-2}$$

FORMAT 5:

$$\left\{ \begin{array}{l} \underline{\text{PAGE-COUNTER}} \\ \underline{\text{LINE-COUNTER}} \end{array} \right\} \left\{ \begin{array}{l} \underline{IN} \\ \underline{OF} \end{array} \right\} \text{report-name-1}$$

FORMAT 6:

$$\text{data-name-3} \left\{ \begin{array}{l} \left\{ \begin{array}{l} \underline{IN} \\ \underline{OF} \end{array} \right\} \text{data-name-4} \left[\left\{ \begin{array}{l} \underline{IN} \\ \underline{OF} \end{array} \right\} \text{report-name-2} \right] \\ \left\{ \begin{array}{l} \underline{IN} \\ \underline{OF} \end{array} \right\} \text{report-name-2} \end{array} \right\}$$

MISCELLANEOUS FORMATS

SUBSCRIPTING:

$$\left\{ \begin{array}{l} \text{condition-name-1} \\ \text{data-name-1} \end{array} \right\} \quad (\quad \left\{ \begin{array}{l} \text{integer-1} \\ \text{data-name-2} [\{ \pm \} \text{integer-2}] \\ \text{index-name-1} [\{ \pm \} \text{integer-3}] \end{array} \right\} \quad \dots \quad)$$

REFERENCE MODIFICATION:

data-name-1 (leftmost-character-position: [length])

IDENTIFIER:

$$\text{data-name-1} \left[\left\{ \begin{array}{l} \underline{\text{IN}} \\ \underline{\text{OF}} \end{array} \right\} \text{data-name-2} \right] \dots \left[\left\{ \begin{array}{l} \underline{\text{IN}} \\ \underline{\text{OF}} \end{array} \right\} \left\{ \begin{array}{l} \text{cd-name-1} \\ \text{file-name-1} \\ \text{report-name-1} \end{array} \right\} \right]$$

[({subscript} ...)] [(leftmost-character-position: [length])]

GENERAL FORMAT FOR NESTED SOURCE PROGRAMS

<u>IDENTIFICATION</u> <u>DIVISION</u>

<u>PROGRAM-ID</u>. program-name-1 [IS <u>INITIAL</u> PROGRAM].

[<u>ENVIRONMENT</u> <u>DIVISION</u>. environment-division-content]

[<u>DATA</u> <u>DIVISION</u>. data-division-content]

[<u>PROCEDURE</u> <u>DIVISION</u>. procedure-division-content]

[[nested-source-program] ...

<u>END</u> <u>PROGRAM</u> program-name-1.]

GENERAL FORMAT FOR NESTED-SOURCE-PROGRAM

IDENTIFICATION DIVISION

PROGRAM-ID. program-name-2 $\left[\text{IS} \left\{ \left| \begin{array}{c} \underline{\text{COMMON}} \\ \underline{\text{INITIAL}} \end{array} \right| \right\} \text{PROGRAM} \right]$.

[ENVIRONMENT DIVISION. environment-division-content]

[DATA DIVISION. data-division-content]

[PROCEDURE DIVISION. procedure-division-content]

[nested-source-program] ...

END PROGRAM program-name-2.

GENERAL FORMAT FOR A SEQUENCE OF SOURCE PROGRAMS

{IDENTIFICATION DIVISION

PROGRAM-ID. program-name-3 [IS INITIAL PROGRAM].

[ENVIRONMENT DIVISION. environment-division-content]

[DATA DIVISION. data-division-content]

[PROCEDURE DIVISION. procedure-division-content]

[nested-source-program] ...

END PROGRAM program-name-3.} ...

IDENTIFICATION DIVISION

PROGRAM-ID. program-name-4 [IS INITIAL PROGRAM].

[ENVIRONMENT DIVISION. environment-division-content]

[DATA DIVISION. data-division-content]

[PROCEDURE DIVISION. procedure-division-content]

[[nested-source-program] ...

END PROGRAM program-name-4.]

APPENDIX III

PROGRAMMING STANDARDS

IDENTIFICATION DIVISION

1. The **AUTHOR** paragraph is required.
2. The **DATE-WRITTEN** and **DATE-COMPILED** paragraphs are not required, but are strongly recommended.
3. Include comments (or the **REMARKS** paragraph in older versions of **COBOL**). These comments should describe the function of the program (briefly) and should clarify any code that is not self-explanatory.

ENVIRONMENT DIVISION

1. List **SELECT** statements in alphabetical order by file name.
2. If a **SELECT** statement cannot be written on one line indent continuation lines at least eight columns.

DATA DIVISION

1. File Description entries should appear in the same order as the corresponding **SELECT** statements.
2. All data names, including file names, should be functionally descriptive.
3. If possible, a data field that appears in more than one structure should have the same name in all structures. Use qualification where necessary to distinguish between occurrences.
4. If it is impractical to use the same name in all occurrences of a data field use similar names; for example:

   PRODUCT-WS: working storage
   PRODUCT-IN: input file
   PRODUCT-OUT: output file
   PRODUCT-PRINT : print record

5. Levels should either be numbered starting with **01** and then in steps of five (**01**, **05**, **10**, **15**, etc.) or consecutively (**01**, **02**, **03**, **04**, etc.). Whichever method you use, be consistent.
6. Successive levels should be indented four columns. For example, start level **05** in column 12, level **10** in column 16, level **15** in column 20, etc.
7. A given level number should always start in the same column.
8. Leave two blank columns between level numbers and data names.
9. Start all **PICTURE** clauses in the same column (such as column 40). Abbreviate **PICTURE** to **PIC**.

PROCEDURE DIVISION

1. Paragraph names should be descriptive of the paragraph's function.
2. Each paragraph should be prefixed by a four-character sequence code. The purpose of this code is to relate the program code to the hierarchical structure of the program, and to help find referenced paragraphs easily. The sequence code should have the format **A999**. The driver paragraph, corresponding to the top level of the hierarchy chart, should begin with the letter **A**. Paragraphs corresponding to the second level of the hierarchy chart should begin with the letter **B**. Third level paragraphs should begin with **C**, and so on. No two sequence codes should be identical, and paragraphs should always be written in the program in order of increasing sequence code.
3. A paragraph name should be the only statement on its line.
4. Avoid the use of the **GO TO** statement if possible.
5. Do not ever under any circumstances use the **ALTER** verb.
6. Separate paragraphs by at least one blank line.
7. Any statement not covered by one of the following rules should begin in column 12.
8. Any statement not covered by one of the following rules should begin in the same column as the statement above it.
9. A statement that requires more than one line should have any continuation lines indented eight columns from the first line.
10. **AT END** or **INVALID KEY** clauses should be indented four columns. For example,

```
        READ INPUT-FILE INTO INPUT-WS
            AT END MOVE 'N' TO MORE-DATA-FLAG.
```

11. **SIZE ERROR** clauses should be indented four columns. For example,

```
        MULTIPLY QUANTITY BY COST GIVING VALUE-OF-SALE
            ON SIZE ERROR MOVE 'Y' TO ERROR-FLAG.
```

12. **PERFORM** statements should be formatted as follows:

```
        PERFORM B010-UPDATE-FILE
            UNTIL MORE-DATA-FLAG = 'N'.


        PERFORM C015-LOAD-TABLE
            VARYING X-TBL FROM 1 BY 1
            UNTIL X-TBL > TABLE-LIMIT.
```

13. In the `IF` statement, statements within the `IF` and `ELSE` clauses should be indented four columns. The `ELSE` is aligned under the corresponding `IF`. For example,

```
IF COST > CREDIT
    MOVE 'N' TO CREDIT-FLAG
ELSE
    MOVE 'Y' TO CREDIT-FLAG.
```

14. If you are using `COBOL-85`, `END` phrases should be aligned under the corresponding verb. For example,

```
READ INPUT-FILE INTO INPUT-WS
    AT END MOVE 'N' TO MORE-DATA-FLAG
END-READ.

MULTIPLY QUANTITY BY COST GIVING VALUE-OF-SALE
    ON SIZE ERROR MOVE 'Y' TO ERROR-FLAG
END-MULTIPLY.

PERFORM
    UNTIL MORE-DATA-FLAG = 'N'
    WRITE OUTPUT-RECORD FROM INPUT-RECORD
    READ INPUT-FILE
        AT END MOVE 'N' TO MORE-DATA-FLAG
    END-READ
END-PERFORM.

IF COST > CREDIT
    MOVE 'N' TO CREDIT-FLAG
ELSE
    MOVE 'Y' TO CREDIT-FLAG
END-IF.
```

15. All statements should end with a period unless they are part of a compound statement.

GENERAL

1. Start the Procedure Division at the top of a page. Most compilers contain some technique for skipping to the top of a page within a listing. For example, you can usually use a / in column seven, and the IBM compiler supports the `EJECT` statement. See your computer's `COBOL` manual for details regarding use of the appropriate mechanism.
2. Design the program before you start to write code.
3. Implement the program to follow your design.
4. Simplify.
5. Clarify.
6. Make code self-explanatory.
7. If you cannot make a section of code self-explanatory, use comments to explain it.
8. *Write to be read by others!*

SAMPLE COBOL FORMATS

Note: *COBOL-85* statements are written in *italics*.

```
IDENTIFICATION DIVISION.
PROGRAM-ID.
    FORMAT-SAMPLE.
AUTHOR.
    D. GOLDEN.
DATE-WRITTEN.
    JUNE 3, 1987.
DATE-COMPILED.

*    THIS PROGRAM PRESENTS SAMPLES OF COBOL CODING FORMATS.
*    IT IS NOT INTENDED TO MAKE SENSE AS A WORKING PROGRAM.

ENVIRONMENT DIVISION.
CONFIGURATION SECTION.
SPECIAL-NAMES.
    C01 IS TO-TOP-OF-PAGE.
INPUT-OUTPUT SECTION.
FILE-CONTROL.
    SELECT INPUT-FILE                ASSIGN TO S-INPUT.
    SELECT REPORT-FILE               ASSIGN TO S-REPORT.

DATA DIVISION.
FILE SECTION.
FD   REPORT-FILE
     LABEL RECORDS ARE STANDARD.
01   REPORT-RECORD.
     05   EMPLOYEE-ID                 PIC X(5).
     05   FILLER                      PIC XXX.
     05   HOURS-WORKED                PIC Z9.9.
     05   FILLER                      PIC XXX.
     05   GROSS-PAY                   PIC $$,$$9.99.

WORKING-STORAGE SECTION.
01   TOTAL-SALARY                     PIC S9(7)V99    VALUE ZERO.
01   MORE-DATA-REMAINS-FLAG           PIC X           VALUE 'Y'.
     88   MORE-DATA-REMAINS                           VALUE 'Y'.
     88   NO-MORE-DATA-REMAINS                        VALUE 'N'.


PROCEDURE DIVISION.
A000-STATEMENT-SAMPLES SECTION.
A010-PARAGRAPH-NAME.
    ACCEPT CATALOG-NUMBER.
    ACCEPT TODAYS-DATE FROM DATE.
    ADD 1 TO LINE-NUMBER.
    ADD REGULAR-PAY OVERTIME-PAY GIVING GROSS-PAY.
    ADD DOLLARS TO SELLER-TOTAL ACCOUNT-TOTAL FINAL-TOTAL.
    CALL 'SUBPROG' USING PRODUCT-RECORD RESULT-FLAG.
    CLOSE INPUT-FILE
          REPORT-FILE.
    COMPUTE WEEKLY-SALARY ROUNDED = HOURLY-RATE * HOURS-WORKED.
    DELETE INDEX-PRODUCT-FILE
        INVALID KEY MOVE 'Y' TO ERROR-FLAG.
    DISPLAY 'DATA-FIELD = ' DATA-FIELD.
    DIVIDE HOURS INTO MILES GIVING MILES-PER-HOUR
        ON SIZE ERROR MOVE 'Y' TO SIZE-ERROR-FLAG.
```

```
DIVIDE TOTAL-SALARY BY EMPLOYEE-COUNT GIVING AVERAGE-SALARY
    ON SIZE ERROR MOVE 'Y' TO SIZE-ERROR-FLAG
END-DIVIDE.
EVALUATE INPUT-CODE
    WHEN '1' PERFORM C010-FUNCTION-1
    WHEN '2' PERFORM C020-FUNCTION-2
    WHEN OTHER MOVE 'Y' TO ERROR-FLAG
END-EVALUATE.
EXHIBIT NAMED EMPLOYEE-NUMBER HOURS-WORKED PAYRATE GROSS-PAY.
EXIT.
GENERATE DETAIL-LINE.
GO TO Z999-EXIT.
IF W-GROSS-PAY IS GREATER THAN EXEMPTION
    SUBTRACT W-EXEMPTION FROM W-GROSS-PAY GIVING W-TAXABLE
    MULTIPLY W-TAXABLE BY C-TAXRATE GIVING W-TAX ROUNDED
ELSE
    MOVE ZERO TO W-TAX.
IF W-GROSS-PAY IS GREATER THAN EXEMPTION
    SUBTRACT W-EXEMPTION FROM W-GROSS-PAY GIVING W-TAXABLE
    MULTIPLY W-TAXABLE BY C-TAXRATE GIVING W-TAX ROUNDED
        ON SIZE ERROR MOVE 'Y' TO ERROR-FLAG
    END-MULTIPLY
ELSE
    MOVE ZERO TO W-TAX
END-IF.
INITIATE OVERTIME-REPORT.
INSPECT AMOUNT-FIELD
    TALLYING SPACE-COUNT FOR LEADING SPACES
    REPLACING LEADING SPACES BY '*'.
MOVE SPACES TO REPORT-RECORD.
MOVE QUANTITY OF TRANSACTION TO QUANTITY OF REPORT-RECORD.
MOVE ENROLLMENT TO SIZE-BY-GRADE-AND-YEAR (7, YEAR-SUBSCRIPT).
MULTIPLY UNIT-PRICE BY QUANTITY GIVING TOTAL-PRICE.
OPEN INPUT ORDER-FILE
    OUTPUT NORMAL-HANDLING-FILE
           SPECIAL-HANDLING-FILE.
PERFORM C010-PROCESS-ONE-RECORD
    UNTIL MORE-DATA-REMAINS-FLAY = 'N'.
PERFORM B030-LOAD-TABLE
    VARYING X-TBL FROM 1 BY 1
    UNTIL X-TBL > TABLE-SIZE.
PERFORM
    VARYING X-TBL FROM 1 BY 1
    UNTIL X-TBL > TABLE-SIZE OR NO-MORE-DATA-REMAINS
    READ INPUT-FILE
        AT END MOVE 'N' TO MORE-DATA-REMAINS-FLAG
    END-READ
    IF MORE-DATA-REMAINS
        MOVE INPUT-RECORD TO TABLE-RECORD (X-TBL)
    END-IF
END-PERFORM.
READ INPUT-FILE
    AT END MOVE 'N' TO MORE-DATA-REMAINS-FLAG.
READ INDEXED-FILE
    INVALID KEY MOVE 'Y' TO KEY-ERROR-FLAG.
REWRITE EMPLOYEE-RECORD FROM EMPLOYEE-WS
    INVALID KEY MOVE 'Y' TO KEY-ERROR-FLAG.
SEARCH LOS-TABLE VARYING COL-INDEX
    WHEN LOS < LOS-TABLE (LOS-INDEX) NEXT SENTENCE.
```

```
SEARCH ALL PRODUCT-TABLE
    AT END MOVE 'N' TO PRODUCT-FOUND-FLAG
    WHEN CURRENT-PRODUCT = PRODUCT (PRODUCT-INDEX)
          MOVE 'Y' TO PRODUCT-FOUND-FLAG.
SET COL-INDEX UP BY 1.
SET COL-INDEX TO 1.
SET GREEN TO TRUE.
SORT SORT-FILE
    ON ASCENDING KEY CUSTOMER-NAME
        DESCENDING KEY PURCHASE-DATE
    USING PURCHASE-FILE
    GIVING SORTED PURCHASES.
SORT SORT-FILE
    ON ASCENDING KEY CUSTOMER-NAME
        DESCENDING KEY PURCHASE-DATE
    INPUT PROCEDURE B010-EDIT-INPUT
    OUTPUT PROCEDURE B020-PRODUCE-REPORT.
STOP RUN.
STRING  CUSTOMER-NAME DELIMITED BY SIZE
        SPACE
        CREDIT-AVAILABLE DELIMITED BY '.'
            INTO CREDIT-RECORD
            WITH POINTER INITIAL-POSITION.
SUBTRACT 40 FROM I-HOURS-WORKED GIVING W-HOURS-OVERTIME.
TERMINATE OVERTIME-REPORT.
UNSTRING ADDRESS-IN-RECORD DELIMITED BY '='
    INTO ADDRESS-LINE-1
        ADDRESS-LINE-2
        ADDRESS-LINE-3
    TALLYING IN FIELDS-FILLED
    ON OVERFLOW MOVE 'Y' TO OVERFLOW-FLAG.
WRITE NEW-MASTER-RECORD.
WRITE REPORT-RECORD AFTER ADVANCING 1 LINE.
```

ANSWERS TO STARRED EXERCISES

There are several acceptable answers to many of these exercises. The one shown here is sometimes better than other possibilities, but only occasionally is the test of goodness completely clear. For instance, it seldom makes any difference whether one writes **ADD A B GIVING C** or **ADD B A GIVING C**. In short, the answers given here are correct, but they often are not the *only* possible correct answers.

CHAPTER 3

```
1. 01  ACCOUNTS.
       05  RECEIVABLE          PIC 9(5)V99.
       05  PAYABLE             PIC 9(5)V99.
       05  PAST-DUE            PIC 9(5)V99.

3. 01  ALPHA-INPUT.
       05  A.
           10  B               PIC X(4).
           10  C               PIC X(5).
       05  D                   PIC X(6).
       05  E                   PIC X(7).

5. 01  NORMAL-LINE-OUT.
       05  IDENT               PIC XXX.
       05  FILLER              PIC XXX.
       05  COSTS.
           10  OUTGOING        PIC 9(4).99.
           10  FILLER          PIC XX.
           10  RETURNING       PIC 9(4).99.
           10  FILLER          PIC XX.
       05  TOTAL-MILES         PIC 9(5).
```

```
7.  01  INVENTORY.
        05  PART.
            10   PREFIX          PIC AA.
            10   BIN-NUMBER      PIC 9(4).
        05  YTD-USAGE.
            10   QTY             PIC 9(6).
            10   DOLLARS         PIC 9(5)V99.
        05  DESCRIPTION          PIC X(15).
        05  CODES.
            10   WHERE-MADE      PIC A.
            10   MFG-PURCH       PIC 9.
            10   HI-LO-USAGE     PIC 9.
        05  QOH                  PIC 9(5).
```

9. The record begins with a **POLICY-NUMBER** of seven alphanumeric characters, which is followed by a three-character **FILLER** item. Then there is a group item consisting of four amounts, each of which has six digits with two decimal places, and each of which is followed by a two-character **FILLER** item. The amounts, in order, are named **PREMIUM, DIVIDEND, INTEREST**, and **AMOUNT-DUE**. The record contains 46 characters, counting the **FILLER**s as character positions.

11. **a.** Add the values of the items named R and S to the value of T and replace the value of T with the sum.

   b. Add the values of R and S, and replace the value of T with the sum. The previous value of T does not enter into the calculation, and is destroyed by the action of this statement.

   c. Add the values of A, B, and C; subtract this sum from the value of D, and replace the value of D with the final result.

   d. Add the values of A, B, and C; subtract the sum from the value of D; replace the value of E with the final result. The value of D remains after the completion of the actions of the statement, but the old value of E is destroyed.

   e. The value of **FACTOR-9** is multiplied by 12.3; the product replaces the old value of **FACTOR-9**.

   f. The value of N is divided by the value of M; the old value of N is replaced by the result.

   g. The value of N is divided by the value of M and the rounded quotient is placed in Q.

13. **a.** `ADD JAN FEB MAR GIVING 1-QUARTER.`

   b. `ADD YEAR-1 TO YEAR-2.`

   c. `ADD 13.45 ABC TO DEF.`

   d. `ADD 13.45 ABC DEF GIVING GHI.`

   e. `SUBTRACT 12 FROM Q-1.`

   f. `SUBTRACT Y-88 Y-89 FROM YEARS.`

   g. `MULTIPLY RATE-ADJUSTMENT BY FINAL-TOTAL ROUNDED.`

   h. `MULTIPLY MONTHLY-USAGE BY 12 GIVING YEAR-TOTAL.`

i. MULTIPLY MILES-PER-HOUR BY HOURS GIVING DISTANCE.

j. DIVIDE YEAR-TOTAL BY 12 GIVING MONTHLY-AVERAGE.

k. DIVIDE OVERLAP-FACTOR INTO MACHINE-UTILIZATION ROUNDED.

l. DIVIDE TOTAL-TIME BY 60 GIVING HOURS REMAINDER MINUTES.

15. a. RESULT   PICTURE 9(4)V99.

    b. RESULT   PICTURE 9(5)V9.

    c. RESULT   PICTURE 9(5)V9(6).

17. IDENTIFICATION DIVISION.
    PROGRAM-ID.
        CH3EX17.

    ENVIRONMENT DIVISION.
    INPUT-OUTPUT SECTION.
    FILE-CONTROL.
        SELECT EMPLOYEE-FILE   ASSIGN TO S-PAYFILE.
        SELECT PAY-REPORT-FILE   ASSIGN TO S-REPORT.

    DATA DIVISION.
    FILE SECTION.
    FD   EMPLOYEE-FILE
        LABEL RECORDS ARE OMITTED.
    01   EMPLOYEE-RECORD.
        05 I-IDENT   PIC X(5).
        05 I-HOURS-WORKED   PIC 99V9.
        05 I-PAY-RATE   PIC 99V99.

    FD   PAY-REPORT-FILE
        LABEL RECORDS ARE OMITTED.
    01   PAY-REPORT-RECORD.
        05 O-IDENT   PIC X(5).
        05 FILLER   PIC XXX.
        05 O-HOURS-WORKED   PIC 99.9.
        05 FILLER   PIC XXX.
        05 O-PAY-RATE   PIC 99.99.
        05 FILLER   PIC XXX.
        05 O-PAY   PIC 999.99.

    WORKING-STORAGE SECTION.
    01 W-OUT-OF-DATA-FLAG   PIC X.

    PROCEDURE DIVISION.
    A000-MAIN-ROUTINE.
        OPEN INPUT EMPLOYEE-FILE
            OUTPUT PAY-REPORT-FILE.
        MOVE 'N' TO W-OUT-OF-DATA-FLAG.
        READ EMPLOYEE-FILE
            AT END MOVE 'Y' TO W-OUT-OF-DATA-FLAG.
        PERFORM B010-PRODUCE-PAY-LINE
            UNTIL W-OUT-OF-DATA-FLAG = 'Y'.
        CLOSE EMPLOYEE-FILE
            PAY-REPORT-FILE.
        STOP RUN.

```
B010-PRODUCE-PAY-LINE.
    MOVE SPACES TO PAY-REPORT-RECORD.
    MULTIPLY I-HOURS-WORKED BY I-PAY-RATE GIVING O-PAY ROUNDED.
    MOVE I-IDENT            TO O-IDENT.
    MOVE I-HOURS-WORKED     TO O-HOURS-WORKED.
    MOVE I-PAY-RATE         TO O-PAY-RATE.
    WRITE PAY-REPORT-RECORD.
    READ EMPLOYEE-FILE
        AT END MOVE 'Y' TO W-OUT-OF-DATA-FLAG.
```

Sample output:

```
12345   40.0   03.00   120.00
23456   43.3   12.34   534.32
23457   43.3   12.36   535.19
55555   01.0   01.00   001.00
```

CHAPTER 4

1. **a.** IF AGE is 18 or greater THEN
               add 1 to LEGAL-ADULT
           ENDIF

   b. IF PART-1-A contains the letter "S" THEN
               print STOCK-ITEM
           ENDIF

   c. IF SIZE-A is greater than 800 THEN
               add 1 to BIG
           ELSE
               add 1 to LITTLE
           ENDIF

   d. IF NAME-A is greater than NAME-B THEN
               move NAME-A to TEMPORARY
           ELSE
               move NAME-B to TEMPORARY
           ENDIF

   e. IF HOURS-WORKED is not equal to 40 THEN
               print "NON-STANDARD HOURS"
           ENDIF

4. PRODUCE COMMISSION FILE:
       get sale record
       PERFORM-UNTIL more-data = 'n'
           set up commission record
           write commission record
           get sale record
       ENDPERFORM
       stop

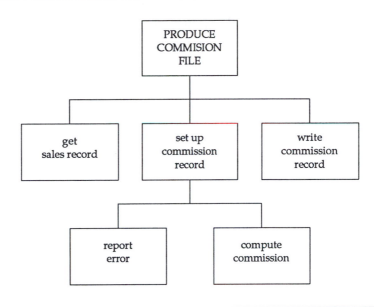

Hierarchy chart for Exercise 4.

Get a sale record:
    read a SALE-RECORD; at end move 'n' to more-data

Set up commission record:
    move SELLER to commission record
    move SALE-PRICE to commission record
    move BASE-PRICE to commission record
    IF PRODUCT-CODE is less than 1 or greater than 5 THEN
        report the error
    ELSE
        compute the commission
    ENDIF

Report error:
    set the commission to zero
    move "ERRONEOUS PRODUCT CODE" to commission record

Compute commission:
    EVALUATE PRODUCT-CODE
        WHEN 1
            commission = 0.15 * SALE-PRICE
        WHEN 2
            commission = 0.40 * (SALE-PRICE - BASE-PRICE)
        WHEN 3
            commission = 0.10 * BASE-PRICE +
                         0.50 * (SALE-PRICE - BASE-PRICE)
        WHEN 4
            commission = 25 + 0.05 * BASE-PRICE
        WHEN 5
            commission = 75
    ENDEVALUATE

We have intentionally omitted a specification for the module "write commission record" because the name of the module is the same as its specification. You may include or omit specification of a module this simple as you choose, but it should always be clear that the module was omitted by intent and not by oversight.

6. Produce tax file:

```
get pay record; at end move 'n' to more-data
PERFORM-UNTIL more-data = 'n'
    move identification to tax record
    move gross pay to tax record
    IF gross pay is greater than 2000 THEN
        tax = 0.04 * (gross pay - 2000)
    ELSE
        tax = 0
    ENDIF
    write tax record
    get pay record; at end move 'n' to more-data
ENDPERFORM
stop
```

8. Report file information:

```
move zero to total
get input record; at end move 'n' to more-data
PERFORM-UNTIL more-data = 'n'
    move IDENT to output record
    move DOLLARS to output record
    move OTHER-INFO to output record
    print output record
    add DOLLARS to total
    get input record; at end move 'n' to more-data
ENDPERFORM
print total
stop
```

CHAPTER 5

1. a.
```
IF AGE IS NOT LESS THAN 18
    ADD 1 TO LEGAL-ADULT.
```

b.
```
IF PART-1-A = 'S'
    PERFORM D050-PROCESS-STOCK-ITEM.
```

c.
```
IF SIZE-A IS GREATER THAN 800
    ADD 1 TO BIG
ELSE
    ADD 1 TO LITTLE.
```

d.
```
IF NAME-A IS GREATER THAN NAME-B
    MOVE NAME-A TO TEMPORARY
ELSE
    MOVE NAME-B TO TEMPORARY.
```

```
e.  IF HOURS-WORKED IS NOT EQUAL TO 40
        PERFORM C035-NON-STANDARD.


f.  IF CODE-X IS NOT NUMERIC
        PERFORM X020-BADE-CODE.


3. ADD ON-HAND ON-ORDER GIVING TEMPORARY.
   IF TEMPORARY IS LESS THAN REORDER-POINT
        MOVE REORDER-QTY TO ORDER-AMOUNT
   ELSE
        MOVE ZERO TO ORDER-AMOUNT.


5. IF      PRODUCT-CODE IS EQUAL TO '1'
        MULTIPLY 0.15 BY SALE-PRICE GIVING COMMISSION
   ELSE IF PRODUCT-CODE IS EQUAL TO '2'
        SUBTRACT BASE-PRICE FROM SALE-PRICE GIVING TEMPORARY
        MULTIPLY 0.40 BY TEMPORARY GIVING COMMISSION
   ELSE IF PRODUCT-CODE IS EQUAL TO '3'
        MULTIPLY 0.10 BY BASE-PRICE GIVING TEMP1
        SUBTRACT BASE-PRICE FROM SALE-PRICE GIVING TEMP2
        MULTIPLY 0.50 BY TEMP2
        ADD TEMP1 TEMP2 GIVING COMMISSION
   ELSE IF PRODUCT-CODE IS EQUAL TO '4'
        MULTIPLY 0.05 BY BASE-PRICE GIVING TEMPORARY
        ADD 10.00 TEMPORARY GIVING COMMISSION
   ELSE IF PRODUCT-CODE IS EQUAL TO '5'
        MOVE 35.00 TO COMMISSION
   ELSE
        MOVE ZERO TO COMMISSION
        MOVE 'X' TO BAD-PRODUCT-CODE-FLAG.
```

COBOL-85

If you are using **COBOL-85** you can use the following **EVALUATE** statement.

```
EVALUATE PRODUCT-CODE
    WHEN '1'  MULTIPLY 0.15 BY SALE-PRICE
    WHEN '2'  SUBTRACT BASE-PRICE FROM SALE-PRICE GIVING
                    TEMPORARY
              MULTIPLY 0.40 BY TEMPORARY GIVING COMMISSION
    WHEN '3'  MULTIPLY 0.10 BY BASE-PRICE GIVING TEMP1
              SUBTRACT BASE-PRICE FROM SALE-PRICE GIVING TEMP2
              MULTIPLY 0.50 BY TEMP2
              ADD TEMP1 TEMP2 GIVING COMMISSION
    WHEN '4'  MULTIPLY 0.05 BY BASE-PRICE GIVING TEMPORARY
              ADD 10.00 TEMPORARY GIVING COMMISSION
    WHEN '5'  MOVE 35.00 TO COMMISSION
    WHEN OTHER
              MOVE ZERO TO COMMISSION
              MOVE 'X' TO BAD-PRODUCT-CODE-FLAG
END-EVALUATE.
```

END COBOL-85

7.

```
IDENTIFICATION DIVISION.
PROGRAM-ID.
    CH5EX7.

ENVIRONMENT DIVISION.
INPUT-OUTPUT SECTION.
FILE-CONTROL.
    SELECT SERVICE-FILE          ASSIGN TO S-SERVICE.
    SELECT REPORT-FILE           ASSIGN TO S-REPORT.

DATA DIVISION.
FILE SECTION.
FD  SERVICE-FILE
    LABEL RECORDS ARE OMITTED.
01  SERVICE-RECORD.
    05  NAME                     PIC X(20).
    05  FILLER                   PIC X(5).
    05  YEARS-OF-SERVICE         PIC 99.
    05  FILLER                   PIC X(53).

FD  REPORT-FILE
    LABEL RECORDS ARE OMITTED.
01  REPORT-RECORD.
    05  NAME-OUT                 PIC X(20).
    05  FILLER                   PIC X(5).
    05  YEARS-OF-SERVICE-OUT     PIC 99.
    05  FILLER                   PIC XXX.
    05  VETERAN-MESSAGE          PIC X(22).

WORKING-STORAGE SECTION.
01  OUT-OF-DATA-FLAG             PIC X VALUE 'N'.

PROCEDURE DIVISION.
A000-MAIN-ROUTINE.
    OPEN INPUT SERVICE-FILE
         OUTPUT REPORT-FILE.
    READ SERVICE-FILE
        AT END MOVE 'Y' TO OUT-OF-DATA-FLAG.
    PERFORM B010-PROCESS-SERVICE-RECORDS
        UNTIL OUT-OF-DATA-FLAG = 'Y'.
    CLOSE SERVICE-FILE
          REPORT-FILE.
    STOP RUN.

B010-PROCESS-SERVICE-RECORDS.
    MOVE SPACES TO REPORT-RECORD.
    MOVE NAME TO NAME-OUT.
    MOVE YEARS-OF-SERVICE TO YEARS-OF-SERVICE-OUT.
    IF YEARS-OF-SERVICE IS GREATER THAN 40
        MOVE 'AN ABC COMPANY VETERAN' TO VETERAN-MESSAGE.
    WRITE REPORT-RECORD.
    READ SERVICE-FILE
        AT END MOVE 'Y' TO OUT-OF-DATA-FLAG.
```

9.

```
IDENTIFICATION DIVISION.
PROGRAM-ID.
    CH5EX9.

ENVIRONMENT DIVISION.
INPUT-OUTPUT SECTION.
FILE-CONTROL.
    SELECT EMPLOYEE-FILE            ASSIGN TO S-EMPLOYEE.
    SELECT REPORT-FILE              ASSIGN TO S-REPORT.

DATA DIVISION.
FILE SECTION.
FD   EMPLOYEE-FILE
     LABEL RECORDS ARE OMITTED.
01   EMPLOYEE-RECORD.
        05   FILLER                 PIC X(44).
        05   IDENT                  PIC X(6).
        05   FILLER                 PIC X(19).
        05   GROSS-PAY              PIC 9(5)V99.
        05   FILLER                 PIC X(4).

FD   REPORT-FILE
     LABEL RECORDS ARE OMITTED.
01   REPORT-RECORD.
        05   IDENT-OUT              PIC X(6).
        05   FILLER                 PIC XXX.
        05   GROSS-PAY-OUT          PIC 9(5).99.
        05   FILLER                 PIC XXX.
        05   TAX                    PIC 9(5).99.

WORKING-STORAGE SECTION.
01   OUT-OF-DATA-FLAG               PIC X VALUE 'N'.
01   TEMPORARY-STORAGE             PIC 9(5)V99.

PROCEDURE DIVISION.
A000-MAIN-ROUTINE.
    OPEN INPUT EMPLOYEE-FILE
        OUTPUT REPORT-FILE.
    READ EMPLOYEE-FILE
        AT END MOVE 'Y' TO OUT-OF-DATA-FLAG.
    PERFORM B010-COMPUTE-TAX
        UNTIL OUT-OF-DATA-FLAG = 'Y'.
    CLOSE EMPLOYEE-FILE
        REPORT-FILE.
    STOP RUN.

B010-COMPUTE-TAX.
    MOVE SPACES TO REPORT-RECORD.
    IF GROSS-PAY IS GREATER THAN 2000.00
        SUBTRACT 2000.00 FROM GROSS-PAY
                GIVING TEMPORARY-STORAGE
        MULTIPLY TEMPORARY-STORAGE BY 0.02 GIVING TAX
    ELSE
        MOVE ZERO TO TAX.
    MOVE IDENT TO IDENT-OUT.
    MOVE GROSS-PAY TO GROSS-PAY-OUT.
    WRITE REPORT-RECORD.
    READ EMPLOYEE-FILE
        AT END MOVE 'Y' TO OUT-OF-DATA-FLAG.
```

11.

```
IDENTIFICATION DIVISION.
PROGRAM-ID.
    CH5EX11.

ENVIRONMENT DIVISION.
INPUT-OUTPUT SECTION.
FILE-CONTROL.
    SELECT INPUT-FILE              ASSIGN TO S-INPUT.
    SELECT REPORT-FILE             ASSIGN TO S-REPORT.

DATA DIVISION.
FILE SECTION.
FD  INPUT-FILE
    LABEL RECORDS ARE OMITTED.
01  INPUT-RECORD.
    05  IDENT                      PIC X(8).
    05  DOLLARS                    PIC 9(5)V99.
    05  OTHER-INFO                 PIC X(75).

FD  REPORT-FILE
    LABEL RECORDS ARE OMITTED.
01  REPORT-RECORD.
    05  IDENT-OUT                  PIC X(8).
    05  FILLER                     PIC XXX.
    05  DOLLARS-OUT                PIC 9(5).99.
    05  FILLER                     PIC XXX.
    05  OTHER-INFO-OUT             PIC X(75).

WORKING-STORAGE SECTION.
01  OUT-OF-DATA-FLAG               PIC X VALUE 'N'.
01  DOLLAR-TOTAL                   PIC 9(7)V99 VALUE ZERO.

PROCEDURE DIVISION.
A000-MAIN-ROUTINE.
    OPEN INPUT INPUT-FILE
        OUTPUT REPORT-FILE.
    READ INPUT-FILE
        AT END MOVE 'Y' TO OUT-OF-DATA-FLAG.
    PERFORM B010-PRINT-INPUT
        UNTIL OUT-OF-DATA-FLAG = 'Y'.
    MOVE SPACES TO REPORT-RECORD.
    MOVE 'TOTAL = ' TO IDENT-OUT.
    MOVE DOLLAR-TOTAL TO DOLLARS-OUT.
    WRITE REPORT-RECORD.
    CLOSE INPUT-FILE
        REPORT-FILE.
    STOP RUN.

B010-PRINT-INPUT.
    MOVE SPACES TO REPORT-RECORD.
    MOVE IDENT TO IDENT-OUT.
    MOVE DOLLARS TO DOLLARS-OUT.
    MOVE OTHER-INFO TO OTHER-INFO-OUT.
    WRITE REPORT-RECORD.
    ADD DOLLARS TO DOLLAR-TOTAL.
    READ INPUT-FILE
        AT END MOVE 'Y' TO OUT-OF-DATA-FLAG.
```

CHAPTER 6

2.

```
IDENTIFICATION DIVISION.
PROGRAM-ID.
    PAYROLL1.
DATE-WRITTEN.
    JULY 14, 1987.

ENVIRONMENT DIVISION.
INPUT-OUTPUT SECTION.
FILE-CONTROL.
    SELECT PAYROLL-FILE     ASSIGN TO S-PAYROLL.
    SELECT REPORT-FILE      ASSIGN TO S-REPORT.

DATA DIVISION.
FILE SECTION.
FD  PAYROLL-FILE
    LABEL RECORDS ARE OMITTED.
01  PAYROLL-RECORD.
    05  I-PAYROLL-NUMBER    PIC X(5).
    05  I-NAME              PIC X(20).
    05  I-HOURS-WORKED      PIC 99V9.
    05  FILLER              PIC X(3).
    05  I-PAYRATE           PIC 99V999.
    05  I-DEPENDENTS        PIC 99.
    05  FILLER              PIC X(42).

FD  REPORT-FILE
    LABEL RECORDS ARE OMITTED.
01  REPORT-RECORD.
    05  O-PAYROLL-NUMBER    PIC X(5).
    05  FILLER              PIC XX.
    05  O-NAME              PIC X(20).
    05  FILLER              PIC XX.
    05  O-HOURS-WORKED      PIC 99.9.
    05  FILLER              PIC XX.
    05  O-PAYRATE           PIC 99.999.
    05  FILLER              PIC XX.
    05  O-DEPENDENTS        PIC 99.
    05  FILLER              PIC XX.
    05  O-GROSS-PAY         PIC 999.99.
    05  FILLER              PIC XX.
    05  O-TAX               PIC 999.99.
    05  FILLER              PIC XX.
    05  O-NET-PAY           PIC 999.99.

WORKING-STORAGE SECTION.
01  C-EXEMPTION             PIC 99V99      VALUE 50.00.
01  C-TAXRATE               PIC  V999      VALUE   .210.
01  W-EXEMPTION-TOTAL       PIC 999V99.
01  W-GROSS-PAY             PIC 999V99.
01  W-NET-PAY               PIC 999V99.
01  W-OUT-OF-RECORDS-FLAG   PIC X          VALUE 'N'.
01  W-OVERTIME-HOURS        PIC  99V9.
01  W-OVERTIME-PAY          PIC 999V99.
01  W-TAX                   PIC 999V99.
01  W-TAXABLE               PIC 999V99.
```

```
PROCEDURE DIVISION.
A000-PRODUCE-PAYROLL-CALC.
    OPEN INPUT PAYROLL-FILE
        OUTPUT REPORT-FILE.
    READ PAYROLL-FILE
            AT END MOVE 'Y' TO W-OUT-OF-RECORDS-FLAG.
    PERFORM B010-CALC-EMP-PAYROLL
        UNTIL W-OUT-OF-RECORDS-FLAG = 'Y'.
    CLOSE PAYROLL-FILE
            REPORT-FILE.
    STOP RUN.

B010-CALC-EMP-PAYROLL.
    MULTIPLY I-HOURS-WORKED BY I-PAYRATE
            GIVING W-GROSS-PAY ROUNDED.
    IF I-HOURS-WORKED IS GREATER THAN 40
        SUBTRACT 40 FROM I-HOURS-WORKED GIVING W-OVERTIME-HOURS
        MULTIPLY 0.5 BY W-OVERTIME-HOURS
        MULTIPLY W-OVERTIME-HOURS BY I-PAYRATE
                GIVING W-OVERTIME-PAY ROUNDED
        ADD W-OVERTIME-PAY TO W-GROSS-PAY.
    MULTIPLY C-EXEMPTION BY I-DEPENDENTS
            GIVING W-EXEMPTIONS-TOTAL.
    IF W-GROSS-PAY IS GREATER THAN W-EXEMPTIONS
        SUBTRACT W-EXEMPTIONS-TOTAL FROM W-GROSS-PAY
                GIVING W-TAXABLE
        MULTIPLY C-TAXRATE BY W-TAXABLE GIVING W-TAX ROUNDED
    ELSE
        MOVE ZERO TO W-TAX.
    SUBTRACT W-TAX FROM W-GROSS-PAY GIVING W-NET-PAY.
    MOVE SPACES                 TO REPORT-RECORD.
    MOVE I-PAYROLL-NUMBER       TO O-PAYROLL-NUMBER.
    MOVE I-NAME                 TO O-NAME.
    MOVE I-HOURS-WORKED         TO O-HOURS-WORKED.
    MOVE I-PAYRATE              TO O-PAYRATE.
    MOVE I-DEPENDENTS           TO O-DEPENDENTS.
    MOVE W-TAX                  TO O-TAX.
    MOVE W-GROSS-PAY            TO O-GROSS-PAY.
    MOVE W-NET-PAY              TO O-NET-PAY.
    WRITE REPORT-RECORD.
    READ PAYROLL-FILE
            AT END MOVE 'Y' TO W-OUT-OF-RECORDS-FLAG.
```

4.

```
IDENTIFICATION DIVISION.
PROGRAM-ID.
    PAYROLL1.
DATE-WRITTEN.
    JULY 14, 1987.

ENVIRONMENT DIVISION.
INPUT-OUTPUT SECTION.
FILE-CONTROL.
    SELECT PAYROLL-FILE     ASSIGN TO S-PAYROLL.
    SELECT REPORT-FILE      ASSIGN TO S-REPORT.
```

```
DATA DIVISION.
FILE SECTION.
FD  PAYROLL-FILE
    LABEL RECORDS ARE OMITTED.
01  PAYROLL-RECORD.
    05  I-PAYROLL-NUMBER      PIC X(5).
    05  I-NAME                PIC X(20).
    05  I-HOURS-WORKED        PIC 99V9.
    05  FILLER                PIC X(3).
    05  I-PAYRATE             PIC 99V999.
    05  I-DEPENDENTS          PIC 99.
    05  FILLER                PIC X(42).

FD  REPORT-FILE
    LABEL RECORDS ARE OMITTED.
01  REPORT-RECORD.
    05  O-PAYROLL-NUMBER      PIC X(5).
    05  FILLER                PIC XX.
    05  O-NAME                PIC X(20).
    05  FILLER                PIC XX.
    05  O-HOURS-WORKED        PIC 99.9.
    05  FILLER                PIC XX.
    05  O-PAYRATE             PIC 99.999.
    05  FILLER                PIC XX.
    05  O-DEPENDENTS          PIC 99.
    05  FILLER                PIC XX.
    05  O-GROSS-PAY           PIC 999.99.
    05  FILLER                PIC XX.
    05  O-TAX                 PIC 999.99.
    05  FILLER                PIC XX.
    05  O-NET-PAY             PIC 999.99.

WORKING-STORAGE SECTION.
01  C-EXEMPTION              PIC 99V99      VALUE 50.00.
01  C-TAXRATE               PIC   V999     VALUE   .210.
01  W-EXEMPTION-TOTAL       PIC 999V99.
01  W-GROSS-PAY             PIC 999V99.
01  W-NET-PAY               PIC 999V99.
01  W-OUT-OF-RECORDS-FLAG   PIC X          VALUE 'N'.
01  W-OVERTIME-HOURS        PIC  99V9.
01  W-OVERTIME-PAY          PIC 999V99.
01  W-RECORD-COUNT          PIC 9(5)       VALUE ZERO.
01  W-TAX                   PIC 999V99.
01  W-TAXABLE               PIC 999V99.

PROCEDURE DIVISION.
A000-PRODUCE-PAYROLL-CALC.
    OPEN INPUT PAYROLL-FILE
        OUTPUT REPORT-FILE.
    PERFORM C010-GET-PAYROLL-REC.
    PERFORM B010-CALC-EMP-PAYROLL
        UNTIL W-OUT-OF-RECORDS-FLAG = 'Y'.
    MOVE SPACES TO REPORT-RECORD.
    MOVE W-RECORD-COUNT TO O-PAYROLL-NUMBER.
    MOVE 'RECORDS PROCESSED' TO O-NAME.
    WRITE REPORT-RECORD.
    CLOSE PAYROLL-FILE
        REPORT-FILE.
    STOP RUN.
```

```
B010-CALC-EMP-PAYROLL.
    ADD 1 TO W-RECORD-COUNT.
    PERFORM C020-COMPUTE-GROSS-PAY.
    PERFORM C030-COMPUTE-EXEMPTIONS.
    PERFORM C040-COMPUTE-TAX
    PERFORM C050-COMPUTE-NET-PAY.
    PERFORM C060-PRINT-OUTPUT.
    PERFORM C010-GET-PAYROLL-REC.

C010-GET-PAYROLL-REC.
    READ PAYROLL-FILE
            AT END MOVE 'Y' TO W-OUT-OF-RECORDS-FLAG.

C020-COMPUTE-GROSS-PAY.
    MULTIPLY I-HOURS-WORKED BY I-PAYRATE
            GIVING W-GROSS-PAY ROUNDED.
    IF I-HOURS-WORKED IS GREATER THAN 40
        SUBTRACT 40 FROM I-HOURS-WORKED GIVING W-OVERTIME-HOURS
        MULTIPLY 0.5 BY W-OVERTIME-HOURS
        MULTIPLY W-OVERTIME-HOURS BY I-PAYRATE
            GIVING W-OVERTIME-PAY ROUNDED
        ADD W-OVERTIME-PAY TO W-GROSS-PAY.

C030-COMPUTE-EXEMPTIONS.
    MULTIPLY C-EXEMPTION BY I-DEPENDENTS
            GIVING W-EXEMPTIONS-TOTAL.

C040-COMPUTE-TAX.
    IF W-GROSS-PAY IS GREATER THAN W-EXEMPTIONS
        SUBTRACT W-EXEMPTIONS-TOTAL FROM W-GROSS-PAY
            GIVING W-TAXABLE
        MULTIPLY C-TAXRATE BY W-TAXABLE GIVING W-TAX ROUNDED
    ELSE
        MOVE ZERO TO W-TAX.

C050-COMPUTE-NET-PAY.
    SUBTRACT W-TAX FROM W-GROSS-PAY GIVING W-NET-PAY.

C060-PRINT-OUTPUT.
    MOVE SPACES              TO REPORT-RECORD.
    MOVE I-PAYROLL-NUMBER    TO O-PAYROLL-NUMBER.
    MOVE I-NAME              TO O-NAME.
    MOVE I-HOURS-WORKED      TO O-HOURS-WORKED.
    MOVE I-PAYRATE           TO O-PAYRATE.
    MOVE I-DEPENDENTS        TO O-DEPENDENTS.
    MOVE W-TAX               TO O-TAX.
    MOVE W-GROSS-PAY         TO O-GROSS-PAY.
    MOVE W-NET-PAY           TO O-NET-PAY.
    WRITE REPORT-RECORD.
```

CHAPTER 7

1. a. ZZ999

   b. $(6)

   c. $ZZ9.99

   d. +(5)

   e. Z9BB999

3.

```
01  I-RECORD.
    05  I-CUST-NO            PIC 9(5).
    05  I-CUST-NAME          PIC X(20).
    05  I-AMT-SALE           PIC S9(4)V99.
    05  I-PRODUCT-CODE       PIC X(6).
    05  FILLER               PIC X(42).
    05  I-RECORD-CODE        PIC X.

01  O-DETAIL-LINE.
    05  O-CUST-NO            PIC 99B999.
    05  FILLER               PIC X(5).
    05  O-CUST-NAME          PIC XBX(19).
    05  FILLER               PIC X(5).
    05  O-AMT-SALE           PIC $$,$$$.99-.
    05  FILLER               PIC X(5).
    05  O-PROD-CODE          PIC X(6).
    05  FILLER               PIC X(5).
    05  O-RECORD-CODE        PIC A.
```

5.

```
01  OUTPUT-LINE.
    05  ID-NUMBER-OUT        PIC X(6).
    05  REQUISITION-OUT      PIC X(6).
    05  FUND-OUT             PIC X(4).
    05  DEPARTMENT-OUT       PIC X(4).
    05  B-OUT                PIC XX.
    05  PURCHASE-ORDER-OUT   PIC X(6).
    05  REFERENCE-OUT        PIC X(18).
    05  FILLER               PIC X.
    05  GROSS-OUT            PIC ZZ,ZZZV99.
    05  FILLER               PIC X.
    05  DISC-OR-DEDUC-OUT    PIC ZZZV99.
    05  FILLER               PIC XX.
    05  AMOUNT-PAYABLE-OUT   PIC ZZZ,ZZV99.
```

7.

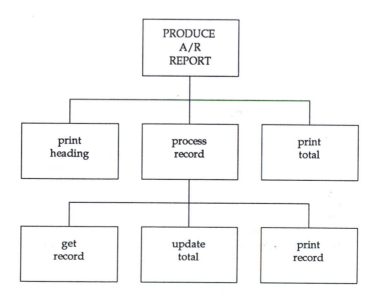

Produce A/R Report:
>   print the heading
>   PERFORM-UNTIL there are no more invoice records
>>   process one invoice record
>   ENDPERFORM
>   print the total

Print Heading:
>   print "ACCOUNTS RECEIVABLE" line
>   print blank line
>   print first column heading line
>   print second column heading line
>   print blank line

Process Record:
>   get the next invoice record
>   IF there is a record to process THEN
>>   update the total
>>   print the output record
>   ENDIF

Print Total:
>   print a blank line
>   move "TOTAL" to the output line
>   move the total to the output line
>   print the output line

Get Record:
>   get an invoice record; at end set the end of file flag

Update Total:
>   add the invoice amount to the total

Print Record:
>   move the invoice fields to the output record
>   print the output record

In the following program several of the smaller modules have been implemented as in-line code rather than as separate paragraphs.

```
IDENTIFICATION DIVISION.
PROGRAM-ID.
    CH7EX7.

ENVIRONMENT DIVISION.
INPUT-OUTPUT SECTION.
FILE-CONTROL.
    SELECT ACCOUNTS-RECEIVABLE-FILE ASSIGN TO S-ARFILE.
    SELECT INVOICE-FILE             ASSIGN TO S-INVCFILE.

DATA DIVISION.
FILE SECTION.
FD  ACCOUNTS-RECEIVABLE-FILE
    LABEL RECORDS ARE OMITTED.
01  ACCOUNTS-RECEIVABLE-RECORD      PIC X(60).
```

```
FD   INVOICE-FILE
     LABEL RECORDS ARE OMITTED.
01   INVOICE-RECORD.
     05   CUSTOMER-NUMBER           PIC X(5).
     05   CUSTOMER-NAME             PIC X(20).
     05   INVOICE-NUMBER            PIC X(5).
     05   INVOICE-DATE              PIC X(6).
     05   INVOICE-AMOUNT            PIC 9(4)V99.

WORKING-STORAGE SECTION.
01   HEADING-LINE-1                 PIC X(60)
         VALUE '              ACCOUNTS RECEIVABLE'.
01   HEADING-LINE-2.
     05   FILLER                    PIC X(31)
         VALUE 'CUSTOMER CUSTOMER'.
     05   FILLER                    PIC X(29)
         VALUE 'INVOICE  INVOICE   INVOICE'.
01   HEADING-LINE-3.
     05   FILLER                    PIC X(31)
         VALUE 'NUMBER   NAME'.
     05   FILLER                    PIC X(29)
         VALUE 'NUMBER   DATE     AMOUNT'.

01   INVOICE-LINE.
     05   CUSTOMER-NUMBER-OUT       PIC X(5).
     05   FILLER                    PIC X(4).
     05   CUSTOMER-NAME-OUT         PIC X(20).
     05   FILLER                    PIC XX.
     05   INVOICE-NUMBER-OUT        PIC X(5).
     05   FILLER                    PIC XXX.
     05   INVOICE-DATE-OUT          PIC XXBXXBXX.
     05   FILLER                    PIC XXX.
     05   INVOICE-AMOUNT-OUT        PIC ZZZ9.99.

01   TOTAL-LINE.
     05   FILLER                    PIC X(36) VALUE SPACES.
     05   FILLER                    PIC X(10) VALUE 'TOTAL'.
     05   INVOICE-TOTAL-OUT         PIC $$$$,$$9.99.

01    INVOICE-TOTAL                 PIC S9(6)V99 VALUE ZERO.

01   MORE-DATA-REMAINING-FLAG       PIC X VALUE 'Y'.
     88   NO-MORE-DATA-REMAINING            VALUE 'N'.
     88   MORE-DATA-REMAINING               VALUE 'Y'.

PROCEDURE DIVISION.
A000-PRODUCE-AR-REPORT.
     OPEN INPUT INVOICE-FILE
         OUTPUT ACCOUNTS-RECEIVABLE-FILE.
     WRITE ACCOUNTS-RECEIVABLE-RECORD FROM HEADING-LINE-1.
     MOVE SPACES TO ACCOUNTS-RECEIVABLE-RECORD.
     WRITE ACCOUNTS-RECEIVABLE-RECORD.
     WRITE ACCOUNTS-RECEIVABLE-RECORD FROM HEADING-LINE-2.
     WRITE ACCOUNTS-RECEIVABLE-RECORD FROM HEADING-LINE-3.
     MOVE SPACES TO ACCOUNTS-RECEIVABLE-RECORD.
     WRITE ACCOUNTS-RECEIVABLE-RECORD.
     PERFORM B010-PROCESS-RECORD
         UNTIL NO-MORE-DATA-REMAINING.
     MOVE SPACES TO ACCOUNTS-RECEIVABLE-RECORD.
     WRITE ACCOUNTS-RECEIVABLE-RECORD.
     MOVE INVOICE-TOTAL TO INVOICE-TOTAL-OUT.
```

```
        WRITE ACCOUNTS-RECEIVABLE-RECORD FROM TOTAL-LINE.
        CLOSE INVOICE-FILE
              ACCOUNTS-RECEIVABLE-FILE.
        STOP RUN.


    B010-PROCESS-RECORD.
        READ INVOICE-FILE
            AT END MOVE 'N' TO MORE-DATA-REMAINING-FLAG.
        IF MORE-DATA-REMAINING
            ADD INVOICE-AMOUNT TO INVOICE-TOTAL
            PERFORM C010-PRINT-RECORD.


    C010-PRINT-RECORD.
        MOVE SPACES TO INVOICE-LINE.
        MOVE CUSTOMER-NUMBER TO CUSTOMER-NUMBER-OUT.
        MOVE CUSTOMER-NAME   TO CUSTOMER-NAME-OUT.
        MOVE INVOICE-NUMBER  TO INVOICE-NUMBER-OUT.
        MOVE INVOICE-DATE    TO INVOICE-DATE-OUT.
        MOVE INVOICE-AMOUNT  TO INVOICE-AMOUNT-OUT.
        WRITE ACCOUNTS-RECEIVABLE-RECORD FROM INVOICE-LINE.
```

9. Add the flag GROSS-PAY-ERROR, and modify paragraphs B020-CALC-EMP-PAYROLL, C020-COMPUTE-GROSS-PAY, and E020-EDIT-PAYROLL-RECORD as shown below.

```
    B020-CALC-EMP-PAYROLL.
        PERFORM C020-COMPUTE-GROSS-PAY.
        IF GROSS-PAY-ERROR = 'N'
            PERFORM C030-COMPUTE-EXEMPTIONS
            PERFORM C040-COMPUTE-TAX
            PERFORM C050-COMPUTE-NET-PAY
            PERFORM C060-PRINT-OUTPUT
        ELSE
            MOVE PAYROLL-RECORD TO BAD-DATA
            MOVE 'GROSS PAY SUSPICIOUSLY LARGE' TO ERROR-MESSAGE
            WRITE REPORT-RECORD FROM ERROR-RECORD.
        PERFORM C010-GET-VALID-PAY-REC.


    C020-COMPUTE-GROSS-PAY.
        MOVE 'N' TO GROSS-PAY-ERROR.
        MULTIPLY I-HOURS-WORKED BY I-PAYRATE
              GIVING W-GROSS-PAY ROUNDED.
        IF I-HOURS-WORKED IS GREATER THAN 40
            SUBTRACT 40 FROM I-HOURS-WORKED GIVING W-OVERTIME-HOURS
            MULTIPLY 0.5 BY W-OVERTIME-HOURS
            MULTIPLY W-OVERTIME-HOURS BY I-PAYRATE
                  GIVING W-OVERTIME-PAY ROUNDED
            ADD W-OVERTIME-PAY TO W-GROSS-PAY.
        IF W-GROSS-PAY IS GREATER THAN 600.00
            MOVE 'Y' TO GROSS-PAY-ERROR.


    E020-EDIT-PAYROLL-RECORD.
        IF      I-PAYROLL-NUMBER IS NOT NUMERIC
            OR  I-HOURS-WORKED   IS NOT NUMERIC
            OR  I-PAYRATE        IS NOT NUMERIC
            OR  I-DEPENDENTS     IS NOT NUMERIC
            MOVE PAYROLL-RECORD TO BAD-DATA
            MOVE 'INVALID DATA IN THIS RECORD' TO ERROR-MESSAGE
            WRITE REPORT-RECORD FROM ERROR-RECORD
        ELSE
            MOVE 'Y' TO W-VALID-PAYROLL-RECORD.
```

11. Fields must be set up in the Working-Storage Section for the two counters (number of input records and number invalid) and the three totals (gross pay, tax, and net pay); they should all be initialized with **VALUE ZERO** clauses. The **IF** statement in **D010-VALID-RECORD-LOOP** should be modified to look something like

```
IF NOT OUT-OF-RECORDS
    ADD 1 TO TOTAL-RECORD-COUNT
    PERFORM E020-EDIT-PAYROLL-RECORD.
```

Counting records with bad data can be done in **E020-EDIT-PAYROLL-RECORD** by placing an **ADD** statement immediately after the **WRITE**, before the **ELSE**. Statements to accumulate the total gross pay, tax, and net pay can be placed at the end of **B020-CALC-EMP-PAYROLL**, just before **PERFORM C010-GET-VALID-PAY-REC**. To print all these counts and totals, define appropriate output lines in Working-Storage, then place **WRITE** statements in **A000-PRODUCE-PAYROLL-CALC** just before the **CLOSE** statement.

12.
```
05  STATE-CODE          PIC XX.
    88  ALABAMA             VALUE '01'.
    88  ALASKA              VALUE '02'.
    88  ARIZONA             VALUE '03'.

    Etc.
```

14.
```
IDENTIFICATION DIVISION.
PROGRAM-ID.
    CH7EX14.

ENVIRONMENT DIVISION.
INPUT-OUTPUT SECTION.
FILE-CONTROL.
    SELECT OUTPUT-FILE          ASSIGN TO S-PICS.

DATA DIVISION.
FILE SECTION.
FD  OUTPUT-FILE
    LABEL RECORDS ARE OMITTED.
01  OUTPUT-RECORD               PIC X(80).

WORKING-STORAGE SECTION.
01  SENDING-1                   PIC 9(4) VALUE 1234.
01  SENDING-2                   PIC 9(4) VALUE 23.
01  SENDING-3                   PIC 9(4) VALUE 23.
01  SENDING-4                   PIC 9(4) VALUE 4.
01  SENDING-5                   PIC 9(4) VALUE 50.
01  SENDING-6                   PIC 9(4) VALUE ZERO.
01  SENDING-7                   PIC 9(4) VALUE 123.
01  SENDING-8                   PIC 9(4) VALUE 2.
01  SENDING-9                   PIC 9(4) VALUE 1234.
01  SENDING-10                  PIC 9(4) VALUE ZERO.
01  SENDING-11                  PIC 9(4) VALUE ZERO.
01  SENDING-12                  PIC 9(4) VALUE 102.

01  LINE-1.
    05  FILLER                  PIC X(50)
        VALUE '9(4)      1234              $9(4)'.
    05  RECEIVING-1             PIC $9(4).
```

```
01   LINE-2.
     05  FILLER                    PIC X(50)
         VALUE '9(4)       0023                        $9(4)'.
     05  RECEIVING-2               PIC $9(4).
01   LINE-3.
     05  FILLER                    PIC X(50)
         VALUE '9(4)       0023                        $ZZ99'.
     05  RECEIVING-3               PIC $ZZ99.
01   LINE-4.
     05  FILLER                    PIC X(50)
         VALUE '9(4)       0004                        $ZZ99'.
     05  RECEIVING-4               PIC $ZZ99.
01   LINE-5.
     05  FILLER                    PIC X(50)
         VALUE '9(4)       0050                        $Z(4)'.
     05  RECEIVING-5               PIC $Z(4).
01   LINE-6.
     05  FILLER                    PIC X(50)
         VALUE '9(4)       0000                        $Z(4)'.
     05  RECEIVING-6               PIC $Z(4).
01   LINE-7.
     05  FILLER                    PIC X(50)
         VALUE '9(4)       0123                        $$999'.
     05  RECEIVING-7               PIC $$999.
01   LINE-8.
     05  FILLER                    PIC X(50)
         VALUE '9(4)       0002                        $$999'.
     05  RECEIVING-8               PIC $$999.
01   LINE-9.
     05  FILLER                    PIC X(50)
         VALUE '9(4)       1234                        $(5)'.
     05  RECEIVING-9               PIC $(5).
01   LINE-10.
     05  FILLER                    PIC X(50)
         VALUE '9(4)       0000                        $$$99'.
     05  RECEIVING-10              PIC $$$99.
01   LINE-11.
     05  FILLER                    PIC X(50)
         VALUE '9(4)       0000                        $(5)'.
     05  RECEIVING-11              PIC $(5).
01   LINE-12.
     05  FILLER                    PIC X(50)
         VALUE '9(4)       0102                        $$$99'.
     05  RECEIVING-12              PIC $$$99.

01   HEADING-1                     PIC X(60) VALUE
     '     SENDING ITEM                     RECEIVING ITEM'.
01   HEADING-2.
     05  FILLER                    PIC X(35)
         VALUE 'PICTURE   SAMPLE DATA'.
     05  FILLER                    PIC X(25)
         VALUE 'PICTURE EDITED RESULT'.
01   BLANK-LINE                    PIC X(60) VALUE SPACES.


PROCEDURE DIVISION.
A000-MAIN-ROUTINE.
     OPEN OUTPUT OUTPUT-FILE.
     WRITE OUTPUT-RECORD FROM HEADING-1.
```

```
WRITE OUTPUT-RECORD FROM HEADING-2.
WRITE OUTPUT-RECORD FROM BLANK-LINE.
MOVE SENDING-1 TO RECEIVING-1.
WRITE OUTPUT-RECORD FROM LINE-1.
WRITE OUTPUT-RECORD FROM BLANK-LINE.
MOVE SENDING-2 TO RECEIVING-2.
WRITE OUTPUT-RECORD FROM LINE-2.
WRITE OUTPUT-RECORD FROM BLANK-LINE.
MOVE SENDING-3 TO RECEIVING-3.
WRITE OUTPUT-RECORD FROM LINE-3.
WRITE OUTPUT-RECORD FROM BLANK-LINE.
MOVE SENDING-4 TO RECEIVING-4.
WRITE OUTPUT-RECORD FROM LINE-4.
WRITE OUTPUT-RECORD FROM BLANK-LINE.
MOVE SENDING-5 TO RECEIVING-5.
WRITE OUTPUT-RECORD FROM LINE-5.
WRITE OUTPUT-RECORD FROM BLANK-LINE.
MOVE SENDING-6 TO RECEIVING-6.
WRITE OUTPUT-RECORD FROM LINE-6.
WRITE OUTPUT-RECORD FROM BLANK-LINE.
WRITE OUTPUT-RECORD FROM BLANK-LINE.
WRITE OUTPUT-RECORD FROM BLANK-LINE.
WRITE OUTPUT-RECORD FROM BLANK-LINE.
WRITE OUTPUT-RECORD FROM BLANK-LINE.
WRITE OUTPUT-RECORD FROM HEADING-1.
WRITE OUTPUT-RECORD FROM HEADING-2.
WRITE OUTPUT-RECORD FROM BLANK-LINE.
MOVE SENDING-7 TO RECEIVING-7.
WRITE OUTPUT-RECORD FROM LINE-7.
WRITE OUTPUT-RECORD FROM BLANK-LINE.
MOVE SENDING-8 TO RECEIVING-8.
WRITE OUTPUT-RECORD FROM LINE-8.
WRITE OUTPUT-RECORD FROM BLANK-LINE.
MOVE SENDING-9 TO RECEIVING-9.
WRITE OUTPUT-RECORD FROM LINE-9.
WRITE OUTPUT-RECORD FROM BLANK-LINE.
MOVE SENDING-10 TO RECEIVING-10.
WRITE OUTPUT-RECORD FROM LINE-10.
WRITE OUTPUT-RECORD FROM BLANK-LINE.
MOVE SENDING-11 TO RECEIVING-11.
WRITE OUTPUT-RECORD FROM LINE-11.
WRITE OUTPUT-RECORD FROM BLANK-LINE.
MOVE SENDING-12 TO RECEIVING-12.
WRITE OUTPUT-RECORD FROM LINE-12.
CLOSE OUTPUT-FILE.
STOP RUN.
```

CHAPTER 8

1. The **ADD** statement in **E010-GET-PAYROLL-RECORD** is executed even when the end-of-file is encountered, so **VALID-RECORD-COUNT** will be one greater than it should be. To correct the problem make the **ADD** statement subordinate to an **IF** statement like the following:

```
IF W-OUT-OF-RECORDS-FLAG = 'N'
    ADD 1 TO VALID-RECORD-COUNT.
```

```
3. IF      MARRIED
        PERFORM D020-MARRIED-ROUTINE
   ELSE IF SINGLE
        PERFORM D010-SINGLE-ROUTINE
   ELSE IF DIVORCED
        PERFORM D030-DIVORCED-ROUTINE
   ELSE IF WIDOWED
        PERFORM D040-WIDOWED-ROUTINE
   ELSE
        PERFORM D050-ERROR-ROUTINE.


5. IF SALARY-CODE = 'W'
        IF GROSS-PAY IS GREATER THAN 500
            PERFORM E050-EXCESSIVE-PAY-POSSIBLE
        ELSE
            NEXT SENTENCE
   ELSE
        IF SALARY-CODE = 'S'
            IF GROSS-PAY IS GREATER THAN 1400
                PERFORM E050-EXCESSIVE-PAY-POSSIBLE
            ELSE
                NEXT SENTENCE
        ELSE
            IF SALARY-CODE = 'M'
                IF GROSS-PAY IS GREATER THAN 4500
                    PERFORM E050-EXCESSIVE-PAY-POSSIBLE
                ELSE
                    NEXT SENTENCE
            ELSE
                PERFORM X030-ERROR-ROUTINE.


7.
IDENTIFICATION DIVISION.
PROGRAM-ID.
    CH8EX7.

ENVIRONMENT DIVISION.
INPUT-OUTPUT SECTION.
FILE-CONTROL.
    SELECT ACCOUNTS-RECEIVABLE-FILE ASSIGN TO S-ARFILE.
    SELECT INVOICE-FILE             ASSIGN TO S-INVCFILE.

DATA DIVISION.
FILE SECTION.
FD  ACCOUNTS-RECEIVABLE-FILE
    LABEL RECORDS ARE OMITTED.
01  ACCOUNTS-RECEIVABLE-RECORD     PIC X(60).

FD  INVOICE-FILE
    LABEL RECORDS ARE OMITTED.
01  INVOICE-RECORD.
    05  CUSTOMER-NUMBER            PIC X(5).
    05  CUSTOMER-NAME              PIC X(20).
    05  INVOICE-NUMBER             PIC X(5).
    05  INVOICE-DATE               PIC X(6).
    05  INVOICE-AMOUNT             PIC 9(4)V99.

WORKING-STORAGE SECTION.
01  HEADING-LINE-1                 PIC X(60)
        VALUE '                 ACCOUNTS RECEIVABLE'.
```

```
01   HEADING-LINE-2.
     05   FILLER                    PIC X(31)
          VALUE 'CUSTOMER CUSTOMER'.
     05   FILLER                    PIC X(29)
          VALUE 'INVOICE    INVOICE    INVOICE'.
01   HEADING-LINE-3.
     05   FILLER                    PIC X(31)
          VALUE 'NUMBER    NAME'.
     05   FILLER                    PIC X(29)
          VALUE 'NUMBER    DATE      AMOUNT'.

01   INVOICE-LINE.
     05   CUSTOMER-NUMBER-OUT       PIC X(5).
     05   FILLER                    PIC X(4).
     05   CUSTOMER-NAME-OUT         PIC X(20).
     05   FILLER                    PIC XX.
     05   INVOICE-NUMBER-OUT        PIC X(5).
     05   FILLER                    PIC XXX.
     05   INVOICE-DATE-OUT          PIC XXBXXBXX.
     05   FILLER                    PIC XXX.
     05   INVOICE-AMOUNT-OUT        PIC ZZZ9.99.

01   TOTAL-LINE.
     05   FILLER                    PIC X(36) VALUE SPACES.
     05   FILLER                    PIC X(10) VALUE 'TOTAL'.
     05   INVOICE-TOTAL-OUT         PIC $$$$,$$9.99.

01   INVOICE-TOTAL                  PIC S9(6)V99 VALUE ZERO.

01   MORE-DATA-REMAINING-FLAG       PIC X VALUE 'Y'.
     88   NO-MORE-DATA-REMAINING         VALUE 'N'.
     88   MORE-DATA-REMAINING            VALUE 'Y'.

01   TOTAL-OVERFLOW-FLAG            PIC X VALUE 'N'.

01   TOTAL-OVERFLOW-MESSAGE         PIC X(52)
     VALUE '    ***** OVERFLOW OCCURRED.    TOTAL INVALID. *****'.

PROCEDURE DIVISION.
A000-PRODUCE-AR-REPORT.
     OPEN INPUT INVOICE-FILE
          OUTPUT ACCOUNTS-RECEIVABLE-FILE.
     WRITE ACCOUNTS-RECEIVABLE-RECORD FROM HEADING-LINE-1.
     MOVE SPACES TO ACCOUNTS-RECEIVABLE-RECORD.
     WRITE ACCOUNTS-RECEIVABLE-RECORD.
     WRITE ACCOUNTS-RECEIVABLE-RECORD FROM HEADING-LINE-2.
     WRITE ACCOUNTS-RECEIVABLE-RECORD FROM HEADING-LINE-3.
     MOVE SPACES TO ACCOUNTS-RECEIVABLE-RECORD.
     WRITE ACCOUNTS-RECEIVABLE-RECORD.
     PERFORM B010-PROCESS-RECORD
          UNTIL NO-MORE-DATA-REMAINING.
     MOVE SPACES TO ACCOUNTS-RECEIVABLE-RECORD.
     WRITE ACCOUNTS-RECEIVABLE-RECORD.
     IF TOTAL-OVERFLOW-FLAG = 'Y'
          WRITE ACCOUNTS-RECEIVABLE-RECORD
                 FROM TOTAL-OVERFLOW-MESSAGE
     ELSE
          MOVE INVOICE-TOTAL TO INVOICE-TOTAL-OUT
          WRITE ACCOUNTS-RECEIVABLE-RECORD FROM TOTAL-LINE.
     CLOSE INVOICE-FILE
          ACCOUNTS-RECEIVABLE-FILE.
     STOP RUN.
```

```
B010-PROCESS-RECORD.
    READ INVOICE-FILE
        AT END MOVE 'N' TO MORE-DATA-REMAINING-FLAG.
    IF MORE-DATA-REMAINING
        PERFORM C020-PROCESS-INVOICE.

C010-PRINT-RECORD.
    MOVE SPACES TO INVOICE-LINE.
    MOVE CUSTOMER-NUMBER TO CUSTOMER-NUMBER-OUT.
    MOVE CUSTOMER-NAME   TO CUSTOMER-NAME-OUT.
    MOVE INVOICE-NUMBER  TO INVOICE-NUMBER-OUT.
    MOVE INVOICE-DATE    TO INVOICE-DATE-OUT.
    MOVE INVOICE-AMOUNT  TO INVOICE-AMOUNT-OUT.
    WRITE ACCOUNTS-RECEIVABLE-RECORD FROM INVOICE-LINE.

C020-PROCESS-INVOICE.
    ADD INVOICE-AMOUNT TO INVOICE-TOTAL
        ON SIZE ERROR MOVE 'Y' TO TOTAL-OVERFLOW-FLAG.
    PERFORM C010-PRINT-RECORD.
```

CHAPTER 9

1. In **A000-PRODUCE-AR-REPORT** delete all lines between the **OPEN** statement and **PERFORM B010-PROCESS-RECORD**. Define a line counter field and initialize it to any value greater than 45. Modify **C010-PRINT-RECORD** to something like the following:

```
C010-PRINT-RECORD.
    IF LINE-COUNT IS NOT LESS THAN 45
        PERFORM D010-PRINT-HEADING.
    MOVE SPACES TO INVOICE-LINE.
    MOVE CUSTOMER-NUMBER TO CUSTOMER-NUMBER-OUT.
    MOVE CUSTOMER-NAME   TO CUSTOMER-NAME-OUT.
    MOVE INVOICE-NUMBER  TO INVOICE-NUMBER-OUT.
    MOVE INVOICE-DATE    TO INVOICE-DATE-OUT.
    MOVE INVOICE-AMOUNT  TO INVOICE-AMOUNT-OUT.
    WRITE ACCOUNTS-RECEIVABLE-RECORD FROM INVOICE-LINE
            AFTER ADVANCING 1 LINE.
    ADD 1 TO LINE-COUNT.

D010-PRINT-HEADING.
    WRITE ACCOUNTS-RECEIVABLE-RECORD FROM HEADING-LINE-1
            AFTER ADVANCING TO-TOP-OF-PAGE.
    WRITE ACCOUNTS-RECEIVABLE-RECORD FROM HEADING-LINE-2
            AFTER ADVANCING 2 LINES.
    WRITE ACCOUNTS-RECEIVABLE-RECORD FROM HEADING-LINE-3
            AFTER ADVANCING 1 LINE.
    MOVE SPACES TO ACCOUNTS-RECEIVABLE-RECORD.
    WRITE ACCOUNTS-RECEIVABLE-RECORD AFTER ADVANCING 1 LINE.
    MOVE 0 TO LINE-COUNT.
```

To allow for the use of the **ADVANCING** clause, define **TO-TOP-OF-PAGE** in the **SPECIAL-NAMES** paragraph and modify the output records in the File Section and the Working-Storage Section to include an additional byte for carriage control.

2. Put two additional MOVEs at the end of D010-PROCESS-ACCOUNT-GROUP and one additional MOVE at the end of C010-PROCESS-SELLER-GROUP, just before PERFORM X010-LINE-OUT. Actually, this is probably a preferable format for general use, since if there are a great many minor totals in each intermediate group it could become clumsy looking ahead to see what the intermediate level is.

4. Define an error message and a sequence error flag in Working-Storage, and initialize the flag with VALUE 'N'. Modify A000-PREPARE-SALES-REPORT as follows:

```
PERFORM B010-PROCESS-ACCOUNT-GROUP
    UNTIL NO-MORE-DATA OR SEQUENCE-ERROR-FLAG = 'Y'.
IF SEQUENCE-ERROR-FLAG = 'Y'
    MOVE SEQUENCE-ERROR-MESSAGE TO DETAIL-LINE
ELSE
    MOVE SPACES TO DETAIL-LINE
    MOVE FINAL-TOTAL TO FINAL-TOTAL-OUT.
```

Modify B010-PROCESS-ACCOUNT-GROUP to the following:

```
B010-PROCESS-ACCOUNT-GROUP.
    MOVE ZERO TO ACCOUNT-TOTAL.
    MOVE ACCOUNT-NUMBER TO PREVIOUS-ACCOUNT-NUMBER.
    PERFORM C010-PROCESS-ACCOUNT-RECORD UNTIL
            ACCOUNT-NUMBER IS NOT EQUAL TO PREVIOUS-ACCOUNT
        OR  NO-MORE-DATA
        OR  SEQUENCE-ERROR-FLAG = 'Y'.
    IF SEQUENCE-ERROR-FLAG = 'N'
        MOVE SPACES TO DETAIL-LINE
        MOVE PREVIOUS-ACCOUNT-NUMBER TO ACCOUNT-NUMBER-OUT
        MOVE ACCOUNT-TOTAL TO ACCOUNT-TOTAL-OUT
        PERFORM X010-LINE-OUT
        ADD ACCOUNT-TOTAL TO FINAL-TOTAL.
```

Finally, at the end of C010-PROCESS-ACCOUNT-RECORD add the following statement:

```
IF MORE-DATA-FLAG = 'Y'
    IF ACCOUNT-NUMBER IS LESS THAN PREVIOUS-ACCOUNT-NUMBER
        MOVE 'Y' TO SEQUENCE-ERROR-FLAG.
```

CHAPTER 10

1. | Decimal | Binary | Hexadecimal |
|---|---|---|
| 7 | 111 | 7 |
| 8 | 1000 | 8 |
| 19 | 10011 | 13 |
| 23 | 10111 | 17 |
| 34 | 100010 | 22 |

3. | Hexadecimal | Binary | Decimal |
|---|---|---|
| 4 | 100 | 4 |
| B | 1011 | 11 |
| 10 | 10000 | 16 |
| 14 | 10100 | 20 |

5. +123

> Packed: 0001 0010 0011 1100
> Zoned: 1111 0001 1111 0010 1100 0011

+1234

> Packed: 0000 0001 0010 0011 0100 1100
> Zoned: 1111 0001 1111 0010 1111 0011 1100 0100

-90345

> Packed: 1001 0000 0011 0100 0101 1101
> Zoned: 1111 1001 1111 0000 1111 0011 1111 0100 1101 0101

-6

> Packed: 0110 1101
> Zoned: 1101 0110

7.

Graphic Symbol	EBCDIC Code	ASCII Code
2	1111 0010	0101 0000
B	1100 0010	0110 0110
M	1101 0100	0111 0111
W	1110 0110	1000 0111
+	0100 1110	0100 0011
(	0100 1101	0100 0000

9.

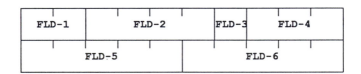

CHAPTER 11

1. Two possibilities:

```
IF COLUMN-23-CODE NOT = '1' AND NOT = '2' AND NOT = '3'
    MOVE 'X' TO INVALID-CODE-FLAG.

IF COLUMN-23-CODE = '1' OR '2' OR '3'
    NEXT SENTENCE
ELSE
    MOVE 'X' TO INVALID-CODE-FLAG.
```

3.
```
IF (SIZE-A > 13 AND SIZE-A < 37) AND SIZE-B < 50
    ADD 1 TO REGULAR-COUNT
ELSE
    ADD 1 TO SPECIAL-COUNT.
```

5. In the Working-Storage Section add appropriate entries to **ERROR-FLAGS** and **ERROR-MESSAGES**. In **C010-EDIT-LINE** add an **IF** statement to test the order number and set the flag if it is not numeric. At the start of **C020-WRITE-MESSAGES** print the error message if the flag is set.

CHAPTER 12

1.
```
open files
set KEY-1, KEY-2, PREVIOUS-KEY-1, and PREVIOUS-KEY-2 to low values
set sequence error flag and duplicate key flag to false
get FILE-1 record
get FILE-2 record
PERFORM-UNTIL (KEY-1 = high values and KEY-2 = high values)
                or a sequence error is detected
                or duplicate keys are detected
    IF  KEY-1  =  KEY-2  THEN
        set  duplicate  key  flag
    ELSE
        IF  KEY-1  is  less  than  KEY-2  THEN
            write  the  FILE-1  record
            get  FILE-1  record
        ELSE
            write  the  FILE-2  record
            get  FILE-2  record
        ENDIF
    ENDIF
ENDPERFORM
IF  a  sequence  error  was  detected  THEN
    write  an  error  message
ENDIF
IF  duplicate  keys  were  detected  THEN
    write  an  error  message
ENDIF
close  files
stop


GET  FILE-X  RECORD:
    read  a  record  from  FILE-X;  at  end  set  KEY-X  to  high  values
    IF  KEY-X  is  less  than  PREVIOUS-KEY-X  THEN
        set  the  sequence  error  flag
    ELSE
        move  KEY-X  to  PREVIOUS-KEY-X
    ENDIF
```

3. The main work is in **B010-MERGE-RECORD**. This logic can be accomplished in many other ways, but make sure that your solution processes duplicates correctly. Try it on the following data.

KEY-1	KEY-2	KEY-3
1	1	2
1	3	2
4	3	3
4	5	5
6	5	6
8	8	7
8	9	10
10	10	10
11	11	11

```
        IDENTIFICATION DIVISION.
        PROGRAM-ID.
            CH12EX3.

*       MERGE WITH SEQUENCE CHECKING

        ENVIRONMENT DIVISION.
        INPUT-OUTPUT SECTION.
        FILE-CONTROL.
            SELECT IN-FILE-1            ASSIGN TO S-FILE1.
            SELECT IN-FILE-2            ASSIGN TO S-FILE2.
            SELECT IN-FILE-3            ASSIGN TO S-FILE3.
            SELECT OUT-FILE             ASSIGN TO S-OUTFILE.

        DATA DIVISION.
        FILE SECTION.

        FD  IN-FILE-1
            LABEL RECORDS ARE OMITTED.
        01  IN-RECORD-1                 PIC X(80).

        FD  IN-FILE-2
            LABEL RECORDS ARE OMITTED.
        01  IN-RECORD-2                 PIC X(80).

        FD  IN-FILE-3
            LABEL RECORDS ARE OMITTED.
        01  IN-RECORD-3                 PIC X(80).

        FD  OUT-FILE
            LABEL RECORDS ARE OMITTED.
        01  OUT-RECORD                  PIC X(80).

        WORKING-STORAGE SECTION.

        01  W-IN-RECORD-1.
            05  KEY-1                   PIC X(5).
            05  REST-OF-RECORD-1        PIC X(75).

        01  W-IN-RECORD-2.
            05  KEY-2                   PIC X(5).
            05  REST-OF-RECORD-2        PIC X(75).

        01  W-IN-RECORD-3.
            05  KEY-3                   PIC X(5).
            05  REST-OF-RECORD-3        PIC X(75).

        01  PREVIOUS-KEY-1              PIC X(5) VALUE LOW-VALUES.
        01  PREVIOUS-KEY-2              PIC X(5) VALUE LOW-VALUES.
        01  PREVIOUS-KEY-3              PIC X(5) VALUE LOW-VALUES.

        01  SEQUENCE-ERROR-FLAG         PIC X VALUE 'N'.
            88  SEQUENCE-ERROR              VALUE 'Y'.


        PROCEDURE DIVISION.
        A000-MERGE-3-FILES.
            OPEN INPUT IN-FILE-1
                       IN-FILE-2
                       IN-FILE-3
                 OUTPUT OUT-FILE.
```

```
        PERFORM X010-READ-1.
        PERFORM X020-READ-2.
        PERFORM X030-READ-3.
        PERFORM B010-MERGE-RECORD
            UNTIL   (KEY-1 = HIGH-VALUES
                AND KEY-2 = HIGH-VALUES
                AND KEY-3 = HIGH-VALUES)
                OR   SEQUENCE-ERROR.
        IF SEQUENCE-ERROR
            DISPLAY 'SEQUENCE ERROR - JOB ABORTED'.
        CLOSE IN-FILE-1
              IN-FILE-2
              IN-FILE-3
              OUT-FILE.
        STOP RUN.

    B010-MERGE-RECORD.
        IF (KEY-1 < KEY-2 AND KEY-1 < KEY-3)
            WRITE OUT-RECORD FROM W-IN-RECORD-1
            PERFORM X010-READ-1
        ELSE
            IF (KEY-2 NOT > KEY-1 AND KEY-2 < KEY-3)
                WRITE OUT-RECORD FROM W-IN-RECORD-2
                PERFORM X020-READ-2
            ELSE
                WRITE OUT-RECORD FROM W-IN-RECORD-3
                PERFORM X030-READ-3.

    X010-READ-1.
        READ IN-FILE-1 INTO W-IN-RECORD-1
            AT END MOVE HIGH-VALUES TO KEY-1.
        IF KEY-1 IS LESS THAN PREVIOUS-KEY-1
            MOVE 'Y' TO SEQUENCE-ERROR-FLAG
        ELSE
            MOVE KEY-1 TO PREVIOUS-KEY-1.

    X020-READ-2.
        READ IN-FILE-2 INTO W-IN-RECORD-2
            AT END MOVE HIGH-VALUES TO KEY-2.
        IF KEY-2 IS LESS THAN PREVIOUS-KEY-2
            MOVE 'Y' TO SEQUENCE-ERROR-FLAG
        ELSE
            MOVE KEY-2 TO PREVIOUS-KEY-2.

    X030-READ-3.
        READ IN-FILE-3 INTO W-IN-RECORD-3
            AT END MOVE HIGH-VALUES TO KEY-3.
        IF KEY-3 IS LESS THAN PREVIOUS-KEY-3
            MOVE 'Y' TO SEQUENCE-ERROR-FLAG
        ELSE
            MOVE KEY-3 TO PREVIOUS-KEY-3.
```

5.

```
IDENTIFICATION DIVISION.
PROGRAM-ID.
    UPDATE2A.

ENVIRONMENT DIVISION.
INPUT-OUTPUT SECTION.
FILE-CONTROL.
    SELECT TRANSACTION-FILE         ASSIGN TO S-TRANS.
    SELECT OLD-MASTER-FILE          ASSIGN TO S-OLDMAST.
    SELECT NEW-MASTER-FILE          ASSIGN TO S-NEWMAST.
    SELECT DELETION-FILE            ASSIGN TO S-DELETION.

DATA DIVISION.

FILE SECTION.

FD  TRANSACTION-FILE
    LABEL RECORDS ARE OMITTED.
01  TRANSACTION-BUFFER              PIC X(80).

FD  OLD-MASTER-FILE
    LABEL RECORDS ARE OMITTED.
01  OLD-MASTER-BUFFER               PIC X(80).

FD  NEW-MASTER-FILE
    LABEL RECORDS ARE OMITTED.
01  NEW-MASTER.
    05  NM-KEY                      PIC X(5).
    05  NM-QUANTITY                 PIC 9(5).
    05  FILLER                      PIC X(70).

FD  DELETION-FILE
    LABEL RECORDS ARE OMITTED.
01  DELETION-REPORT.
    05  CARRIAGE-CONTROL            PIC X.
    05  DELETION-LINE               PIC X(132).

WORKING-STORAGE SECTION.

01  OLD-MASTER.
    05  OM-KEY                      PIC X(5).
    05  OM-QUANTITY                 PIC 9(5).
    05  FILLER                      PIC X(70).

01  TRANSACTION.
    05  TR-KEY                      PIC X(5).
    05  TR-QUANTITY                 PIC 9(5).
    05  TR-TRANSACTION-CODE         PIC X.
        88  ADDITION                        VALUE '1'.
        88  ADJUSTMENT                      VALUE '2'.
        88  RECEIPT                         VALUE '3'.
        88  SHIPMENT                        VALUE '4'.
        88  DELETION                        VALUE '5'.
    05  FILLER                      PIC X(69).

01  HOLD-MASTER                     PIC X(80).

01  NEED-MASTER-FLAG                PIC X VALUE 'Y'.
    88  NEED-MASTER                         VALUE 'Y'.
```

```
       PROCEDURE DIVISION.
       A000-UPDATE-FILE.
           OPEN INPUT TRANSACTION-FILE
                      OLD-MASTER-FILE
               OUTPUT NEW-MASTER-FILE
                      DELETION-FILE.
           PERFORM C010-GET-TRANSACTION.
           PERFORM C020-GET-MASTER.
           PERFORM B010-UPDATE-LOGIC
               UNTIL OM-KEY = HIGH-VALUES  AND  TR-KEY = HIGH-VALUES.
           CLOSE TRANSACTION-FILE
                 OLD-MASTER-FILE
                 NEW-MASTER-FILE
                 DELETION-FILE.
           STOP RUN.

       B010-UPDATE-LOGIC.
           IF OM-KEY IS LESS THAN TR-KEY
               WRITE NEW-MASTER FROM OLD-MASTER
               PERFORM C020-GET-MASTER
           ELSE
               IF OM-KEY = TR-KEY
                   IF DELETION
                       MOVE OLD-MASTER TO DELETION-LINE
                       WRITE DELETION-REPORT AFTER ADVANCING 1 LINE
                       PERFORM C010-GET-TRANSACTION
                       PERFORM C020-GET-MASTER
                   ELSE
                       PERFORM C030-UPDATE-MASTER
                       PERFORM C010-GET-TRANSACTION
               ELSE
                   PERFORM D010-ADD-MASTER
                   PERFORM C010-GET-TRANSACTION.

       C010-GET-TRANSACTION.
           READ TRANSACTION-FILE INTO TRANSACTION
               AT END MOVE HIGH-VALUES TO TR-KEY.

       C020-GET-MASTER.
           IF NEED-MASTER
               READ OLD-MASTER-FILE INTO OLD-MASTER
                   AT END MOVE HIGH-VALUES TO OM-KEY
           ELSE
               MOVE HOLD-MASTER TO OLD-MASTER
               MOVE 'Y' TO NEED-MASTER-FLAG.

       C030-UPDATE-MASTER.
           DISPLAY ' OM ', OM-KEY, ' TR ', TR-KEY.

       D010-ADD-MASTER.
           MOVE OLD-MASTER TO HOLD-MASTER.
           MOVE 'N' TO NEED-MASTER-FLAG.
           MOVE  TR-KEY TO OM-KEY.
           MOVE TR-QUANTITY TO OM-QUANTITY.
           DISPLAY ' OM ', OM-KEY, ' NM ', TR-KEY.

   ******************* END OF PROGRAM *****************************
```

Notice what the changes involve. In the Working-Storage Section we define a place to hold a master record temporarily, and a flag to tell whether there is anything in this storage area. In the Procedure Division, instead of automatically writing the new master we execute **D010-ADD-MASTER** when an **ADDITION** transaction is processed. This paragraph saves the old master, sets the flag so that we know there is something in the hold area, and creates a new master. If the next transaction has the same key as this master, it is applied to the new master. Eventually, when the program gets another master record, we get the record from the hold area instead of reading one from the file and the flag is reset. Code such as this can be used to apply as many transaction records as necessary (including none) to a newly created master record.

6. In the Working-Storage Section, rename **SEQUENCE-ERROR-FLAG** as **MASTER-SEQUENCE-ERROR-FLAG** and initialize it with a **VALUE 'N'** clause; add definitions for **XACT-SEQUENCE-ERROR-FLAG** and **XACT-SEQUENCE-ERROR-COUNT**, initialized to zero; change **TERMINATION-MSG** to show 100 errors; and add appropriate definitions for **MASTER-SEQUENCE-MSG** and **XACT-SEQUENCE-MSG**. Then make the following changes in the Procedure Division.

```
PERFORM B010-UPDATE-LOGIC
    UNTIL (OM-KEY = HIGH-VALUES  AND  TR-KEY = HIGH-VALUES)
            OR ERROR-COUNT IS GREATER THAN 100
            OR MASTER-SEQUENCE-ERROR-FLAG = 'Y'
            OR XACT-SEQUENCE-ERROR-COUNT IS GREATER THAN 10.
IF      ERROR-COUNT IS GREATER THAN 100
    MOVE TERMINATION-MSG TO LOG-LINE
    WRITE LOG-RECORD AFTER ADVANCING 1 LINE
ELSE IF MASTER-SEQUENCE-ERROR-FLAG = 'Y'
    MOVE MASTER-SEQUENCE-MSG TO LOG-LINE
    WRITE LOG-RECORD AFTER ADVANCING 1 LINE
ELSE IF XACT-SEQUENCE-ERROR-COUNT IS GREATER THAN 10
    MOVE XACT-SEQUENCE-MSG TO LOG-LINE
    WRITE LOG-RECORD AFTER ADVANCING 1 LINE.
```

Change **X010-GET-VALID-TRANSACTION** to test **XACT-SEQUENCE-ERROR-COUNT** instead of **ERROR-COUNT**.

Change **X020-GET-VALID-MASTER** as follows:

```
X020-GET-VALID-MASTER.
    READ OLD-MASTER-FILE INTO OLD-MASTER
        AT END MOVE HIGH-VALUES TO OM-KEY.
    IF OM-KEY IS LESS THAN OM-KEY-PREVIOUS
        MOVE 'Y' TO MASTER-SEQUENCE-ERROR-FLAG
    ELSE
        MOVE OM-KEY TO OM-KEY-PREVIOUS.
```

Change **Y010-READ-TRANSACTION** to increment **XACT-SEQUENCE-ERROR-COUNT** instead of **ERROR-COUNT**.

Delete **Y020-READ-MASTER**.

CHAPTER 13

1. ADD SET-UP (13) UNIT-TIME (13) GIVING JOB-TIME.

3. ADD AMOUNT TO SALES (SELLER-NUMBER).

5.
```
        MOVE ZERO TO TOTAL.
        PERFORM D030-TOTALLER
            VARYING S-DAY FROM 1 BY 1
                    UNTIL S-DAY > 5.
        DIVIDE TOTAL BY 5 GIVING AVERAGE-TIME.
        .
        .
        .

    D030-TOTALLER.
        ADD A-TIME (S-DAY) TO TOTAL.
```

7.
```
        MOVE 1 TO BIG-SELLER.
        MOVE SALES (1) TO BIG-SALES.
        PERFORM C020-FIND-BIG
            VARYING SELLER FROM 2 BY 1
                    UNTIL SELLER > 50.
        DISPLAY BIG-SELLER, ' ', BIG-SALES.
        .
        .
        .

    C020-FIND-BIG.
        IF SALES (SELLER) > BIG-SALES
            MOVE SELLER TO BIG-SELLER
            MOVE SALES (SELLER) TO BIG-SALES.
```

9.
```
WORKING-STORAGE SECTION.

01   STUDENT-NAME-VALUES.
     05   FILLER   PIC X(25) VALUE 'ANDERSON, JAMES G.        '.
     05   FILLER   PIC X(25) VALUE 'BRIDGES, SUSAN H.         '.
     05   FILLER   PIC X(25) VALUE 'BROWN, WILLIAM F.         '.
     05   FILLER   PIC X(25) VALUE 'CASHMAN, FREDERICK P.     '.
        .
        .
        .

01   STUDENT-NAME-TABLE REDEFINES STUDENT-NAME-VALUES.
     05   STUDENT-NAME   PIC X(25) OCCURS 40 TIMES.
```

11.
```
    PERFORM C050-WRITE-A-LINE
        VARYING GRADE FROM 1 BY 1
                UNTIL GRADE > 12.
        .
        .
        .

C050-WRITE-A-LINE.
    MOVE GRADE TO GRADE-OUT.
    MOVE SIZE-BY-GRADE-AND-YEAR (GRADE, 3) TO ENROLLMENT-OUT.
    WRITE OUTPUT-LINE.
```

13.

```
    PERFORM C050-WRITE-A-LINE
        VARYING GRADE FROM 1 BY 1
                UNTIL GRADE > 12.
        .
        .
        .
C050-WRITE-A-LINE.
    MOVE GRADE TO GRADE-OUT.
    ADD SIZE-BY-GRADE-AND-YEAR (GRADE, 1)
        SIZE-BY-GRADE-AND-YEAR (GRADE, 2)
        SIZE-BY-GRADE-AND-YEAR (GRADE, 3)
        SIZE-BY-GRADE-AND-YEAR (GRADE, 4)
        GIVING TOTAL-ENROLLMENT.
    DIVIDE TOTAL-ENROLLMENT BY 4
        GIVING TOTAL-ENROLLMENT-OUT ROUNDED.
    WRITE OUTPUT-LINE.
```

15.

```
    READ YEAR-IN-FILE
        AT END MOVE 'N' TO MORE-DATA-REMAINS-FLAG.
    MOVE 1 TO BIG-GRADE.
    MOVE SIZE-BY-GRADE-AND-YEAR (1, YEAR) TO BIG-ENROLLMENT.
    PERFORM C030-FIND-BIG
        VARYING GRADE FROM 2 BY 1
                UNTIL GRADE > 12.
    MOVE YEAR TO YEAR-OUT.
    MOVE BIG-GRADE TO BIG-GRADE-OUT.
    MOVE BIG-ENROLLMENT TO BIG-ENROLLMENT-OUT.
    WRITE OUTPUT-LINE.
        .
        .
        .
C030-FIND-BIG.
    IF SIZE-BY-GRADE-AND-YEAR (GRADE, YEAR) > BIG-ENROLLMENT
        MOVE GRADE TO BIG-GRADE
        MOVE SIZE-BY-GRADE-AND-YEAR (GRADE, YEAR)
                TO BIG-ENROLLMENT.
```

17. Add the following to Working-Storage.

```
01  OVERFLOW-FLAG                   PIC X VALUE 'N'.
    88   NO-OVERFLOW                      VALUE 'N'.

01  OVERFLOW-MESSAGE.
    05   FILLER                      PIC X(34)
        VALUE 'TABLE OVERFLOW.  RUN TERMINATED.  '.
    05   FILLER                      PIC X(37)
        VALUE 'MODIFY PROGRAM TO ALLOW FOR AT LEAST '.
    05   NEW-TABLE-SIZE              PIC ZZ,ZZ9.
    05   FILLER                      PIC X(8) VALUE 'ENTRIES.'.
```

Change the Procedure Division as follows.

```
A000-VALIDATE-ORDERS.
    PERFORM B020-LOAD-VALID-NUMBER.
    IF NO-OVERFLOW
        PERFORM A010-CONTINUE-VALIDATION.
    STOP RUN.
```

```
A010-CONTINUE-VALIDATION.
    OPEN INPUT ORDER-FILE
         OUTPUT NORMAL-HANDLING-FILE
                SPECIAL-HANDLING-FILE.
    MOVE 'Y' TO MORE-DATA-REMAINS-FLAG.
    READ ORDER-FILE
         AT END MOVE 'N' TO MORE-DATA-REMAINS-FLAG.
    PERFORM B010-VALIDATE-ONE-LINE
         UNTIL NO-MORE-DATA-REMAINS.
    CLOSE ORDER-FILE
          NORMAL-HANDLING-FILE
          SPECIAL-HANDLING-FILE.
     .
     .
     .

B020-LOAD-VALID-NUMBER.
    OPEN INPUT CATALOG-FILE.
    MOVE 'Y' TO MORE-DATA-REMAINS-FLAG.
    MOVE ZERO TO X-CATALOG.
    READ CATALOG-FILE
         AT END MOVE 'N' TO MORE-DATA-REMAINS-FLAG.
    PERFORM C030-LOAD-CATALOG-RECORD
         UNTIL  NO-MORE-DATA-REMAINS.
    CLOSE CATALOG-FILE.
    IF X-CATALOG > VALID-NUMBER-MAX
        MOVE X-CATALOG TO NEW-TABLE-SIZE
        DISPLAY OVERFLOW-MESSAGE
        MOVE 'Y' TO OVERFLOW-FLAG
    ELSE
        MOVE X-CATALOG TO VALID-NUMBER-MAX.
     .
     .
     .

C030-LOAD-CATALOG-RECORD.
    ADD 1 TO X-CATALOG.
    IF X-CATALOG NOT > VALID-NUMBER-MAX
        MOVE MASTER-CATALOG-NUMBER TO VALID-NUMBER (X-CATALOG).
    READ CATALOG-FILE
         AT END MOVE 'N' TO MORE-DATA-REMAINS-FLAG.
```

CHAPTER 15

1. Items **c** and **d** assume that STRING-TALLY and COUNTER have the initial
    values of zero.

    a. `INSPECT ITEM-A REPLACING ALL ' ' BY '0'.`

    b. `INSPECT ITEM-B REPLACING FIRST 'A' BY '2'.`

    c. `INSPECT ITEM-C TALLYING STRING-TALLY FOR LEADING '*'.`

    d. `INSPECT ITEM-D TALLYING COUNTER FOR LEADING '*'`
        `            REPLACING LEADING '*' BY '0'.`

    e. `INSPECT ITEM-E`
        `        REPLACING CHARACTERS BY '9' BEFORE INITIAL 'X'.`

3.

```
IDENTIFICATION DIVISION.
PROGRAM-ID.
    CH15EX3.

ENVIRONMENT DIVISION.
INPUT-OUTPUT SECTION.
FILE-CONTROL.
    SELECT CUSTOMER-FILE        ASSIGN TO S-CUSTFILE.
    SELECT LETTER-FILE          ASSIGN TO S-LETTERS.

DATA DIVISION.
FILE SECTION.
FD  CUSTOMER-FILE
    LABEL RECORDS ARE OMITTED.
01  CUSTOMER-RECORD.
    05  CUSTOMER-NAME.
        10  LAST-NAME           PIC X(15).
        10  FIRST-NAME          PIC X(15).
        10  TITLE               PIC X(5).
    05  CUSTOMER-ADDRESS.
        10  HOUSE-NUMBER        PIC X(5).
        10  STREET-NAME         PIC X(15).
        10  CITY                PIC X(15).
        10  STATE               PIC X(15).
        10  ZIP                 PIC X(5).
    05  REST-OF-RECORD          PIC X(10).

FD  LETTER-FILE
    LABEL RECORDS ARE OMITTED.
01  LETTER-RECORD               PIC X(80).

WORKING-STORAGE SECTION.

01  MORE-DATA-REMAINS-FLAG      PIC X VALUE 'Y'.
    88  NO-MORE-DATA-REMAINS          VALUE 'N'.

01  INITIAL-POSITION            PIC 99.


PROCEDURE DIVISION.
A000-PRINT-LETTERS.
    OPEN INPUT CUSTOMER-FILE
         OUTPUT LETTER-FILE.
    READ CUSTOMER-FILE
        AT END MOVE 'N' TO MORE-DATA-REMAINS-FLAG.
    PERFORM B010-PRINT-HEADING
        UNTIL NO-MORE-DATA-REMAINS.
    CLOSE CUSTOMER-FILE
          LETTER-FILE.
    STOP RUN.

B010-PRINT-HEADING.
    MOVE SPACES TO LETTER-RECORD.
    MOVE 2 TO INITIAL-POSITION.
    STRING
        TITLE           DELIMITED BY SPACE
        SPACE           DELIMITED BY SIZE
        FIRST-NAME      DELIMITED BY SPACE
        SPACE           DELIMITED BY SIZE
        LAST-NAME       DELIMITED BY SPACE
```

```
            INTO LETTER-RECORD
            WITH POINTER INITIAL-POSITION.
WRITE LETTER-RECORD AFTER ADVANCING 5 LINES.
MOVE SPACES TO LETTER-RECORD.
MOVE 2 TO INITIAL-POSITION.
STRING
    HOUSE-NUMBER  DELIMITED BY SPACE
    SPACE         DELIMITED BY SIZE
    STREET-NAME   DELIMITED BY SPACE
        INTO LETTER-RECORD
        WITH POINTER INITIAL-POSITION.
WRITE LETTER-RECORD AFTER ADVANCING 1 LINE.
MOVE SPACES TO LETTER-RECORD.
MOVE 2 TO INITIAL-POSITION.
STRING
    CITY DELIMITED BY SPACE
    ', ' DELIMITED BY SIZE
    STATE DELIMITED BY SPACE
    SPACE DELIMITED BY SIZE
    ZIP DELIMITED BY SIZE
        INTO LETTER-RECORD
        WITH POINTER INITIAL-POSITION.
WRITE LETTER-RECORD AFTER ADVANCING 1 LINE.
MOVE SPACES TO LETTER-RECORD.
MOVE 2 TO INITIAL-POSITION.
STRING
    'Dear ' DELIMITED BY SIZE
    TITLE DELIMITED BY SPACE
    SPACE DELIMITED BY SIZE
    LAST-NAME DELIMITED BY SPACE
        INTO LETTER-RECORD
        WITH POINTER INITIAL-POSITION.
WRITE LETTER-RECORD AFTER ADVANCING 3 LINES.
READ CUSTOMER-FILE
    AT END MOVE 'N' TO MORE-DATA-REMAINS-FLAG.
```

CHAPTER 16

2.

```
IDENTIFICATION DIVISION.
PROGRAM-ID.
    ONELEVEL.

ENVIRONMENT DIVISION.
INPUT-OUTPUT SECTION.
FILE-CONTROL.
    SELECT ACCOUNT-FILE        ASSIGN TO S-ACCOUNT.
    SELECT REPORT-FILE         ASSIGN TO S-REPORT.

DATA DIVISION.

FILE SECTION.

FD  ACCOUNT-FILE
    LABEL RECORDS ARE OMITTED.
01  ACCOUNT-RECORD.
    05  ACCOUNT-NUMBER         PIC X(5).
    05  SALE-AMOUNT            PIC 9(5)V99.
    05  FILLER                PIC X(68).
```

```
FD   REPORT-FILE
     LABEL RECORDS ARE OMITTED
     REPORT IS SALES-REPORT.

WORKING-STORAGE SECTION.

01   MORE-DATA-FLAG              PIC X VALUE 'Y'.
     88  NO-MORE-DATA                   VALUE 'N'.

REPORT SECTION.

RD   SALES-REPORT
     CONTROLS ARE FINAL
                   ACCOUNT-NUMBER
     PAGE LIMIT IS 60 LINES
          HEADING       1
          FIRST DETAIL  4
          LAST DETAIL   55
          FOOTING       60.
01   TYPE IS PAGE HEADING LINE IS 1.
     05   COLUMN 1               PIC X(48)
          VALUE 'ACCOUNT    TOTAL             FINAL TOTAL'.
     05   COLUMN 45              PIC X(04) VALUE 'PAGE'.
     05   COLUMN 49              PIC Z(6)9
               SOURCE IS PAGE-COUNTER.

01   ACCOUNT-LINE TYPE DETAIL
          PIC 9(6)V99 SOURCE IS SALE-AMOUNT.

01   TYPE CONTROL FOOTING ACCOUNT-NUMBER LINE PLUS 1.
     05   COLUMN 1               PIC Z(4)9
               SOURCE IS ACCOUNT-NUMBER.
     05   COLUMN 9               PIC $$$$,$$9.99 SUM SALE-AMOUNT.

01   TYPE CONTROL FOOTING FINAL LINE PLUS 1.
     05   COLUMN 28              PIC $$$$,$$9.99 SUM SALE-AMOUNT.


PROCEDURE DIVISION.
A000-PREPARE-SALES-REPORT.
     OPEN INPUT ACCOUNT-FILE
          OUTPUT REPORT-FILE.
     INITIATE SALES-REPORT.
     READ ACCOUNT-FILE
          AT END MOVE 'N' TO MORE-DATA-FLAG.
     PERFORM B010-PROCESS-ACCOUNT-GROUP
          UNTIL NO-MORE-DATA.
     TERMINATE SALES-REPORT.
     CLOSE ACCOUNT-FILE
          REPORT-FILE.
     STOP RUN.


B010-PROCESS-ACCOUNT-GROUP.
     GENERATE ACCOUNT-LINE.
     READ ACCOUNT-FILE
          AT END MOVE 'N' TO MORE-DATA-FLAG.
```

INDEX